CHAPTER 9

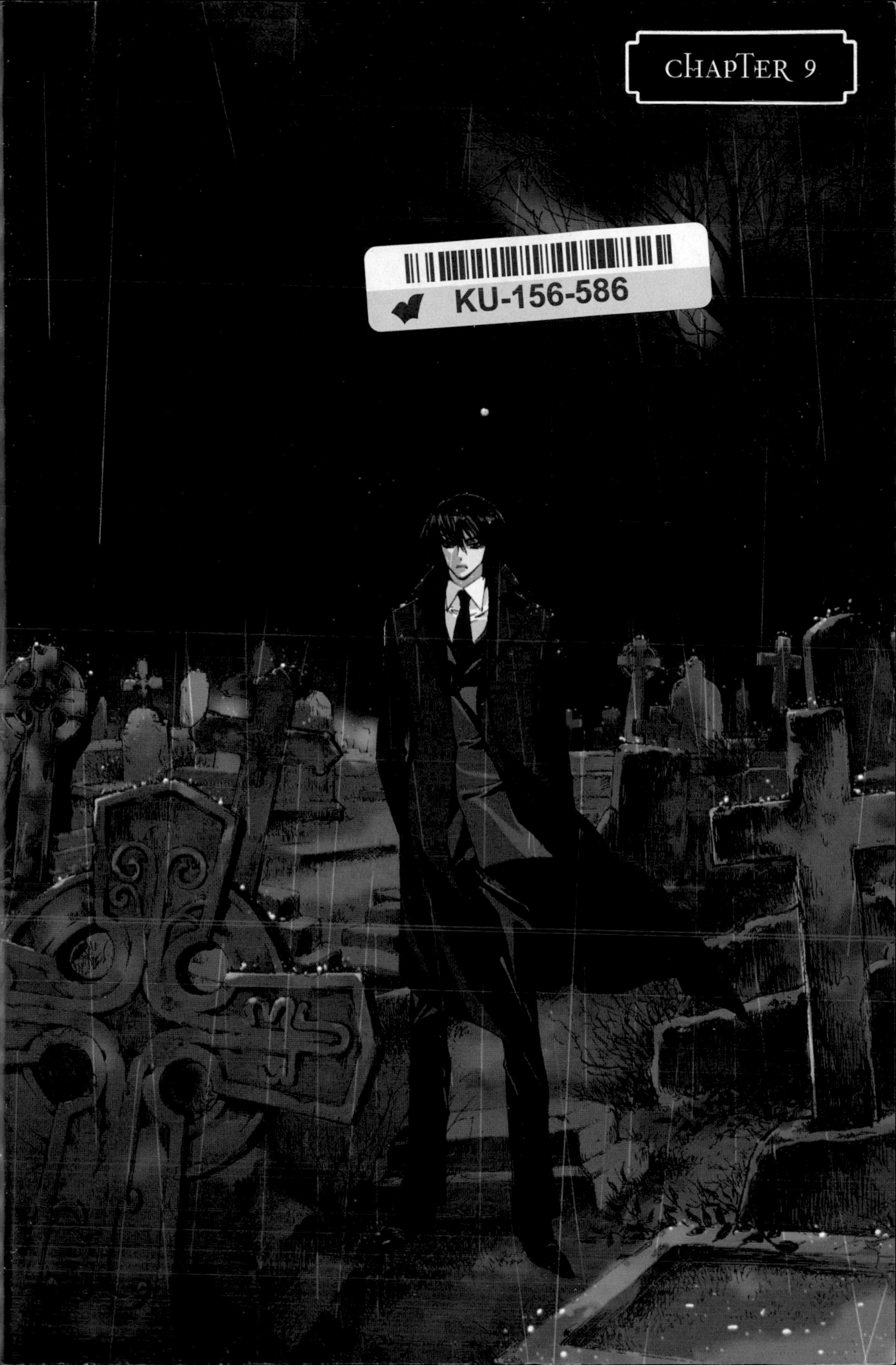

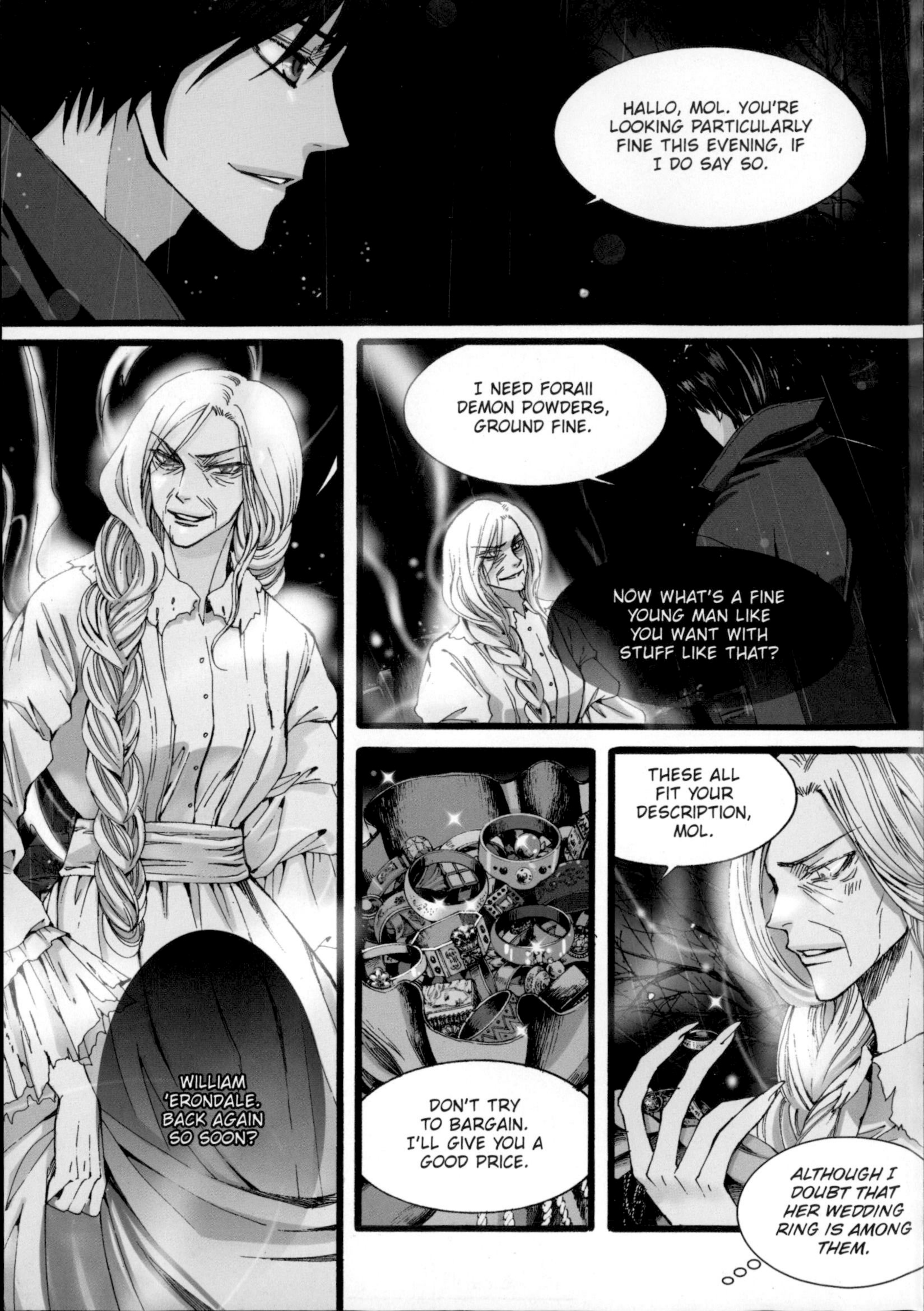
HALLO, MOL. YOU'RE LOOKING PARTICULARLY FINE THIS EVENING, IF I DO SAY SO.
WILLIAM 'ERONDALE. BACK AGAIN SO SOON?
I NEED FORAII DEMON POWDERS, GROUND FINE.
NOW WHAT'S A FINE YOUNG MAN LIKE YOU WANT WITH STUFF LIKE THAT?
DON'T TRY TO BARGAIN. I'LL GIVE YOU A GOOD PRICE.
THESE ALL FIT YOUR DESCRIPTION, MOL.
ALTHOUGH I DOUBT THAT HER WEDDING RING IS AMONG THEM.

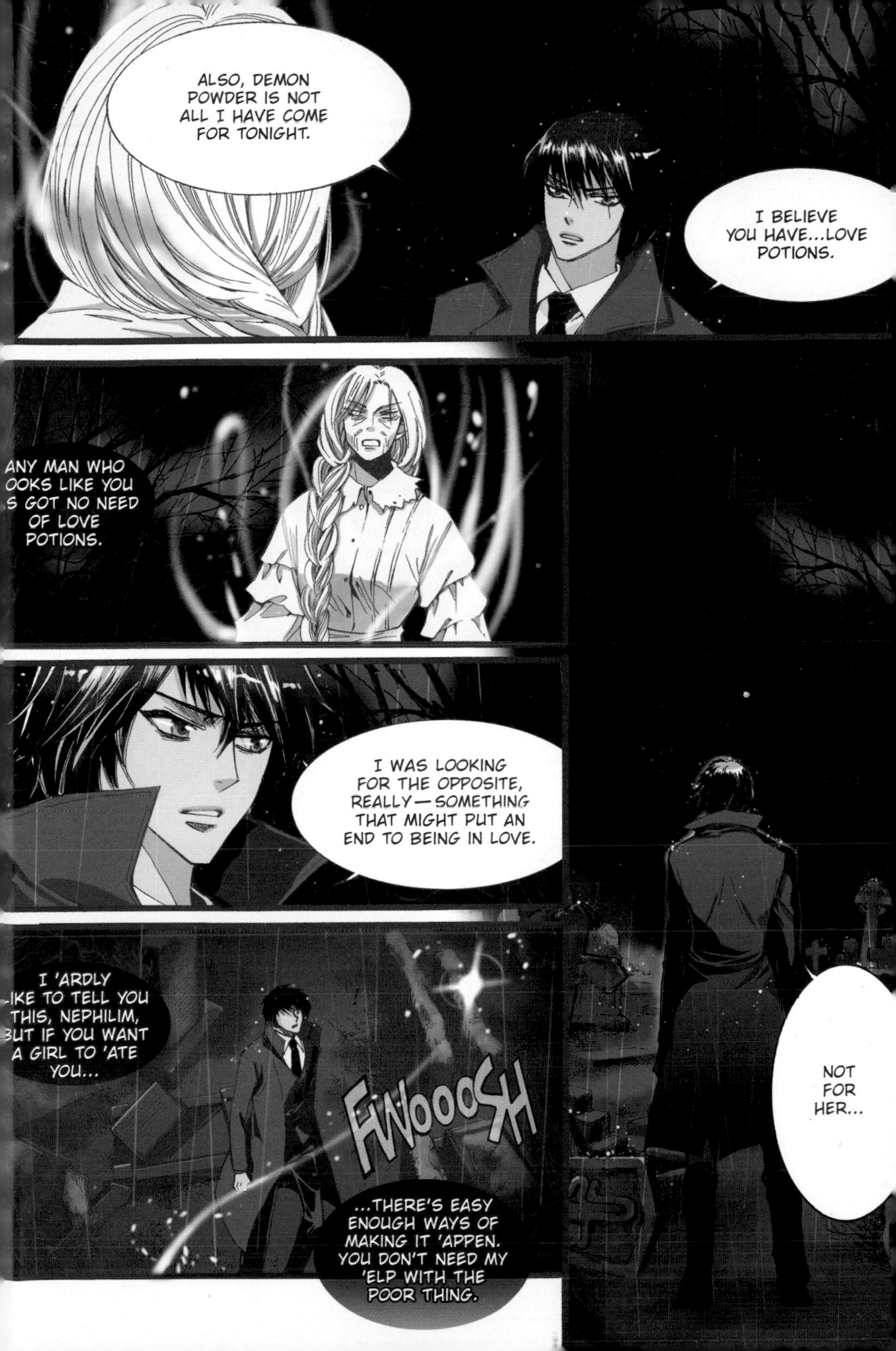
ALSO, DEMON POWDER IS NOT ALL I HAVE COME FOR TONIGHT.
I BELIEVE YOU HAVE...LOVE POTIONS.
ANY MAN WHO OOKS LIKE YOU S GOT NO NEED OF LOVE POTIONS.
I WAS LOOKING FOR THE OPPOSITE, REALLY—SOMETHING THAT MIGHT PUT AN END TO BEING IN LOVE.
I 'ARDLY IKE TO TELL YOU THIS, NEPHILIM, UT IF YOU WANT A GIRL TO 'ATE YOU...
FWOOOSH
...THERE'S EASY ENOUGH WAYS OF MAKING IT 'APPEN. YOU DON'T NEED MY 'ELP WITH THE POOR THING.
NOT FOR HER...

FOR ME...

SO THIS IS WESTMINSTER ABBEY?

I'VE BECOME VERY FOND OF JEM OVER THE PAST FORTNIGHT.

WILL HAS BEEN STUDIOUSLY AVOIDING ME, CHARLOTTE AND HENRY HAVE BEEN CAUGHT UP IN ISSUES OF CLAVE AND COUNCIL AND THE RUNNING OF THE INSTITUTE—AND EVEN JESSAMINE HAS SEEMED PREOCCUPIED.

HENRY JAMES
OM
Novelist
New York 1843
London 1916

THOMAS STEARNS
ELIOT
OM
BORN 26 SEPTEMBER 1888
DIED 4 JANUARY 1965

POETS' CORNER.

I KNOW WE ARE IN A HURRY TO GET TO THE COUNCIL MEETING, BUT I WANTED YOU TO SEE THIS.

BUT JEM WAS ALWAYS THERE.

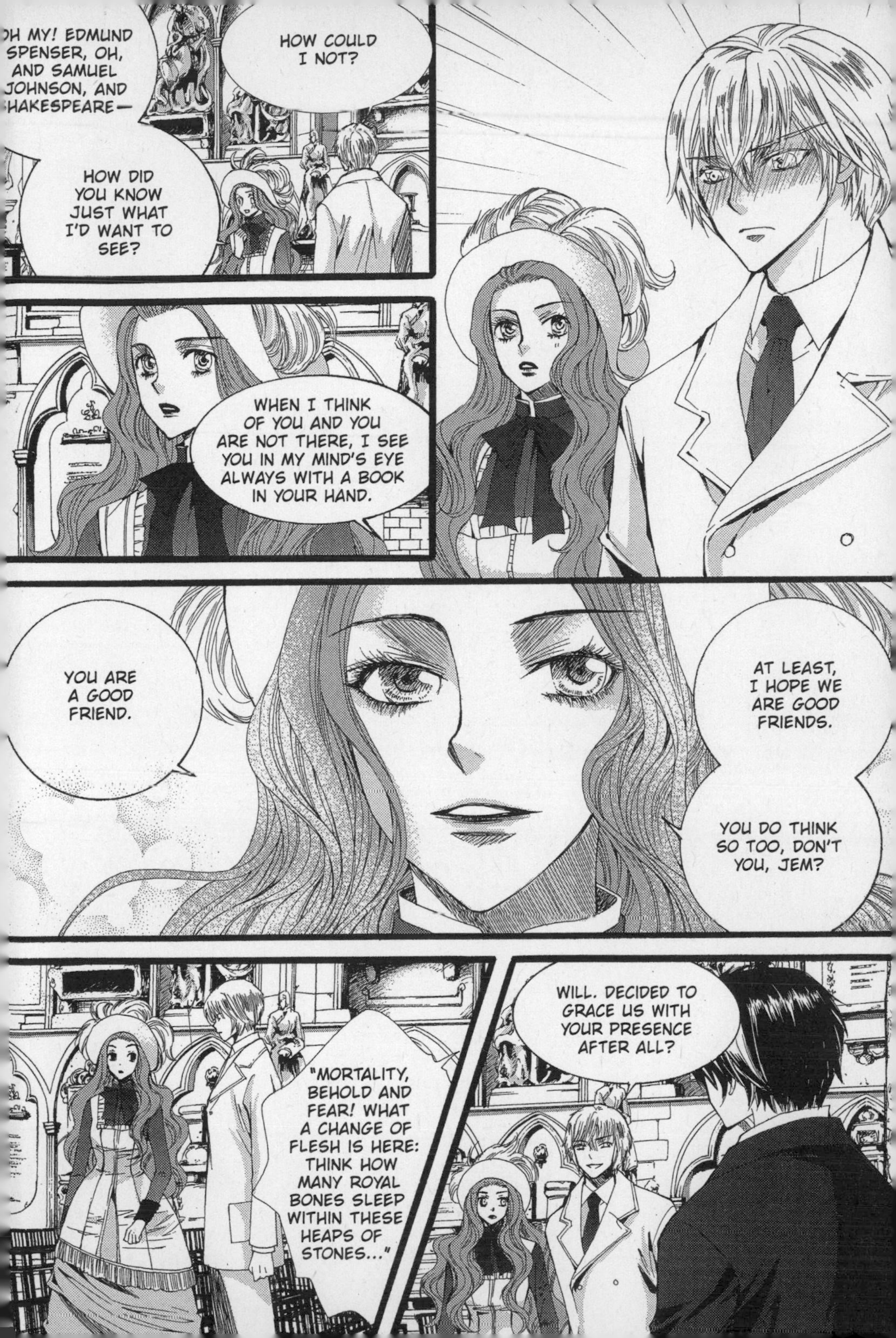
OH MY! EDMUND SPENSER, OH, AND SAMUEL JOHNSON, AND SHAKESPEARE—
HOW DID YOU KNOW JUST WHAT I'D WANT TO SEE?
HOW COULD I NOT?
WHEN I THINK OF YOU AND YOU ARE NOT THERE, I SEE YOU IN MY MIND'S EYE ALWAYS WITH A BOOK IN YOUR HAND.
YOU ARE A GOOD FRIEND.
AT LEAST, I HOPE WE ARE GOOD FRIENDS.
YOU DO THINK SO TOO, DON'T YOU, JEM?
"MORTALITY, BEHOLD AND FEAR! WHAT A CHANGE OF FLESH IS HERE: THINK HOW MANY ROYAL BONES SLEEP WITHIN THESE HEAPS OF STONES..."
WILL. DECIDED TO GRACE US WITH YOUR PRESENCE AFTER ALL?

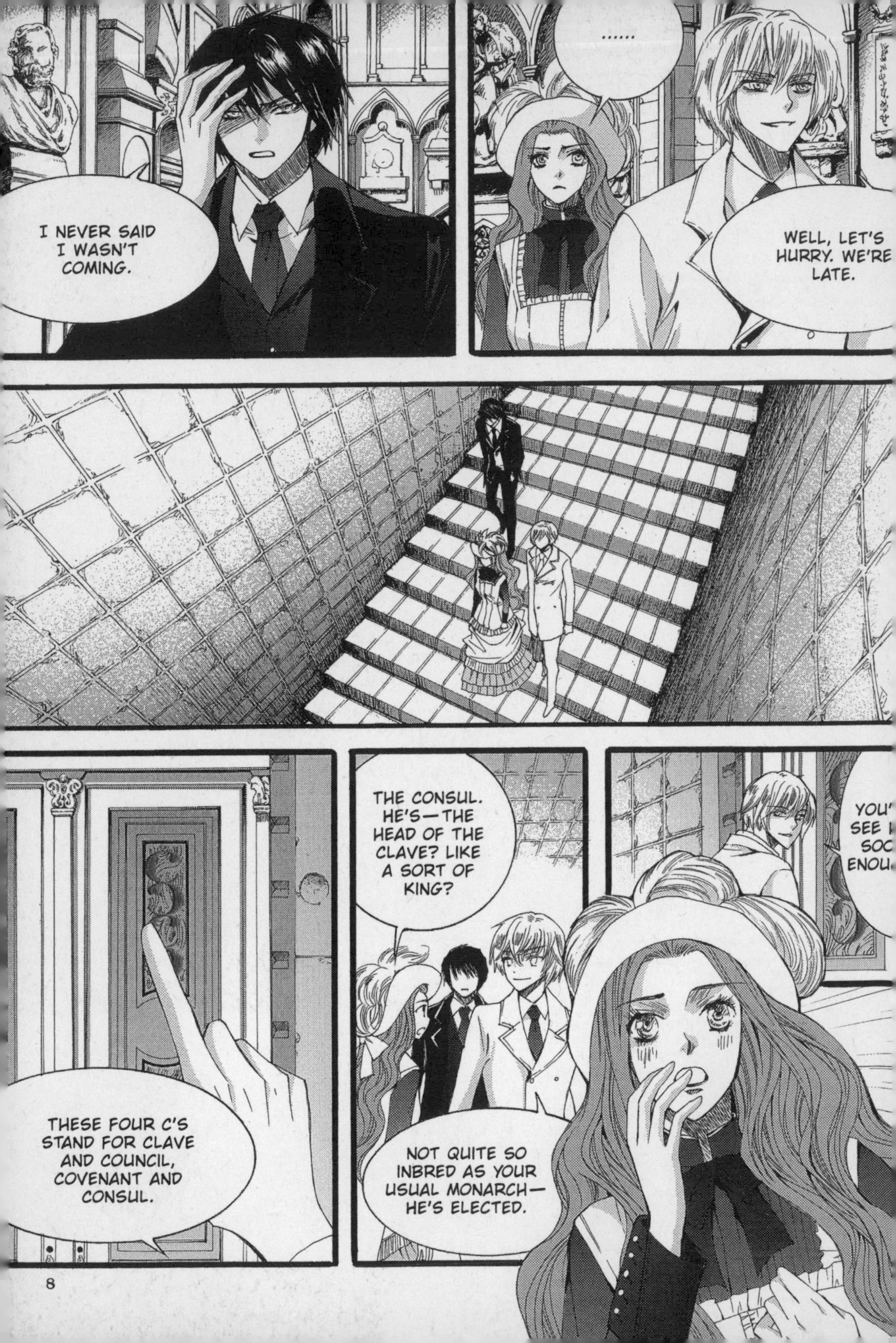
I NEVER SAID I WASN'T COMING.
......
WELL, LET'S HURRY. WE'RE LATE.
THESE FOUR C'S STAND FOR CLAVE AND COUNCIL, COVENANT AND CONSUL.
THE CONSUL. HE'S—THE HEAD OF THE CLAVE? LIKE A SORT OF KING?
NOT QUITE SO INBRED AS YOUR USUAL MONARCH—HE'S ELECTED.

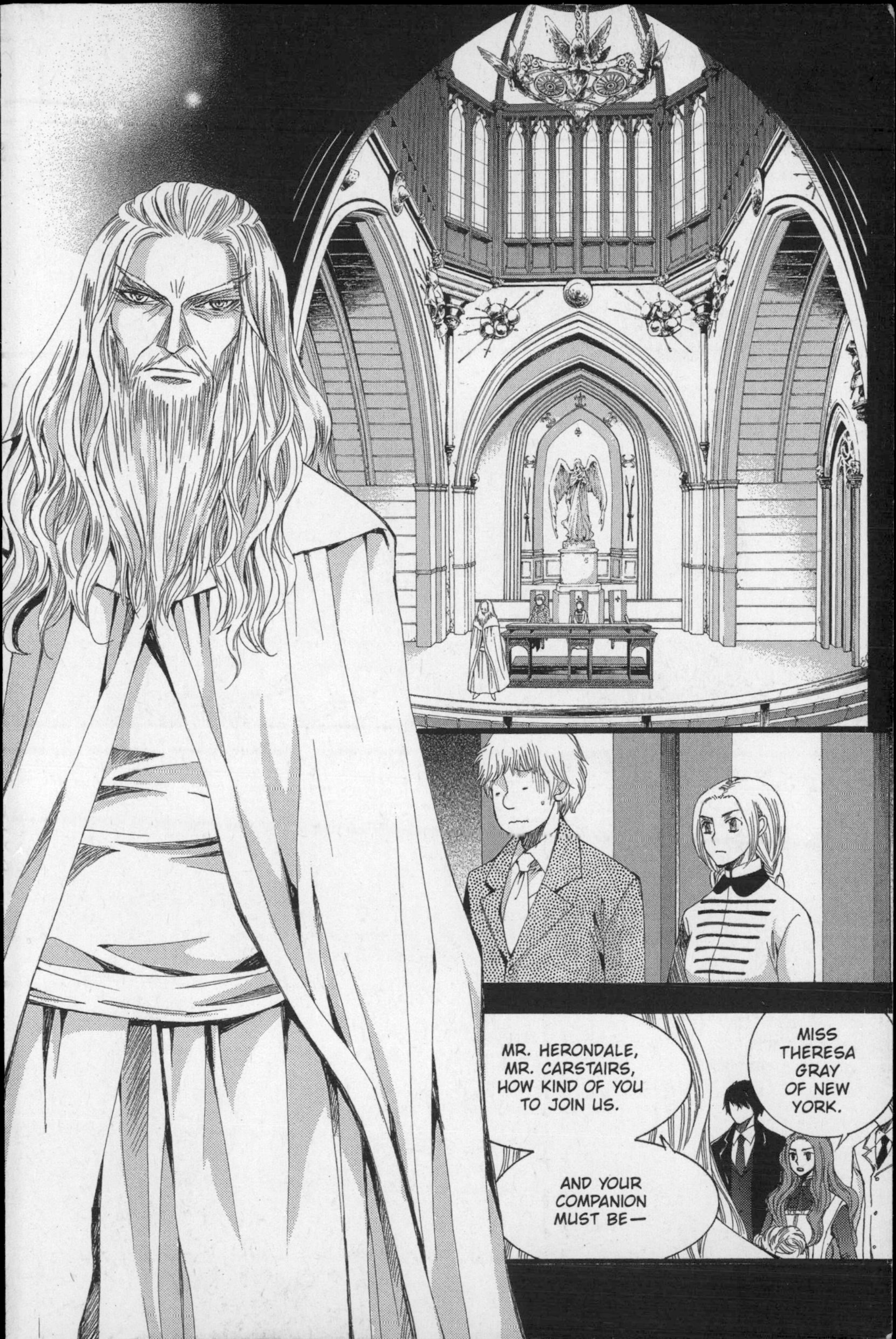
MR. HERONDALE, MR. CARSTAIRS, HOW KIND OF YOU TO JOIN US.
AND YOUR COMPANION MUST BE—
MISS THERESA GRAY OF NEW YORK.

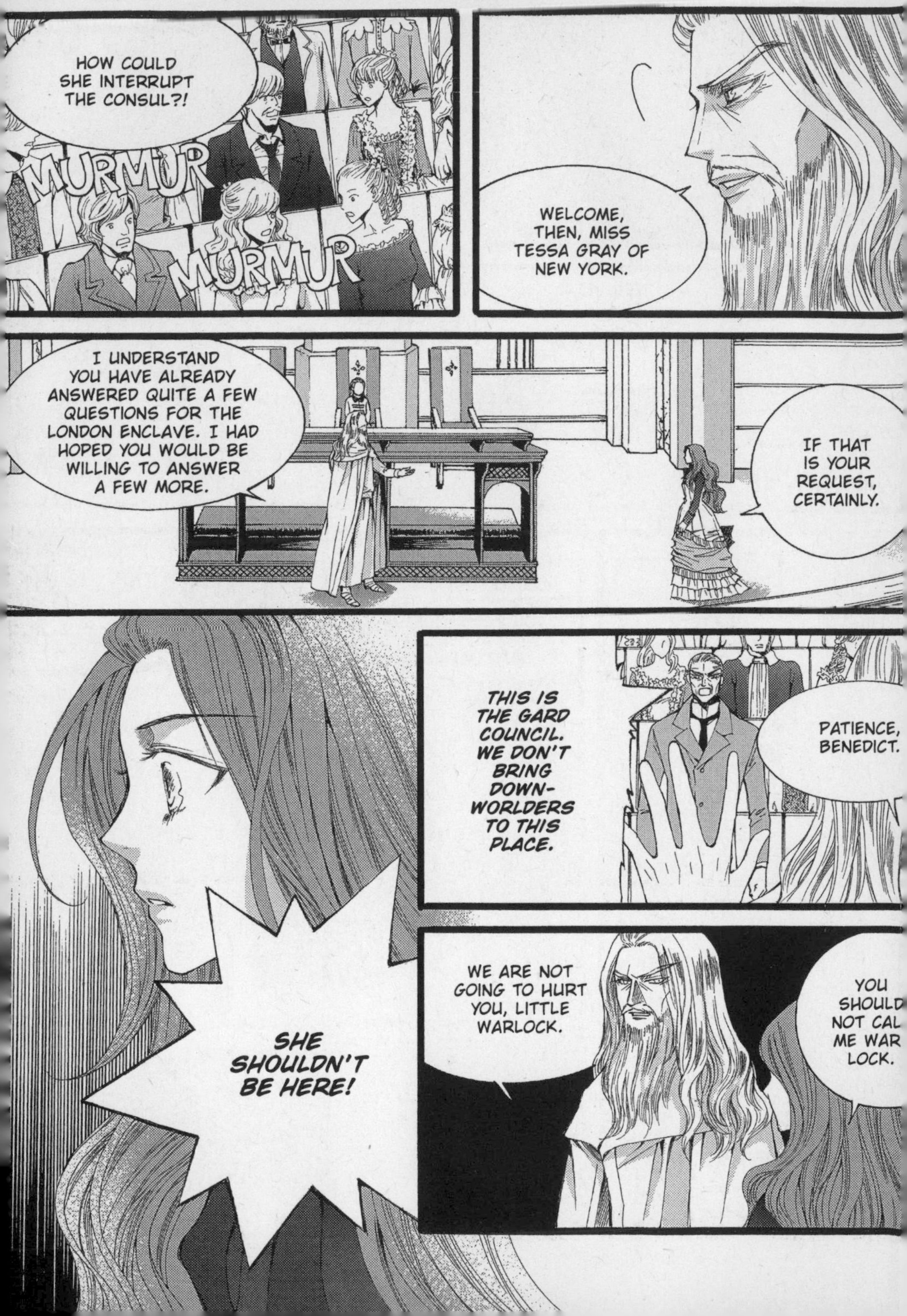
HOW COULD SHE INTERRUPT THE CONSUL?!
MURMUR
MURMUR
WELCOME, THEN, MISS TESSA GRAY OF NEW YORK.
I UNDERSTAND YOU HAVE ALREADY ANSWERED QUITE A FEW QUESTIONS FOR THE LONDON ENCLAVE. I HAD HOPED YOU WOULD BE WILLING TO ANSWER A FEW MORE.
IF THAT IS YOUR REQUEST, CERTAINLY.
THIS IS THE GARD COUNCIL. WE DON'T BRING DOWN-WORLDERS TO THIS PLACE.
PATIENCE, BENEDICT.
SHE SHOULDN'T BE HERE!
WE ARE NOT GOING TO HURT YOU, LITTLE WARLOCK.
YOU SHOULD NOT CAL ME WAR LOCK.

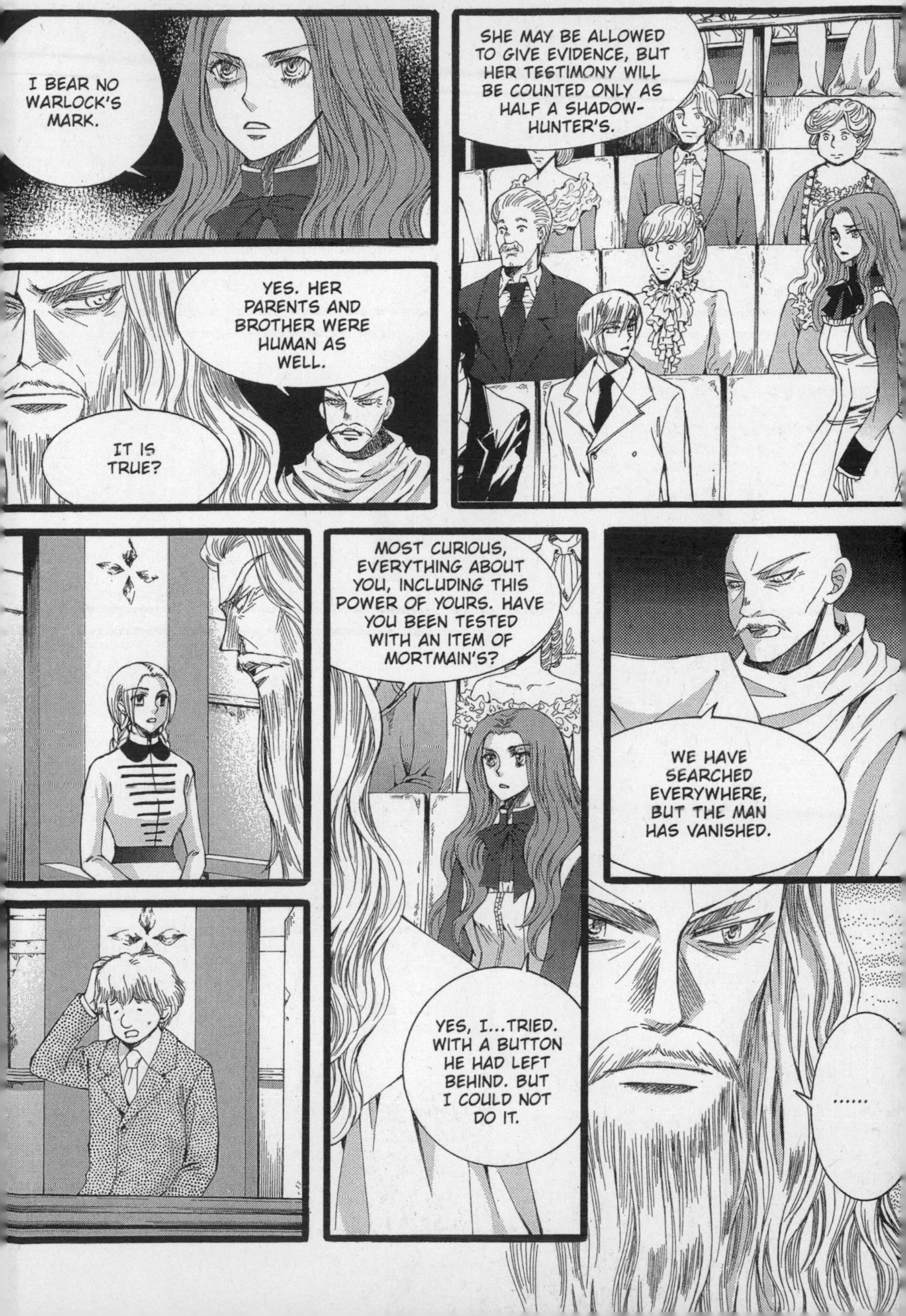
I BEAR NO WARLOCK'S MARK.
SHE MAY BE ALLOWED TO GIVE EVIDENCE, BUT HER TESTIMONY WILL BE COUNTED ONLY AS HALF A SHADOW-HUNTER'S.
YES. HER PARENTS AND BROTHER WERE HUMAN AS WELL.
IT IS TRUE?
MOST CURIOUS, EVERYTHING ABOUT YOU, INCLUDING THIS POWER OF YOURS. HAVE YOU BEEN TESTED WITH AN ITEM OF MORTMAIN'S?
WE HAVE SEARCHED EVERYWHERE, BUT THE MAN HAS VANISHED.
YES, I...TRIED. WITH A BUTTON HE HAD LEFT BEHIND. BUT I COULD NOT DO IT.
......

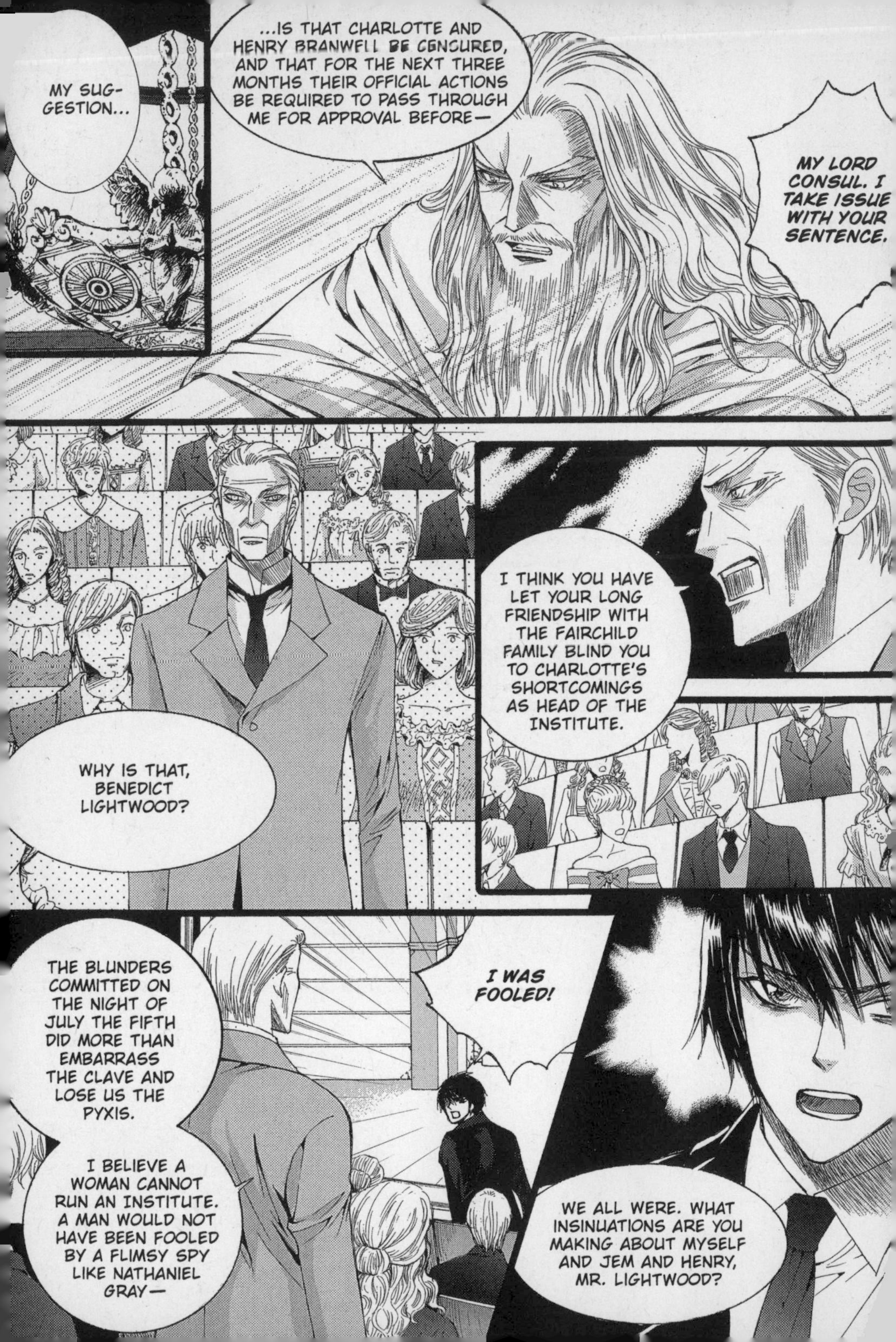
MY SUG-GESTION...
...IS THAT CHARLOTTE AND HENRY BRANWELL BE CENSURED, AND THAT FOR THE NEXT THREE MONTHS THEIR OFFICIAL ACTIONS BE REQUIRED TO PASS THROUGH ME FOR APPROVAL BEFORE—
MY LORD CONSUL. I TAKE ISSUE WITH YOUR SENTENCE.
WHY IS THAT, BENEDICT LIGHTWOOD?
I THINK YOU HAVE LET YOUR LONG FRIENDSHIP WITH THE FAIRCHILD FAMILY BLIND YOU TO CHARLOTTE'S SHORTCOMINGS AS HEAD OF THE INSTITUTE.
THE BLUNDERS COMMITTED ON THE NIGHT OF JULY THE FIFTH DID MORE THAN EMBARRASS THE CLAVE AND LOSE US THE PYXIS.
I BELIEVE A WOMAN CANNOT RUN AN INSTITUTE. A MAN WOULD NOT HAVE BEEN FOOLED BY A FLIMSY SPY LIKE NATHANIEL GRAY—
I WAS FOOLED!
WE ALL WERE. WHAT INSINUATIONS ARE YOU MAKING ABOUT MYSELF AND JEM AND HENRY, MR. LIGHTWOOD?

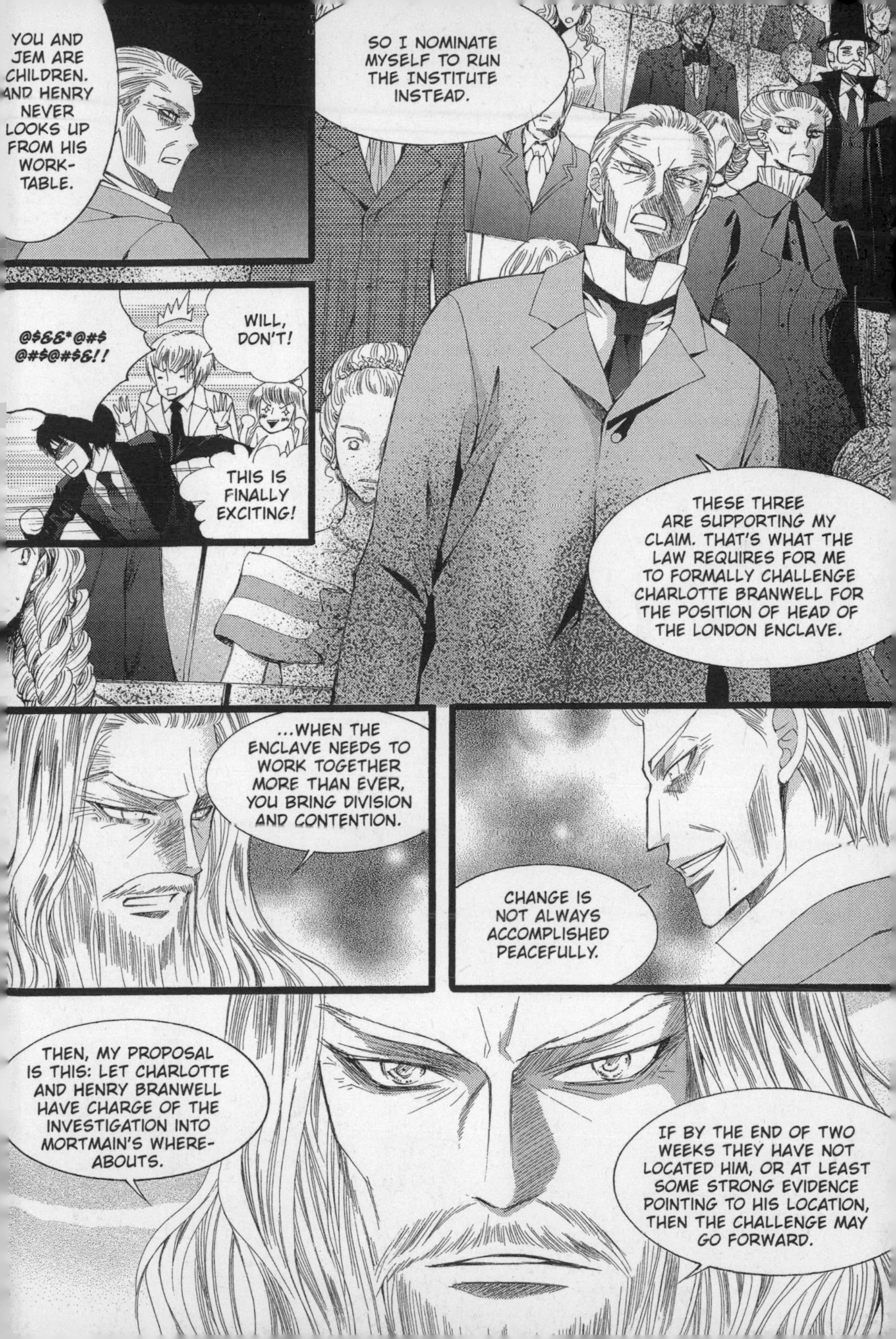
YOU AND JEM ARE CHILDREN. AND HENRY NEVER LOOKS UP FROM HIS WORK-TABLE.
SO I NOMINATE MYSELF TO RUN THE INSTITUTE INSTEAD.
@$&&*@#$ @#$@#$&!!
WILL, DON'T!
THIS IS FINALLY EXCITING!
THESE THREE ARE SUPPORTING MY CLAIM. THAT'S WHAT THE LAW REQUIRES FOR ME TO FORMALLY CHALLENGE CHARLOTTE BRANWELL FOR THE POSITION OF HEAD OF THE LONDON ENCLAVE.
...WHEN THE ENCLAVE NEEDS TO WORK TOGETHER MORE THAN EVER, YOU BRING DIVISION AND CONTENTION.
CHANGE IS NOT ALWAYS ACCOMPLISHED PEACEFULLY.
THEN, MY PROPOSAL IS THIS: LET CHARLOTTE AND HENRY BRANWELL HAVE CHARGE OF THE INVESTIGATION INTO MORTMAIN'S WHERE-ABOUTS.
IF BY THE END OF TWO WEEKS THEY HAVE NOT LOCATED HIM, OR AT LEAST SOME STRONG EVIDENCE POINTING TO HIS LOCATION, THEN THE CHALLENGE MAY GO FORWARD.

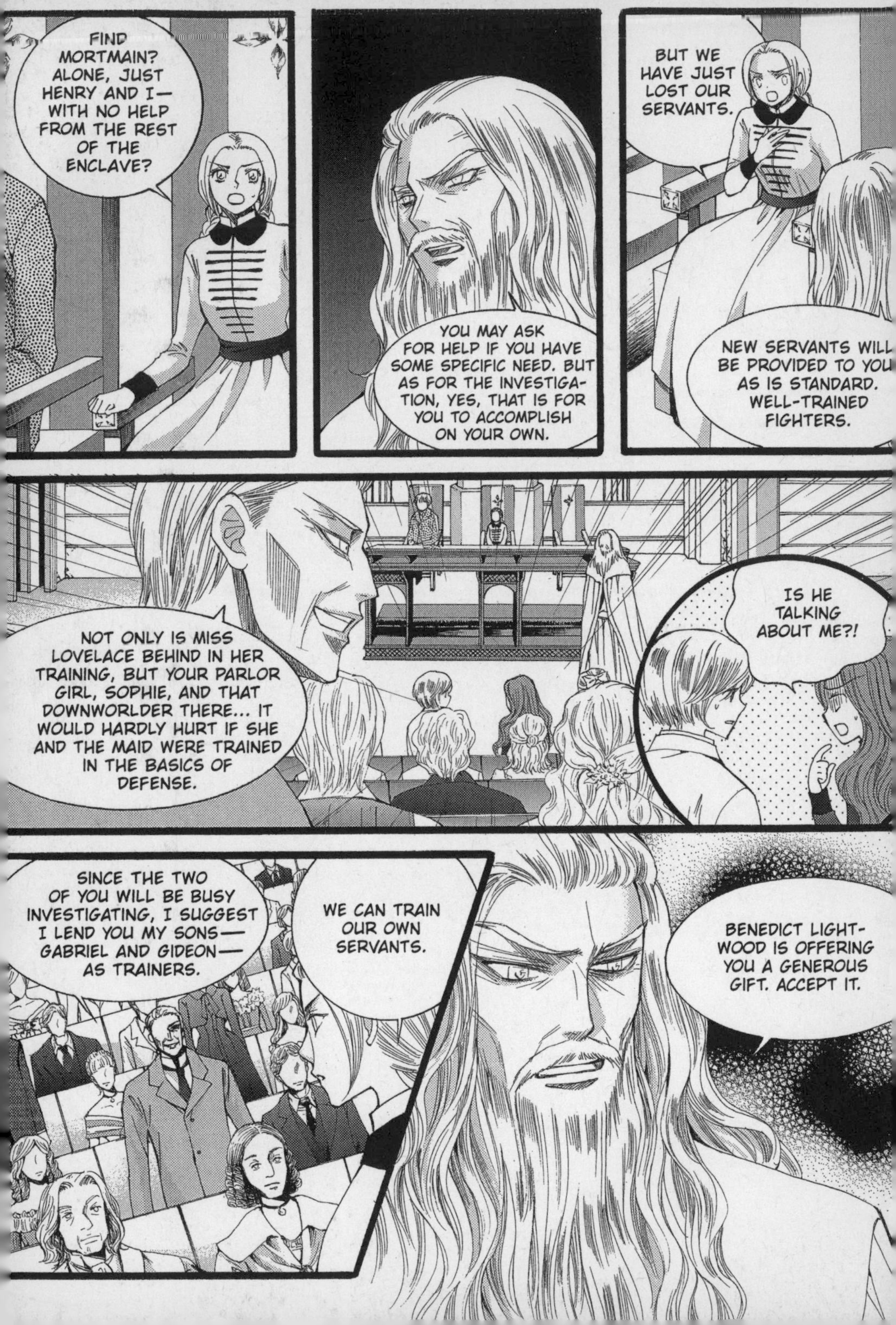
FIND MORTMAIN? ALONE, JUST HENRY AND I— WITH NO HELP FROM THE REST OF THE ENCLAVE?
YOU MAY ASK FOR HELP IF YOU HAVE SOME SPECIFIC NEED. BUT AS FOR THE INVESTIGATION, YES, THAT IS FOR YOU TO ACCOMPLISH ON YOUR OWN.
BUT WE HAVE JUST LOST OUR SERVANTS.
NEW SERVANTS WILL BE PROVIDED TO YOU AS IS STANDARD. WELL-TRAINED FIGHTERS.
NOT ONLY IS MISS LOVELACE BEHIND IN HER TRAINING, BUT YOUR PARLOR GIRL, SOPHIE, AND THAT DOWNWORLDER THERE... IT WOULD HARDLY HURT IF SHE AND THE MAID WERE TRAINED IN THE BASICS OF DEFENSE.
IS HE TALKING ABOUT ME?!
SINCE THE TWO OF YOU WILL BE BUSY INVESTIGATING, I SUGGEST I LEND YOU MY SONS— GABRIEL AND GIDEON— AS TRAINERS.
WE CAN TRAIN OUR OWN SERVANTS.
BENEDICT LIGHTWOOD IS OFFERING YOU A GENEROUS GIFT. ACCEPT IT.

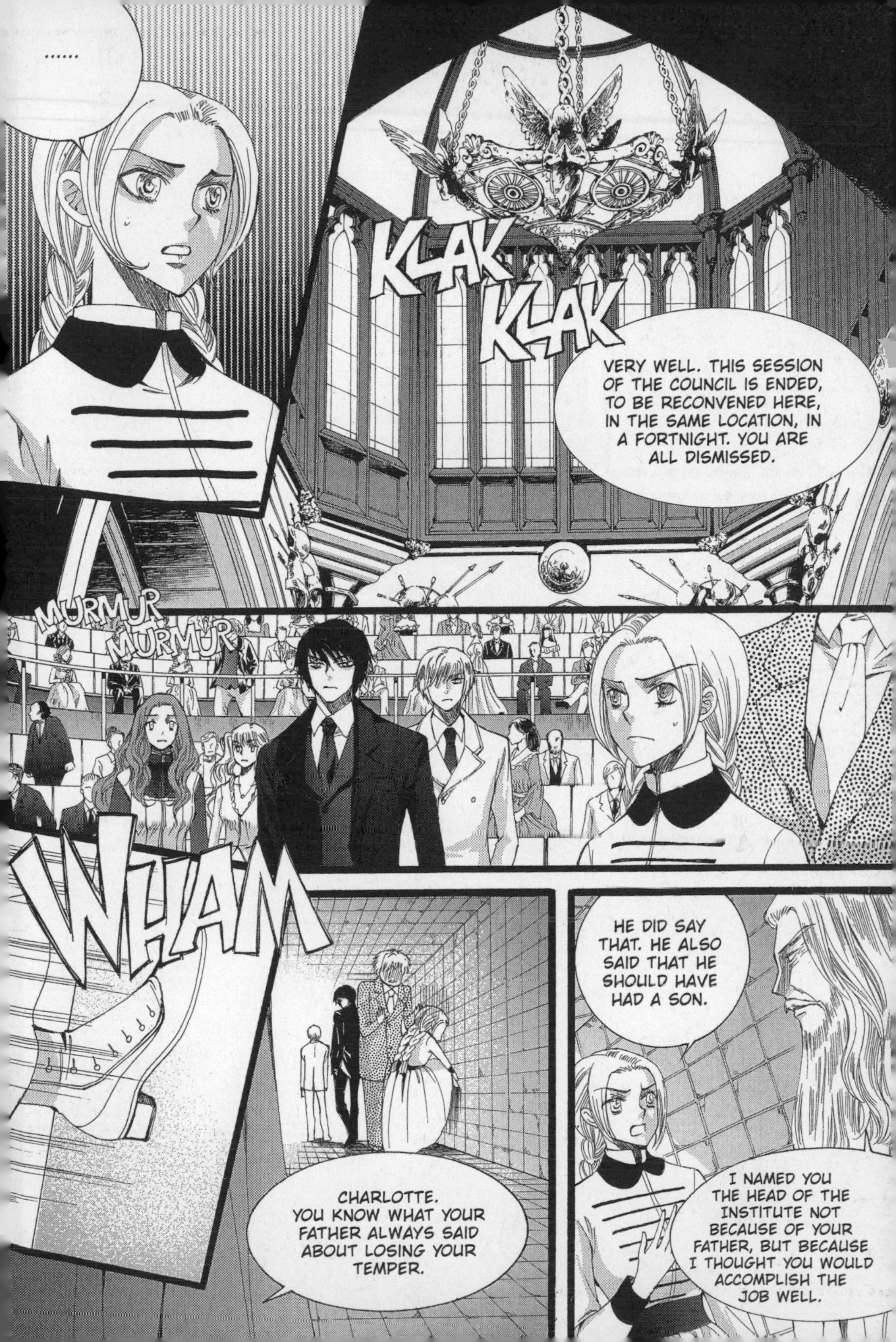
......
KLAK KLAK
VERY WELL. THIS SESSION OF THE COUNCIL IS ENDED, TO BE RECONVENED HERE, IN THE SAME LOCATION, IN A FORTNIGHT. YOU ARE ALL DISMISSED.
MURMUR MURMUR
WHAM
CHARLOTTE. YOU KNOW WHAT YOUR FATHER ALWAYS SAID ABOUT LOSING YOUR TEMPER.
HE DID SAY THAT. HE ALSO SAID THAT HE SHOULD HAVE HAD A SON.
I NAMED YOU THE HEAD OF THE INSTITUTE NOT BECAUSE OF YOUR FATHER, BUT BECAUSE I THOUGHT YOU WOULD ACCOMPLISH THE JOB WELL.

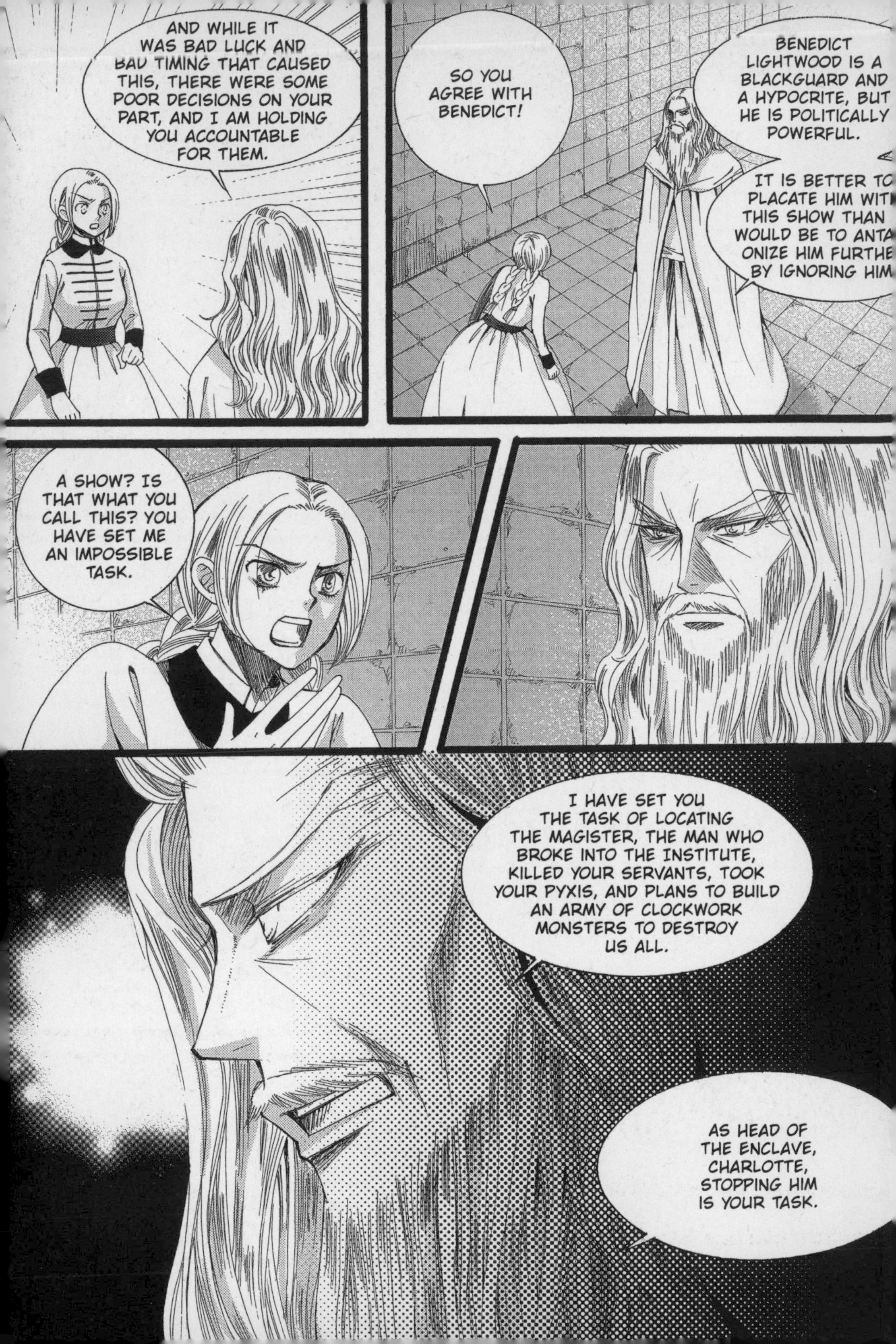
AND WHILE IT WAS BAD LUCK AND BAD TIMING THAT CAUSED THIS, THERE WERE SOME POOR DECISIONS ON YOUR PART, AND I AM HOLDING YOU ACCOUNTABLE FOR THEM.
SO YOU AGREE WITH BENEDICT!
BENEDICT LIGHTWOOD IS A BLACKGUARD AND A HYPOCRITE, BUT HE IS POLITICALLY POWERFUL.
IT IS BETTER TO PLACATE HIM WITH THIS SHOW THAN WOULD BE TO ANTAG ONIZE HIM FURTHE BY IGNORING HIM
A SHOW? IS THAT WHAT YOU CALL THIS? YOU HAVE SET ME AN IMPOSSIBLE TASK.
I HAVE SET YOU THE TASK OF LOCATING THE MAGISTER, THE MAN WHO BROKE INTO THE INSTITUTE, KILLED YOUR SERVANTS, TOOK YOUR PYXIS, AND PLANS TO BUILD AN ARMY OF CLOCKWORK MONSTERS TO DESTROY US ALL.
AS HEAD OF THE ENCLAVE, CHARLOTTE, STOPPING HIM IS YOUR TASK.

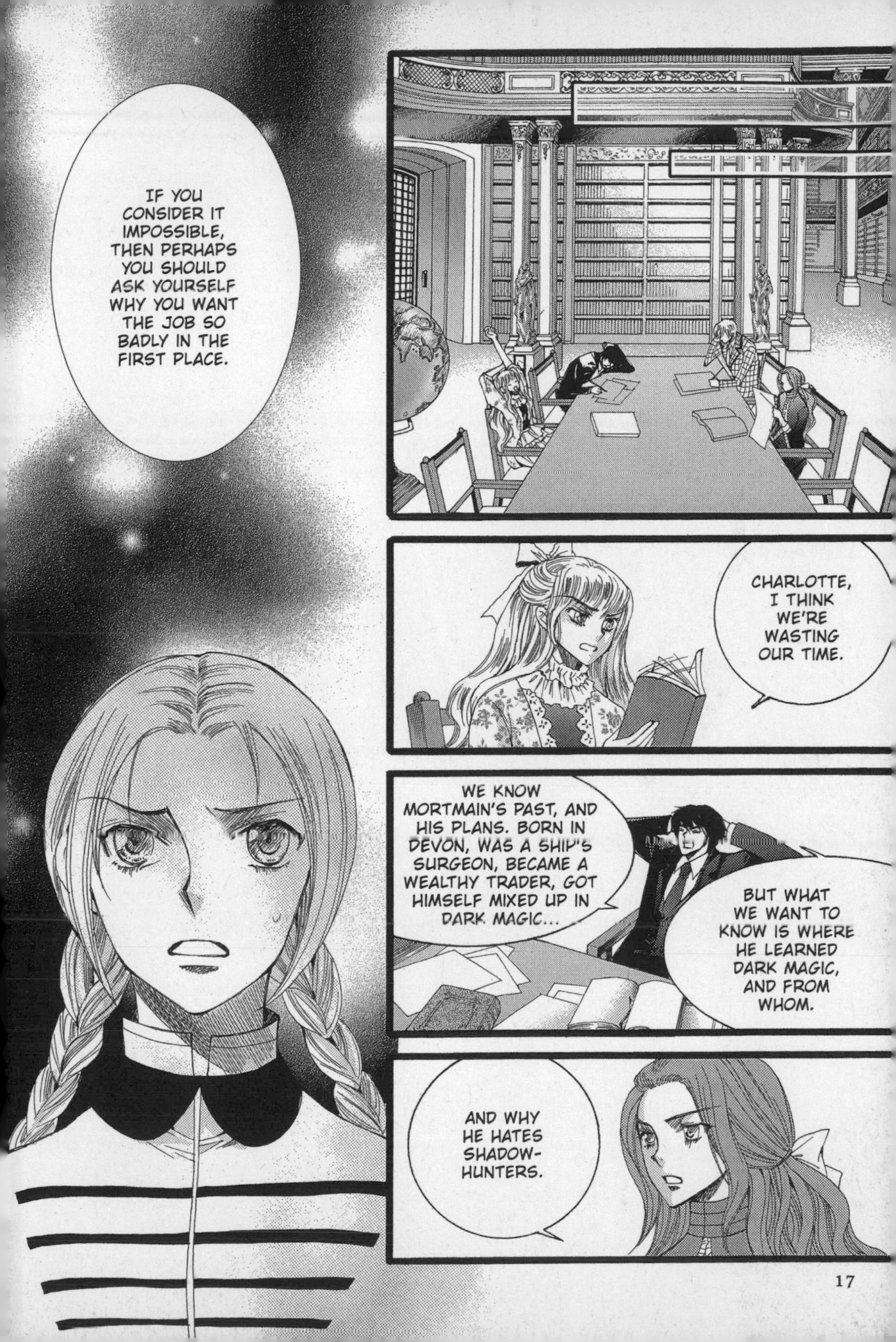
IF YOU CONSIDER IT IMPOSSIBLE, THEN PERHAPS YOU SHOULD ASK YOURSELF WHY YOU WANT THE JOB SO BADLY IN THE FIRST PLACE.
CHARLOTTE, I THINK WE'RE WASTING OUR TIME.
WE KNOW MORTMAIN'S PAST, AND HIS PLANS. BORN IN DEVON, WAS A SHIP'S SURGEON, BECAME A WEALTHY TRADER, GOT HIMSELF MIXED UP IN DARK MAGIC...
BUT WHAT WE WANT TO KNOW IS WHERE HE LEARNED DARK MAGIC, AND FROM WHOM.
AND WHY HE HATES SHADOW-HUNTERS.

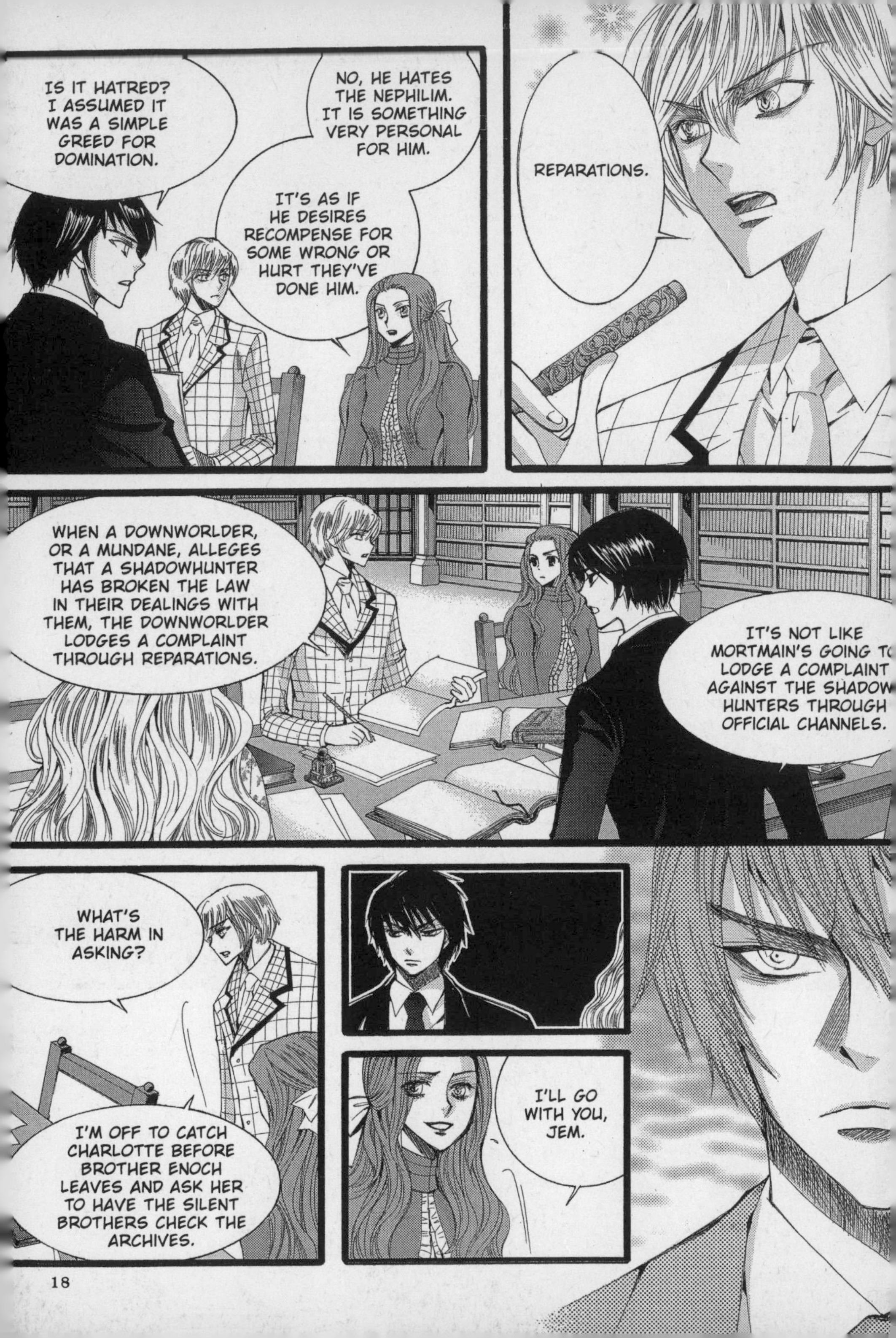

IS IT HATRED? I ASSUMED IT WAS A SIMPLE GREED FOR DOMINATION.
NO, HE HATES THE NEPHILIM. IT IS SOMETHING VERY PERSONAL FOR HIM.
IT'S AS IF HE DESIRES RECOMPENSE FOR SOME WRONG OR HURT THEY'VE DONE HIM.
REPARATIONS.
WHEN A DOWNWORLDER, OR A MUNDANE, ALLEGES THAT A SHADOWHUNTER HAS BROKEN THE LAW IN THEIR DEALINGS WITH THEM, THE DOWNWORLDER LODGES A COMPLAINT THROUGH REPARATIONS.
IT'S NOT LIKE MORTMAIN'S GOING T LODGE A COMPLAINT AGAINST THE SHADOW HUNTERS THROUGH OFFICIAL CHANNELS.
WHAT'S THE HARM IN ASKING?
I'M OFF TO CATCH CHARLOTTE BEFORE BROTHER ENOCH LEAVES AND ASK HER TO HAVE THE SILENT BROTHERS CHECK THE ARCHIVES.
I'LL GO WITH YOU, JEM.

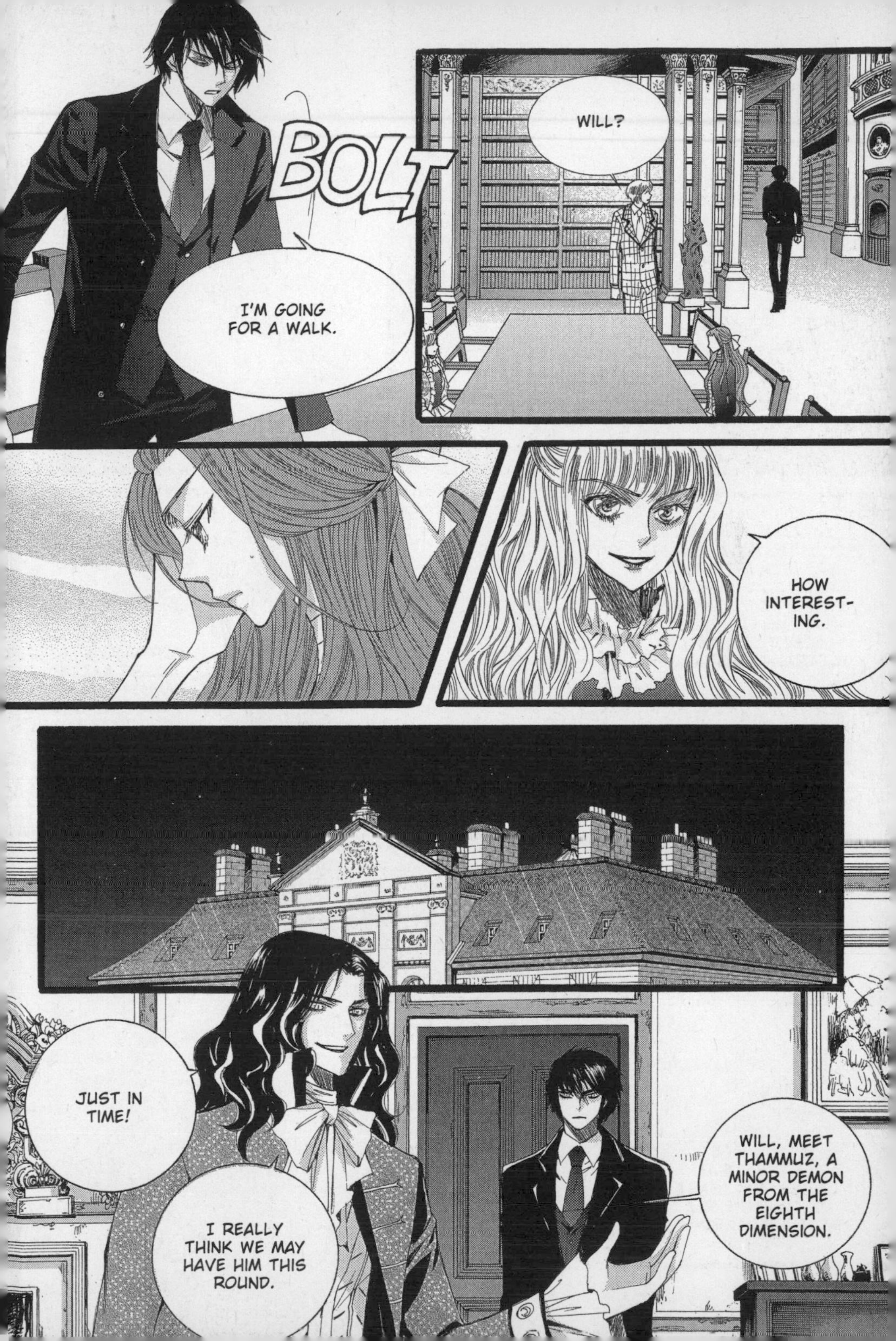
BOLT
I'M GOING FOR A WALK.
WILL?
HOW INTEREST-ING.
JUST IN TIME!
I REALLY THINK WE MAY HAVE HIM THIS ROUND.
WILL, MEET THAMMUZ, A MINOR DEMON FROM THE EIGHTH DIMENSION.

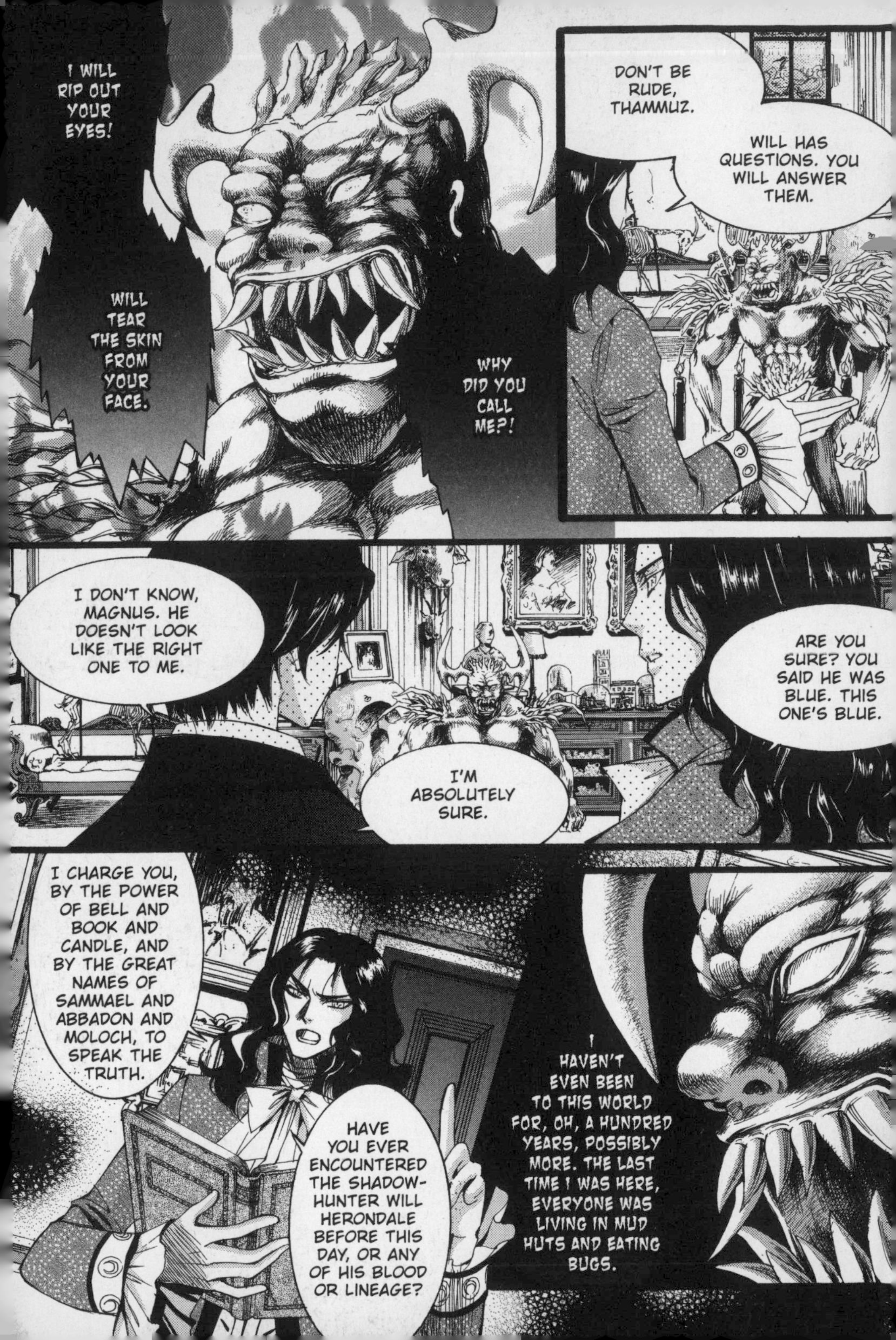
I WILL RIP OUT YOUR EYES!
WILL TEAR THE SKIN FROM YOUR FACE.
WHY DID YOU CALL ME?!
DON'T BE RUDE, THAMMUZ.
WILL HAS QUESTIONS. YOU WILL ANSWER THEM.
I DON'T KNOW, MAGNUS. HE DOESN'T LOOK LIKE THE RIGHT ONE TO ME.
ARE YOU SURE? YOU SAID HE WAS BLUE. THIS ONE'S BLUE.
I'M ABSOLUTELY SURE.
I CHARGE YOU, BY THE POWER OF BELL AND BOOK AND CANDLE, AND BY THE GREAT NAMES OF SAMMAEL AND ABBADON AND MOLOCH, TO SPEAK THE TRUTH.
HAVE YOU EVER ENCOUNTERED THE SHADOW-HUNTER WILL HERONDALE BEFORE THIS DAY, OR ANY OF HIS BLOOD OR LINEAGE?
I HAVEN'T EVEN BEEN TO THIS WORLD FOR, OH, A HUNDRED YEARS, POSSIBLY MORE. THE LAST TIME I WAS HERE, EVERYONE WAS LIVING IN MUD HUTS AND EATING BUGS.

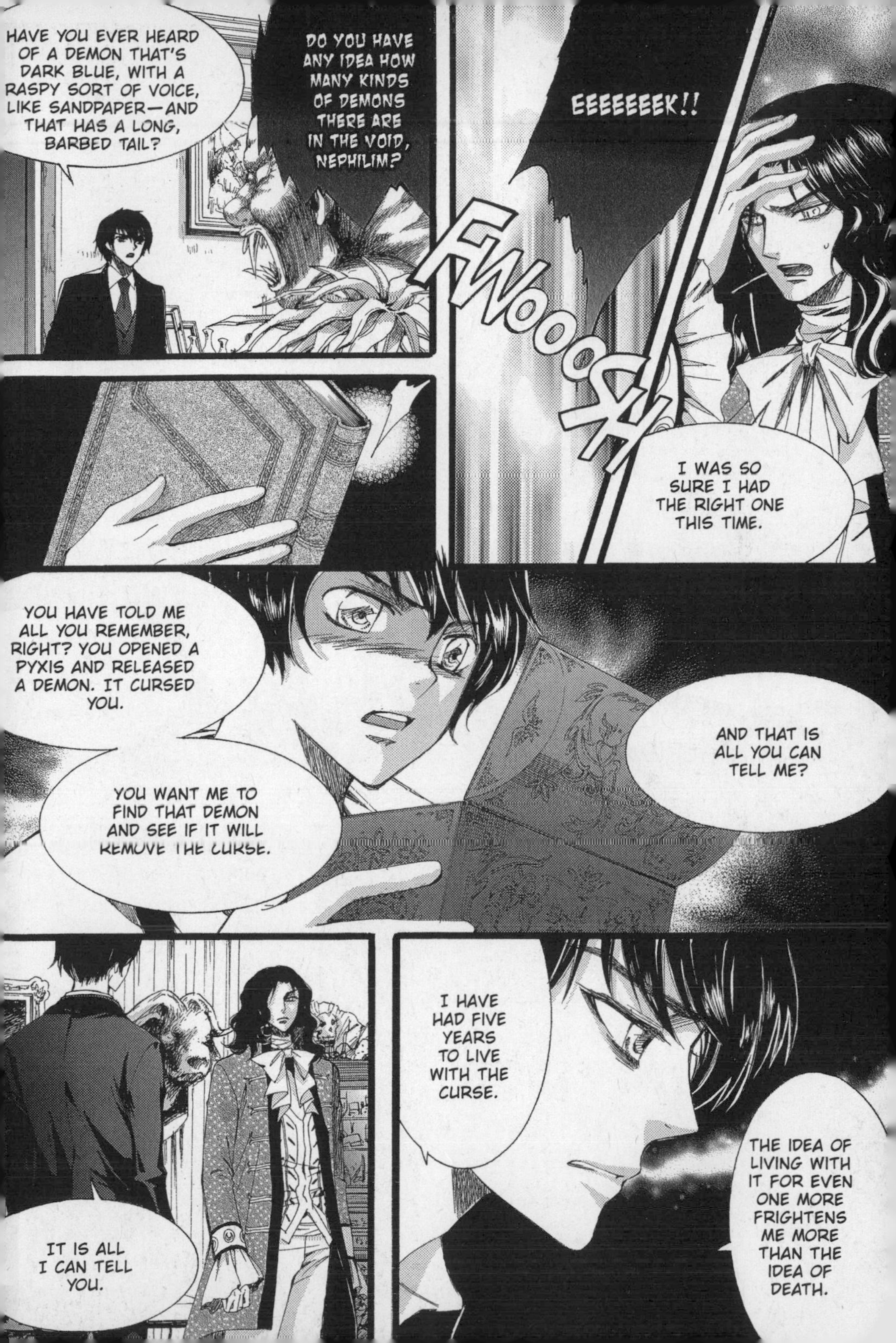
HAVE YOU EVER HEARD OF A DEMON THAT'S DARK BLUE, WITH A RASPY SORT OF VOICE, LIKE SANDPAPER—AND THAT HAS A LONG, BARBED TAIL?
DO YOU HAVE ANY IDEA HOW MANY KINDS OF DEMONS THERE ARE IN THE VOID, NEPHILIM?
EEEEEEEK!!
FWOOOSH
I WAS SO SURE I HAD THE RIGHT ONE THIS TIME.
YOU HAVE TOLD ME ALL YOU REMEMBER, RIGHT? YOU OPENED A PYXIS AND RELEASED A DEMON. IT CURSED YOU.
YOU WANT ME TO FIND THAT DEMON AND SEE IF IT WILL REMOVE THE CURSE.
AND THAT IS ALL YOU CAN TELL ME?
IT IS ALL I CAN TELL YOU.
I HAVE HAD FIVE YEARS TO LIVE WITH THE CURSE.
THE IDEA OF LIVING WITH IT FOR EVEN ONE MORE FRIGHTENS ME MORE THAN THE IDEA OF DEATH.

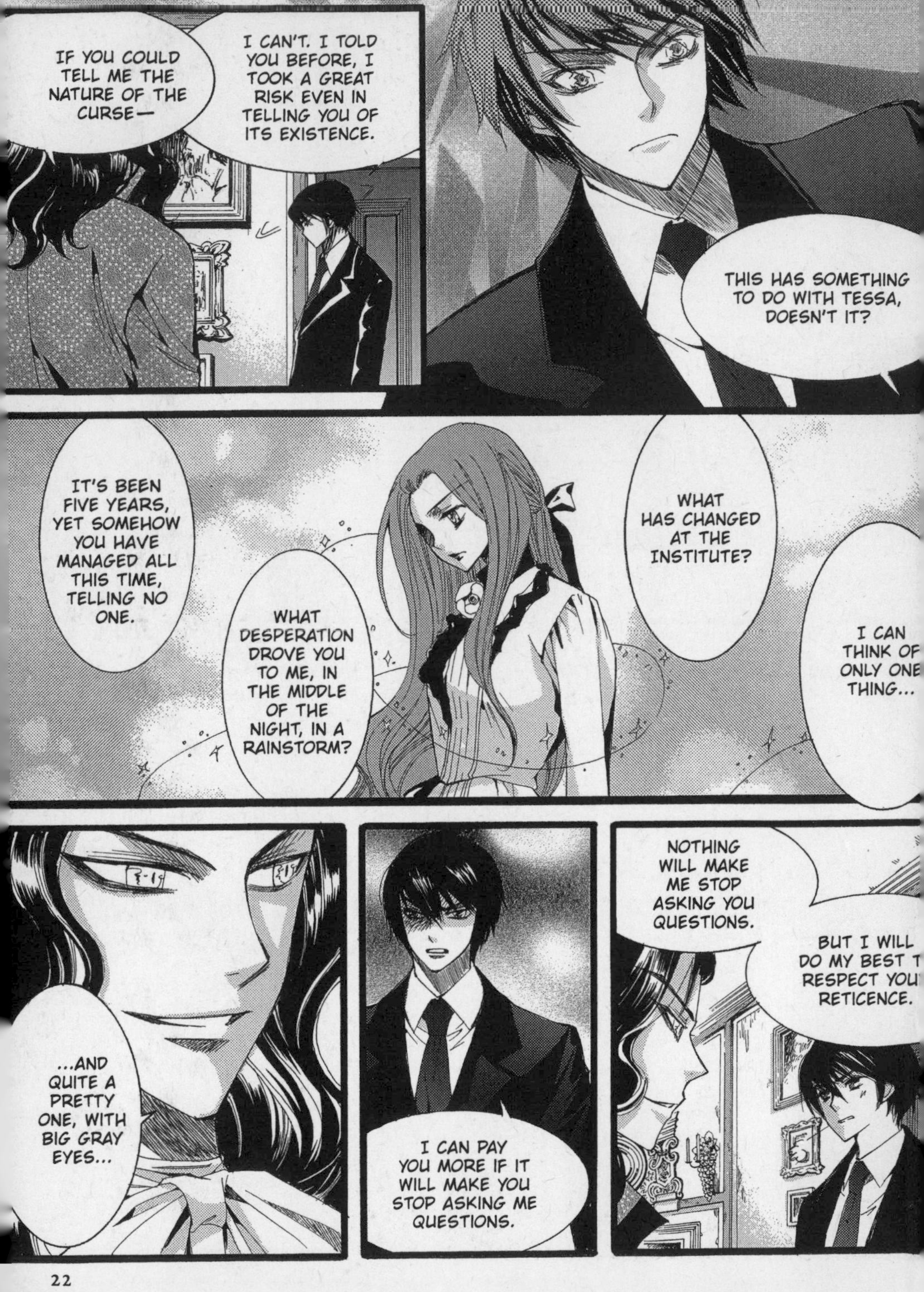
IF YOU COULD TELL ME THE NATURE OF THE CURSE—
I CAN'T. I TOLD YOU BEFORE, I TOOK A GREAT RISK EVEN IN TELLING YOU OF ITS EXISTENCE.
THIS HAS SOMETHING TO DO WITH TESSA, DOESN'T IT?
IT'S BEEN FIVE YEARS, YET SOMEHOW YOU HAVE MANAGED ALL THIS TIME, TELLING NO ONE.
WHAT DESPERATION DROVE YOU TO ME, IN THE MIDDLE OF THE NIGHT, IN A RAINSTORM?
WHAT HAS CHANGED AT THE INSTITUTE?
I CAN THINK OF ONLY ONE THING...
...AND QUITE A PRETTY ONE, WITH BIG GRAY EYES...
I CAN PAY YOU MORE IF IT WILL MAKE YOU STOP ASKING ME QUESTIONS.
NOTHING WILL MAKE ME STOP ASKING YOU QUESTIONS.
BUT I WILL DO MY BEST T RESPECT YOU RETICENCE.

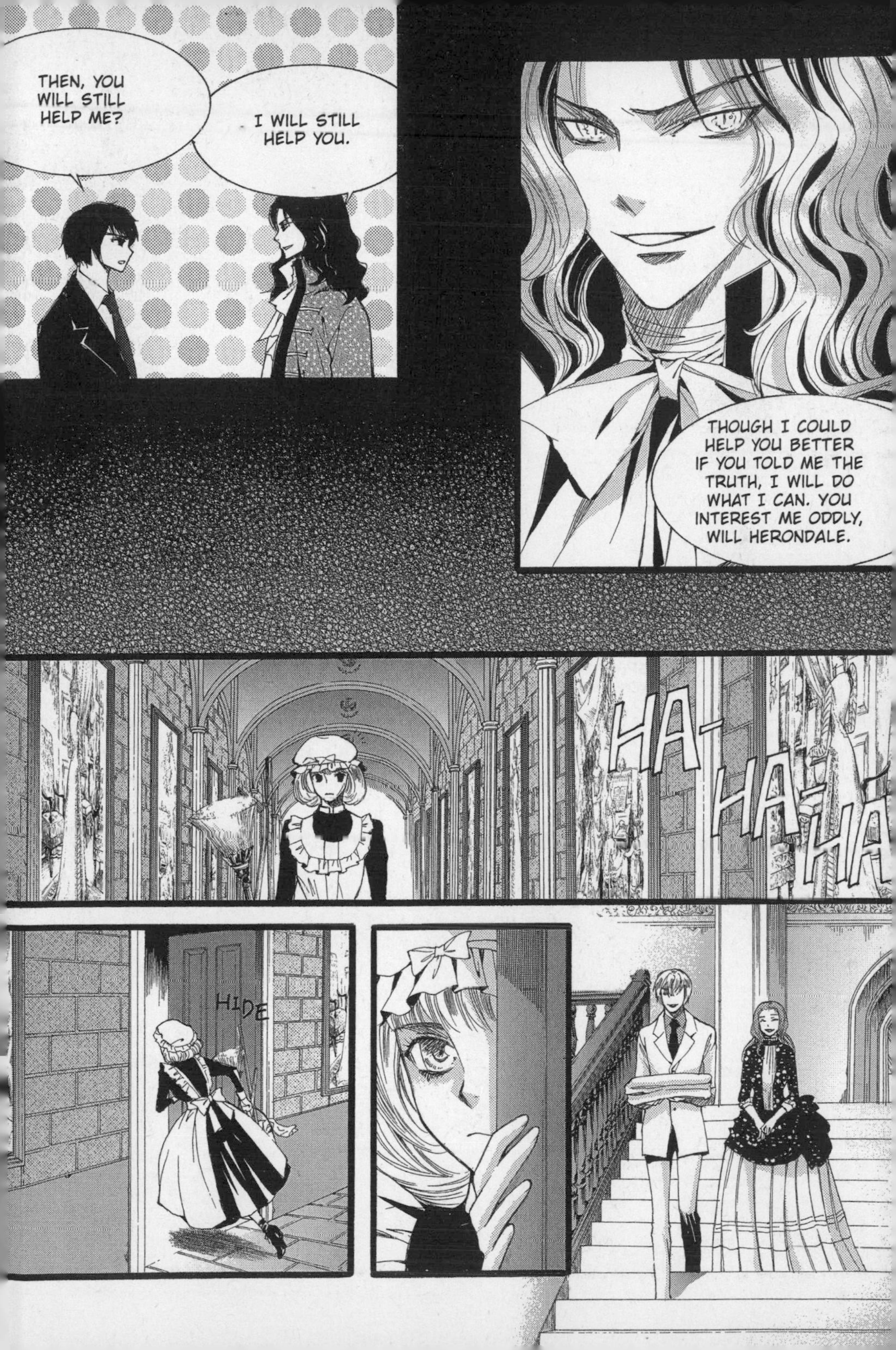
THEN, YOU WILL STILL HELP ME?
I WILL STILL HELP YOU.
THOUGH I COULD HELP YOU BETTER IF YOU TOLD ME THE TRUTH, I WILL DO WHAT I CAN. YOU INTEREST ME ODDLY, WILL HERONDALE.
HA-HA-HA-HA
HIDE

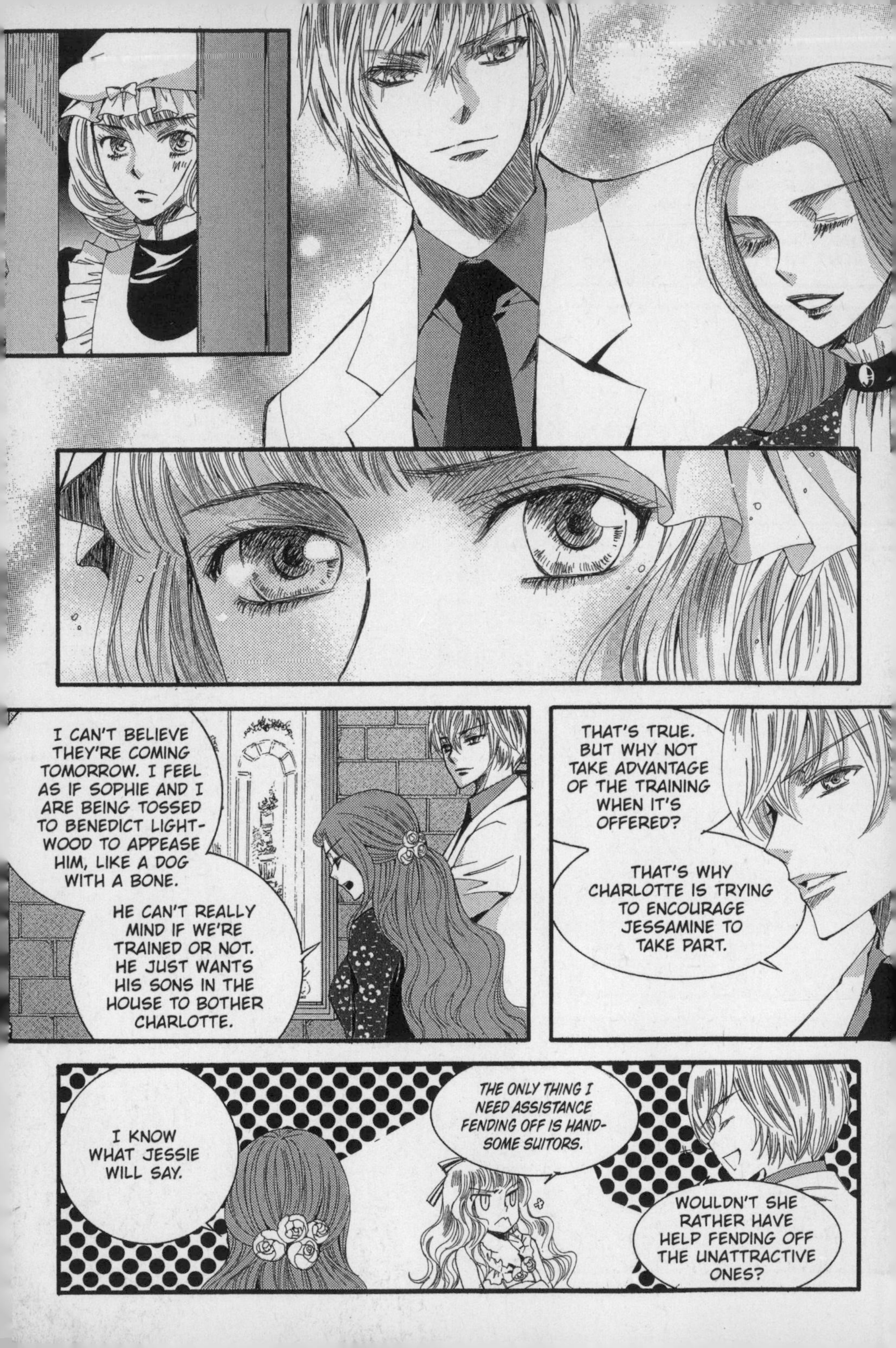
I CAN'T BELIEVE THEY'RE COMING TOMORROW. I FEEL AS IF SOPHIE AND I ARE BEING TOSSED TO BENEDICT LIGHT-WOOD TO APPEASE HIM, LIKE A DOG WITH A BONE.
HE CAN'T REALLY MIND IF WE'RE TRAINED OR NOT. HE JUST WANTS HIS SONS IN THE HOUSE TO BOTHER CHARLOTTE.
THAT'S TRUE. BUT WHY NOT TAKE ADVANTAGE OF THE TRAINING WHEN IT'S OFFERED?
THAT'S WHY CHARLOTTE IS TRYING TO ENCOURAGE JESSAMINE TO TAKE PART.
I KNOW WHAT JESSIE WILL SAY.
THE ONLY THING I NEED ASSISTANCE FENDING OFF IS HAND-SOME SUITORS.
WOULDN'T SHE RATHER HAVE HELP FENDING OFF THE UNATTRACTIVE ONES?

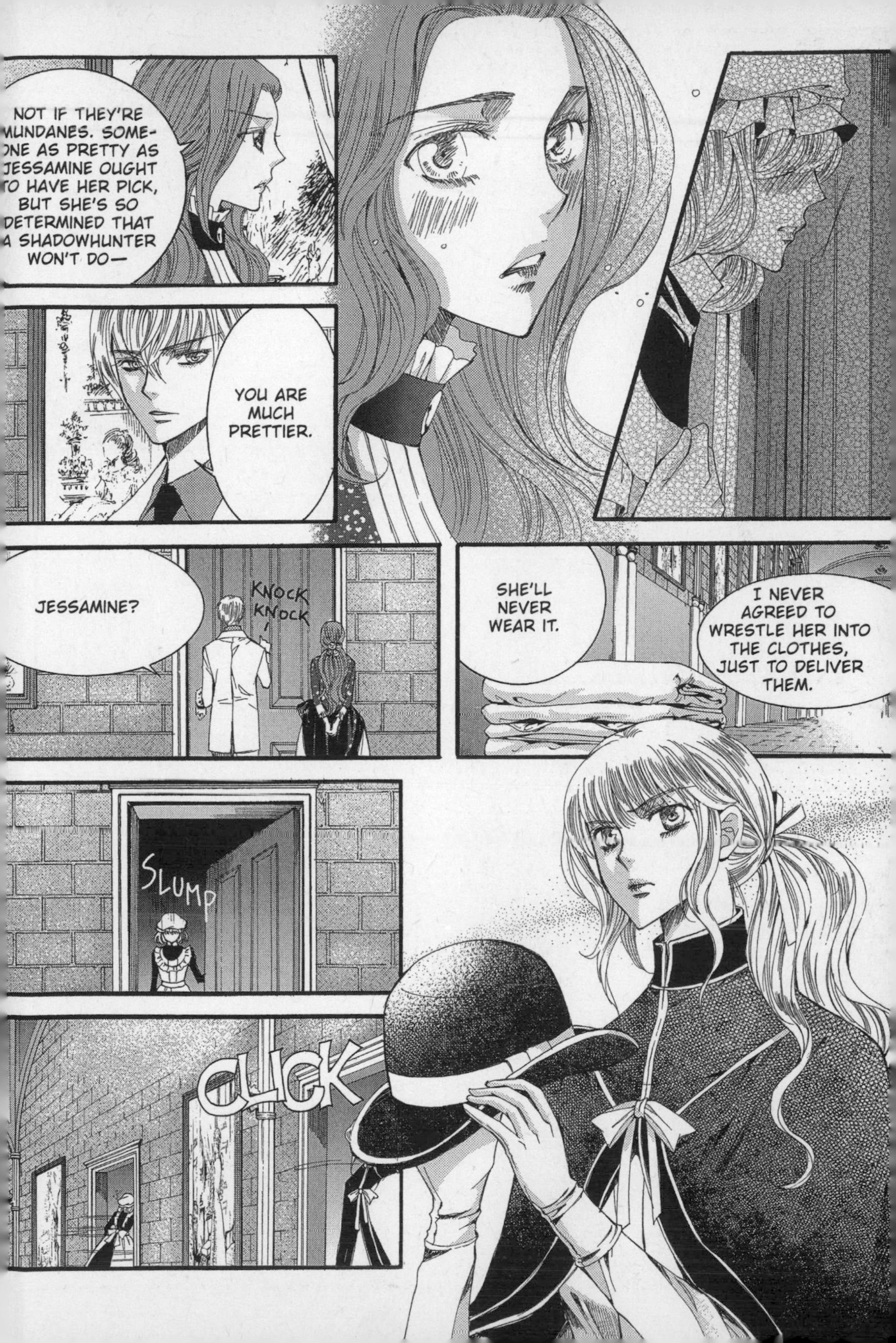
NOT IF THEY'RE MUNDANES. SOME-ONE AS PRETTY AS JESSAMINE OUGHT TO HAVE HER PICK, BUT SHE'S SO DETERMINED THAT A SHADOWHUNTER WON'T DO—
YOU ARE MUCH PRETTIER.
JESSAMINE?
KNOCK KNOCK
SHE'LL NEVER WEAR IT.
I NEVER AGREED TO WRESTLE HER INTO THE CLOTHES, JUST TO DELIVER THEM.
SLUMP
CLICK

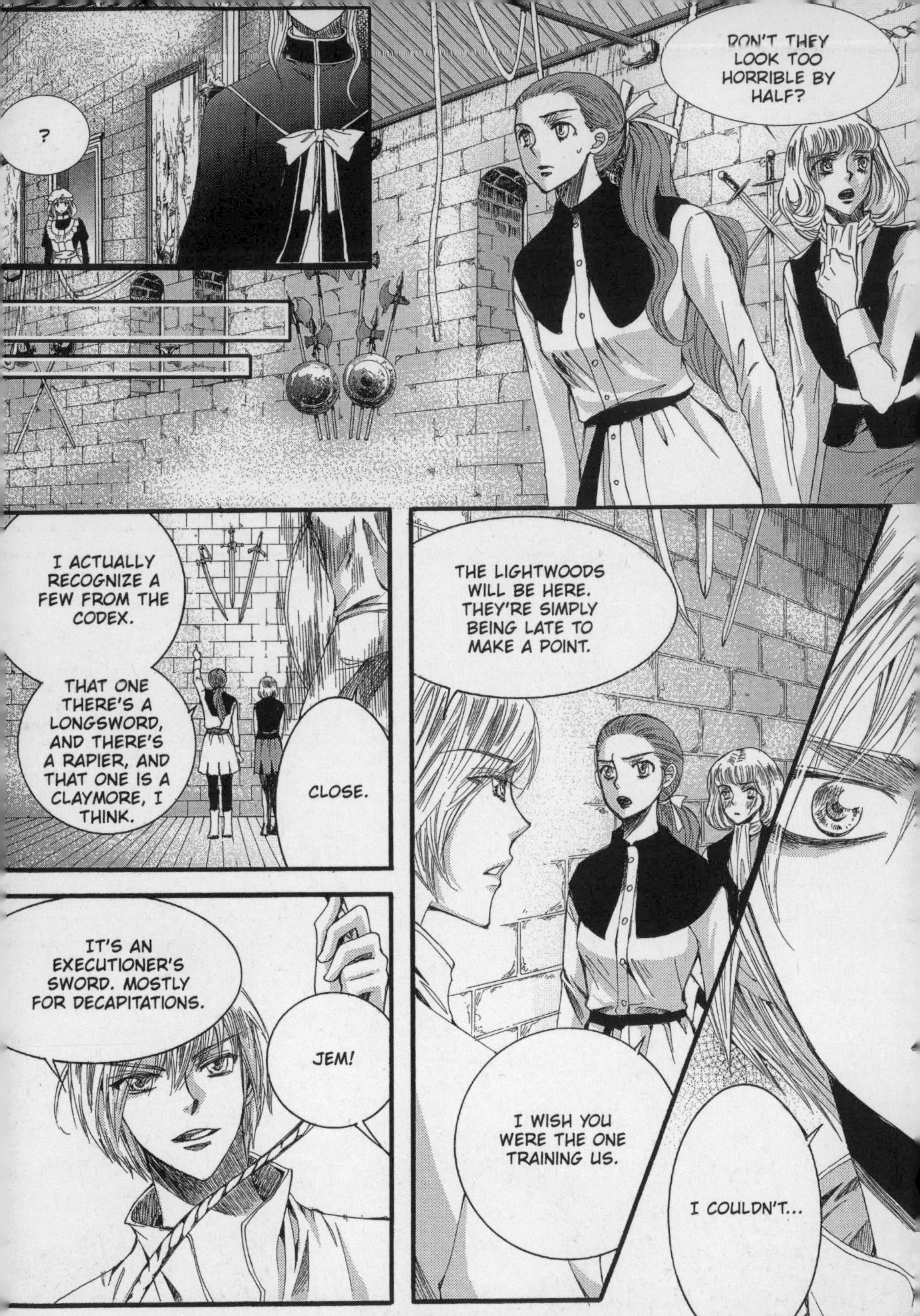
?
DON'T THEY LOOK TOO HORRIBLE BY HALF?
I ACTUALLY RECOGNIZE A FEW FROM THE CODEX.
THAT ONE THERE'S A LONGSWORD, AND THERE'S A RAPIER, AND THAT ONE IS A CLAYMORE, I THINK.
CLOSE.
THE LIGHTWOODS WILL BE HERE. THEY'RE SIMPLY BEING LATE TO MAKE A POINT.
IT'S AN EXECUTIONER'S SWORD. MOSTLY FOR DECAPITATIONS.
JEM!
I WISH YOU WERE THE ONE TRAINING US.
I COULDN'T...

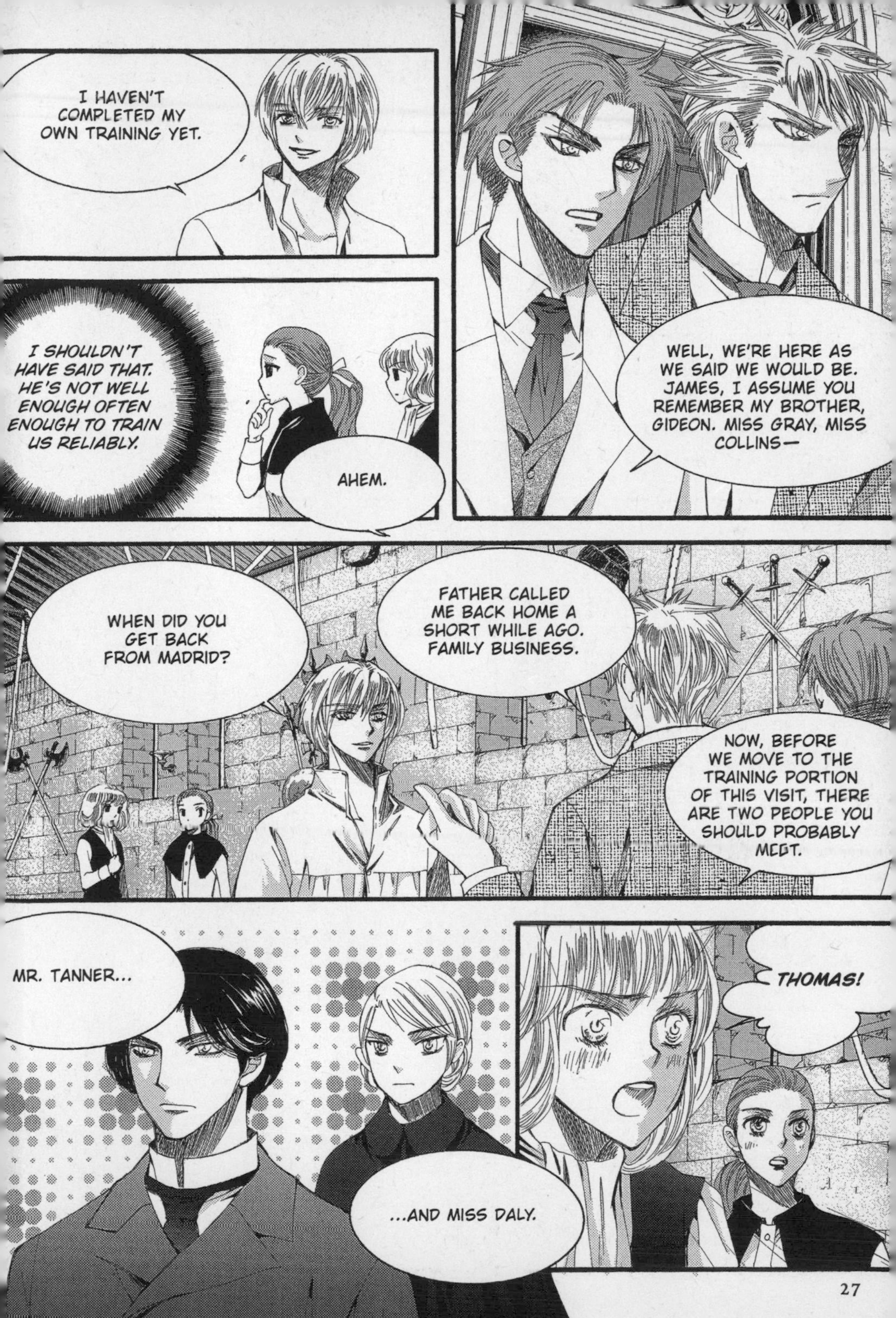
I HAVEN'T COMPLETED MY OWN TRAINING YET.
I SHOULDN'T HAVE SAID THAT. HE'S NOT WELL ENOUGH OFTEN ENOUGH TO TRAIN US RELIABLY.
AHEM.
WELL, WE'RE HERE AS WE SAID WE WOULD BE. JAMES, I ASSUME YOU REMEMBER MY BROTHER, GIDEON. MISS GRAY, MISS COLLINS—
WHEN DID YOU GET BACK FROM MADRID?
FATHER CALLED ME BACK HOME A SHORT WHILE AGO. FAMILY BUSINESS.
NOW, BEFORE WE MOVE TO THE TRAINING PORTION OF THIS VISIT, THERE ARE TWO PEOPLE YOU SHOULD PROBABLY MEET.
MR. TANNER...
...AND MISS DALY.
THOMAS!

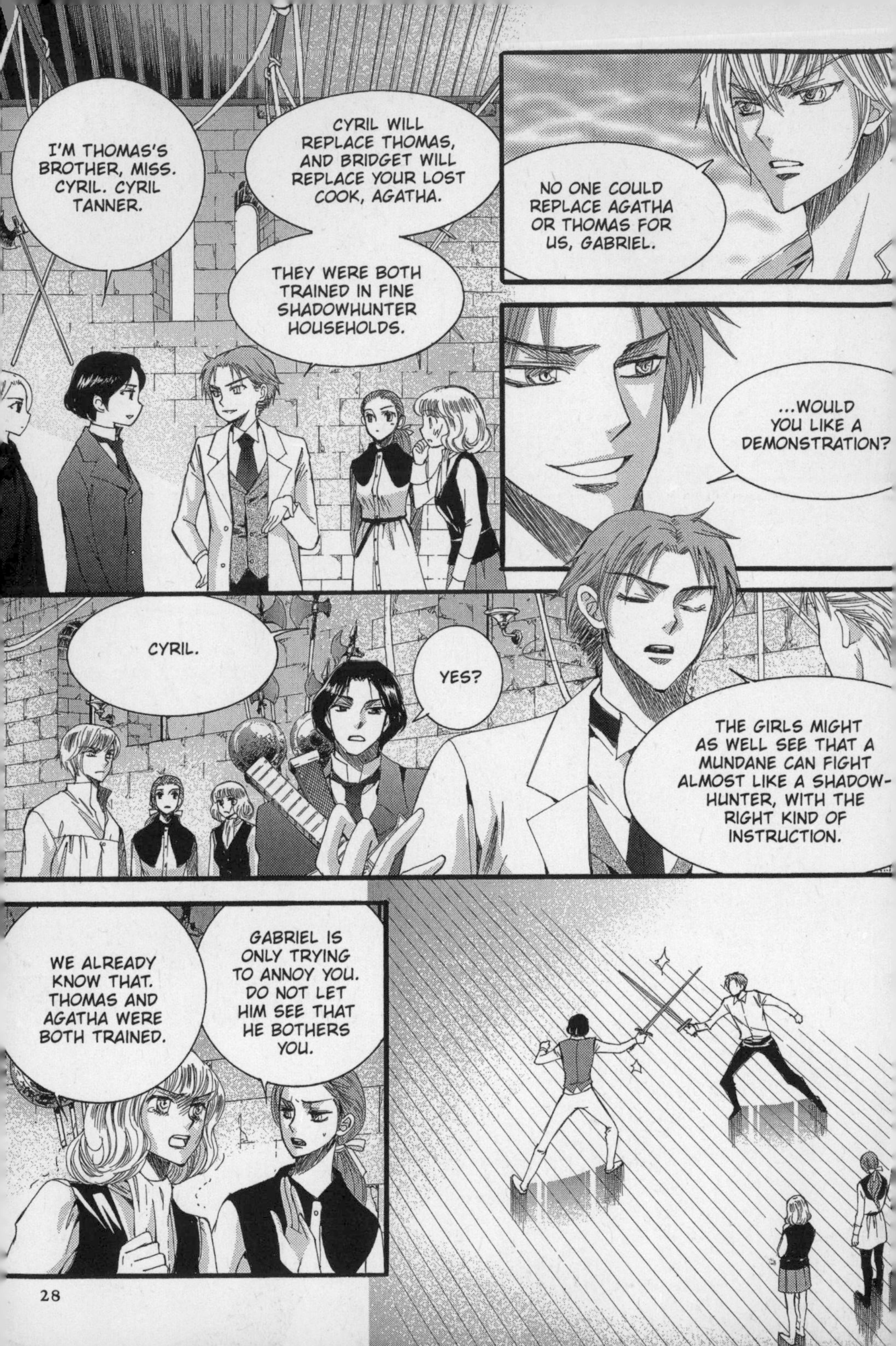
I'M THOMAS'S BROTHER, MISS. CYRIL. CYRIL TANNER.
CYRIL WILL REPLACE THOMAS, AND BRIDGET WILL REPLACE YOUR LOST COOK, AGATHA.
THEY WERE BOTH TRAINED IN FINE SHADOWHUNTER HOUSEHOLDS.
NO ONE COULD REPLACE AGATHA OR THOMAS FOR US, GABRIEL.
...WOULD YOU LIKE A DEMONSTRATION?
CYRIL.
YES?
THE GIRLS MIGHT AS WELL SEE THAT A MUNDANE CAN FIGHT ALMOST LIKE A SHADOW-HUNTER, WITH THE RIGHT KIND OF INSTRUCTION.
WE ALREADY KNOW THAT. THOMAS AND AGATHA WERE BOTH TRAINED.
GABRIEL IS ONLY TRYING TO ANNOY YOU. DO NOT LET HIM SEE THAT HE BOTHERS YOU.

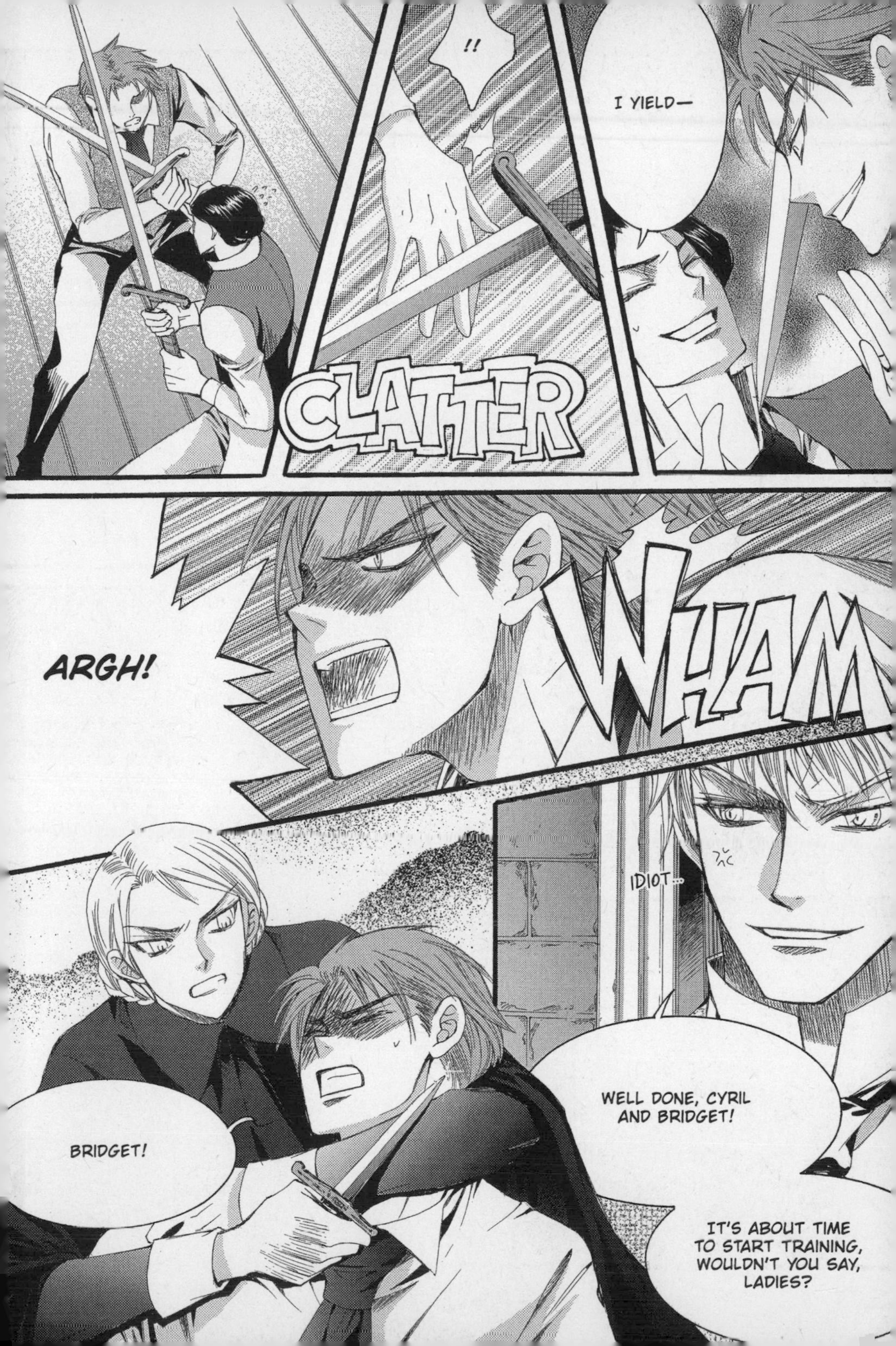
!!
I YIELD—
CLATTER
WHAM
ARGH!
IDIOT...
WELL DONE, CYRIL AND BRIDGET!
BRIDGET!
IT'S ABOUT TIME TO START TRAINING, WOULDN'T YOU SAY, LADIES?

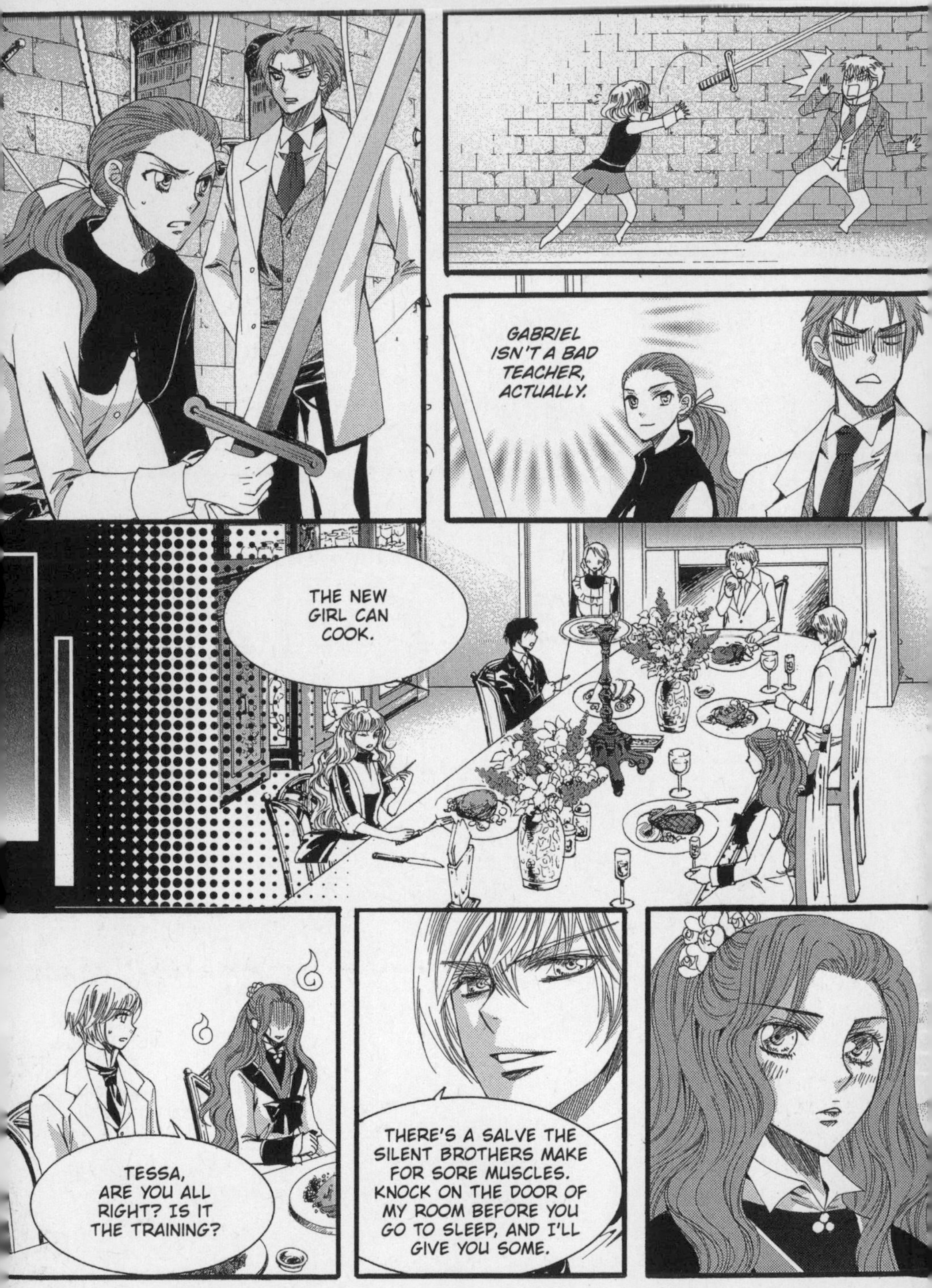
GABRIEL ISN'T A BAD TEACHER, ACTUALLY.
THE NEW GIRL CAN COOK.
TESSA, ARE YOU ALL RIGHT? IS IT THE TRAINING?
THERE'S A SALVE THE SILENT BROTHERS MAKE FOR SORE MUSCLES. KNOCK ON THE DOOR OF MY ROOM BEFORE YOU GO TO SLEEP, AND I'LL GIVE YOU SOME.

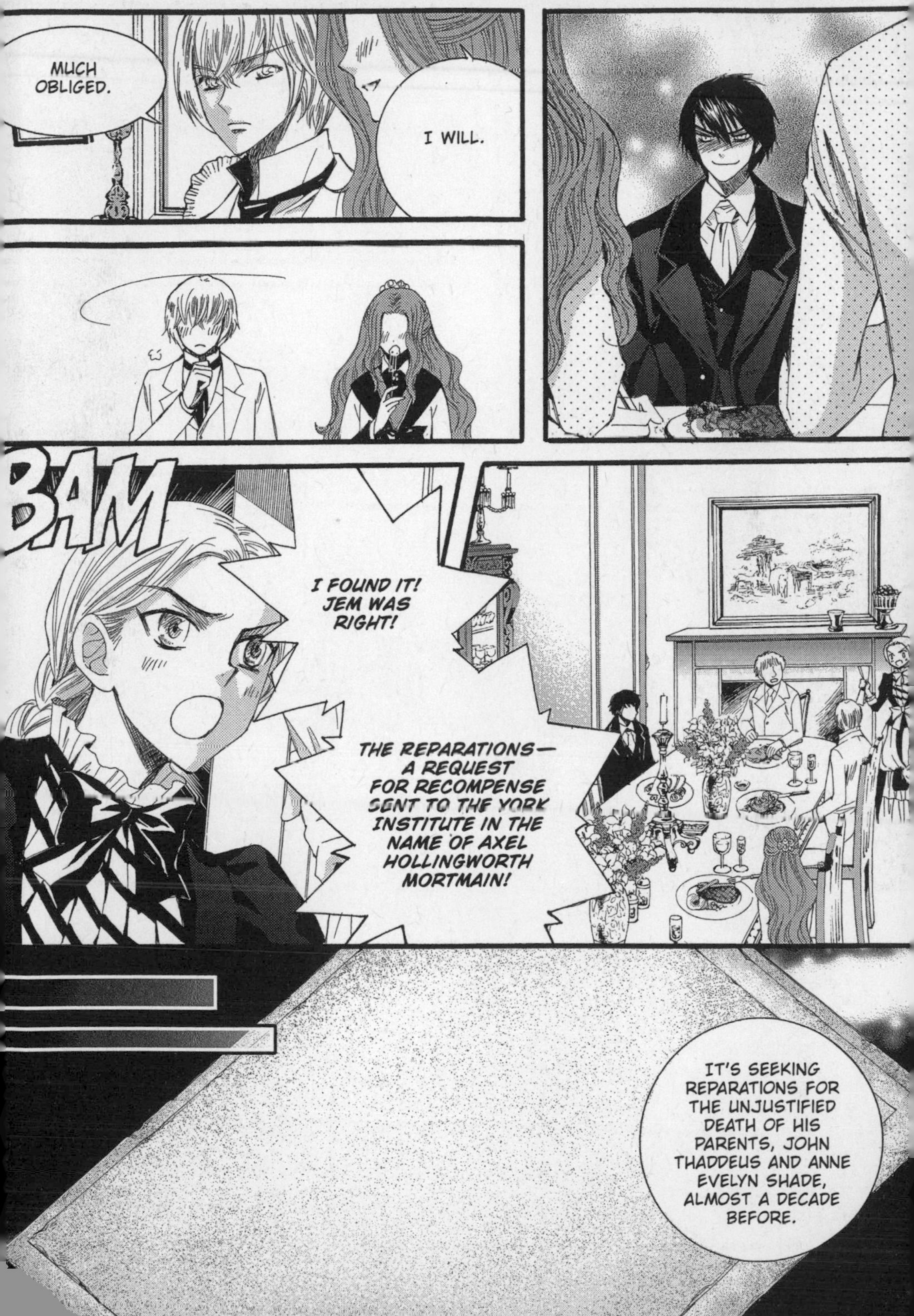

MUCH OBLIGED.
I WILL.
BAM
I FOUND IT! JEM WAS RIGHT!
THE REPARATIONS— A REQUEST FOR RECOMPENSE SENT TO THE YORK INSTITUTE IN THE NAME OF AXEL HOLLINGWORTH MORTMAIN!
IT'S SEEKING REPARATIONS FOR THE UNJUSTIFIED DEATH OF HIS PARENTS, JOHN THADDEUS AND ANNE EVELYN SHADE, ALMOST A DECADE BEFORE.

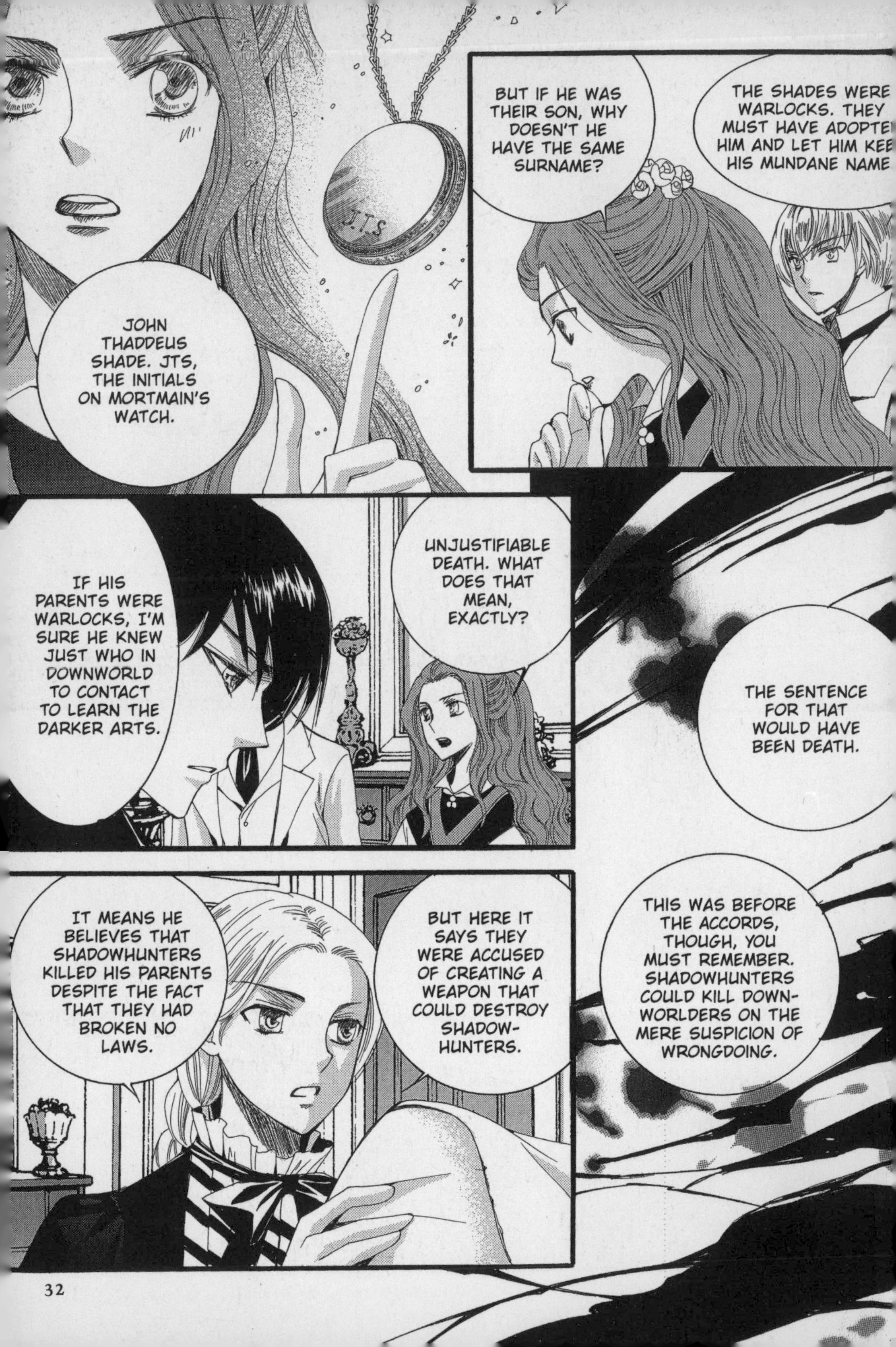
J.T.S.
JOHN THADDEUS SHADE. JTS, THE INITIALS ON MORTMAIN'S WATCH.
BUT IF HE WAS THEIR SON, WHY DOESN'T HE HAVE THE SAME SURNAME?
THE SHADES WERE WARLOCKS. THEY MUST HAVE ADOPTE HIM AND LET HIM KEE HIS MUNDANE NAME
IF HIS PARENTS WERE WARLOCKS, I'M SURE HE KNEW JUST WHO IN DOWNWORLD TO CONTACT TO LEARN THE DARKER ARTS.
UNJUSTIFIABLE DEATH. WHAT DOES THAT MEAN, EXACTLY?
THE SENTENCE FOR THAT WOULD HAVE BEEN DEATH.
IT MEANS HE BELIEVES THAT SHADOWHUNTERS KILLED HIS PARENTS DESPITE THE FACT THAT THEY HAD BROKEN NO LAWS.
BUT HERE IT SAYS THEY WERE ACCUSED OF CREATING A WEAPON THAT COULD DESTROY SHADOW-HUNTERS.
THIS WAS BEFORE THE ACCORDS, THOUGH, YOU MUST REMEMBER. SHADOWHUNTERS COULD KILL DOWN-WORLDERS ON THE MERE SUSPICION OF WRONGDOING.

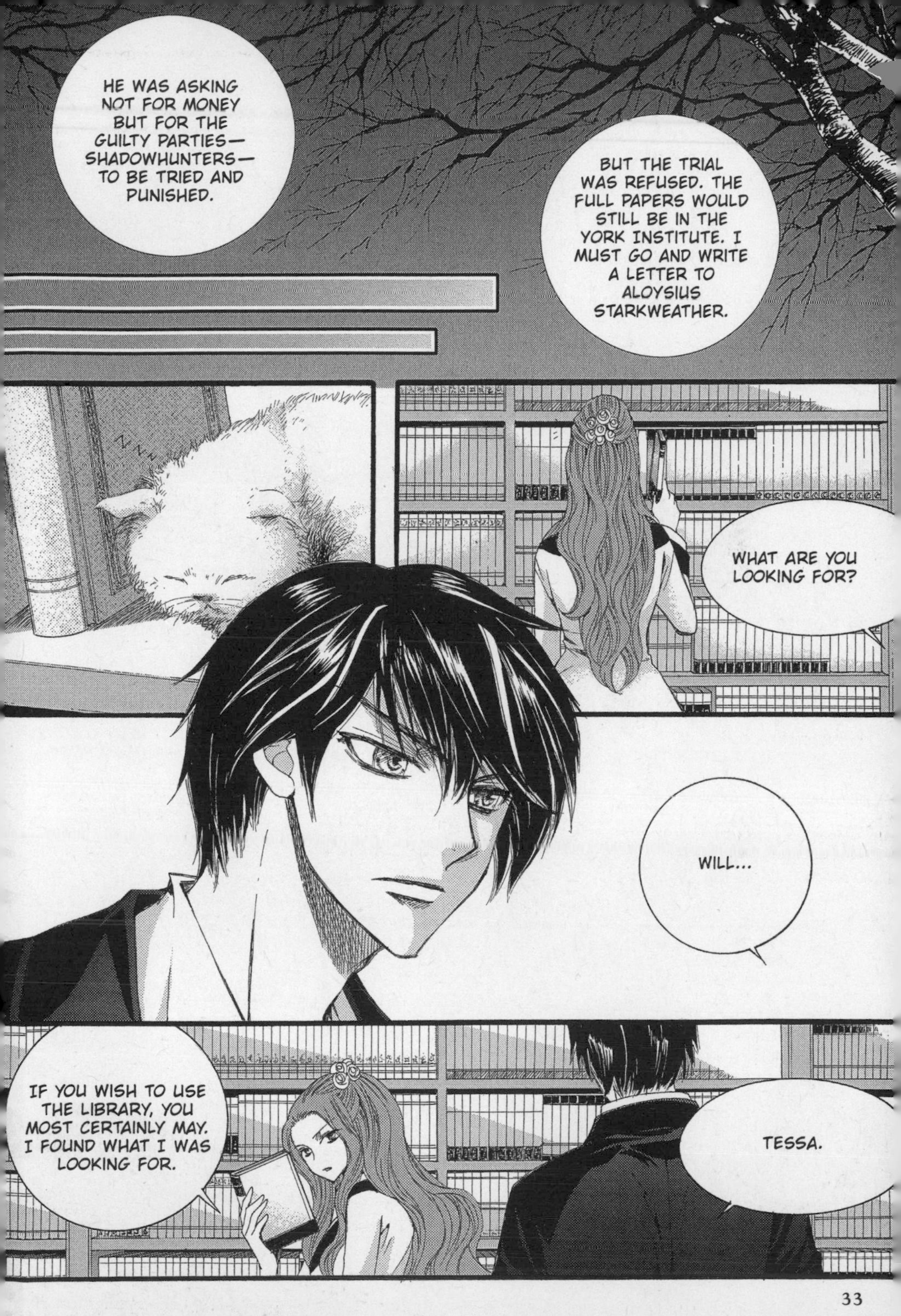
HE WAS ASKING NOT FOR MONEY BUT FOR THE GUILTY PARTIES—SHADOWHUNTERS—TO BE TRIED AND PUNISHED.
BUT THE TRIAL WAS REFUSED. THE FULL PAPERS WOULD STILL BE IN THE YORK INSTITUTE. I MUST GO AND WRITE A LETTER TO ALOYSIUS STARKWEATHER.
WHAT ARE YOU LOOKING FOR?
WILL...
IF YOU WISH TO USE THE LIBRARY, YOU MOST CERTAINLY MAY. I FOUND WHAT I WAS LOOKING FOR.
TESSA.

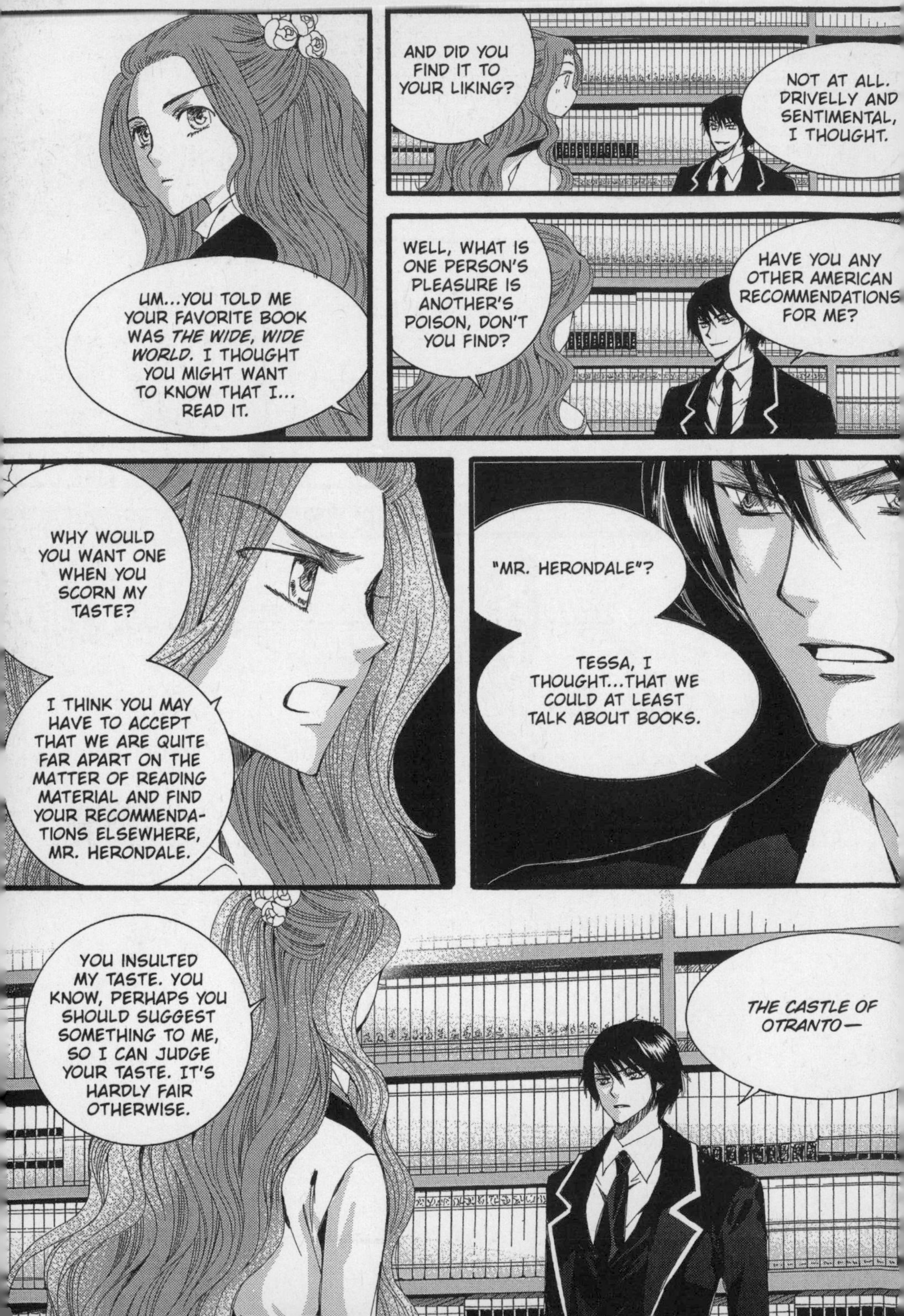
UM...YOU TOLD ME YOUR FAVORITE BOOK WAS *THE WIDE, WIDE WORLD*. I THOUGHT YOU MIGHT WANT TO KNOW THAT I... READ IT.
AND DID YOU FIND IT TO YOUR LIKING?
NOT AT ALL. DRIVELLY AND SENTIMENTAL, I THOUGHT.
WELL, WHAT IS ONE PERSON'S PLEASURE IS ANOTHER'S POISON, DON'T YOU FIND?
HAVE YOU ANY OTHER AMERICAN RECOMMENDATIONS FOR ME?
WHY WOULD YOU WANT ONE WHEN YOU SCORN MY TASTE?
I THINK YOU MAY HAVE TO ACCEPT THAT WE ARE QUITE FAR APART ON THE MATTER OF READING MATERIAL AND FIND YOUR RECOMMENDATIONS ELSEWHERE, MR. HERONDALE.
"MR. HERONDALE"?
TESSA, I THOUGHT...THAT WE COULD AT LEAST TALK ABOUT BOOKS.
YOU INSULTED MY TASTE. YOU KNOW, PERHAPS YOU SHOULD SUGGEST SOMETHING TO ME, SO I CAN JUDGE YOUR TASTE. IT'S HARDLY FAIR OTHERWISE.
THE CASTLE OF OTRANTO—

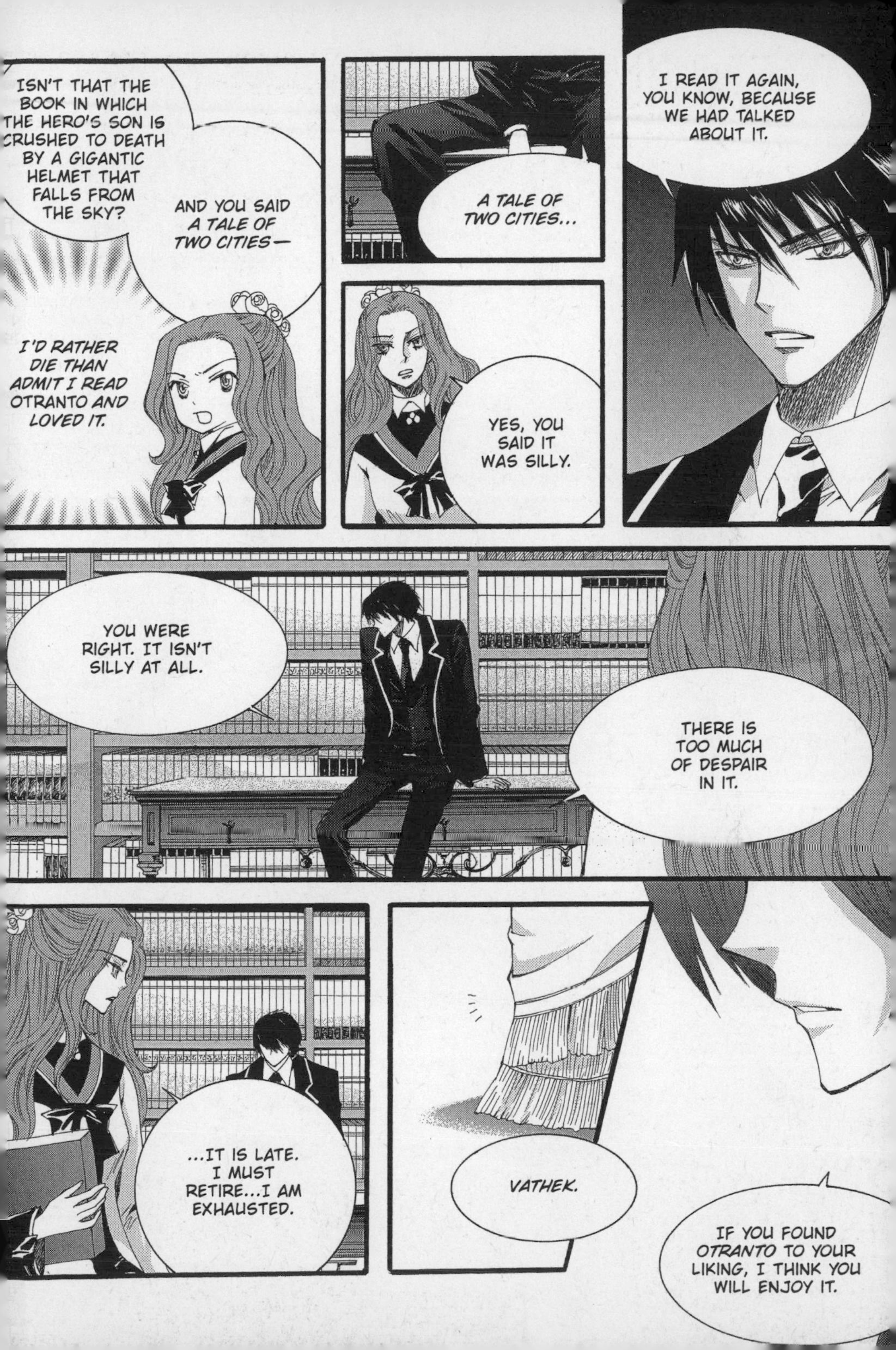
ISN'T THAT THE BOOK IN WHICH THE HERO'S SON IS CRUSHED TO DEATH BY A GIGANTIC HELMET THAT FALLS FROM THE SKY?
AND YOU SAID A TALE OF TWO CITIES—
I'D RATHER DIE THAN ADMIT I READ OTRANTO AND LOVED IT.
A TALE OF TWO CITIES...
YES, YOU SAID IT WAS SILLY.
I READ IT AGAIN, YOU KNOW, BECAUSE WE HAD TALKED ABOUT IT.
YOU WERE RIGHT. IT ISN'T SILLY AT ALL.
THERE IS TOO MUCH OF DESPAIR IN IT.
...IT IS LATE. I MUST RETIRE...I AM EXHAUSTED.
VATHEK.
IF YOU FOUND OTRANTO TO YOUR LIKING, I THINK YOU WILL ENJOY IT.

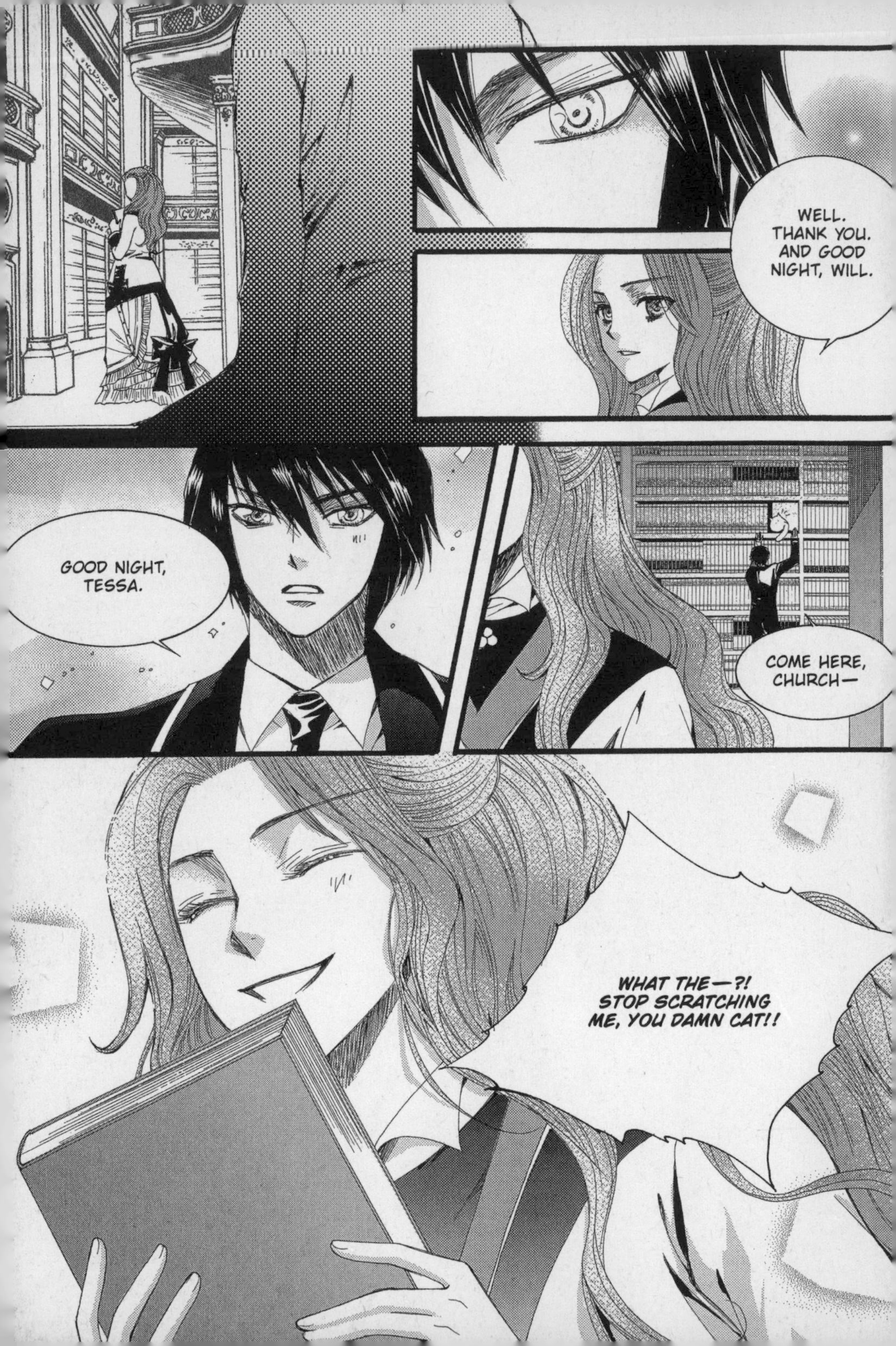
WELL. THANK YOU. AND GOOD NIGHT, WILL.
GOOD NIGHT, TESSA.
COME HERE, CHURCH—
WHAT THE—?! STOP SCRATCHING ME, YOU DAMN CAT!!

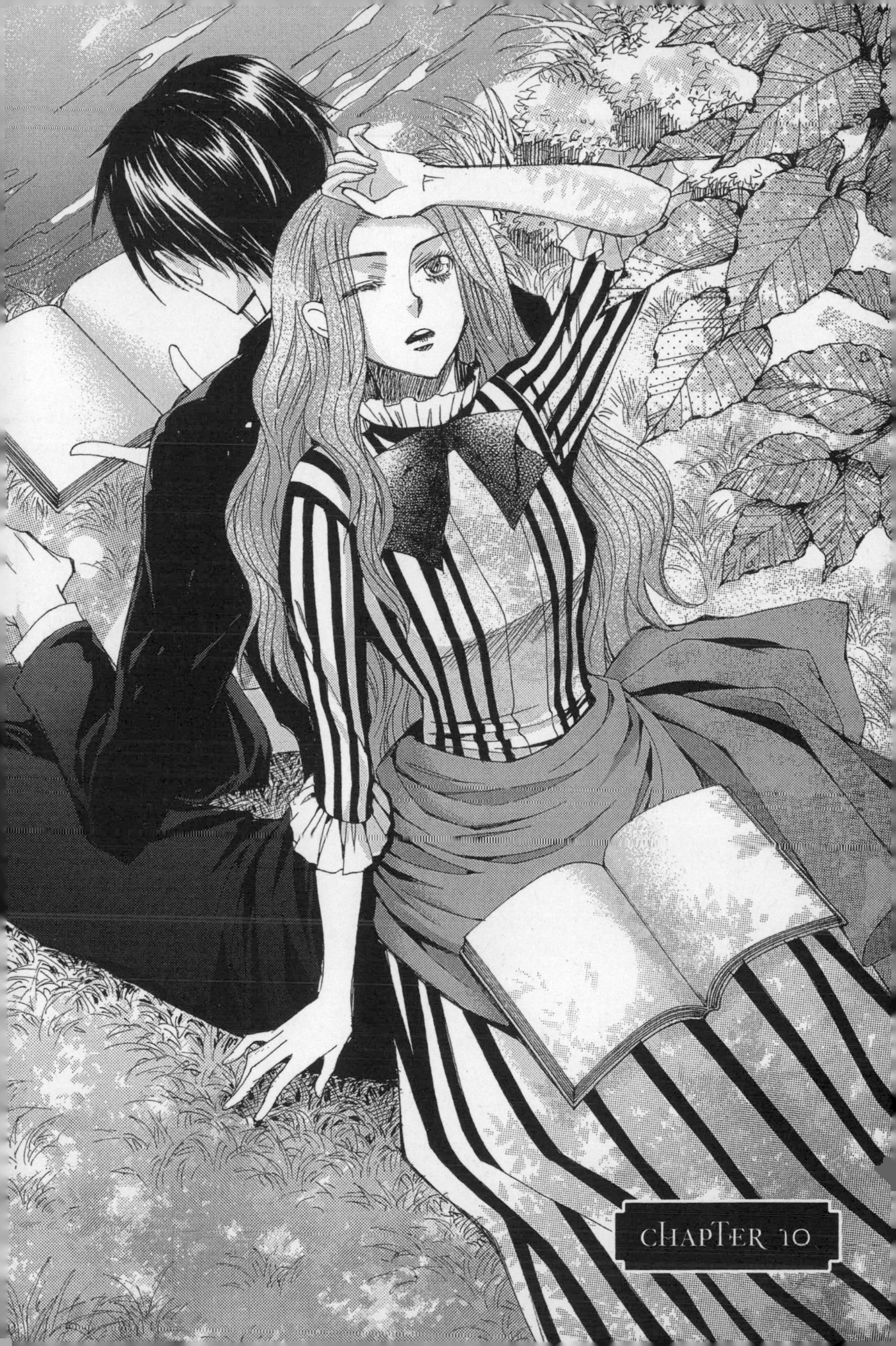
CHAPTER 10

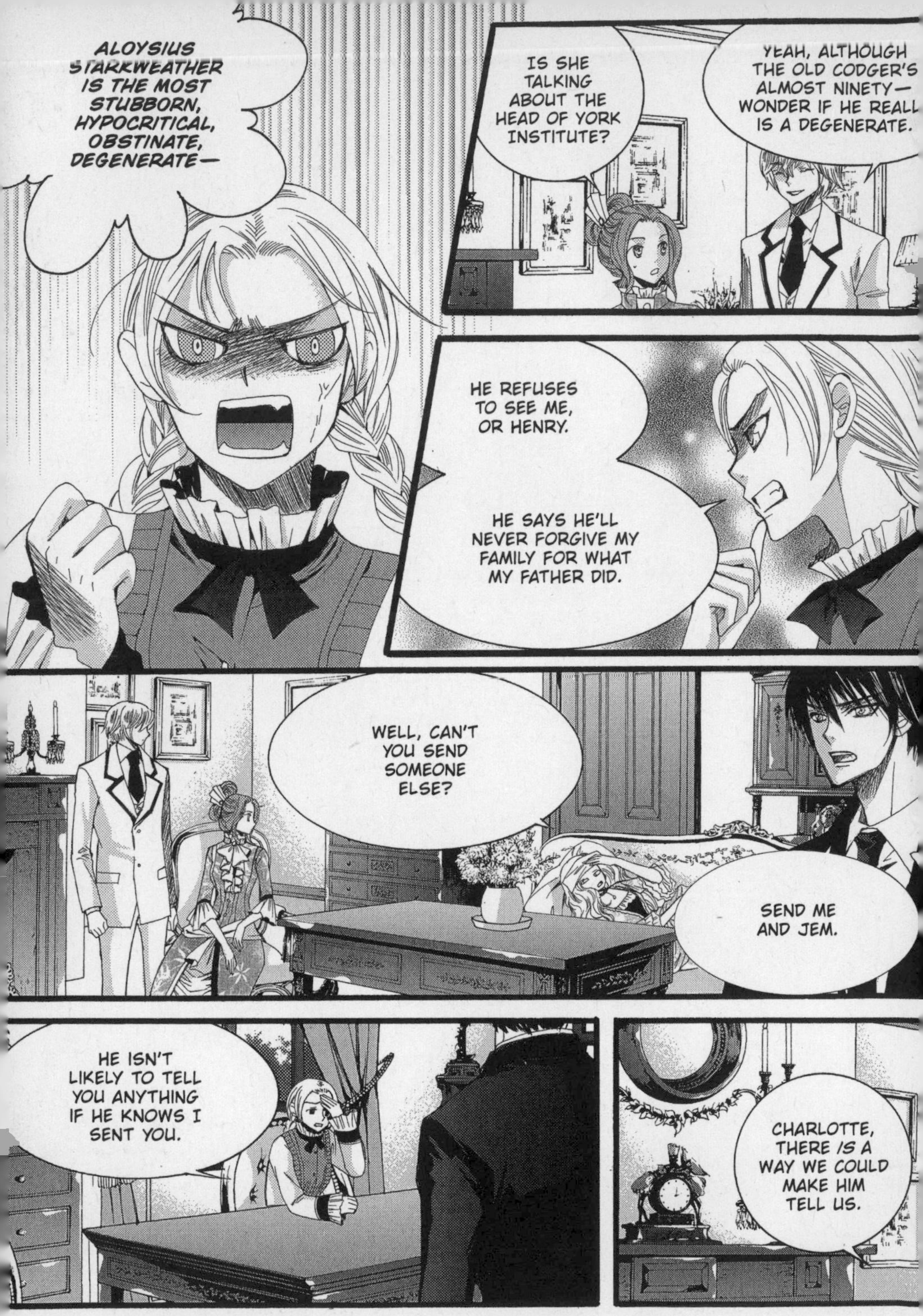
ALOYSIUS STARKWEATHER IS THE MOST STUBBORN, HYPOCRITICAL, OBSTINATE, DEGENERATE—
IS SHE TALKING ABOUT THE HEAD OF YORK INSTITUTE?
YEAH, ALTHOUGH THE OLD CODGER'S ALMOST NINETY—WONDER IF HE REALL IS A DEGENERATE.
HE REFUSES TO SEE ME, OR HENRY.
HE SAYS HE'LL NEVER FORGIVE MY FAMILY FOR WHAT MY FATHER DID.
WELL, CAN'T YOU SEND SOMEONE ELSE?
SEND ME AND JEM.
HE ISN'T LIKELY TO TELL YOU ANYTHING IF HE KNOWS I SENT YOU.
CHARLOTTE, THERE IS A WAY WE COULD MAKE HIM TELL US.

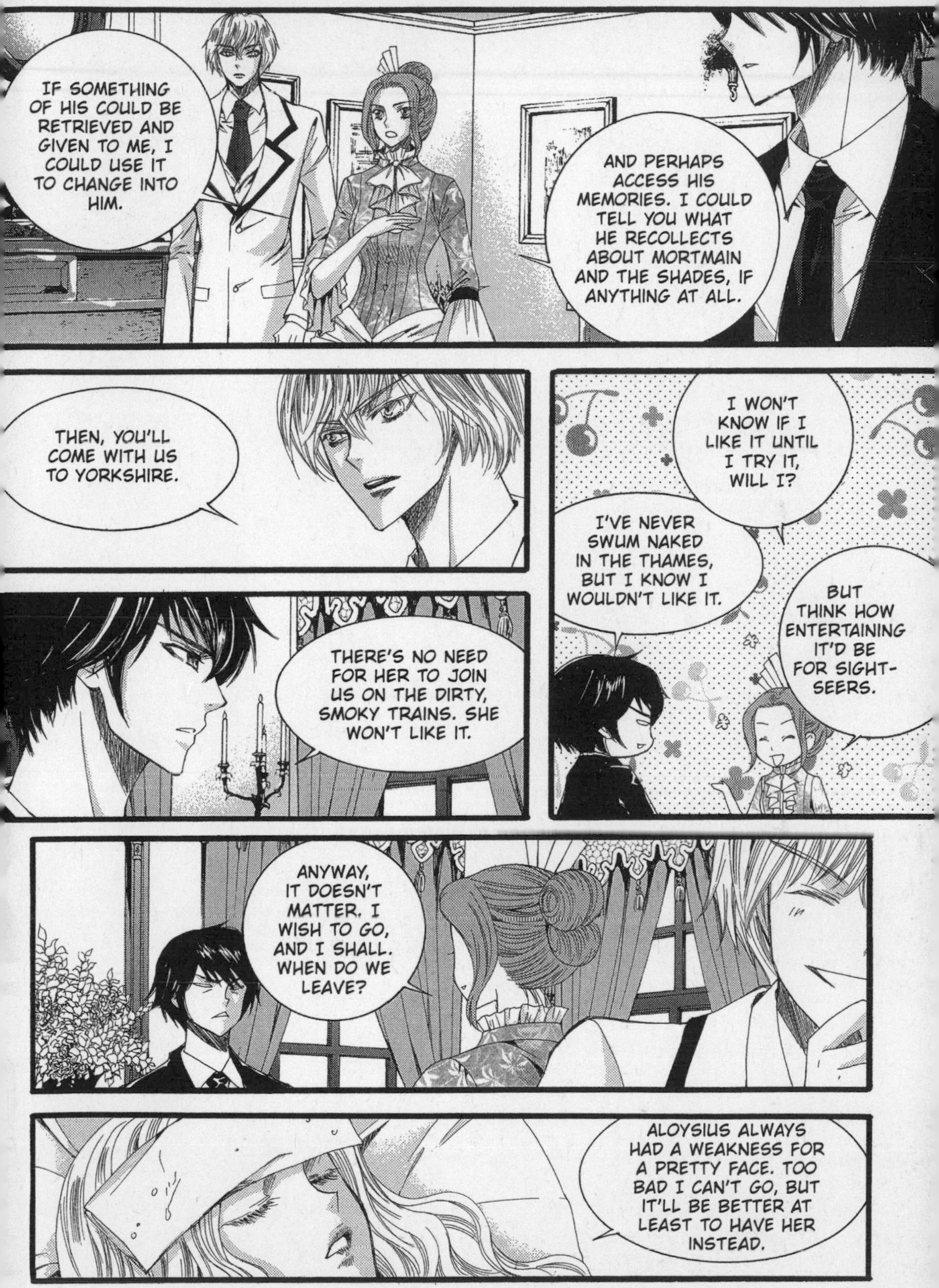
IF SOMETHING OF HIS COULD BE RETRIEVED AND GIVEN TO ME, I COULD USE IT TO CHANGE INTO HIM.
AND PERHAPS ACCESS HIS MEMORIES. I COULD TELL YOU WHAT HE RECOLLECTS ABOUT MORTMAIN AND THE SHADES, IF ANYTHING AT ALL.
THEN, YOU'LL COME WITH US TO YORKSHIRE.
THERE'S NO NEED FOR HER TO JOIN US ON THE DIRTY, SMOKY TRAINS. SHE WON'T LIKE IT.
I WON'T KNOW IF I LIKE IT UNTIL I TRY IT, WILL I?
I'VE NEVER SWUM NAKED IN THE THAMES, BUT I KNOW I WOULDN'T LIKE IT.
BUT THINK HOW ENTERTAINING IT'D BE FOR SIGHT-SEERS.
ANYWAY, IT DOESN'T MATTER. I WISH TO GO, AND I SHALL. WHEN DO WE LEAVE?
ALOYSIUS ALWAYS HAD A WEAKNESS FOR A PRETTY FACE. TOO BAD I CAN'T GO, BUT IT'LL BE BETTER AT LEAST TO HAVE HER INSTEAD.

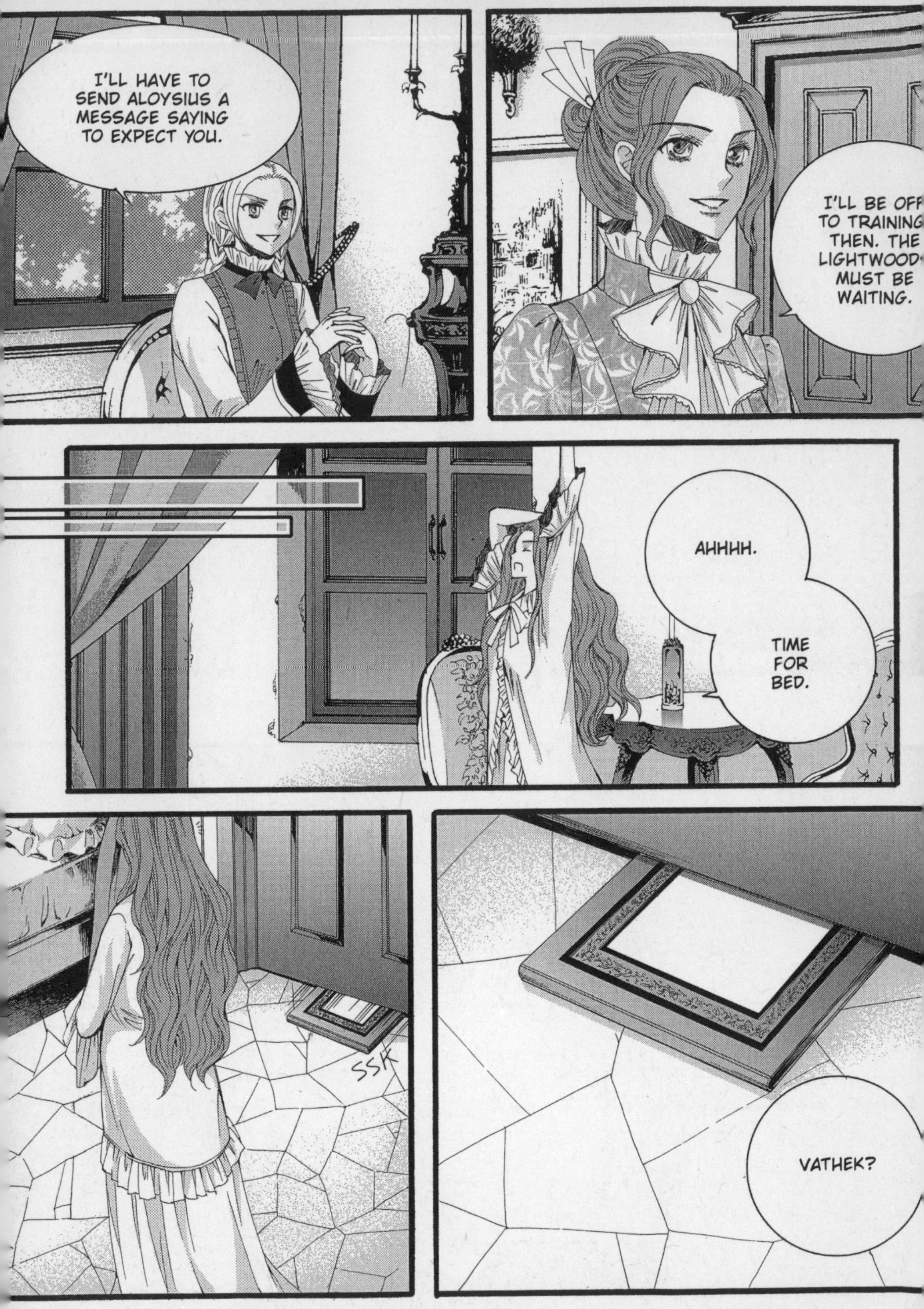
I'LL HAVE TO SEND ALOYSIUS A MESSAGE SAYING TO EXPECT YOU.
I'LL BE OFF TO TRAINING THEN. THE LIGHTWOOD MUST BE WAITING.
AHHHH.
TIME FOR BED.
SSK
VATHEK?

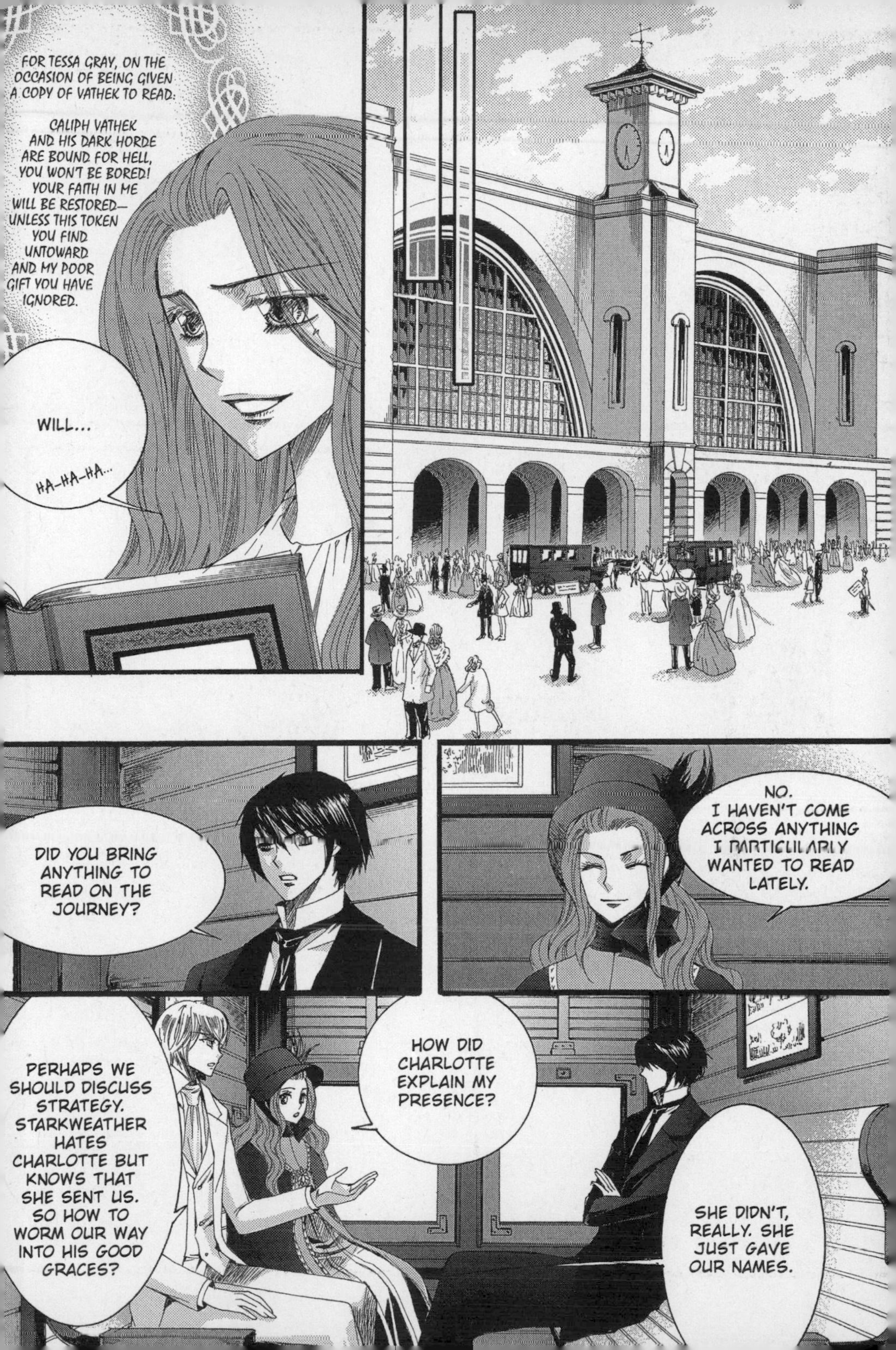
FOR TESSA GRAY, ON THE OCCASION OF BEING GIVEN A COPY OF VATHEK TO READ:
CALIPH VATHEK AND HIS DARK HORDE ARE BOUND FOR HELL, YOU WON'T BE BORED! YOUR FAITH IN ME WILL BE RESTORED— UNLESS THIS TOKEN YOU FIND UNTOWARD AND MY POOR GIFT YOU HAVE IGNORED.
WILL...
HA-HA-HA...
DID YOU BRING ANYTHING TO READ ON THE JOURNEY?
NO. I HAVEN'T COME ACROSS ANYTHING I PARTICULARLY WANTED TO READ LATELY.
PERHAPS WE SHOULD DISCUSS STRATEGY. STARKWEATHER HATES CHARLOTTE BUT KNOWS THAT SHE SENT US. SO HOW TO WORM OUR WAY INTO HIS GOOD GRACES?
HOW DID CHARLOTTE EXPLAIN MY PRESENCE?
SHE DIDN'T, REALLY. SHE JUST GAVE OUR NAMES.

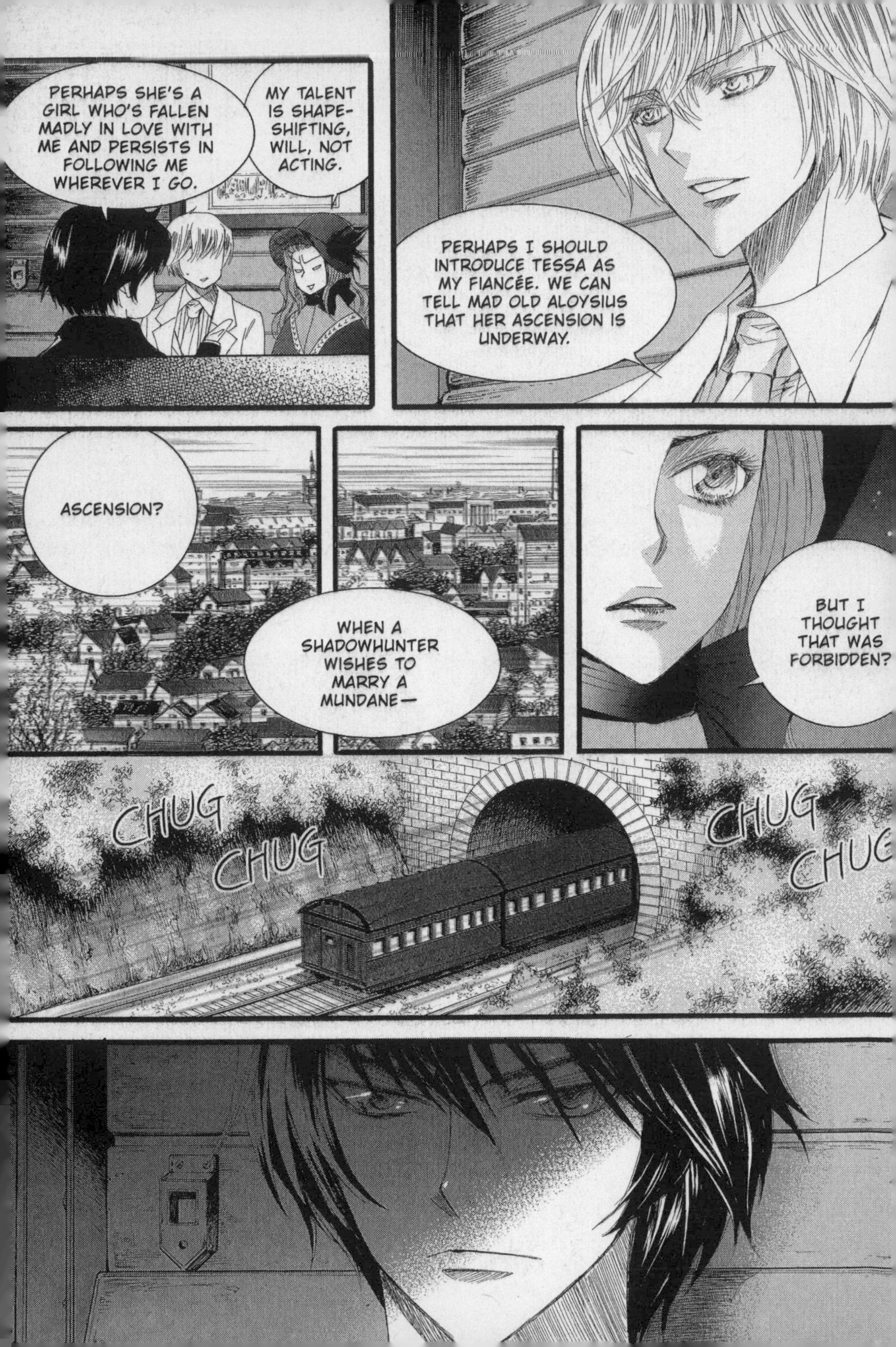
PERHAPS SHE'S A GIRL WHO'S FALLEN MADLY IN LOVE WITH ME AND PERSISTS IN FOLLOWING ME WHEREVER I GO.
MY TALENT IS SHAPE-SHIFTING, WILL, NOT ACTING.
PERHAPS I SHOULD INTRODUCE TESSA AS MY FIANCÉE. WE CAN TELL MAD OLD ALOYSIUS THAT HER ASCENSION IS UNDERWAY.
ASCENSION?
WHEN A SHADOWHUNTER WISHES TO MARRY A MUNDANE—
BUT I THOUGHT THAT WAS FORBIDDEN?
CHUG CHUG
CHUG CHUG

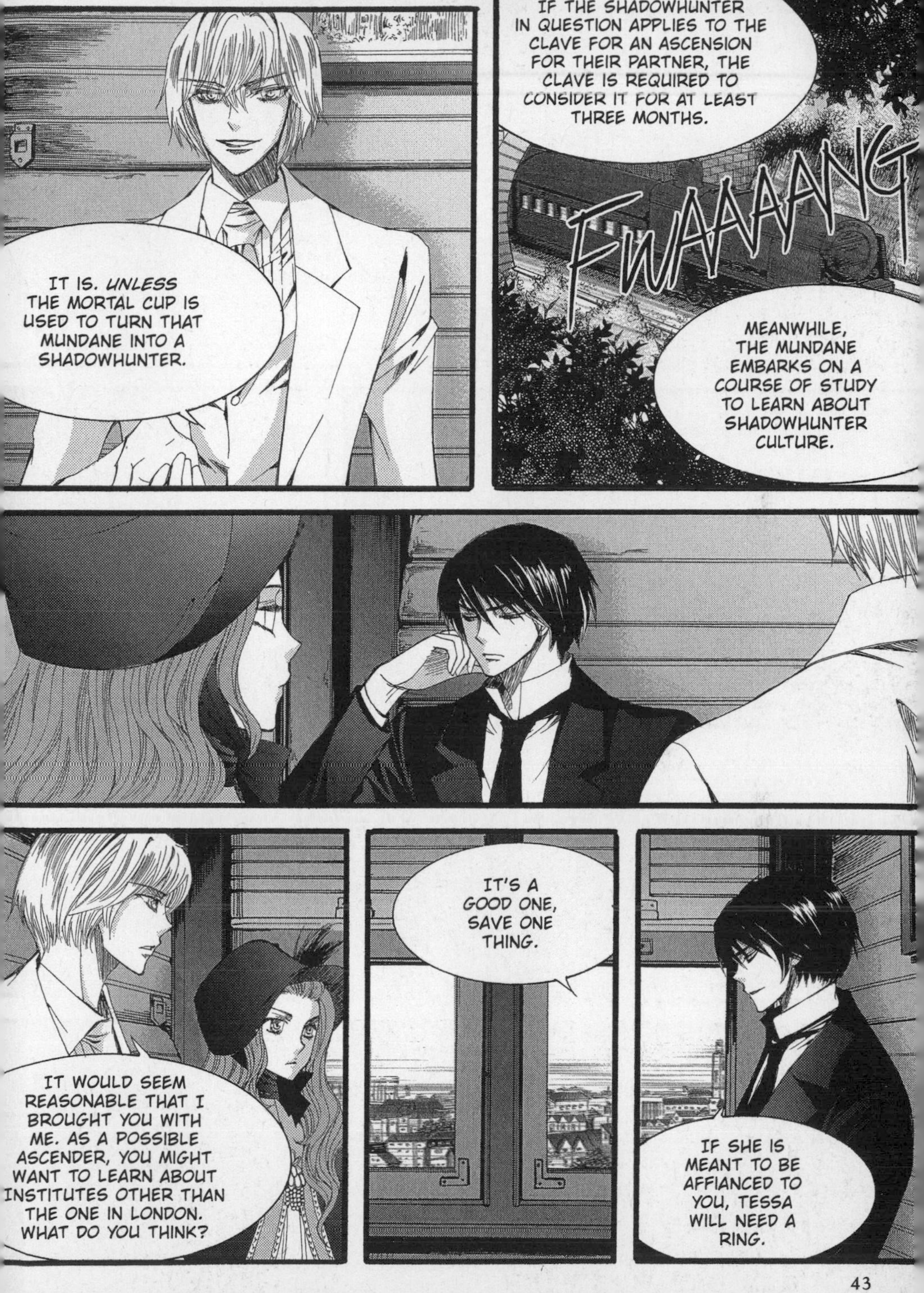
IT IS. *UNLESS* THE MORTAL CUP IS USED TO TURN THAT MUNDANE INTO A SHADOWHUNTER.
IF THE SHADOWHUNTER IN QUESTION APPLIES TO THE CLAVE FOR AN ASCENSION FOR THEIR PARTNER, THE CLAVE IS REQUIRED TO CONSIDER IT FOR AT LEAST THREE MONTHS.
FWAAAANG
MEANWHILE, THE MUNDANE EMBARKS ON A COURSE OF STUDY TO LEARN ABOUT SHADOWHUNTER CULTURE.
IT WOULD SEEM REASONABLE THAT I BROUGHT YOU WITH ME. AS A POSSIBLE ASCENDER, YOU MIGHT WANT TO LEARN ABOUT INSTITUTES OTHER THAN THE ONE IN LONDON. WHAT DO YOU THINK?
IT'S A GOOD ONE, SAVE ONE THING.
IF SHE IS MEANT TO BE AFFIANCED TO YOU, TESSA WILL NEED A RING.

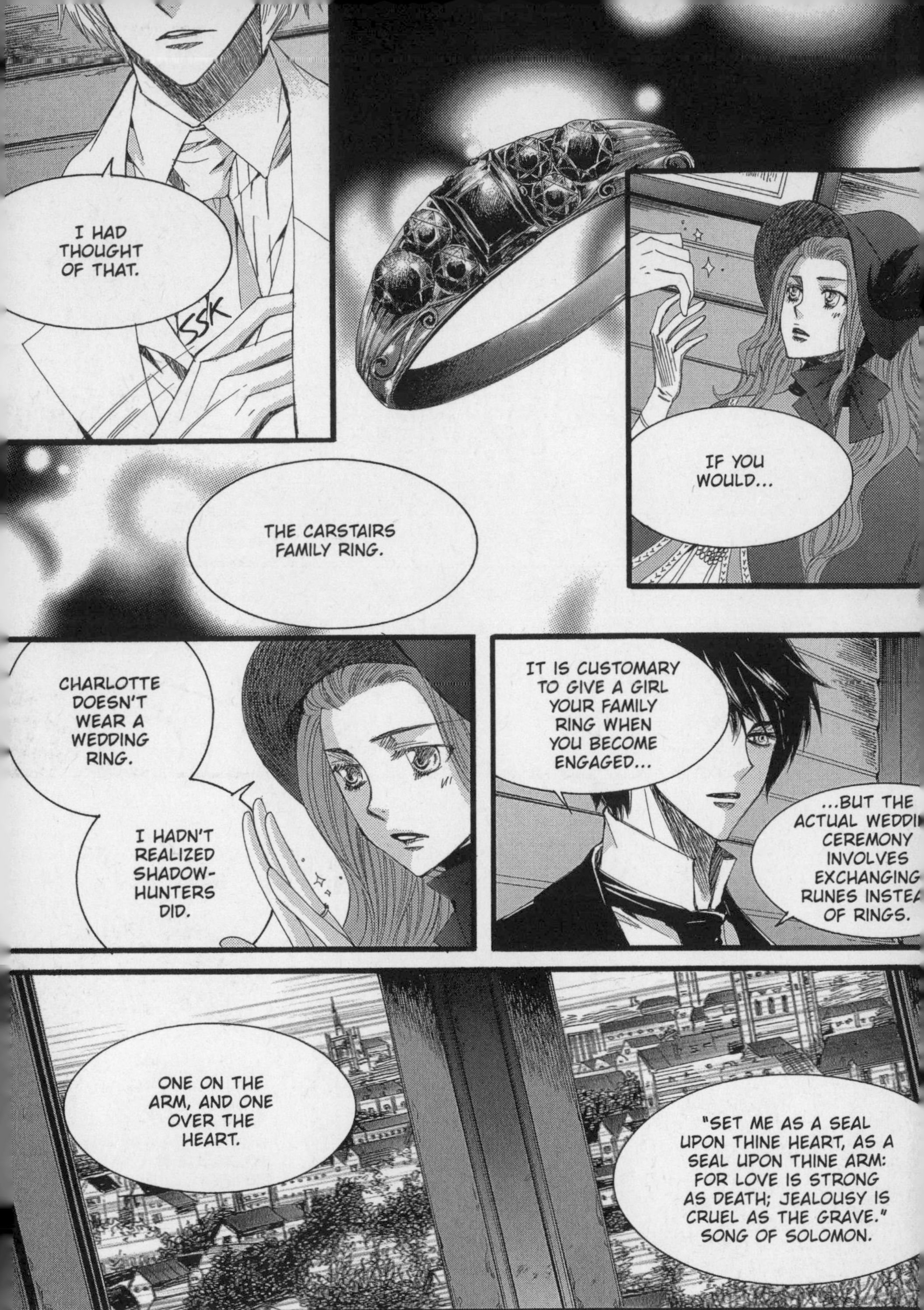
I HAD THOUGHT OF THAT.
SSK
IF YOU WOULD...
THE CARSTAIRS FAMILY RING.
CHARLOTTE DOESN'T WEAR A WEDDING RING.
I HADN'T REALIZED SHADOW-HUNTERS DID.
IT IS CUSTOMARY TO GIVE A GIRL YOUR FAMILY RING WHEN YOU BECOME ENGAGED...
...BUT THE ACTUAL WEDDI
CEREMONY INVOLVES EXCHANGING RUNES INSTE
OF RINGS.
ONE ON THE ARM, AND ONE OVER THE HEART.
"SET ME AS A SEAL UPON THINE HEART, AS A SEAL UPON THINE ARM: FOR LOVE IS STRONG AS DEATH; JEALOUSY IS CRUEL AS THE GRAVE." SONG OF SOLOMON.

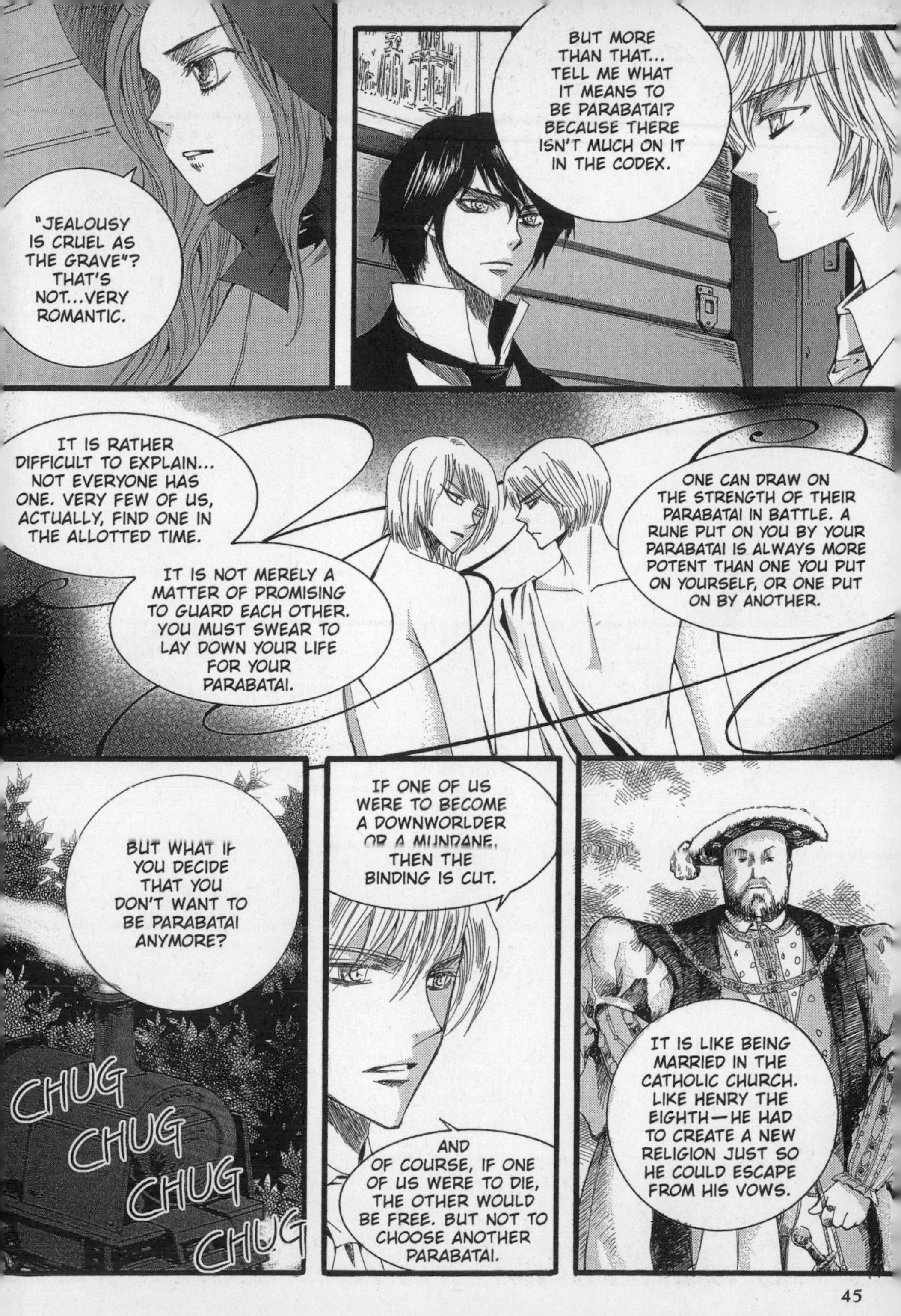
"JEALOUSY IS CRUEL AS THE GRAVE"? THAT'S NOT...VERY ROMANTIC.
BUT MORE THAN THAT... TELL ME WHAT IT MEANS TO BE PARABATAI? BECAUSE THERE ISN'T MUCH ON IT IN THE CODEX.
IT IS RATHER DIFFICULT TO EXPLAIN... NOT EVERYONE HAS ONE. VERY FEW OF US, ACTUALLY, FIND ONE IN THE ALLOTTED TIME.
IT IS NOT MERELY A MATTER OF PROMISING TO GUARD EACH OTHER. YOU MUST SWEAR TO LAY DOWN YOUR LIFE FOR YOUR PARABATAI.
ONE CAN DRAW ON THE STRENGTH OF THEIR PARABATAI IN BATTLE. A RUNE PUT ON YOU BY YOUR PARABATAI IS ALWAYS MORE POTENT THAN ONE YOU PUT ON YOURSELF, OR ONE PUT ON BY ANOTHER.
BUT WHAT IF YOU DECIDE THAT YOU DON'T WANT TO BE PARABATAI ANYMORE?
CHUG CHUG CHUG CHUG
IF ONE OF US WERE TO BECOME A DOWNWORLDER OR A MUNDANE, THEN THE BINDING IS CUT.
AND OF COURSE, IF ONE OF US WERE TO DIE, THE OTHER WOULD BE FREE. BUT NOT TO CHOOSE ANOTHER PARABATAI.
IT IS LIKE BEING MARRIED IN THE CATHOLIC CHURCH. LIKE HENRY THE EIGHTH—HE HAD TO CREATE A NEW RELIGION JUST SO HE COULD ESCAPE FROM HIS VOWS.

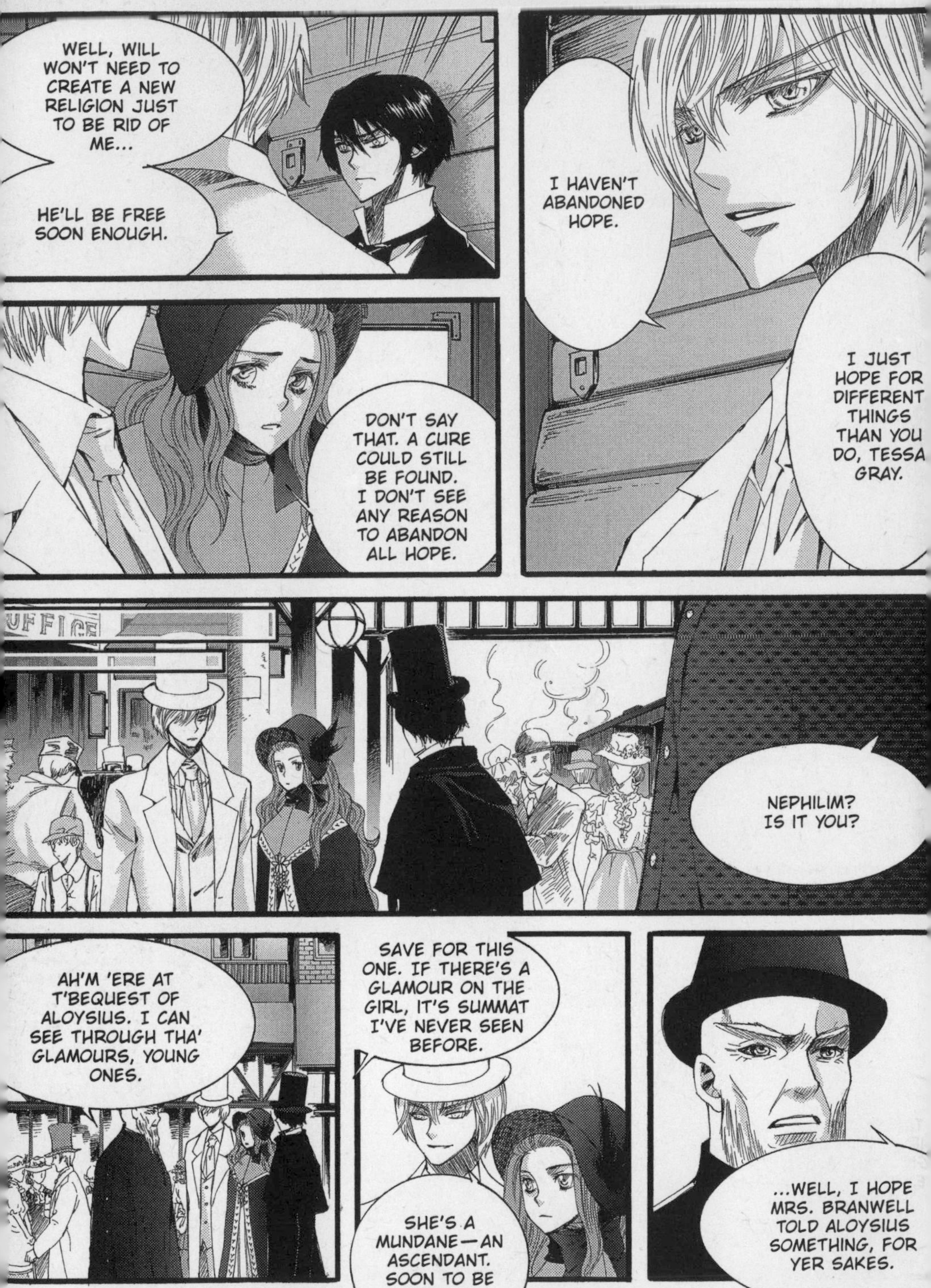
WELL, WILL WON'T NEED TO CREATE A NEW RELIGION JUST TO BE RID OF ME...
HE'LL BE FREE SOON ENOUGH.
I HAVEN'T ABANDONED HOPE.
DON'T SAY THAT. A CURE COULD STILL BE FOUND. I DON'T SEE ANY REASON TO ABANDON ALL HOPE.
I JUST HOPE FOR DIFFERENT THINGS THAN YOU DO, TESSA GRAY.
UFFICE
NEPHILIM? IS IT YOU?
AH'M 'ERE AT T'BEQUEST OF ALOYSIUS. I CAN SEE THROUGH THA' GLAMOURS, YOUNG ONES.
SAVE FOR THIS ONE. IF THERE'S A GLAMOUR ON THE GIRL, IT'S SUMMAT I'VE NEVER SEEN BEFORE.
SHE'S A MUNDANE—AN ASCENDANT. SOON TO BE MY WIFE.
...WELL, I HOPE MRS. BRANWELL TOLD ALOYSIUS SOMETHING, FOR YER SAKES.

YOUNG HERONDALE, ARE YOU? HALF-MUNDANE, HALF-WELSH, AND THE WORST TRAITS OF BOTH, I'VE HEARD.

AND JAMES CARSTAIRS. ANOTHER INSTITUTE BRAT.

I'VE HALF A MIND TO TELL THE LOT OF YOU TO GO TO BLAZES. THAT CHARLOTTE FAIRCHILD, FOISTING YOU ALL ON ME WITH NARY A BY-YOUR-LEAVE.

NONE OF THAT FAMILY EVER HAD A BIT O' MANNERS. I COULD DO WITHOUT HER FATHER, AND I CAN DO WITHOUT

!!

THIS IS TESSA GRAY, SIR. SHE IS A MUNDANE GIRL, BUT SHE IS THE BETROTHED OF ME, AND AN ASCENDANT.

A MUNDANE, YOU SAY?

WELL, TIMES HAVE—YES, I SUPPOSE THEN—

47

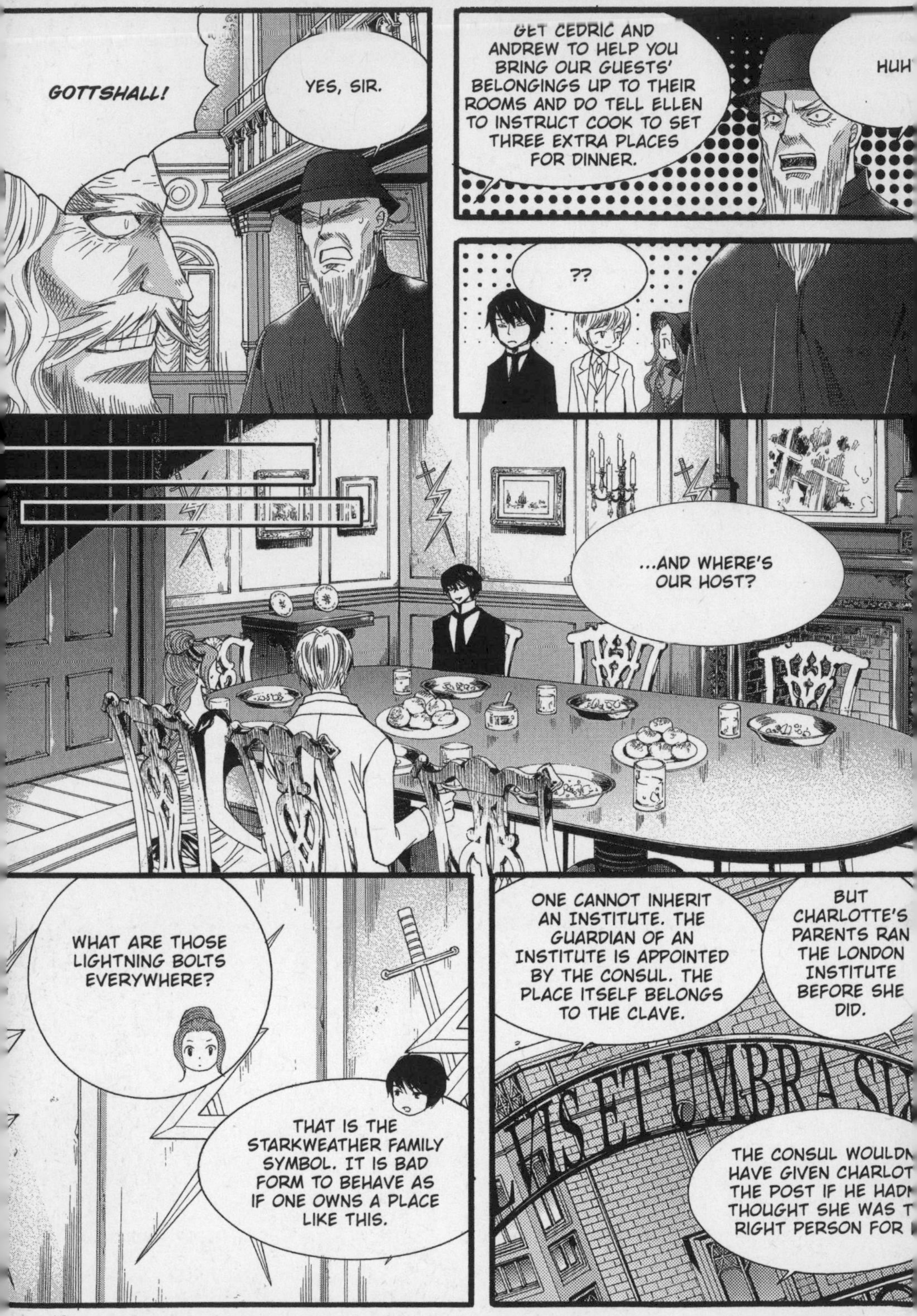
GOTTSHALL!
YES, SIR.
GET CEDRIC AND ANDREW TO HELP YOU BRING OUR GUESTS' BELONGINGS UP TO THEIR ROOMS AND DO TELL ELLEN TO INSTRUCT COOK TO SET THREE EXTRA PLACES FOR DINNER.
HUH
??
...AND WHERE'S OUR HOST?
WHAT ARE THOSE LIGHTNING BOLTS EVERYWHERE?
THAT IS THE STARKWEATHER FAMILY SYMBOL. IT IS BAD FORM TO BEHAVE AS IF ONE OWNS A PLACE LIKE THIS.
ONE CANNOT INHERIT AN INSTITUTE. THE GUARDIAN OF AN INSTITUTE IS APPOINTED BY THE CONSUL. THE PLACE ITSELF BELONGS TO THE CLAVE.
BUT CHARLOTTE'S PARENTS RAN THE LONDON INSTITUTE BEFORE SHE DID.
THE CONSUL WOULDN HAVE GIVEN CHARLOT THE POST IF HE HADN THOUGHT SHE WAS T RIGHT PERSON FOR

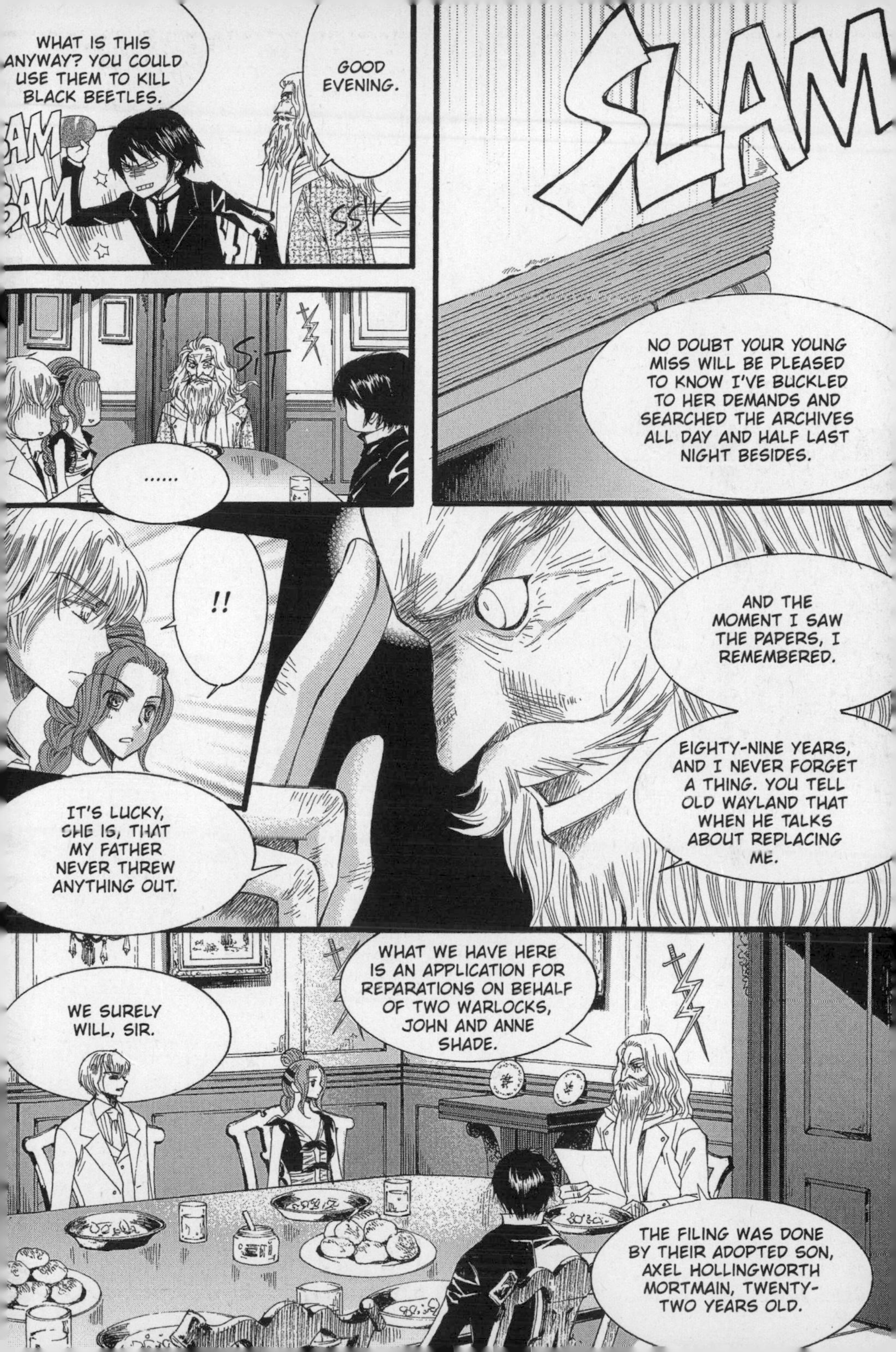
WHAT IS THIS ANYWAY? YOU COULD USE THEM TO KILL BLACK BEETLES.
GOOD EVENING.
SSK
SLAM
SIT
......
NO DOUBT YOUR YOUNG MISS WILL BE PLEASED TO KNOW I'VE BUCKLED TO HER DEMANDS AND SEARCHED THE ARCHIVES ALL DAY AND HALF LAST NIGHT BESIDES.
!!
AND THE MOMENT I SAW THE PAPERS, I REMEMBERED.
EIGHTY-NINE YEARS, AND I NEVER FORGET A THING. YOU TELL OLD WAYLAND THAT WHEN HE TALKS ABOUT REPLACING ME.
IT'S LUCKY, SHE IS, THAT MY FATHER NEVER THREW ANYTHING OUT.
WE SURELY WILL, SIR.
WHAT WE HAVE HERE IS AN APPLICATION FOR REPARATIONS ON BEHALF OF TWO WARLOCKS, JOHN AND ANNE SHADE.
THE FILING WAS DONE BY THEIR ADOPTED SON, AXEL HOLLINGWORTH MORTMAIN, TWENTY-TWO YEARS OLD.

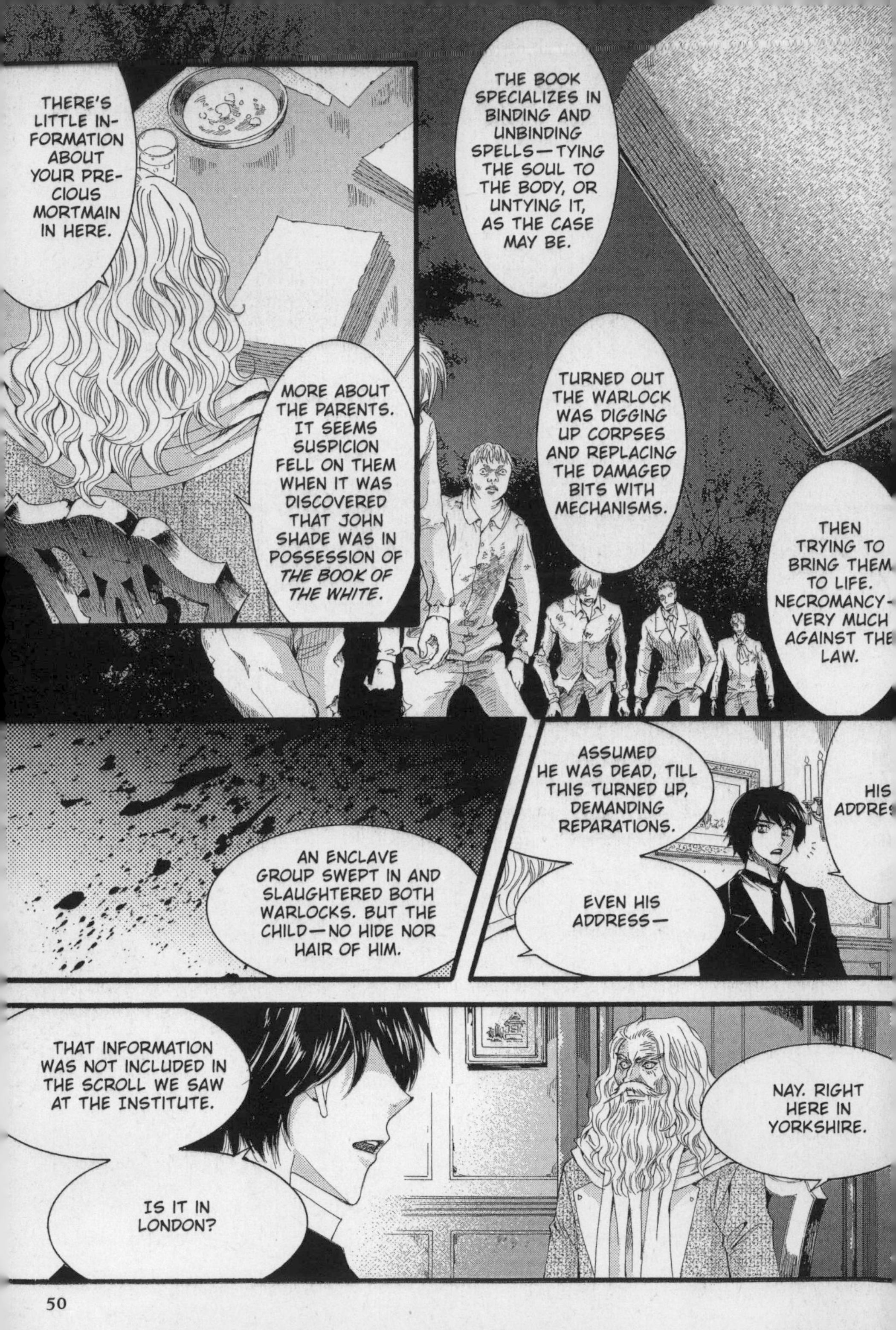
THERE'S LITTLE INFORMATION ABOUT YOUR PRECIOUS MORTMAIN IN HERE.
MORE ABOUT THE PARENTS. IT SEEMS SUSPICION FELL ON THEM WHEN IT WAS DISCOVERED THAT JOHN SHADE WAS IN POSSESSION OF *THE BOOK OF THE WHITE.*
THE BOOK SPECIALIZES IN BINDING AND UNBINDING SPELLS—TYING THE SOUL TO THE BODY, OR UNTYING IT, AS THE CASE MAY BE.
TURNED OUT THE WARLOCK WAS DIGGING UP CORPSES AND REPLACING THE DAMAGED BITS WITH MECHANISMS.
THEN TRYING TO BRING THEM TO LIFE. NECROMANCY- VERY MUCH AGAINST THE LAW.
AN ENCLAVE GROUP SWEPT IN AND SLAUGHTERED BOTH WARLOCKS. BUT THE CHILD—NO HIDE NOR HAIR OF HIM.
ASSUMED HE WAS DEAD, TILL THIS TURNED UP, DEMANDING REPARATIONS.
EVEN HIS ADDRESS—
HIS ADDRE
THAT INFORMATION WAS NOT INCLUDED IN THE SCROLL WE SAW AT THE INSTITUTE.
IS IT IN LONDON?
NAY. RIGHT HERE IN YORKSHIRE.

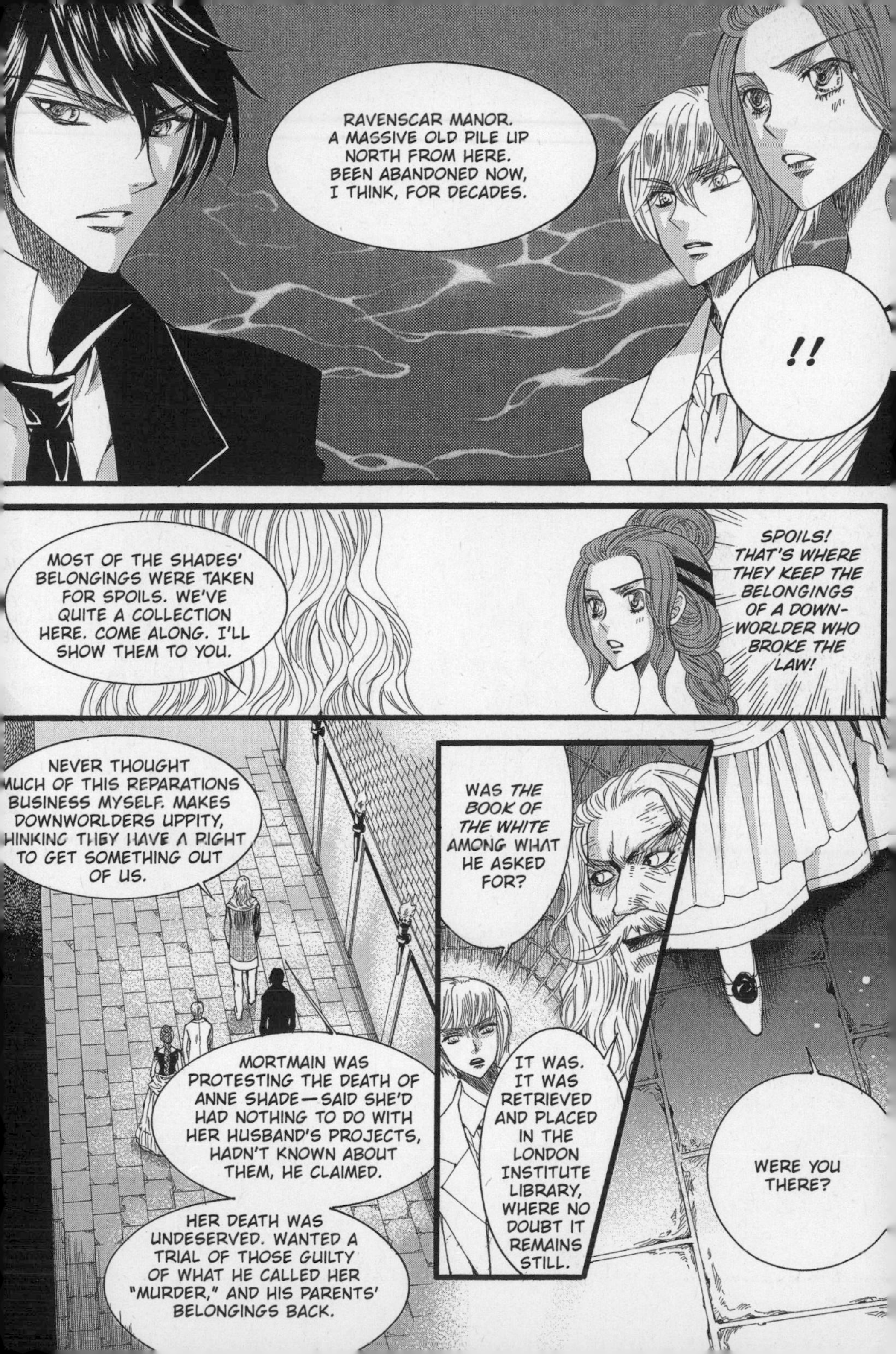
RAVENSCAR MANOR. A MASSIVE OLD PILE UP NORTH FROM HERE. BEEN ABANDONED NOW, I THINK, FOR DECADES.
!!
MOST OF THE SHADES' BELONGINGS WERE TAKEN FOR SPOILS. WE'VE QUITE A COLLECTION HERE. COME ALONG. I'LL SHOW THEM TO YOU.
SPOILS! THAT'S WHERE THEY KEEP THE BELONGINGS OF A DOWN-WORLDER WHO BROKE THE LAW!
NEVER THOUGHT MUCH OF THIS REPARATIONS BUSINESS MYSELF. MAKES DOWNWORLDERS UPPITY, THINKING THEY HAVE A RIGHT TO GET SOMETHING OUT OF US.
MORTMAIN WAS PROTESTING THE DEATH OF ANNE SHADE—SAID SHE'D HAD NOTHING TO DO WITH HER HUSBAND'S PROJECTS, HADN'T KNOWN ABOUT THEM, HE CLAIMED.
HER DEATH WAS UNDESERVED. WANTED A TRIAL OF THOSE GUILTY OF WHAT HE CALLED HER "MURDER," AND HIS PARENTS' BELONGINGS BACK.
WAS *THE BOOK OF THE WHITE* AMONG WHAT HE ASKED FOR?
IT WAS. IT WAS RETRIEVED AND PLACED IN THE LONDON INSTITUTE LIBRARY, WHERE NO DOUBT IT REMAINS STILL.
WERE YOU THERE?

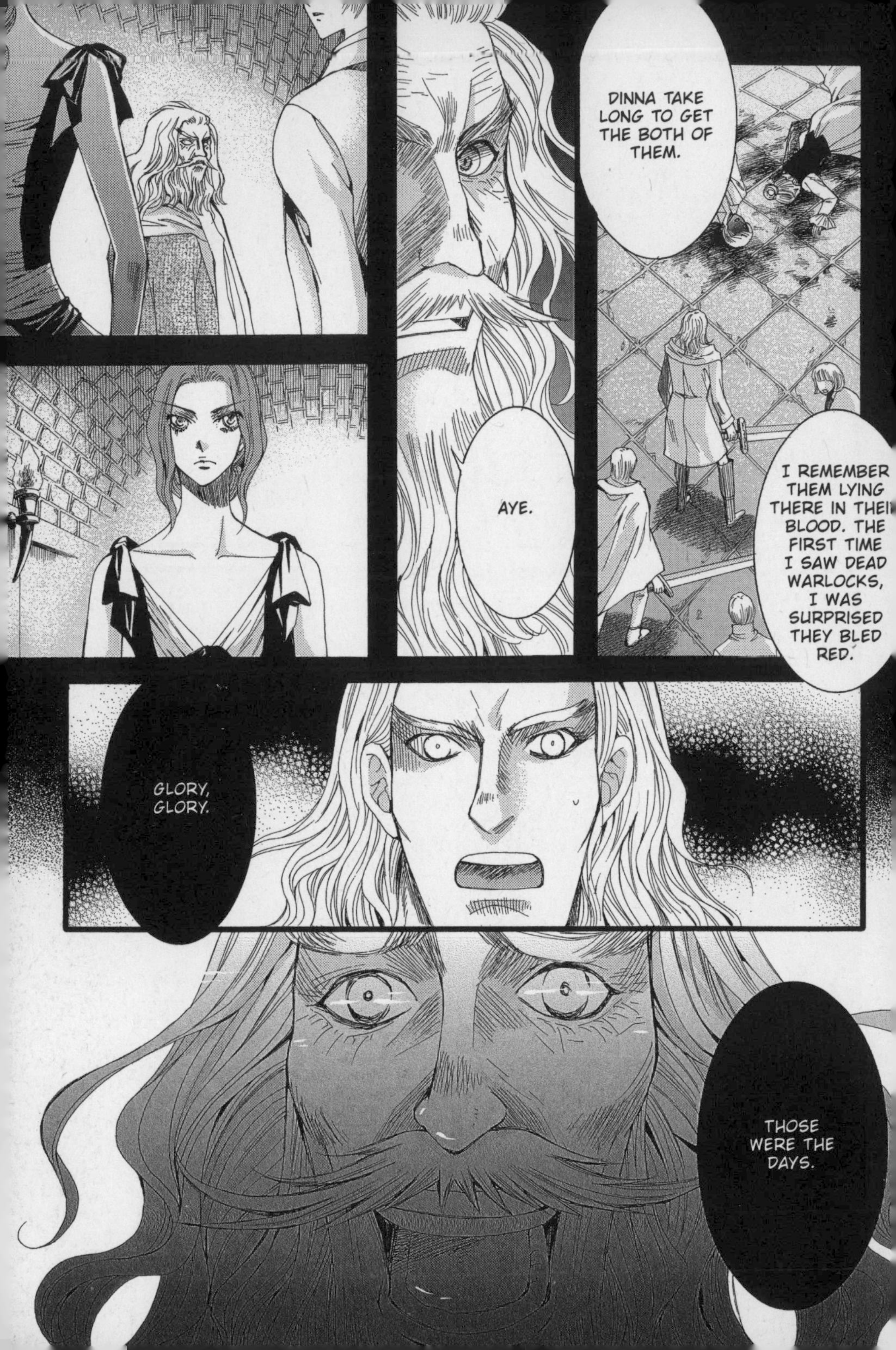
DINNA TAKE LONG TO GET THE BOTH OF THEM.
AYE.
I REMEMBER THEM LYING THERE IN THEI BLOOD. THE FIRST TIME I SAW DEAD WARLOCKS, I WAS SURPRISED THEY BLED RED.
GLORY, GLORY.
THOSE WERE THE DAYS.

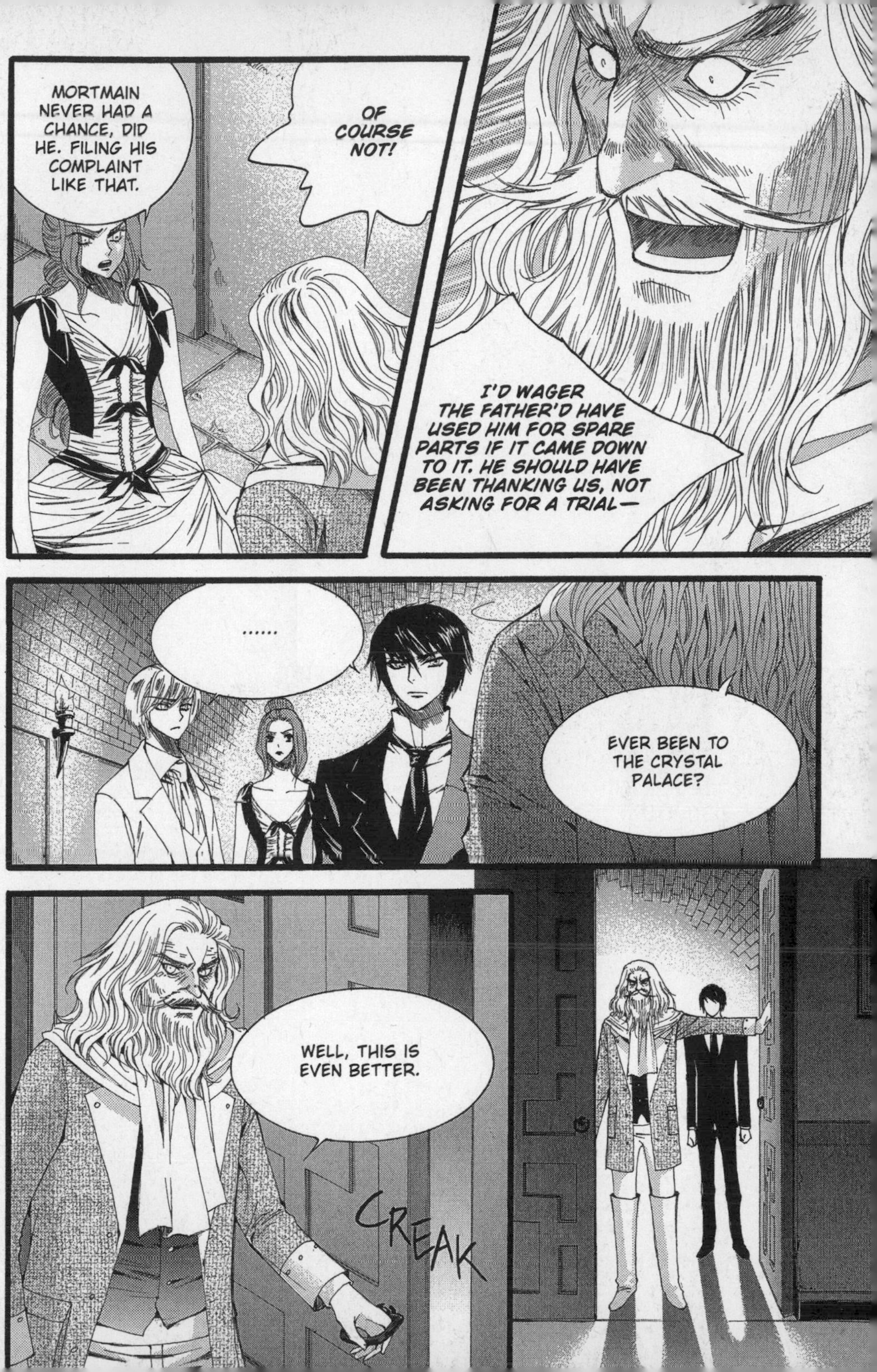
MORTMAIN NEVER HAD A CHANCE, DID HE. FILING HIS COMPLAINT LIKE THAT.
OF COURSE NOT!
I'D WAGER THE FATHER'D HAVE USED HIM FOR SPARE PARTS IF IT CAME DOWN TO IT. HE SHOULD HAVE BEEN THANKING US, NOT ASKING FOR A TRIAL—
......
EVER BEEN TO THE CRYSTAL PALACE?
WELL, THIS IS EVEN BETTER.
CREAK

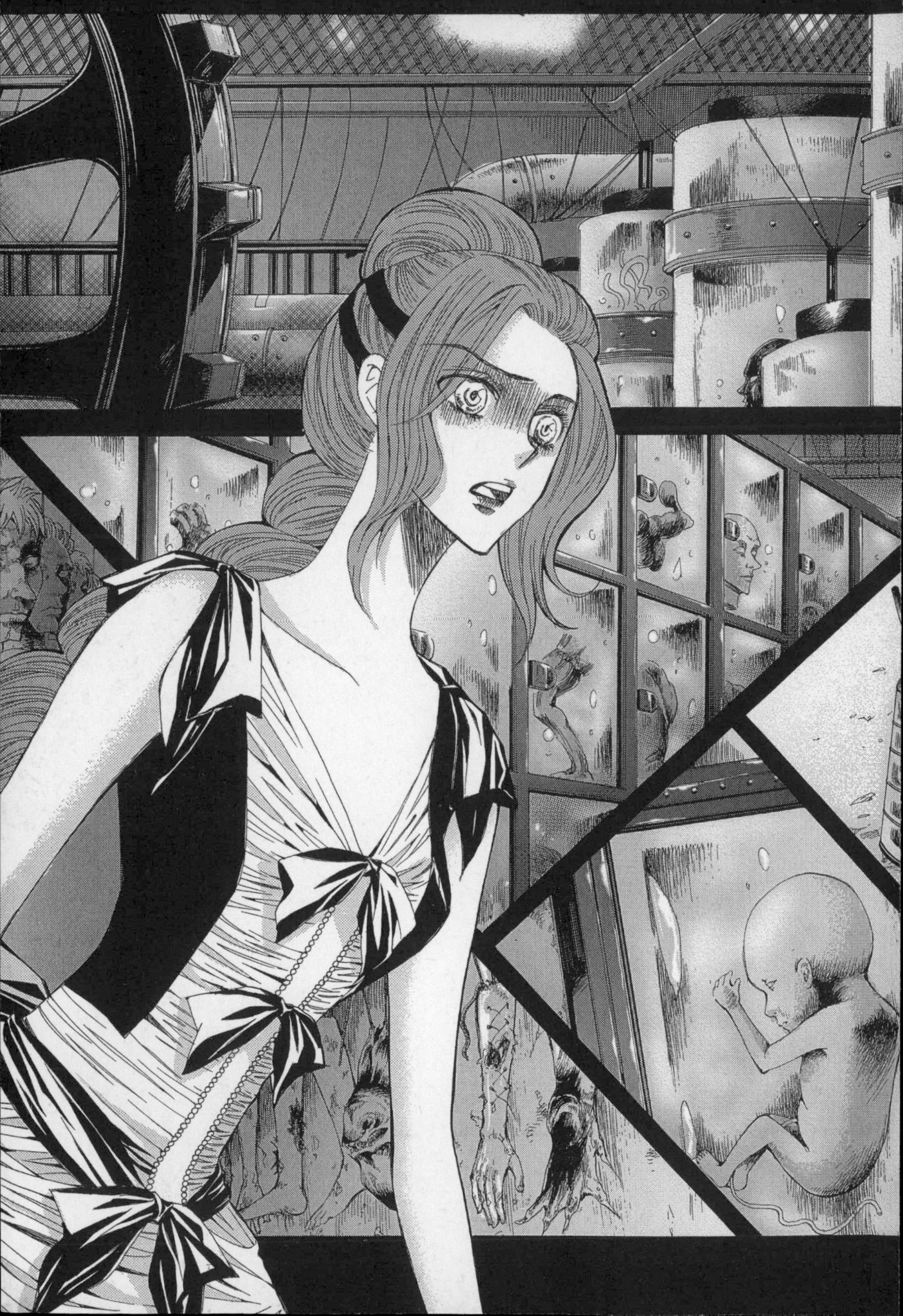

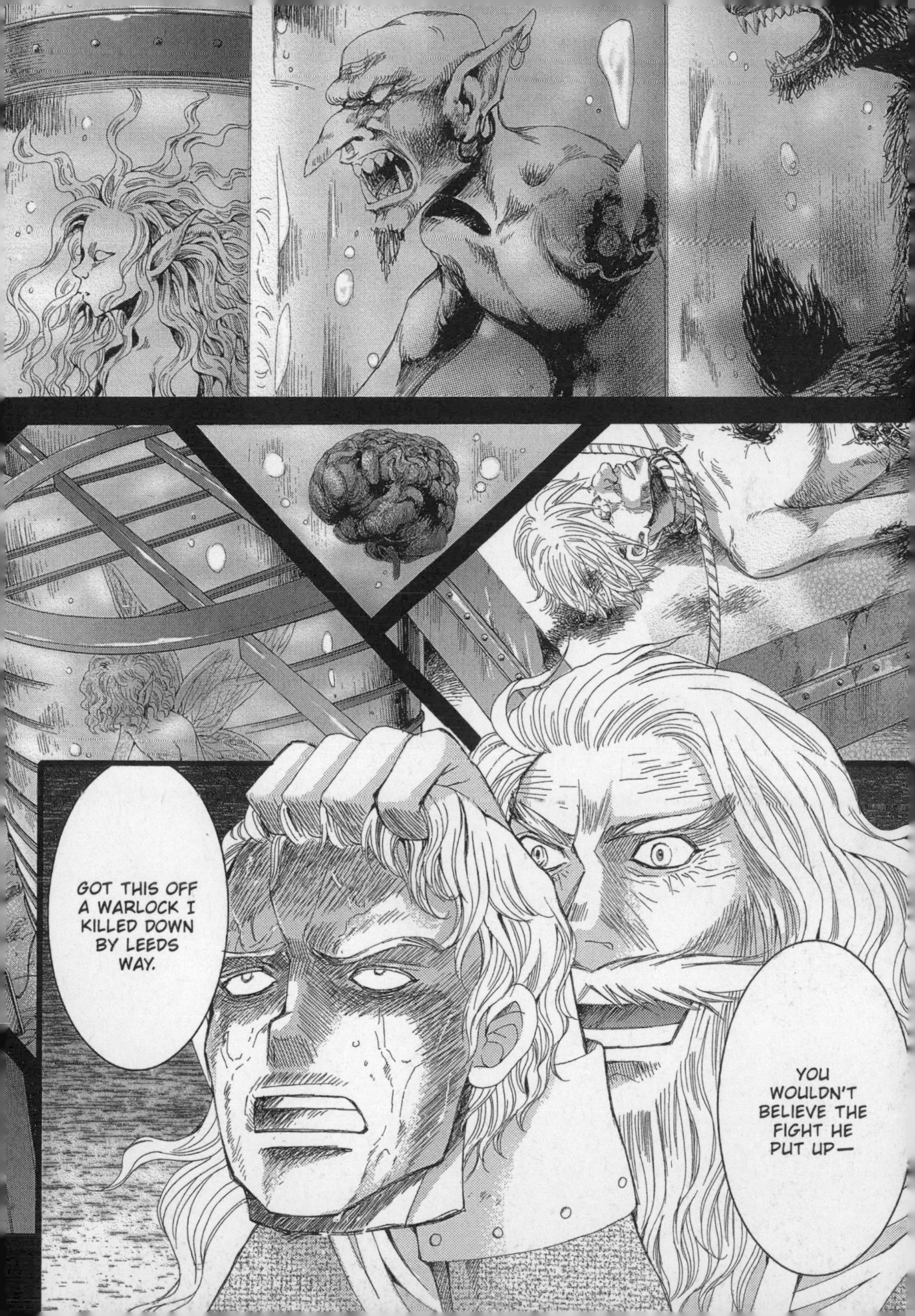
GOT THIS OFF A WARLOCK I KILLED DOWN BY LEEDS WAY.
YOU WOULDN'T BELIEVE THE FIGHT HE PUT UP—

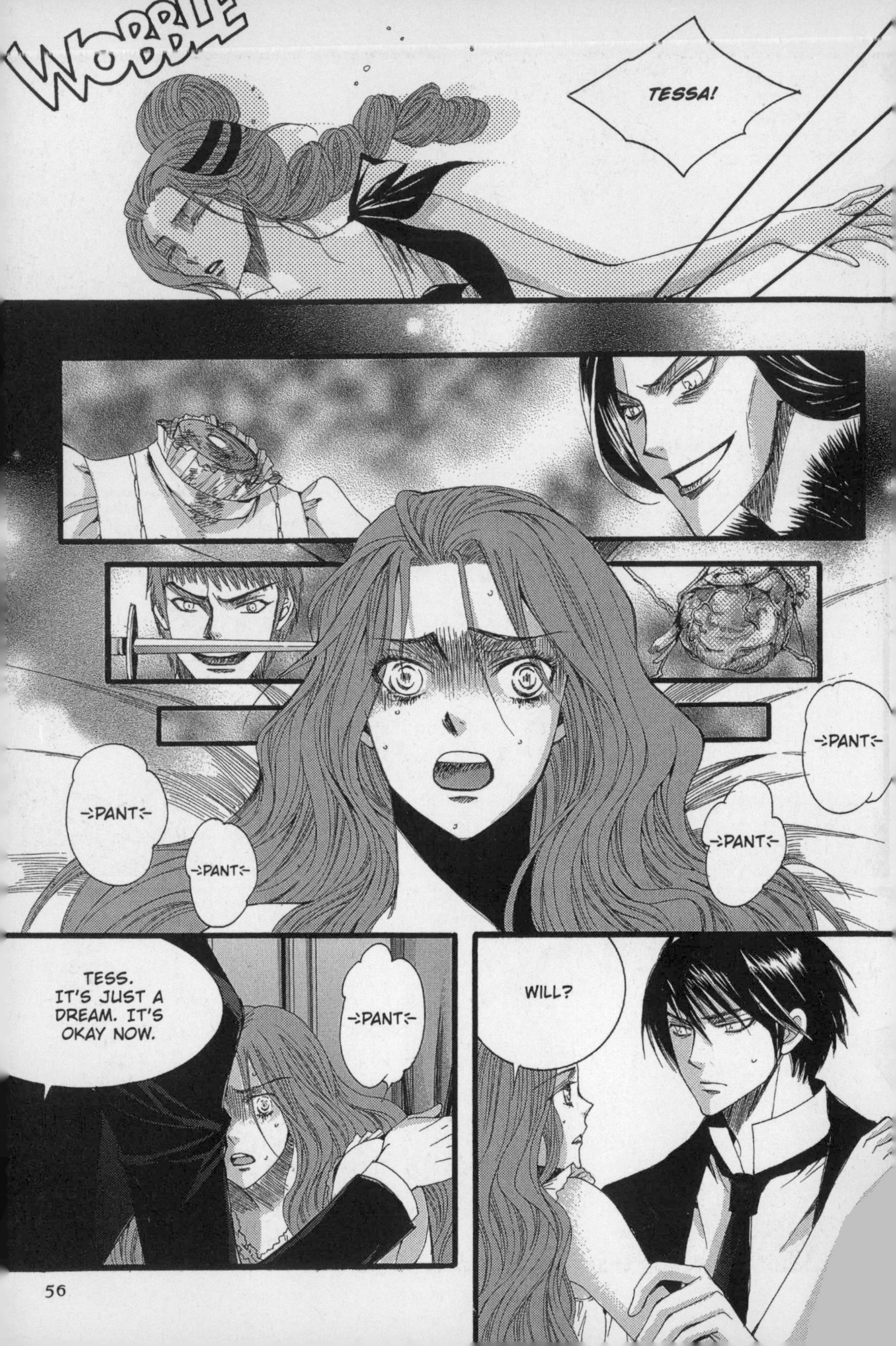
WOBBLE
TESSA!
PANT
PANT
PANT
PANT
TESS. IT'S JUST A DREAM. IT'S OKAY NOW.
PANT
WILL?

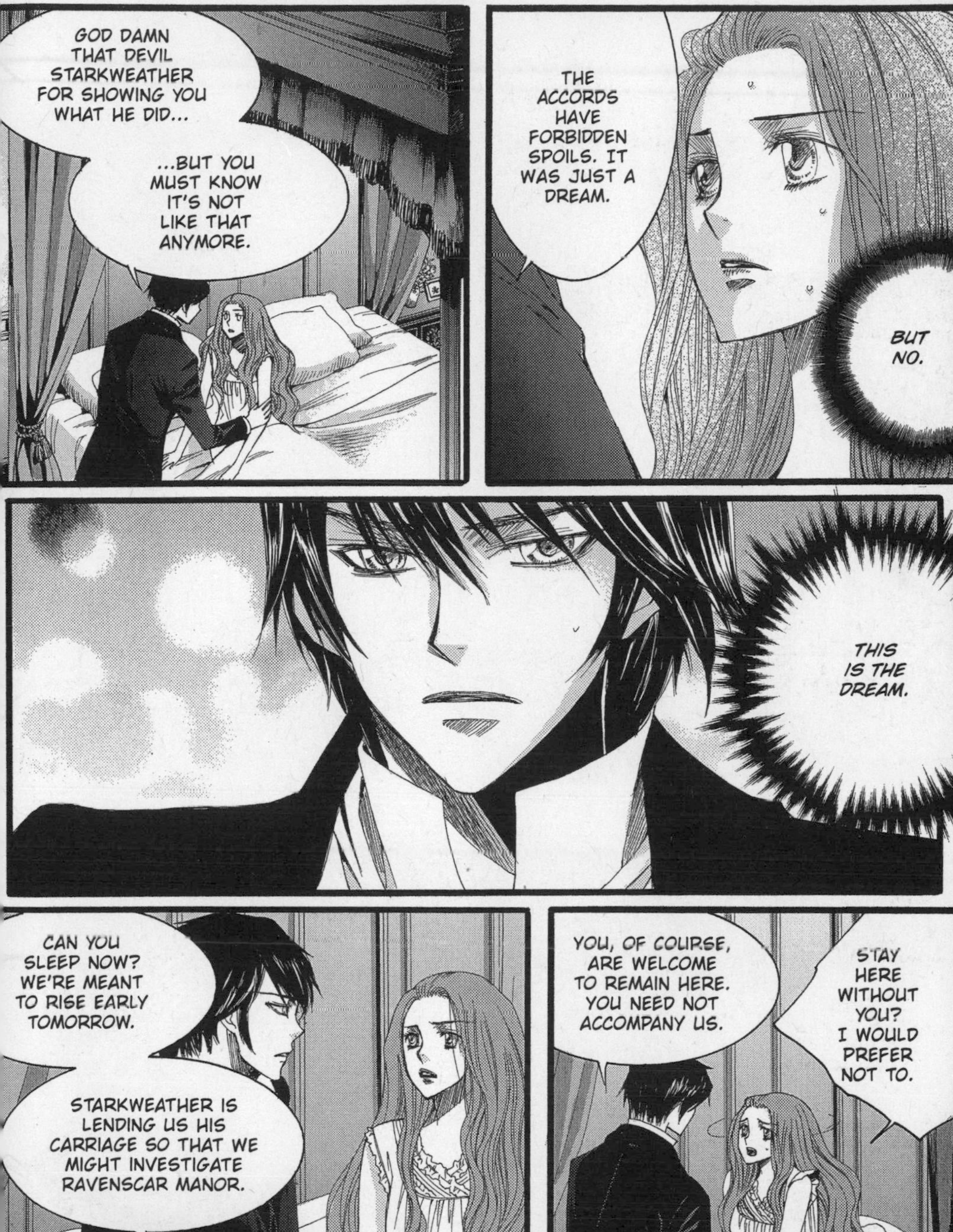
GOD DAMN THAT DEVIL STARKWEATHER FOR SHOWING YOU WHAT HE DID...
...BUT YOU MUST KNOW IT'S NOT LIKE THAT ANYMORE.
THE ACCORDS HAVE FORBIDDEN SPOILS. IT WAS JUST A DREAM.
BUT NO.
THIS IS THE DREAM.
CAN YOU SLEEP NOW? WE'RE MEANT TO RISE EARLY TOMORROW.
STARKWEATHER IS LENDING US HIS CARRIAGE SO THAT WE MIGHT INVESTIGATE RAVENSCAR MANOR.
YOU, OF COURSE, ARE WELCOME TO REMAIN HERE. YOU NEED NOT ACCOMPANY US.
STAY HERE WITHOUT YOU? I WOULD PREFER NOT TO.

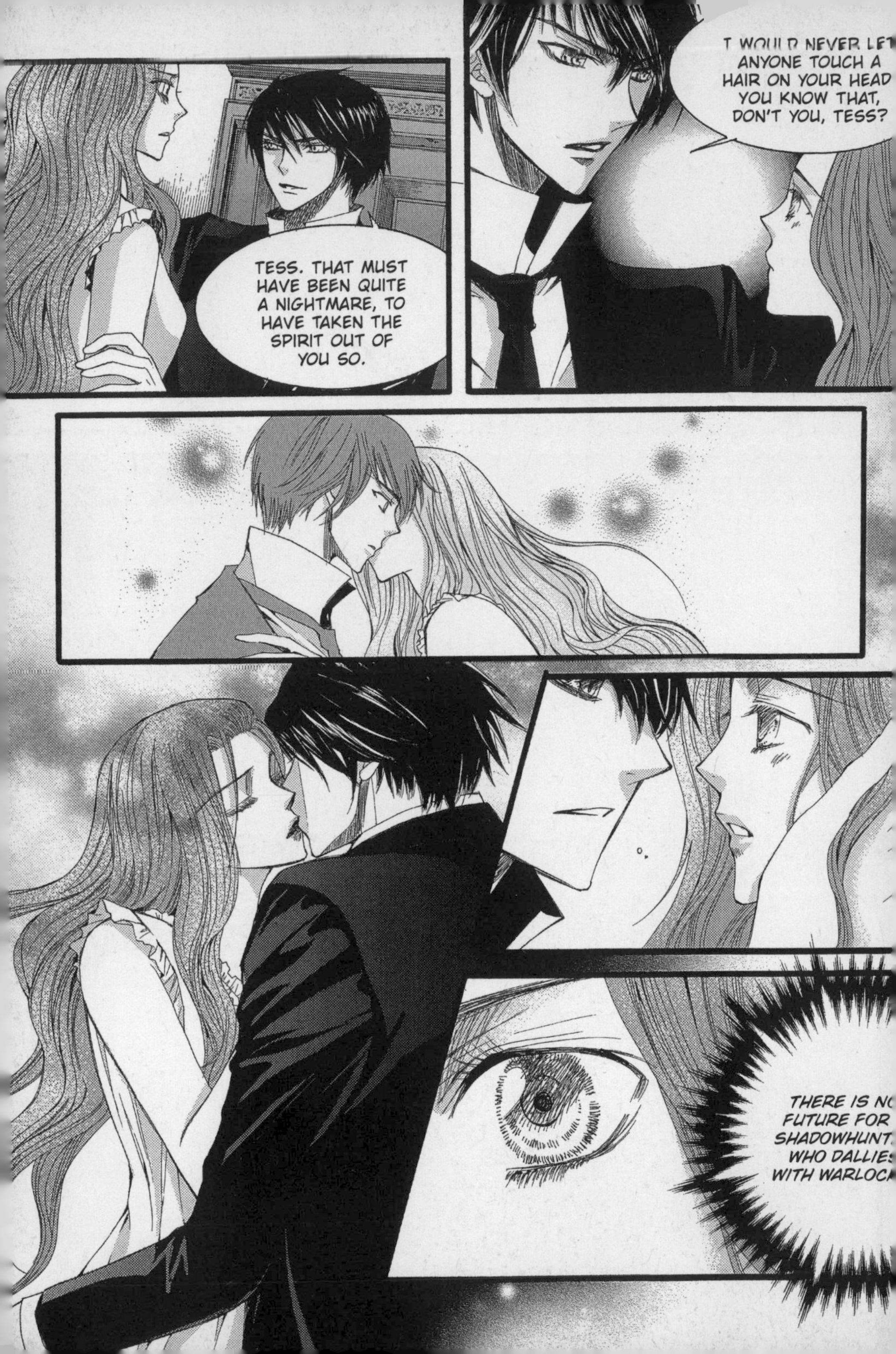
TESS. THAT MUST HAVE BEEN QUITE A NIGHTMARE, TO HAVE TAKEN THE SPIRIT OUT OF YOU SO.
I WOULD NEVER LET ANYONE TOUCH A HAIR ON YOUR HEAD YOU KNOW THAT, DON'T YOU, TESS?
THERE IS N FUTURE FOR SHADOWHUNT WHO DALLIE WITH WARLOC

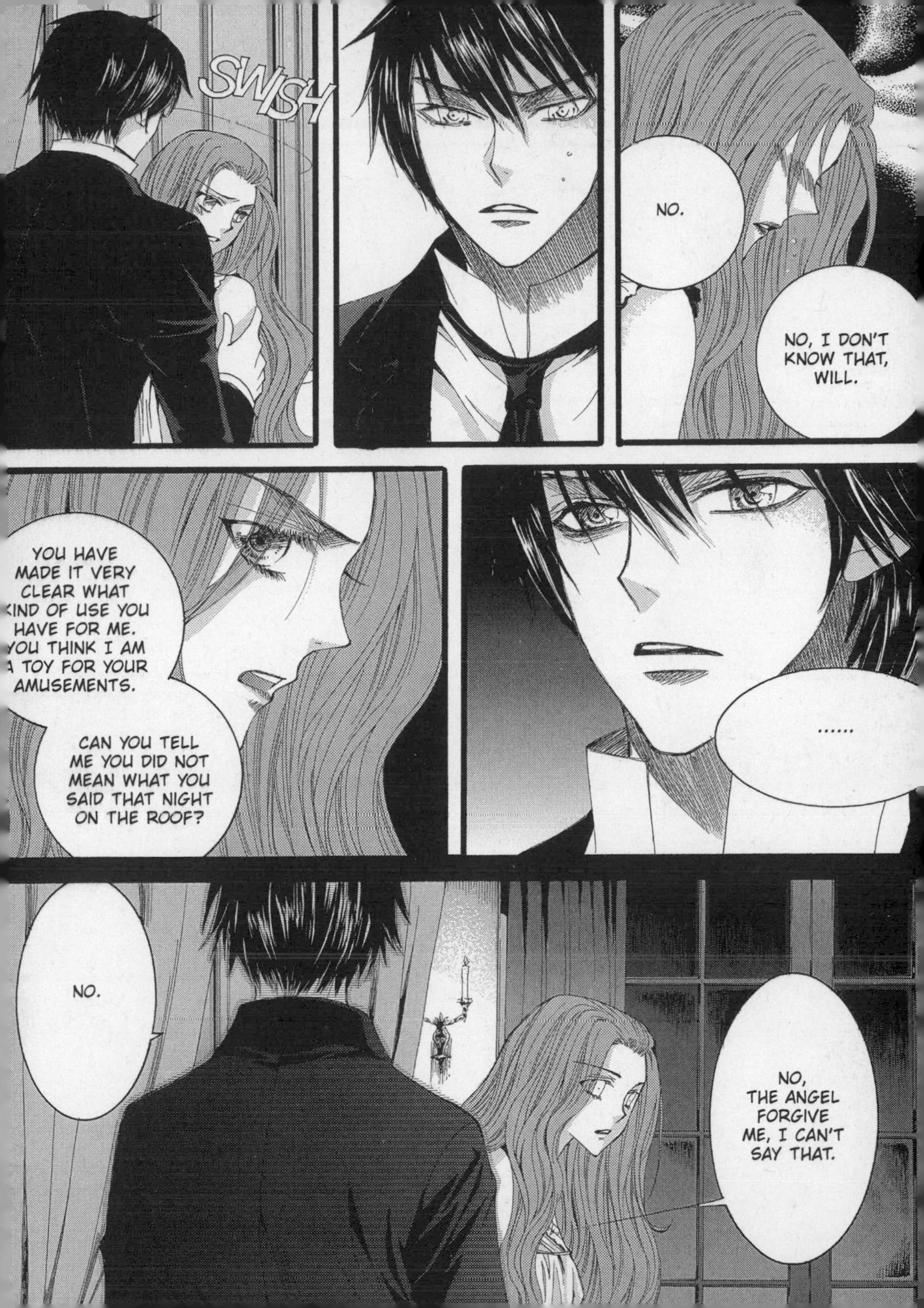
SWISH
NO.
NO, I DON'T KNOW THAT, WILL.
YOU HAVE MADE IT VERY CLEAR WHAT KIND OF USE YOU HAVE FOR ME. YOU THINK I AM A TOY FOR YOUR AMUSEMENTS.
CAN YOU TELL ME YOU DID NOT MEAN WHAT YOU SAID THAT NIGHT ON THE ROOF?
......
NO.
NO, THE ANGEL FORGIVE ME, I CAN'T SAY THAT.

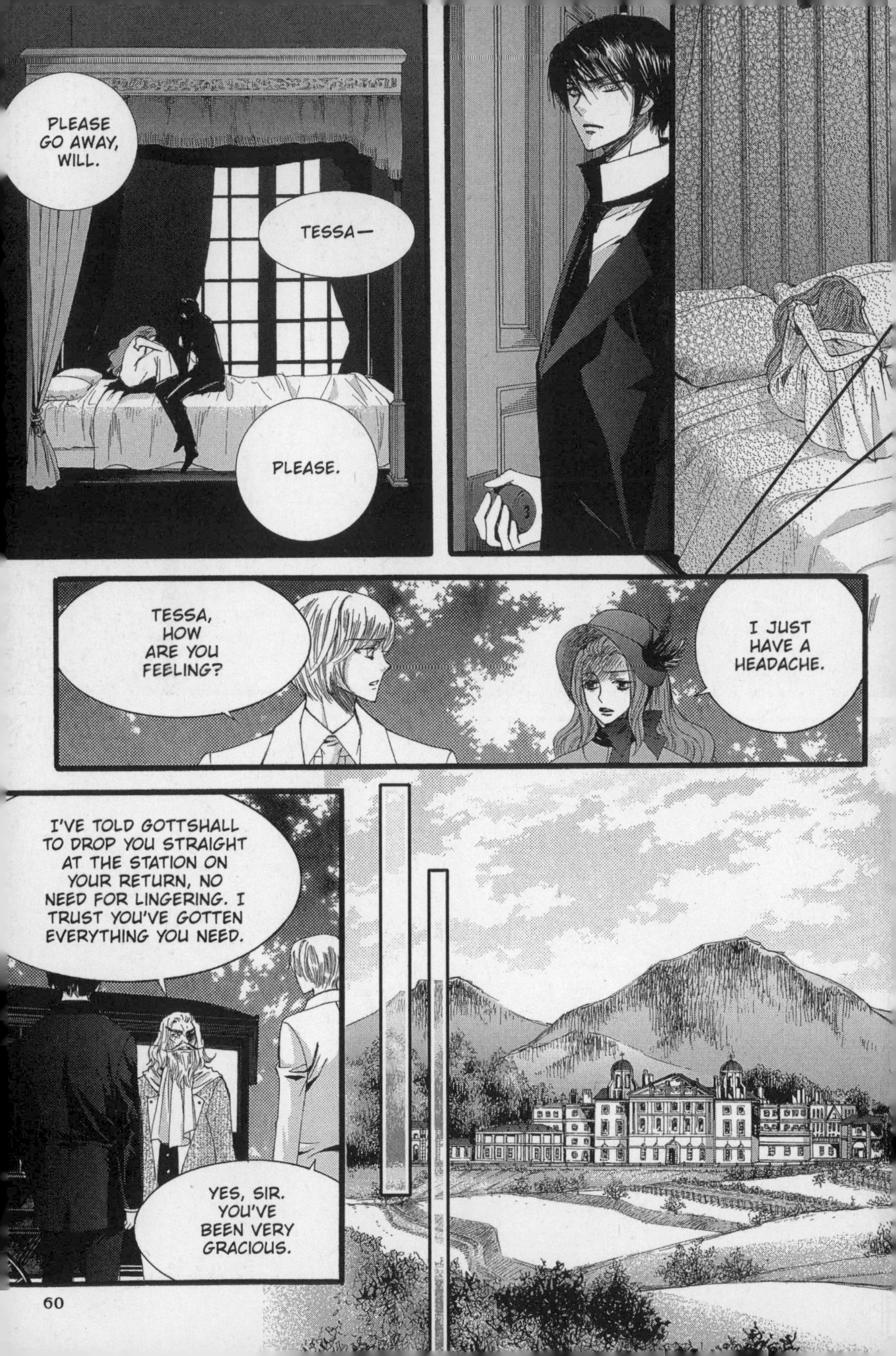
PLEASE GO AWAY, WILL.
TESSA—
PLEASE.
TESSA, HOW ARE YOU FEELING?
I JUST HAVE A HEADACHE.
I'VE TOLD GOTTSHALL TO DROP YOU STRAIGHT AT THE STATION ON YOUR RETURN, NO NEED FOR LINGERING. I TRUST YOU'VE GOTTEN EVERYTHING YOU NEED.
YES, SIR. YOU'VE BEEN VERY GRACIOUS.

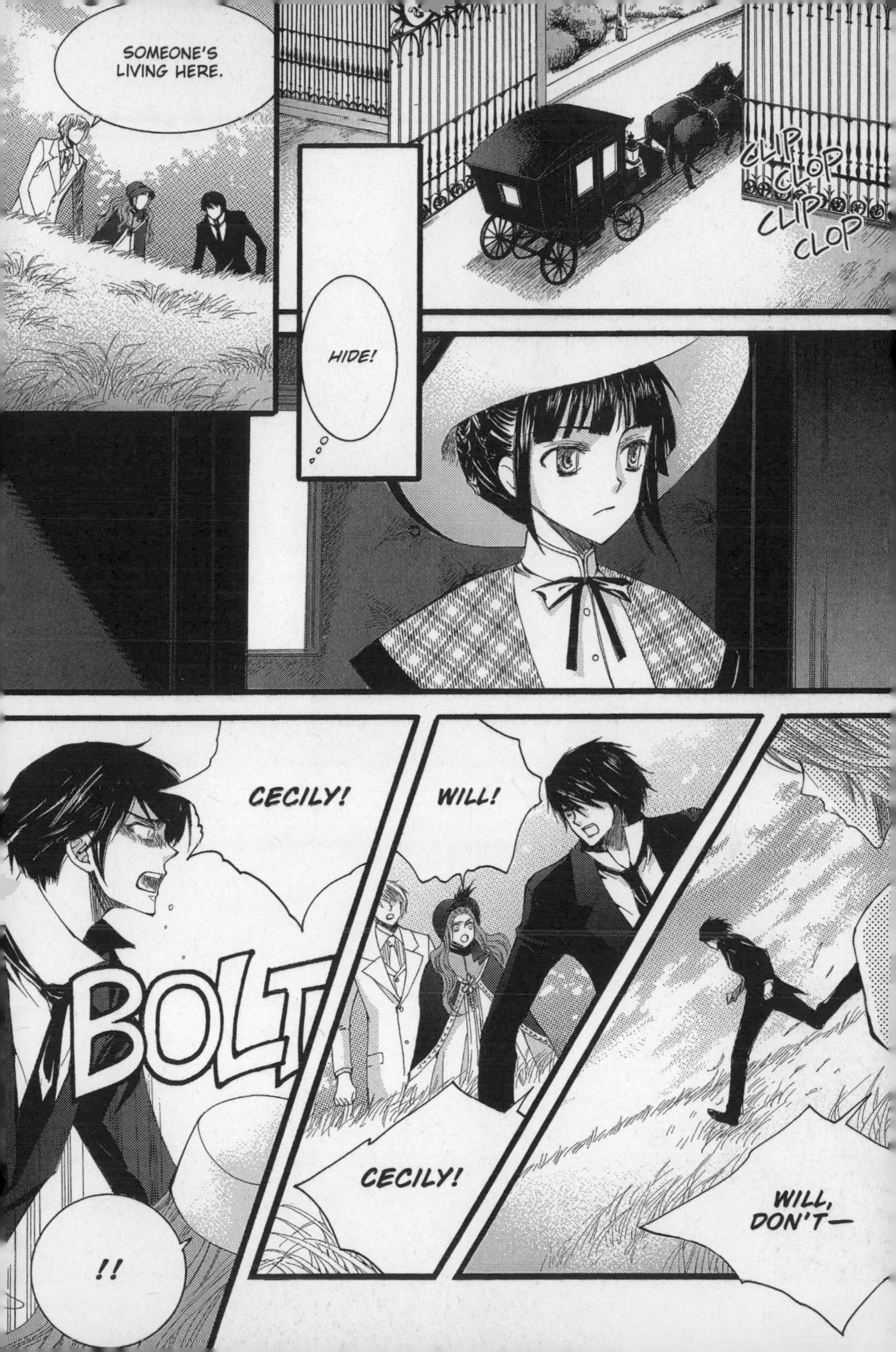
SOMEONE'S LIVING HERE.
CLIP CLOP CLIP CLOP
HIDE!
CECILY!
WILL!
BOLT
CECILY!
WILL, DON'T—
!!

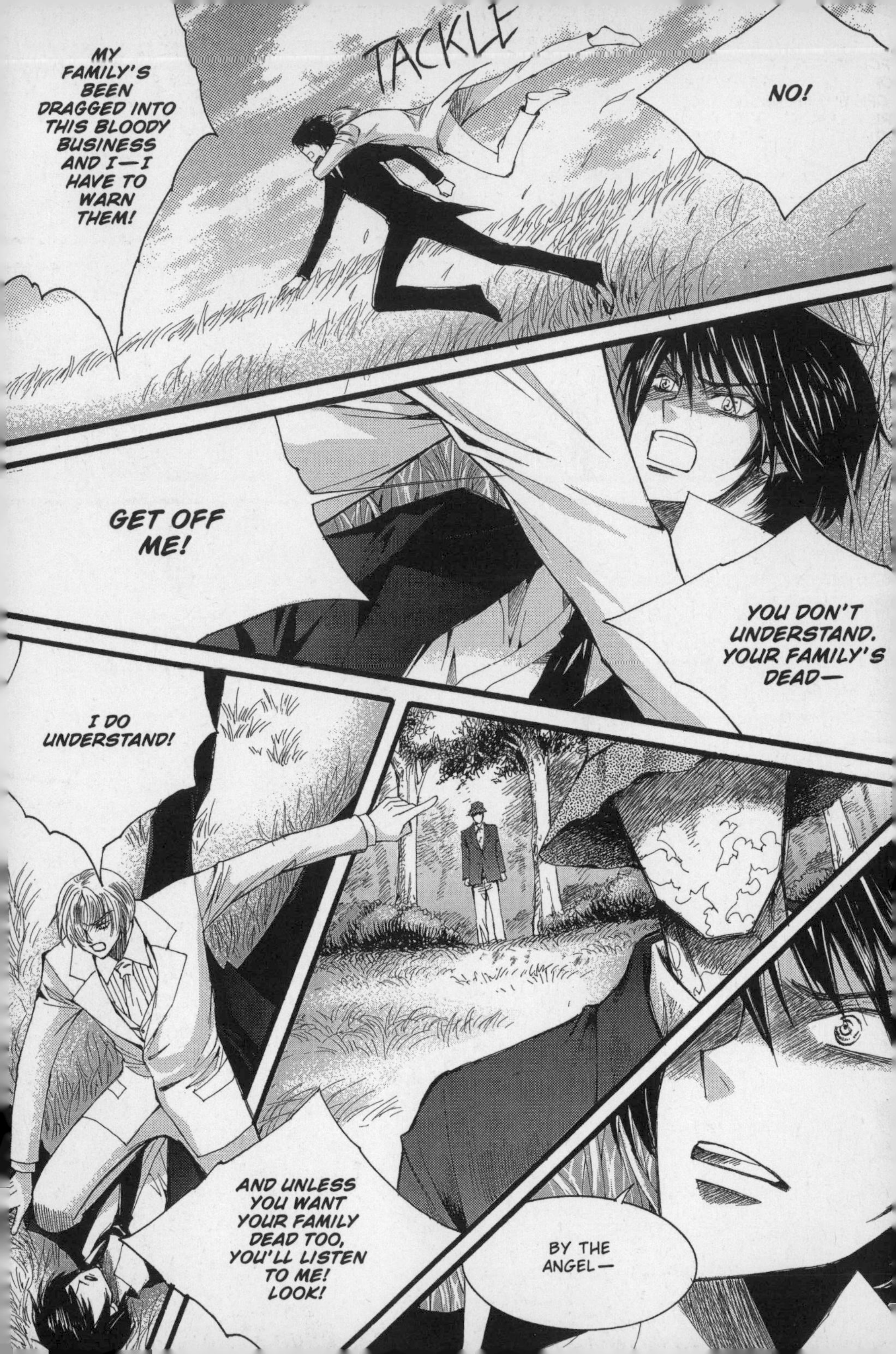

TACKLE
MY FAMILY'S BEEN DRAGGED INTO THIS BLOODY BUSINESS AND I—I HAVE TO WARN THEM!
NO!
GET OFF ME!
YOU DON'T UNDERSTAND. YOUR FAMILY'S DEAD—
I DO UNDERSTAND!
AND UNLESS YOU WANT YOUR FAMILY DEAD TOO, YOU'LL LISTEN TO ME! LOOK!
BY THE ANGEL—

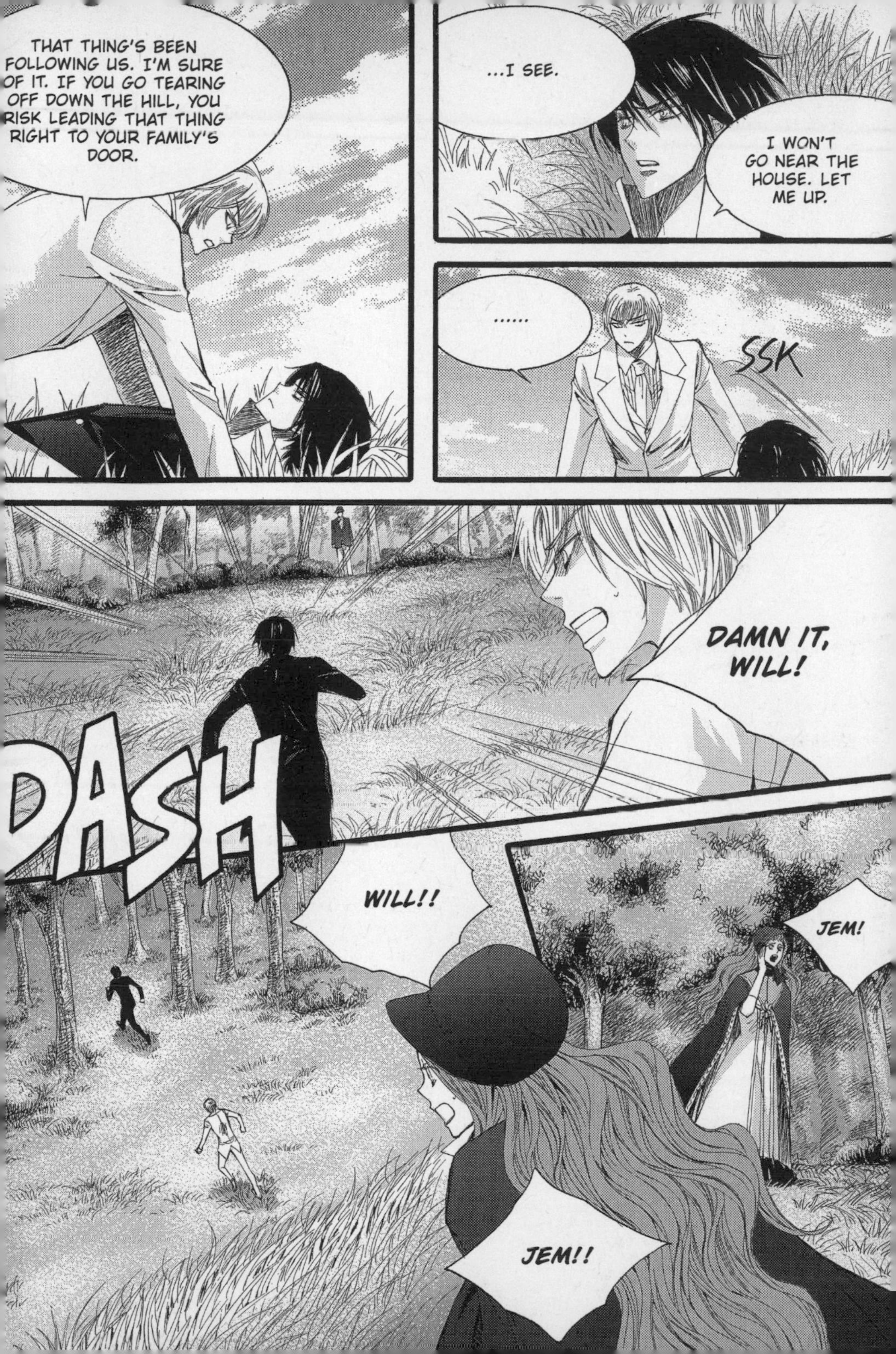
THAT THING'S BEEN FOLLOWING US. I'M SURE OF IT. IF YOU GO TEARING OFF DOWN THE HILL, YOU RISK LEADING THAT THING RIGHT TO YOUR FAMILY'S DOOR.
...I SEE.
I WON'T GO NEAR THE HOUSE. LET ME UP.
......
SSK
DAMN IT, WILL!
DASH
WILL!!
JEM!
JEM!!

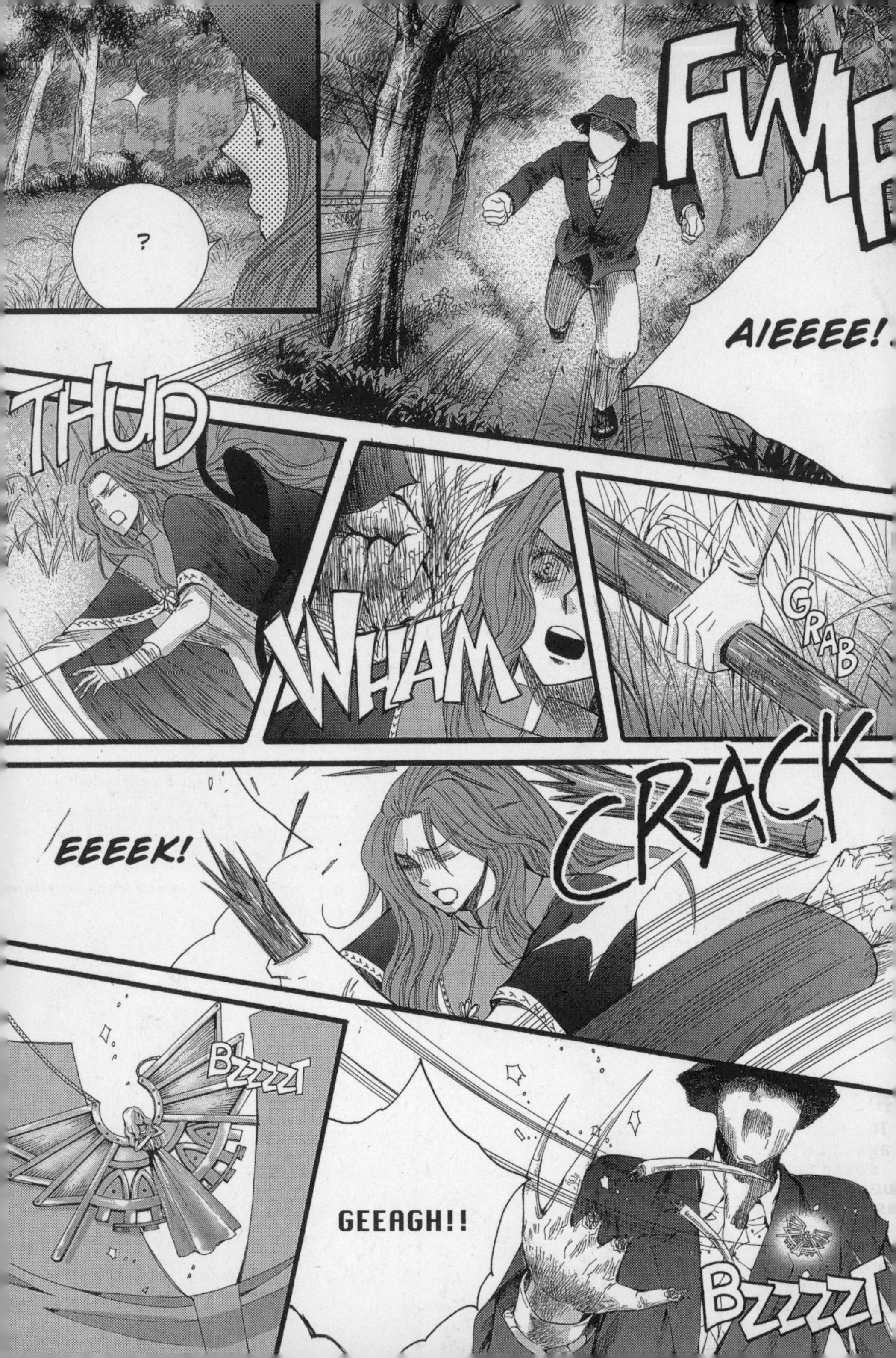
?
FWIP
AIEEEE!
THUD
WHAM
GRAB
CRACK
EEEEK!
BZZZZT
GEEAGH!!
BZZZZT

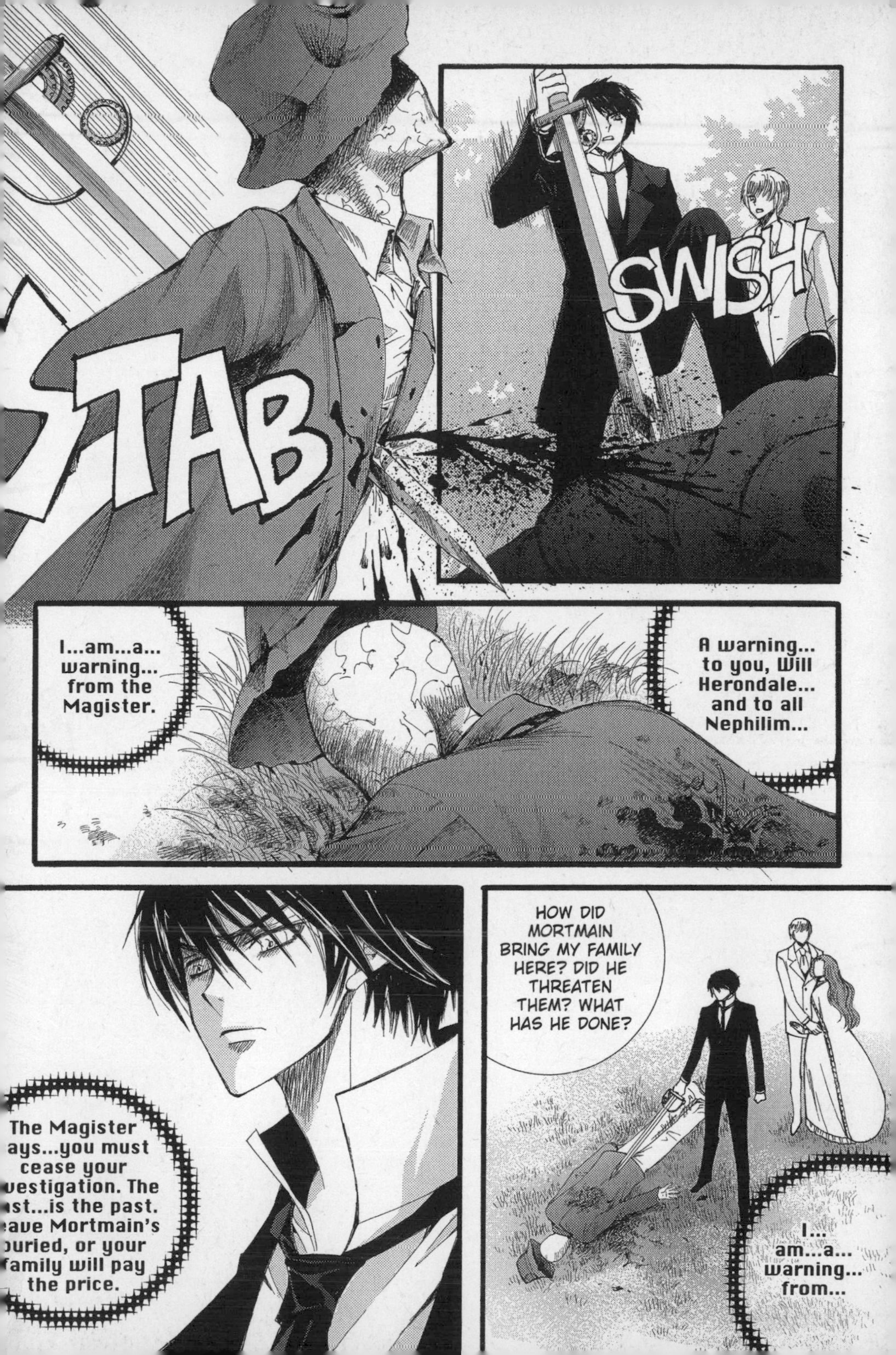
TAB
SWISH
I...am...a... warning... from the Magister.
A warning... to you, Will Herondale... and to all Nephilim...
The Magister ays...you must cease your vestigation. The ast...is the past. eave Mortmain's buried, or your family will pay the price.
HOW DID MORTMAIN BRING MY FAMILY HERE? DID HE THREATEN THEM? WHAT HAS HE DONE?
I... am...a... warning... from...

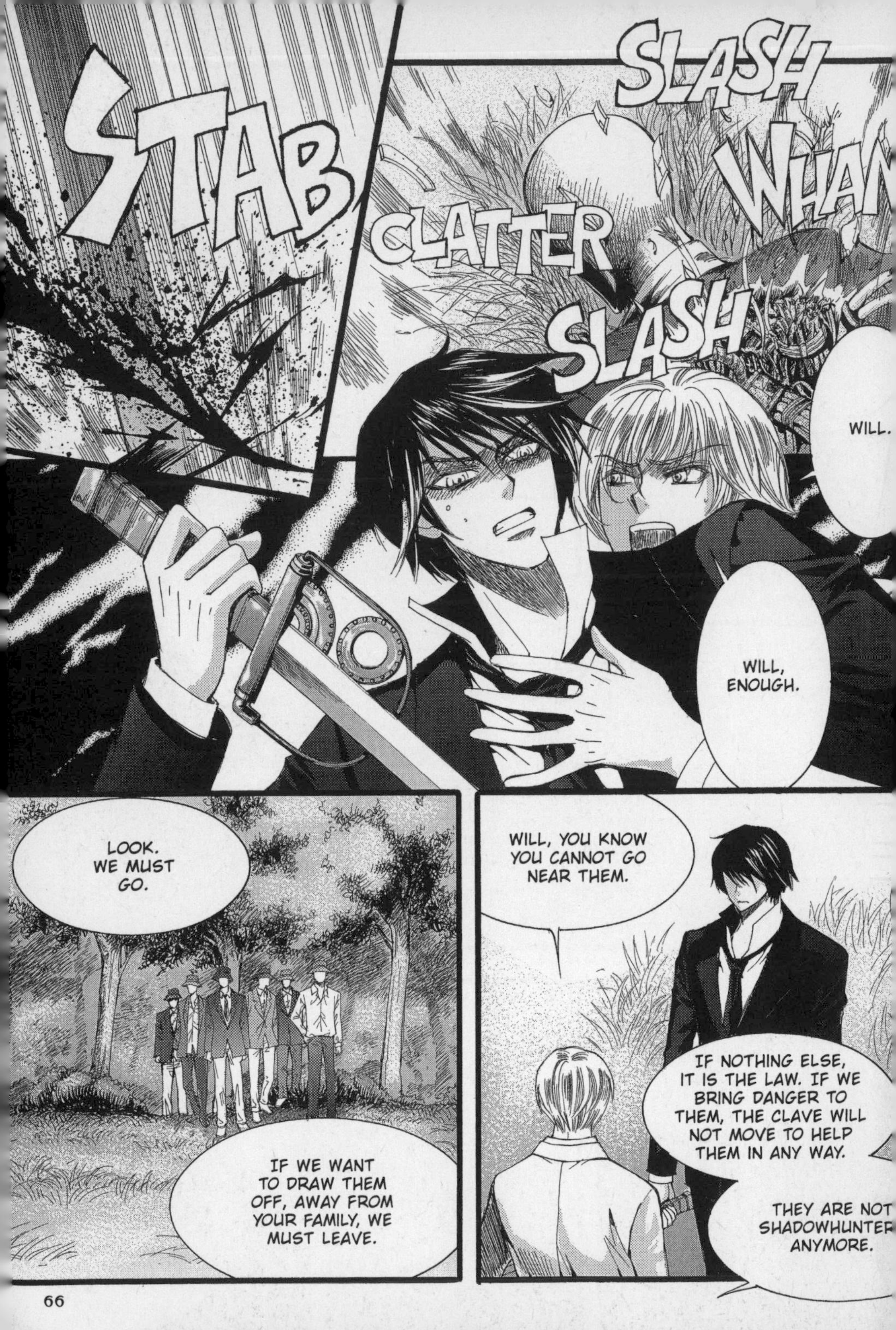
STAB
SLASH
CLATTER
WHA
SLASH
WILL.
WILL, ENOUGH.
LOOK. WE MUST GO.
IF WE WANT TO DRAW THEM OFF, AWAY FROM YOUR FAMILY, WE MUST LEAVE.
WILL, YOU KNOW YOU CANNOT GO NEAR THEM.
IF NOTHING ELSE, IT IS THE LAW. IF WE BRING DANGER TO THEM, THE CLAVE WILL NOT MOVE TO HELP THEM IN ANY WAY.
THEY ARE NOT SHADOWHUNTER ANYMORE.

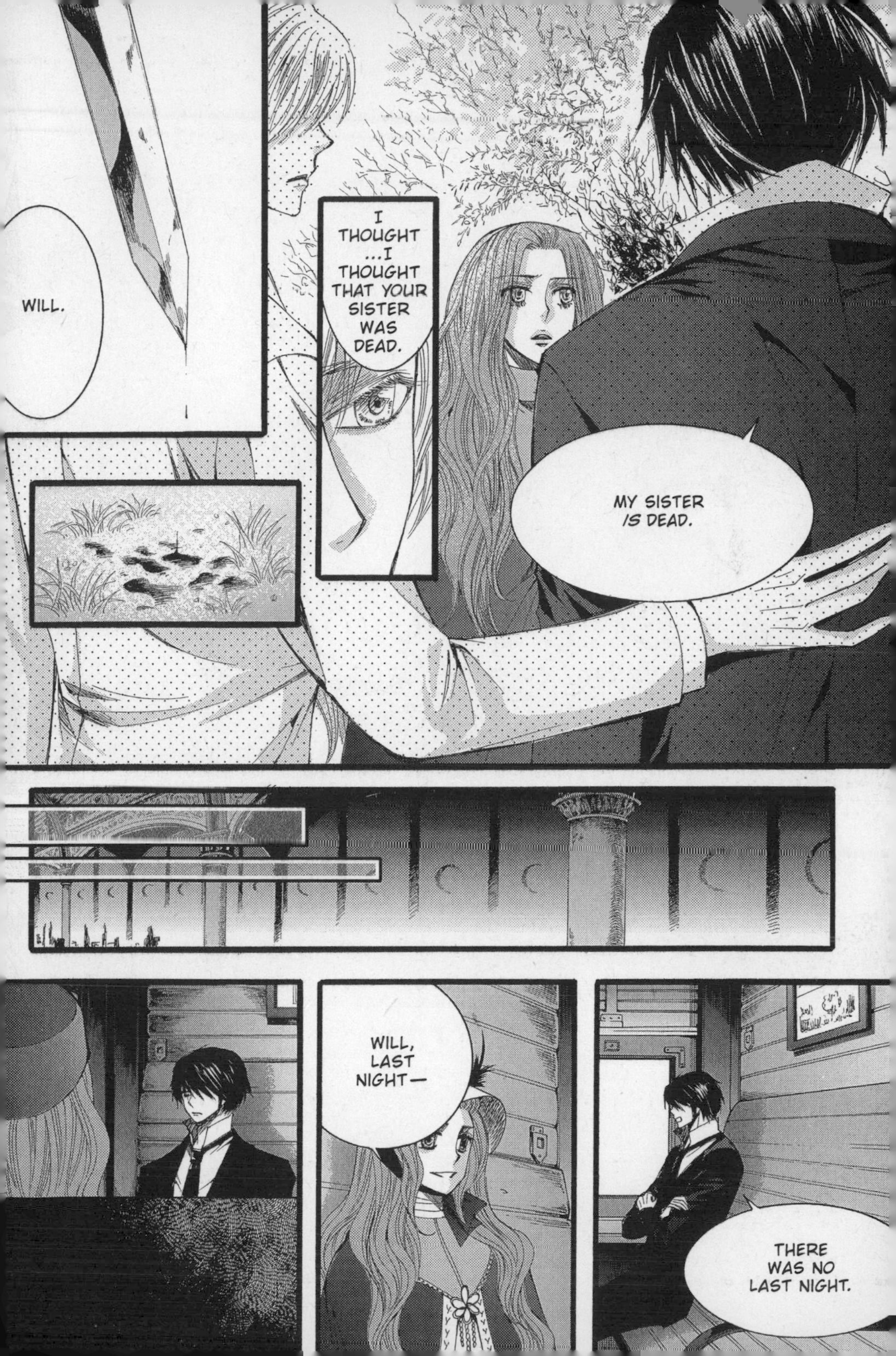
WILL.
I THOUGHT ...I THOUGHT THAT YOUR SISTER WAS DEAD.
MY SISTER IS DEAD.
WILL, LAST NIGHT—
THERE WAS NO LAST NIGHT.

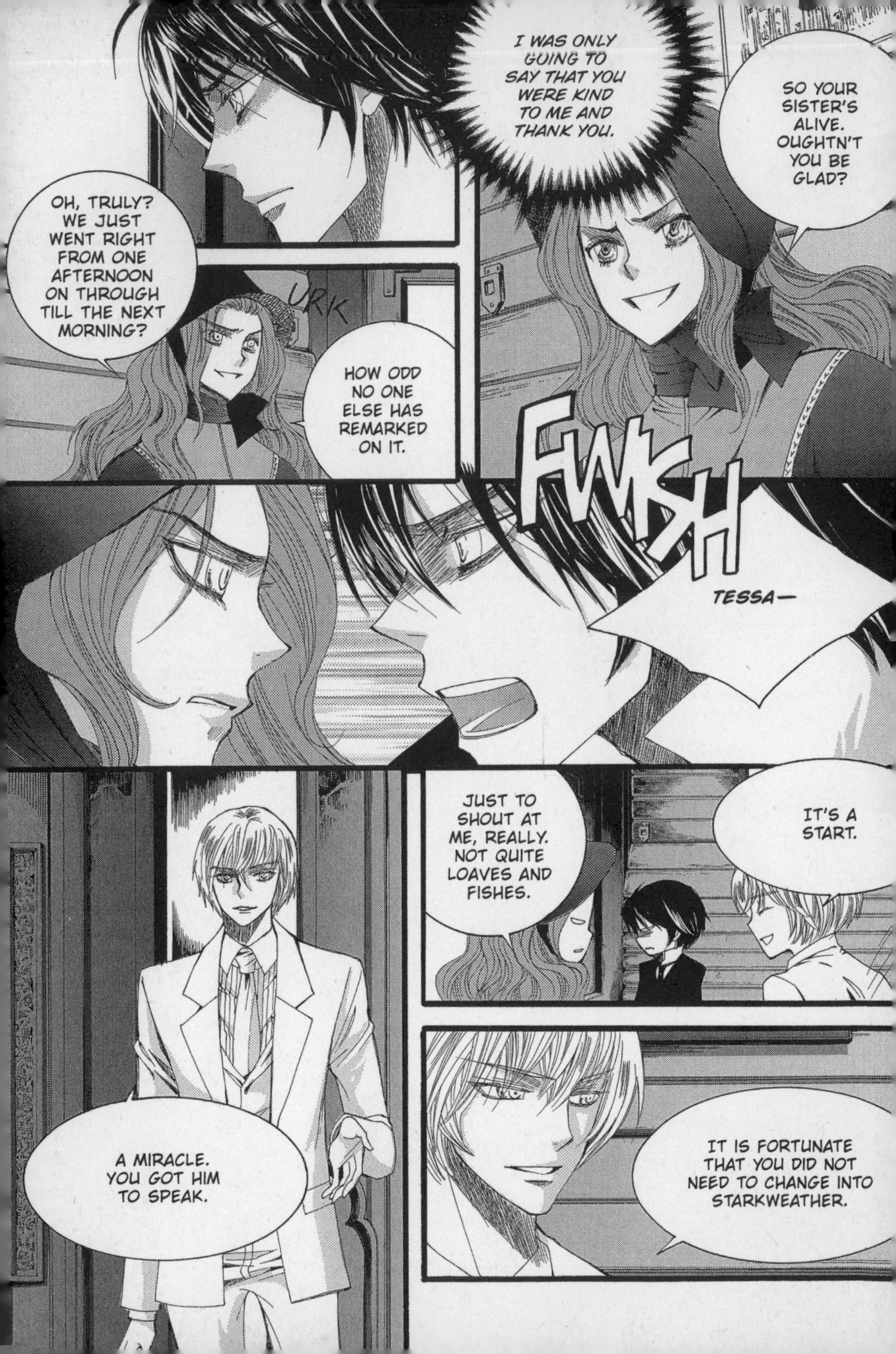
I WAS ONLY GOING TO SAY THAT YOU WERE KIND TO ME AND THANK YOU.
SO YOUR SISTER'S ALIVE. OUGHTN'T YOU BE GLAD?
OH, TRULY? WE JUST WENT RIGHT FROM ONE AFTERNOON ON THROUGH TILL THE NEXT MORNING?
URK
HOW ODD NO ONE ELSE HAS REMARKED ON IT.
FWISH
TESSA—
A MIRACLE. YOU GOT HIM TO SPEAK.
JUST TO SHOUT AT ME, REALLY. NOT QUITE LOAVES AND FISHES.
IT'S A START.
IT IS FORTUNATE THAT YOU DID NOT NEED TO CHANGE INTO STARKWEATHER.

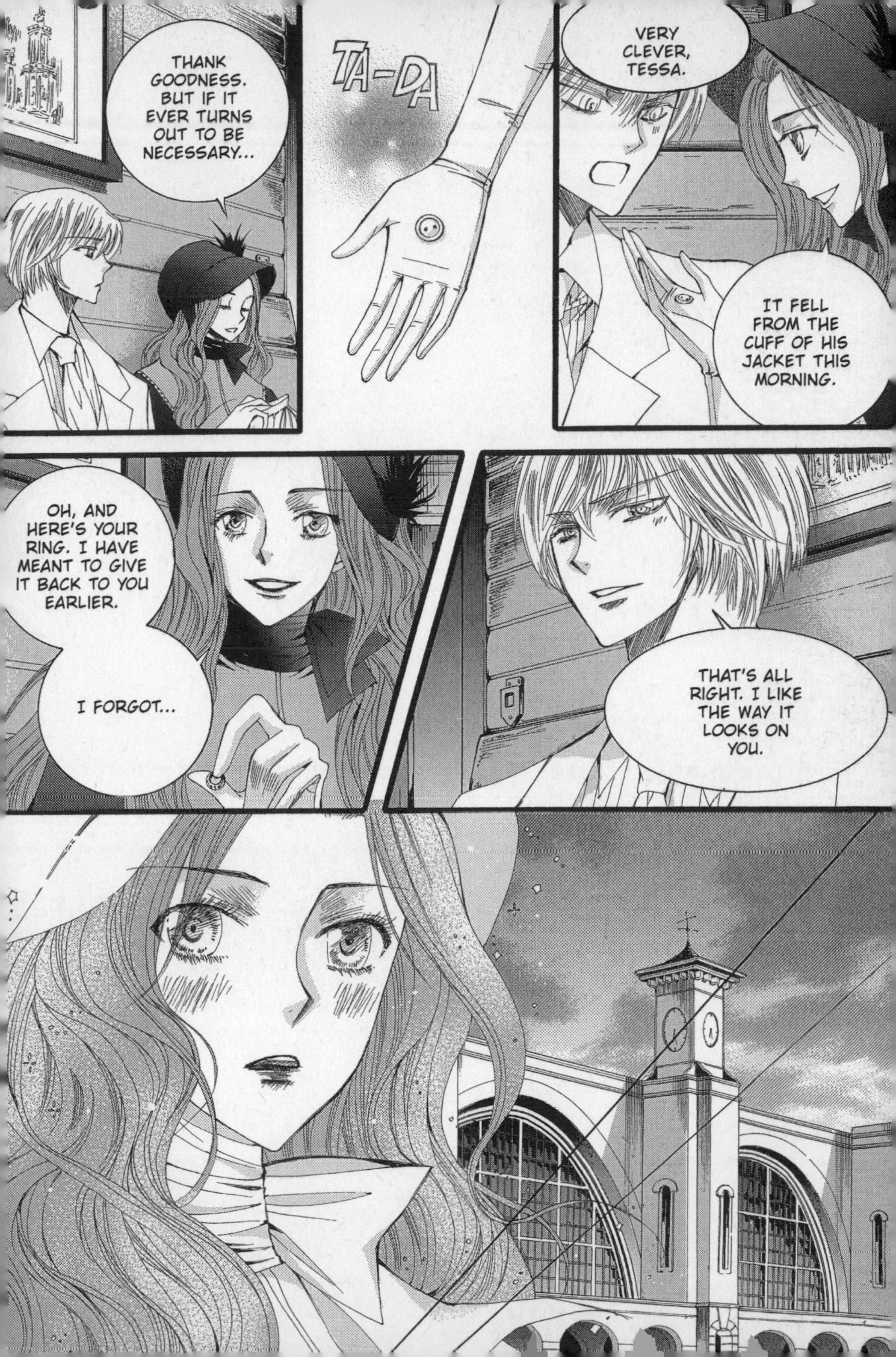
THANK GOODNESS. BUT IF IT EVER TURNS OUT TO BE NECESSARY...
TA-DA
VERY CLEVER, TESSA.
IT FELL FROM THE CUFF OF HIS JACKET THIS MORNING.
OH, AND HERE'S YOUR RING. I HAVE MEANT TO GIVE IT BACK TO YOU EARLIER.
I FORGOT...
THAT'S ALL RIGHT. I LIKE THE WAY IT LOOKS ON YOU.

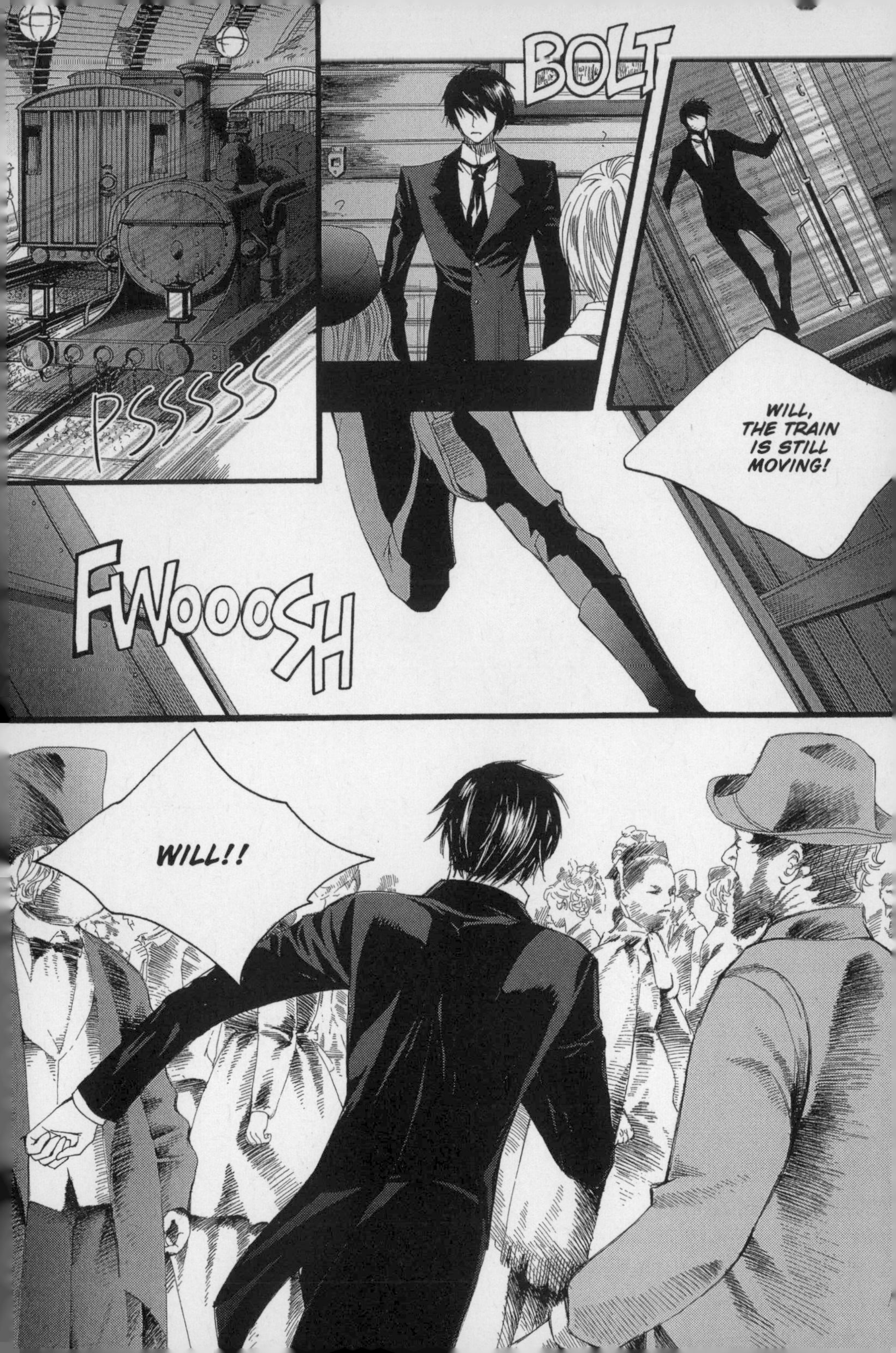
PSSSSS
BOLT
WILL, THE TRAIN IS STILL MOVING!
FWOOOSH
WILL!!

THE INFERNAL DEVICES
CLOCKWORK PRINCE

CHAPTER 11

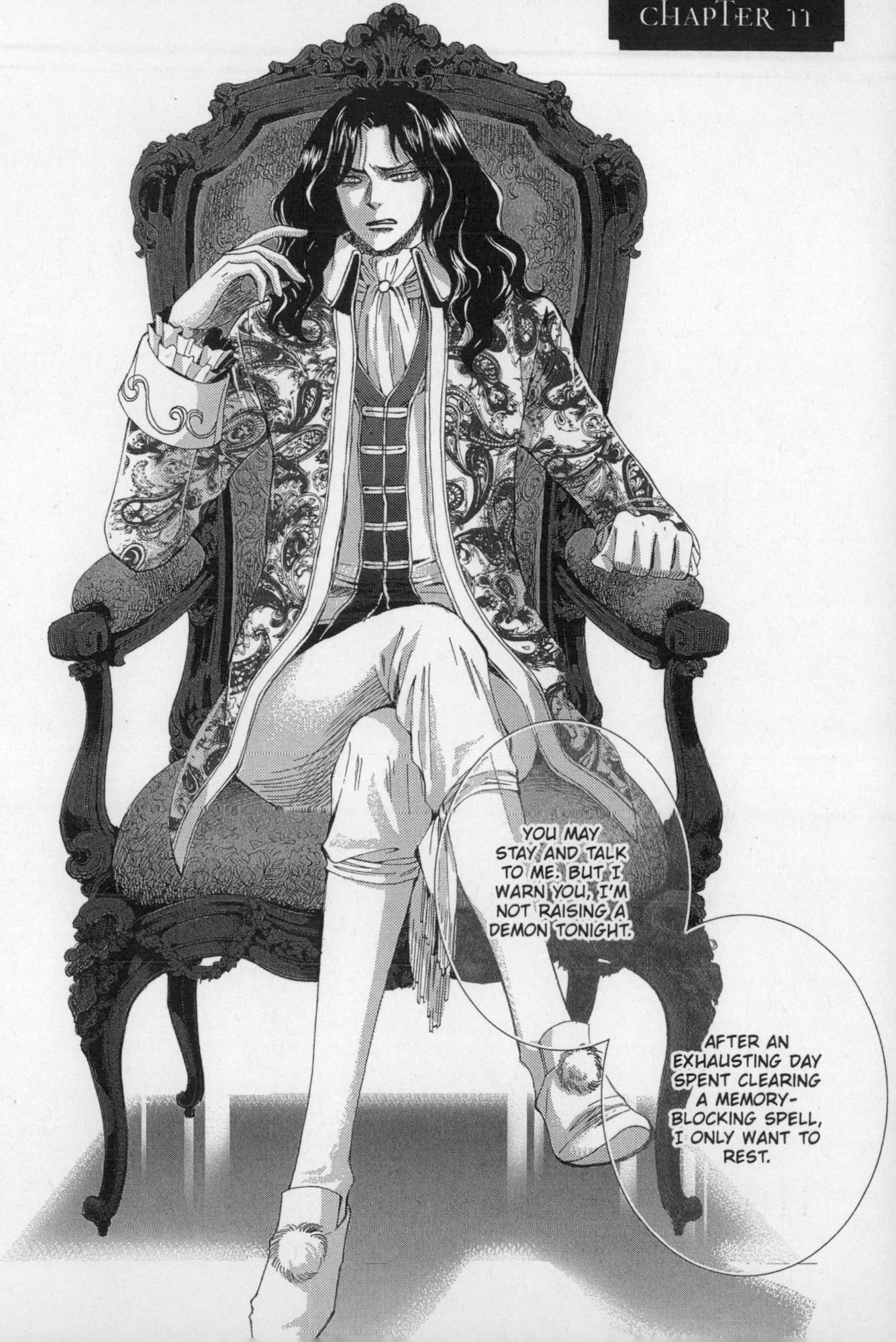
YOU MAY STAY AND TALK TO ME. BUT I WARN YOU, I'M NOT RAISING A DEMON TONIGHT.
AFTER AN EXHAUSTING DAY SPENT CLEARING A MEMORY-BLOCKING SPELL, I ONLY WANT TO REST.

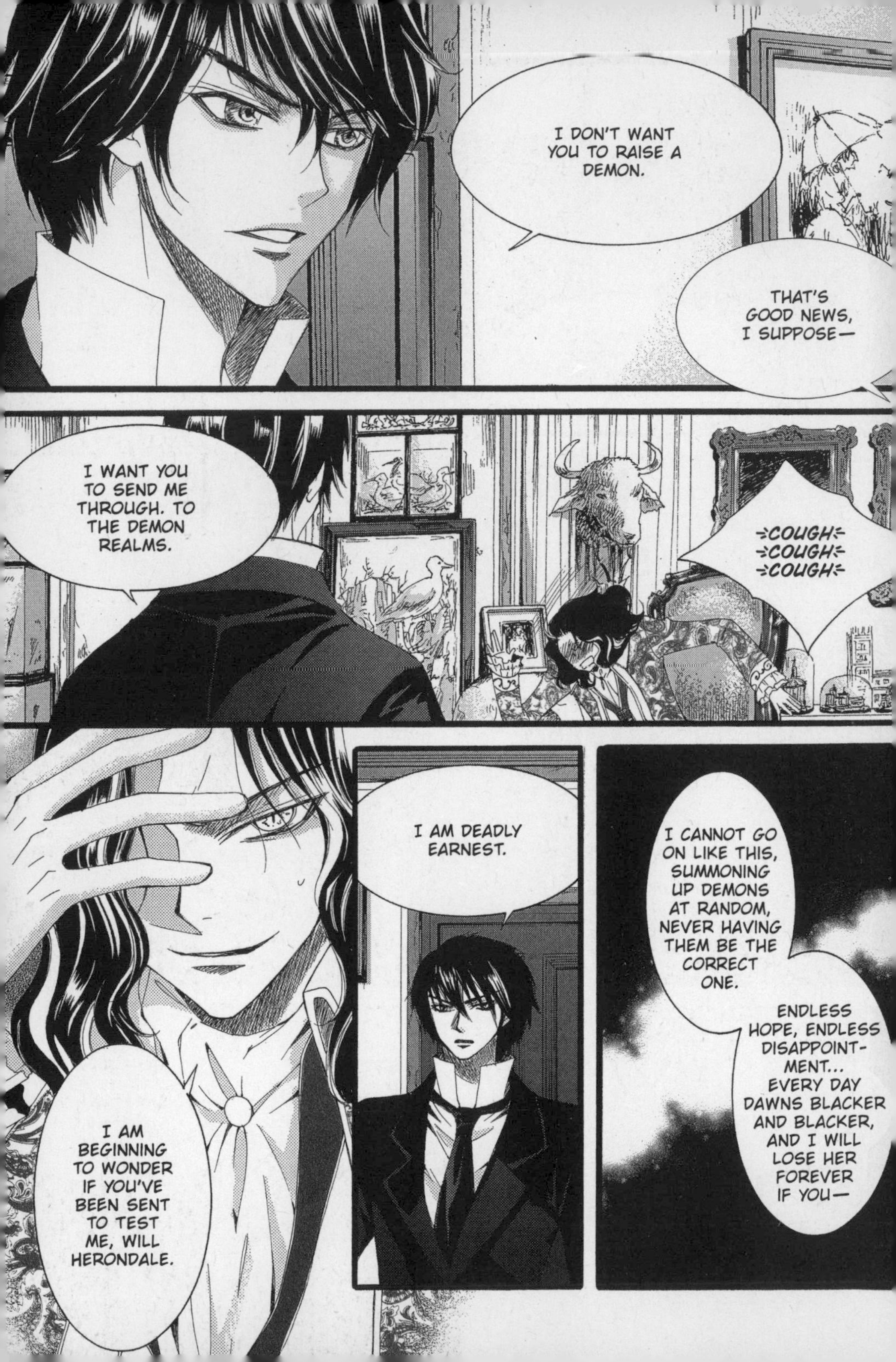

I DON'T WANT YOU TO RAISE A DEMON.
THAT'S GOOD NEWS, I SUPPOSE—
I WANT YOU TO SEND ME THROUGH. TO THE DEMON REALMS.
≠COUGH≠ ≠COUGH≠ ≠COUGH≠
I AM DEADLY EARNEST.
I CANNOT GO ON LIKE THIS, SUMMONING UP DEMONS AT RANDOM, NEVER HAVING THEM BE THE CORRECT ONE.
ENDLESS HOPE, ENDLESS DISAPPOINT-MENT... EVERY DAY DAWNS BLACKER AND BLACKER, AND I WILL LOSE HER FOREVER IF YOU—
I AM BEGINNING TO WONDER IF YOU'VE BEEN SENT TO TEST ME, WILL HERONDALE.

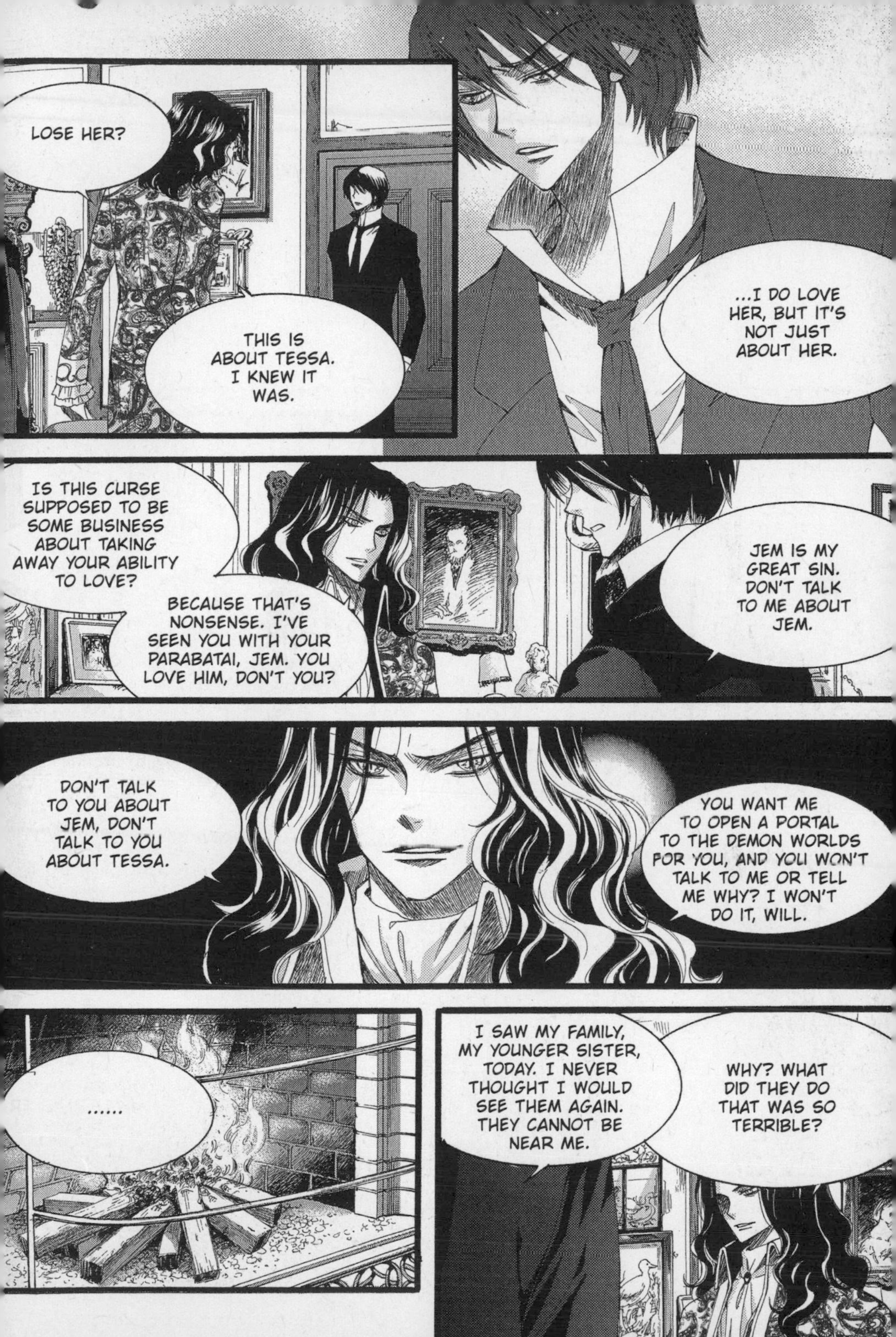
LOSE HER?
THIS IS ABOUT TESSA. I KNEW IT WAS.
...I DO LOVE HER, BUT IT'S NOT JUST ABOUT HER.
IS THIS CURSE SUPPOSED TO BE SOME BUSINESS ABOUT TAKING AWAY YOUR ABILITY TO LOVE?
BECAUSE THAT'S NONSENSE. I'VE SEEN YOU WITH YOUR PARABATAI, JEM. YOU LOVE HIM, DON'T YOU?
JEM IS MY GREAT SIN. DON'T TALK TO ME ABOUT JEM.
DON'T TALK TO YOU ABOUT JEM, DON'T TALK TO YOU ABOUT TESSA.
YOU WANT ME TO OPEN A PORTAL TO THE DEMON WORLDS FOR YOU, AND YOU WON'T TALK TO ME OR TELL ME WHY? I WON'T DO IT, WILL.
......
I SAW MY FAMILY, MY YOUNGER SISTER, TODAY. I NEVER THOUGHT I WOULD SEE THEM AGAIN. THEY CANNOT BE NEAR ME.
WHY? WHAT DID THEY DO THAT WAS SO TERRIBLE?

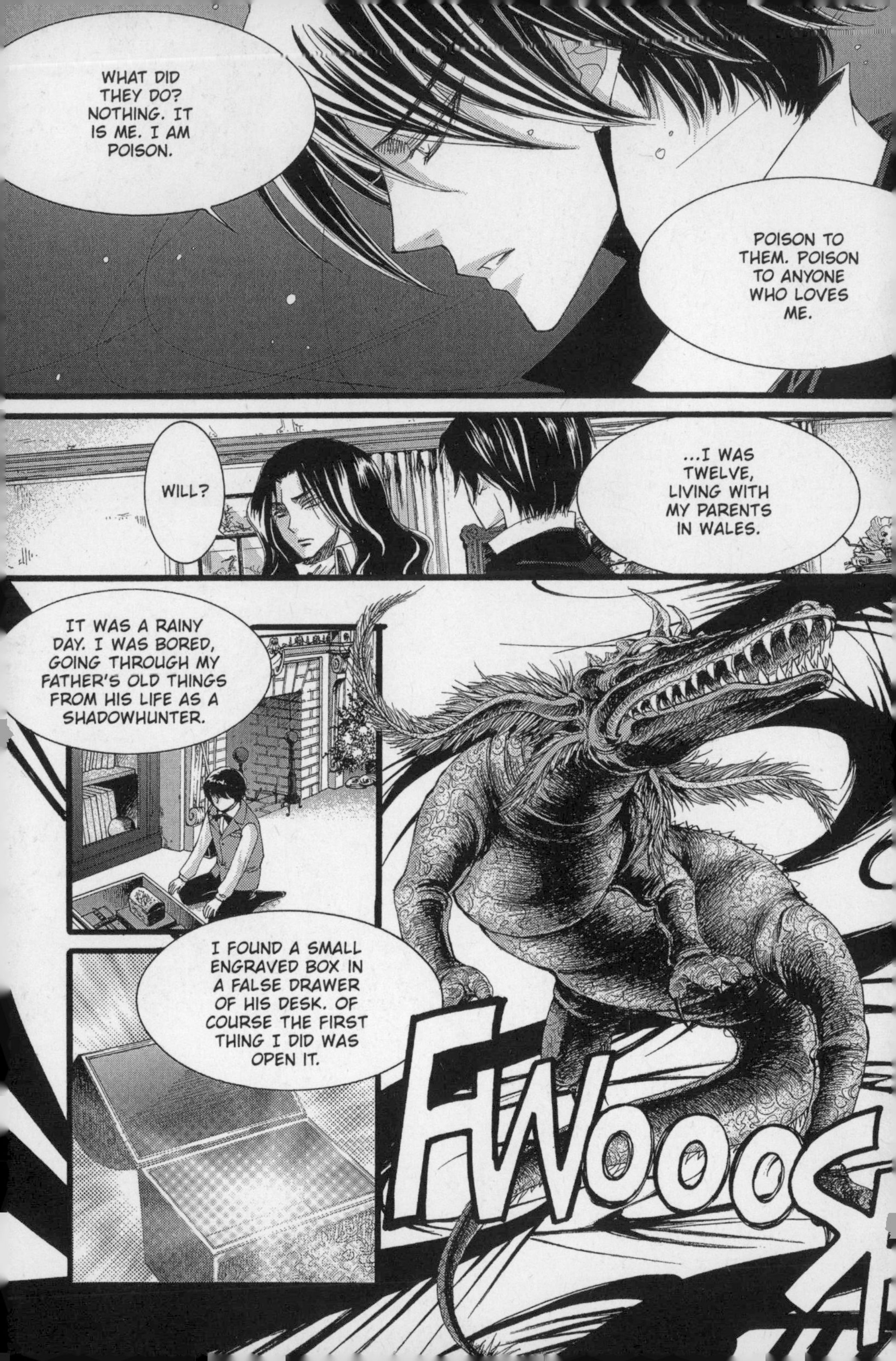
WHAT DID THEY DO? NOTHING. IT IS ME. I AM POISON.
POISON TO THEM. POISON TO ANYONE WHO LOVES ME.
WILL?
...I WAS TWELVE, LIVING WITH MY PARENTS IN WALES.
IT WAS A RAINY DAY. I WAS BORED, GOING THROUGH MY FATHER'S OLD THINGS FROM HIS LIFE AS A SHADOWHUNTER.
I FOUND A SMALL ENGRAVED BOX IN A FALSE DRAWER OF HIS DESK. OF COURSE THE FIRST THING I DID WAS OPEN IT.
FWOOOSH

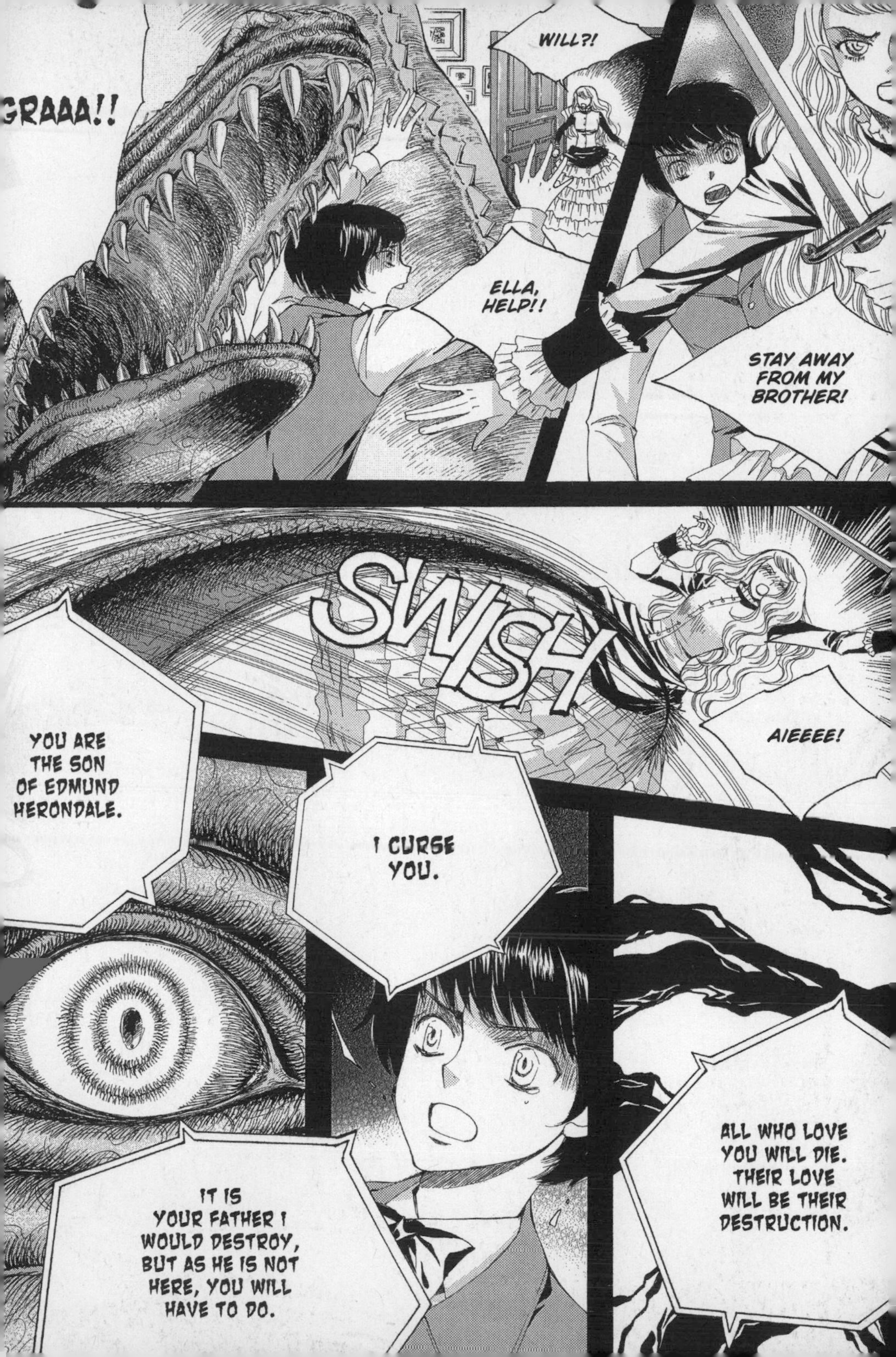
GRAAA!!
WILL?!
ELLA, HELP!!
STAY AWAY FROM MY BROTHER!
SWISH
AIEEEE!
YOU ARE THE SON OF EDMUND HERONDALE.
I CURSE YOU.
IT IS YOUR FATHER I WOULD DESTROY, BUT AS HE IS NOT HERE, YOU WILL HAVE TO DO.
ALL WHO LOVE YOU WILL DIE. THEIR LOVE WILL BE THEIR DESTRUCTION.

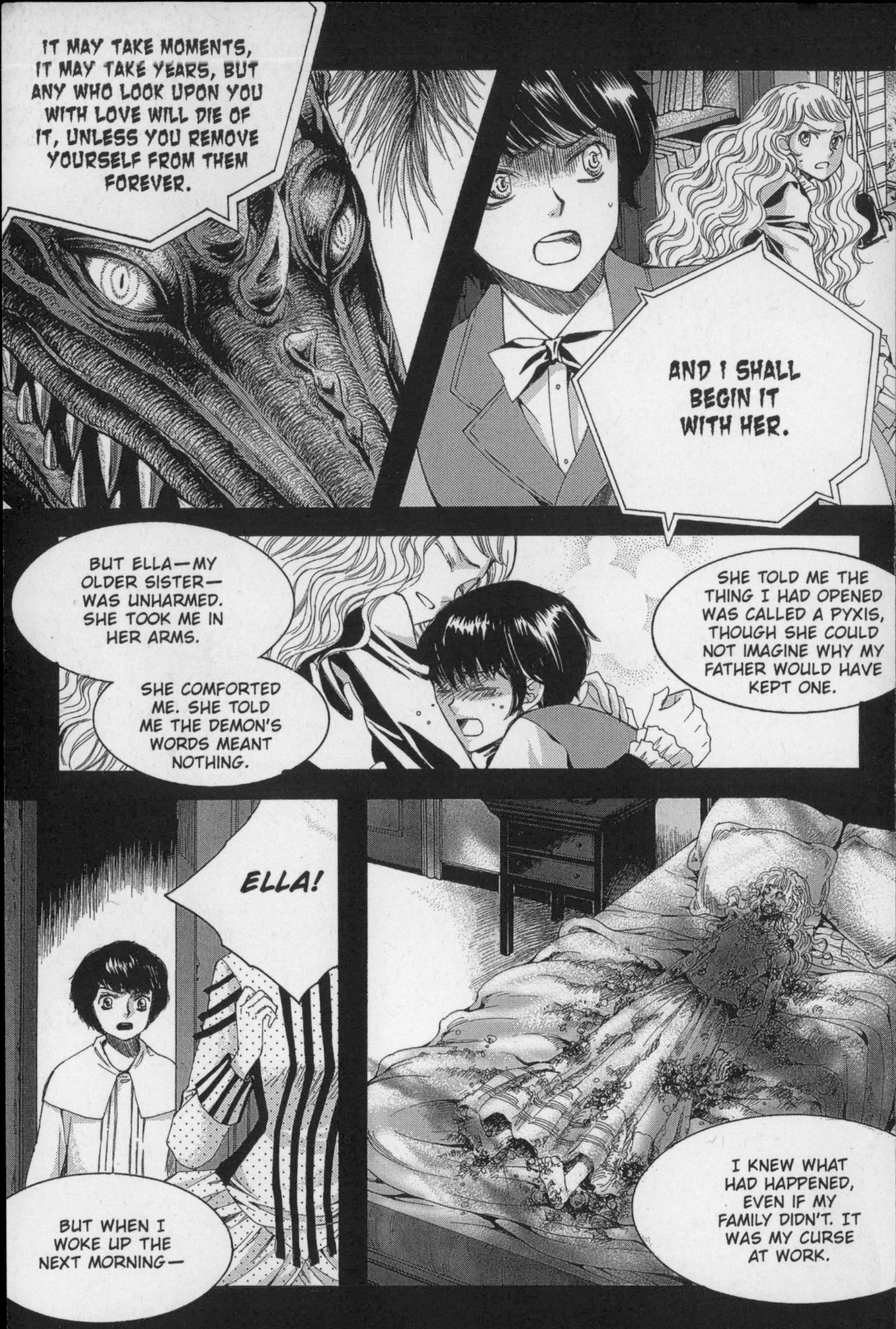
IT MAY TAKE MOMENTS, IT MAY TAKE YEARS, BUT ANY WHO LOOK UPON YOU WITH LOVE WILL DIE OF IT, UNLESS YOU REMOVE YOURSELF FROM THEM FOREVER.
AND I SHALL BEGIN IT WITH HER.
BUT ELLA—MY OLDER SISTER—WAS UNHARMED. SHE TOOK ME IN HER ARMS.
SHE COMFORTED ME. SHE TOLD ME THE DEMON'S WORDS MEANT NOTHING.
SHE TOLD ME THE THING I HAD OPENED WAS CALLED A PYXIS, THOUGH SHE COULD NOT IMAGINE WHY MY FATHER WOULD HAVE KEPT ONE.
ELLA!
BUT WHEN I WOKE UP THE NEXT MORNING—
I KNEW WHAT HAD HAPPENED, EVEN IF MY FAMILY DIDN'T. IT WAS MY CURSE AT WORK.

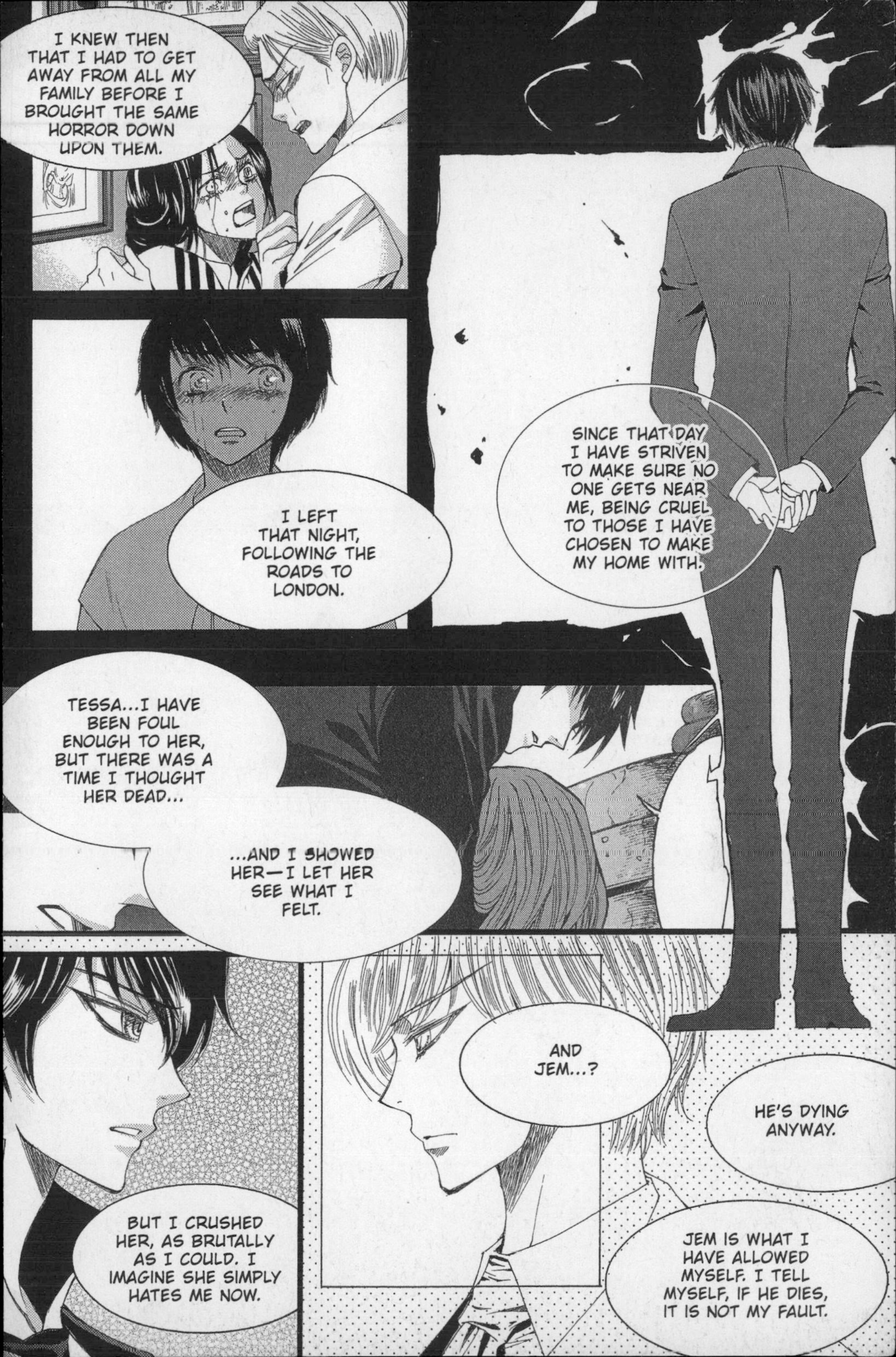
I KNEW THEN THAT I HAD TO GET AWAY FROM ALL MY FAMILY BEFORE I BROUGHT THE SAME HORROR DOWN UPON THEM.
I LEFT THAT NIGHT, FOLLOWING THE ROADS TO LONDON.
SINCE THAT DAY I HAVE STRIVEN TO MAKE SURE NO ONE GETS NEAR ME, BEING CRUEL TO THOSE I HAVE CHOSEN TO MAKE MY HOME WITH.
TESSA...I HAVE BEEN FOUL ENOUGH TO HER, BUT THERE WAS A TIME I THOUGHT HER DEAD...
...AND I SHOWED HER—I LET HER SEE WHAT I FELT.
BUT I CRUSHED HER, AS BRUTALLY AS I COULD. I IMAGINE SHE SIMPLY HATES ME NOW.
AND JEM...?
HE'S DYING ANYWAY.
JEM IS WHAT I HAVE ALLOWED MYSELF. I TELL MYSELF, IF HE DIES, IT IS NOT MY FAULT.

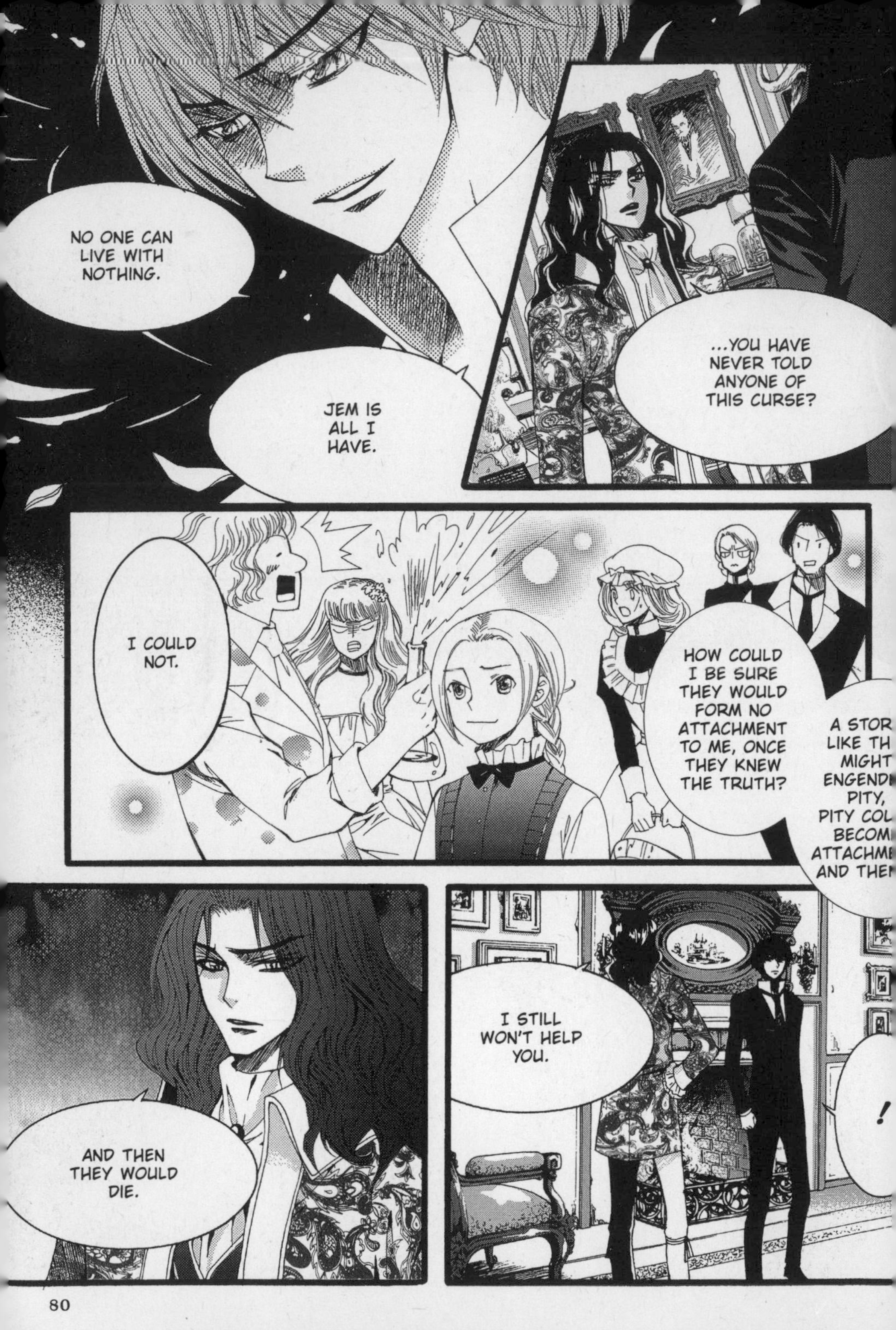
NO ONE CAN LIVE WITH NOTHING.
JEM IS ALL I HAVE.
...YOU HAVE NEVER TOLD ANYONE OF THIS CURSE?
I COULD NOT.
HOW COULD I BE SURE THEY WOULD FORM NO ATTACHMENT TO ME, ONCE THEY KNEW THE TRUTH?
A STOR LIKE TH MIGHT ENGEND PITY, PITY COU BECOM ATTACHM AND THE
AND THEN THEY WOULD DIE.
I STILL WON'T HELP YOU.
!

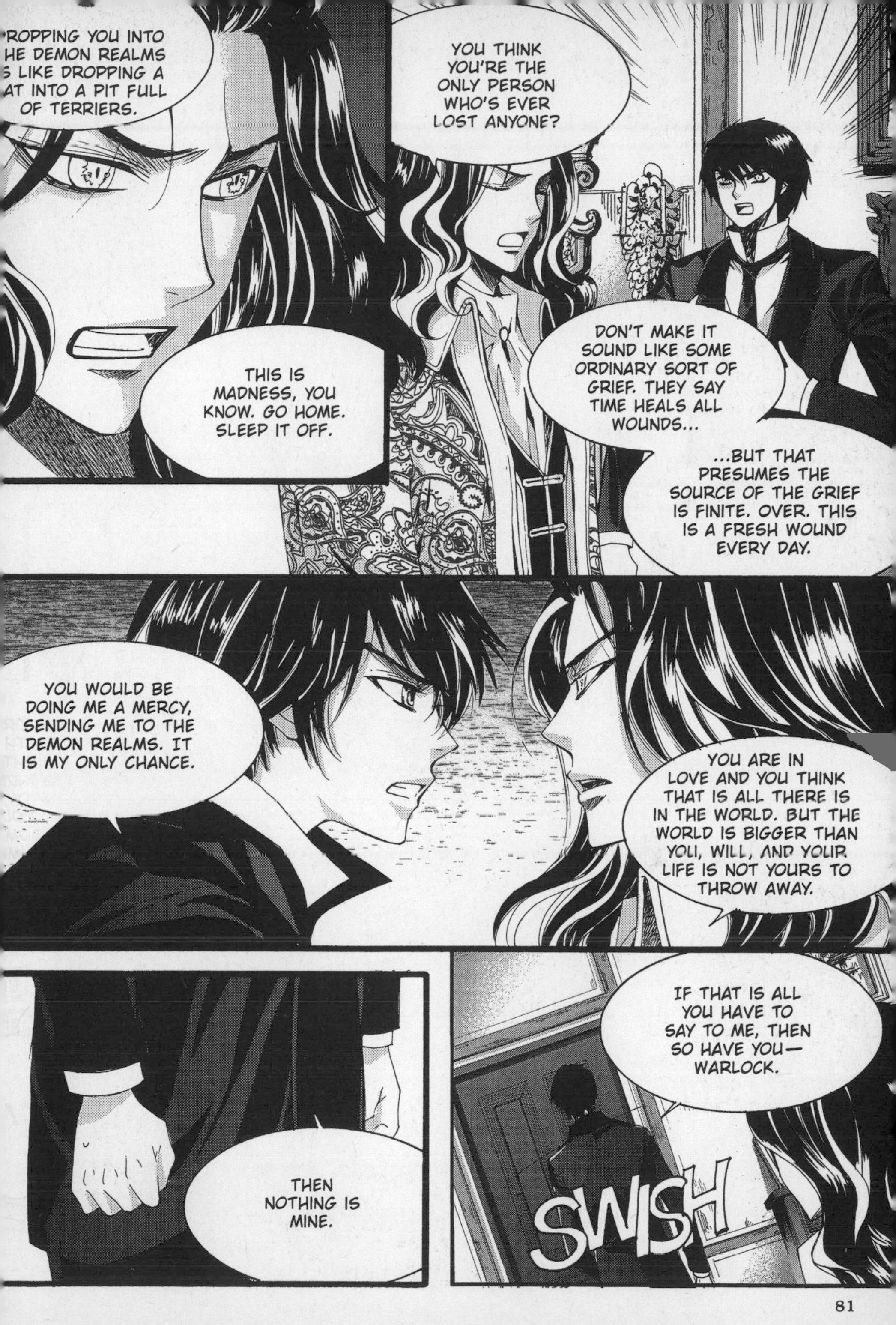
ROPPING YOU INTO HE DEMON REALMS S LIKE DROPPING A AT INTO A PIT FULL OF TERRIERS.
YOU THINK YOU'RE THE ONLY PERSON WHO'S EVER LOST ANYONE?
THIS IS MADNESS, YOU KNOW. GO HOME. SLEEP IT OFF.
DON'T MAKE IT SOUND LIKE SOME ORDINARY SORT OF GRIEF. THEY SAY TIME HEALS ALL WOUNDS...
...BUT THAT PRESUMES THE SOURCE OF THE GRIEF IS FINITE. OVER. THIS IS A FRESH WOUND EVERY DAY.
YOU WOULD BE DOING ME A MERCY, SENDING ME TO THE DEMON REALMS. IT IS MY ONLY CHANCE.
YOU ARE IN LOVE AND YOU THINK THAT IS ALL THERE IS IN THE WORLD. BUT THE WORLD IS BIGGER THAN YOU, WILL, AND YOUR LIFE IS NOT YOURS TO THROW AWAY.
THEN NOTHING IS MINE.
IF THAT IS ALL YOU HAVE TO SAY TO ME, THEN SO HAVE YOU— WARLOCK.
SWISH

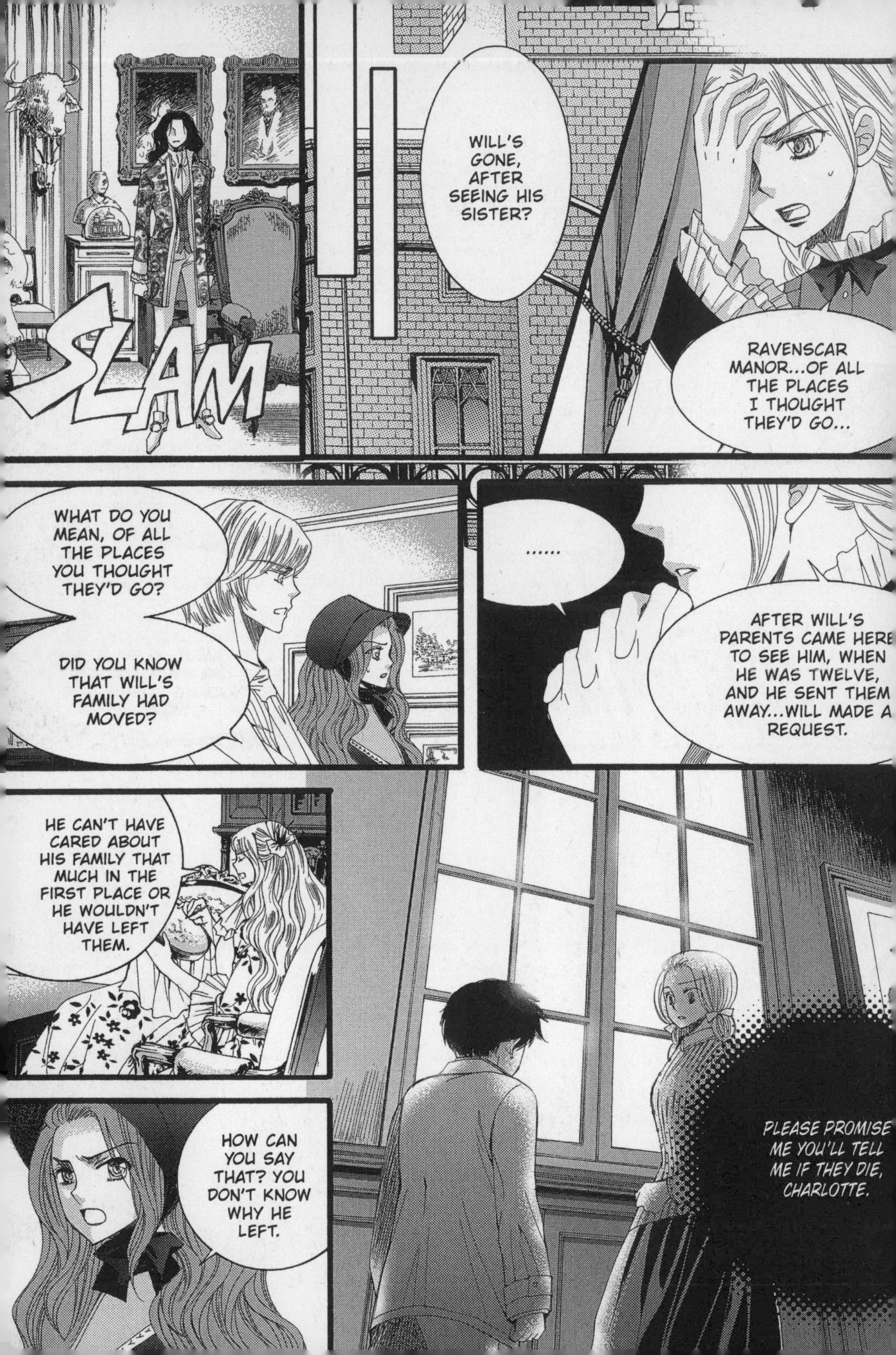
SLAM
WILL'S GONE, AFTER SEEING HIS SISTER?
RAVENSCAR MANOR...OF ALL THE PLACES I THOUGHT THEY'D GO...
WHAT DO YOU MEAN, OF ALL THE PLACES YOU THOUGHT THEY'D GO?
DID YOU KNOW THAT WILL'S FAMILY HAD MOVED?
......
AFTER WILL'S PARENTS CAME HERE TO SEE HIM, WHEN HE WAS TWELVE, AND HE SENT THEM AWAY...WILL MADE A REQUEST.
HE CAN'T HAVE CARED ABOUT HIS FAMILY THAT MUCH IN THE FIRST PLACE OR HE WOULDN'T HAVE LEFT THEM.
HOW CAN YOU SAY THAT? YOU DON'T KNOW WHY HE LEFT.
PLEASE PROMISE ME YOU'LL TELL ME IF THEY DIE, CHARLOTTE.

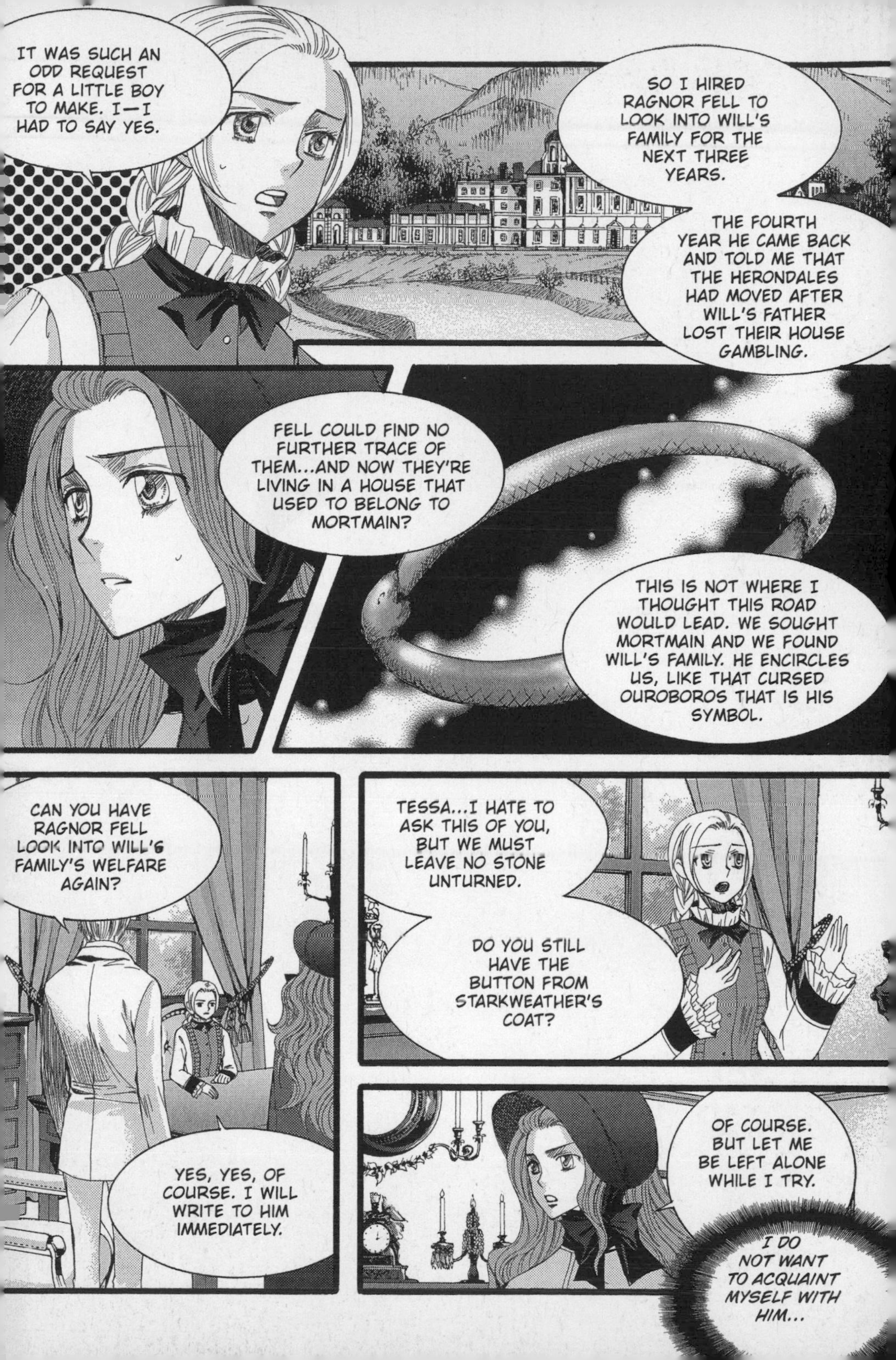
IT WAS SUCH AN ODD REQUEST FOR A LITTLE BOY TO MAKE. I—I HAD TO SAY YES.
SO I HIRED RAGNOR FELL TO LOOK INTO WILL'S FAMILY FOR THE NEXT THREE YEARS.
THE FOURTH YEAR HE CAME BACK AND TOLD ME THAT THE HERONDALES HAD MOVED AFTER WILL'S FATHER LOST THEIR HOUSE GAMBLING.
FELL COULD FIND NO FURTHER TRACE OF THEM...AND NOW THEY'RE LIVING IN A HOUSE THAT USED TO BELONG TO MORTMAIN?
THIS IS NOT WHERE I THOUGHT THIS ROAD WOULD LEAD. WE SOUGHT MORTMAIN AND WE FOUND WILL'S FAMILY. HE ENCIRCLES US, LIKE THAT CURSED OUROBOROS THAT IS HIS SYMBOL.
CAN YOU HAVE RAGNOR FELL LOOK INTO WILL'S FAMILY'S WELFARE AGAIN?
YES, YES, OF COURSE. I WILL WRITE TO HIM IMMEDIATELY.
TESSA...I HATE TO ASK THIS OF YOU, BUT WE MUST LEAVE NO STONE UNTURNED.
DO YOU STILL HAVE THE BUTTON FROM STARKWEATHER'S COAT?
OF COURSE. BUT LET ME BE LEFT ALONE WHILE I TRY.
I DO NOT WANT TO ACQUAINT MYSELF WITH HIM...

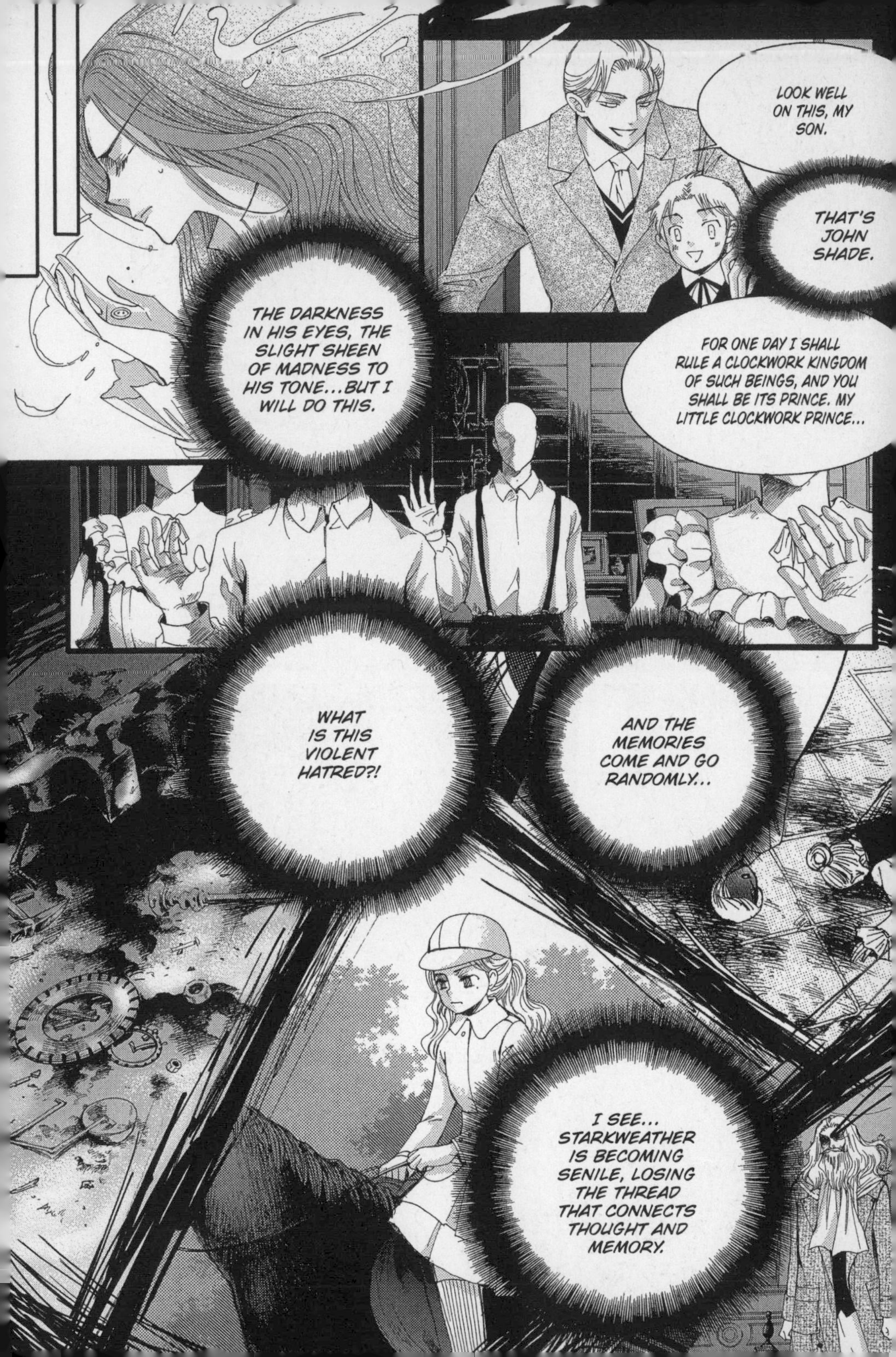
LOOK WELL ON THIS, MY SON.
THAT'S JOHN SHADE.
THE DARKNESS IN HIS EYES, THE SLIGHT SHEEN OF MADNESS TO HIS TONE...BUT I WILL DO THIS.
FOR ONE DAY I SHALL RULE A CLOCKWORK KINGDOM OF SUCH BEINGS, AND YOU SHALL BE ITS PRINCE. MY LITTLE CLOCKWORK PRINCE...
WHAT IS THIS VIOLENT HATRED?!
AND THE MEMORIES COME AND GO RANDOMLY...
I SEE... STARKWEATHER IS BECOMING SENILE, LOSING THE THREAD THAT CONNECTS THOUGHT AND MEMORY.

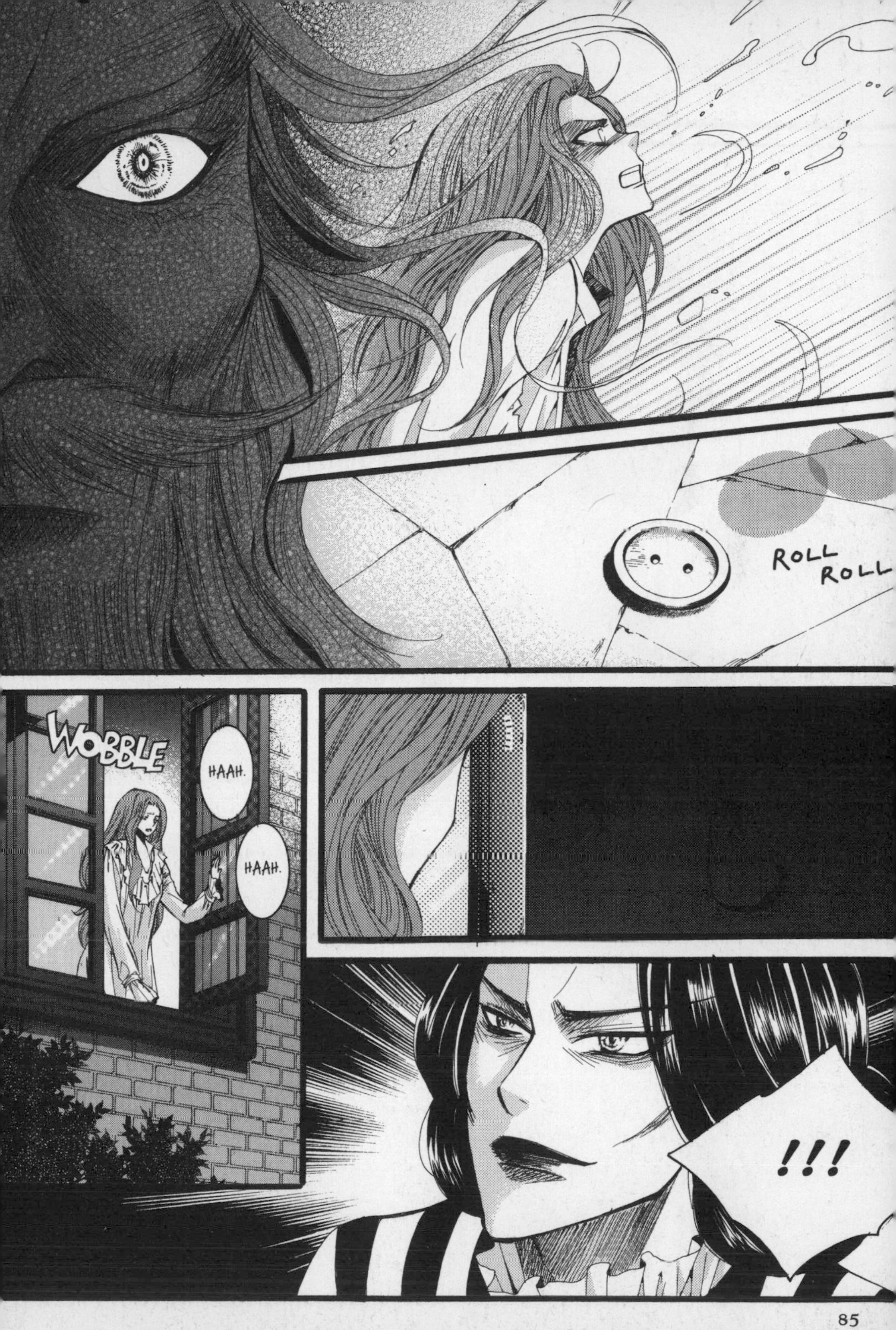
ROLL
ROLL
WOBBLE
HAAH.
HAAH.
!!!

I'D BETTER REIN IN MY DAY-DREAMING...

...OR I'LL END UP AS MAD AS OLD STARK-WEATHER.

I TOLD CHARLOTTE ABOUT STARKWEATHER'S MEMORIES OF THE SHADE FAMILY, BUT SHE LOOKED DISAPPOINTED WHEN I SAID I HAD DISCOVERED NOTHING ABOUT RAVENSCAR MANOR.

THANK YOU SO MUCH FOR YOUR HELP, TESSA.

MAIL FOR ME? THANK YO SOPHIE.

A LETTER FOR YOU, MISS.

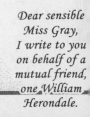

Dear sensible Miss Gray, I write to you on behalf of a mutual friend, one William Herondale.

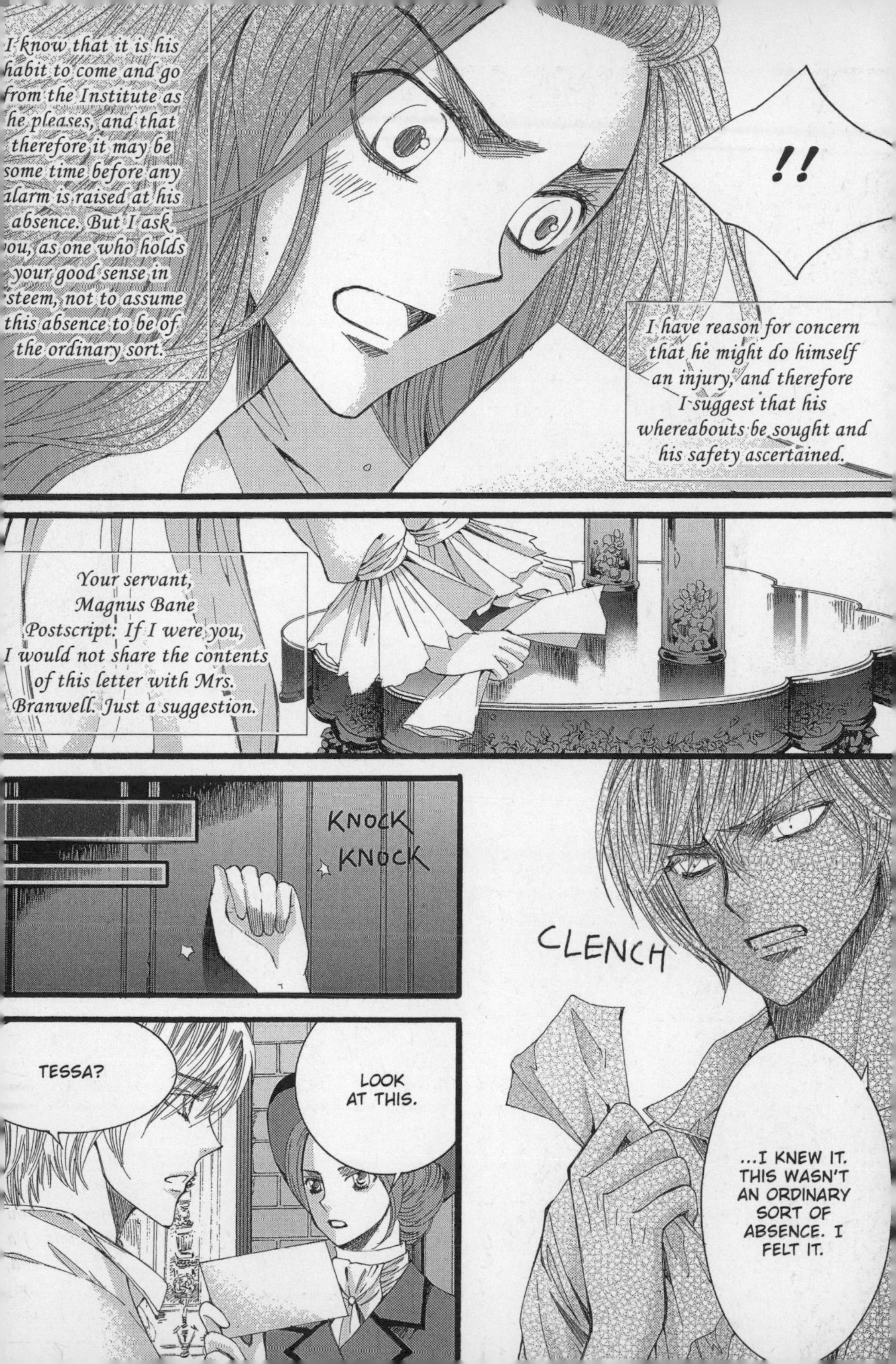

I know that it is his
habit to come and go
from the Institute as
he pleases, and that
therefore it may be
some time before any
alarm is raised at his
absence. But I ask
ou, as one who holds
your good sense in
steem, not to assume
this absence to be of
the ordinary sort.
!!
I have reason for concern that he might do himself an injury, and therefore I suggest that his whereabouts be sought and his safety ascertained.
Your servant, Magnus Bane
Postscript: If I were you, I would not share the contents of this letter with Mrs. Branwell. Just a suggestion.
KNOCK KNOCK
CLENCH
TESSA?
LOOK AT THIS.
...I KNEW IT. THIS WASN'T AN ORDINARY SORT OF ABSENCE. I FELT IT.

WAIT FOR ME IN YOUR ROOM. I WILL GET DRESSED AND BE THERE MOMENTARILY.

THIS IS WILL'S ROOM.

GRACIOUS. I'VE NEVER BEEN IN HERE.

I WAS STARTING TO IMAGINE HE SLEPT UPSIDE DOWN, LIKE A BAT.

HA-HA...

WAIT HERE. I NEED TO FIND SOMETHING.

THE LETTERS I WROTE TO NATE FROM THE DARK HOUSE?!

DROP DROP

WHAT AR[E] THEY DO[ING] HERE?[!]

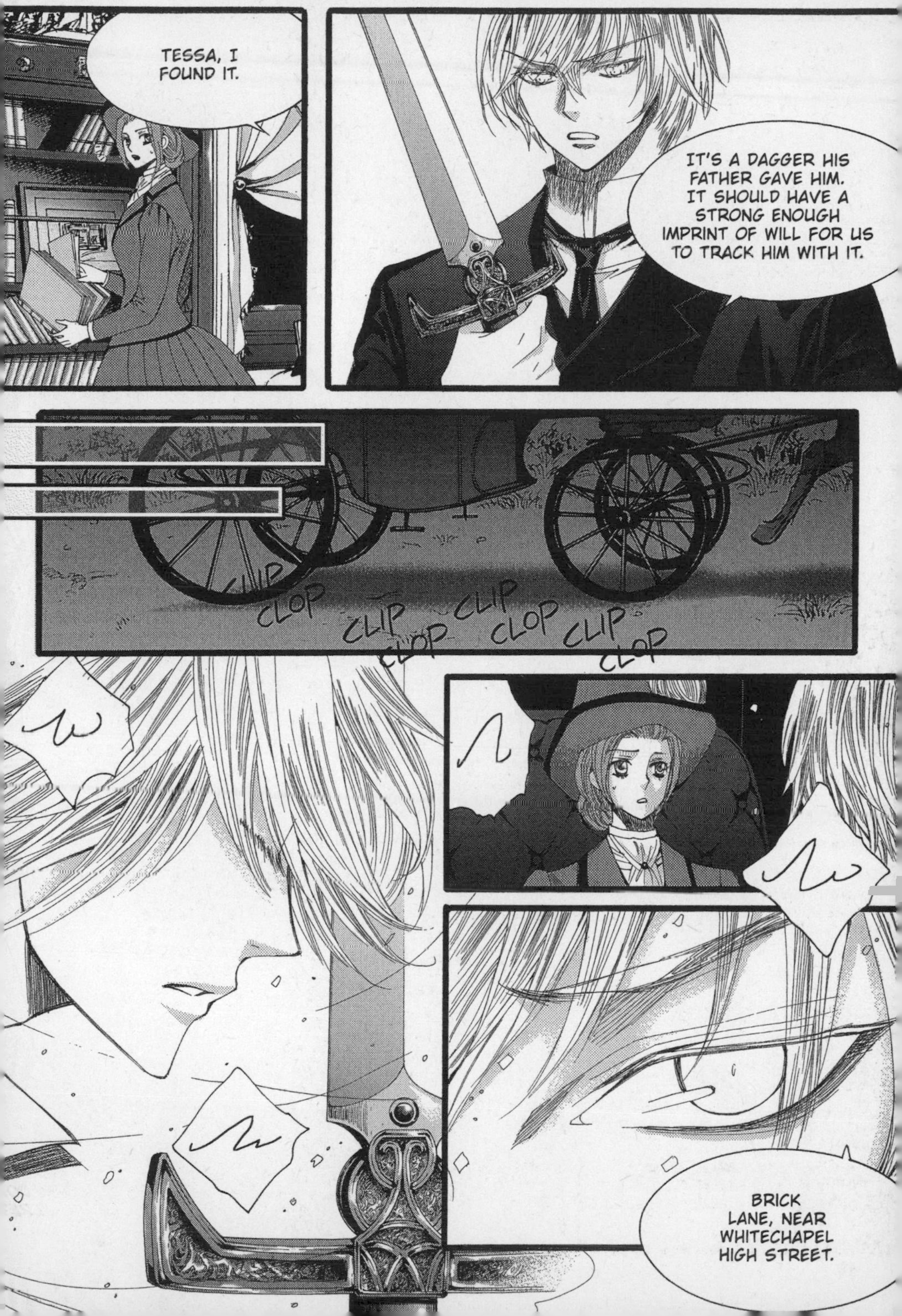
TESSA, I FOUND IT.
IT'S A DAGGER HIS FATHER GAVE HIM. IT SHOULD HAVE A STRONG ENOUGH IMPRINT OF WILL FOR US TO TRACK HIM WITH IT.
CLIP CLOP CLIP CLOP CLIP CLOP CLIP CLOP
BRICK LANE, NEAR WHITECHAPEL HIGH STREET.

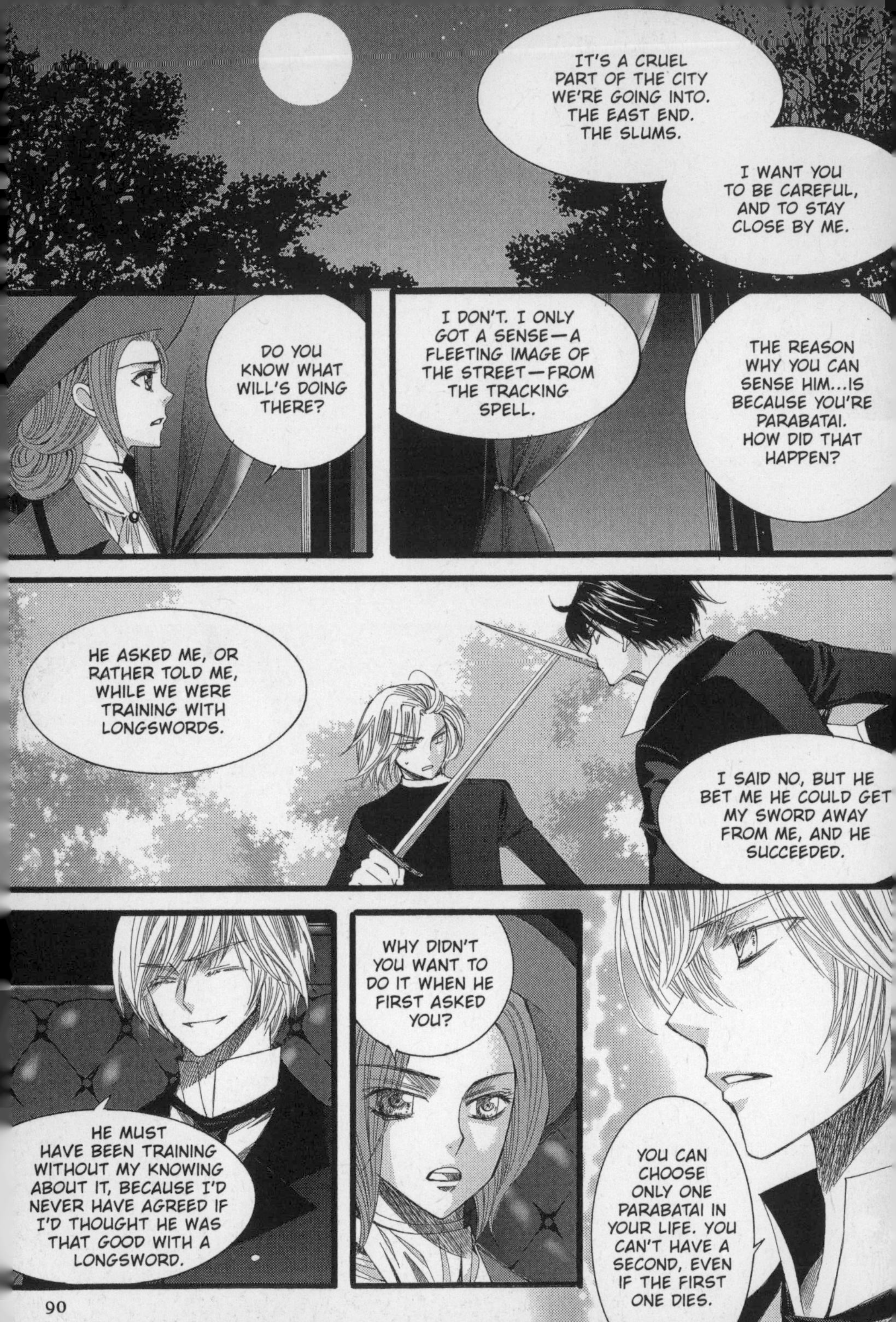
IT'S A CRUEL PART OF THE CITY WE'RE GOING INTO. THE EAST END. THE SLUMS.
I WANT YOU TO BE CAREFUL, AND TO STAY CLOSE BY ME.
DO YOU KNOW WHAT WILL'S DOING THERE?
I DON'T. I ONLY GOT A SENSE—A FLEETING IMAGE OF THE STREET—FROM THE TRACKING SPELL.
THE REASON WHY YOU CAN SENSE HIM...IS BECAUSE YOU'RE PARABATAI. HOW DID THAT HAPPEN?
HE ASKED ME, OR RATHER TOLD ME, WHILE WE WERE TRAINING WITH LONGSWORDS.
I SAID NO, BUT HE BET ME HE COULD GET MY SWORD AWAY FROM ME, AND HE SUCCEEDED.
HE MUST HAVE BEEN TRAINING WITHOUT MY KNOWING ABOUT IT, BECAUSE I'D NEVER HAVE AGREED IF I'D THOUGHT HE WAS THAT GOOD WITH A LONGSWORD.
WHY DIDN'T YOU WANT TO DO IT WHEN HE FIRST ASKED YOU?
YOU CAN CHOOSE ONLY ONE PARABATAI IN YOUR LIFE. YOU CAN'T HAVE A SECOND, EVEN IF THE FIRST ONE DIES.

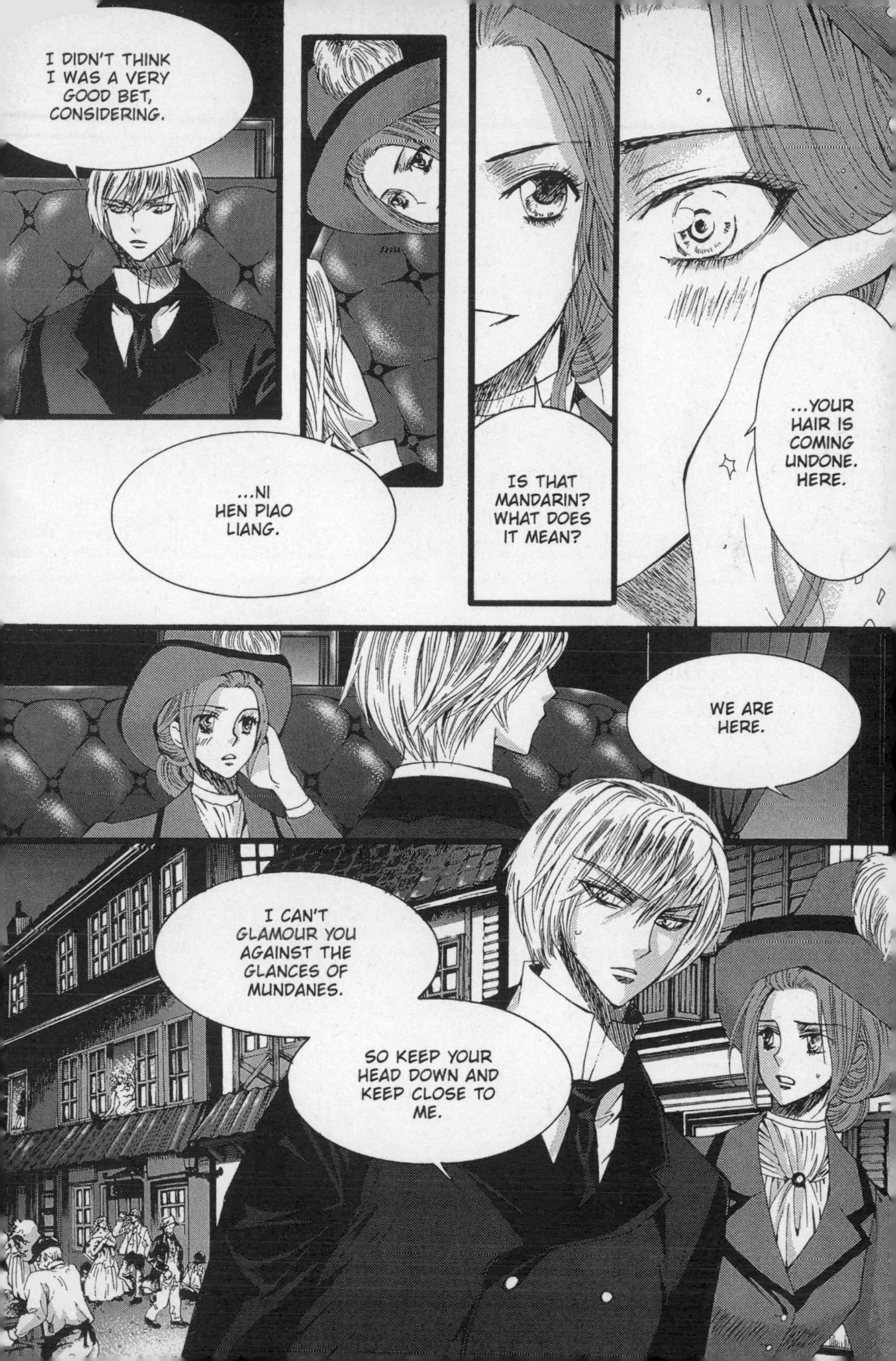
I DIDN'T THINK I WAS A VERY GOOD BET, CONSIDERING.
...NI HEN PIAO LIANG.
IS THAT MANDARIN? WHAT DOES IT MEAN?
...YOUR HAIR IS COMING UNDONE. HERE.
WE ARE HERE.
I CAN'T GLAMOUR YOU AGAINST THE GLANCES OF MUNDANES.
SO KEEP YOUR HEAD DOWN AND KEEP CLOSE TO ME.

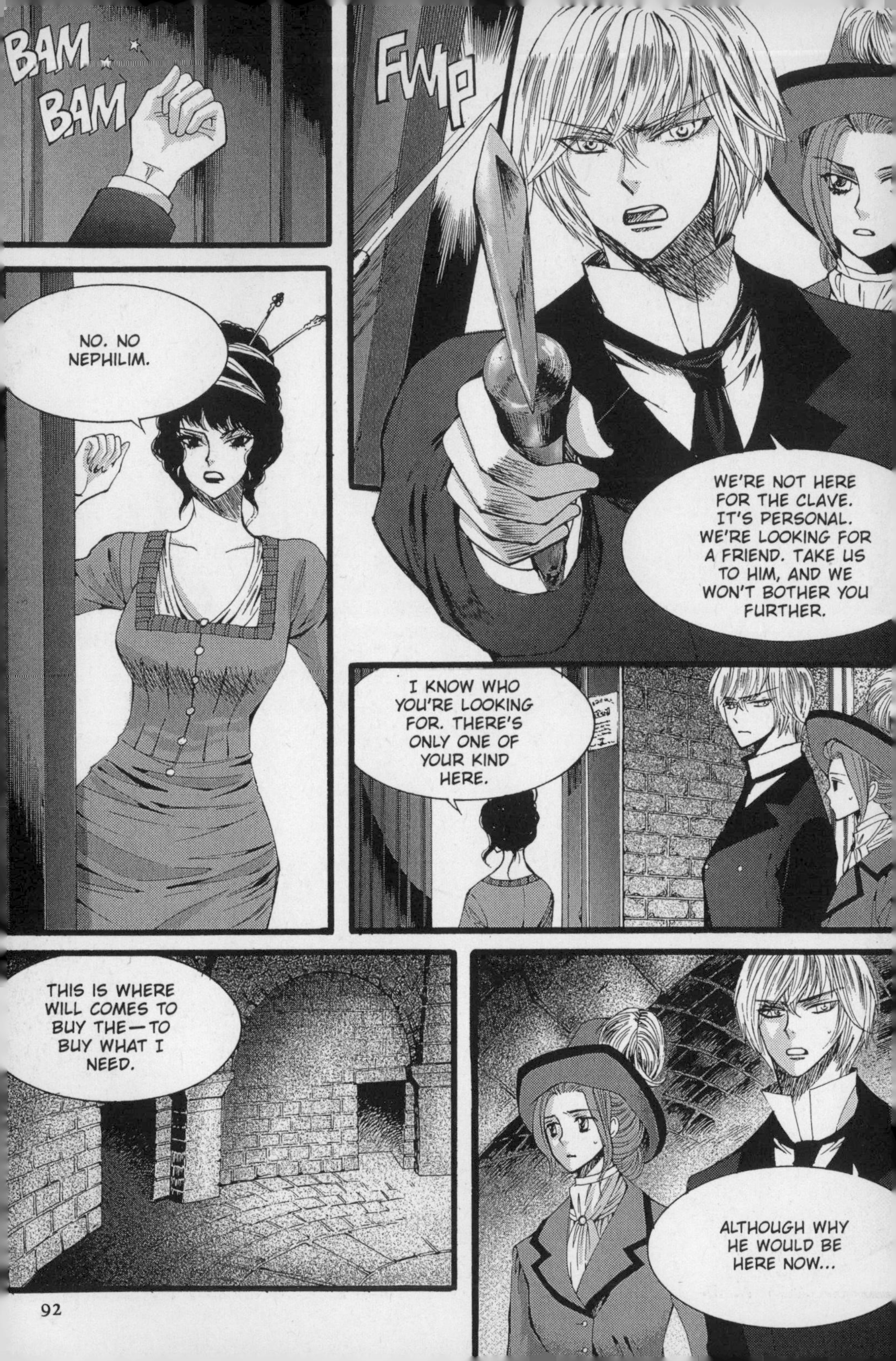

BAM BAM
FWP
NO. NO NEPHILIM.
WE'RE NOT HERE FOR THE CLAVE. IT'S PERSONAL. WE'RE LOOKING FOR A FRIEND. TAKE US TO HIM, AND WE WON'T BOTHER YOU FURTHER.
I KNOW WHO YOU'RE LOOKING FOR. THERE'S ONLY ONE OF YOUR KIND HERE.
THIS IS WHERE WILL COMES TO BUY THE—TO BUY WHAT I NEED.
ALTHOUGH WHY HE WOULD BE HERE NOW...

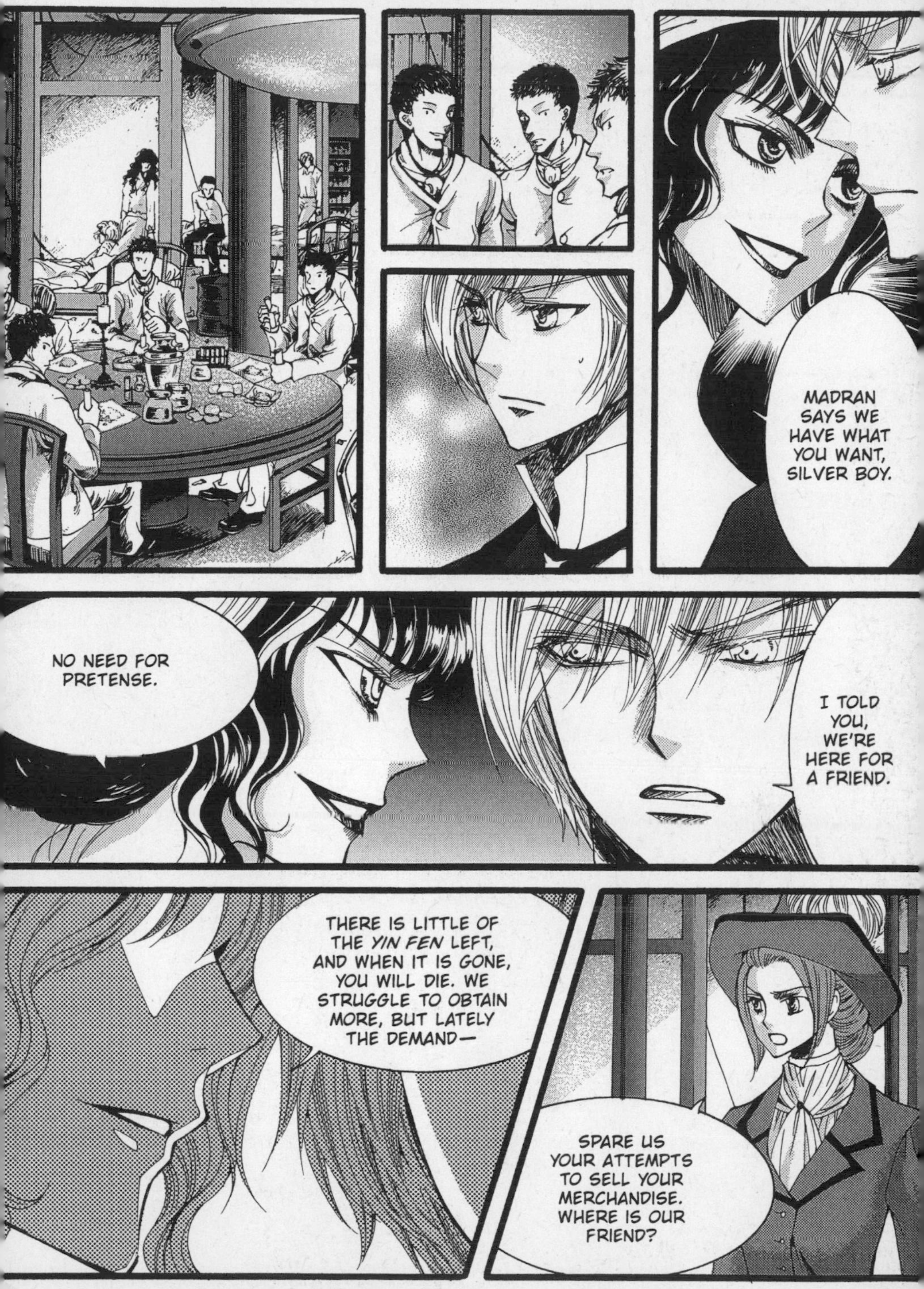
MADRAN SAYS WE HAVE WHAT YOU WANT, SILVER BOY.
NO NEED FOR PRETENSE.
I TOLD YOU, WE'RE HERE FOR A FRIEND.
THERE IS LITTLE OF THE *YIN FEN* LEFT, AND WHEN IT IS GONE, YOU WILL DIE. WE STRUGGLE TO OBTAIN MORE, BUT LATELY THE DEMAND—
SPARE US YOUR ATTEMPTS TO SELL YOUR MERCHANDISE. WHERE IS OUR FRIEND?

...THERE.

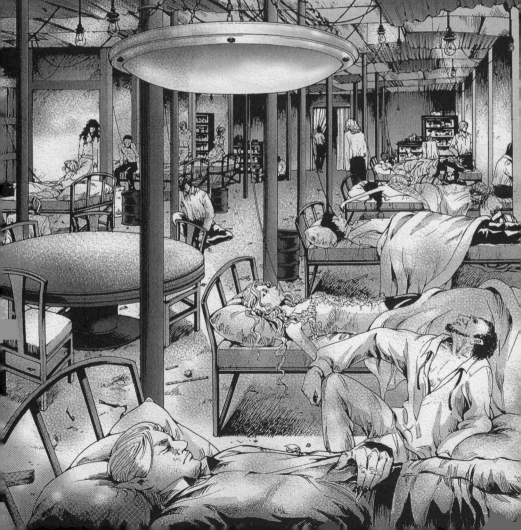

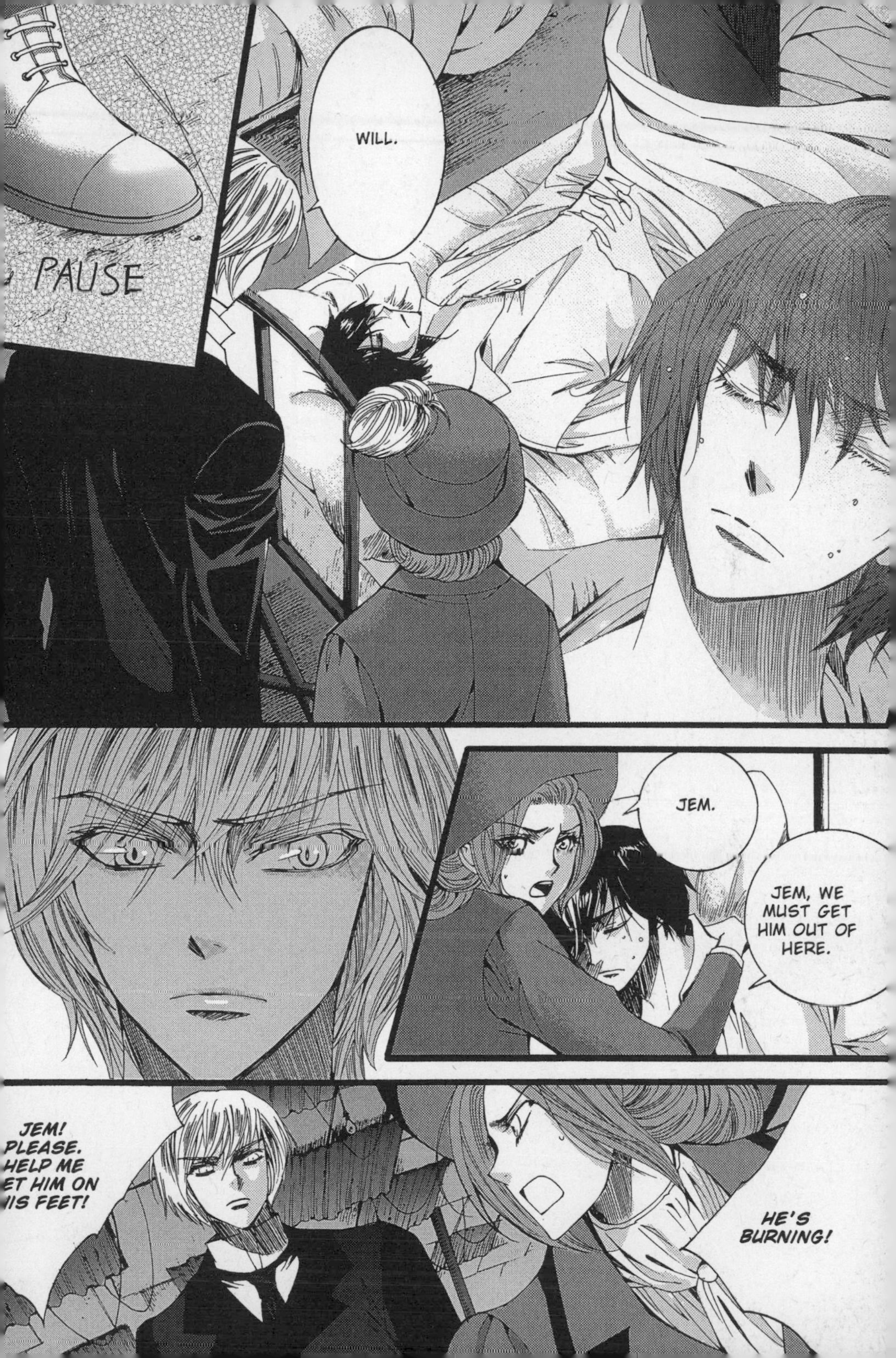
WILL.
PAUSE
JEM.
JEM, WE MUST GET HIM OUT OF HERE.
JEM! PLEASE. HELP ME GET HIM ON HIS FEET!
HE'S BURNING!

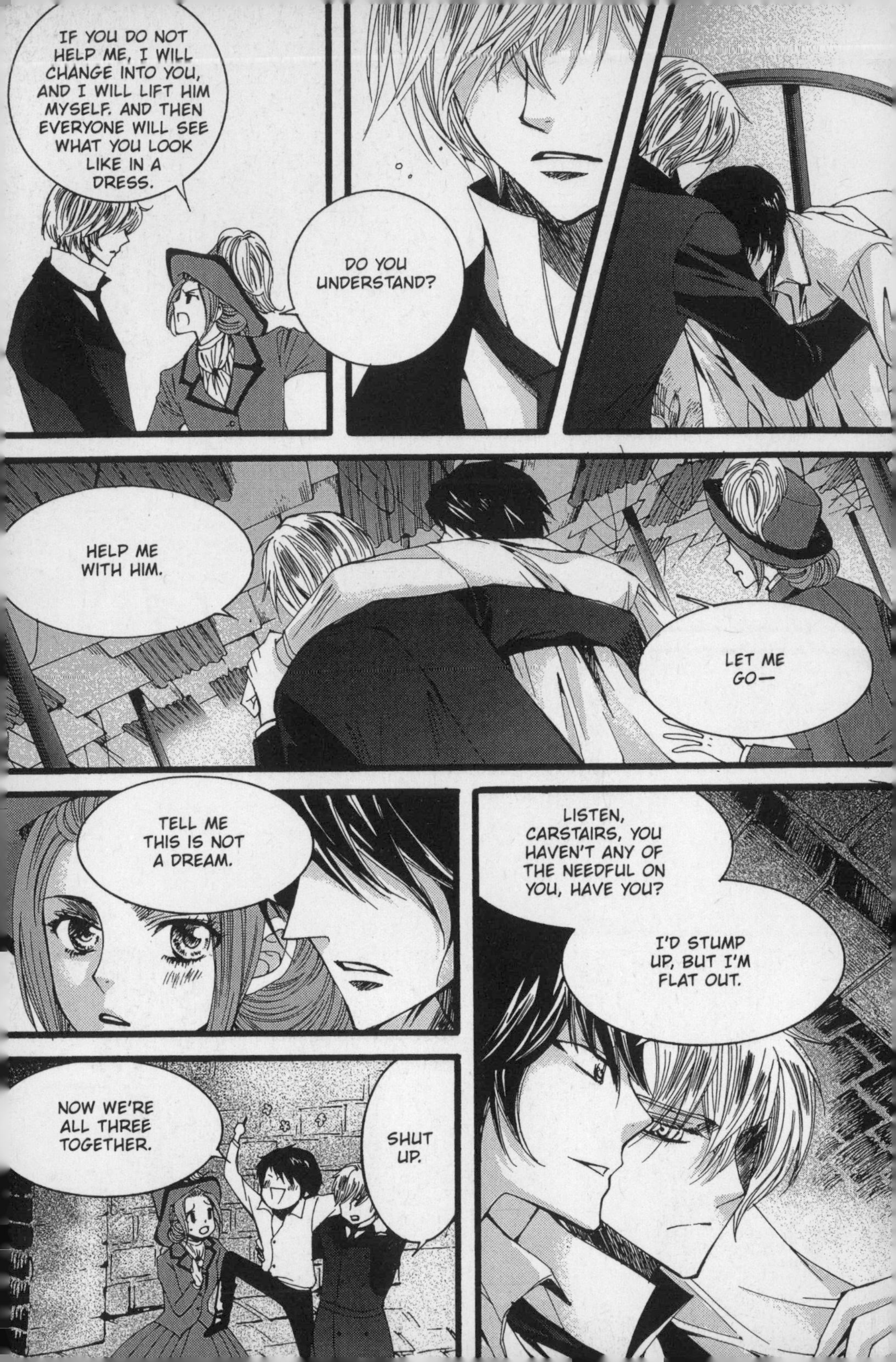
IF YOU DO NOT HELP ME, I WILL CHANGE INTO YOU, AND I WILL LIFT HIM MYSELF. AND THEN EVERYONE WILL SEE WHAT YOU LOOK LIKE IN A DRESS.
DO YOU UNDERSTAND?
HELP ME WITH HIM.
LET ME GO—
TELL ME THIS IS NOT A DREAM.
LISTEN, CARSTAIRS, YOU HAVEN'T ANY OF THE NEEDFUL ON YOU, HAVE YOU?
I'D STUMP UP, BUT I'M FLAT OUT.
NOW WE'RE ALL THREE TOGETHER.
SHUT UP.

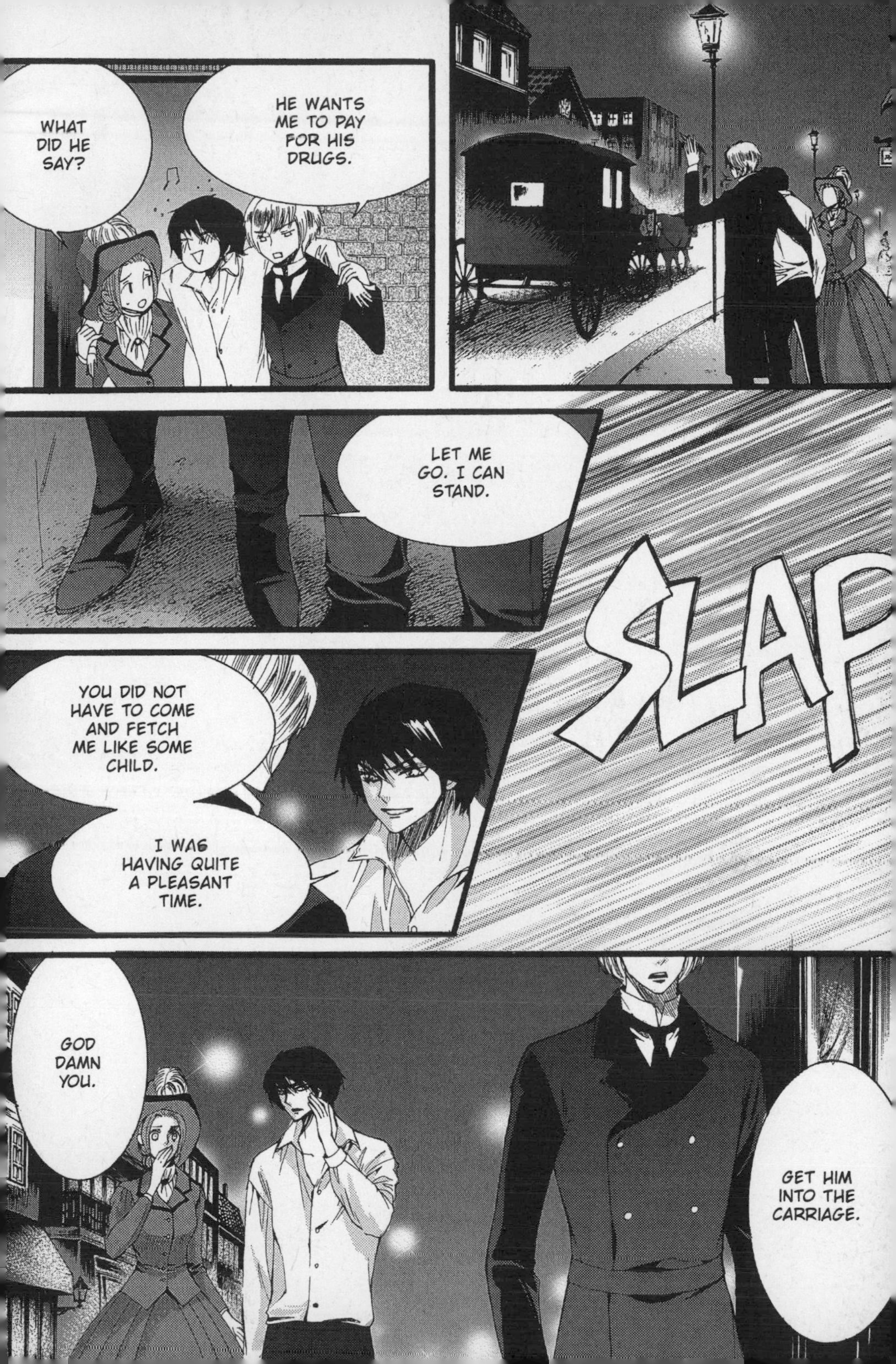
WHAT DID HE SAY?
HE WANTS ME TO PAY FOR HIS DRUGS.
LET ME GO. I CAN STAND.
YOU DID NOT HAVE TO COME AND FETCH ME LIKE SOME CHILD.
I WAS HAVING QUITE A PLEASANT TIME.
SLAP
GOD DAMN YOU.
GET HIM INTO THE CARRIAGE.

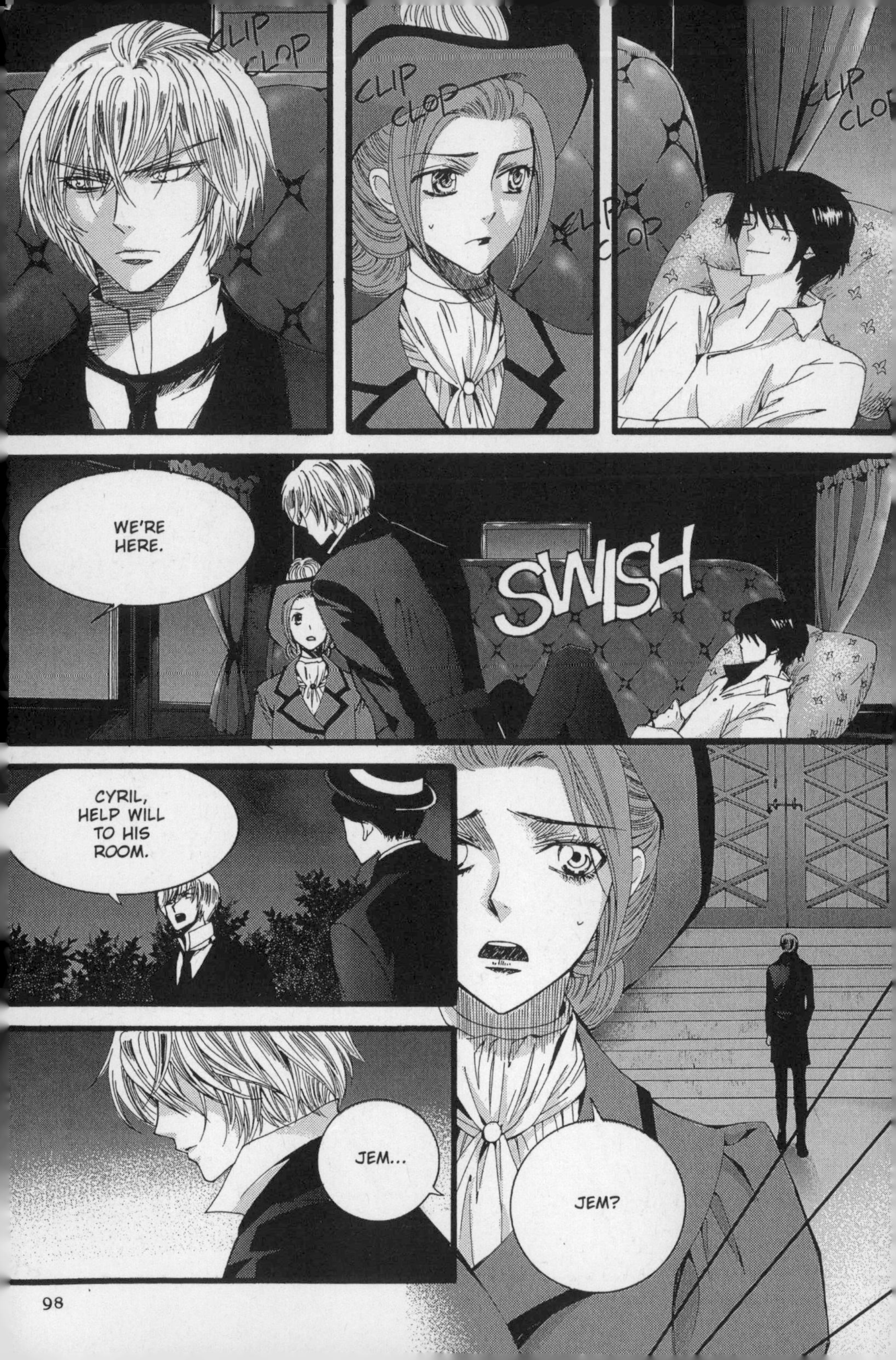
CLIP CLOP
CLIP CLOP
CLIP CLOP
CLIP CLOP
WE'RE HERE.
SWISH
CYRIL, HELP WILL TO HIS ROOM.
JEM...
JEM?

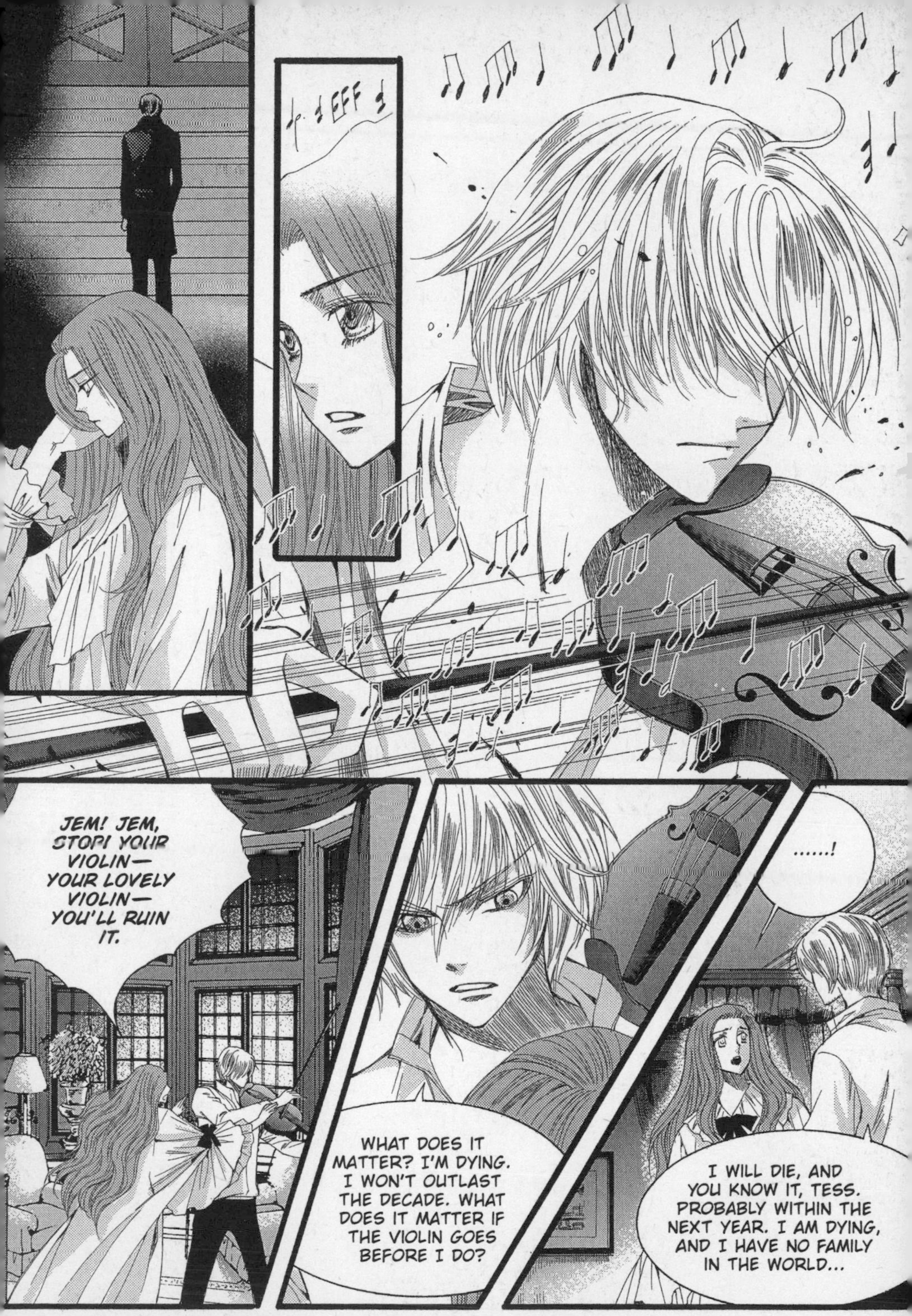
JEM! JEM, STOP! YOUR VIOLIN— YOUR LOVELY VIOLIN— YOU'LL RUIN IT.
WHAT DOES IT MATTER? I'M DYING. I WON'T OUTLAST THE DECADE. WHAT DOES IT MATTER IF THE VIOLIN GOES BEFORE I DO?
......!
I WILL DIE, AND YOU KNOW IT, TESS. PROBABLY WITHIN THE NEXT YEAR. I AM DYING, AND I HAVE NO FAMILY IN THE WORLD...

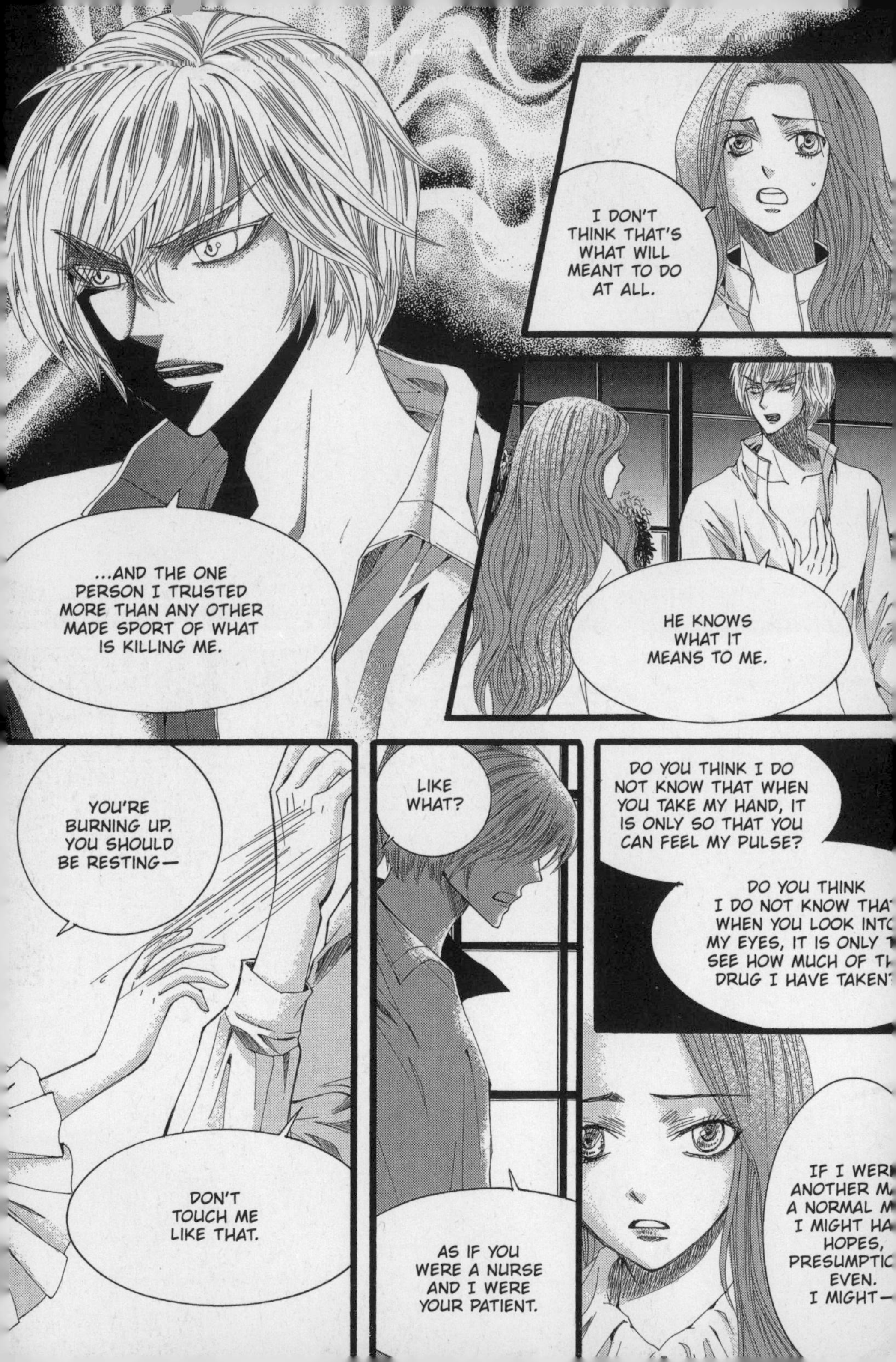
...AND THE ONE PERSON I TRUSTED MORE THAN ANY OTHER MADE SPORT OF WHAT IS KILLING ME.
I DON'T THINK THAT'S WHAT WILL MEANT TO DO AT ALL.
HE KNOWS WHAT IT MEANS TO ME.
YOU'RE BURNING UP. YOU SHOULD BE RESTING—
DON'T TOUCH ME LIKE THAT.
LIKE WHAT?
AS IF YOU WERE A NURSE AND I WERE YOUR PATIENT.
DO YOU THINK I DO NOT KNOW THAT WHEN YOU TAKE MY HAND, IT IS ONLY SO THAT YOU CAN FEEL MY PULSE?
DO YOU THINK I DO NOT KNOW THA WHEN YOU LOOK INT MY EYES, IT IS ONLY T SEE HOW MUCH OF TH DRUG I HAVE TAKEN
IF I WER ANOTHER M A NORMAL M I MIGHT HA HOPES, PRESUMPTIC EVEN. I MIGHT—

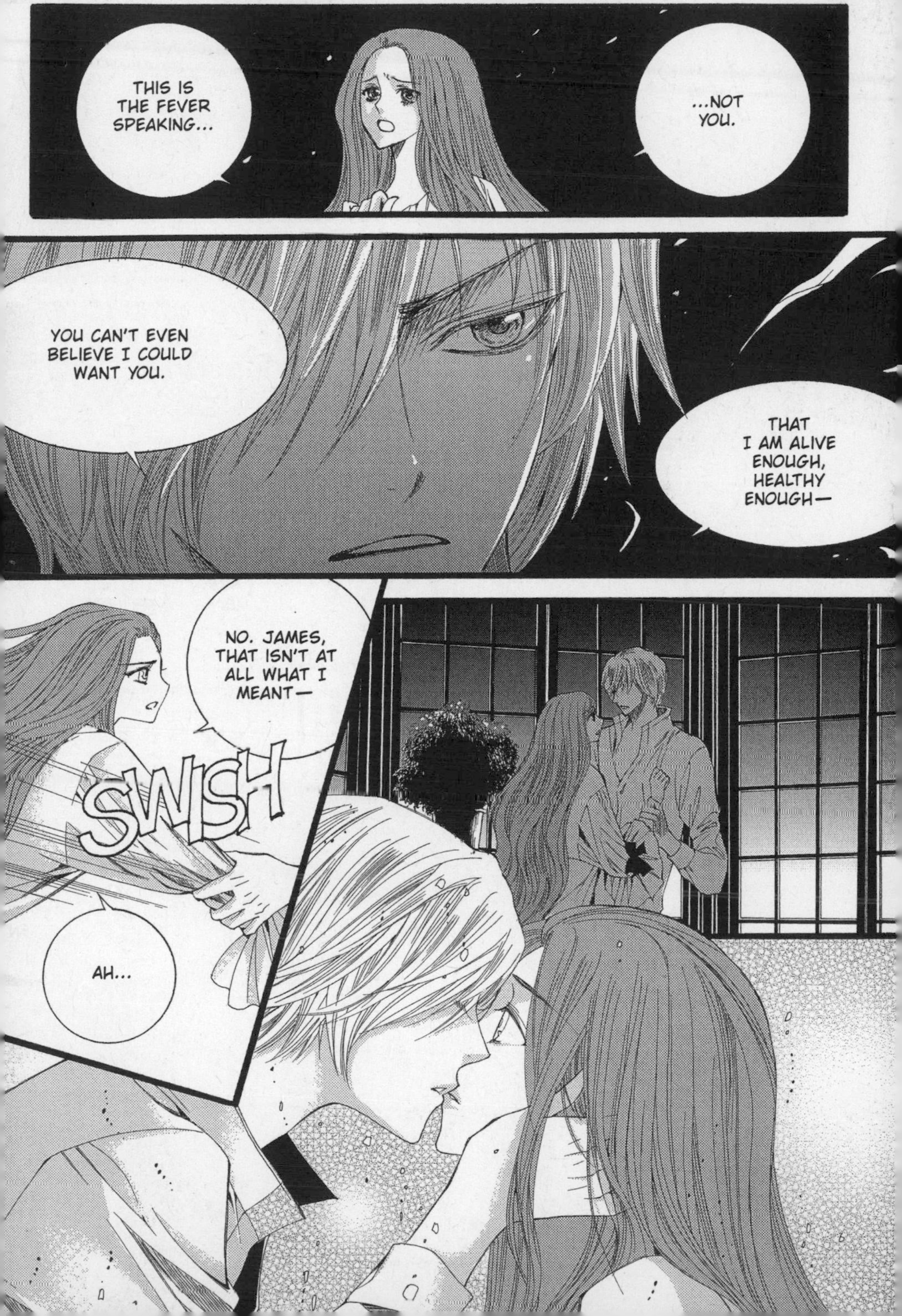
THIS IS THE FEVER SPEAKING...
...NOT YOU.
YOU CAN'T EVEN BELIEVE I COULD WANT YOU.
THAT I AM ALIVE ENOUGH, HEALTHY ENOUGH—
NO. JAMES, THAT ISN'T AT ALL WHAT I MEANT—
SWISH
AH...

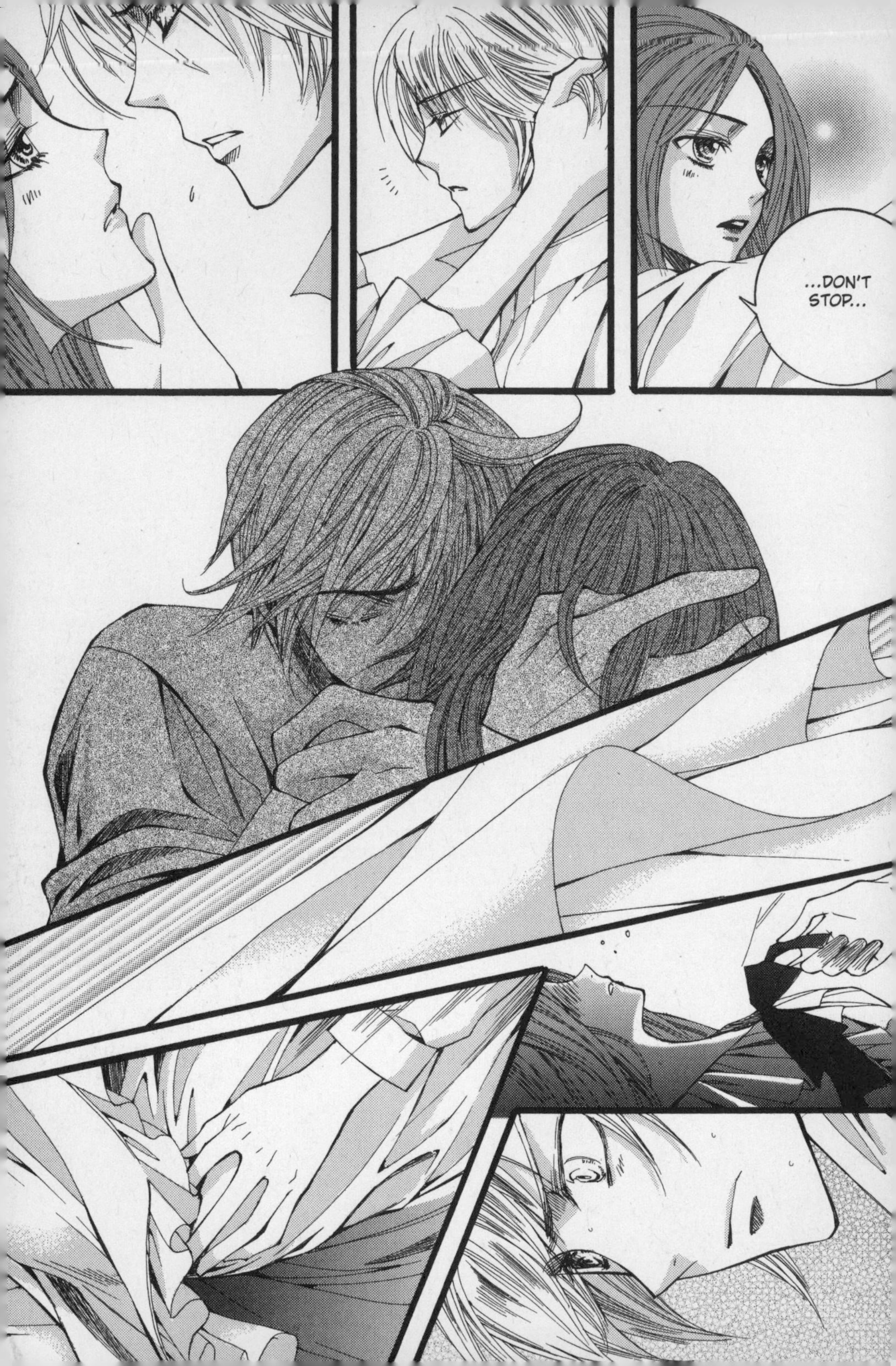
...DON'T
STOP...

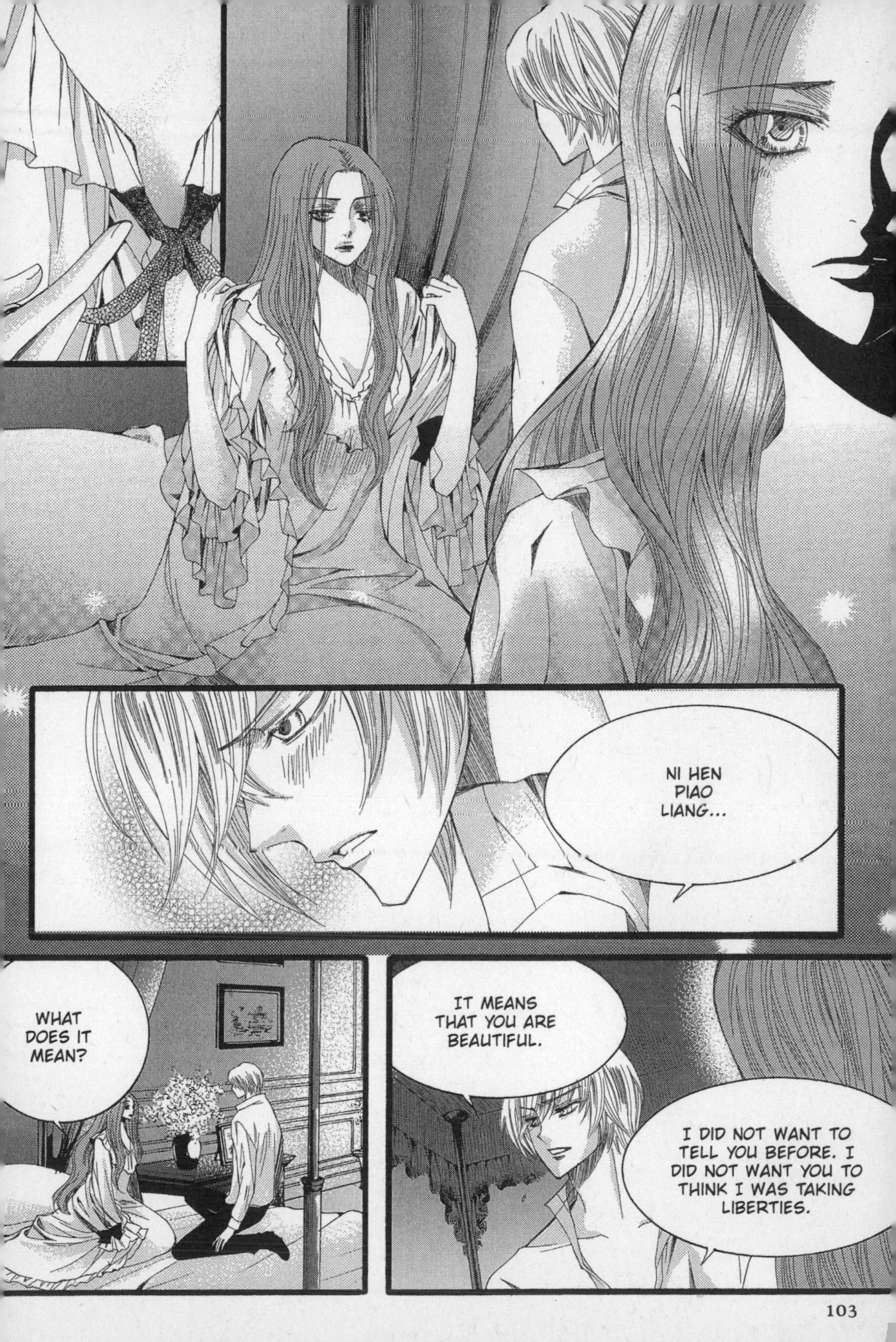
NI HEN PIAO LIANG...
WHAT DOES IT MEAN?
IT MEANS THAT YOU ARE BEAUTIFUL.
I DID NOT WANT TO TELL YOU BEFORE. I DID NOT WANT YOU TO THINK I WAS TAKING LIBERTIES.

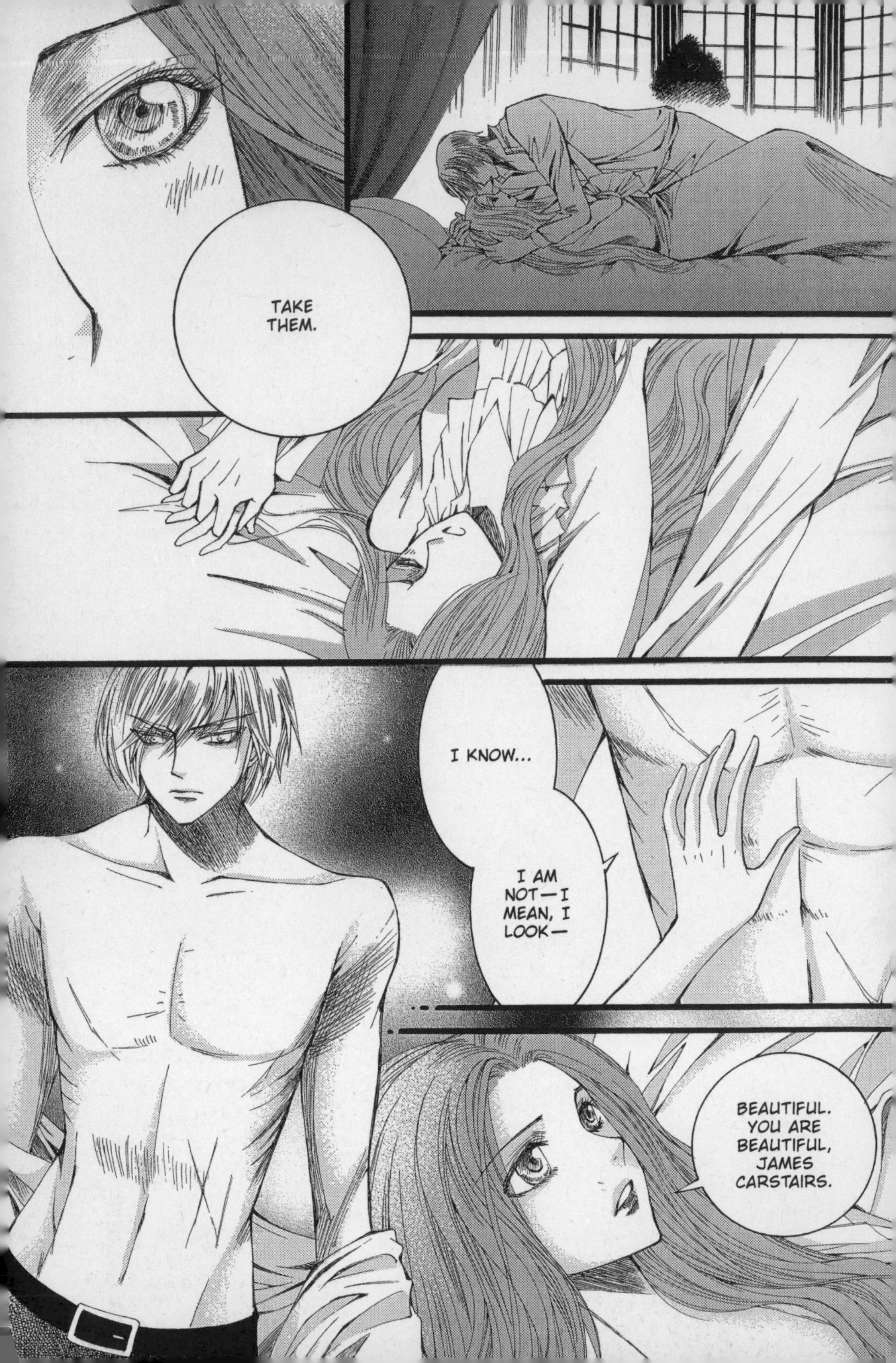
TAKE THEM.
I KNOW...
I AM NOT—I MEAN, I LOOK—
BEAUTIFUL. YOU ARE BEAUTIFUL, JAMES CARSTAIRS.

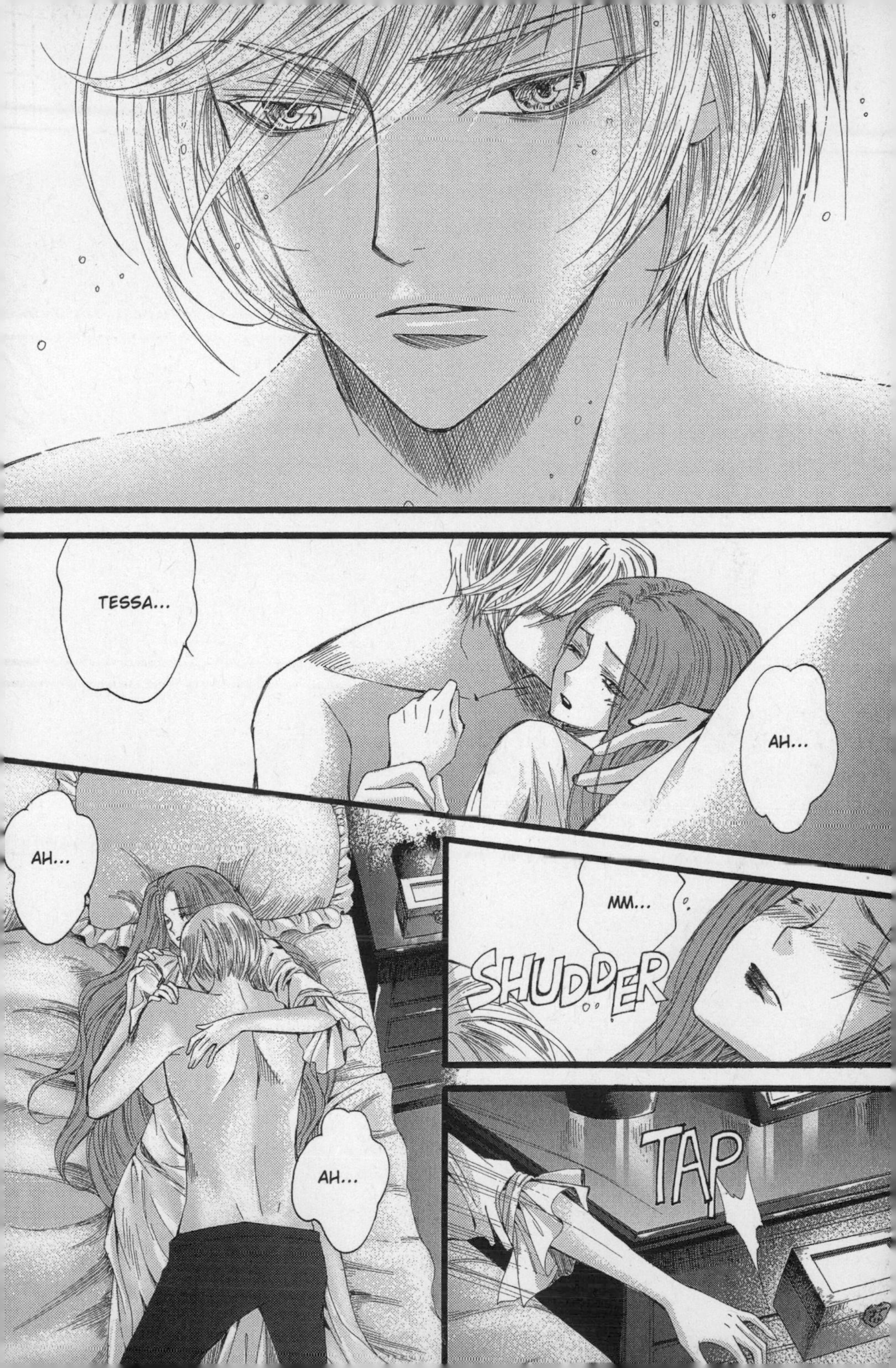
TESSA...
AH...
AH...
MM...
SHUDDER
AH...
TAP

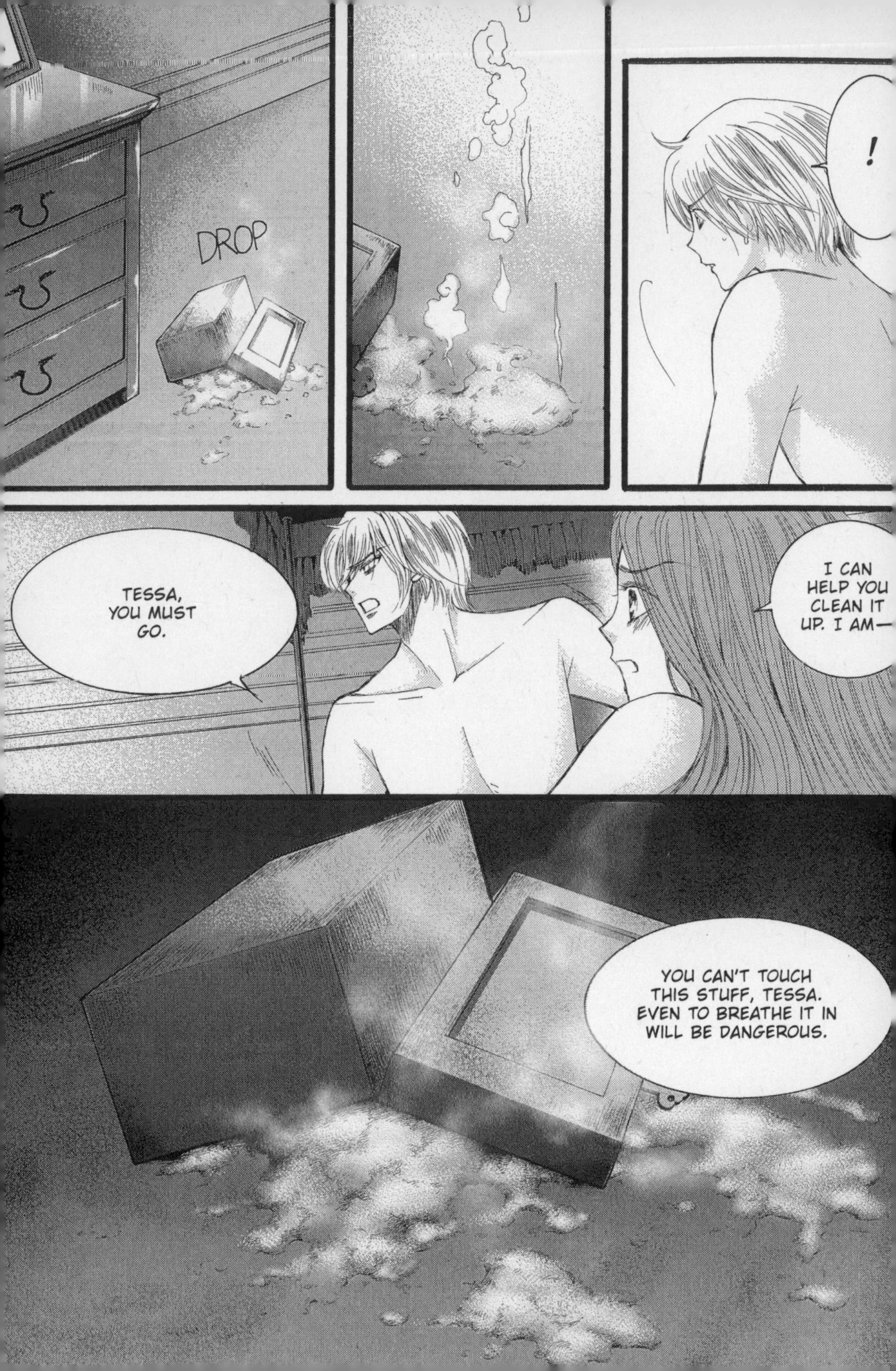
DROP
!
TESSA, YOU MUST GO.
I CAN HELP YOU CLEAN IT UP. I AM—
YOU CAN'T TOUCH THIS STUFF, TESSA. EVEN TO BREATHE IT IN WILL BE DANGEROUS.

THE INFERNAL DEVICES
CLOCKWORK PRINCE

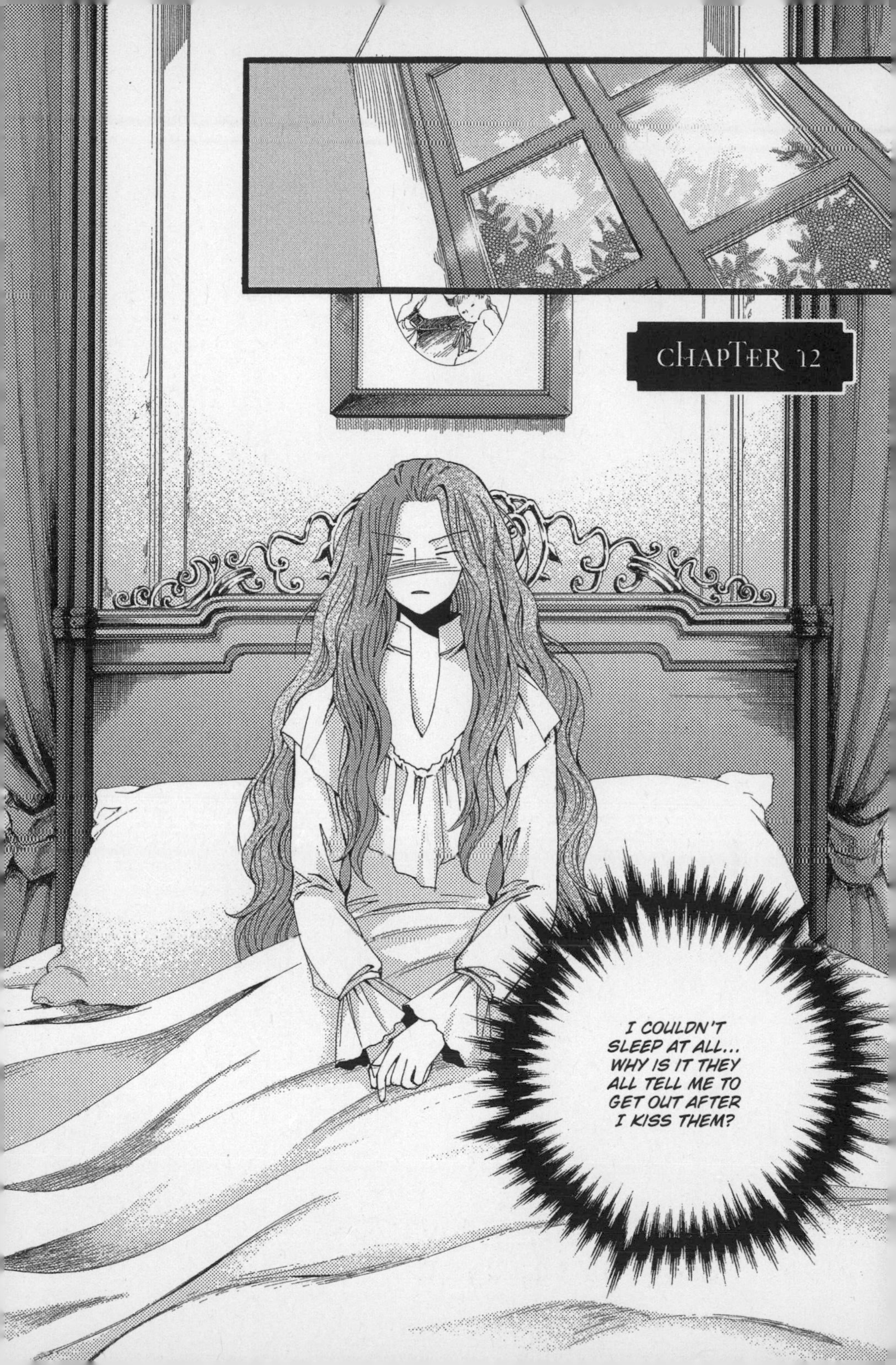
CHAPTER 12
I COULDN'T SLEEP AT ALL... WHY IS IT THEY ALL TELL ME TO GET OUT AFTER I KISS THEM?

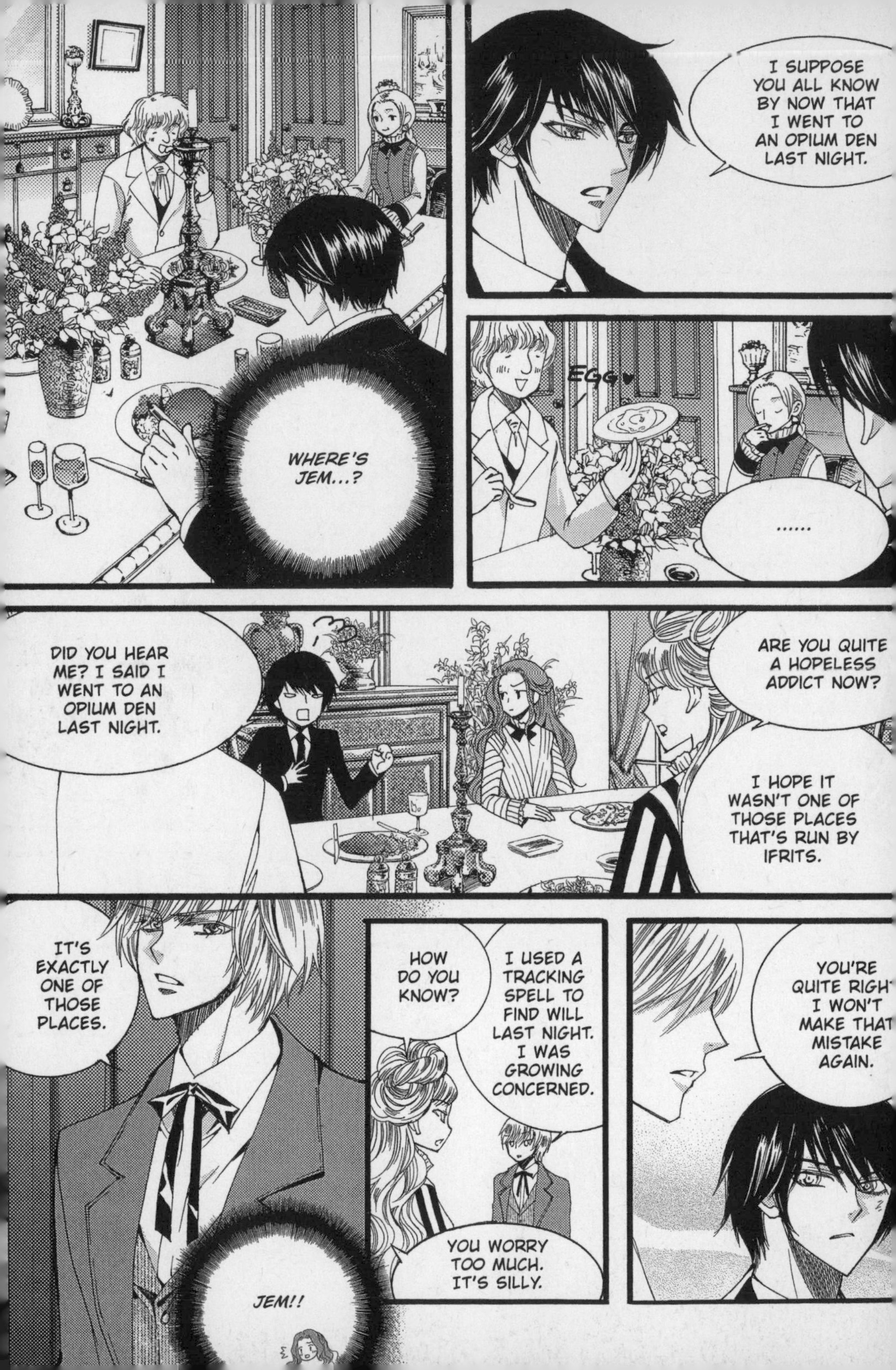
WHERE'S JEM...?
I SUPPOSE YOU ALL KNOW BY NOW THAT I WENT TO AN OPIUM DEN LAST NIGHT.
EGG♥
......
DID YOU HEAR ME? I SAID I WENT TO AN OPIUM DEN LAST NIGHT.
ARE YOU QUITE A HOPELESS ADDICT NOW?
I HOPE IT WASN'T ONE OF THOSE PLACES THAT'S RUN BY IFRITS.
IT'S EXACTLY ONE OF THOSE PLACES.
HOW DO YOU KNOW?
I USED A TRACKING SPELL TO FIND WILL LAST NIGHT. I WAS GROWING CONCERNED.
YOU WORRY TOO MUCH. IT'S SILLY.
YOU'RE QUITE RIGHT. I WON'T MAKE THAT MISTAKE AGAIN.
JEM!!

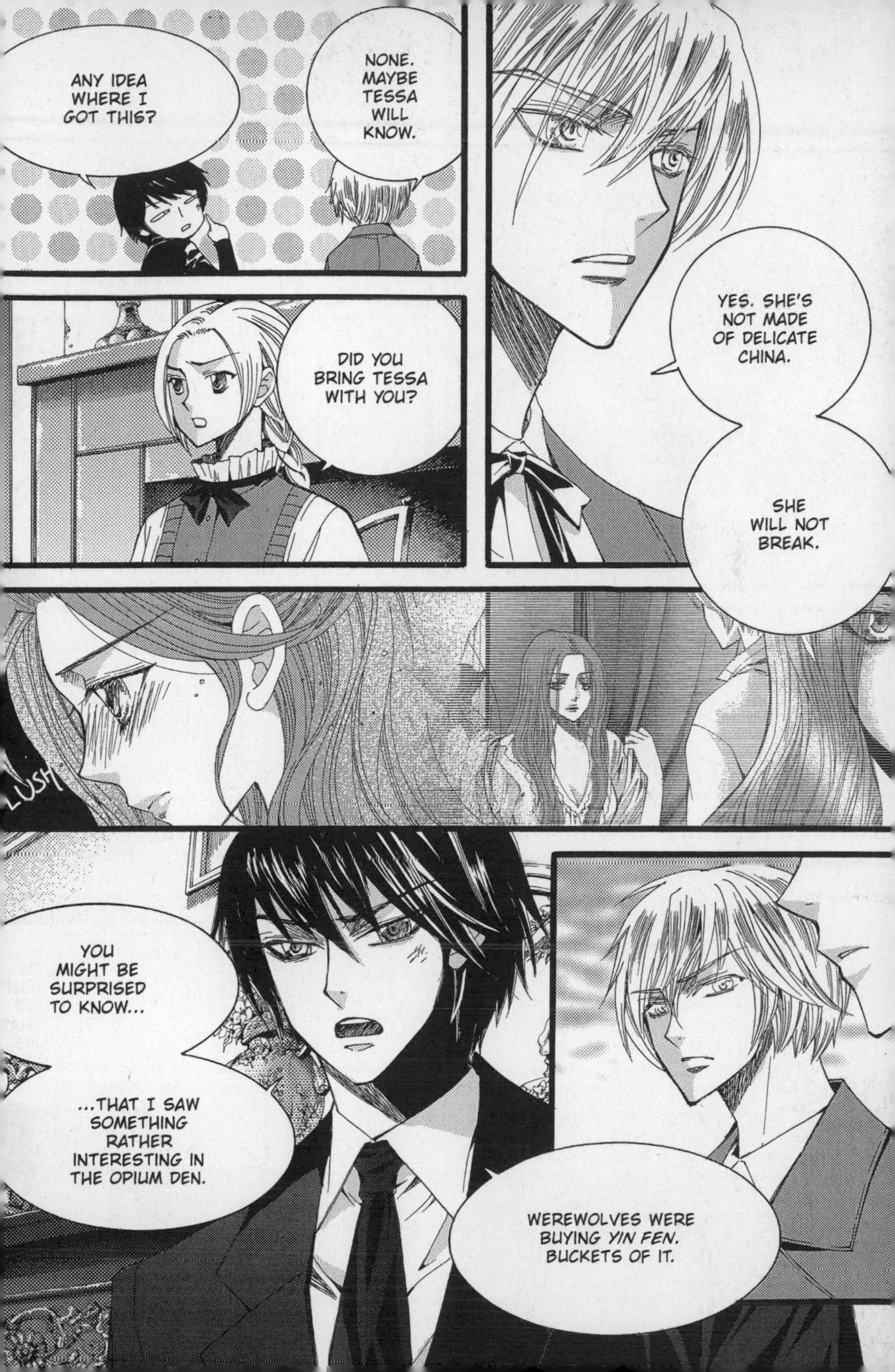

ANY IDEA WHERE I GOT THIS?
NONE. MAYBE TESSA WILL KNOW.
DID YOU BRING TESSA WITH YOU?
YES. SHE'S NOT MADE OF DELICATE CHINA.
SHE WILL NOT BREAK.
LUSH
YOU MIGHT BE SURPRISED TO KNOW...
...THAT I SAW SOMETHING RATHER INTERESTING IN THE OPIUM DEN.
WEREWOLVES WERE BUYING *YIN FEN*. BUCKETS OF IT.

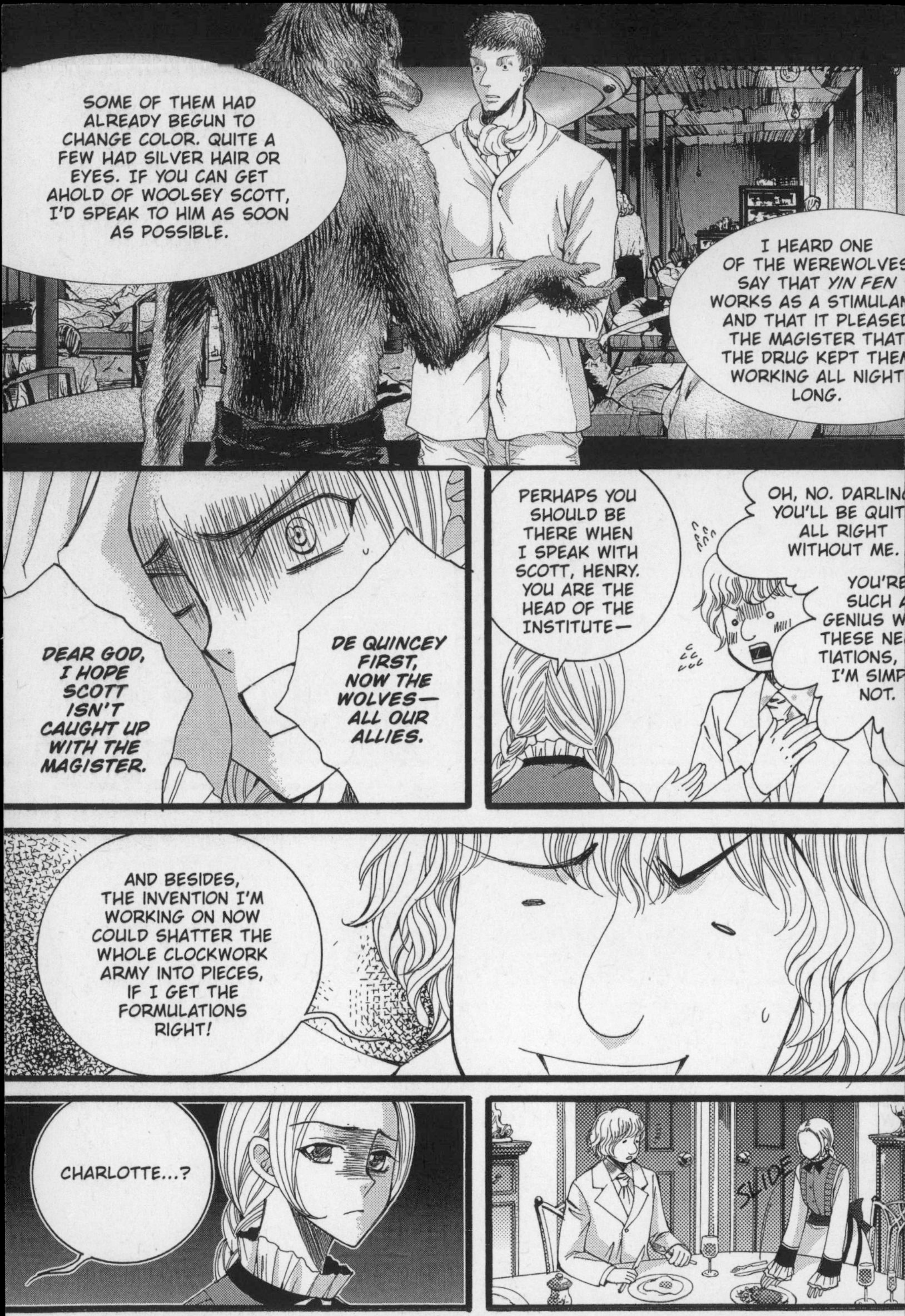
SOME OF THEM HAD ALREADY BEGUN TO CHANGE COLOR. QUITE A FEW HAD SILVER HAIR OR EYES. IF YOU CAN GET AHOLD OF WOOLSEY SCOTT, I'D SPEAK TO HIM AS SOON AS POSSIBLE.
I HEARD ONE OF THE WEREWOLVES SAY THAT YIN FEN WORKS AS A STIMULAN AND THAT IT PLEASED THE MAGISTER THAT THE DRUG KEPT THEM WORKING ALL NIGHT LONG.
DE QUINCEY FIRST, NOW THE WOLVES— ALL OUR ALLIES.
DEAR GOD, I HOPE SCOTT ISN'T CAUGHT UP WITH THE MAGISTER.
PERHAPS YOU SHOULD BE THERE WHEN I SPEAK WITH SCOTT, HENRY. YOU ARE THE HEAD OF THE INSTITUTE—
OH, NO. DARLING YOU'LL BE QUIT ALL RIGHT WITHOUT ME.
YOU'RE SUCH A GENIUS W THESE NE TIATIONS, I'M SIMP NOT.
AND BESIDES, THE INVENTION I'M WORKING ON NOW COULD SHATTER THE WHOLE CLOCKWORK ARMY INTO PIECES, IF I GET THE FORMULATIONS RIGHT!
CHARLOTTE...?
SLIDE

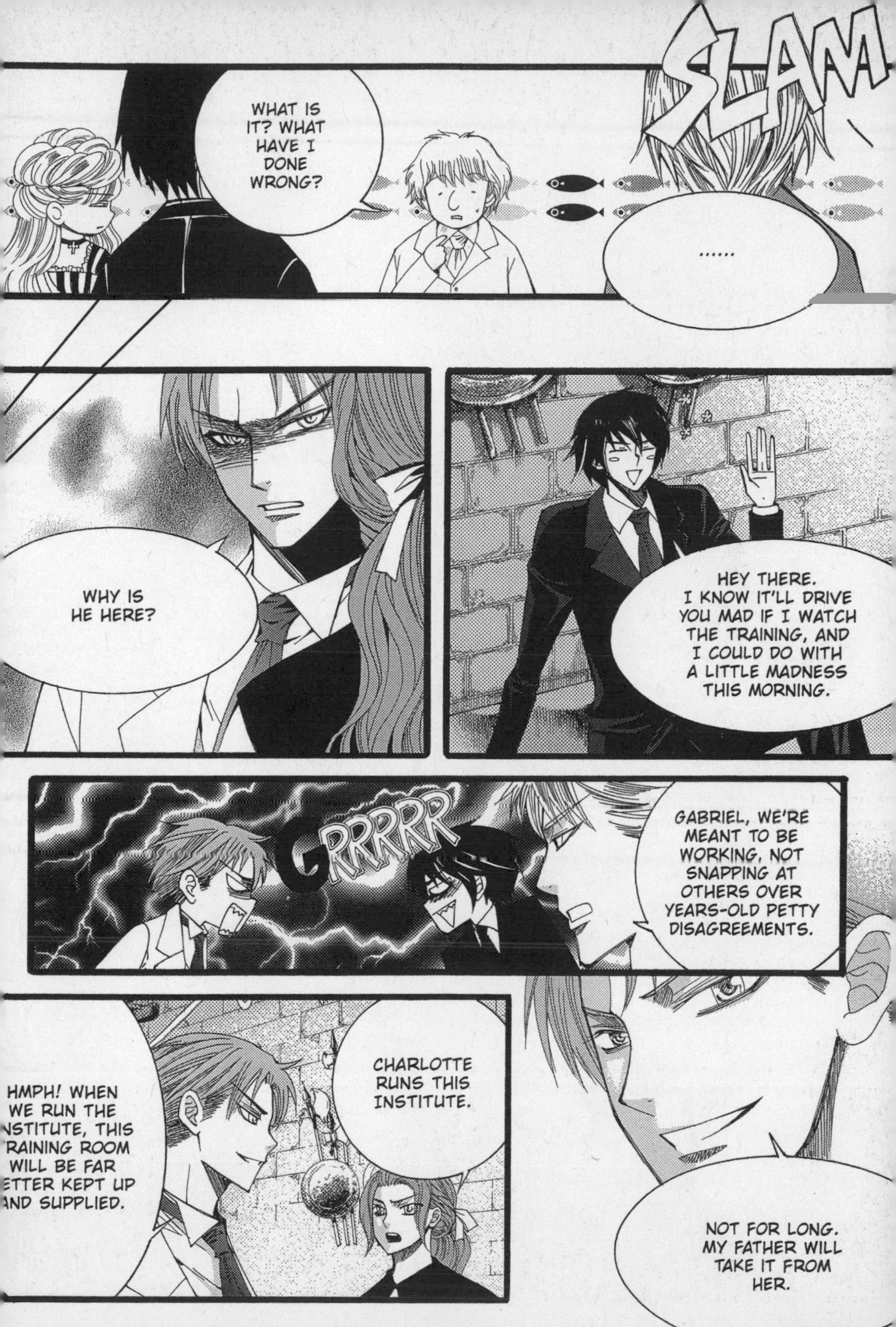
SLAM
WHAT IS IT? WHAT HAVE I DONE WRONG?
......
WHY IS HE HERE?
HEY THERE. I KNOW IT'LL DRIVE YOU MAD IF I WATCH THE TRAINING, AND I COULD DO WITH A LITTLE MADNESS THIS MORNING.
GRRRRR
GABRIEL, WE'RE MEANT TO BE WORKING, NOT SNAPPING AT OTHERS OVER YEARS-OLD PETTY DISAGREEMENTS.
HMPH! WHEN WE RUN THE NSTITUTE, THIS RAINING ROOM WILL BE FAR ETTER KEPT UP AND SUPPLIED.
CHARLOTTE RUNS THIS INSTITUTE.
NOT FOR LONG. MY FATHER WILL TAKE IT FROM HER.

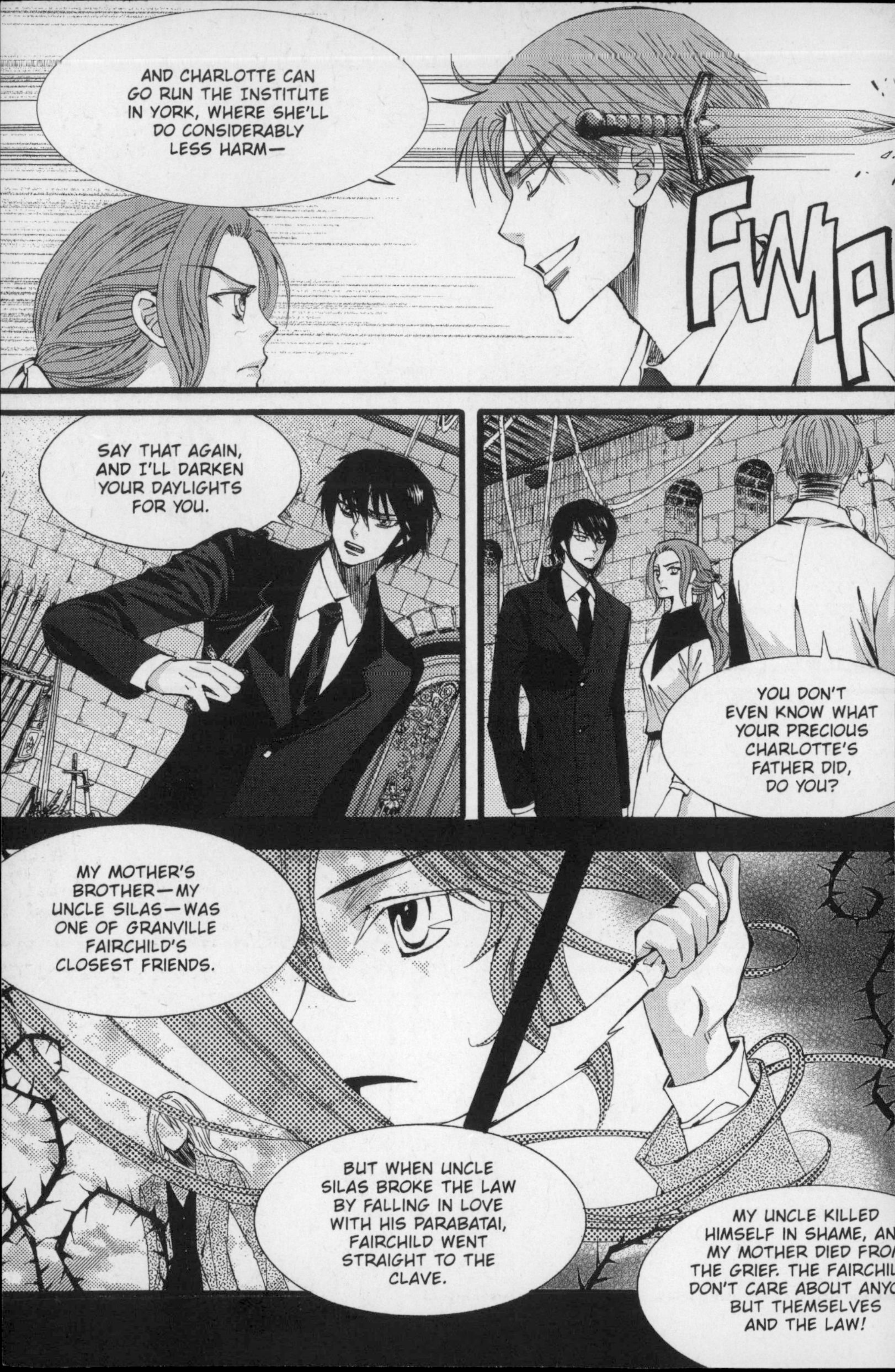
AND CHARLOTTE CAN GO RUN THE INSTITUTE IN YORK, WHERE SHE'LL DO CONSIDERABLY LESS HARM—
FWP
SAY THAT AGAIN, AND I'LL DARKEN YOUR DAYLIGHTS FOR YOU.
YOU DON'T EVEN KNOW WHAT YOUR PRECIOUS CHARLOTTE'S FATHER DID, DO YOU?
MY MOTHER'S BROTHER—MY UNCLE SILAS—WAS ONE OF GRANVILLE FAIRCHILD'S CLOSEST FRIENDS.
BUT WHEN UNCLE SILAS BROKE THE LAW BY FALLING IN LOVE WITH HIS PARABATAI, FAIRCHILD WENT STRAIGHT TO THE CLAVE.
MY UNCLE KILLED HIMSELF IN SHAME, AN MY MOTHER DIED FROM THE GRIEF. THE FAIRCHIL DON'T CARE ABOUT ANYO BUT THEMSELVES AND THE LAW!

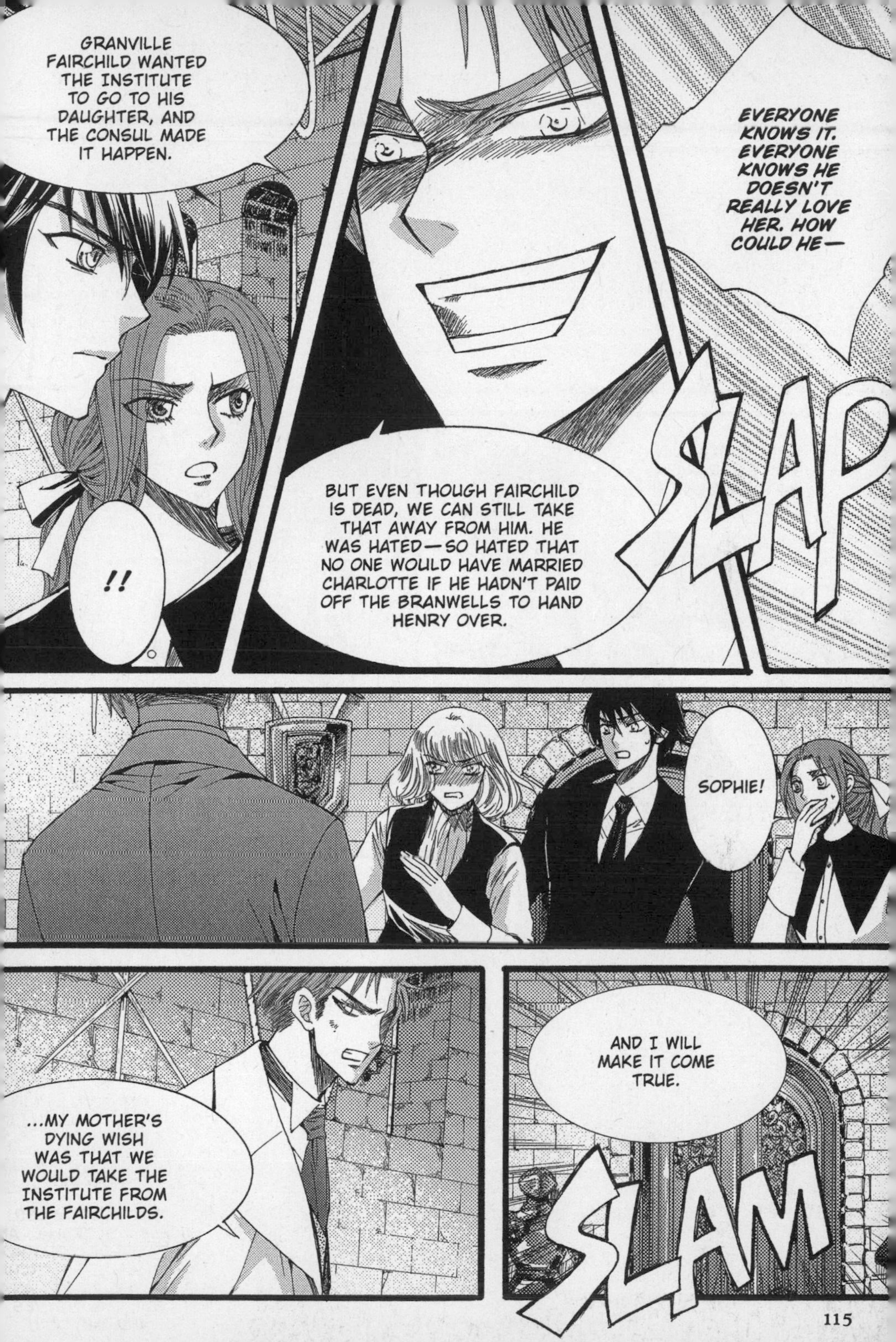
GRANVILLE FAIRCHILD WANTED THE INSTITUTE TO GO TO HIS DAUGHTER, AND THE CONSUL MADE IT HAPPEN.
EVERYONE KNOWS IT. EVERYONE KNOWS HE DOESN'T REALLY LOVE HER. HOW COULD HE—
!!
BUT EVEN THOUGH FAIRCHILD IS DEAD, WE CAN STILL TAKE THAT AWAY FROM HIM. HE WAS HATED—SO HATED THAT NO ONE WOULD HAVE MARRIED CHARLOTTE IF HE HADN'T PAID OFF THE BRANWELLS TO HAND HENRY OVER.
SLAP
SOPHIE!
...MY MOTHER'S DYING WISH WAS THAT WE WOULD TAKE THE INSTITUTE FROM THE FAIRCHILDS.
AND I WILL MAKE IT COME TRUE.
SLAM

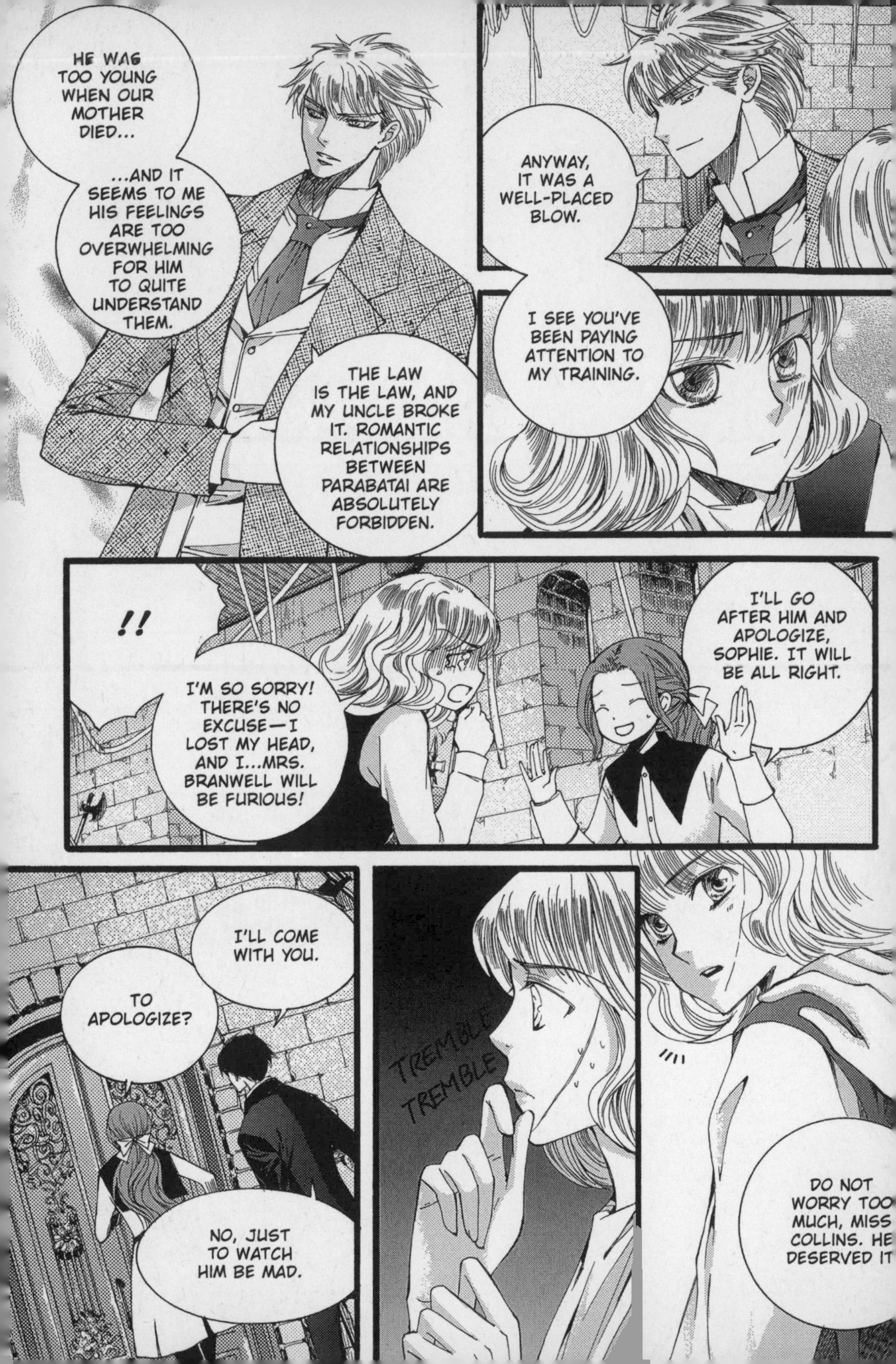
HE WAS TOO YOUNG WHEN OUR MOTHER DIED...
...AND IT SEEMS TO ME HIS FEELINGS ARE TOO OVERWHELMING FOR HIM TO QUITE UNDERSTAND THEM.
THE LAW IS THE LAW, AND MY UNCLE BROKE IT. ROMANTIC RELATIONSHIPS BETWEEN PARABATAI ARE ABSOLUTELY FORBIDDEN.
ANYWAY, IT WAS A WELL-PLACED BLOW.
I SEE YOU'VE BEEN PAYING ATTENTION TO MY TRAINING.
!!
I'M SO SORRY! THERE'S NO EXCUSE—I LOST MY HEAD, AND I...MRS. BRANWELL WILL BE FURIOUS!
I'LL GO AFTER HIM AND APOLOGIZE, SOPHIE. IT WILL BE ALL RIGHT.
I'LL COME WITH YOU.
TO APOLOGIZE?
NO, JUST TO WATCH HIM BE MAD.
TREMBLE TREMBLE
DO NOT WORRY TOO MUCH, MISS COLLINS. HE DESERVED IT

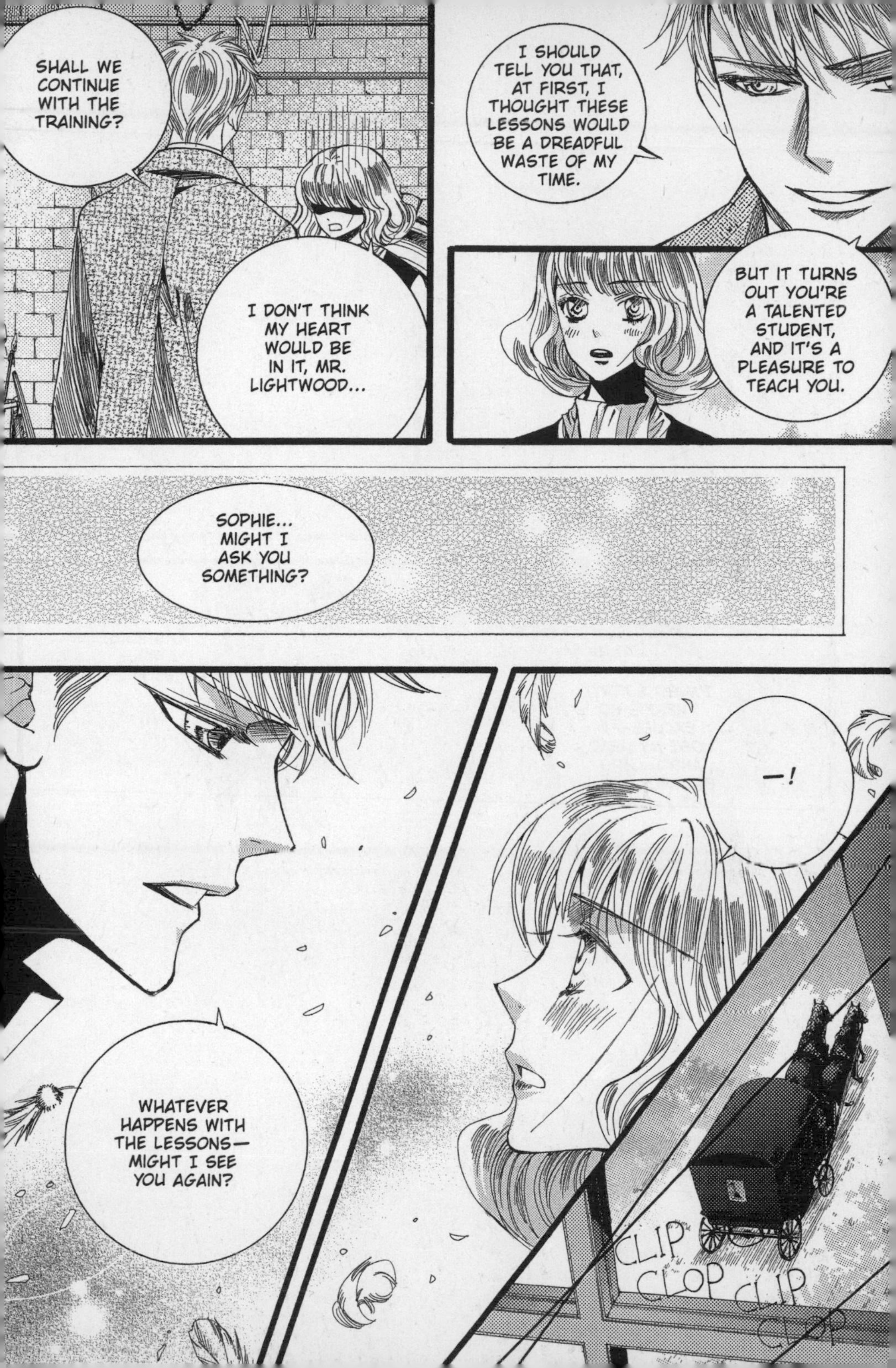

SHALL WE CONTINUE WITH THE TRAINING?
I DON'T THINK MY HEART WOULD BE IN IT, MR. LIGHTWOOD...
I SHOULD TELL YOU THAT, AT FIRST, I THOUGHT THESE LESSONS WOULD BE A DREADFUL WASTE OF MY TIME.
BUT IT TURNS OUT YOU'RE A TALENTED STUDENT, AND IT'S A PLEASURE TO TEACH YOU.
SOPHIE... MIGHT I ASK YOU SOMETHING?
WHATEVER HAPPENS WITH THE LESSONS—MIGHT I SEE YOU AGAIN?
—!
CLIP CLOP CLIP CLOP

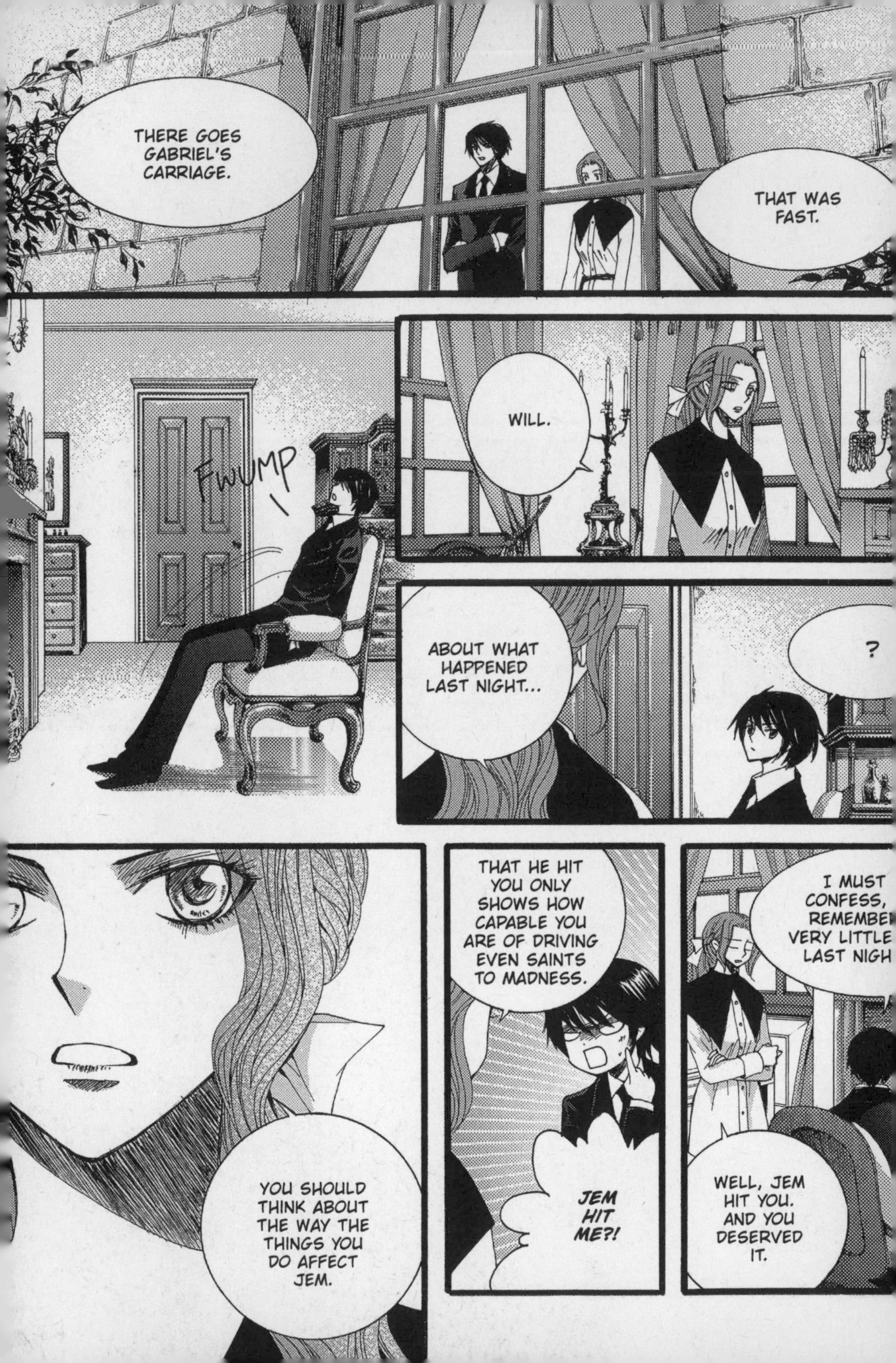
THERE GOES GABRIEL'S CARRIAGE.
THAT WAS FAST.
FWUMP
WILL.
ABOUT WHAT HAPPENED LAST NIGHT...
?
I MUST CONFESS, REMEMBE VERY LITTLE LAST NIGH
WELL, JEM HIT YOU. AND YOU DESERVED IT.
JEM HIT ME?!
THAT HE HIT YOU ONLY SHOWS HOW CAPABLE YOU ARE OF DRIVING EVEN SAINTS TO MADNESS.
YOU SHOULD THINK ABOUT THE WAY THE THINGS YOU DO AFFECT JEM.

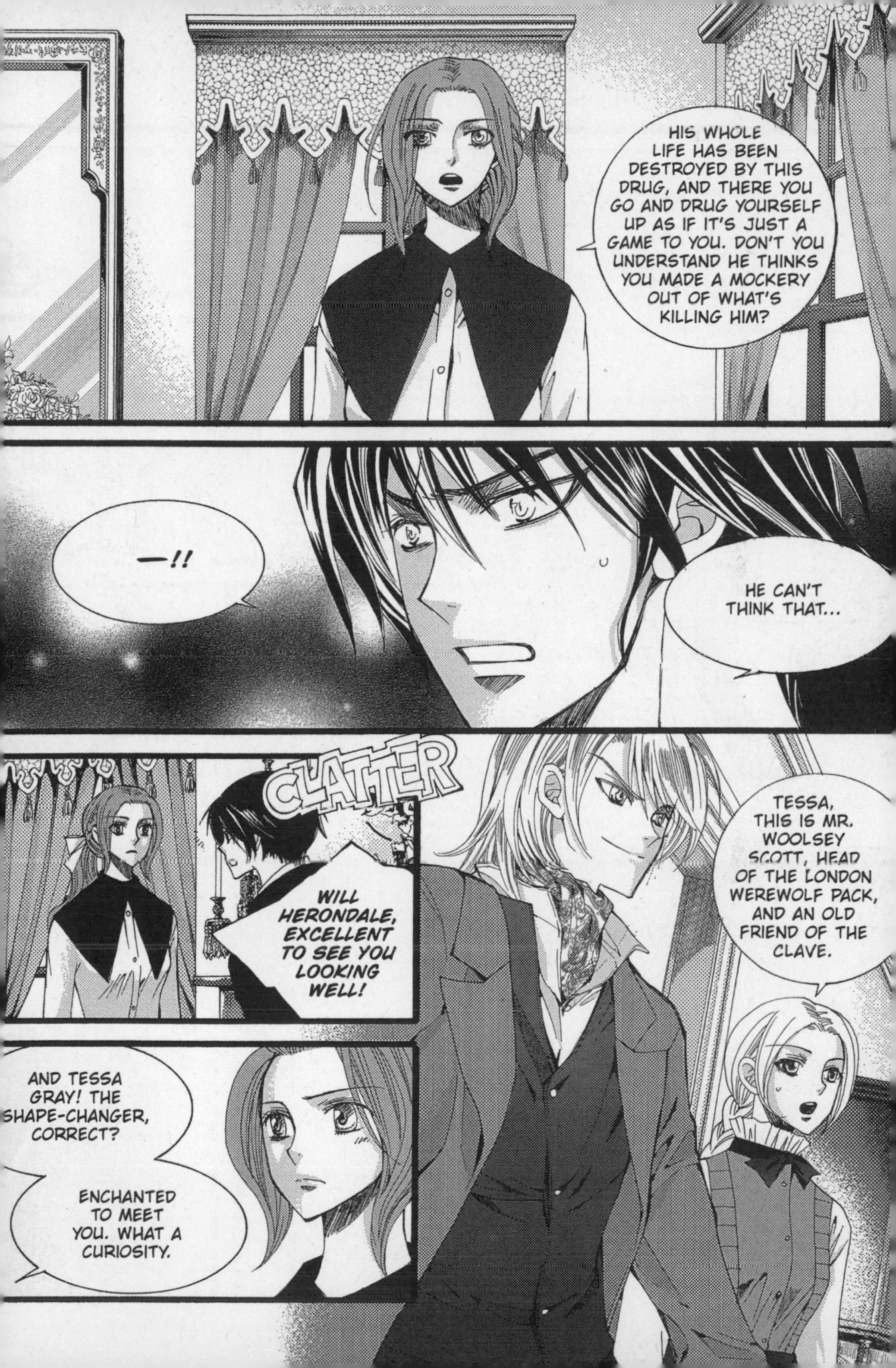
HIS WHOLE LIFE HAS BEEN DESTROYED BY THIS DRUG, AND THERE YOU GO AND DRUG YOURSELF UP AS IF IT'S JUST A GAME TO YOU. DON'T YOU UNDERSTAND HE THINKS YOU MADE A MOCKERY OUT OF WHAT'S KILLING HIM?
—!!
HE CAN'T THINK THAT...
CLATTER
WILL HERONDALE, EXCELLENT TO SEE YOU LOOKING WELL!
TESSA, THIS IS MR. WOOLSEY SCOTT, HEAD OF THE LONDON WEREWOLF PACK, AND AN OLD FRIEND OF THE CLAVE.
AND TESSA GRAY! THE SHAPE-CHANGER, CORRECT?
ENCHANTED TO MEET YOU. WHAT A CURIOSITY.

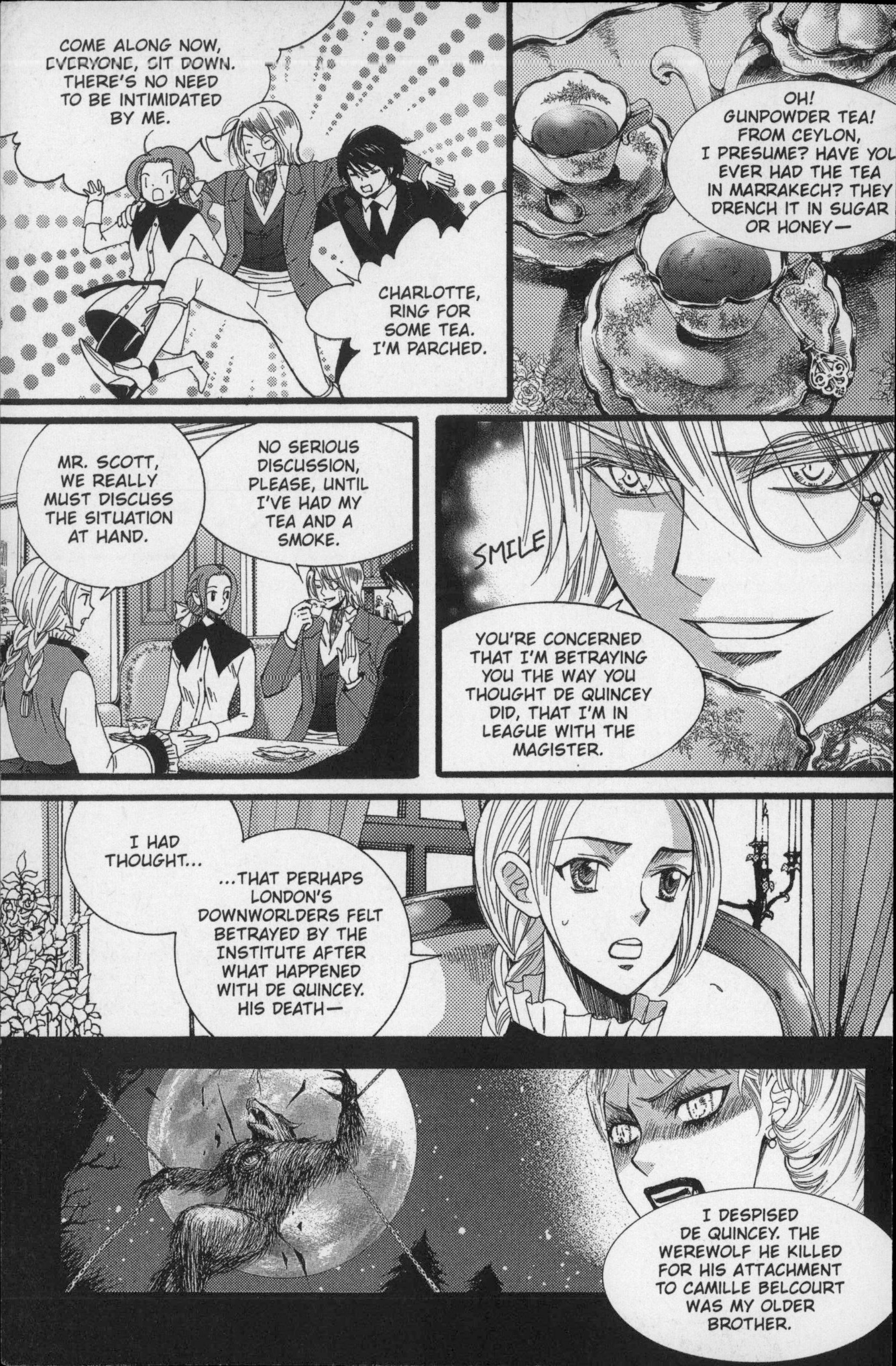
COME ALONG NOW, EVERYONE, SIT DOWN. THERE'S NO NEED TO BE INTIMIDATED BY ME.
CHARLOTTE, RING FOR SOME TEA. I'M PARCHED.
OH! GUNPOWDER TEA! FROM CEYLON, I PRESUME? HAVE YOU EVER HAD THE TEA IN MARRAKECH? THEY DRENCH IT IN SUGAR OR HONEY—
MR. SCOTT, WE REALLY MUST DISCUSS THE SITUATION AT HAND.
NO SERIOUS DISCUSSION, PLEASE, UNTIL I'VE HAD MY TEA AND A SMOKE.
SMILE
YOU'RE CONCERNED THAT I'M BETRAYING YOU THE WAY YOU THOUGHT DE QUINCEY DID, THAT I'M IN LEAGUE WITH THE MAGISTER.
I HAD THOUGHT...
...THAT PERHAPS LONDON'S DOWNWORLDERS FELT BETRAYED BY THE INSTITUTE AFTER WHAT HAPPENED WITH DE QUINCEY. HIS DEATH—
I DESPISED DE QUINCEY. THE WEREWOLF HE KILLED FOR HIS ATTACHMENT TO CAMILLE BELCOURT WAS MY OLDER BROTHER.

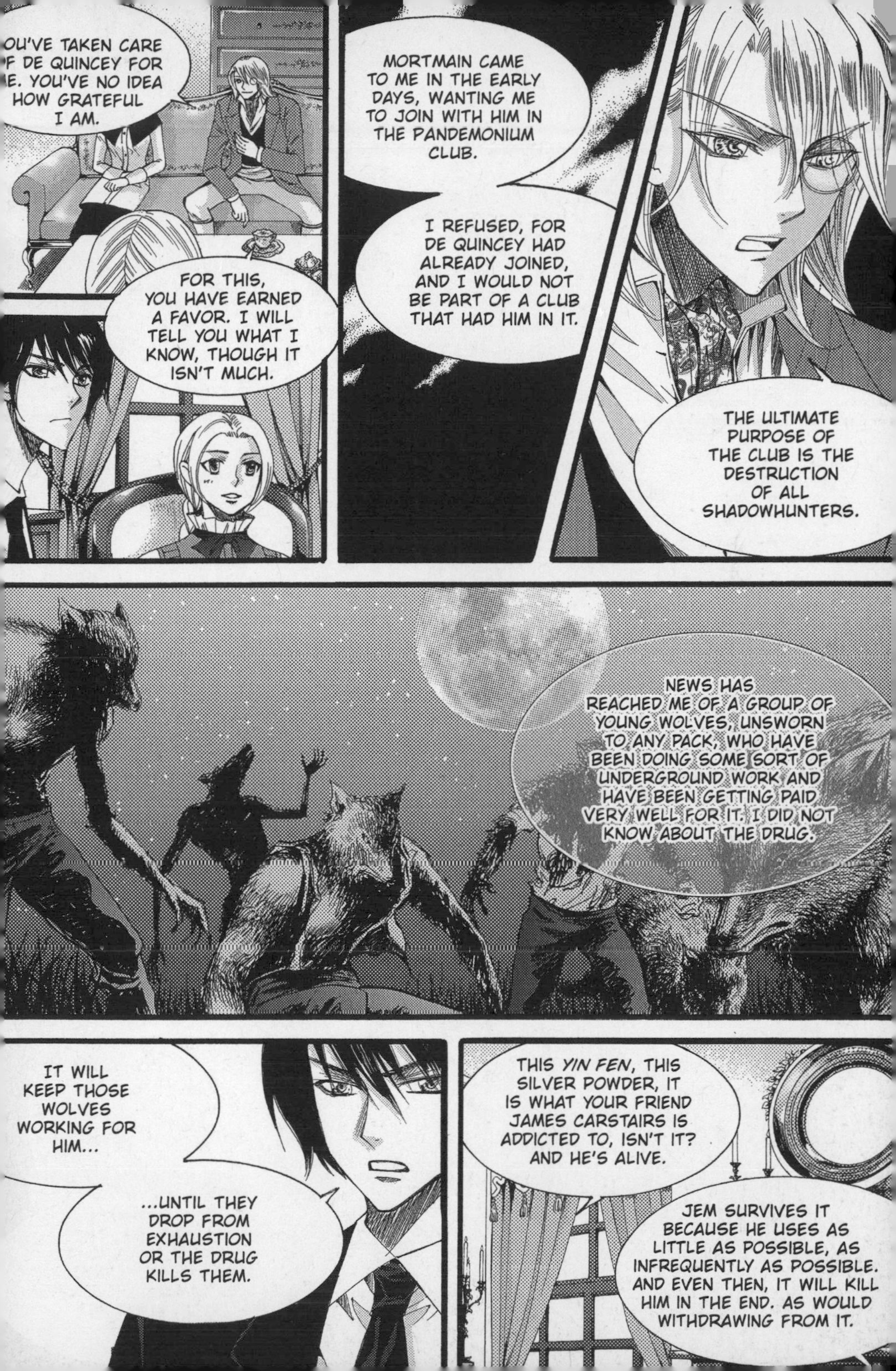
OU'VE TAKEN CARE F DE QUINCEY FOR E. YOU'VE NO IDEA HOW GRATEFUL I AM.
FOR THIS, YOU HAVE EARNED A FAVOR. I WILL TELL YOU WHAT I KNOW, THOUGH IT ISN'T MUCH.
MORTMAIN CAME TO ME IN THE EARLY DAYS, WANTING ME TO JOIN WITH HIM IN THE PANDEMONIUM CLUB.
I REFUSED, FOR DE QUINCEY HAD ALREADY JOINED, AND I WOULD NOT BE PART OF A CLUB THAT HAD HIM IN IT.
THE ULTIMATE PURPOSE OF THE CLUB IS THE DESTRUCTION OF ALL SHADOWHUNTERS.
NEWS HAS REACHED ME OF A GROUP OF YOUNG WOLVES, UNSWORN TO ANY PACK, WHO HAVE BEEN DOING SOME SORT OF UNDERGROUND WORK AND HAVE BEEN GETTING PAID VERY WELL FOR IT. I DID NOT KNOW ABOUT THE DRUG.
IT WILL KEEP THOSE WOLVES WORKING FOR HIM...
...UNTIL THEY DROP FROM EXHAUSTION OR THE DRUG KILLS THEM.
THIS *YIN FEN*, THIS SILVER POWDER, IT IS WHAT YOUR FRIEND JAMES CARSTAIRS IS ADDICTED TO, ISN'T IT? AND HE'S ALIVE.
JEM SURVIVES IT BECAUSE HE USES AS LITTLE AS POSSIBLE, AS INFREQUENTLY AS POSSIBLE. AND EVEN THEN, IT WILL KILL HIM IN THE END. AS WOULD WITHDRAWING FROM IT.

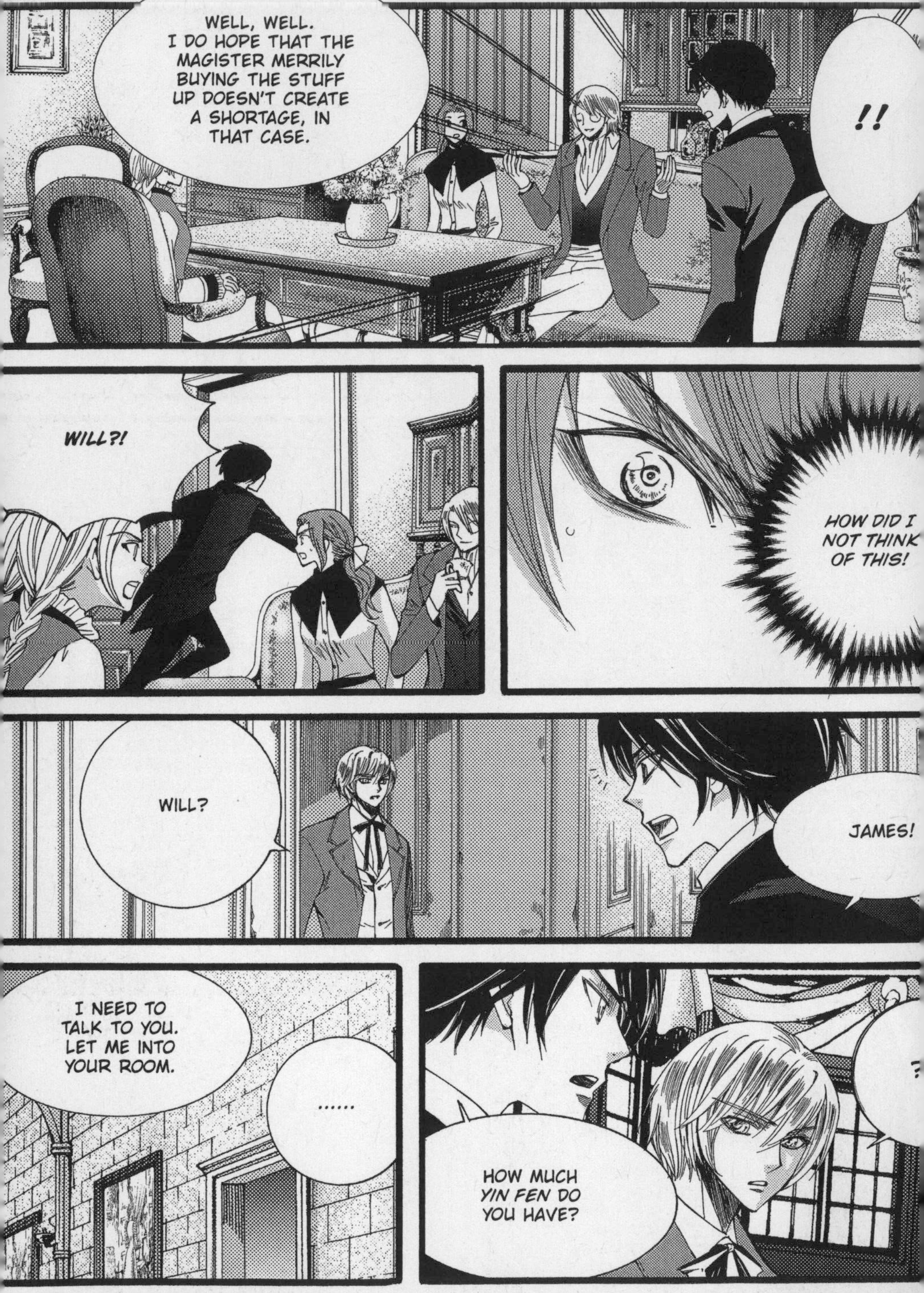
WELL, WELL. I DO HOPE THAT THE MAGISTER MERRILY BUYING THE STUFF UP DOESN'T CREATE A SHORTAGE, IN THAT CASE.
!!
HOW DID I NOT THINK OF THIS!
WILL?!
JAMES!
WILL?
I NEED TO TALK TO YOU. LET ME INTO YOUR ROOM.
......
HOW MUCH YIN FEN DO YOU HAVE?
?

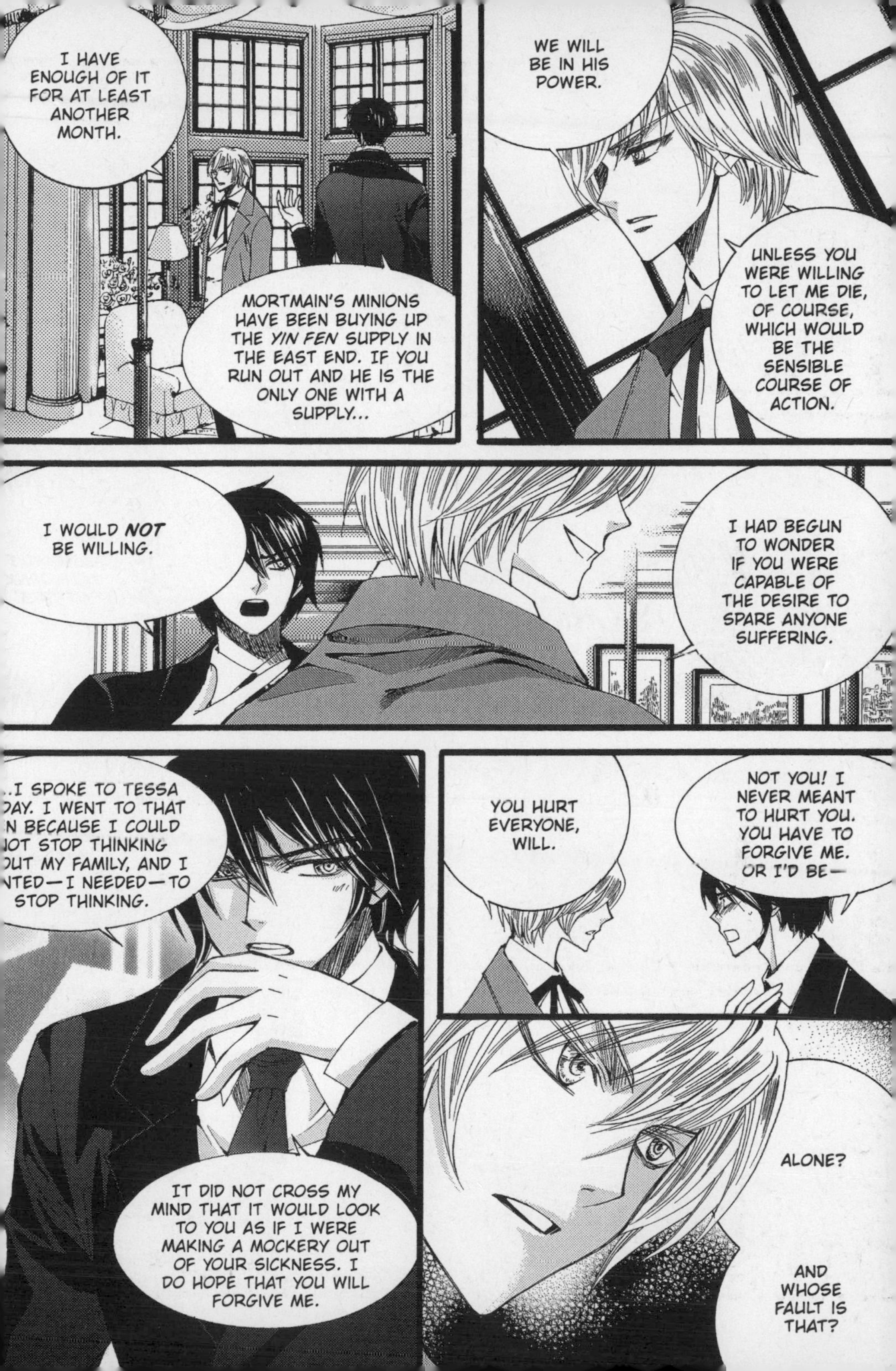
I HAVE ENOUGH OF IT FOR AT LEAST ANOTHER MONTH.
MORTMAIN'S MINIONS HAVE BEEN BUYING UP THE *YIN FEN* SUPPLY IN THE EAST END. IF YOU RUN OUT AND HE IS THE ONLY ONE WITH A SUPPLY...
WE WILL BE IN HIS POWER.
UNLESS YOU WERE WILLING TO LET ME DIE, OF COURSE, WHICH WOULD BE THE SENSIBLE COURSE OF ACTION.
I WOULD **NOT** BE WILLING.
I HAD BEGUN TO WONDER IF YOU WERE CAPABLE OF THE DESIRE TO SPARE ANYONE SUFFERING.
..I SPOKE TO TESSA DAY. I WENT TO THAT N BECAUSE I COULD NOT STOP THINKING OUT MY FAMILY, AND I NTED—I NEEDED—TO STOP THINKING.
IT DID NOT CROSS MY MIND THAT IT WOULD LOOK TO YOU AS IF I WERE MAKING A MOCKERY OUT OF YOUR SICKNESS. I DO HOPE THAT YOU WILL FORGIVE ME.
YOU HURT EVERYONE, WILL.
NOT YOU! I NEVER MEANT TO HURT YOU. YOU HAVE TO FORGIVE ME. OR I'D BE—
ALONE?
AND WHOSE FAULT IS THAT?

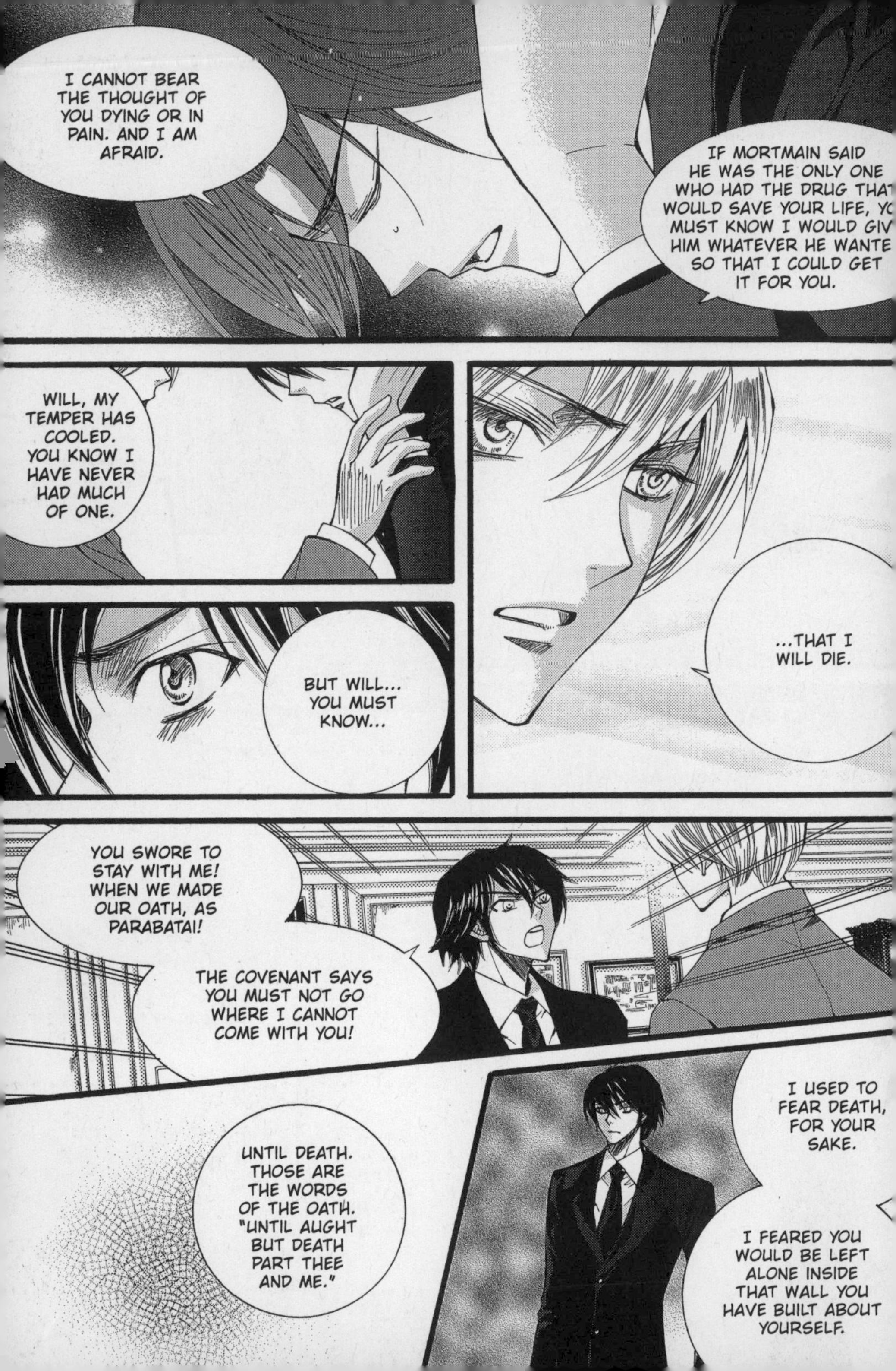
I CANNOT BEAR THE THOUGHT OF YOU DYING OR IN PAIN. AND I AM AFRAID.
IF MORTMAIN SAID HE WAS THE ONLY ONE WHO HAD THE DRUG THAT WOULD SAVE YOUR LIFE, YOU MUST KNOW I WOULD GIVE HIM WHATEVER HE WANTED SO THAT I COULD GET IT FOR YOU.
WILL, MY TEMPER HAS COOLED. YOU KNOW I HAVE NEVER HAD MUCH OF ONE.
BUT WILL... YOU MUST KNOW...
...THAT I WILL DIE.
YOU SWORE TO STAY WITH ME! WHEN WE MADE OUR OATH, AS PARABATAI!
THE COVENANT SAYS YOU MUST NOT GO WHERE I CANNOT COME WITH YOU!
UNTIL DEATH. THOSE ARE THE WORDS OF THE OATH. "UNTIL AUGHT BUT DEATH PART THEE AND ME."
I USED TO FEAR DEATH, FOR YOUR SAKE.
I FEARED YOU WOULD BE LEFT ALONE INSIDE THAT WALL YOU HAVE BUILT ABOUT YOURSELF.

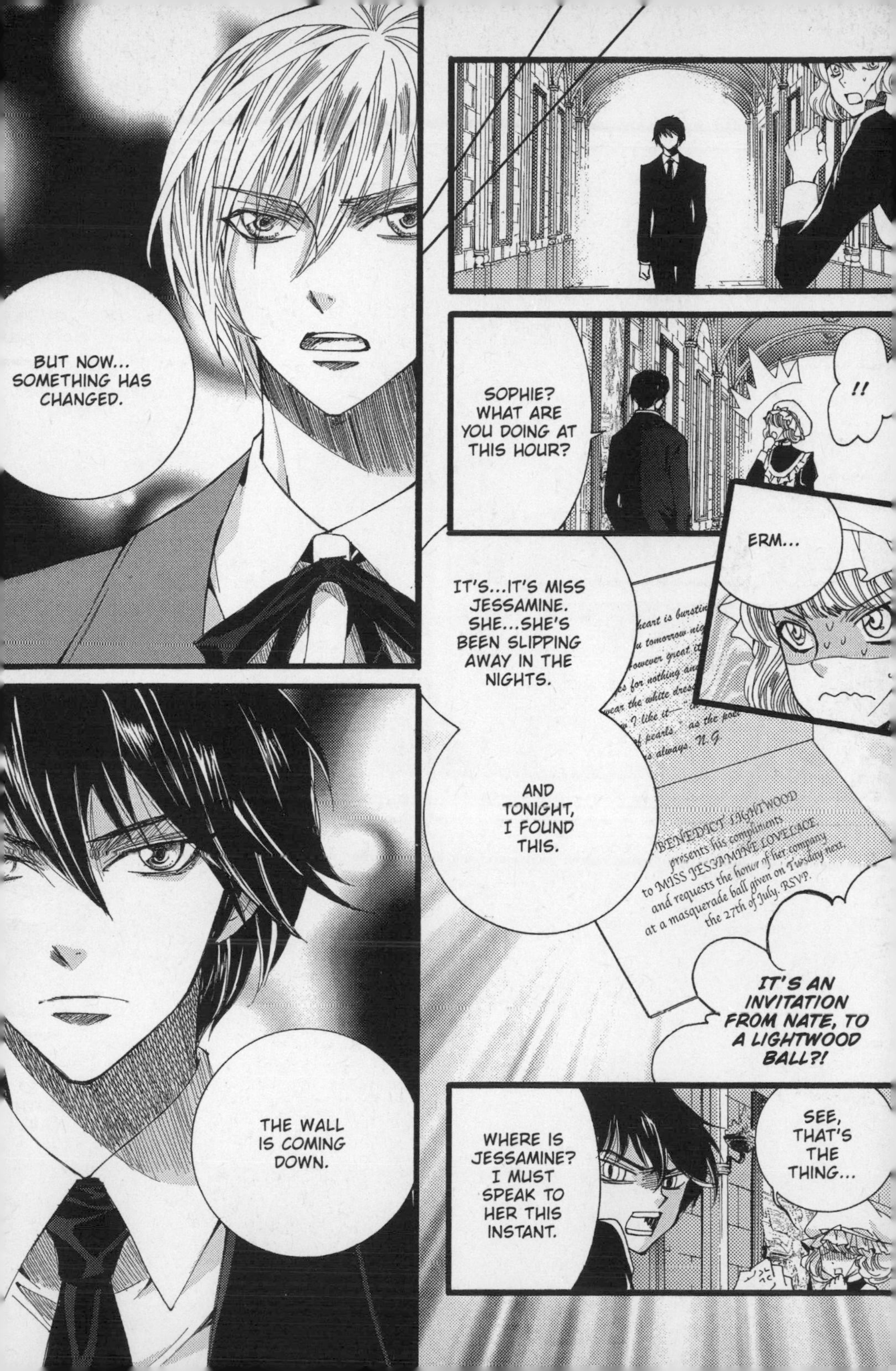
BUT NOW... SOMETHING HAS CHANGED.
THE WALL IS COMING DOWN.
SOPHIE? WHAT ARE YOU DOING AT THIS HOUR?
!!
ERM...
IT'S...IT'S MISS JESSAMINE. SHE...SHE'S BEEN SLIPPING AWAY IN THE NIGHTS.
AND TONIGHT, I FOUND THIS.
BENEDICT LIGHTWOOD presents his compliments to MISS JESSAMINE LOVELACE and requests the honor of her company at a masquerade ball given on Tuesday next, the 27th of July. RSVP.
IT'S AN INVITATION FROM NATE, TO A LIGHTWOOD BALL?!
WHERE IS JESSAMINE? I MUST SPEAK TO HER THIS INSTANT.
SEE, THAT'S THE THING...

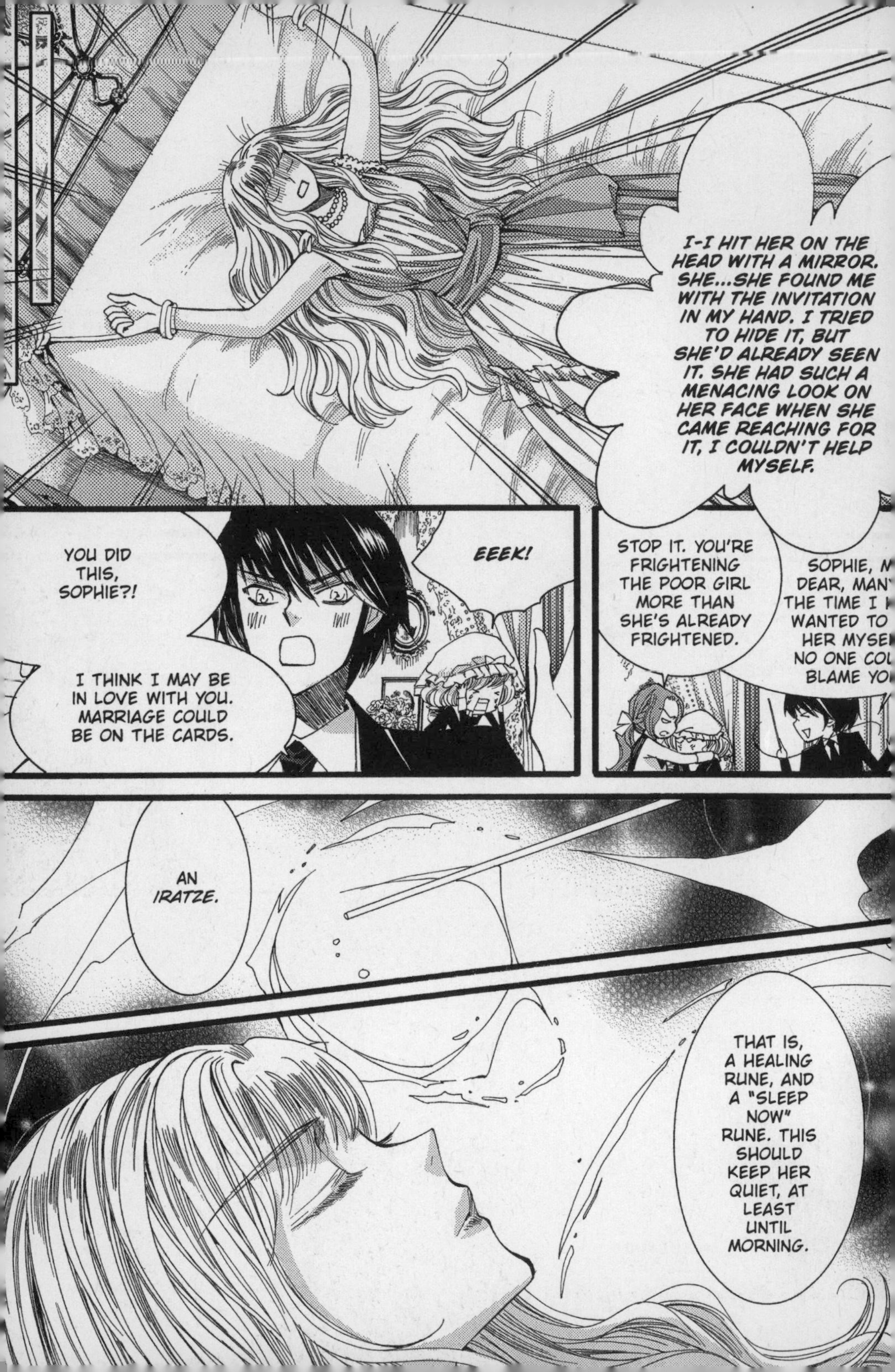
I-I HIT HER ON THE HEAD WITH A MIRROR. SHE...SHE FOUND ME WITH THE INVITATION IN MY HAND. I TRIED TO HIDE IT, BUT SHE'D ALREADY SEEN IT. SHE HAD SUCH A MENACING LOOK ON HER FACE WHEN SHE CAME REACHING FOR IT, I COULDN'T HELP MYSELF.
SOPHIE, M DEAR, MAN THE TIME I WANTED TO HER MYSE NO ONE CO BLAME YO
STOP IT. YOU'RE FRIGHTENING THE POOR GIRL MORE THAN SHE'S ALREADY FRIGHTENED.
EEEK!
YOU DID THIS, SOPHIE?!
I THINK I MAY BE IN LOVE WITH YOU. MARRIAGE COULD BE ON THE CARDS.
AN IRATZE.
THAT IS, A HEALING RUNE, AND A "SLEEP NOW" RUNE. THIS SHOULD KEEP HER QUIET, AT LEAST UNTIL MORNING.

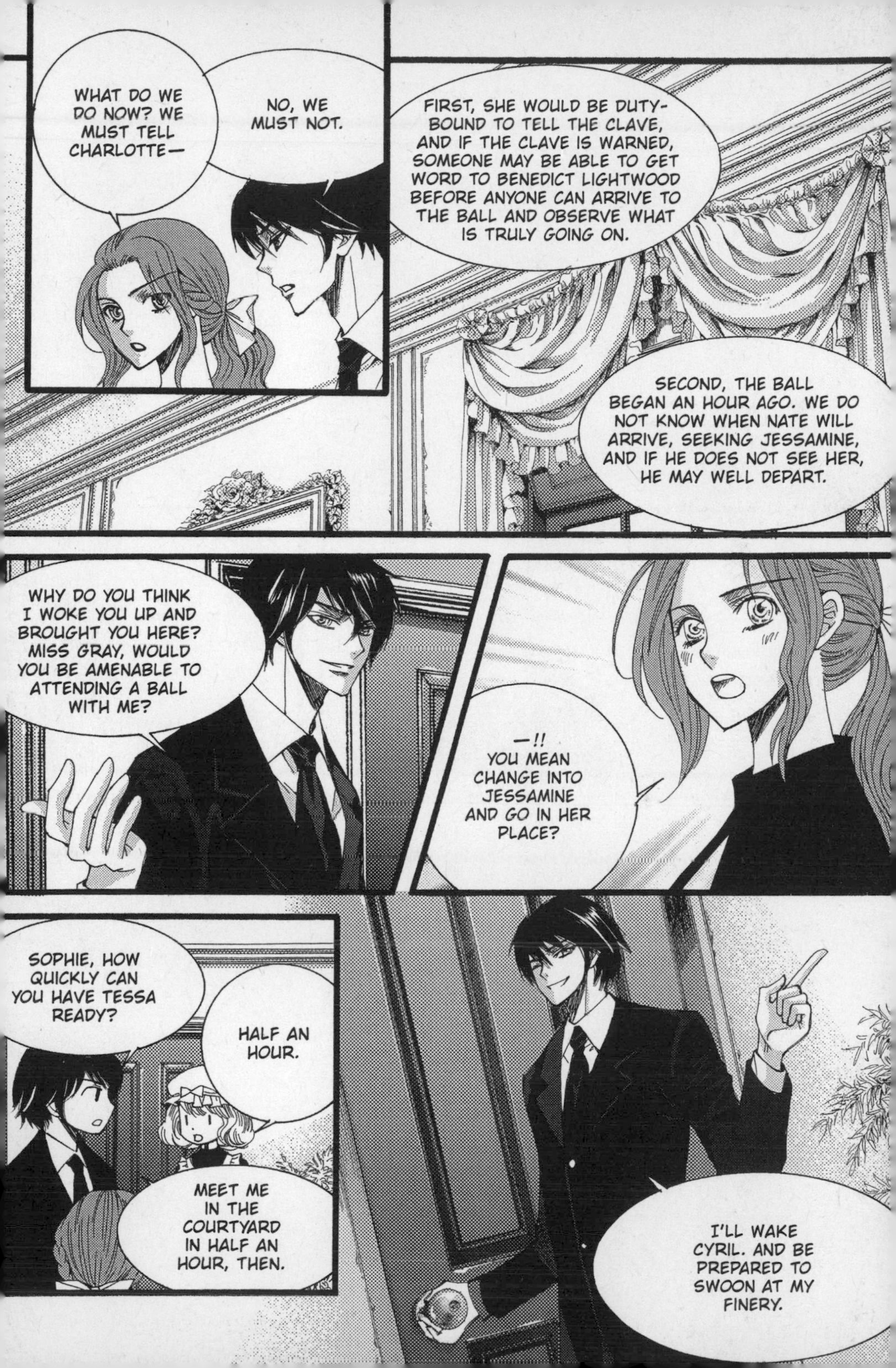
WHAT DO WE DO NOW? WE MUST TELL CHARLOTTE—
NO, WE MUST NOT.
FIRST, SHE WOULD BE DUTY-BOUND TO TELL THE CLAVE, AND IF THE CLAVE IS WARNED, SOMEONE MAY BE ABLE TO GET WORD TO BENEDICT LIGHTWOOD BEFORE ANYONE CAN ARRIVE TO THE BALL AND OBSERVE WHAT IS TRULY GOING ON.
SECOND, THE BALL BEGAN AN HOUR AGO. WE DO NOT KNOW WHEN NATE WILL ARRIVE, SEEKING JESSAMINE, AND IF HE DOES NOT SEE HER, HE MAY WELL DEPART.
WHY DO YOU THINK I WOKE YOU UP AND BROUGHT YOU HERE? MISS GRAY, WOULD YOU BE AMENABLE TO ATTENDING A BALL WITH ME?
—!! YOU MEAN CHANGE INTO JESSAMINE AND GO IN HER PLACE?
SOPHIE, HOW QUICKLY CAN YOU HAVE TESSA READY?
HALF AN HOUR.
MEET ME IN THE COURTYARD IN HALF AN HOUR, THEN.
I'LL WAKE CYRIL. AND BE PREPARED TO SWOON AT MY FINERY.

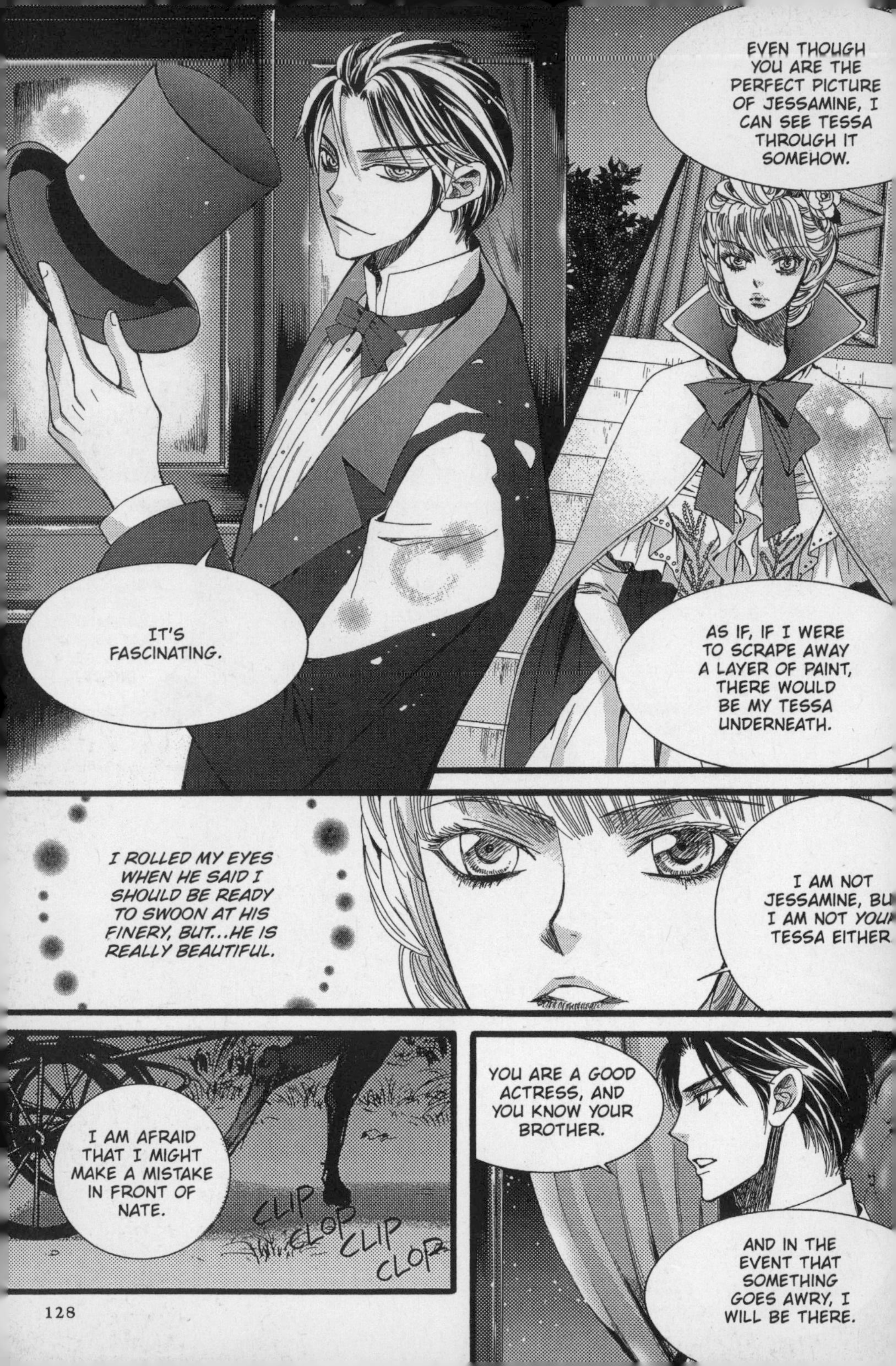
EVEN THOUGH YOU ARE THE PERFECT PICTURE OF JESSAMINE, I CAN SEE TESSA THROUGH IT SOMEHOW.
IT'S FASCINATING.
AS IF, IF I WERE TO SCRAPE AWAY A LAYER OF PAINT, THERE WOULD BE MY TESSA UNDERNEATH.
I ROLLED MY EYES WHEN HE SAID I SHOULD BE READY TO SWOON AT HIS FINERY, BUT...HE IS REALLY BEAUTIFUL.
I AM NOT JESSAMINE, BU I AM NOT YOU TESSA EITHER
I AM AFRAID THAT I MIGHT MAKE A MISTAKE IN FRONT OF NATE.
CLIP CLOP CLIP CLOP
YOU ARE A GOOD ACTRESS, AND YOU KNOW YOUR BROTHER.
AND IN THE EVENT THAT SOMETHING GOES AWRY, I WILL BE THERE.

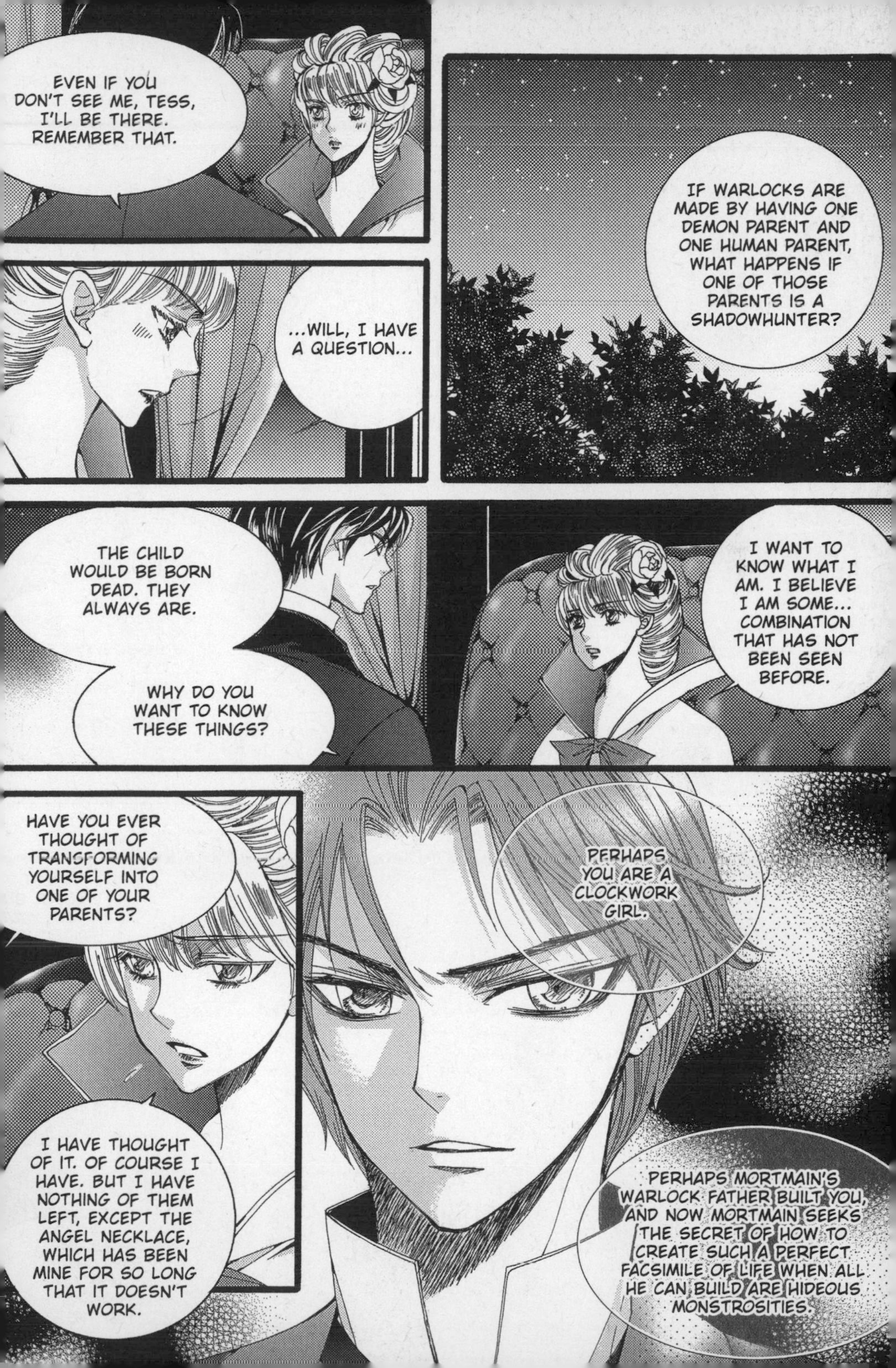
EVEN IF YOU DON'T SEE ME, TESS, I'LL BE THERE. REMEMBER THAT.
...WILL, I HAVE A QUESTION...
IF WARLOCKS ARE MADE BY HAVING ONE DEMON PARENT AND ONE HUMAN PARENT, WHAT HAPPENS IF ONE OF THOSE PARENTS IS A SHADOWHUNTER?
THE CHILD WOULD BE BORN DEAD. THEY ALWAYS ARE.
WHY DO YOU WANT TO KNOW THESE THINGS?
I WANT TO KNOW WHAT I AM. I BELIEVE I AM SOME... COMBINATION THAT HAS NOT BEEN SEEN BEFORE.
HAVE YOU EVER THOUGHT OF TRANSFORMING YOURSELF INTO ONE OF YOUR PARENTS?
I HAVE THOUGHT OF IT. OF COURSE I HAVE. BUT I HAVE NOTHING OF THEM LEFT, EXCEPT THE ANGEL NECKLACE, WHICH HAS BEEN MINE FOR SO LONG THAT IT DOESN'T WORK.
PERHAPS YOU ARE A CLOCKWORK GIRL.
PERHAPS MORTMAIN'S WARLOCK FATHER BUILT YOU, AND NOW MORTMAIN SEEKS THE SECRET OF HOW TO CREATE SUCH A PERFECT FACSIMILE OF LIFE WHEN ALL HE CAN BUILD ARE HIDEOUS MONSTROSITIES.

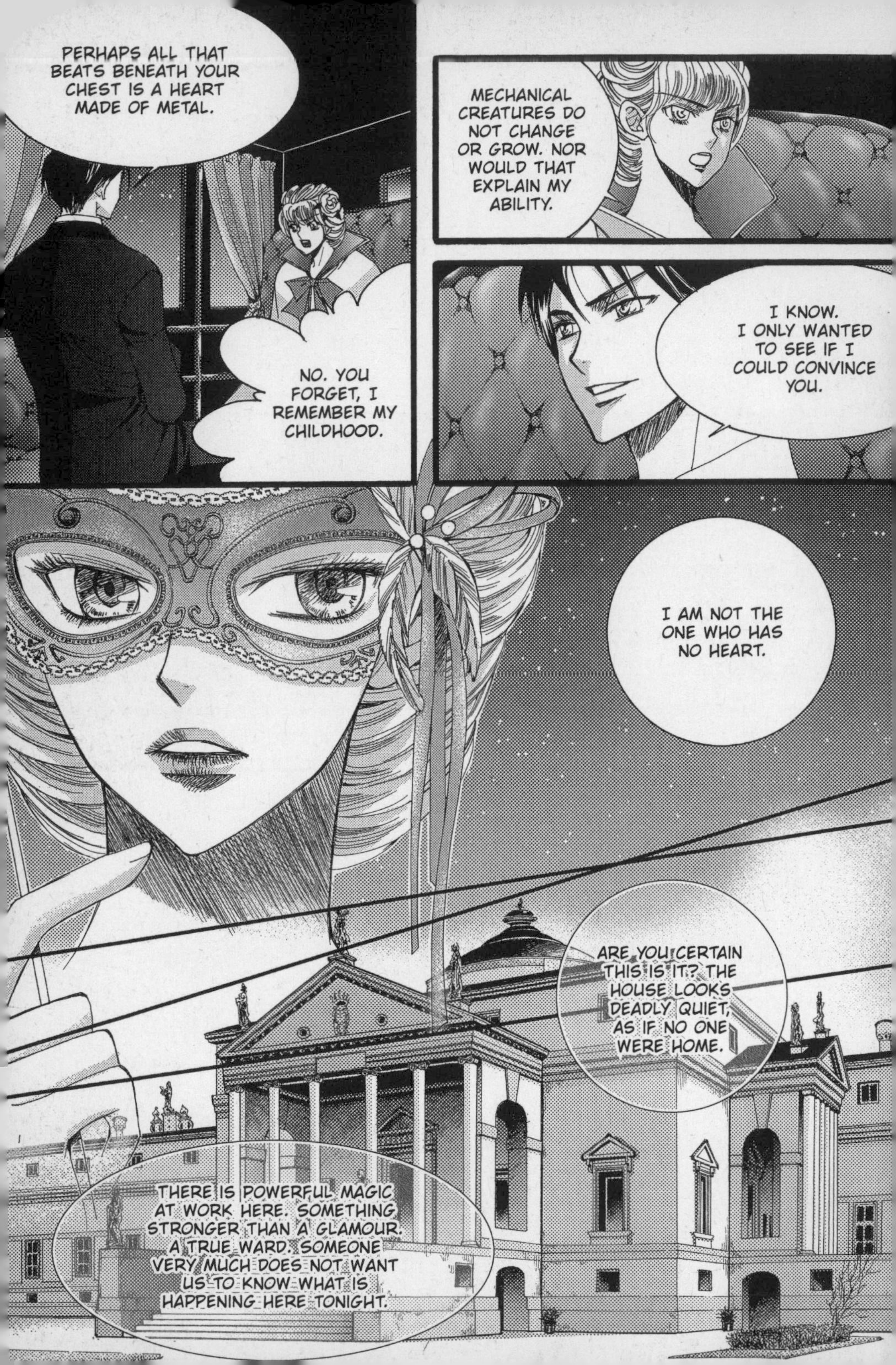
PERHAPS ALL THAT BEATS BENEATH YOUR CHEST IS A HEART MADE OF METAL.
MECHANICAL CREATURES DO NOT CHANGE OR GROW. NOR WOULD THAT EXPLAIN MY ABILITY.
NO. YOU FORGET, I REMEMBER MY CHILDHOOD.
I KNOW. I ONLY WANTED TO SEE IF I COULD CONVINCE YOU.
I AM NOT THE ONE WHO HAS NO HEART.
ARE YOU CERTAIN THIS IS IT? THE HOUSE LOOKS DEADLY QUIET, AS IF NO ONE WERE HOME.
THERE IS POWERFUL MAGIC AT WORK HERE. SOMETHING STRONGER THAN A GLAMOUR. A TRUE WARD. SOMEONE VERY MUCH DOES NOT WANT US TO KNOW WHAT IS HAPPENING HERE TONIGHT.

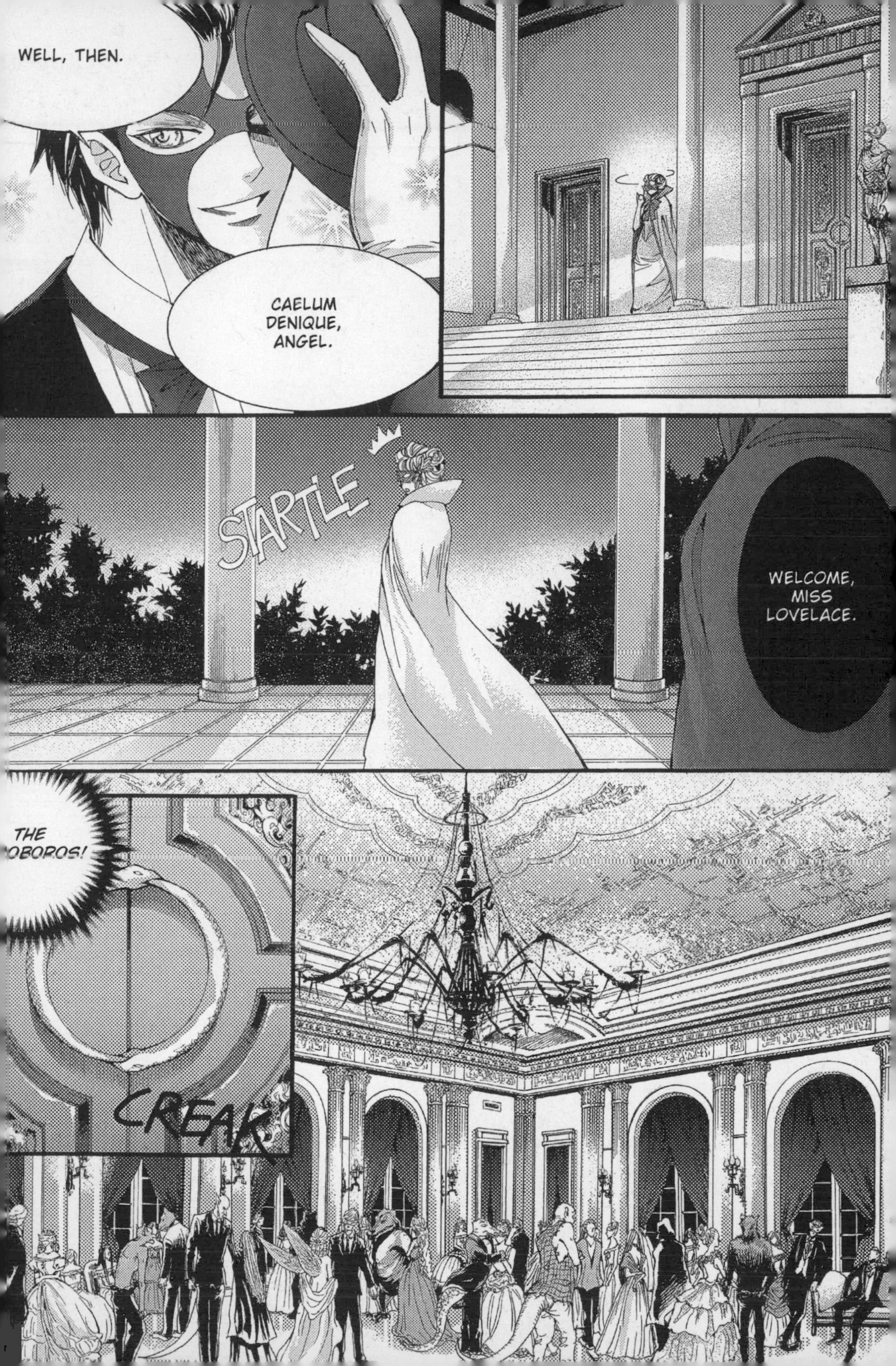

WELL, THEN.
CAELUM DENIQUE, ANGEL.
STARTLE
WELCOME, MISS LOVELACE.
THE OBOROS!
CREAK

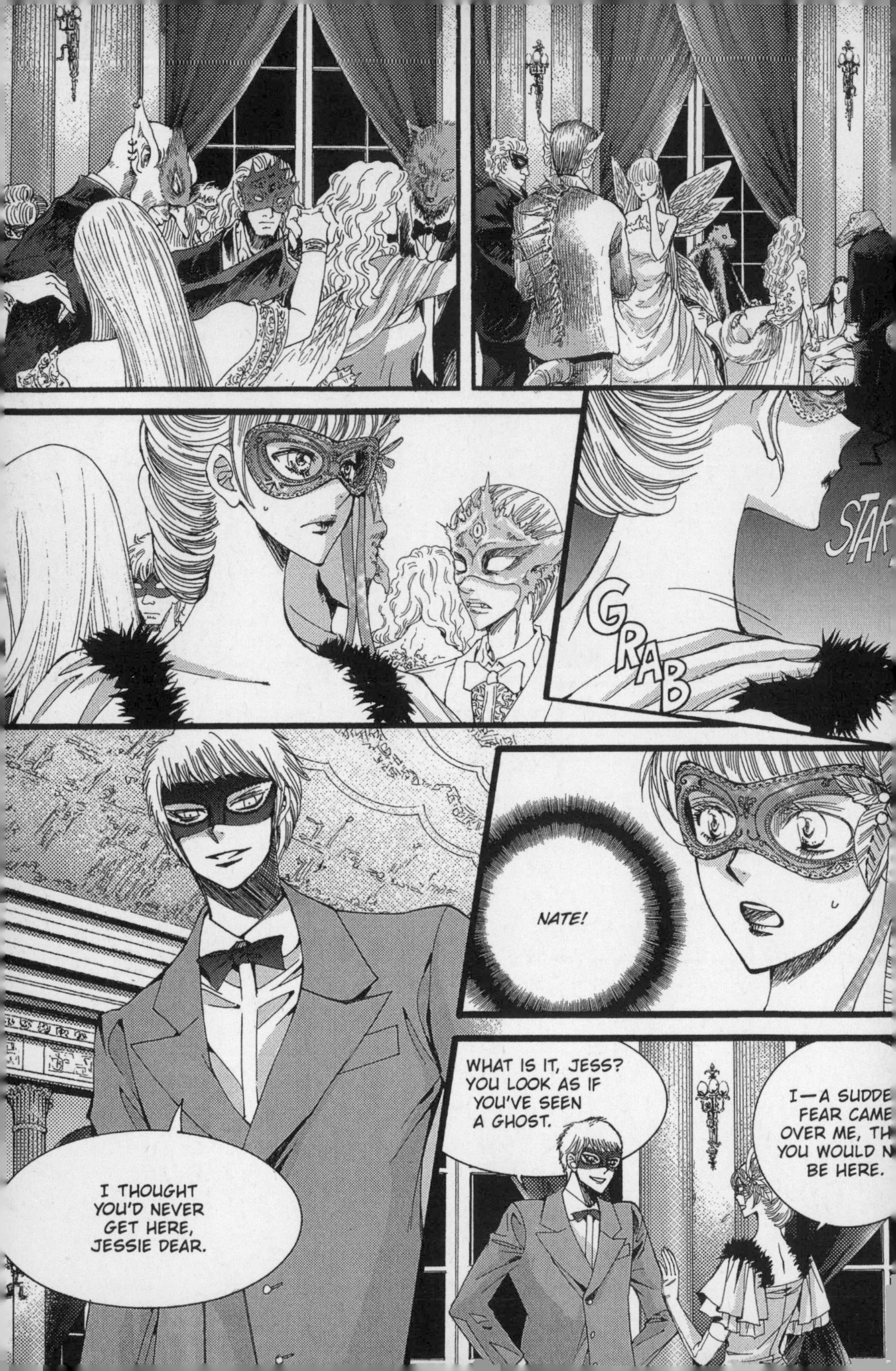

STAR
GRAB
NATE!
I THOUGHT YOU'D NEVER GET HERE, JESSIE DEAR.
WHAT IS IT, JESS? YOU LOOK AS IF YOU'VE SEEN A GHOST.
I—A SUDDE FEAR CAME OVER ME, TH YOU WOULD N BE HERE.

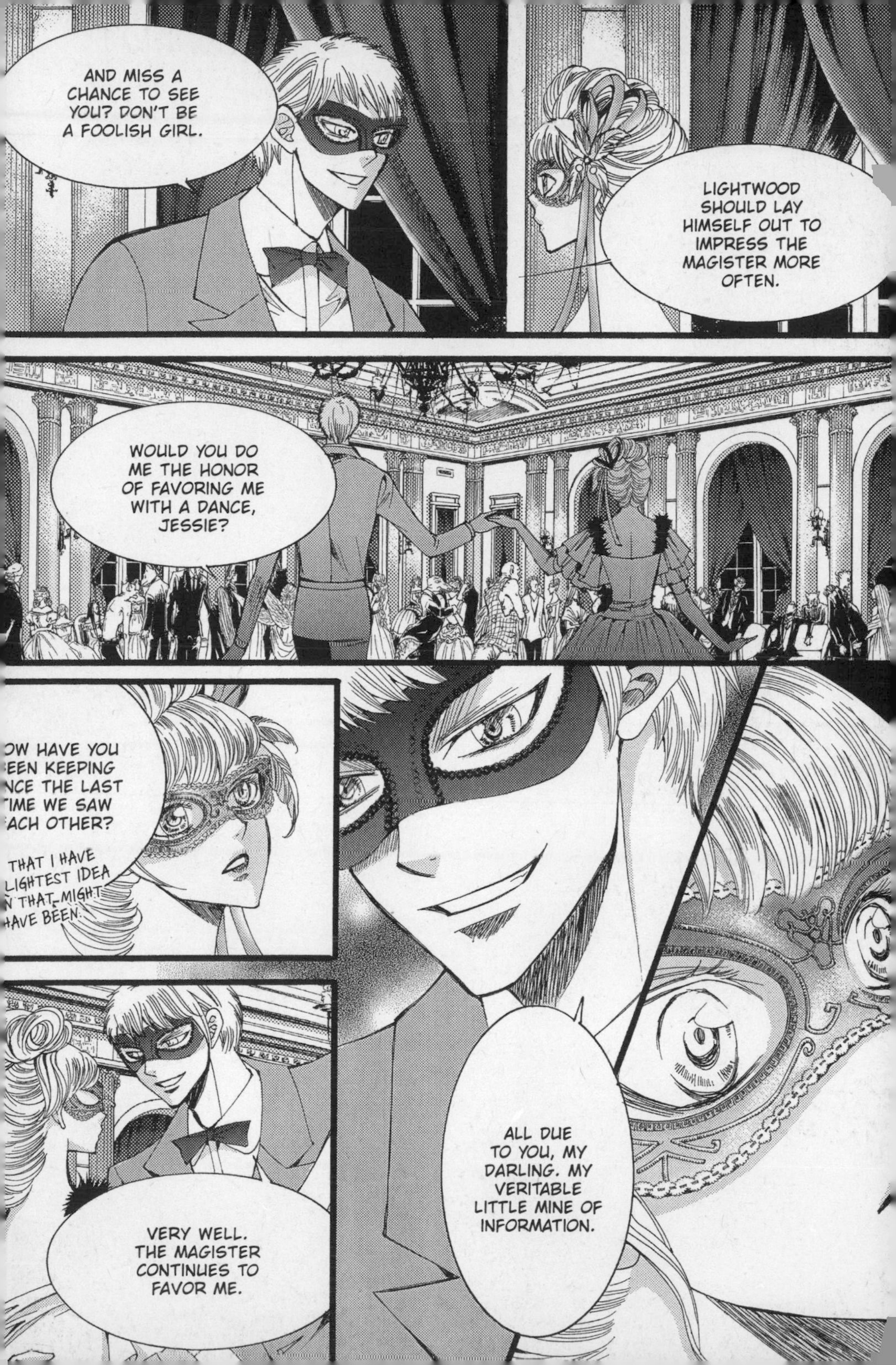
AND MISS A CHANCE TO SEE YOU? DON'T BE A FOOLISH GIRL.
LIGHTWOOD SHOULD LAY HIMSELF OUT TO IMPRESS THE MAGISTER MORE OFTEN.
WOULD YOU DO ME THE HONOR OF FAVORING ME WITH A DANCE, JESSIE?
OW HAVE YOU EEN KEEPING NCE THE LAST TIME WE SAW ACH OTHER?
THAT I HAVE LIGHTEST IDEA N THAT MIGHT HAVE BEEN.
VERY WELL. THE MAGISTER CONTINUES TO FAVOR ME.
ALL DUE TO YOU, MY DARLING. MY VERITABLE LITTLE MINE OF INFORMATION.

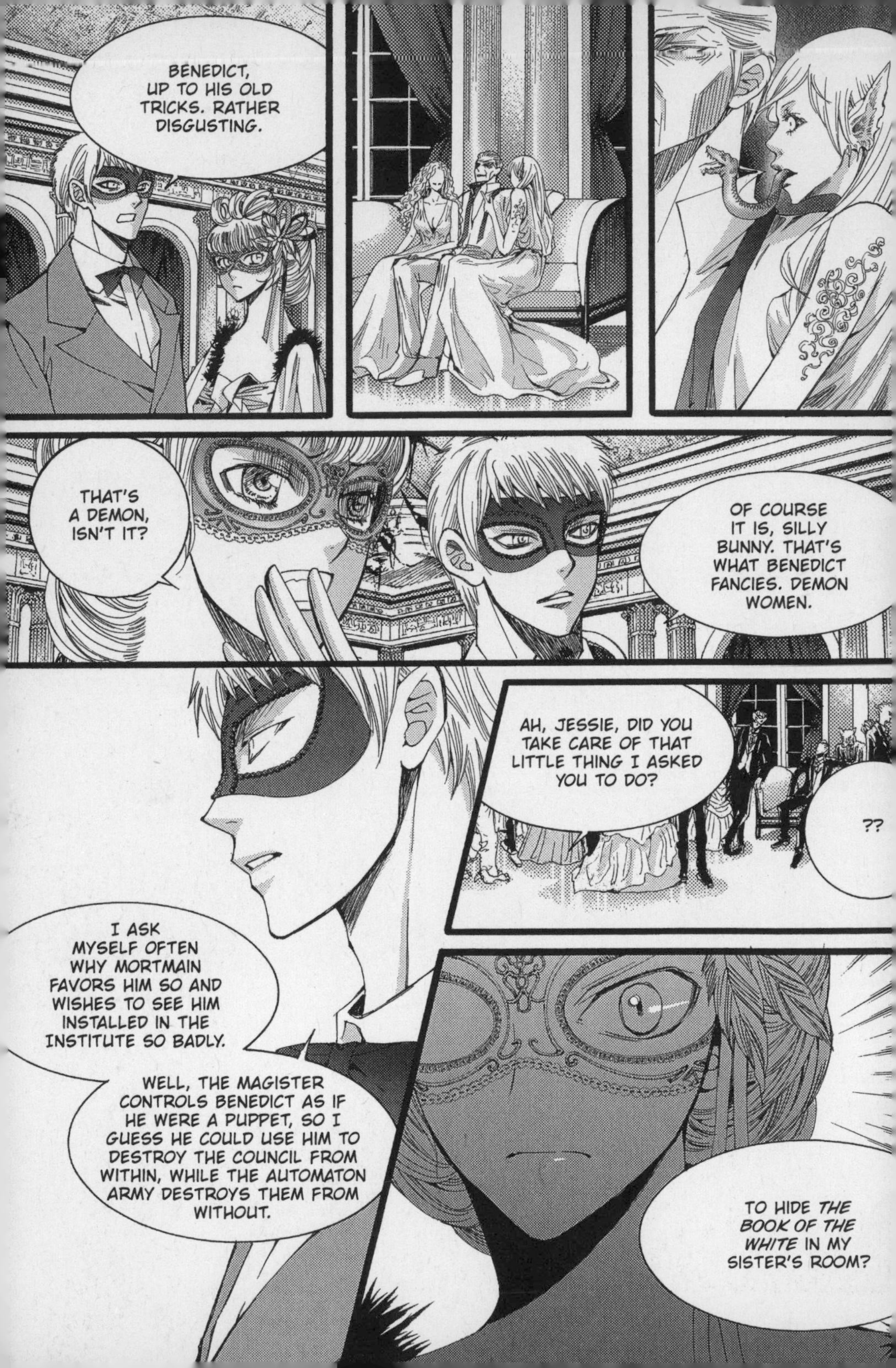
BENEDICT, UP TO HIS OLD TRICKS. RATHER DISGUSTING.
THAT'S A DEMON, ISN'T IT?
OF COURSE IT IS, SILLY BUNNY. THAT'S WHAT BENEDICT FANCIES. DEMON WOMEN.
I ASK MYSELF OFTEN WHY MORTMAIN FAVORS HIM SO AND WISHES TO SEE HIM INSTALLED IN THE INSTITUTE SO BADLY.
WELL, THE MAGISTER CONTROLS BENEDICT AS IF HE WERE A PUPPET, SO I GUESS HE COULD USE HIM TO DESTROY THE COUNCIL FROM WITHIN, WHILE THE AUTOMATON ARMY DESTROYS THEM FROM WITHOUT.
AH, JESSIE, DID YOU TAKE CARE OF THAT LITTLE THING I ASKED YOU TO DO?
??
TO HIDE *THE BOOK OF THE WHITE* IN MY SISTER'S ROOM?

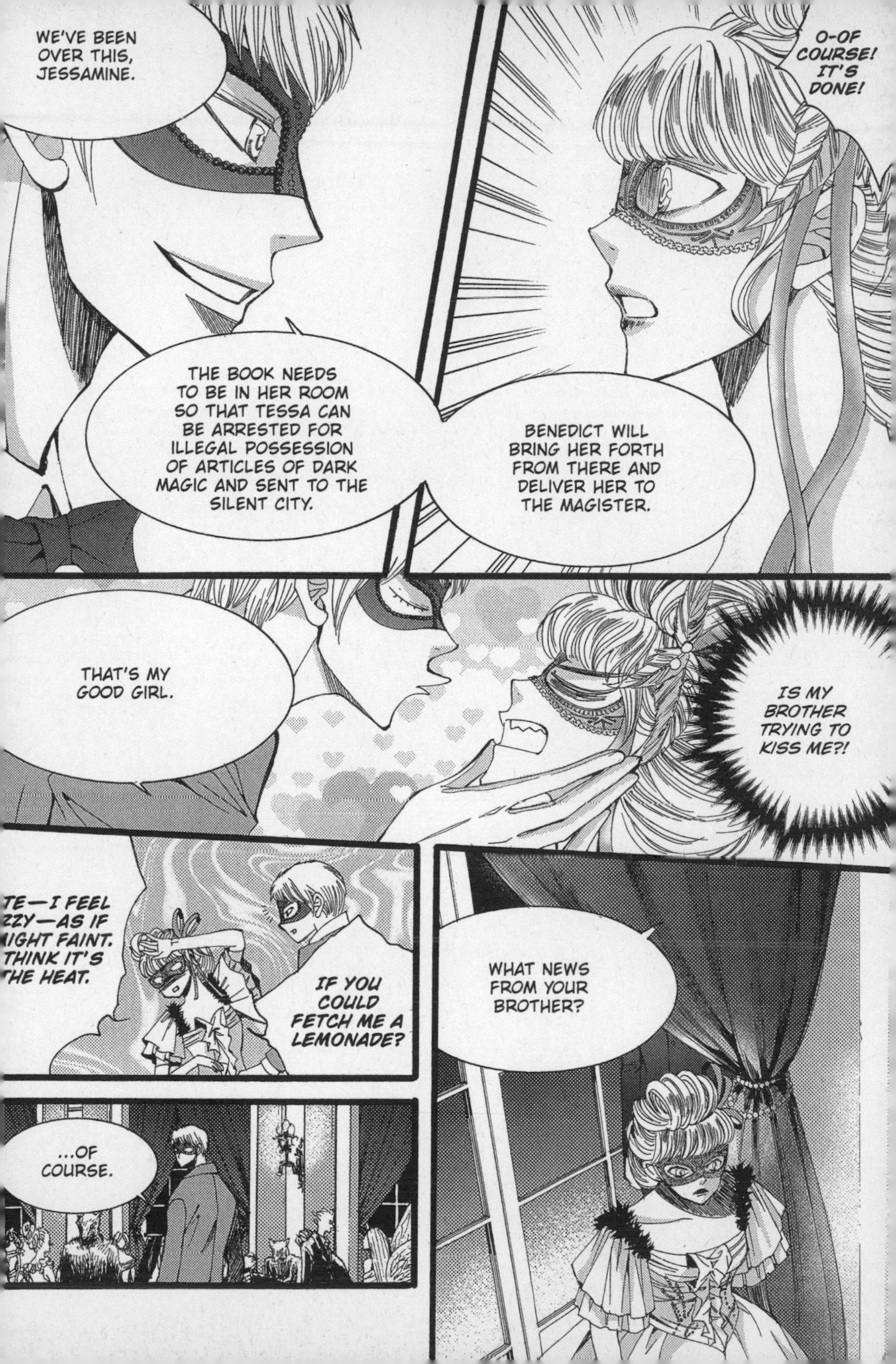
WE'VE BEEN OVER THIS, JESSAMINE.
O-OF COURSE! IT'S DONE!
THE BOOK NEEDS TO BE IN HER ROOM SO THAT TESSA CAN BE ARRESTED FOR ILLEGAL POSSESSION OF ARTICLES OF DARK MAGIC AND SENT TO THE SILENT CITY.
BENEDICT WILL BRING HER FORTH FROM THERE AND DELIVER HER TO THE MAGISTER.
THAT'S MY GOOD GIRL.
IS MY BROTHER TRYING TO KISS ME?!
TE—I FEEL ZZY—AS IF IGHT FAINT. THINK IT'S THE HEAT.
IF YOU COULD FETCH ME A LEMONADE?
WHAT NEWS FROM YOUR BROTHER?
...OF COURSE.

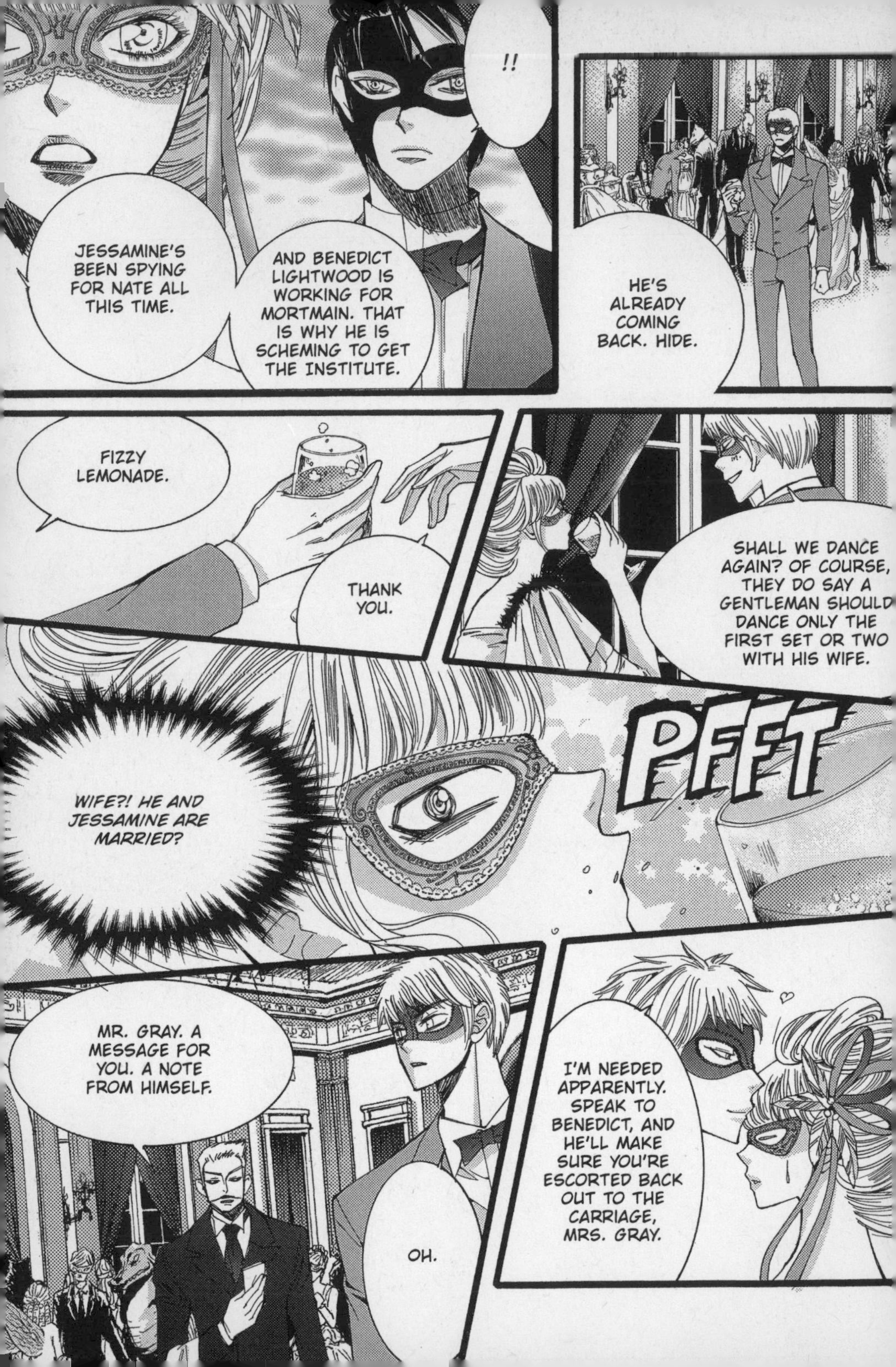
!!
JESSAMINE'S BEEN SPYING FOR NATE ALL THIS TIME.
AND BENEDICT LIGHTWOOD IS WORKING FOR MORTMAIN. THAT IS WHY HE IS SCHEMING TO GET THE INSTITUTE.
HE'S ALREADY COMING BACK. HIDE.
FIZZY LEMONADE.
THANK YOU.
SHALL WE DANCE AGAIN? OF COURSE, THEY DO SAY A GENTLEMAN SHOULD DANCE ONLY THE FIRST SET OR TWO WITH HIS WIFE.
WIFE?! HE AND JESSAMINE ARE MARRIED?
PFFT
MR. GRAY. A MESSAGE FOR YOU. A NOTE FROM HIMSELF.
OH.
I'M NEEDED APPARENTLY. SPEAK TO BENEDICT, AND HE'LL MAKE SURE YOU'RE ESCORTED BACK OUT TO THE CARRIAGE, MRS. GRAY.

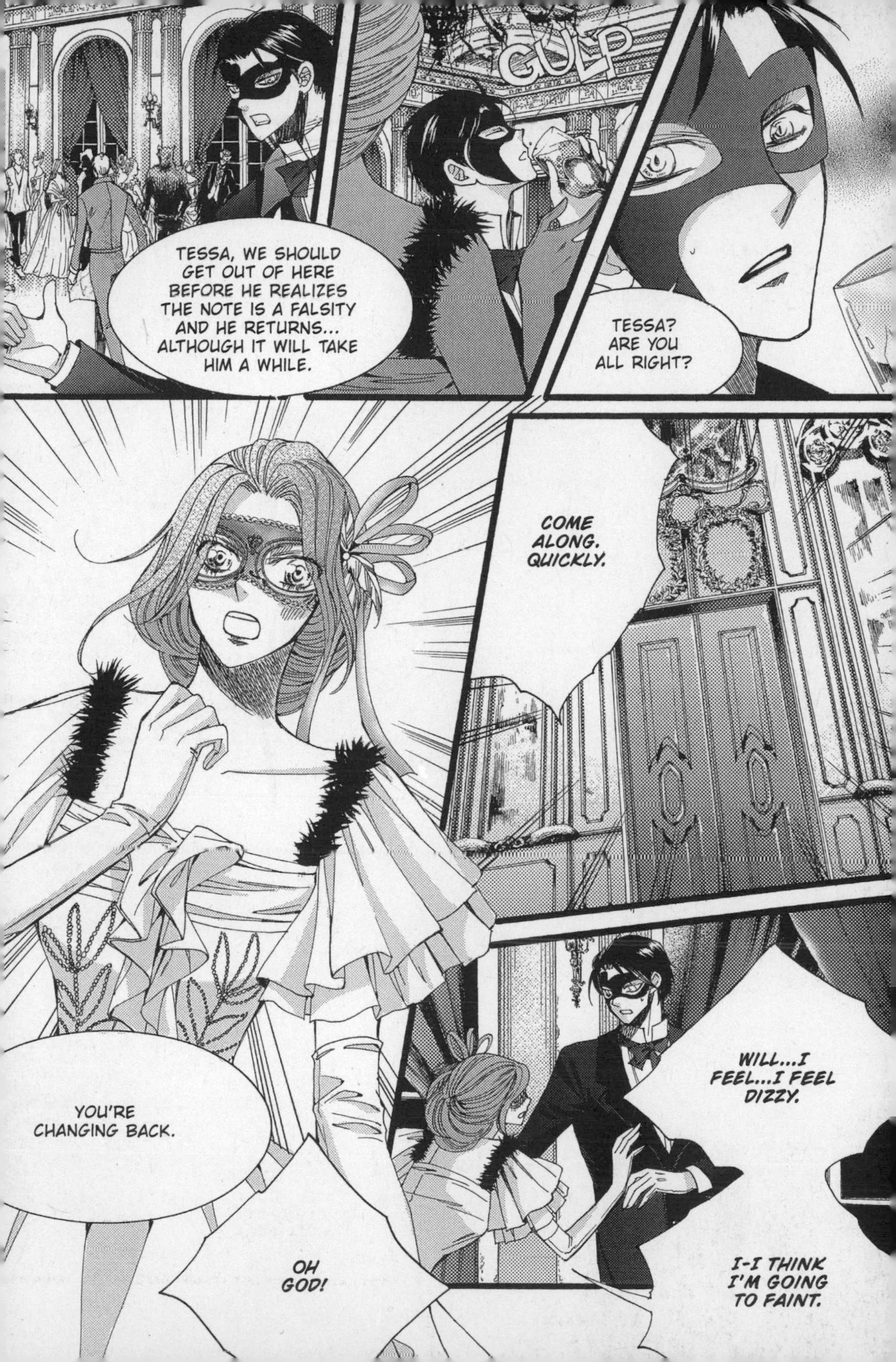

TESSA, WE SHOULD GET OUT OF HERE BEFORE HE REALIZES THE NOTE IS A FALSITY AND HE RETURNS... ALTHOUGH IT WILL TAKE HIM A WHILE.
GULP
TESSA? ARE YOU ALL RIGHT?
COME ALONG. QUICKLY.
YOU'RE CHANGING BACK.
OH GOD!
WILL...I FEEL...I FEEL DIZZY.
I-I THINK I'M GOING TO FAINT.

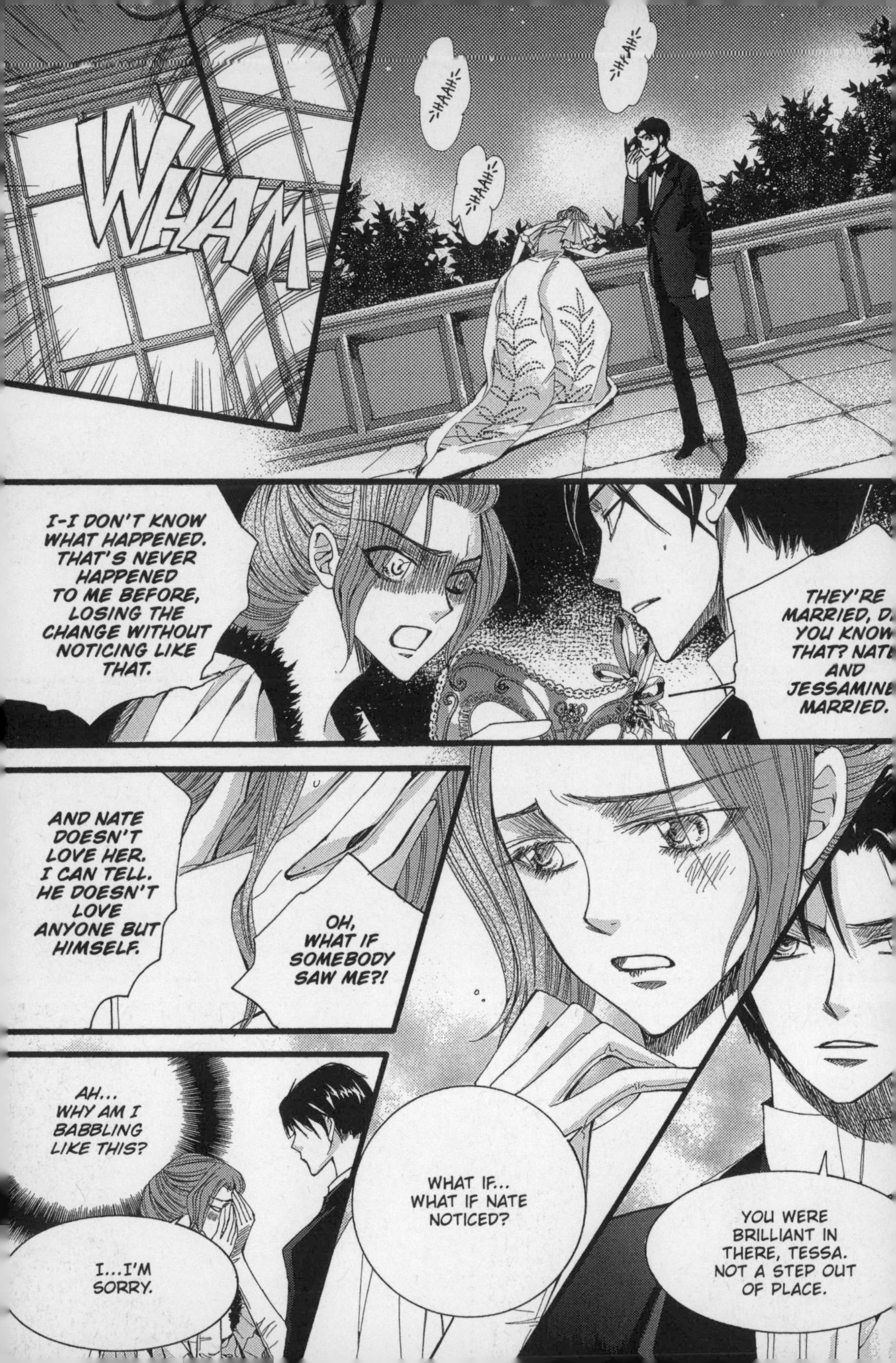
WHAM
HAAH
HAAH
H-AH
I-I DON'T KNOW WHAT HAPPENED. THAT'S NEVER HAPPENED TO ME BEFORE, LOSING THE CHANGE WITHOUT NOTICING LIKE THAT.
THEY'RE MARRIED, D... YOU KNOW THAT? NATE AND JESSAMINE MARRIED.
AND NATE DOESN'T LOVE HER. I CAN TELL. HE DOESN'T LOVE ANYONE BUT HIMSELF.
OH, WHAT IF SOMEBODY SAW ME?!
AH... WHY AM I BABBLING LIKE THIS?
I...I'M SORRY.
WHAT IF... WHAT IF NATE NOTICED?
YOU WERE BRILLIANT IN THERE, TESSA. NOT A STEP OUT OF PLACE.

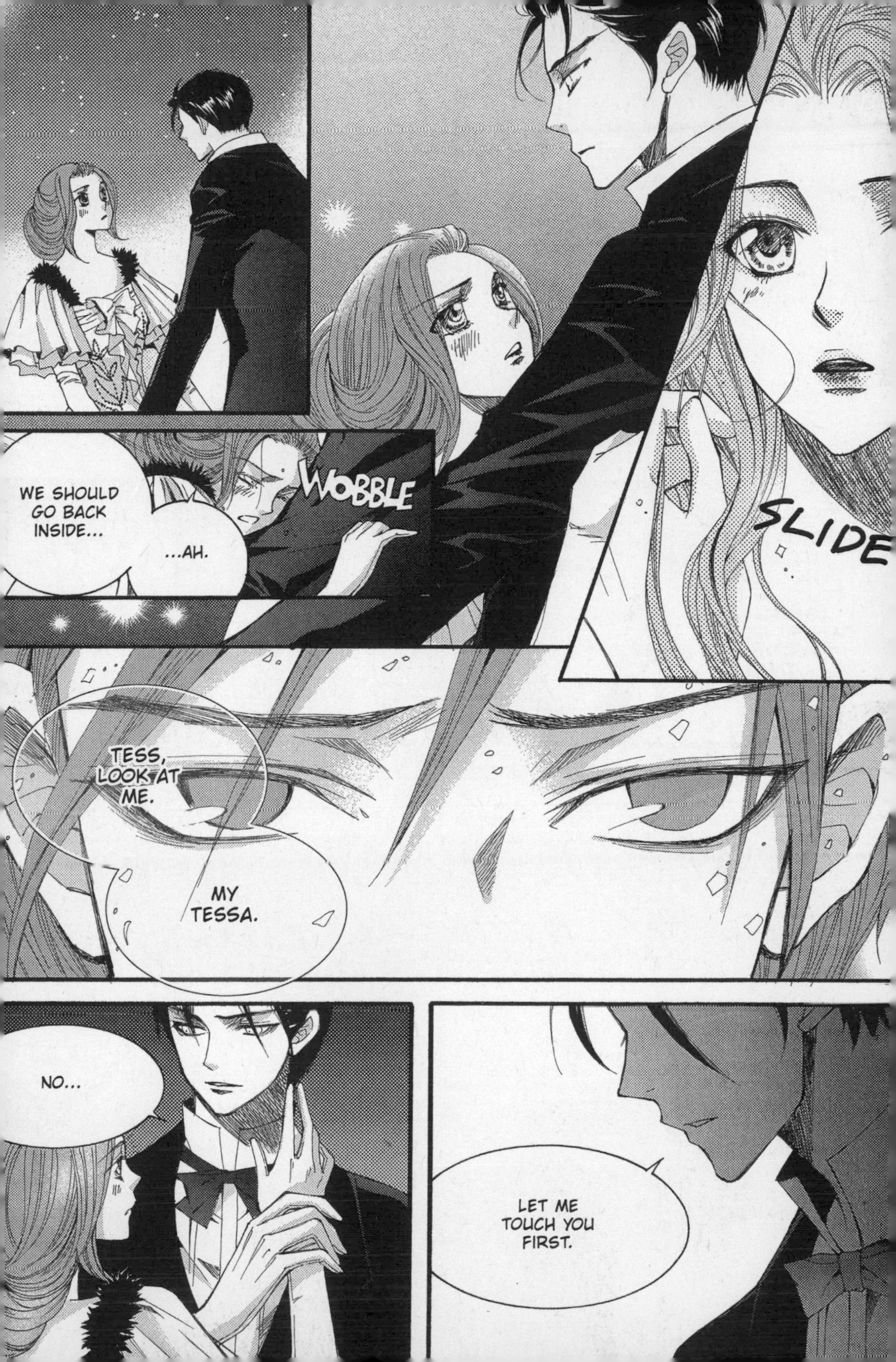

WE SHOULD GO BACK INSIDE...
...AH.
WOBBLE
SLIDE
TESS, LOOK AT ME.
MY TESSA.
NO...
LET ME TOUCH YOU FIRST.

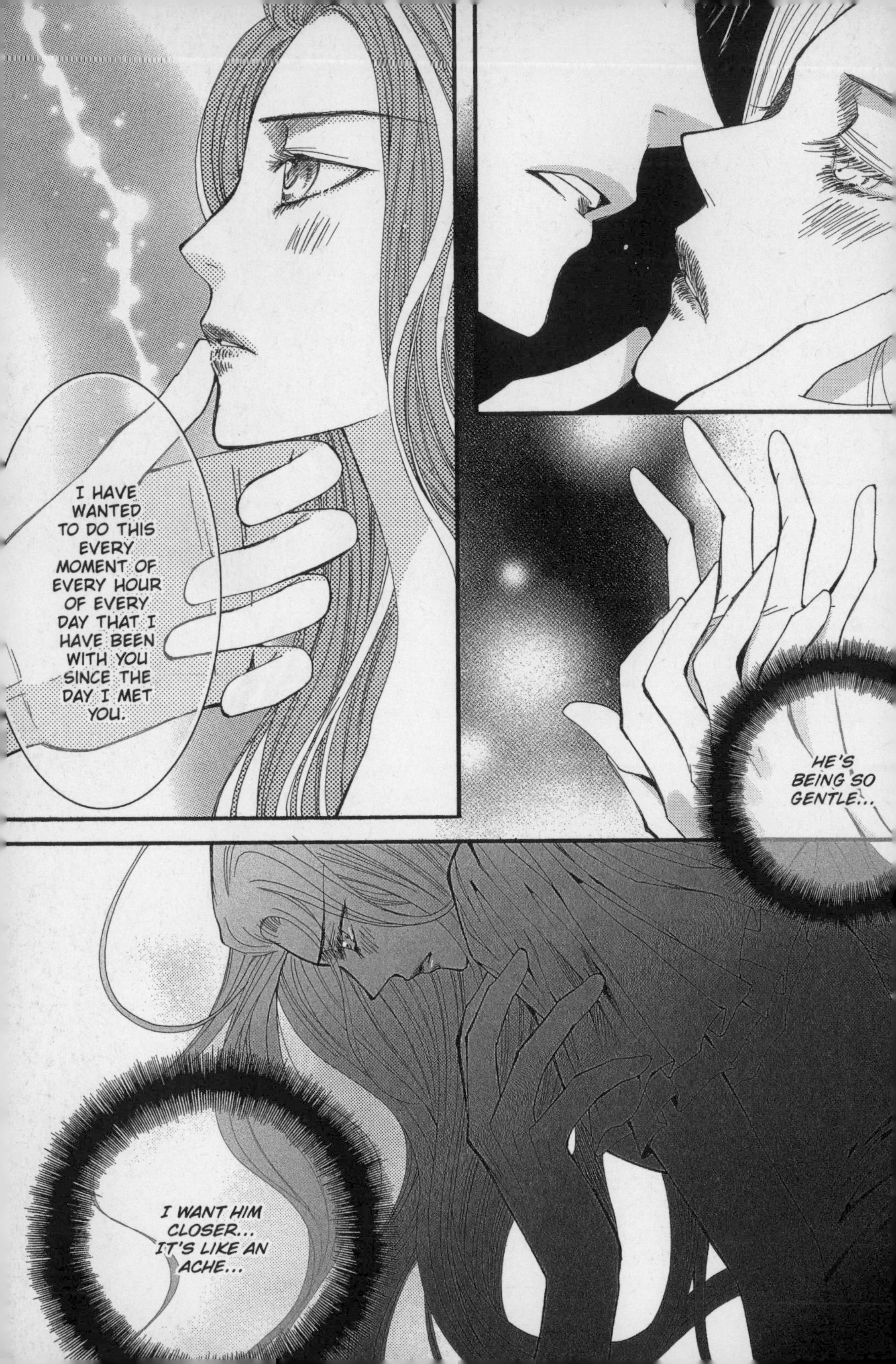
I HAVE WANTED TO DO THIS EVERY MOMENT OF EVERY HOUR OF EVERY DAY THAT I HAVE BEEN WITH YOU SINCE THE DAY I MET YOU.
HE'S BEING SO GENTLE...
I WANT HIM CLOSER... IT'S LIKE AN ACHE...

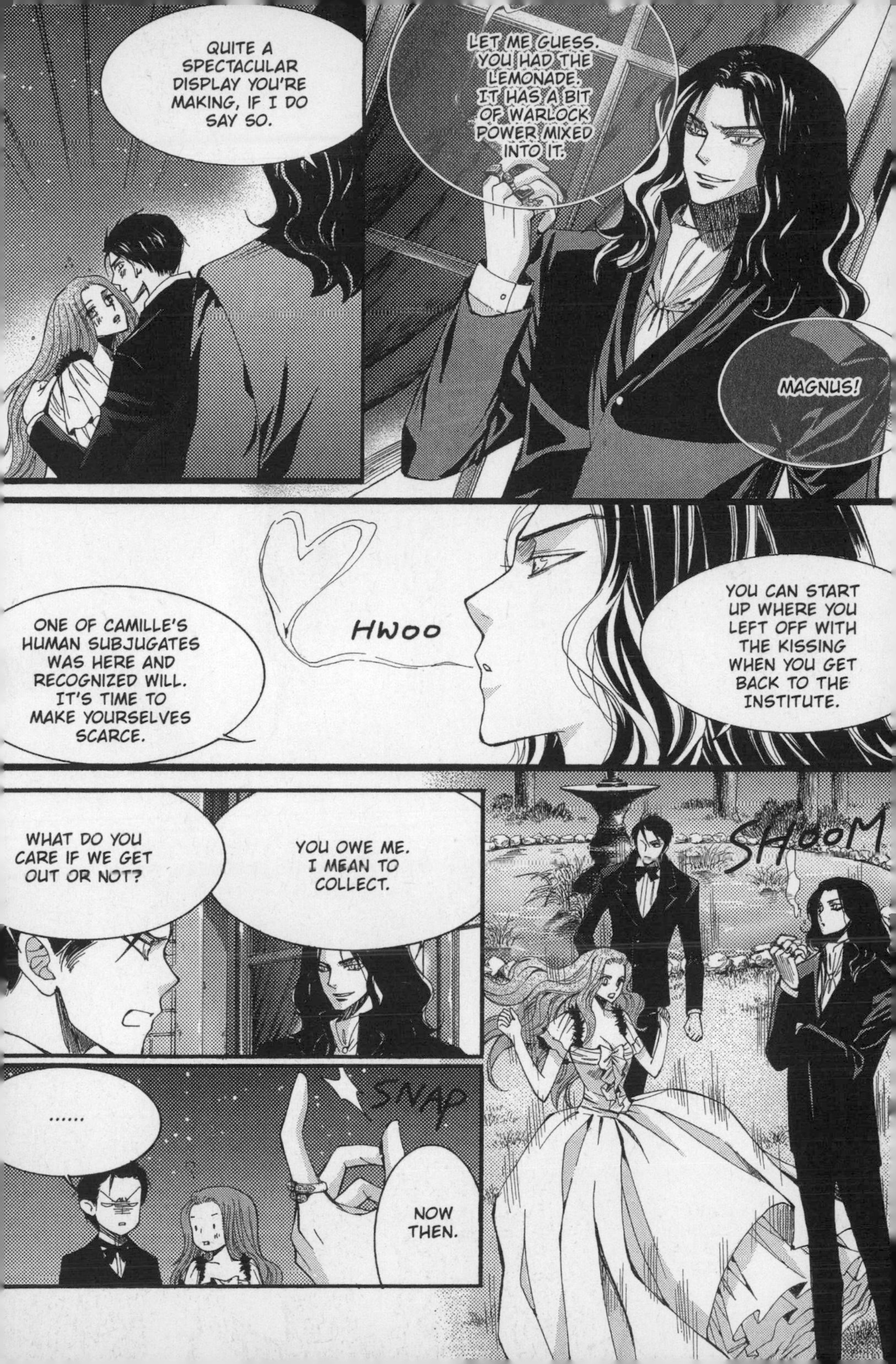
QUITE A SPECTACULAR DISPLAY YOU'RE MAKING, IF I DO SAY SO.
LET ME GUESS. YOU HAD THE LEMONADE. IT HAS A BIT OF WARLOCK POWER MIXED INTO IT.
MAGNUS!
ONE OF CAMILLE'S HUMAN SUBJUGATES WAS HERE AND RECOGNIZED WILL. IT'S TIME TO MAKE YOURSELVES SCARCE.
HWOO
YOU CAN START UP WHERE YOU LEFT OFF WITH THE KISSING WHEN YOU GET BACK TO THE INSTITUTE.
WHAT DO YOU CARE IF WE GET OUT OR NOT?
YOU OWE ME. I MEAN TO COLLECT.
......
SNAP
NOW THEN.
SHOOM

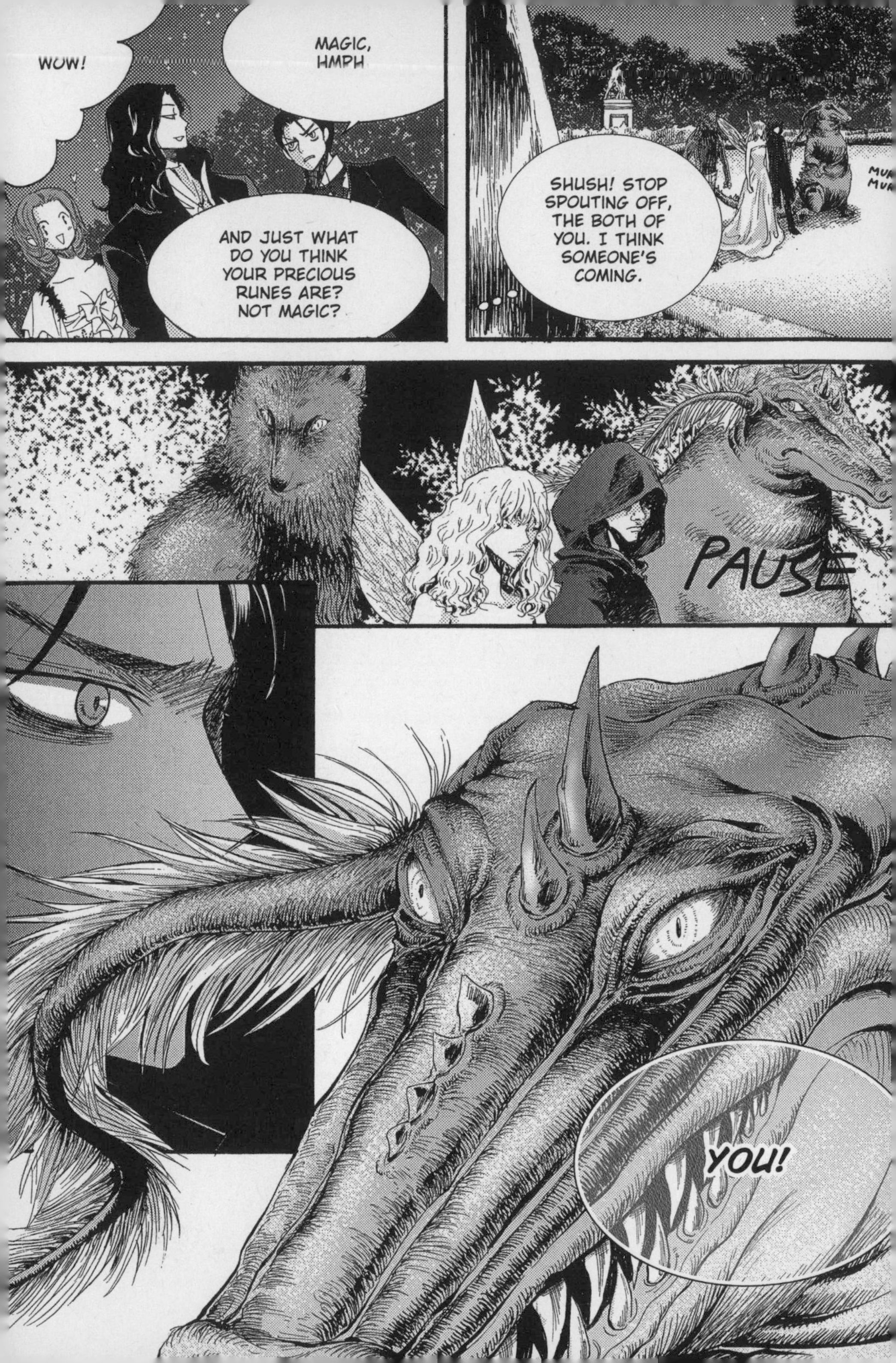
WOW!
MAGIC, HMPH
AND JUST WHAT DO YOU THINK YOUR PRECIOUS RUNES ARE? NOT MAGIC?
SHUSH! STOP SPOUTING OFF, THE BOTH OF YOU. I THINK SOMEONE'S COMING.
PAUSE
YOU!

THE INFERNAL DEVICES
CLOCKWORK PRINCE

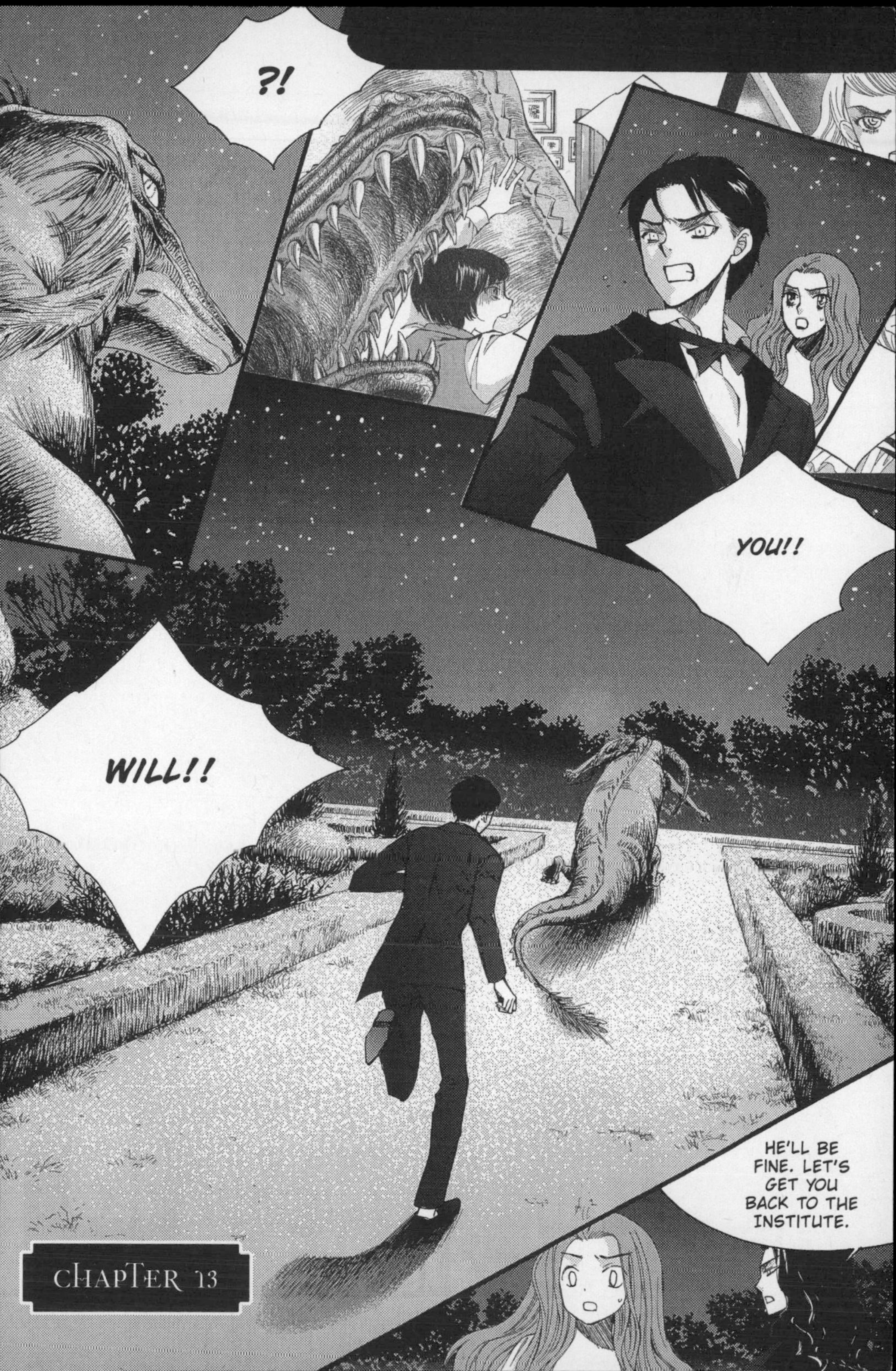

?!
YOU!!
WILL!!
HE'LL BE FINE. LET'S GET YOU BACK TO THE INSTITUTE.
CHAPTER 13

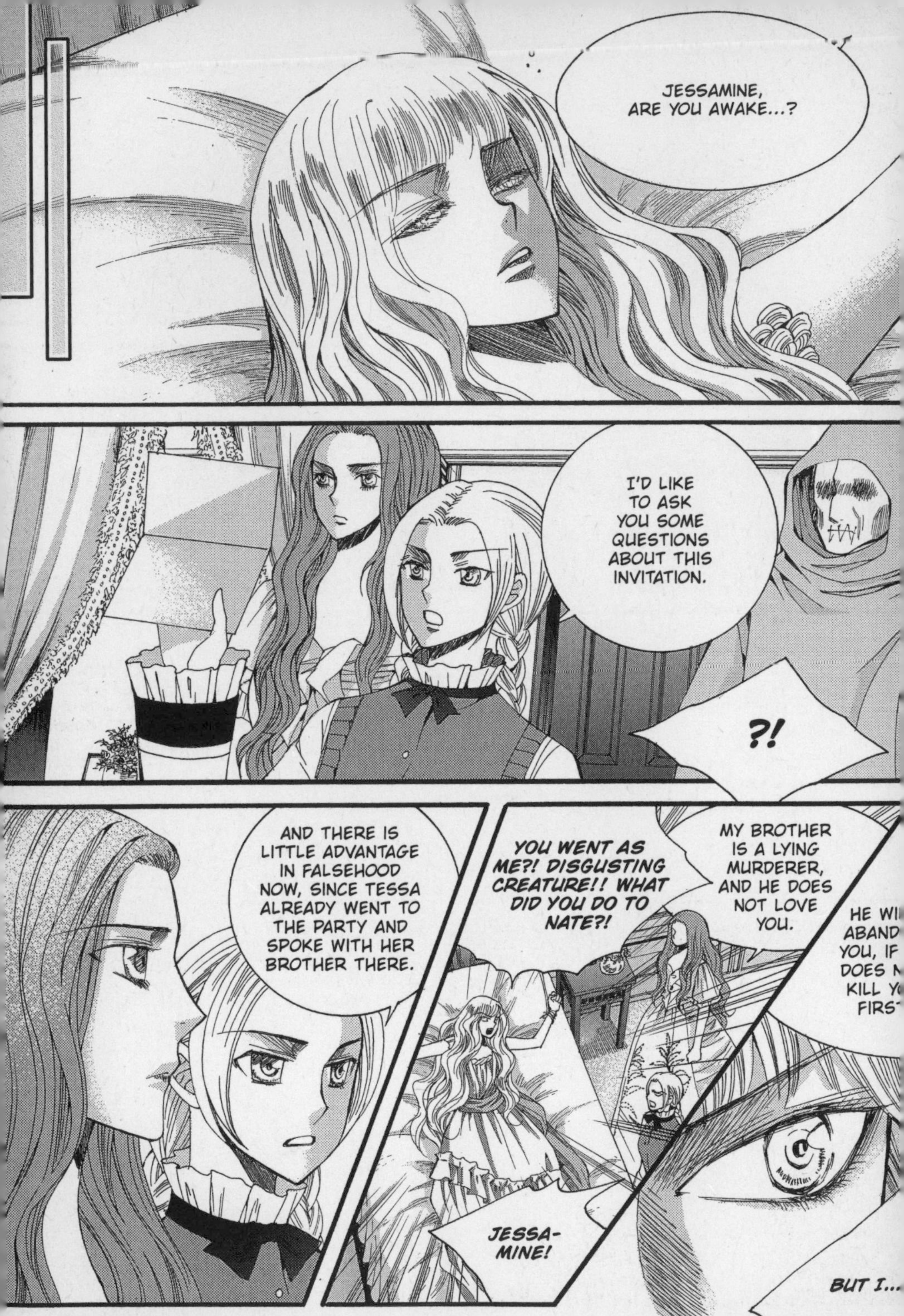
JESSAMINE, ARE YOU AWAKE...?
I'D LIKE TO ASK YOU SOME QUESTIONS ABOUT THIS INVITATION.
?!
AND THERE IS LITTLE ADVANTAGE IN FALSEHOOD NOW, SINCE TESSA ALREADY WENT TO THE PARTY AND SPOKE WITH HER BROTHER THERE.
YOU WENT AS ME?! DISGUSTING CREATURE!! WHAT DID YOU DO TO NATE?!
JESSA-MINE!
MY BROTHER IS A LYING MURDERER, AND HE DOES NOT LOVE YOU.
BUT I...

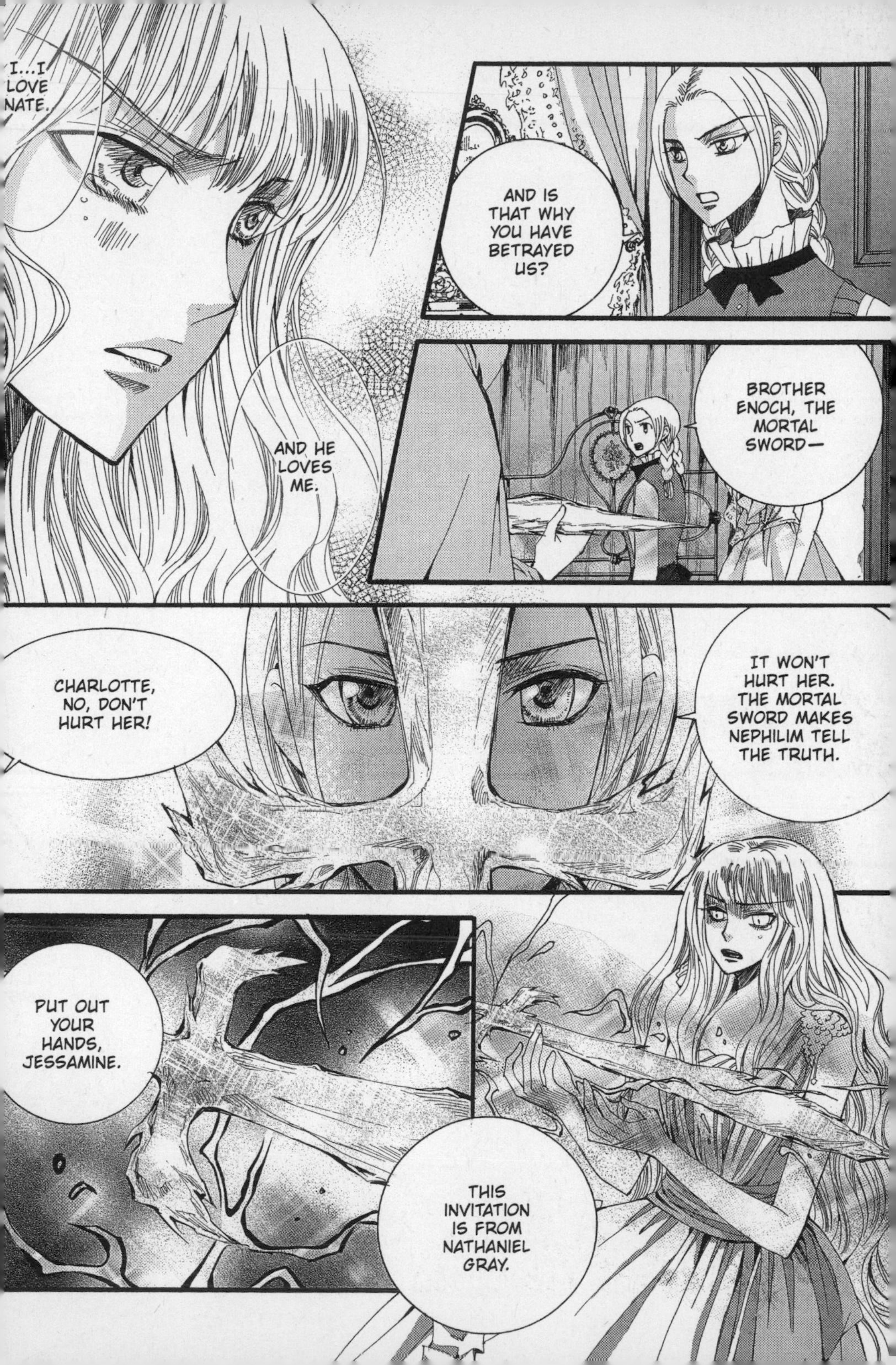
I...I LOVE NATE.
AND IS THAT WHY YOU HAVE BETRAYED US?
AND HE LOVES ME.
BROTHER ENOCH, THE MORTAL SWORD—
CHARLOTTE, NO, DON'T HURT HER!
IT WON'T HURT HER. THE MORTAL SWORD MAKES NEPHILIM TELL THE TRUTH.
PUT OUT YOUR HANDS, JESSAMINE.
THIS INVITATION IS FROM NATHANIEL GRAY.

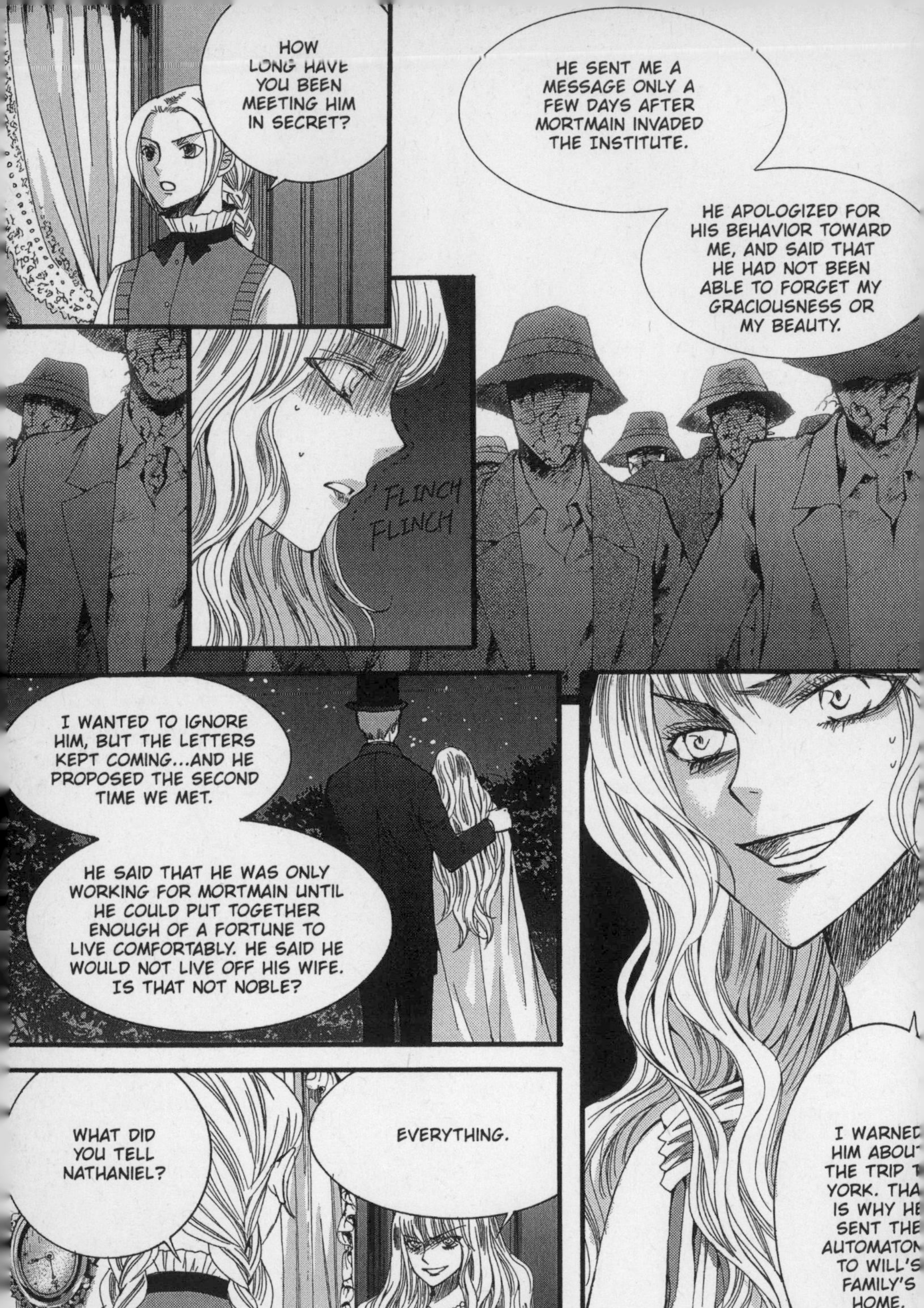
HOW LONG HAVE YOU BEEN MEETING HIM IN SECRET?
HE SENT ME A MESSAGE ONLY A FEW DAYS AFTER MORTMAIN INVADED THE INSTITUTE.
HE APOLOGIZED FOR HIS BEHAVIOR TOWARD ME, AND SAID THAT HE HAD NOT BEEN ABLE TO FORGET MY GRACIOUSNESS OR MY BEAUTY.
FLINCH FLINCH
I WANTED TO IGNORE HIM, BUT THE LETTERS KEPT COMING...AND HE PROPOSED THE SECOND TIME WE MET.
HE SAID THAT HE WAS ONLY WORKING FOR MORTMAIN UNTIL HE COULD PUT TOGETHER ENOUGH OF A FORTUNE TO LIVE COMFORTABLY. HE SAID HE WOULD NOT LIVE OFF HIS WIFE. IS THAT NOT NOBLE?
WHAT DID YOU TELL NATHANIEL?
EVERYTHING.
I WARNED HIM ABOUT THE TRIP TO YORK. THAT IS WHY HE SENT THE AUTOMATONS TO WILL'S FAMILY'S HOME.

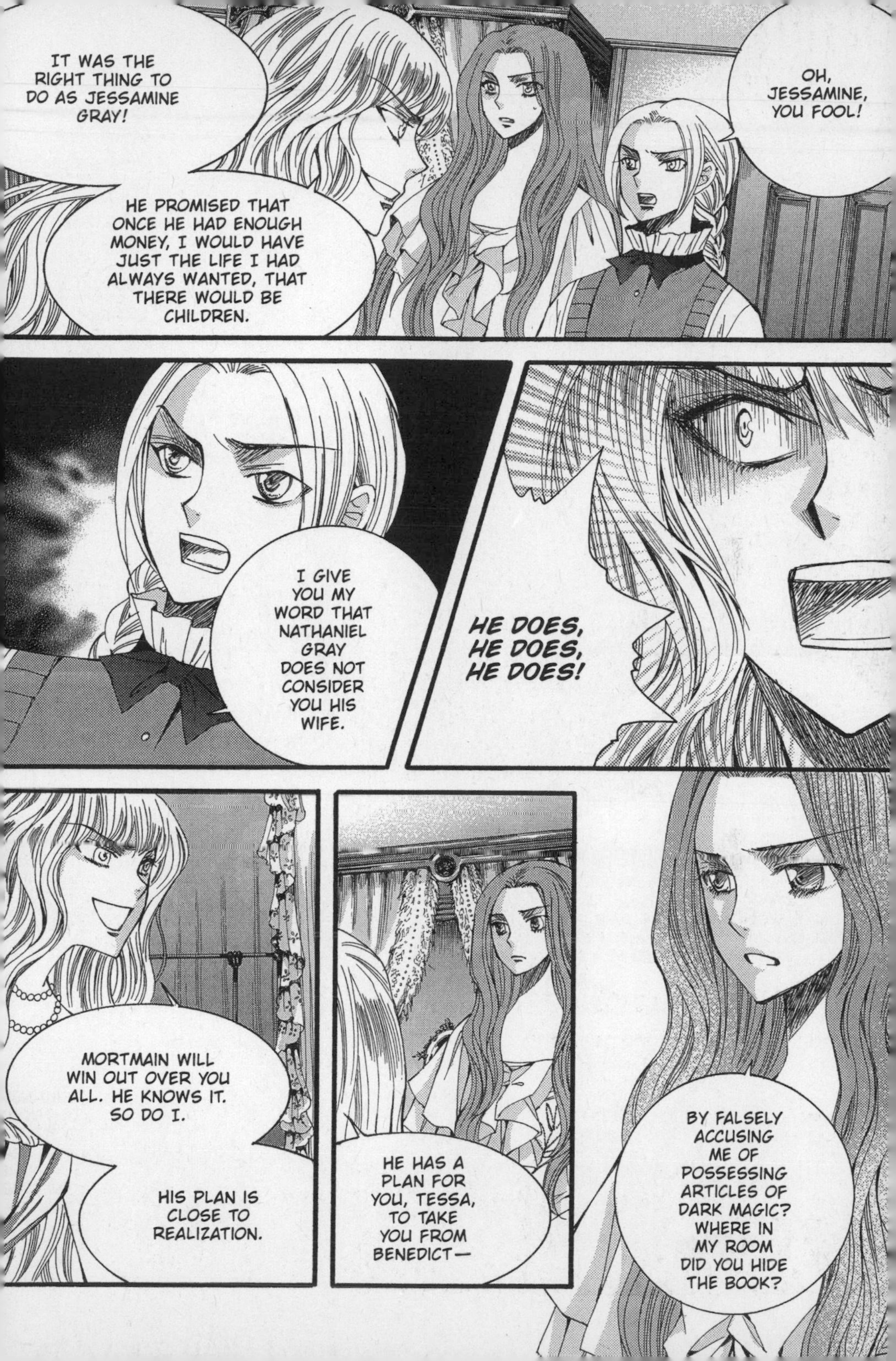
IT WAS THE RIGHT THING TO DO AS JESSAMINE GRAY!
HE PROMISED THAT ONCE HE HAD ENOUGH MONEY, I WOULD HAVE JUST THE LIFE I HAD ALWAYS WANTED, THAT THERE WOULD BE CHILDREN.
OH, JESSAMINE, YOU FOOL!
I GIVE YOU MY WORD THAT NATHANIEL GRAY DOES NOT CONSIDER YOU HIS WIFE.
HE DOES, HE DOES, HE DOES!
MORTMAIN WILL WIN OUT OVER YOU ALL. HE KNOWS IT. SO DO I.
HIS PLAN IS CLOSE TO REALIZATION.
HE HAS A PLAN FOR YOU, TESSA, TO TAKE YOU FROM BENEDICT—
BY FALSELY ACCUSING ME OF POSSESSING ARTICLES OF DARK MAGIC? WHERE IN MY ROOM DID YOU HIDE THE BOOK?

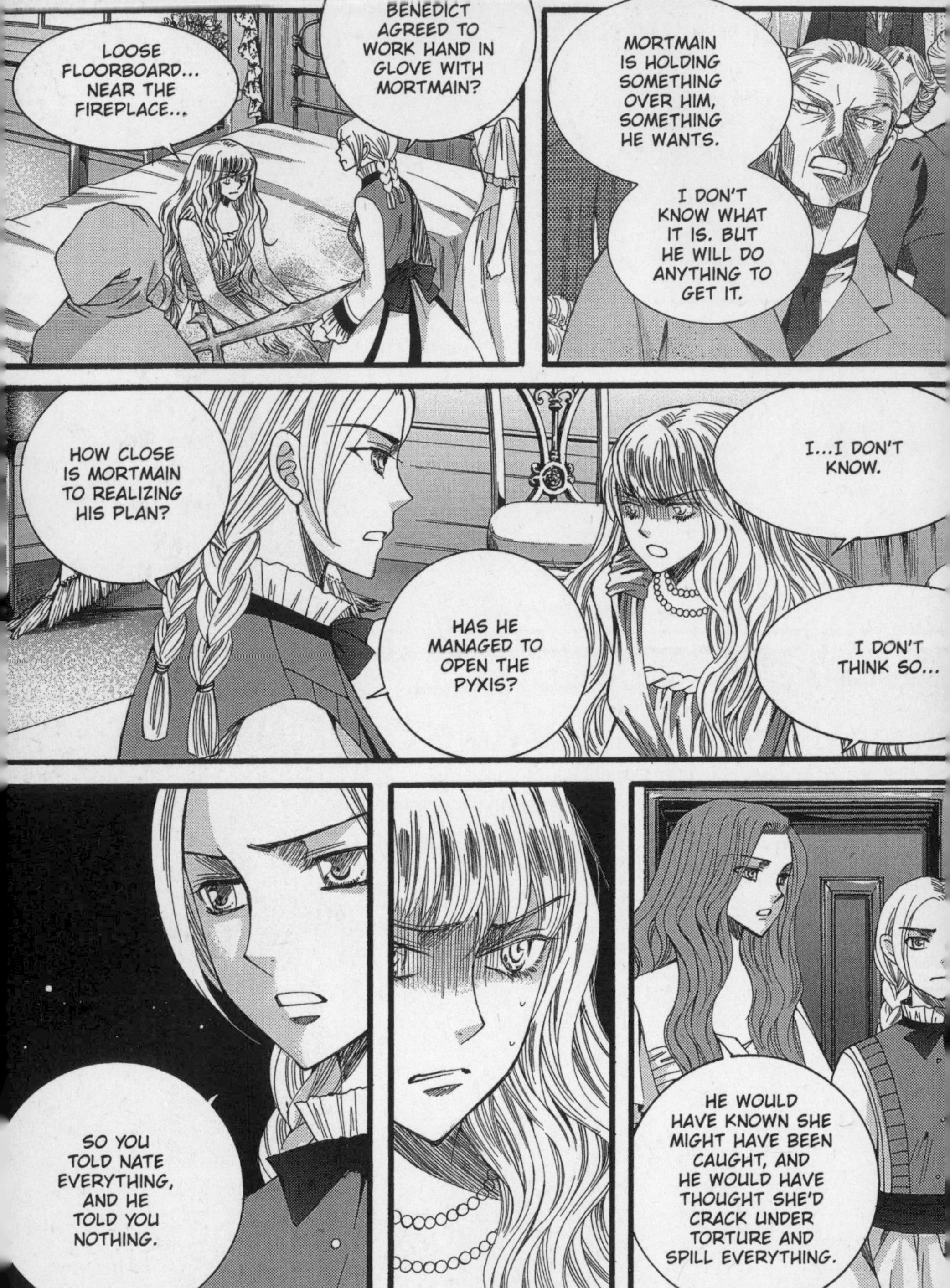

LOOSE FLOORBOARD... NEAR THE FIREPLACE...
WHY HAS BENEDICT AGREED TO WORK HAND IN GLOVE WITH MORTMAIN?
MORTMAIN IS HOLDING SOMETHING OVER HIM, SOMETHING HE WANTS.
I DON'T KNOW WHAT IT IS. BUT HE WILL DO ANYTHING TO GET IT.
HOW CLOSE IS MORTMAIN TO REALIZING HIS PLAN?
I...I DON'T KNOW.
HAS HE MANAGED TO OPEN THE PYXIS?
I DON'T THINK SO...
SO YOU TOLD NATE EVERYTHING, AND HE TOLD YOU NOTHING.
HE WOULD HAVE KNOWN SHE MIGHT HAVE BEEN CAUGHT, AND HE WOULD HAVE THOUGHT SHE'D CRACK UNDER TORTURE AND SPILL EVERYTHING.

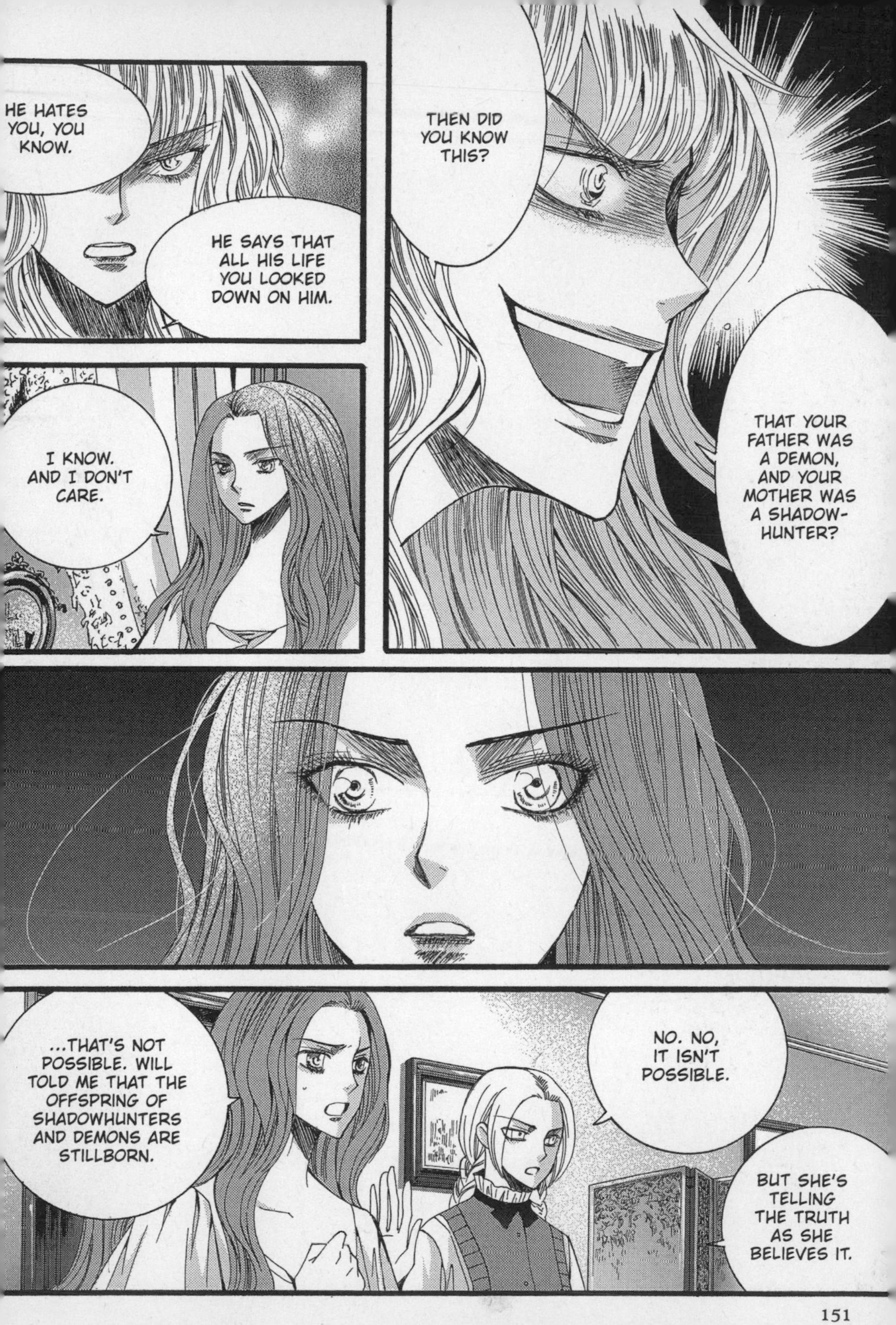
HE HATES YOU, YOU KNOW.
HE SAYS THAT ALL HIS LIFE YOU LOOKED DOWN ON HIM.
I KNOW. AND I DON'T CARE.
THEN DID YOU KNOW THIS?
THAT YOUR FATHER WAS A DEMON, AND YOUR MOTHER WAS A SHADOW-HUNTER?
...THAT'S NOT POSSIBLE. WILL TOLD ME THAT THE OFFSPRING OF SHADOWHUNTERS AND DEMONS ARE STILLBORN.
NO. NO, IT ISN'T POSSIBLE.
BUT SHE'S TELLING THE TRUTH AS SHE BELIEVES IT.

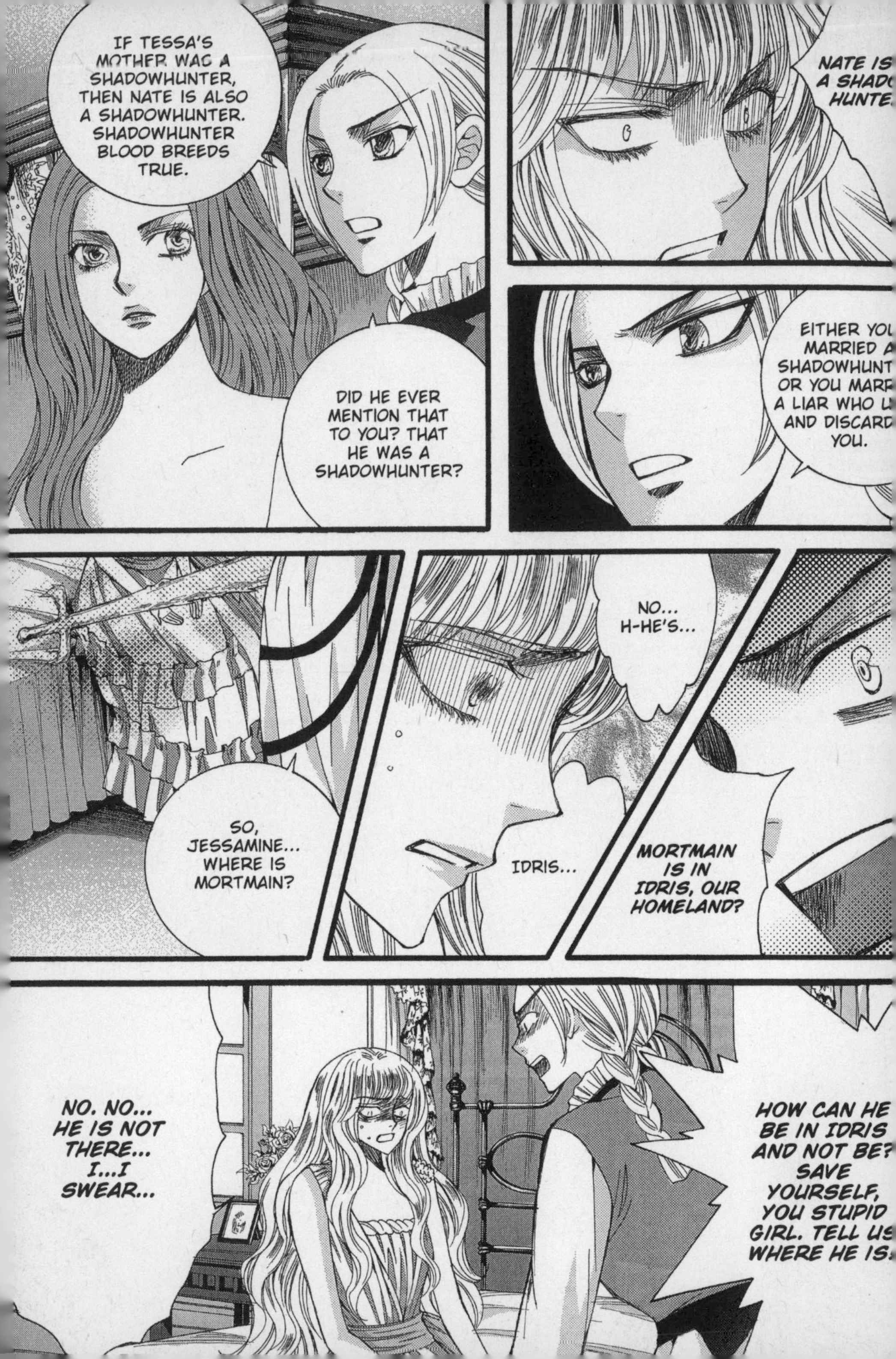
IF TESSA'S MOTHER WAS A SHADOWHUNTER, THEN NATE IS ALSO A SHADOWHUNTER. SHADOWHUNTER BLOOD BREEDS TRUE.
DID HE EVER MENTION THAT TO YOU? THAT HE WAS A SHADOWHUNTER?
NATE IS A SHAD HUNTE
EITHER YOU MARRIED A SHADOWHUNT OR YOU MARR A LIAR WHO U AND DISCARD YOU.
SO, JESSAMINE... WHERE IS MORTMAIN?
NO... H-HE'S...
IDRIS...
MORTMAIN IS IN IDRIS, OUR HOMELAND?
NO. NO... HE IS NOT THERE... I...I SWEAR...
HOW CAN HE BE IN IDRIS AND NOT BE? SAVE YOURSELF, YOU STUPID GIRL. TELL US WHERE HE IS.

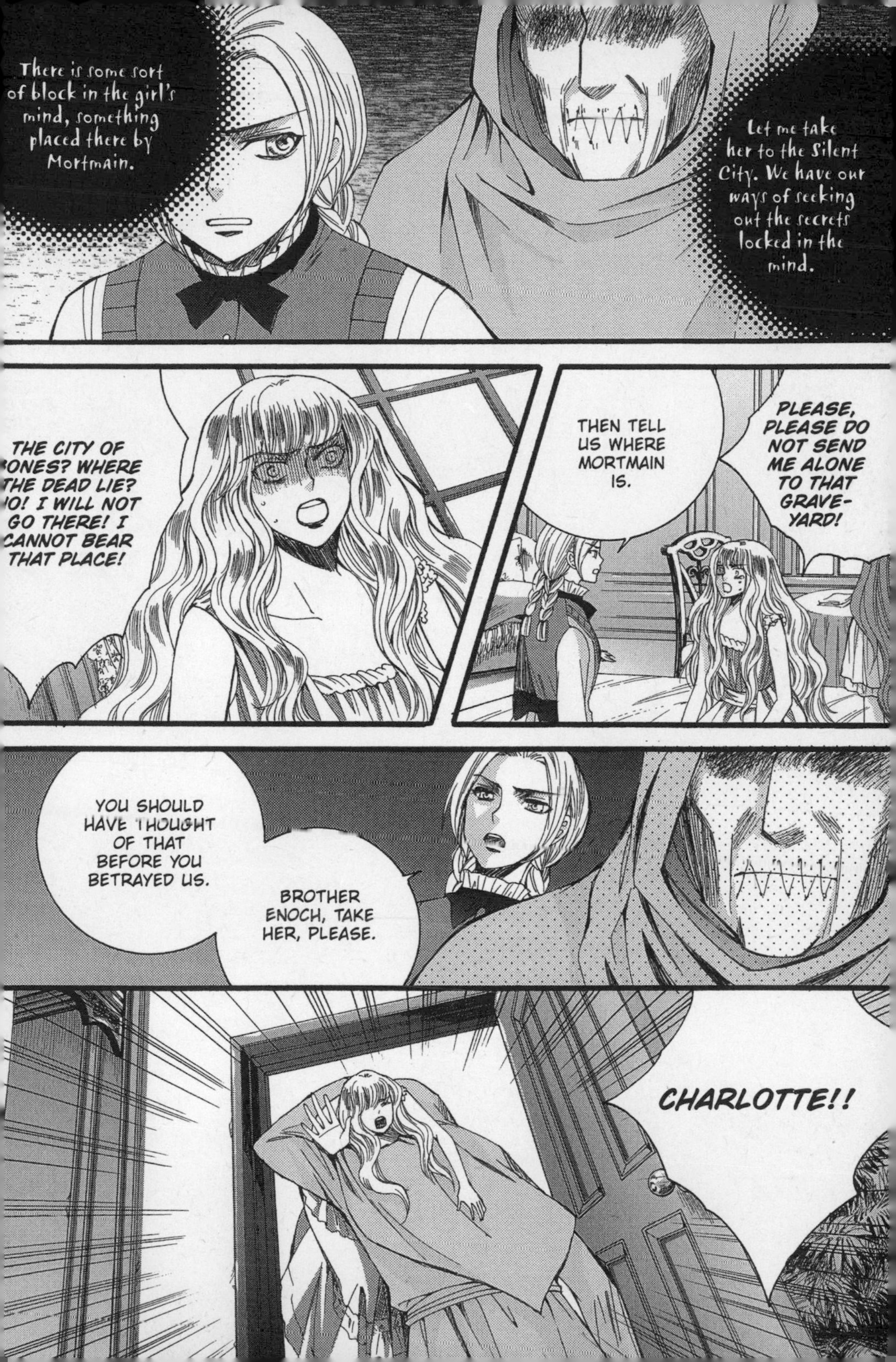
There is some sort of block in the girl's mind, something placed there by Mortmain.
Let me take her to the Silent City. We have our ways of seeking out the secrets locked in the mind.
THE CITY OF ONES? WHERE THE DEAD LIE? O! I WILL NOT GO THERE! I CANNOT BEAR THAT PLACE!
THEN TELL US WHERE MORTMAIN IS.
PLEASE, PLEASE DO NOT SEND ME ALONE TO THAT GRAVE-YARD!
YOU SHOULD HAVE THOUGHT OF THAT BEFORE YOU BETRAYED US.
BROTHER ENOCH, TAKE HER, PLEASE.
CHARLOTTE!!

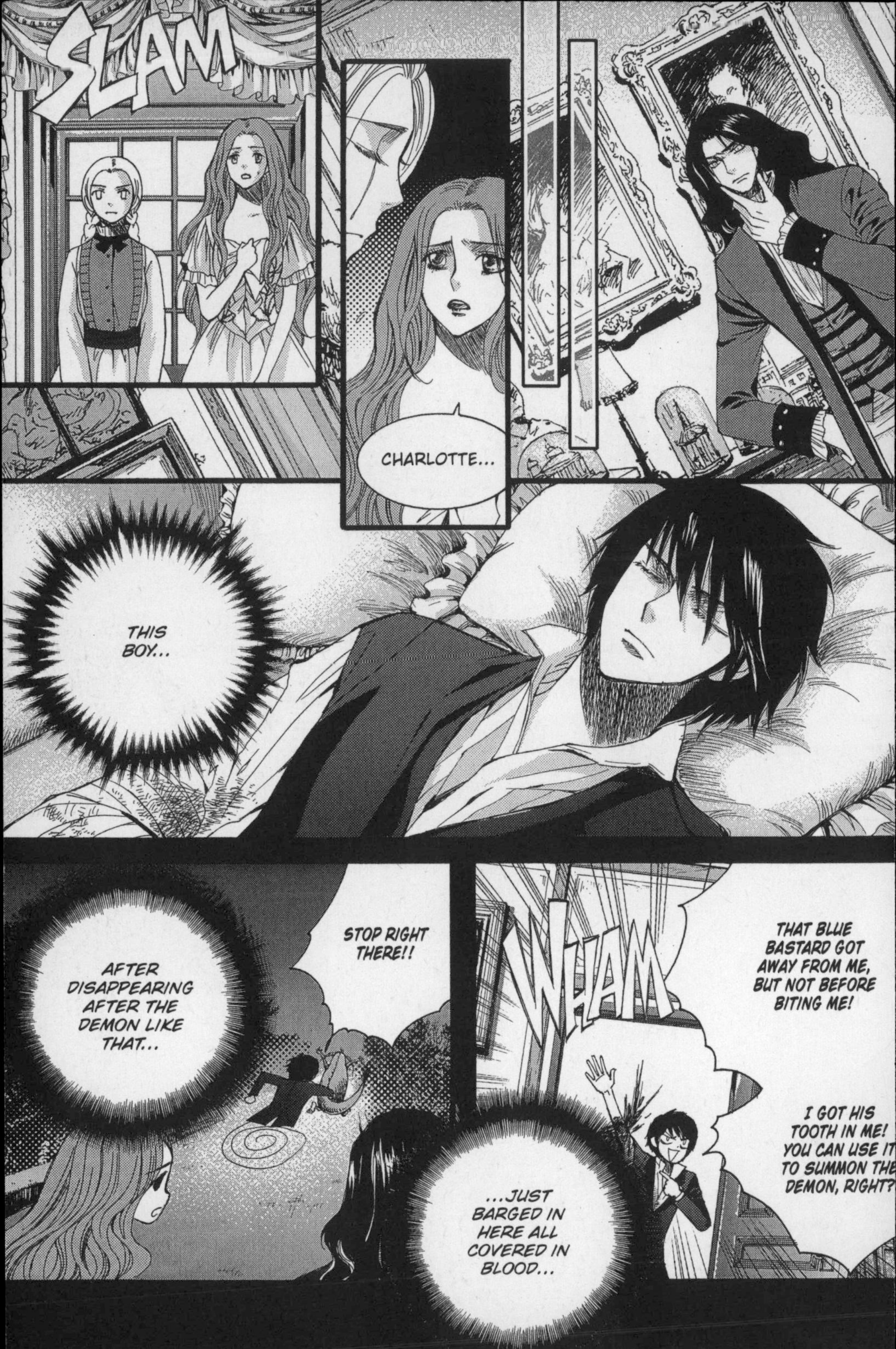
SLAM
CHARLOTTE...
THIS BOY...
AFTER DISAPPEARING AFTER THE DEMON LIKE THAT...
STOP RIGHT THERE!!
...JUST BARGED IN HERE ALL COVERED IN BLOOD...
WHAM
THAT BLUE BASTARD GOT AWAY FROM ME, BUT NOT BEFORE BITING ME!
I GOT HIS TOOTH IN ME! YOU CAN USE IT TO SUMMON THE DEMON, RIGHT?

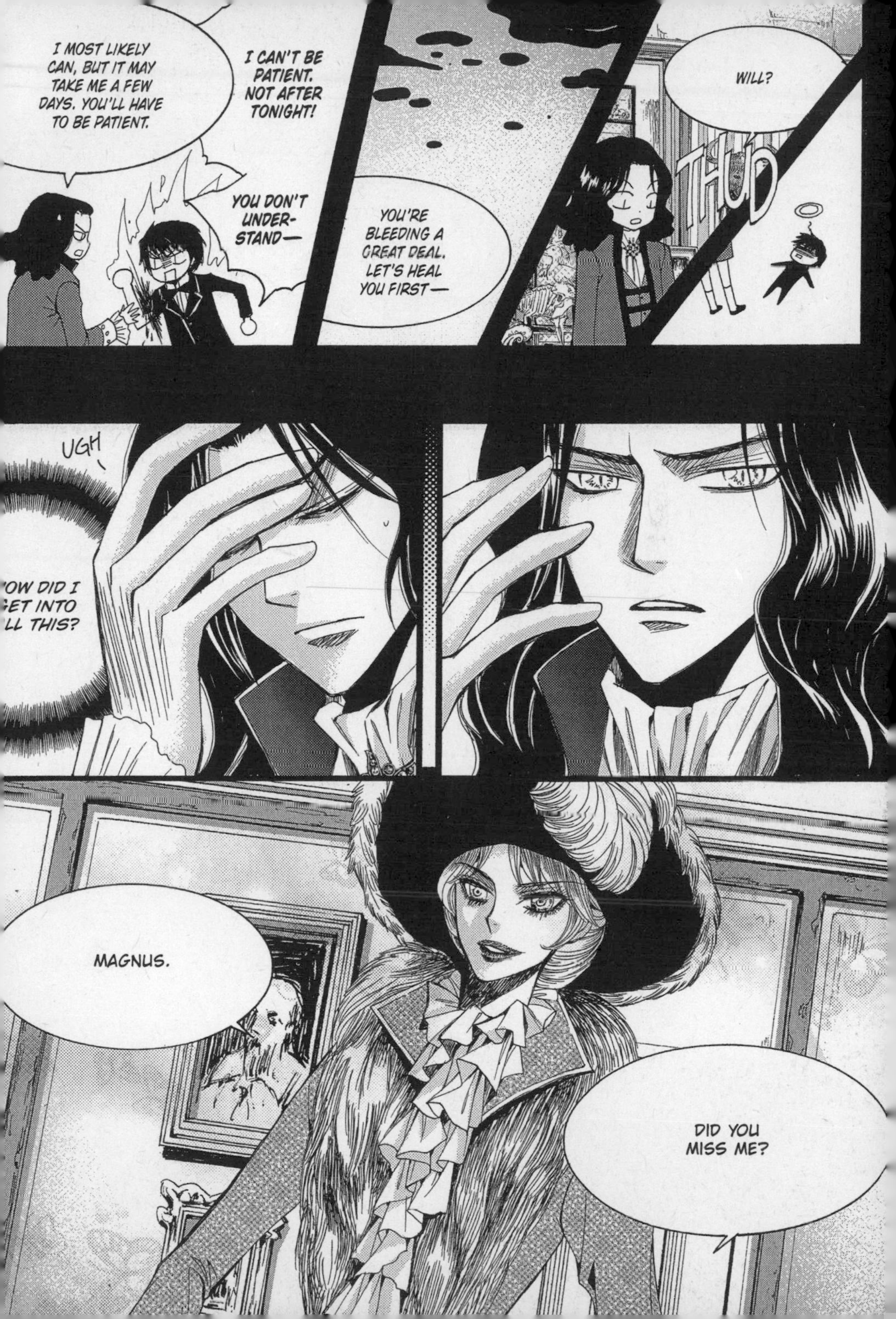
I MOST LIKELY CAN, BUT IT MAY TAKE ME A FEW DAYS. YOU'LL HAVE TO BE PATIENT.
I CAN'T BE PATIENT. NOT AFTER TONIGHT!
YOU DON'T UNDER-STAND—
YOU'RE BLEEDING A GREAT DEAL. LET'S HEAL YOU FIRST—
WILL?
THUD
UGH
OW DID I ET INTO LL THIS?
MAGNUS.
DID YOU MISS ME?

YOU SENT NO MESSAGE. ALTHOUGH THAT DOESN'T MEAN I DIDN'T KEEP TRACK OF YOU.

ALL DONE WITH YOUR RUSSIAN LOVER?

AND THAT MADE YOU JEALOUS?

CAMILLE.

DID YOU WANT ME TO BE?

HE IS DEAD. SO HE HARDLY REPRESENTS COMPETITION FOR YOU.

YOU MUST LET ME HAVE MY LITTLE DIVERSIONS, MAGNUS.

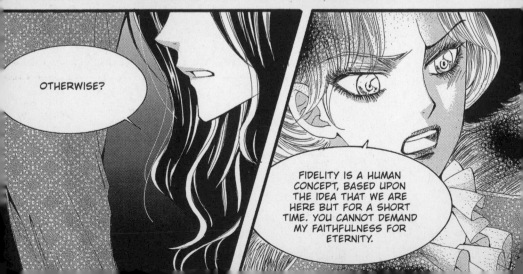

OTHERWISE?

FIDELITY IS A HUMAN CONCEPT, BASED UPON THE IDEA THAT WE ARE HERE BUT FOR A SHORT TIME. YOU CANNOT DEMAND MY FAITHFULNESS FOR ETERNITY.

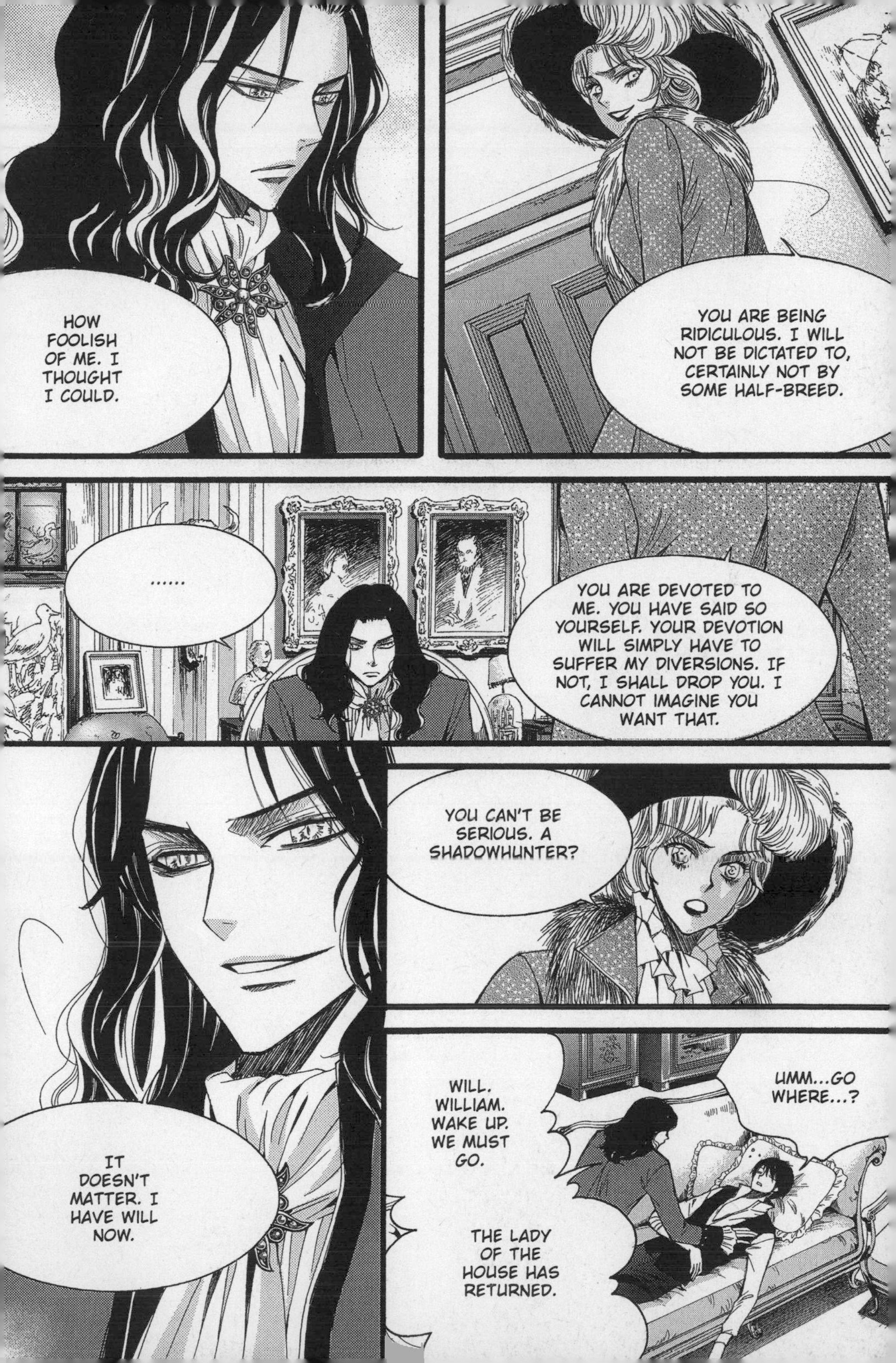
HOW FOOLISH OF ME. I THOUGHT I COULD.
YOU ARE BEING RIDICULOUS. I WILL NOT BE DICTATED TO, CERTAINLY NOT BY SOME HALF-BREED.
......
YOU ARE DEVOTED TO ME. YOU HAVE SAID SO YOURSELF. YOUR DEVOTION WILL SIMPLY HAVE TO SUFFER MY DIVERSIONS. IF NOT, I SHALL DROP YOU. I CANNOT IMAGINE YOU WANT THAT.
IT DOESN'T MATTER. I HAVE WILL NOW.
YOU CAN'T BE SERIOUS. A SHADOWHUNTER?
WILL. WILLIAM. WAKE UP. WE MUST GO.
UMM...GO WHERE...?
THE LADY OF THE HOUSE HAS RETURNED.

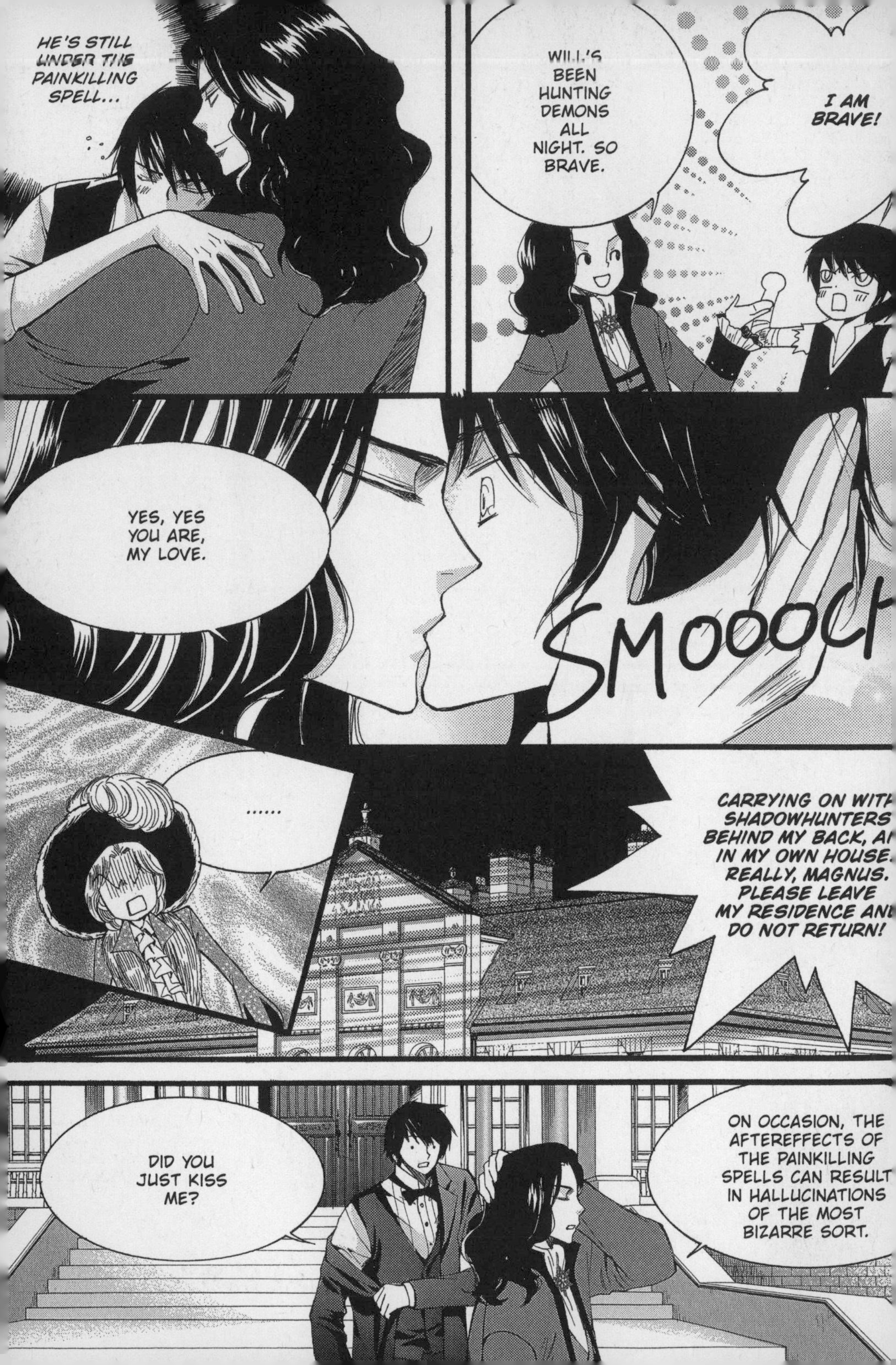

HE'S STILL UNDER THE PAINKILLING SPELL...
WILL'S BEEN HUNTING DEMONS ALL NIGHT. SO BRAVE.
I AM BRAVE!
YES, YES YOU ARE, MY LOVE.
SMOOOCH
......
CARRYING ON WITH SHADOWHUNTERS BEHIND MY BACK, AND IN MY OWN HOUSE. REALLY, MAGNUS. PLEASE LEAVE MY RESIDENCE AND DO NOT RETURN!
DID YOU JUST KISS ME?
ON OCCASION, THE AFTEREFFECTS OF THE PAINKILLING SPELLS CAN RESULT IN HALLUCINATIONS OF THE MOST BIZARRE SORT.

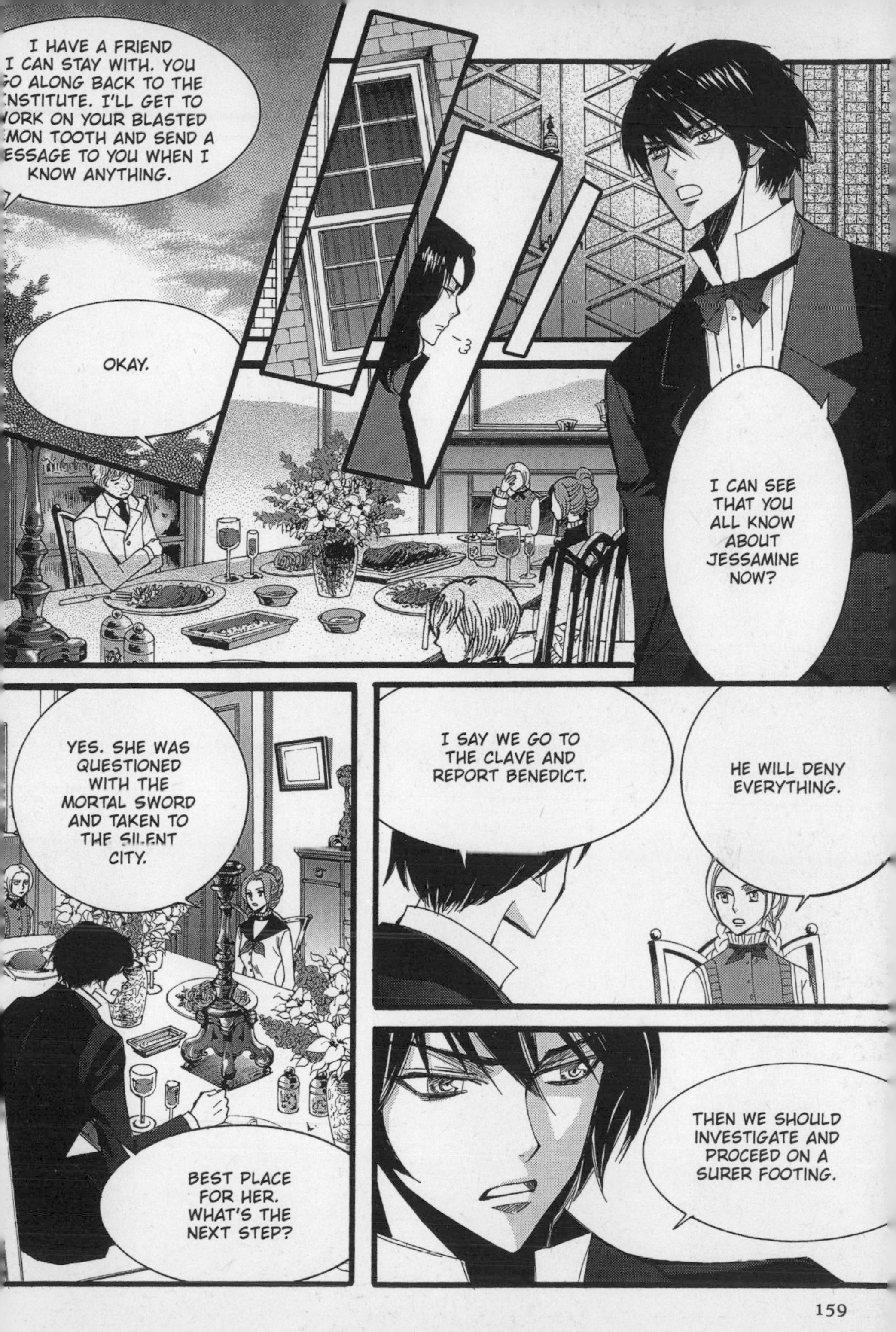
I HAVE A FRIEND I CAN STAY WITH. YOU GO ALONG BACK TO THE INSTITUTE. I'LL GET TO WORK ON YOUR BLASTED MON TOOTH AND SEND A ESSAGE TO YOU WHEN I KNOW ANYTHING.
OKAY.
I CAN SEE THAT YOU ALL KNOW ABOUT JESSAMINE NOW?
YES. SHE WAS QUESTIONED WITH THE MORTAL SWORD AND TAKEN TO THE SILENT CITY.
BEST PLACE FOR HER. WHAT'S THE NEXT STEP?
I SAY WE GO TO THE CLAVE AND REPORT BENEDICT.
HE WILL DENY EVERYTHING.
THEN WE SHOULD INVESTIGATE AND PROCEED ON A SURER FOOTING.

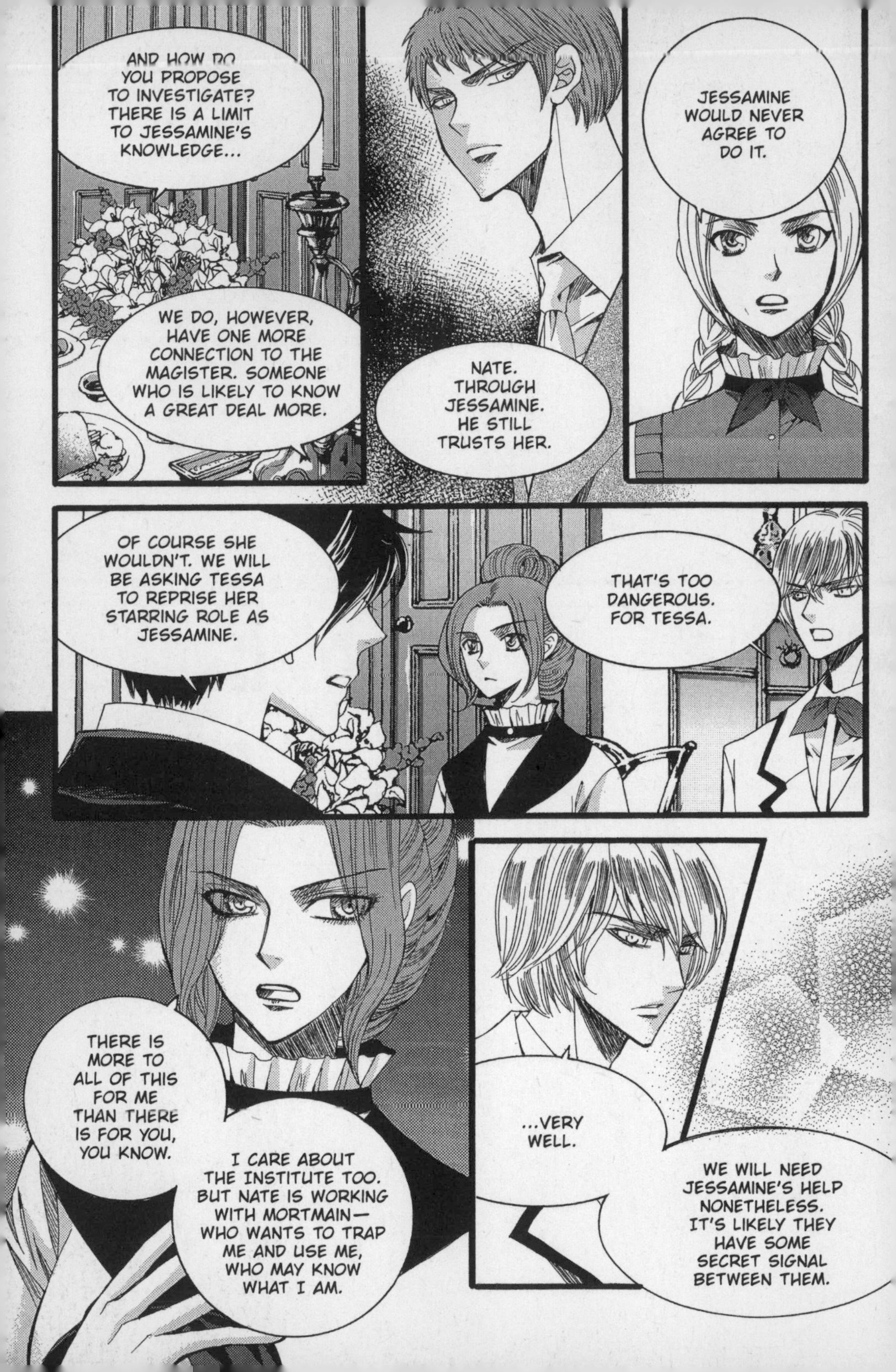

AND HOW DO YOU PROPOSE TO INVESTIGATE? THERE IS A LIMIT TO JESSAMINE'S KNOWLEDGE...
WE DO, HOWEVER, HAVE ONE MORE CONNECTION TO THE MAGISTER. SOMEONE WHO IS LIKELY TO KNOW A GREAT DEAL MORE.
NATE. THROUGH JESSAMINE. HE STILL TRUSTS HER.
JESSAMINE WOULD NEVER AGREE TO DO IT.
OF COURSE SHE WOULDN'T. WE WILL BE ASKING TESSA TO REPRISE HER STARRING ROLE AS JESSAMINE.
THAT'S TOO DANGEROUS. FOR TESSA.
THERE IS MORE TO ALL OF THIS FOR ME THAN THERE IS FOR YOU, YOU KNOW.
I CARE ABOUT THE INSTITUTE TOO. BUT NATE IS WORKING WITH MORTMAIN— WHO WANTS TO TRAP ME AND USE ME, WHO MAY KNOW WHAT I AM.
...VERY WELL.
WE WILL NEED JESSAMINE'S HELP NONETHELESS. IT'S LIKELY THEY HAVE SOME SECRET SIGNAL BETWEEN THEM.

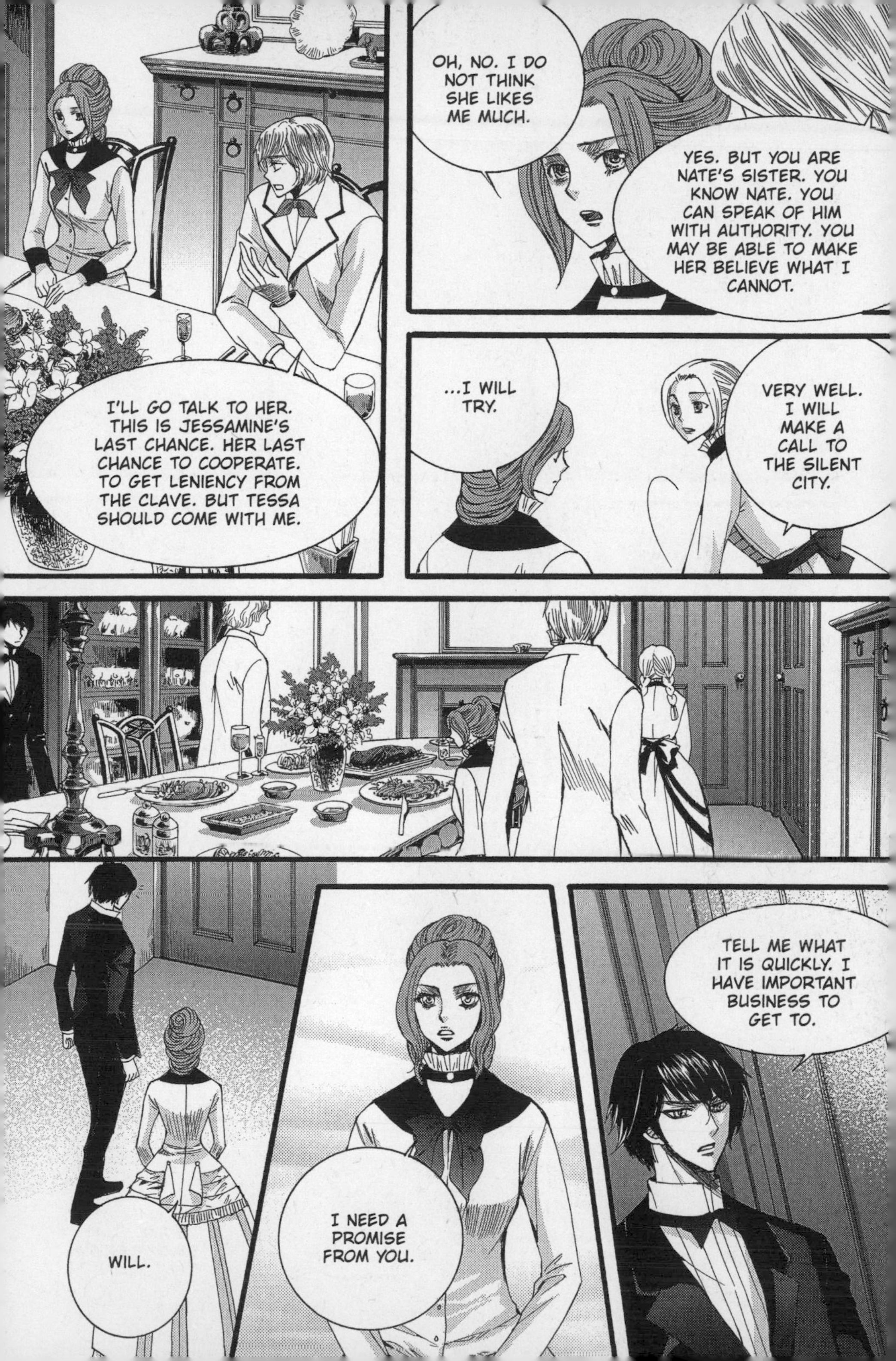
I'LL GO TALK TO HER. THIS IS JESSAMINE'S LAST CHANCE. HER LAST CHANCE TO COOPERATE. TO GET LENIENCY FROM THE CLAVE. BUT TESSA SHOULD COME WITH ME.
OH, NO. I DO NOT THINK SHE LIKES ME MUCH.
YES. BUT YOU ARE NATE'S SISTER. YOU KNOW NATE. YOU CAN SPEAK OF HIM WITH AUTHORITY. YOU MAY BE ABLE TO MAKE HER BELIEVE WHAT I CANNOT.
...I WILL TRY.
VERY WELL. I WILL MAKE A CALL TO THE SILENT CITY.
WILL.
I NEED A PROMISE FROM YOU.
TELL ME WHAT IT IS QUICKLY. I HAVE IMPORTANT BUSINESS TO GET TO.

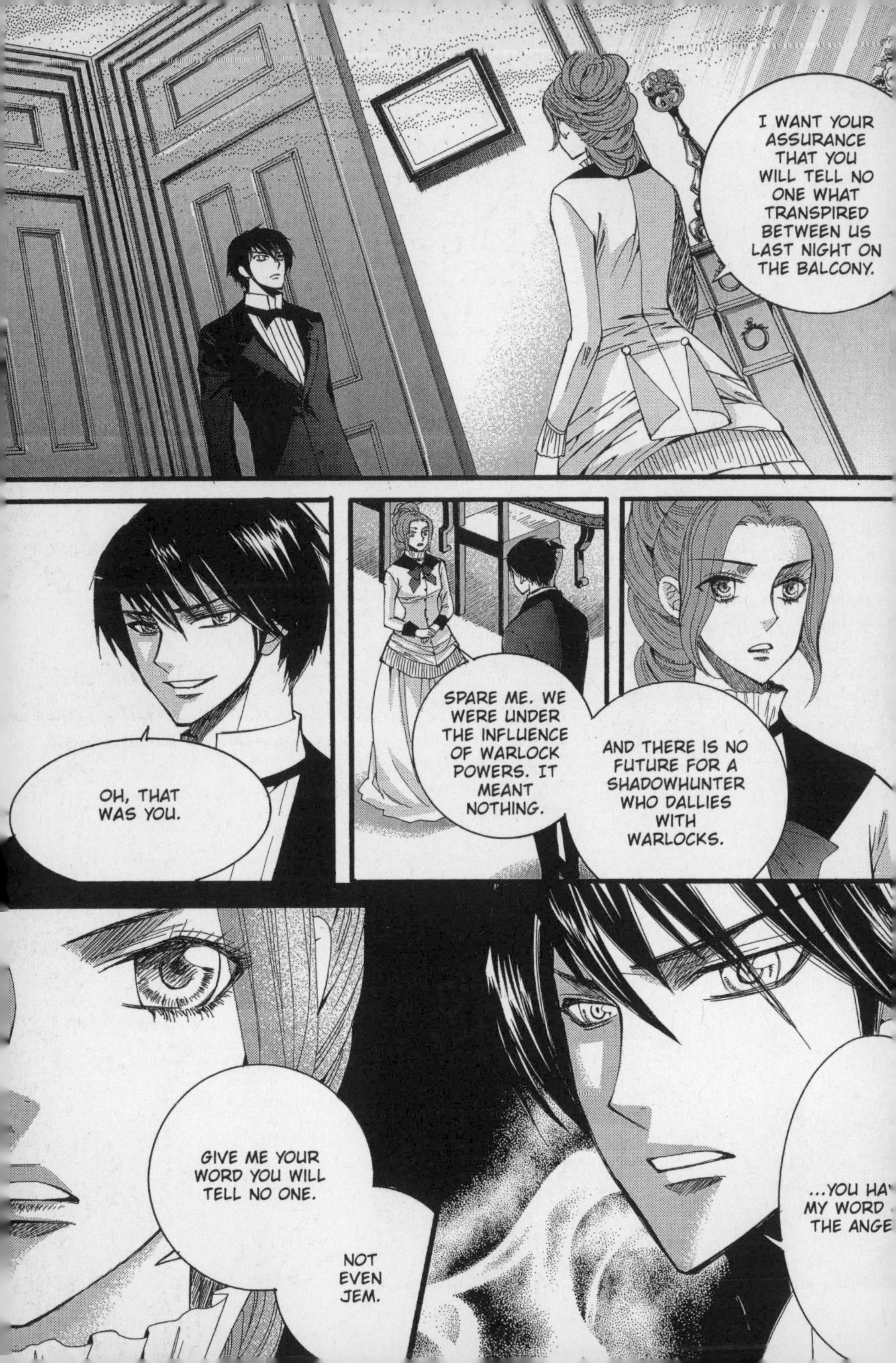
I WANT YOUR ASSURANCE THAT YOU WILL TELL NO ONE WHAT TRANSPIRED BETWEEN US LAST NIGHT ON THE BALCONY.
OH, THAT WAS YOU.
SPARE ME. WE WERE UNDER THE INFLUENCE OF WARLOCK POWERS. IT MEANT NOTHING.
AND THERE IS NO FUTURE FOR A SHADOWHUNTER WHO DALLIES WITH WARLOCKS.
GIVE ME YOUR WORD YOU WILL TELL NO ONE.
NOT EVEN JEM.
...YOU HA
MY WORD
THE ANGE

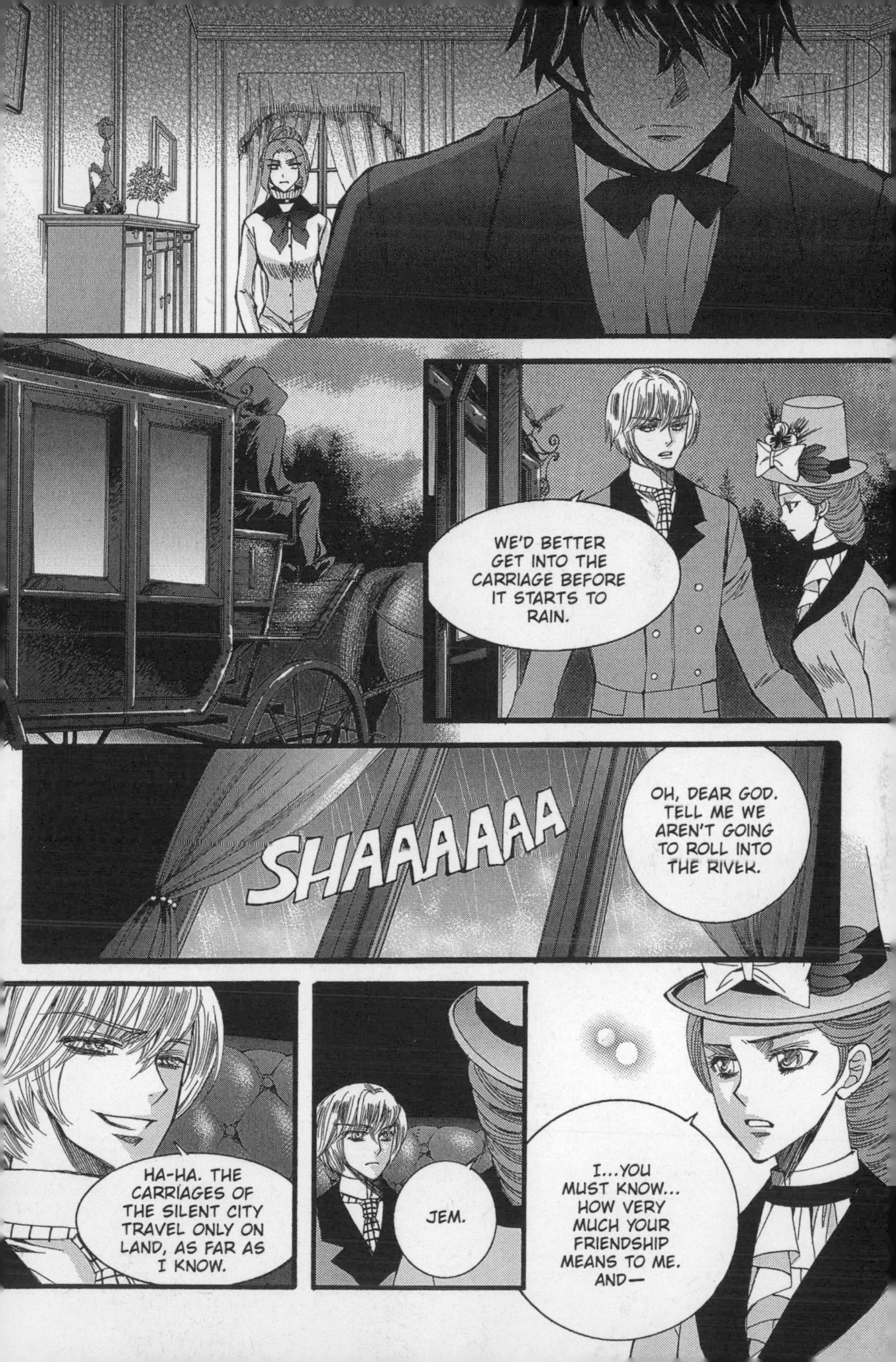
WE'D BETTER GET INTO THE CARRIAGE BEFORE IT STARTS TO RAIN.
SHAAAAAA
OH, DEAR GOD. TELL ME WE AREN'T GOING TO ROLL INTO THE RIVER.
HA-HA. THE CARRIAGES OF THE SILENT CITY TRAVEL ONLY ON LAND, AS FAR AS I KNOW.
JEM.
I...YOU MUST KNOW... HOW VERY MUCH YOUR FRIENDSHIP MEANS TO ME. AND—

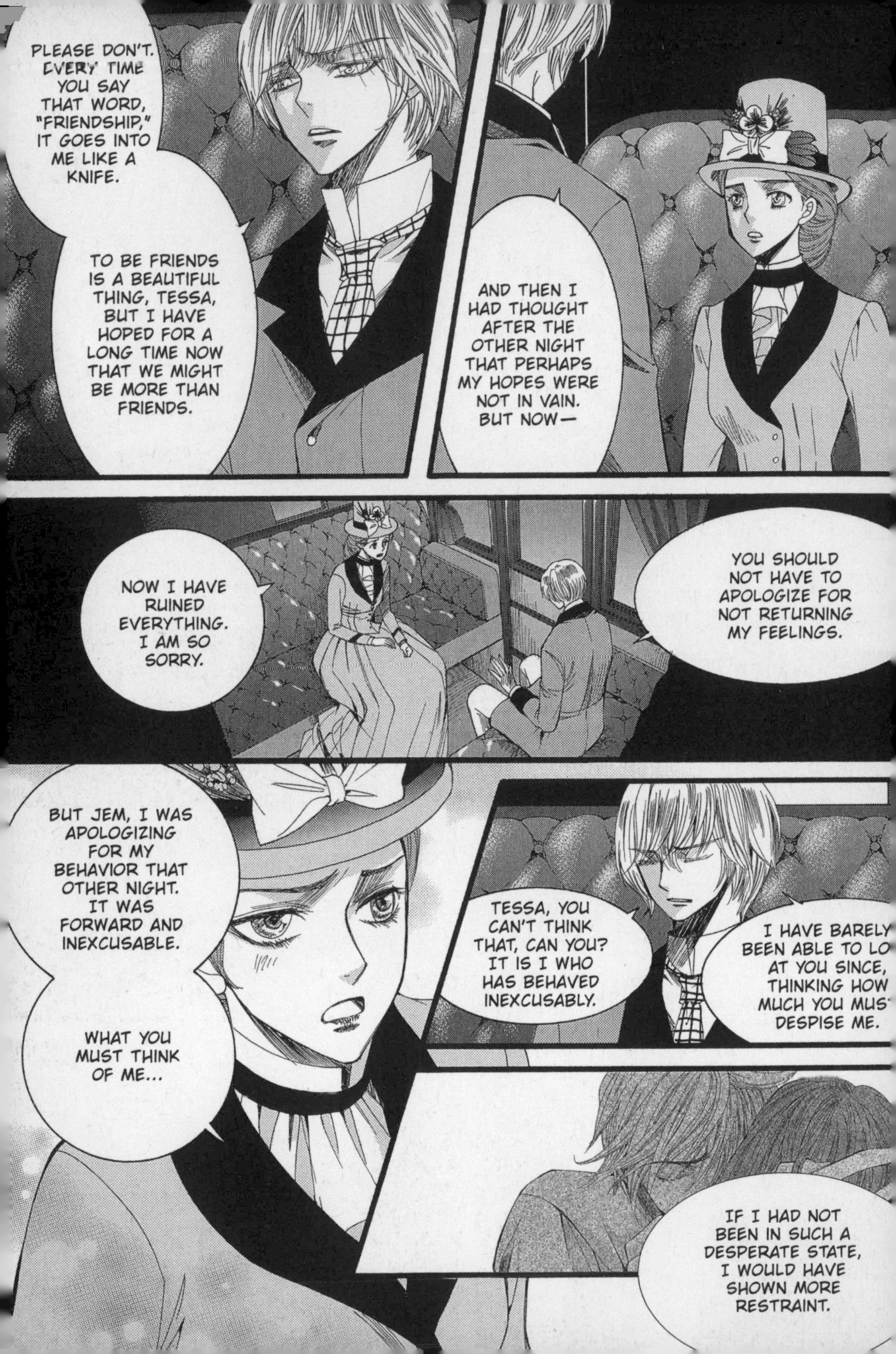
PLEASE DON'T. EVERY TIME YOU SAY THAT WORD, "FRIENDSHIP," IT GOES INTO ME LIKE A KNIFE.
TO BE FRIENDS IS A BEAUTIFUL THING, TESSA, BUT I HAVE HOPED FOR A LONG TIME NOW THAT WE MIGHT BE MORE THAN FRIENDS.
AND THEN I HAD THOUGHT AFTER THE OTHER NIGHT THAT PERHAPS MY HOPES WERE NOT IN VAIN. BUT NOW—
NOW I HAVE RUINED EVERYTHING. I AM SO SORRY.
YOU SHOULD NOT HAVE TO APOLOGIZE FOR NOT RETURNING MY FEELINGS.
BUT JEM, I WAS APOLOGIZING FOR MY BEHAVIOR THAT OTHER NIGHT. IT WAS FORWARD AND INEXCUSABLE.
WHAT YOU MUST THINK OF ME...
TESSA, YOU CAN'T THINK THAT, CAN YOU? IT IS I WHO HAS BEHAVED INEXCUSABLY.
I HAVE BARELY BEEN ABLE TO LO AT YOU SINCE, THINKING HOW MUCH YOU MUS DESPISE ME.
IF I HAD NOT BEEN IN SUCH A DESPERATE STATE, I WOULD HAVE SHOWN MORE RESTRAINT.

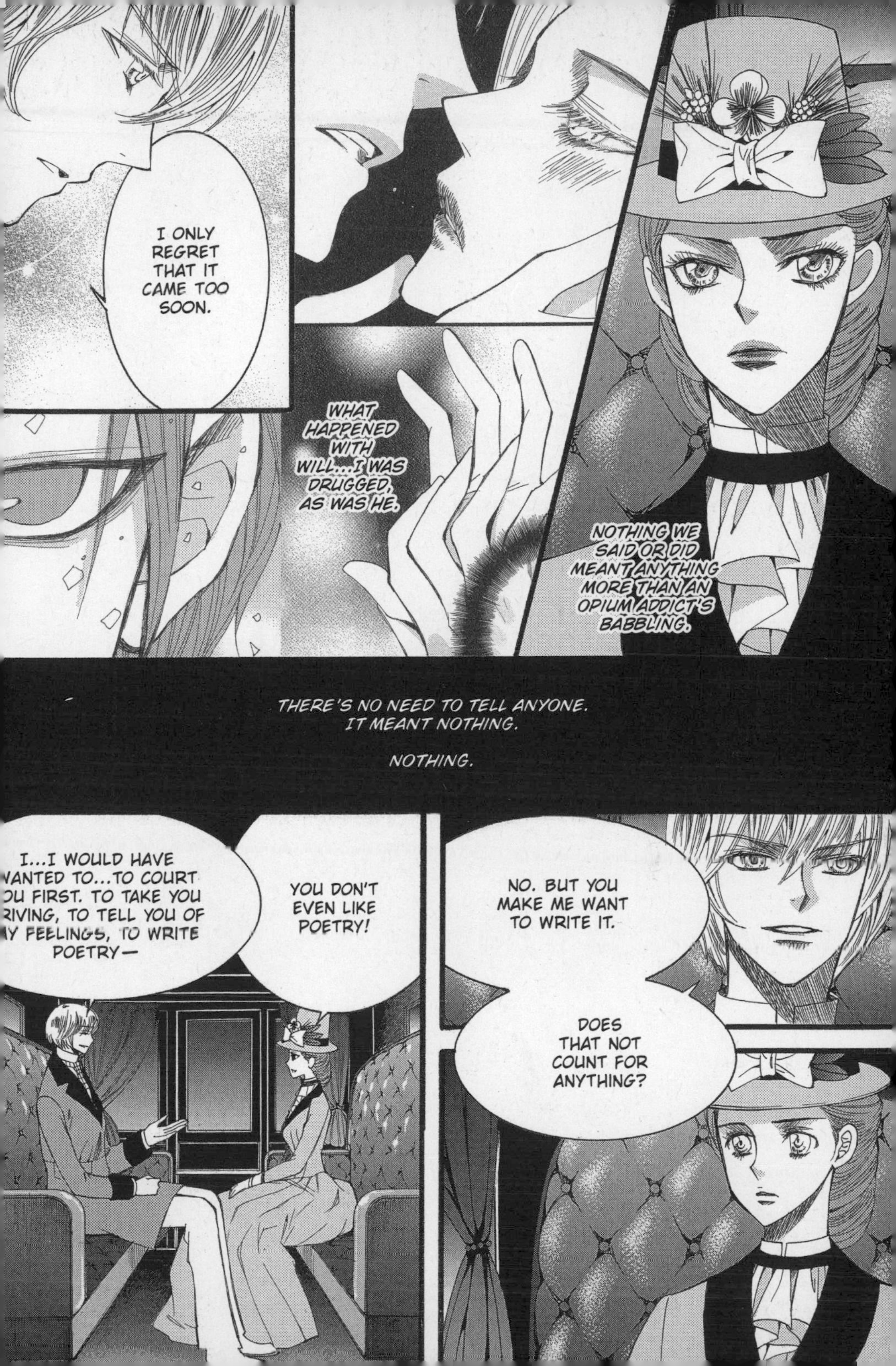
I ONLY REGRET THAT IT CAME TOO SOON.
WHAT HAPPENED WITH WILL...I WAS DRUGGED, AS WAS HE.
NOTHING WE SAID OR DID MEANT ANYTHING MORE THAN AN OPIUM ADDICT'S BABBLING.
THERE'S NO NEED TO TELL ANYONE.
IT MEANT NOTHING.
NOTHING.
I...I WOULD HAVE VANTED TO...TO COURT OU FIRST. TO TAKE YOU RIVING, TO TELL YOU OF Y FEELINGS, TO WRITE POETRY—
YOU DON'T EVEN LIKE POETRY!
NO. BUT YOU MAKE ME WANT TO WRITE IT.
DOES THAT NOT COUNT FOR ANYTHING?

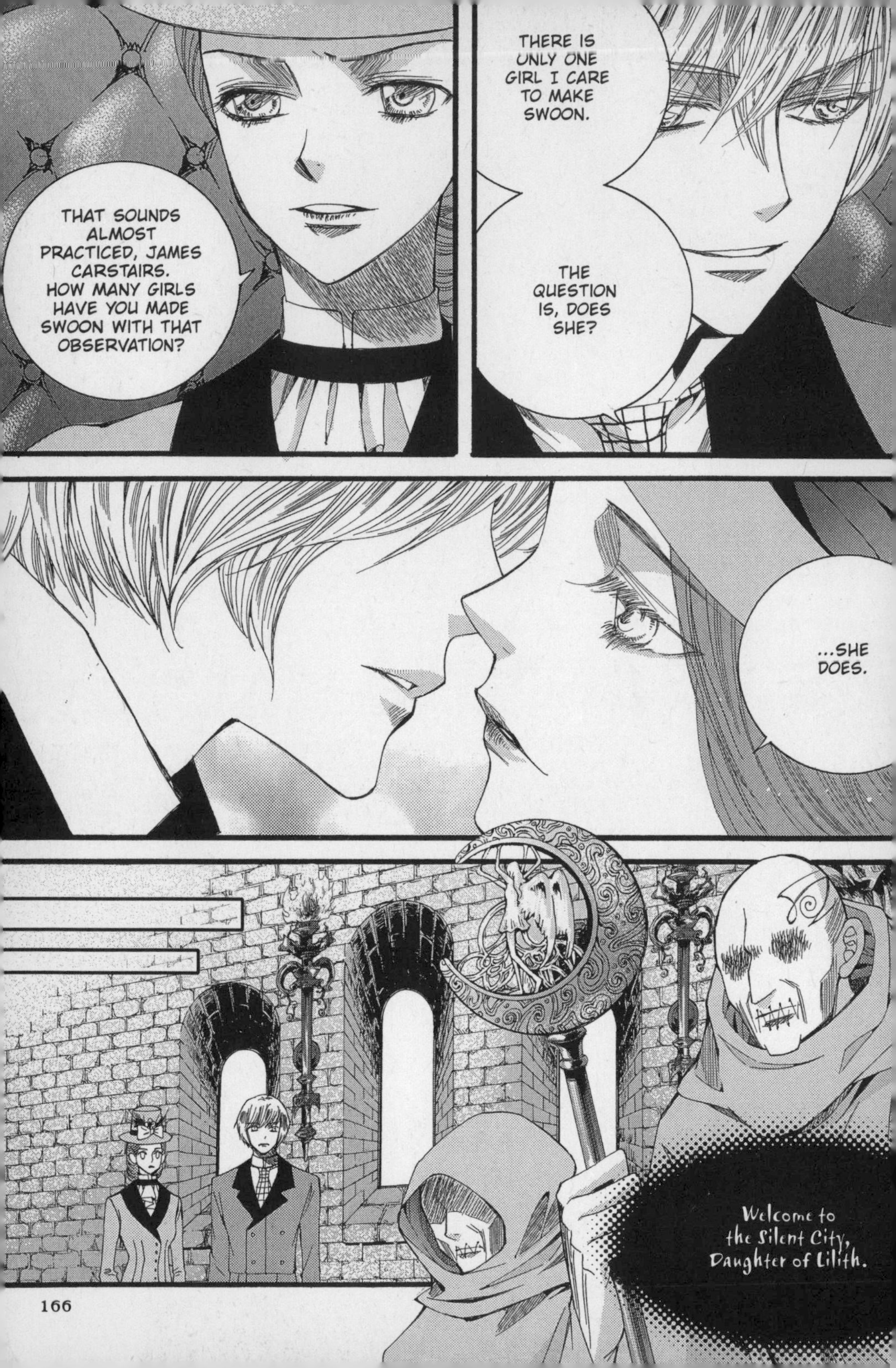
THAT SOUNDS ALMOST PRACTICED, JAMES CARSTAIRS. HOW MANY GIRLS HAVE YOU MADE SWOON WITH THAT OBSERVATION?
THERE IS ONLY ONE GIRL I CARE TO MAKE SWOON.
THE QUESTION IS, DOES SHE?
...SHE DOES.
Welcome to the Silent City, Daughter of Lilith.

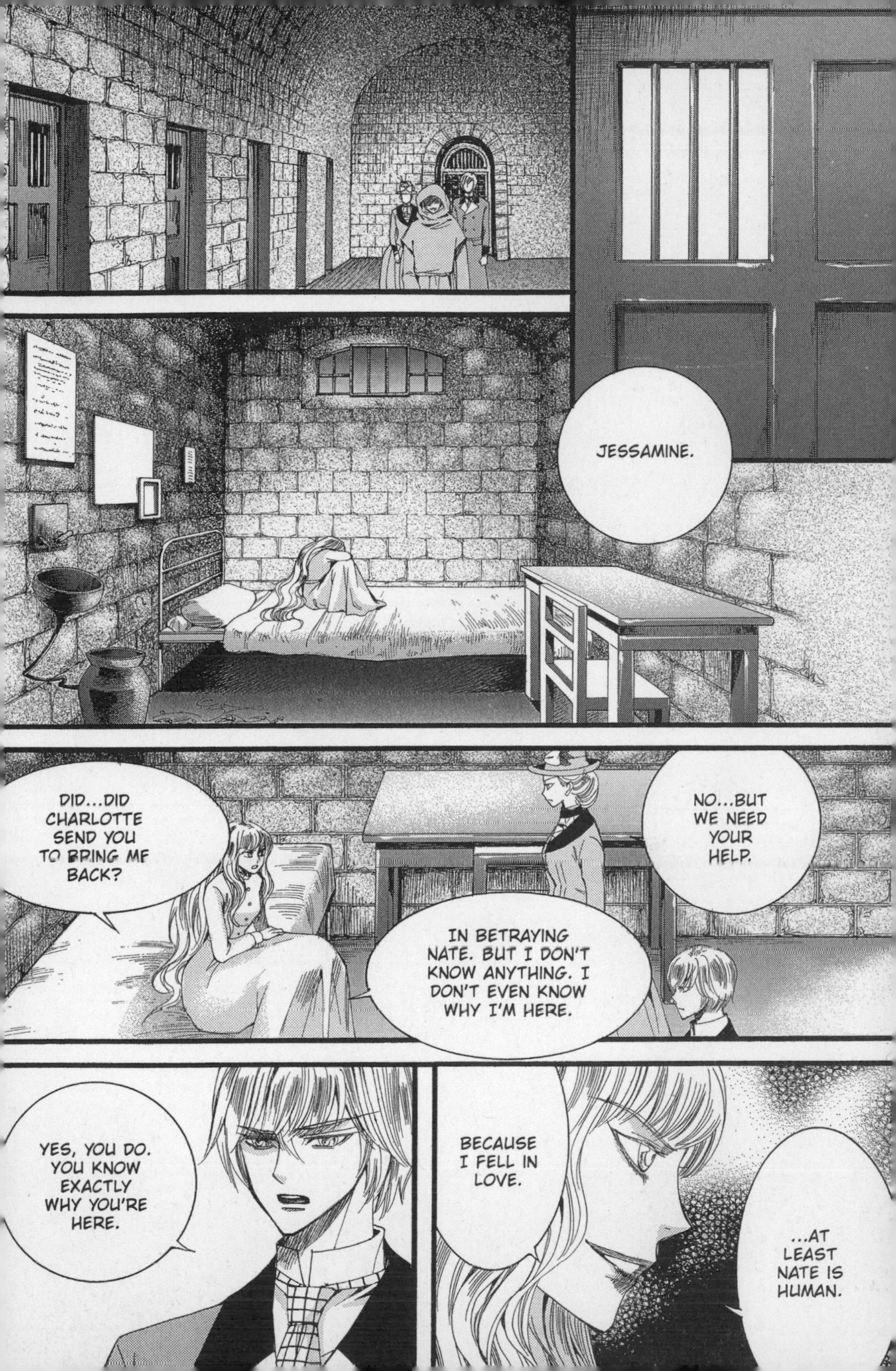
JESSAMINE.
DID...DID CHARLOTTE SEND YOU TO BRING ME BACK?
NO...BUT WE NEED YOUR HELP.
IN BETRAYING NATE. BUT I DON'T KNOW ANYTHING. I DON'T EVEN KNOW WHY I'M HERE.
YES, YOU DO. YOU KNOW EXACTLY WHY YOU'RE HERE.
BECAUSE I FELL IN LOVE.
...AT LEAST NATE IS HUMAN.

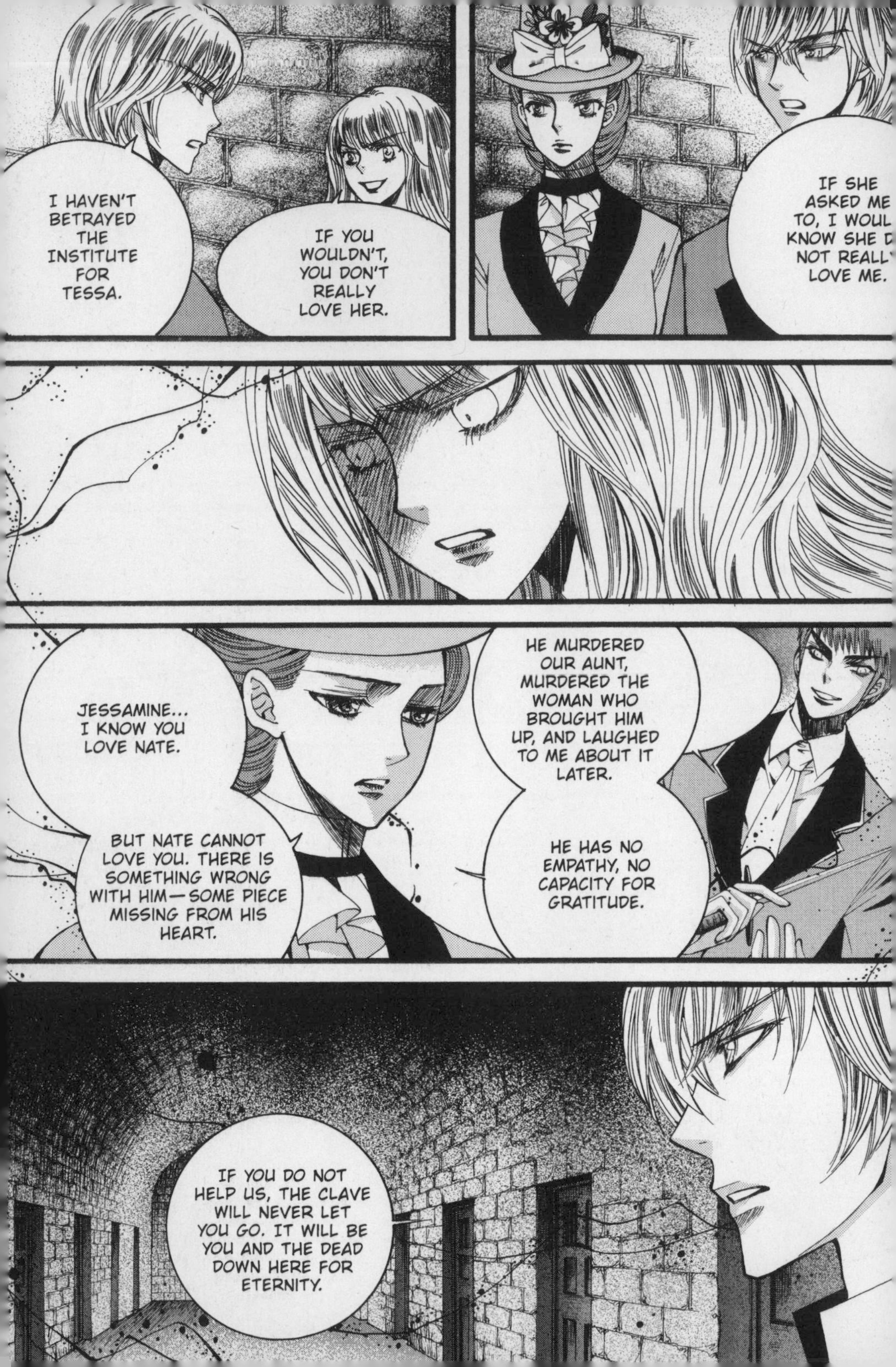
I HAVEN'T BETRAYED THE INSTITUTE FOR TESSA.
IF YOU WOULDN'T, YOU DON'T REALLY LOVE HER.
IF SHE ASKED ME TO, I WOUL KNOW SHE D NOT REALL LOVE ME.
JESSAMINE... I KNOW YOU LOVE NATE.
BUT NATE CANNOT LOVE YOU. THERE IS SOMETHING WRONG WITH HIM—SOME PIECE MISSING FROM HIS HEART.
HE MURDERED OUR AUNT, MURDERED THE WOMAN WHO BROUGHT HIM UP, AND LAUGHED TO ME ABOUT IT LATER.
HE HAS NO EMPATHY, NO CAPACITY FOR GRATITUDE.
IF YOU DO NOT HELP US, THE CLAVE WILL NEVER LET YOU GO. IT WILL BE YOU AND THE DEAD DOWN HERE FOR ETERNITY.

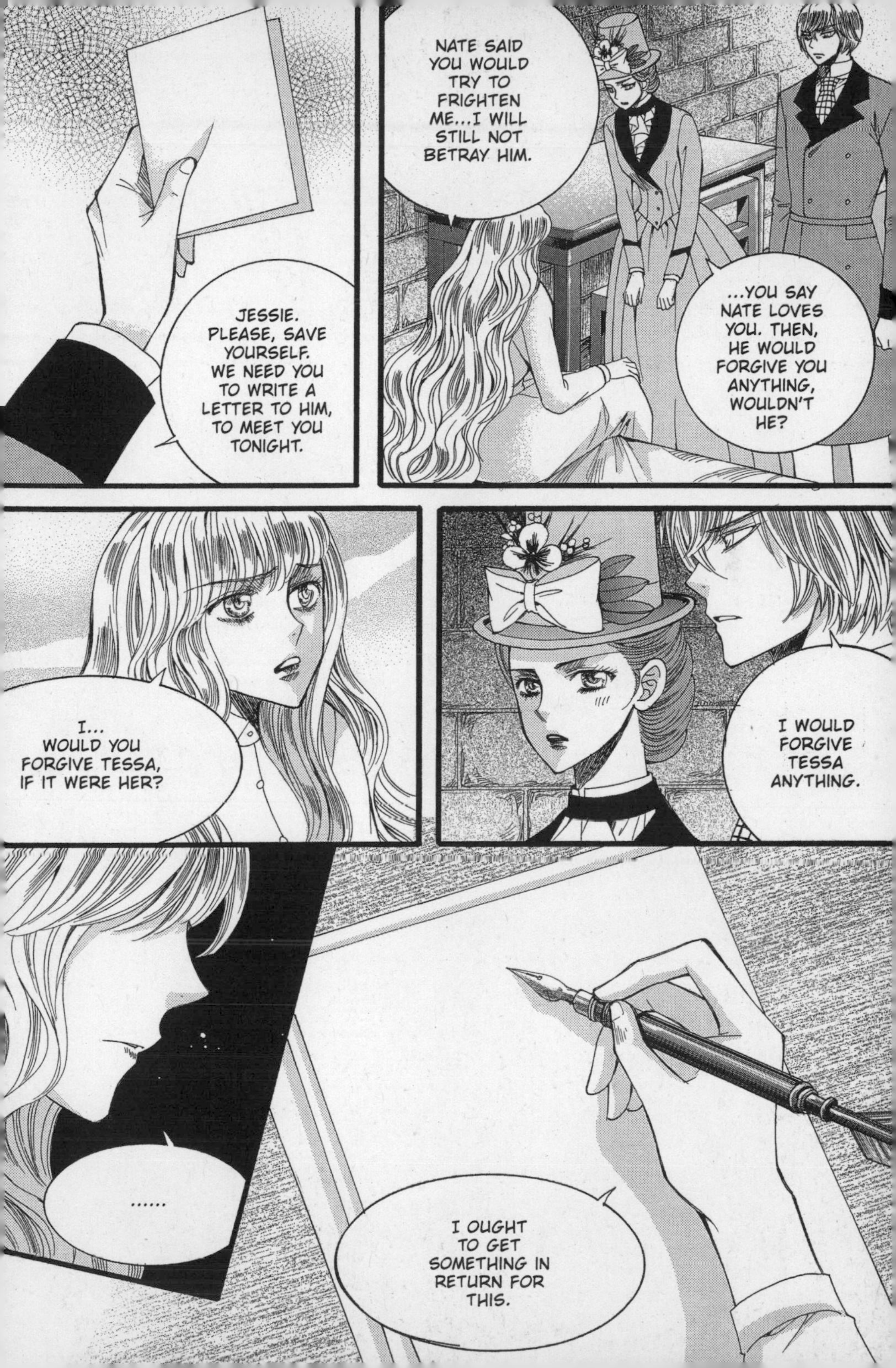
JESSIE. PLEASE, SAVE YOURSELF. WE NEED YOU TO WRITE A LETTER TO HIM, TO MEET YOU TONIGHT.
NATE SAID YOU WOULD TRY TO FRIGHTEN ME...I WILL STILL NOT BETRAY HIM.
...YOU SAY NATE LOVES YOU. THEN, HE WOULD FORGIVE YOU ANYTHING, WOULDN'T HE?
I... WOULD YOU FORGIVE TESSA, IF IT WERE HER?
I WOULD FORGIVE TESSA ANYTHING.
......
I OUGHT TO GET SOMETHING IN RETURN FOR THIS.

WHEN I MEET HIM AT NIGHT, I AM ALWAYS DRESSED AS A BOY.

THE BOYS' CLOTHES I WEAR ARE BEHIND THE DOLL'S HOUSE IN MY ROOM. TAKE CARE MOVING IT.

I...

CHARLOTTE SENT ME TO TELL YOU WE'RE WAITING IN THE DRAWING ROOM.

TESSA, CHARLOTTE SENT ME TO GIVE YOU—

WHAT WAS THAT ABOUT?

WELL, THOSE CLOTHES ARE A BIT TIGHT, YOU SEE.

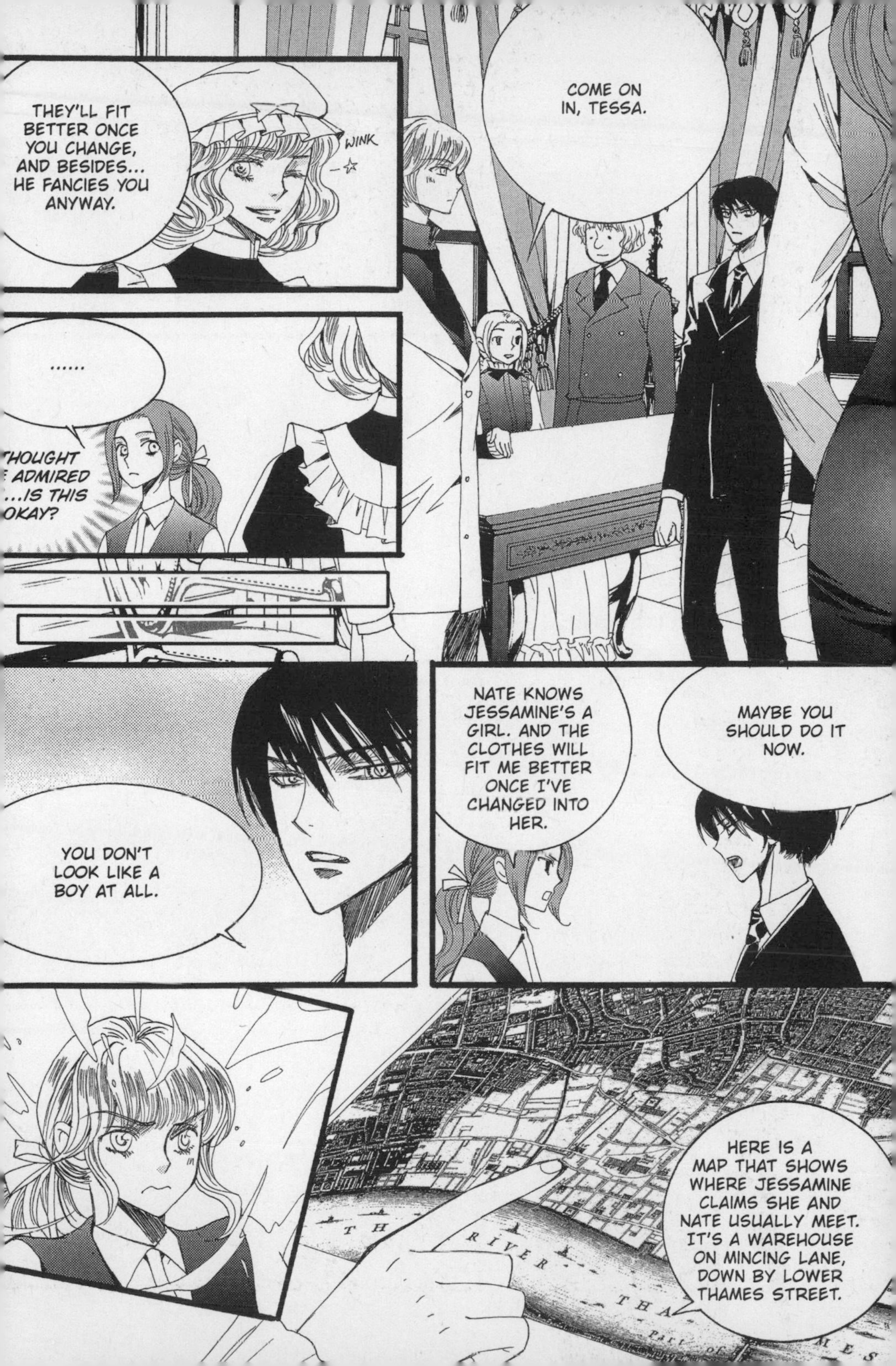
THEY'LL FIT BETTER ONCE YOU CHANGE, AND BESIDES... HE FANCIES YOU ANYWAY.
WINK
COME ON IN, TESSA.
......
THOUGHT
ADMIRED
...IS THIS
OKAY?
YOU DON'T LOOK LIKE A BOY AT ALL.
NATE KNOWS JESSAMINE'S A GIRL. AND THE CLOTHES WILL FIT ME BETTER ONCE I'VE CHANGED INTO HER.
MAYBE YOU SHOULD DO IT NOW.
HERE IS A MAP THAT SHOWS WHERE JESSAMINE CLAIMS SHE AND NATE USUALLY MEET. IT'S A WAREHOUSE ON MINCING LANE, DOWN BY LOWER THAMES STREET.
RIVER

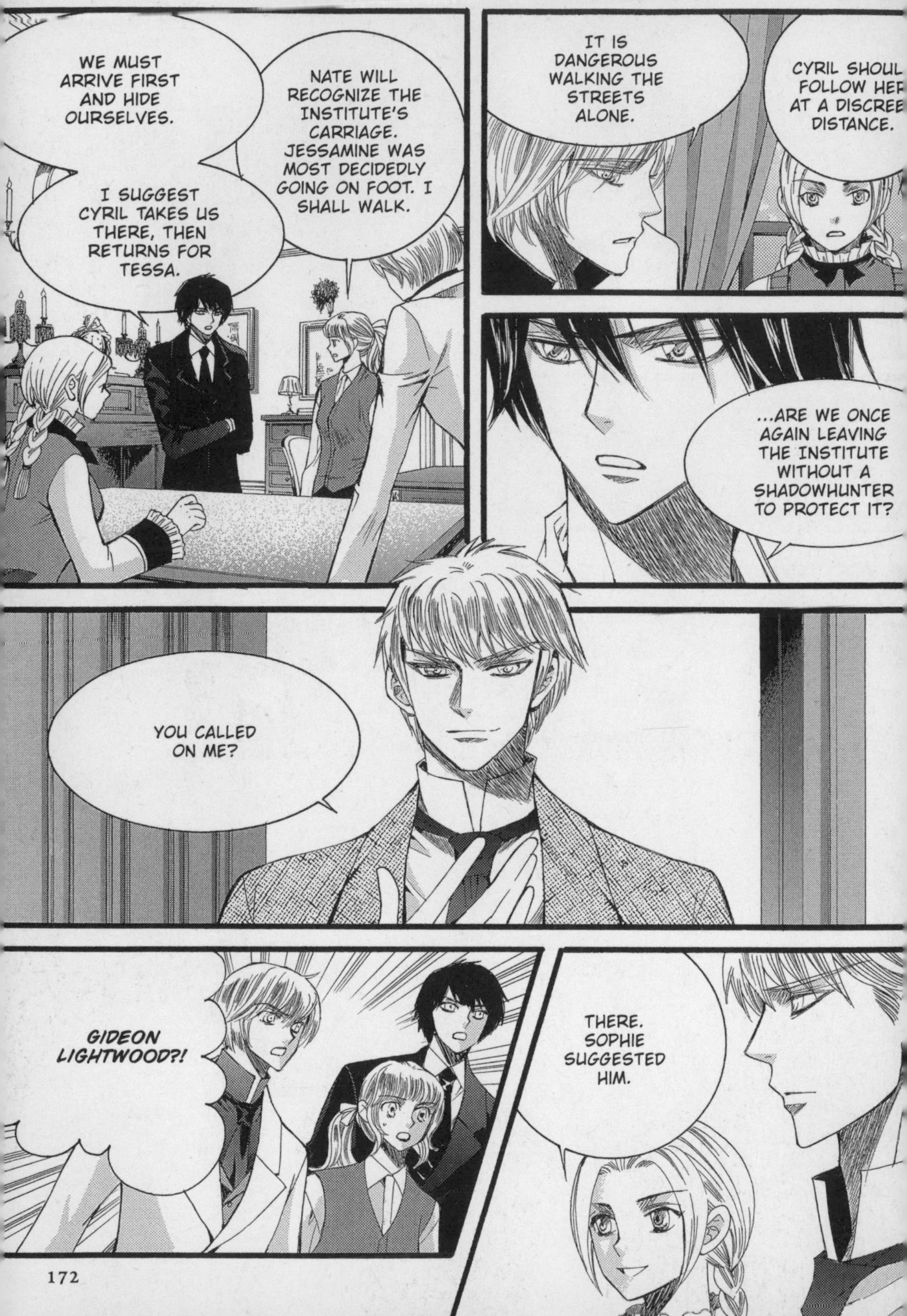

WE MUST ARRIVE FIRST AND HIDE OURSELVES.
I SUGGEST CYRIL TAKES US THERE, THEN RETURNS FOR TESSA.
NATE WILL RECOGNIZE THE INSTITUTE'S CARRIAGE. JESSAMINE WAS MOST DECIDEDLY GOING ON FOOT. I SHALL WALK.
IT IS DANGEROUS WALKING THE STREETS ALONE.
CYRIL SHOUL FOLLOW HER AT A DISCREE DISTANCE.
...ARE WE ONCE AGAIN LEAVING THE INSTITUTE WITHOUT A SHADOWHUNTER TO PROTECT IT?
YOU CALLED ON ME?
GIDEON LIGHTWOOD?!
THERE. SOPHIE SUGGESTED HIM.

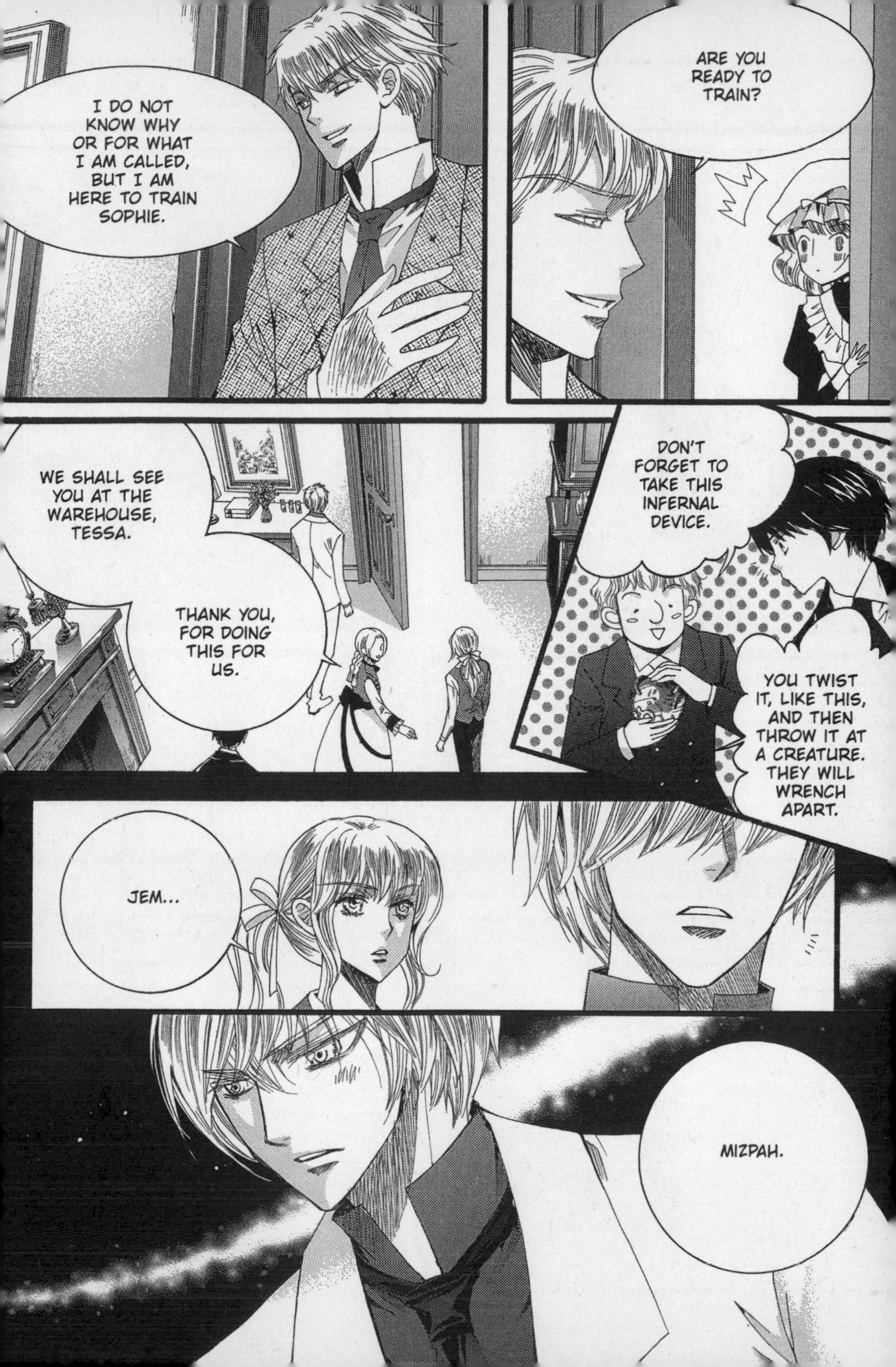
I DO NOT KNOW WHY OR FOR WHAT I AM CALLED, BUT I AM HERE TO TRAIN SOPHIE.
ARE YOU READY TO TRAIN?
WE SHALL SEE YOU AT THE WAREHOUSE, TESSA.
THANK YOU, FOR DOING THIS FOR US.
DON'T FORGET TO TAKE THIS INFERNAL DEVICE.
YOU TWIST IT, LIKE THIS, AND THEN THROW IT AT A CREATURE. THEY WILL WRENCH APART.
JEM...
MIZPAH.

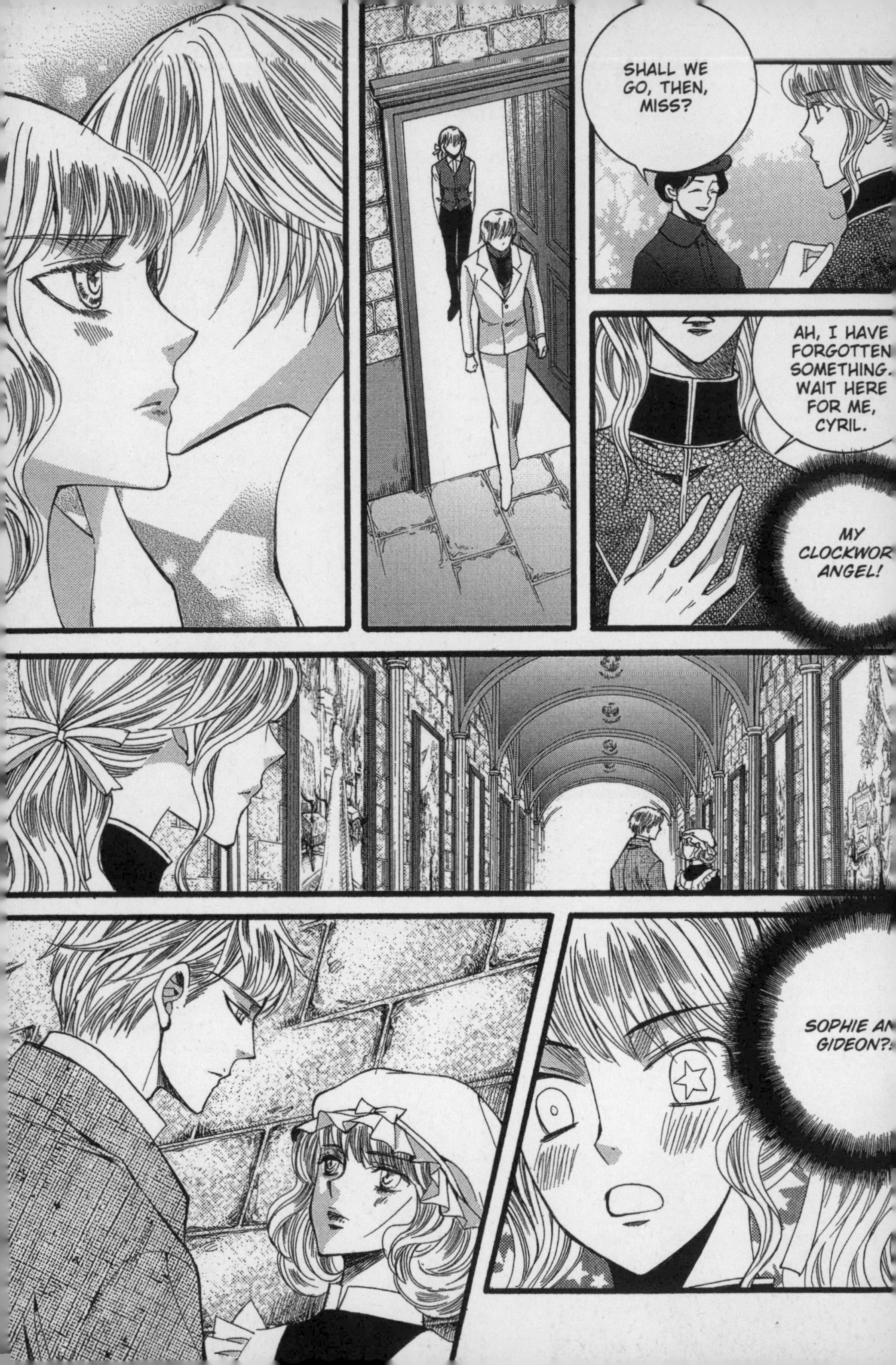
SHALL WE GO, THEN, MISS?
AH, I HAVE FORGOTTEN SOMETHING. WAIT HERE FOR ME, CYRIL.
MY CLOCKWOR ANGEL!
SOPHIE AN GIDEON?!

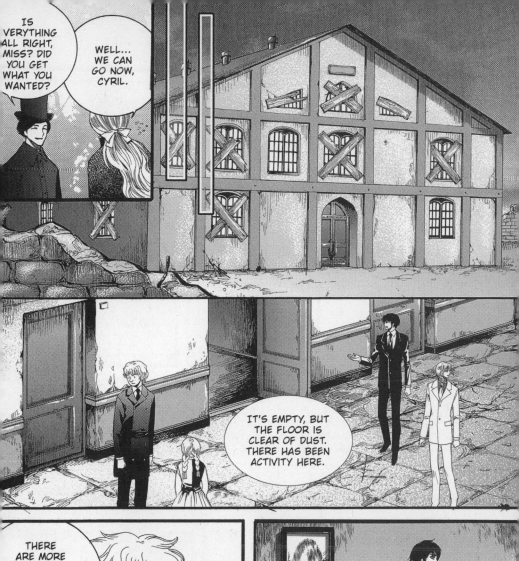

IS VERYTHING ALL RIGHT, MISS? DID YOU GET WHAT YOU WANTED?

WELL... WE CAN GO NOW, CYRIL.

IT'S EMPTY, BUT THE FLOOR IS CLEAR OF DUST. THERE HAS BEEN ACTIVITY HERE.

THERE ARE MORE OFFICES THAT WAY. CHARLOTTE AND I WILL SEARCH THEM.

WILL, JEM, YOU EXAMINE THE SECOND FLOOR.

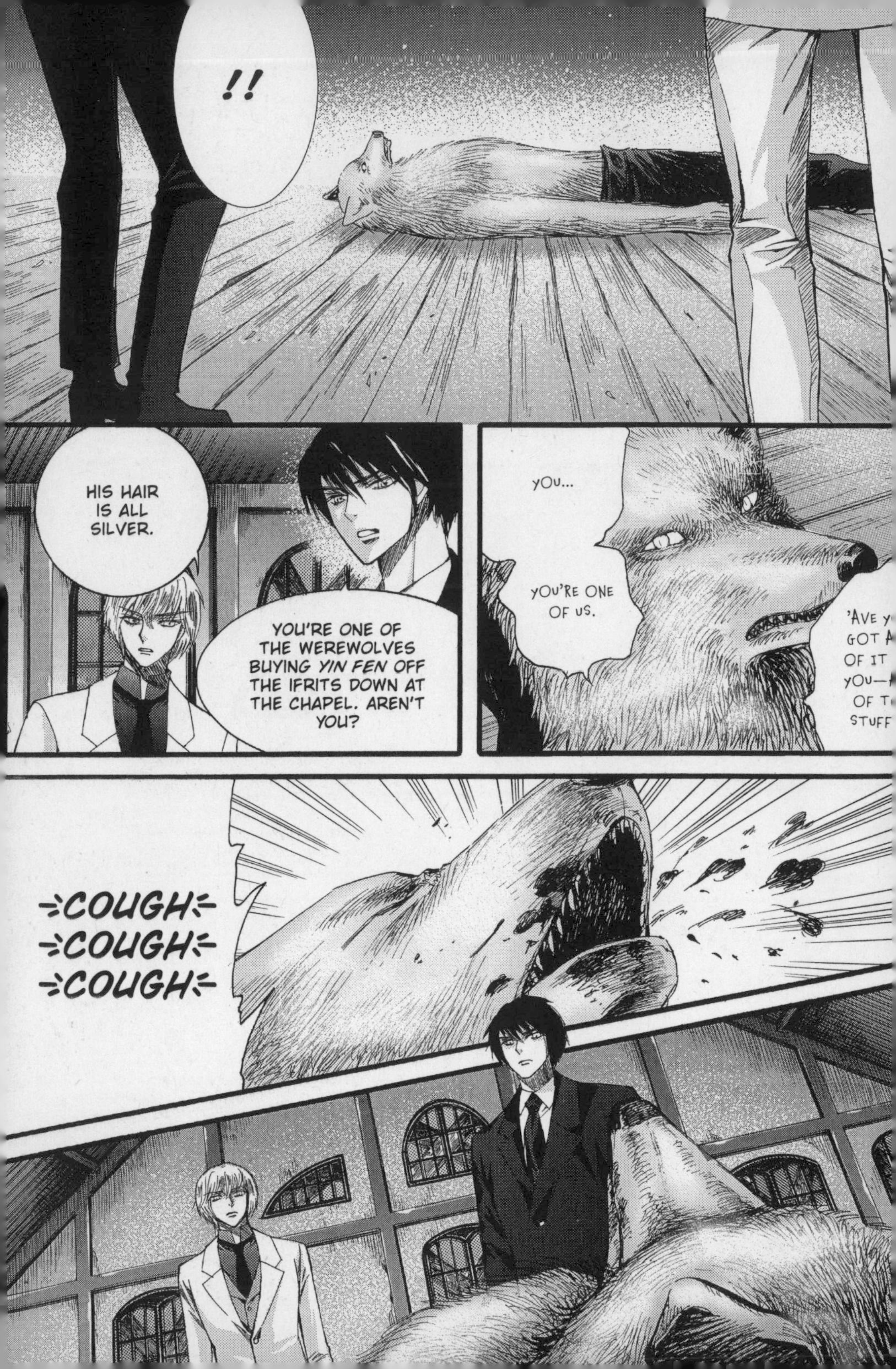
!!
HIS HAIR IS ALL SILVER.
YOU'RE ONE OF THE WEREWOLVES BUYING *YIN FEN* OFF THE IFRITS DOWN AT THE CHAPEL. AREN'T YOU?
YOU...
YOU'RE ONE OF US.
'AVE
GOT
OF IT
YOU—
OF
STUFF
COUGH
COUGH
COUGH

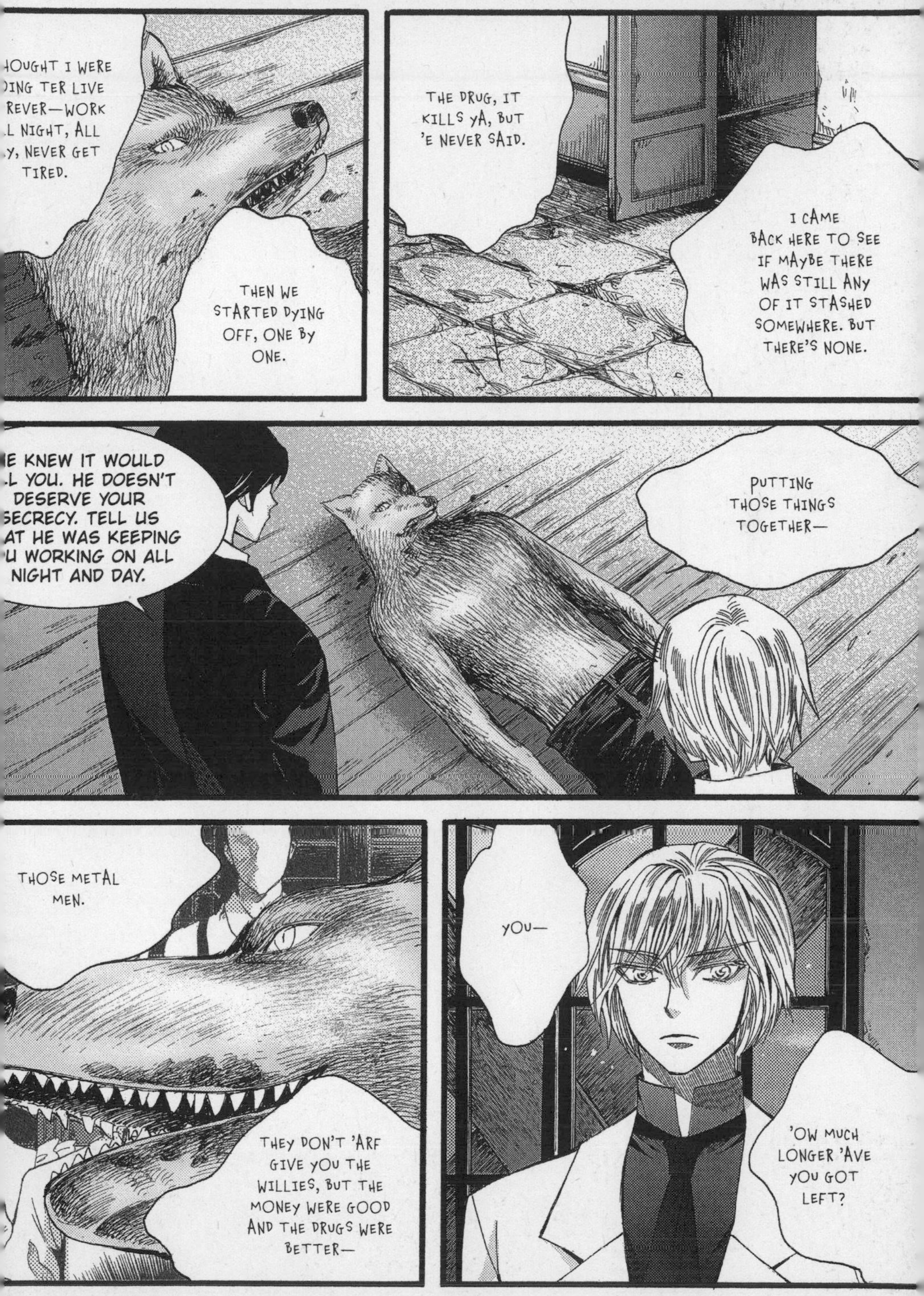

HOUGHT I WERE
DING TER LIVE
REVER—WORK
L NIGHT, ALL
Y, NEVER GET
TIRED.
THEN WE STARTED DYING OFF, ONE BY ONE.
THE DRUG, IT KILLS YA, BUT 'E NEVER SAID.
I CAME BACK HERE TO SEE IF MAYBE THERE WAS STILL ANY OF IT STASHED SOMEWHERE. BUT THERE'S NONE.
E KNEW IT WOULD
L YOU. HE DOESN'T
DESERVE YOUR
SECRECY. TELL US
AT HE WAS KEEPING
U WORKING ON ALL
NIGHT AND DAY.
PUTTING THOSE THINGS TOGETHER—
THOSE METAL MEN.
THEY DON'T 'ARF GIVE YOU THE WILLIES, BUT THE MONEY WERE GOOD AND THE DRUGS WERE BETTER—
YOU—
'OW MUCH LONGER 'AVE YOU GOT LEFT?

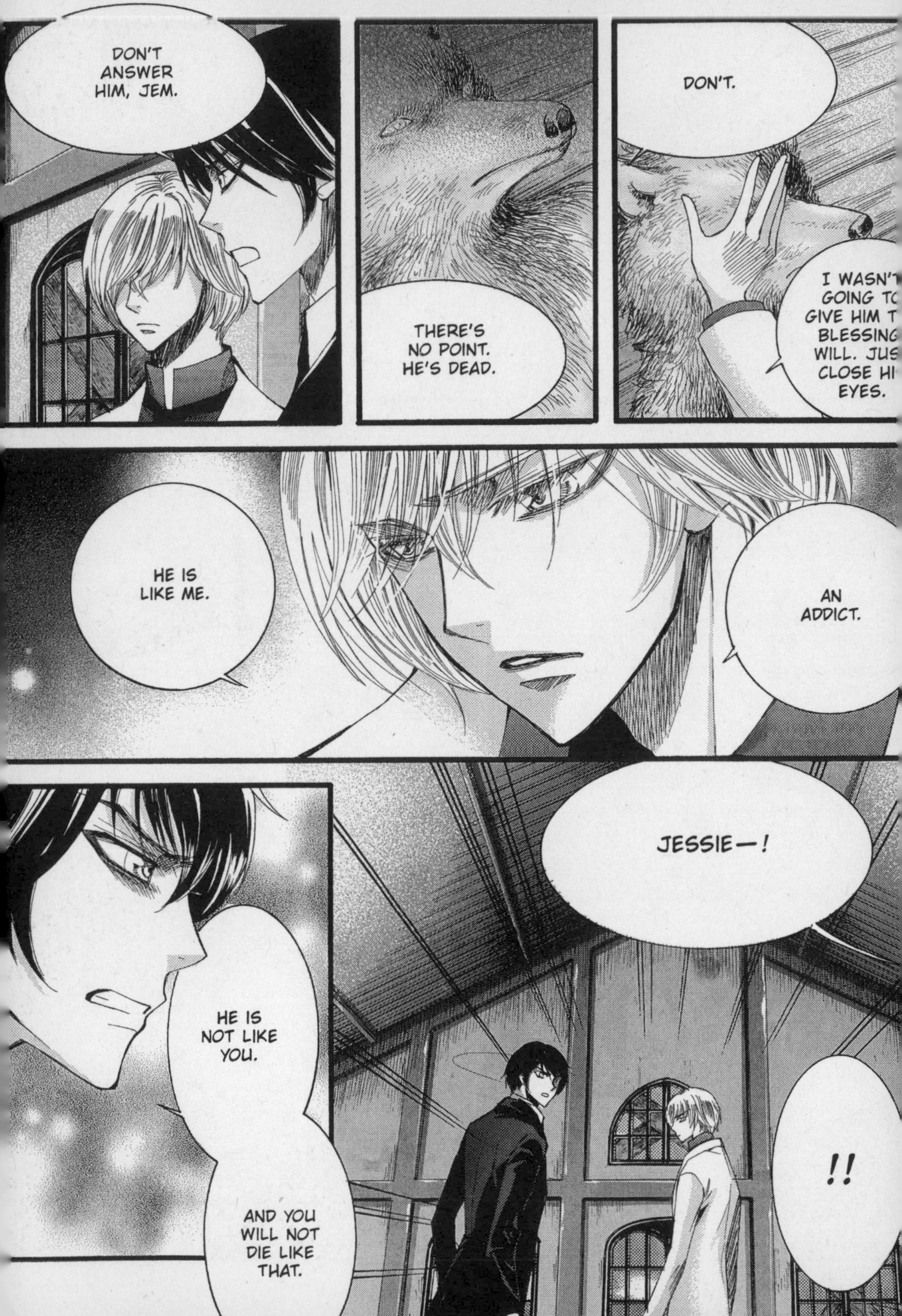
DON'T ANSWER HIM, JEM.
THERE'S NO POINT. HE'S DEAD.
DON'T.
I WASN'T GOING TO GIVE HIM THE BLESSING WILL. JUST CLOSE HIS EYES.
HE IS LIKE ME.
AN ADDICT.
JESSIE—!
HE IS NOT LIKE YOU.
AND YOU WILL NOT DIE LIKE THAT.
!!

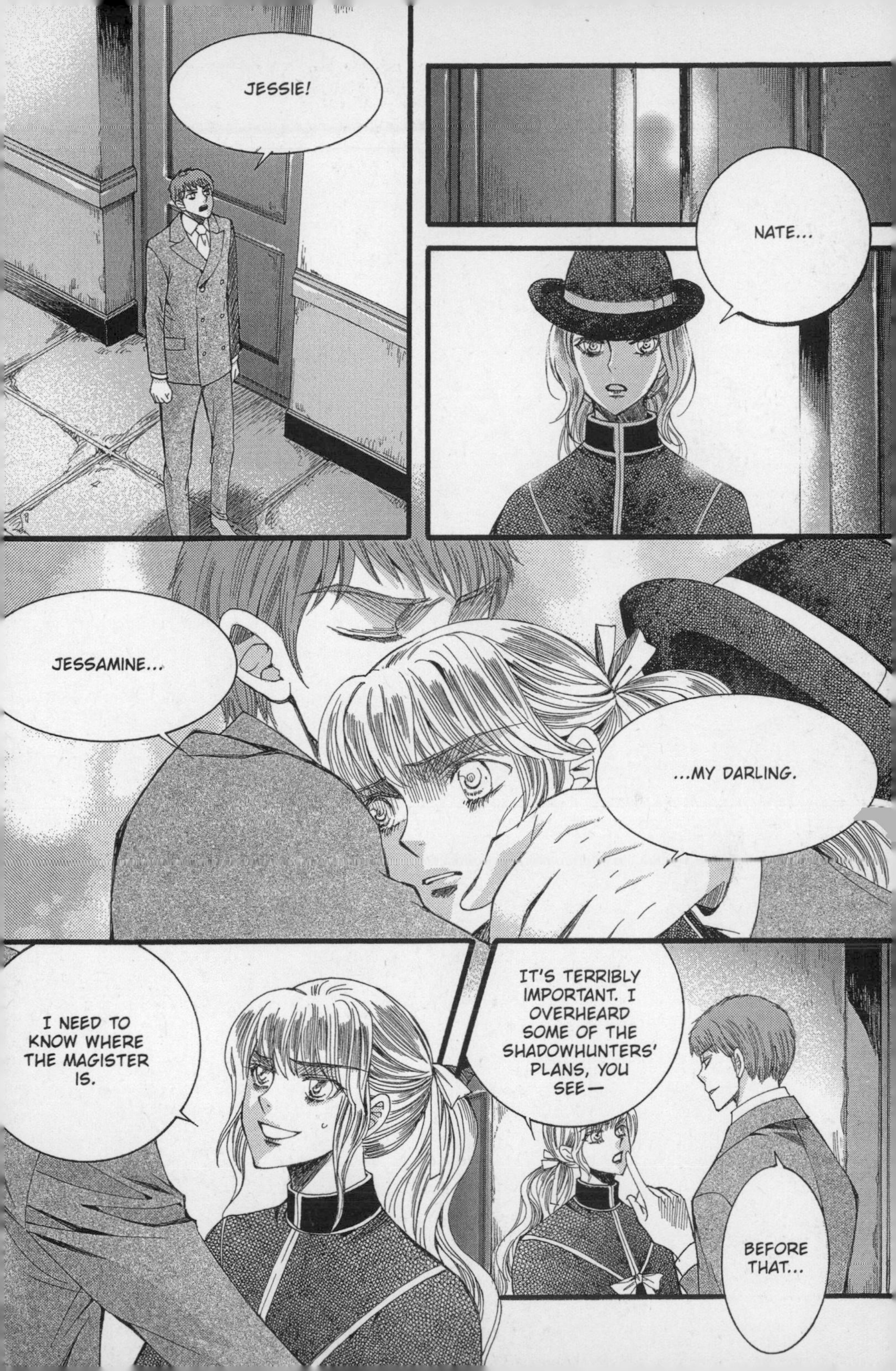
JESSIE!
NATE...
JESSAMINE...
...MY DARLING.
I NEED TO KNOW WHERE THE MAGISTER IS.
IT'S TERRIBLY IMPORTANT. I OVERHEARD SOME OF THE SHADOWHUNTERS' PLANS, YOU SEE—
BEFORE THAT...

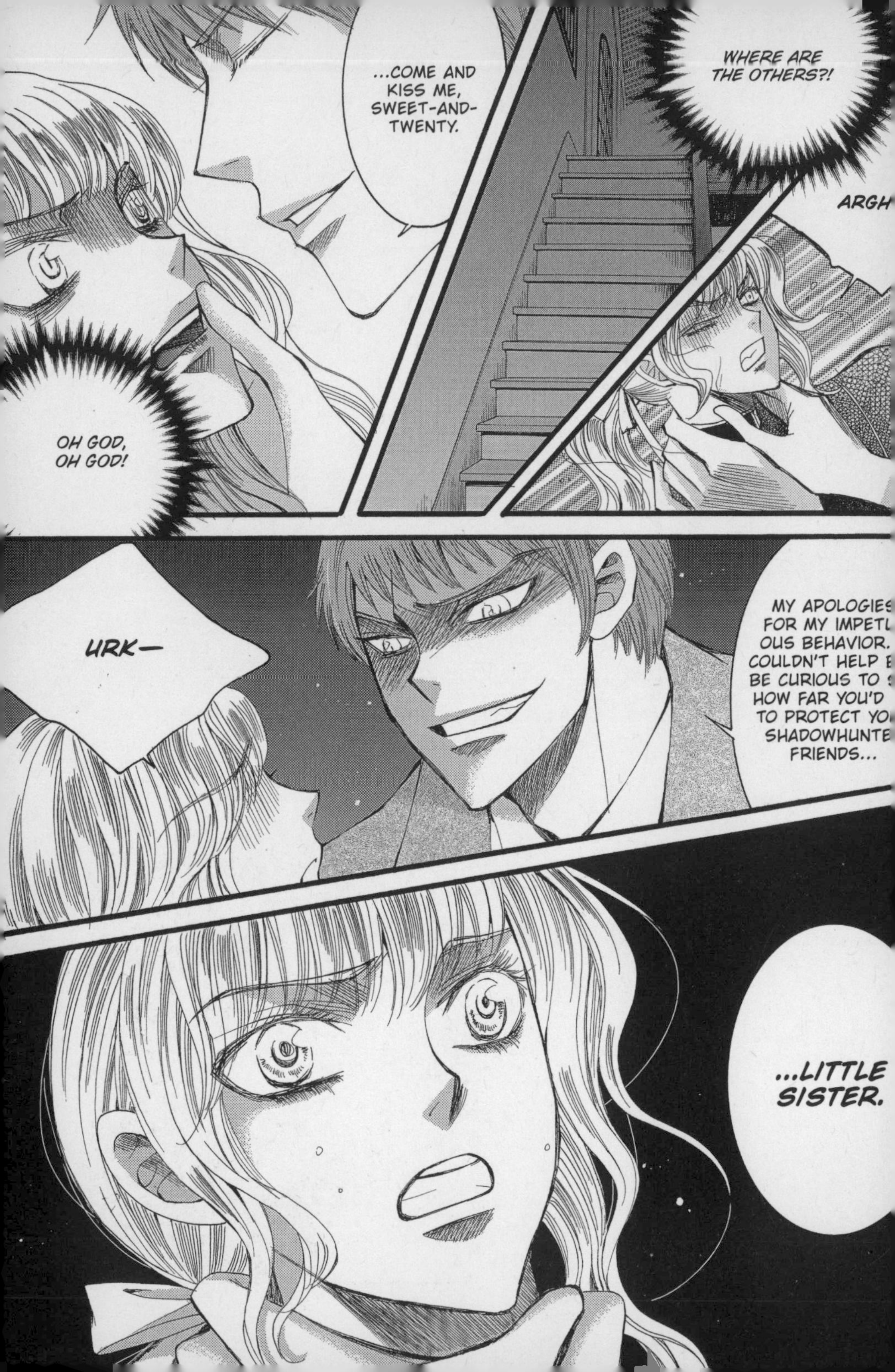

...COME AND KISS ME, SWEET-AND-TWENTY.
OH GOD, OH GOD!
WHERE ARE THE OTHERS?!
ARGH
URK—
MY APOLOGIES FOR MY IMPETU OUS BEHAVIOR. COULDN'T HELP B BE CURIOUS TO S HOW FAR YOU'D TO PROTECT YO SHADOWHUNTE FRIENDS...
...LITTLE SISTER.

THE INFERNAL DEVICES
CLOCKWORK PRINCE

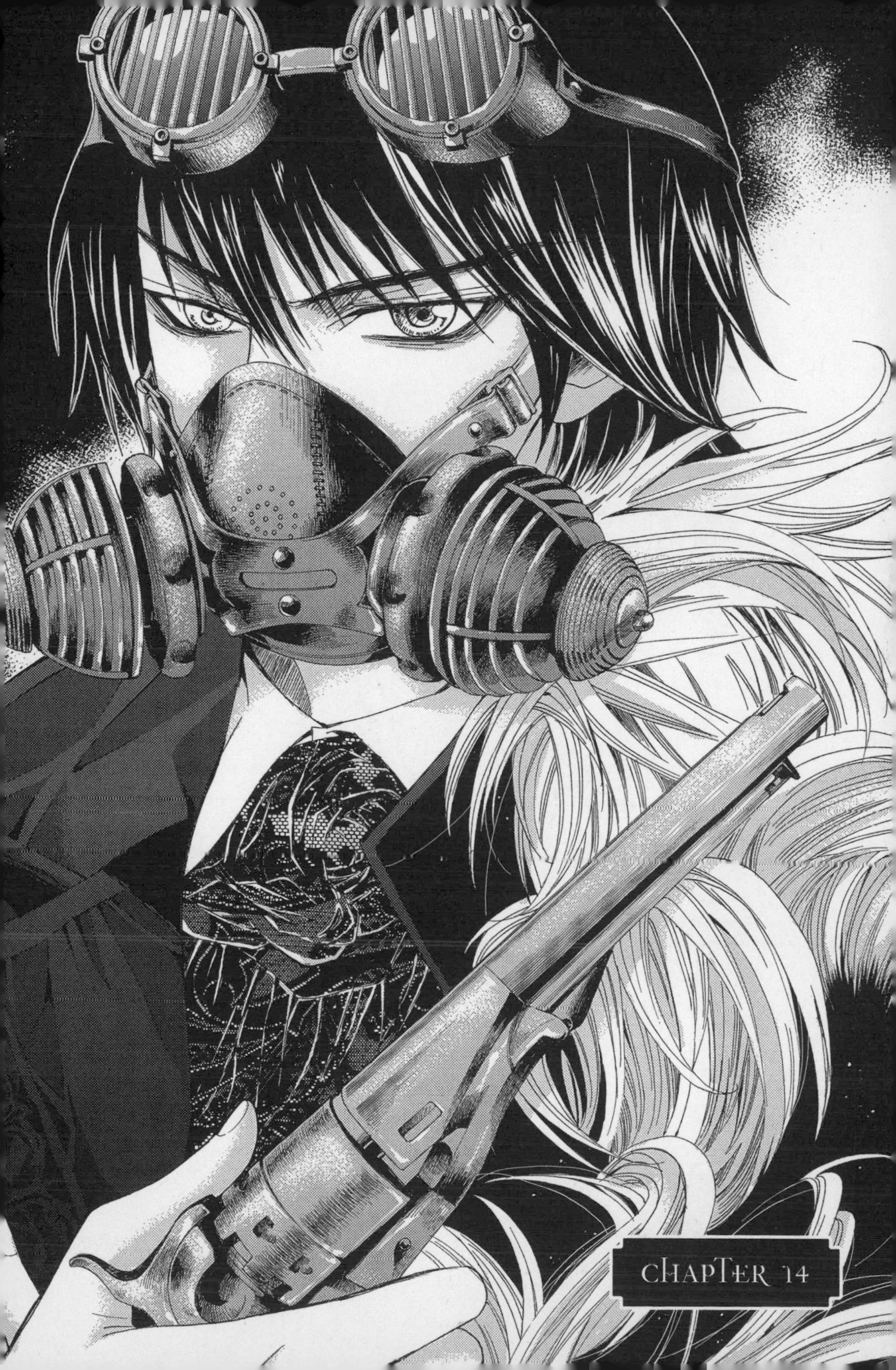
CHAPTER 14

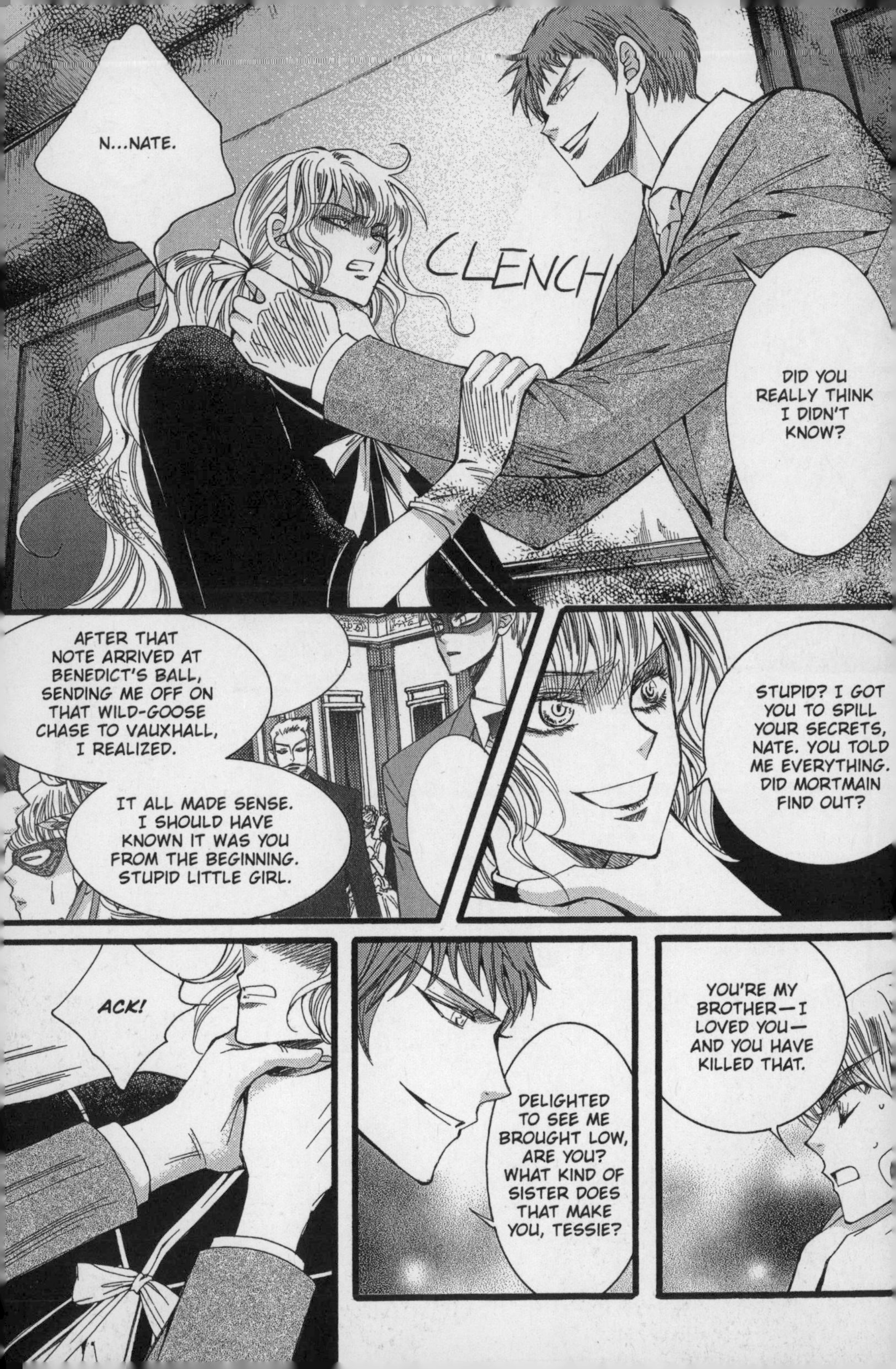
N...NATE.
CLENCH
DID YOU REALLY THINK I DIDN'T KNOW?
AFTER THAT NOTE ARRIVED AT BENEDICT'S BALL, SENDING ME OFF ON THAT WILD-GOOSE CHASE TO VAUXHALL, I REALIZED.
IT ALL MADE SENSE. I SHOULD HAVE KNOWN IT WAS YOU FROM THE BEGINNING. STUPID LITTLE GIRL.
STUPID? I GOT YOU TO SPILL YOUR SECRETS, NATE. YOU TOLD ME EVERYTHING. DID MORTMAIN FIND OUT?
ACK!
DELIGHTED TO SEE ME BROUGHT LOW, ARE YOU? WHAT KIND OF SISTER DOES THAT MAKE YOU, TESSIE?
YOU'RE MY BROTHER—I LOVED YOU—AND YOU HAVE KILLED THAT.

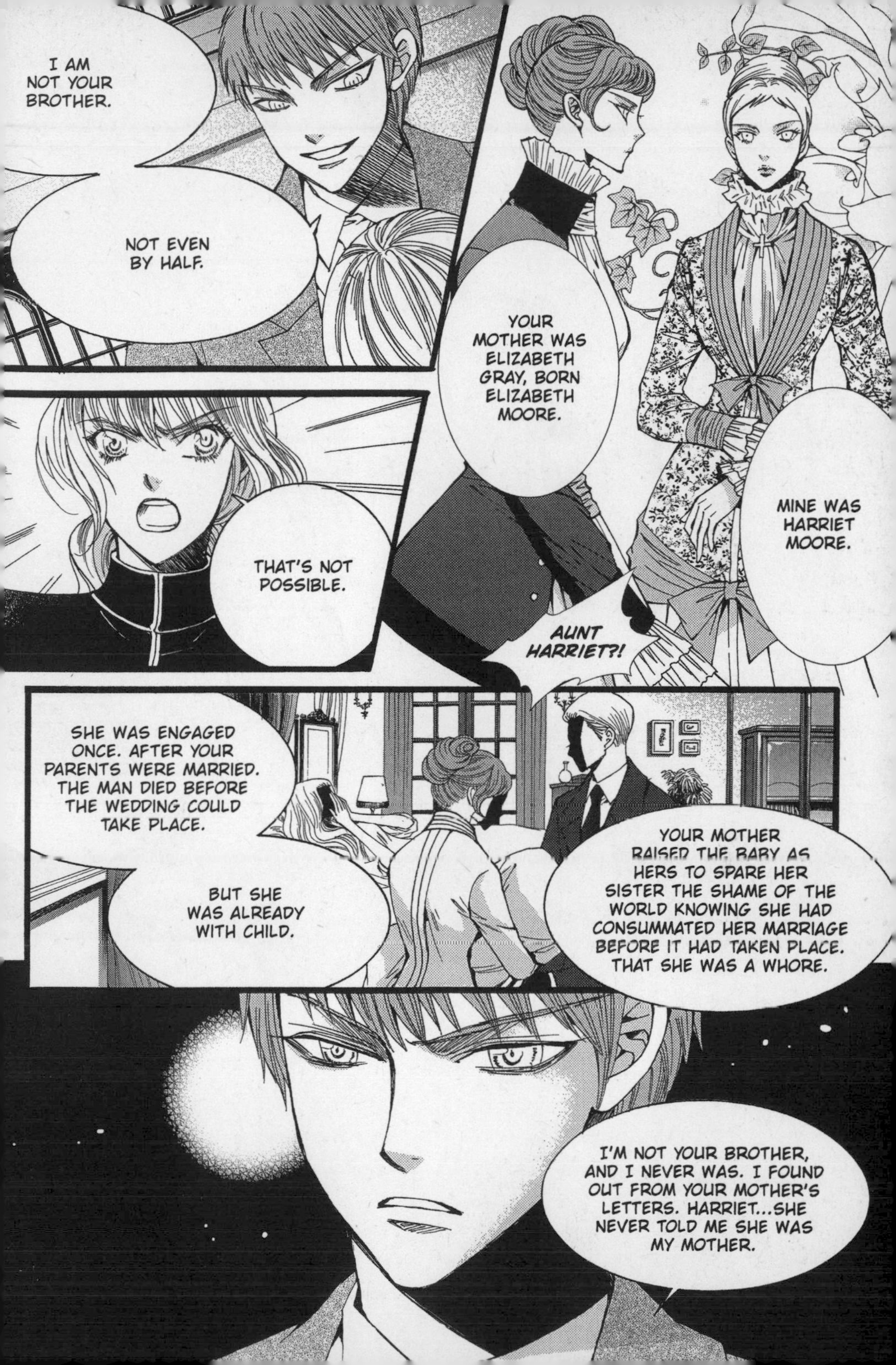
I AM NOT YOUR BROTHER.
NOT EVEN BY HALF.
YOUR MOTHER WAS ELIZABETH GRAY, BORN ELIZABETH MOORE.
MINE WAS HARRIET MOORE.
THAT'S NOT POSSIBLE.
AUNT HARRIET?!
SHE WAS ENGAGED ONCE. AFTER YOUR PARENTS WERE MARRIED. THE MAN DIED BEFORE THE WEDDING COULD TAKE PLACE.
BUT SHE WAS ALREADY WITH CHILD.
YOUR MOTHER RAISED THE BABY AS HERS TO SPARE HER SISTER THE SHAME OF THE WORLD KNOWING SHE HAD CONSUMMATED HER MARRIAGE BEFORE IT HAD TAKEN PLACE. THAT SHE WAS A WHORE.
I'M NOT YOUR BROTHER, AND I NEVER WAS. I FOUND OUT FROM YOUR MOTHER'S LETTERS. HARRIET...SHE NEVER TOLD ME SHE WAS MY MOTHER.

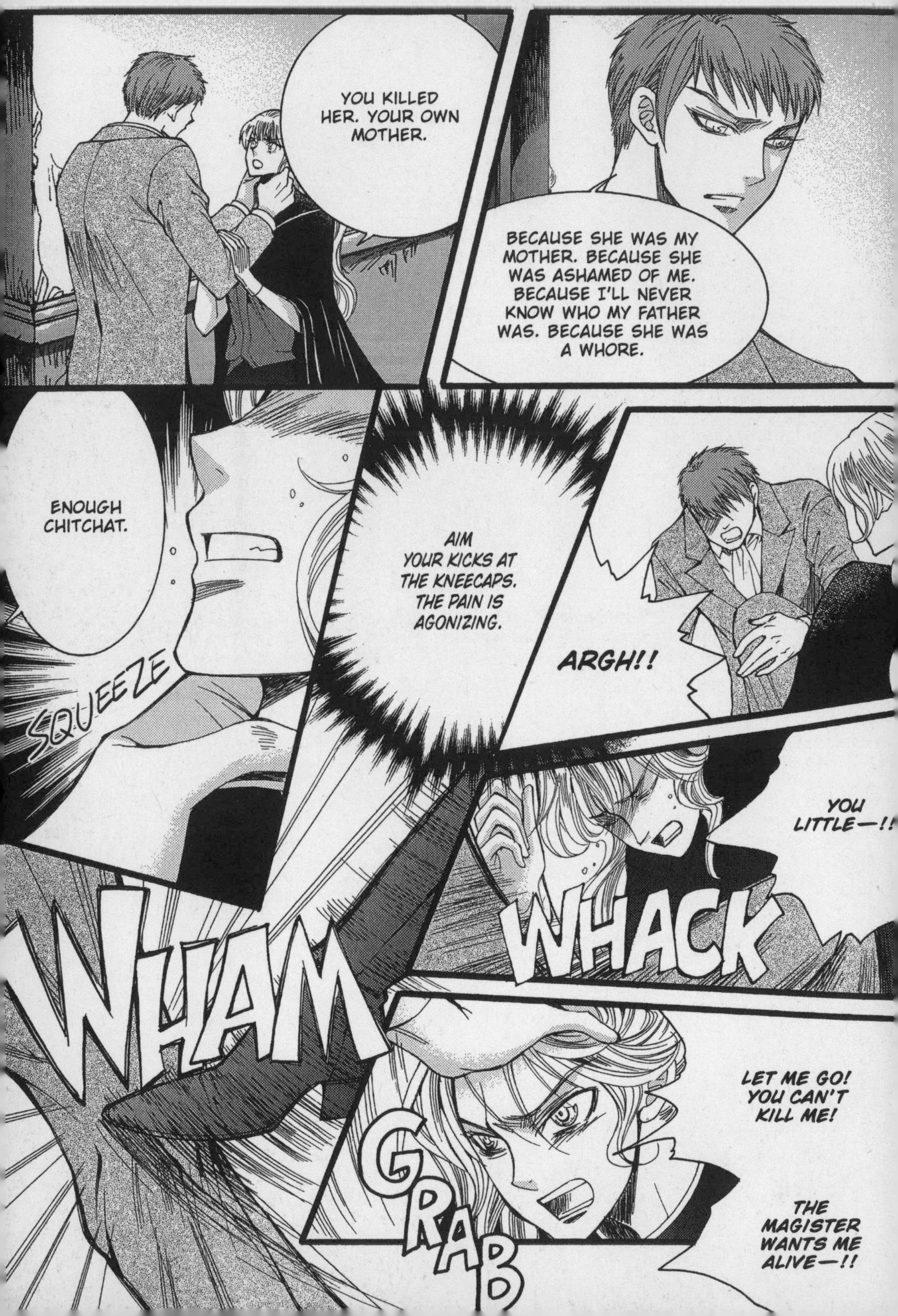
YOU KILLED HER. YOUR OWN MOTHER.
BECAUSE SHE WAS MY MOTHER. BECAUSE SHE WAS ASHAMED OF ME. BECAUSE I'LL NEVER KNOW WHO MY FATHER WAS. BECAUSE SHE WAS A WHORE.
ENOUGH CHITCHAT.
SQUEEZE
AIM YOUR KICKS AT THE KNEECAPS. THE PAIN IS AGONIZING.
ARGH!!
WHAM
YOU LITTLE—!!
WHACK
LET ME GO! YOU CAN'T KILL ME!
THE MAGISTER WANTS ME ALIVE—!!
GRAB

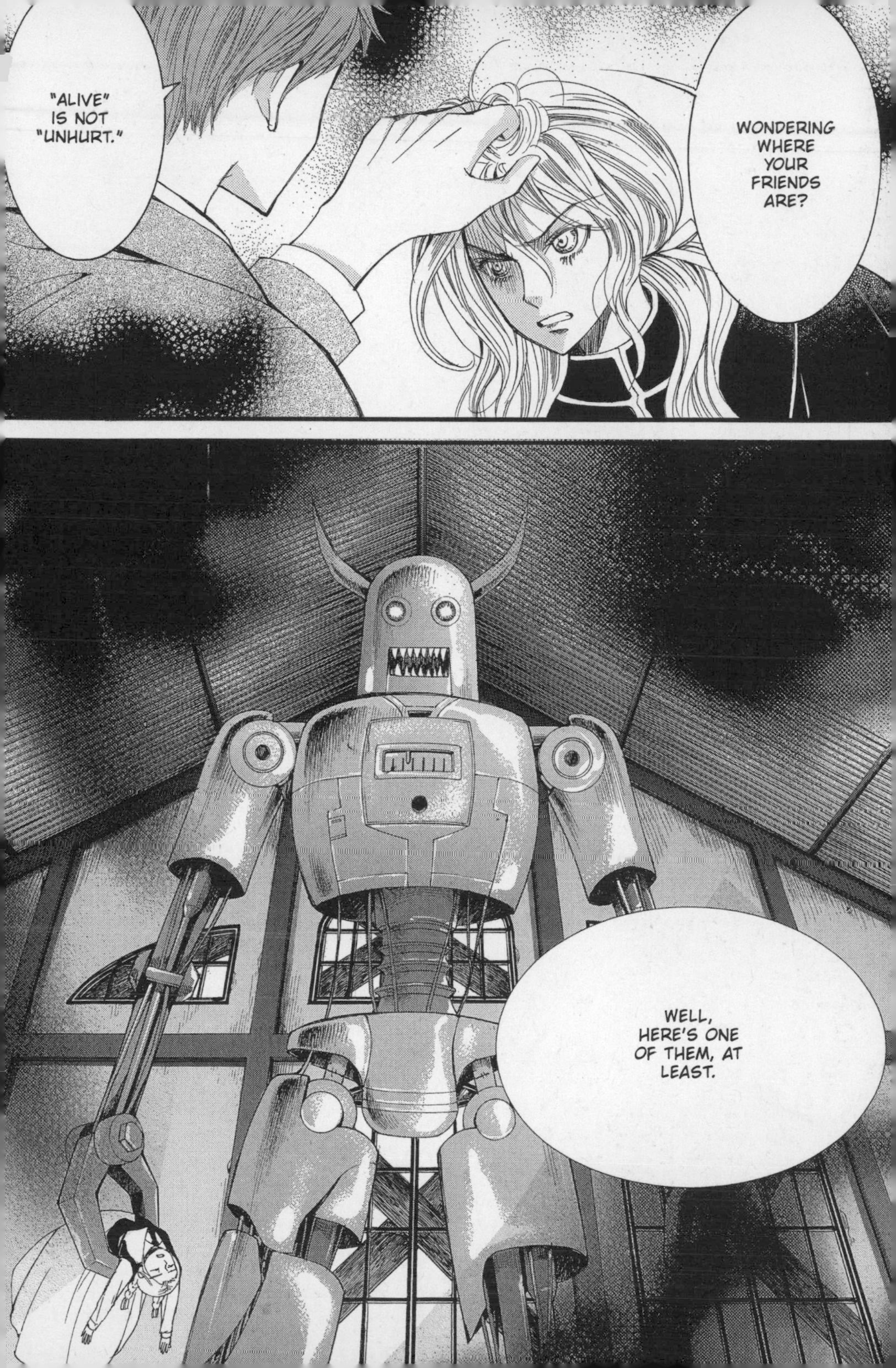
WONDERING WHERE YOUR FRIENDS ARE?
"ALIVE" IS NOT "UNHURT."
WELL, HERE'S ONE OF THEM, AT LEAST.

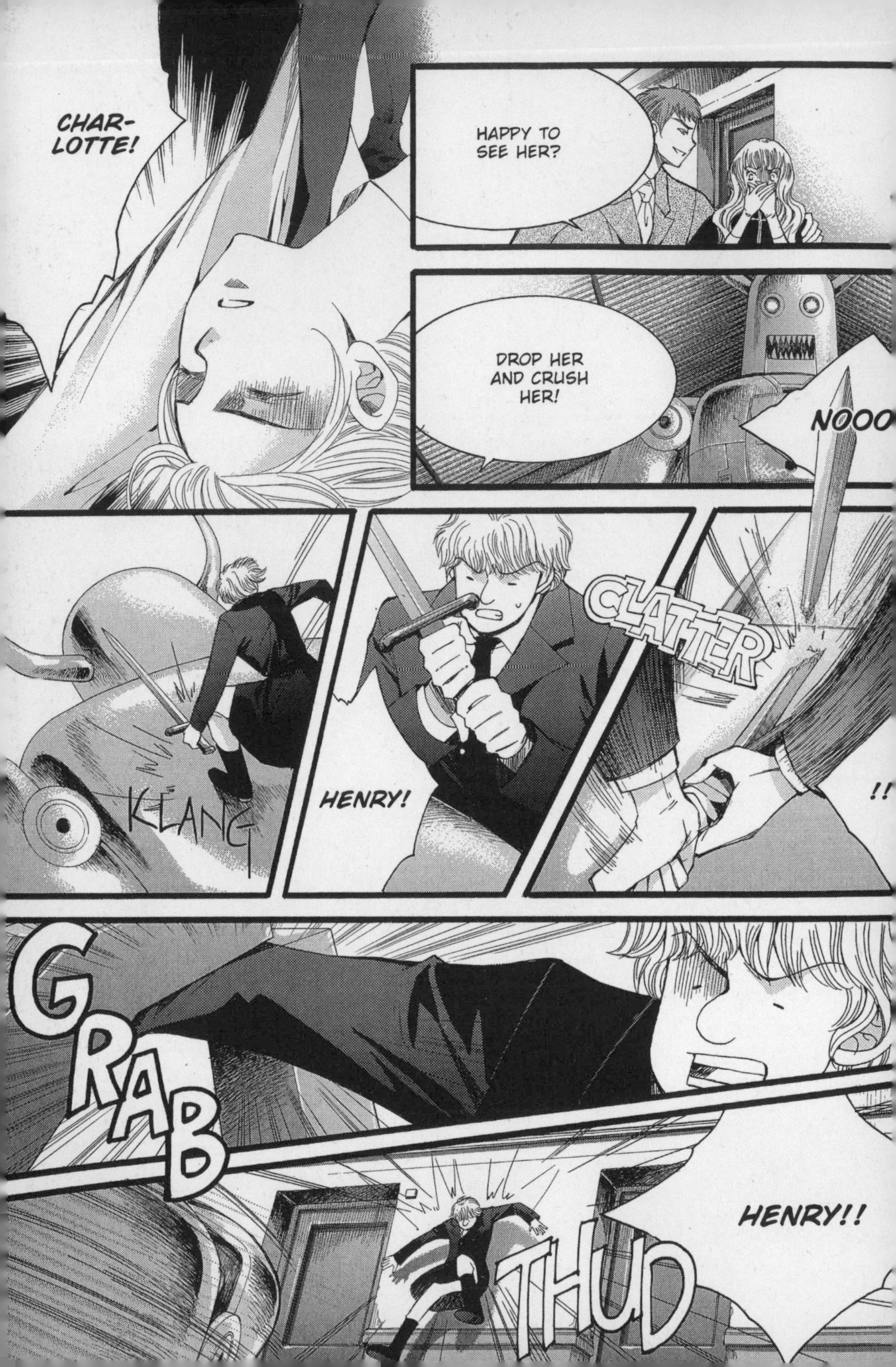
HAPPY TO SEE HER?
DROP HER AND CRUSH HER!
NOOO
CHAR-LOTTE!
!!
CLATTER
HENRY!
KLANG
GRAB
HENRY!!
THUD

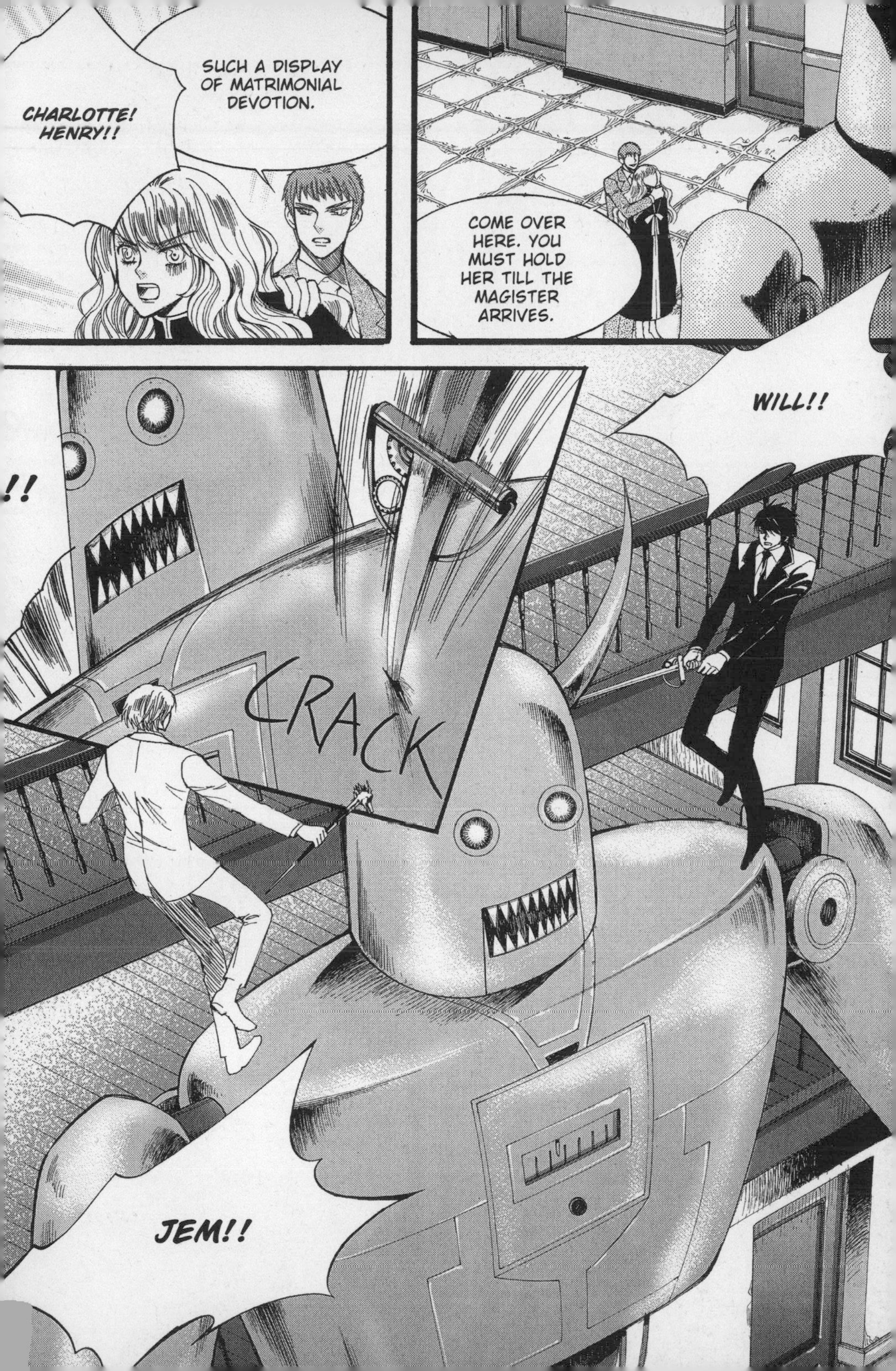
CHARLOTTE! HENRY!!
SUCH A DISPLAY OF MATRIMONIAL DEVOTION.
COME OVER HERE. YOU MUST HOLD HER TILL THE MAGISTER ARRIVES.
!!
WILL!!
CRACK
JEM!!

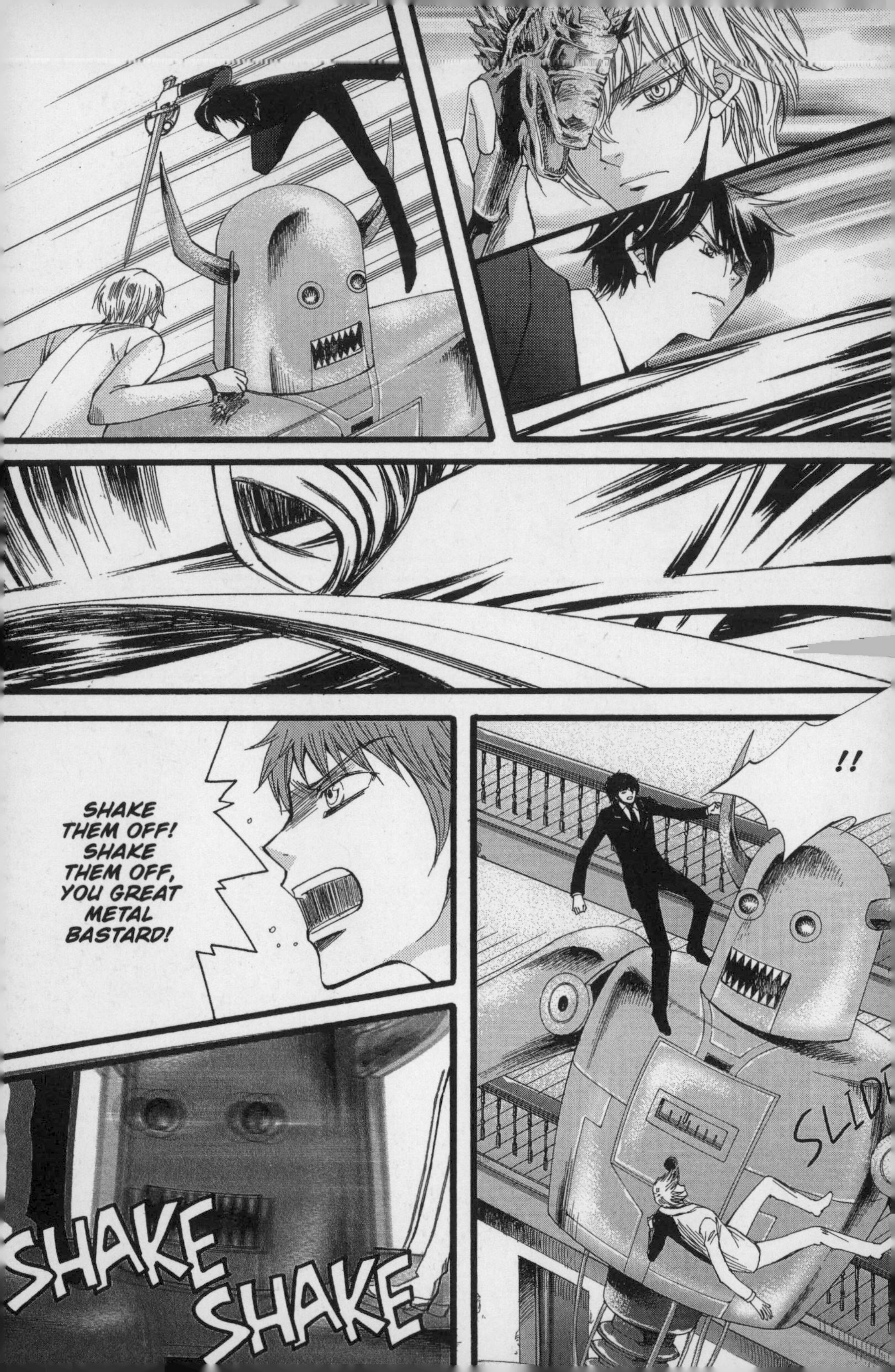
!!
SHAKE THEM OFF! SHAKE THEM OFF, YOU GREAT METAL BASTARD!
SHAKE SHAKE
SLIDE

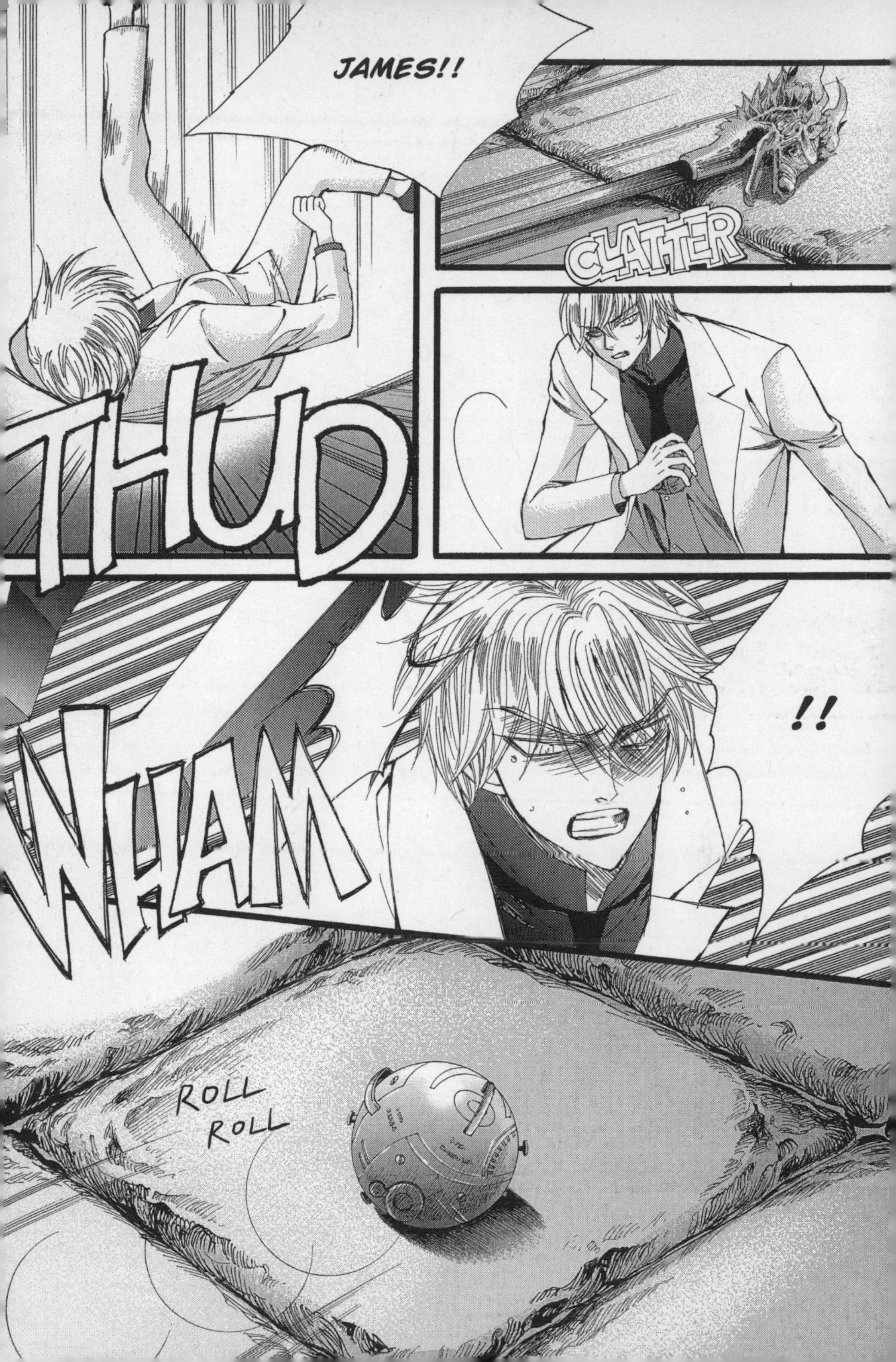
JAMES!!
CLATTER
THUD
!!
WHAM
ROLL
ROLL

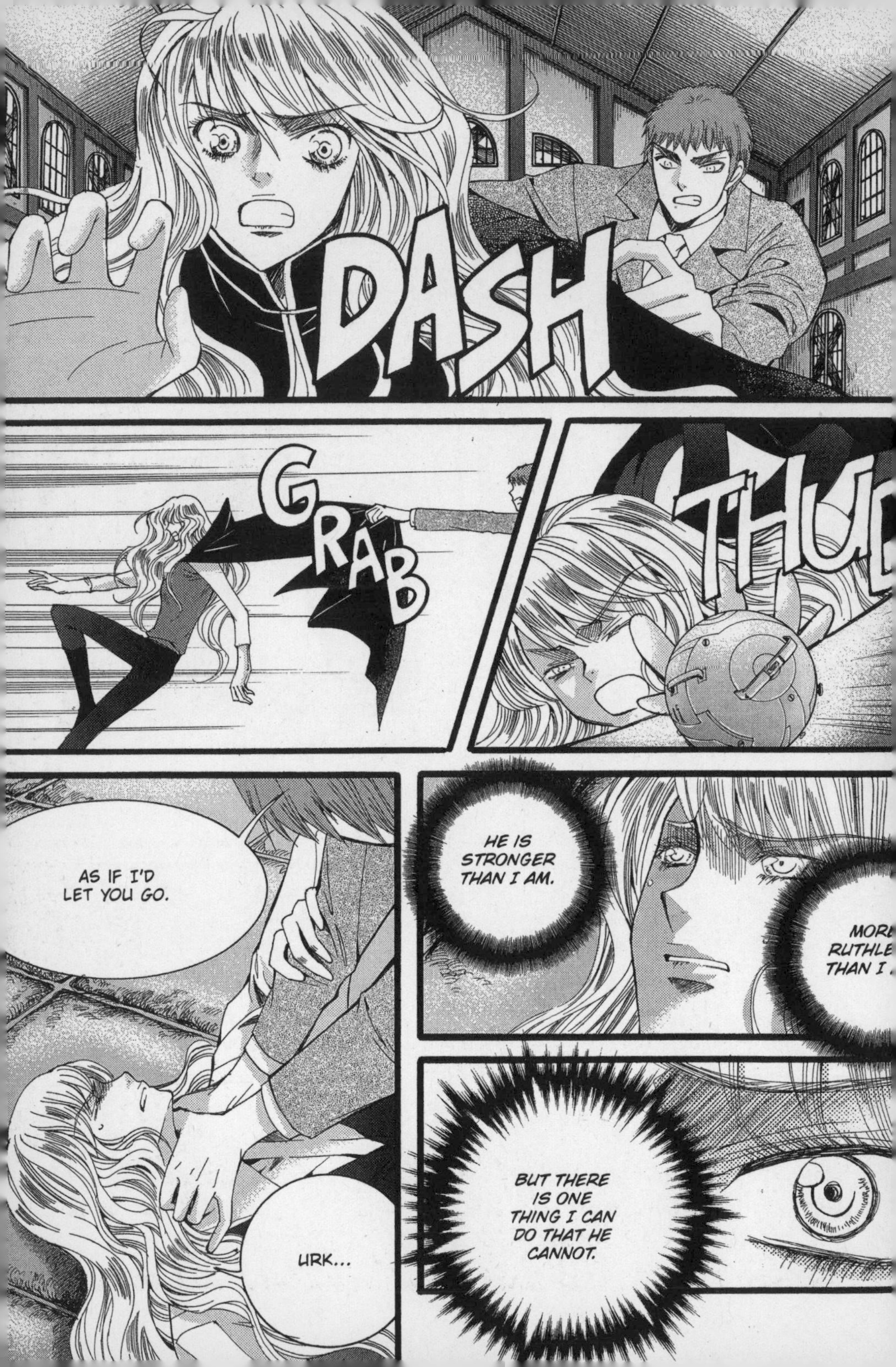
DASH
GRAB
THU
AS IF I'D LET YOU GO.
URK...
HE IS STRONGER THAN I AM.
MORE RUTHLE THAN I
BUT THERE IS ONE THING I CAN DO THAT HE CANNOT.

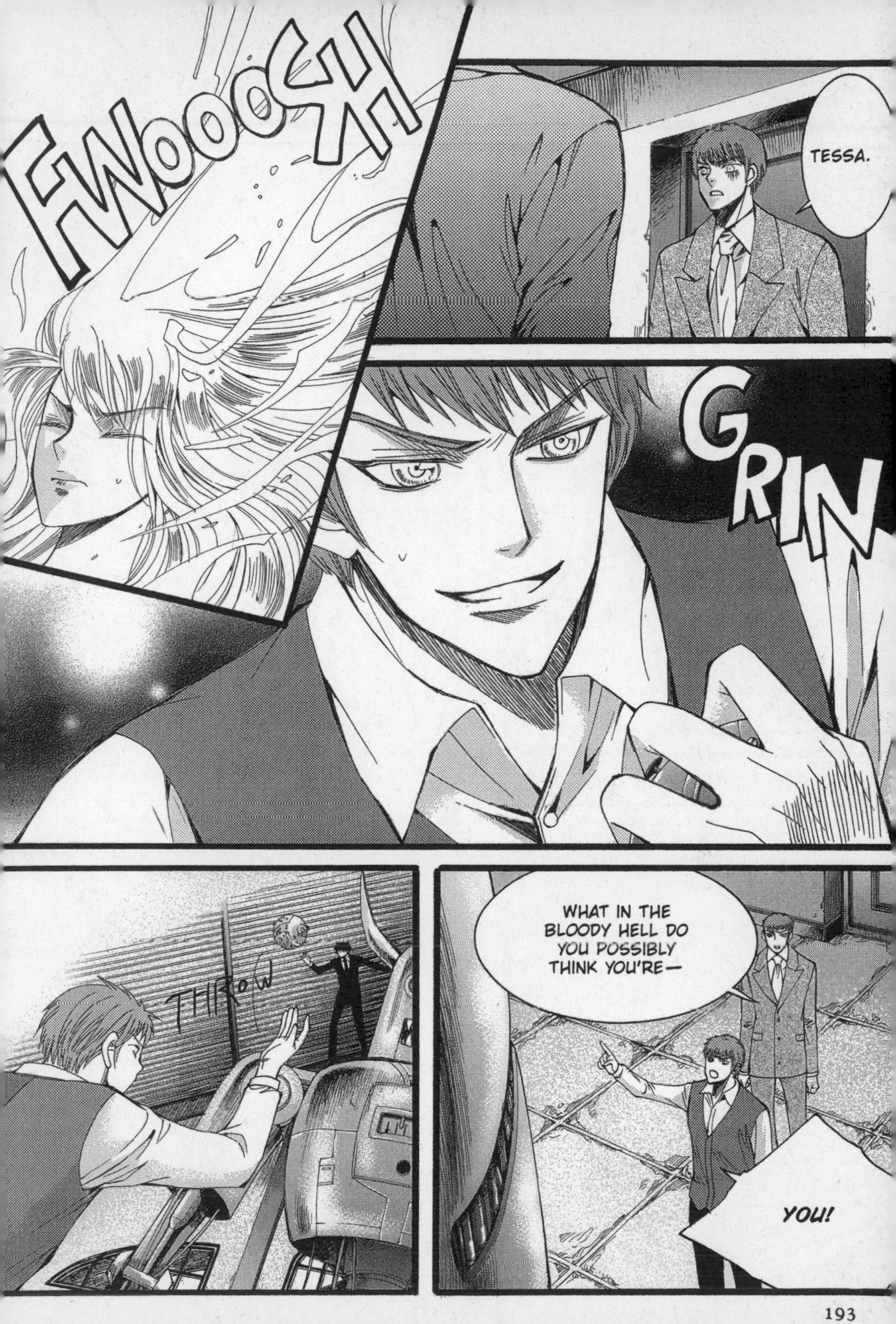
FWOOOSH
TESSA.
GRIN
THROW
WHAT IN THE BLOODY HELL DO YOU POSSIBLY THINK YOU'RE—
YOU!

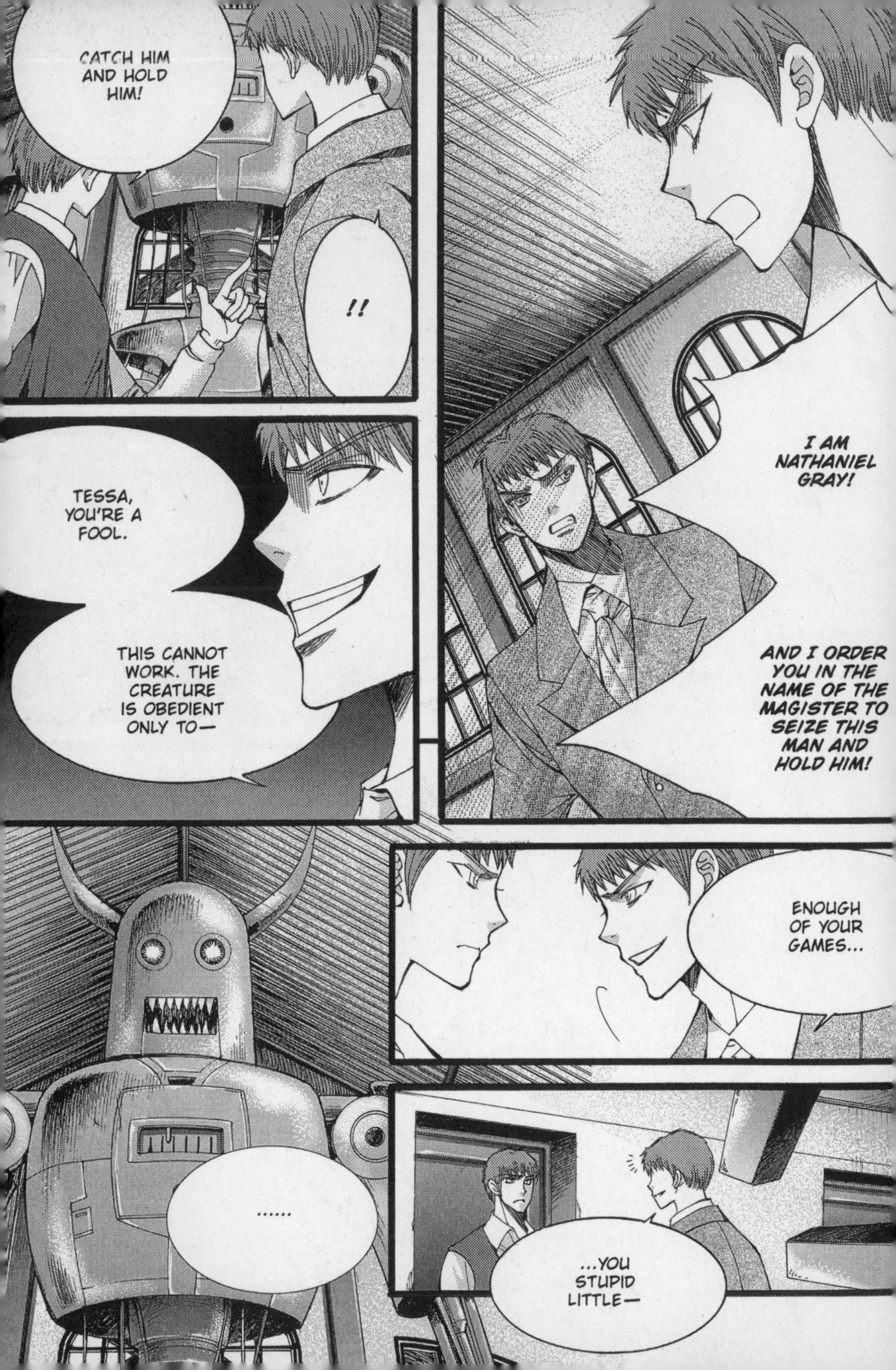
CATCH HIM AND HOLD HIM!
!!
TESSA, YOU'RE A FOOL.
THIS CANNOT WORK. THE CREATURE IS OBEDIENT ONLY TO—
I AM NATHANIEL GRAY!
AND I ORDER YOU IN THE NAME OF THE MAGISTER TO SEIZE THIS MAN AND HOLD HIM!
ENOUGH OF YOUR GAMES...
......
...YOU STUPID LITTLE—

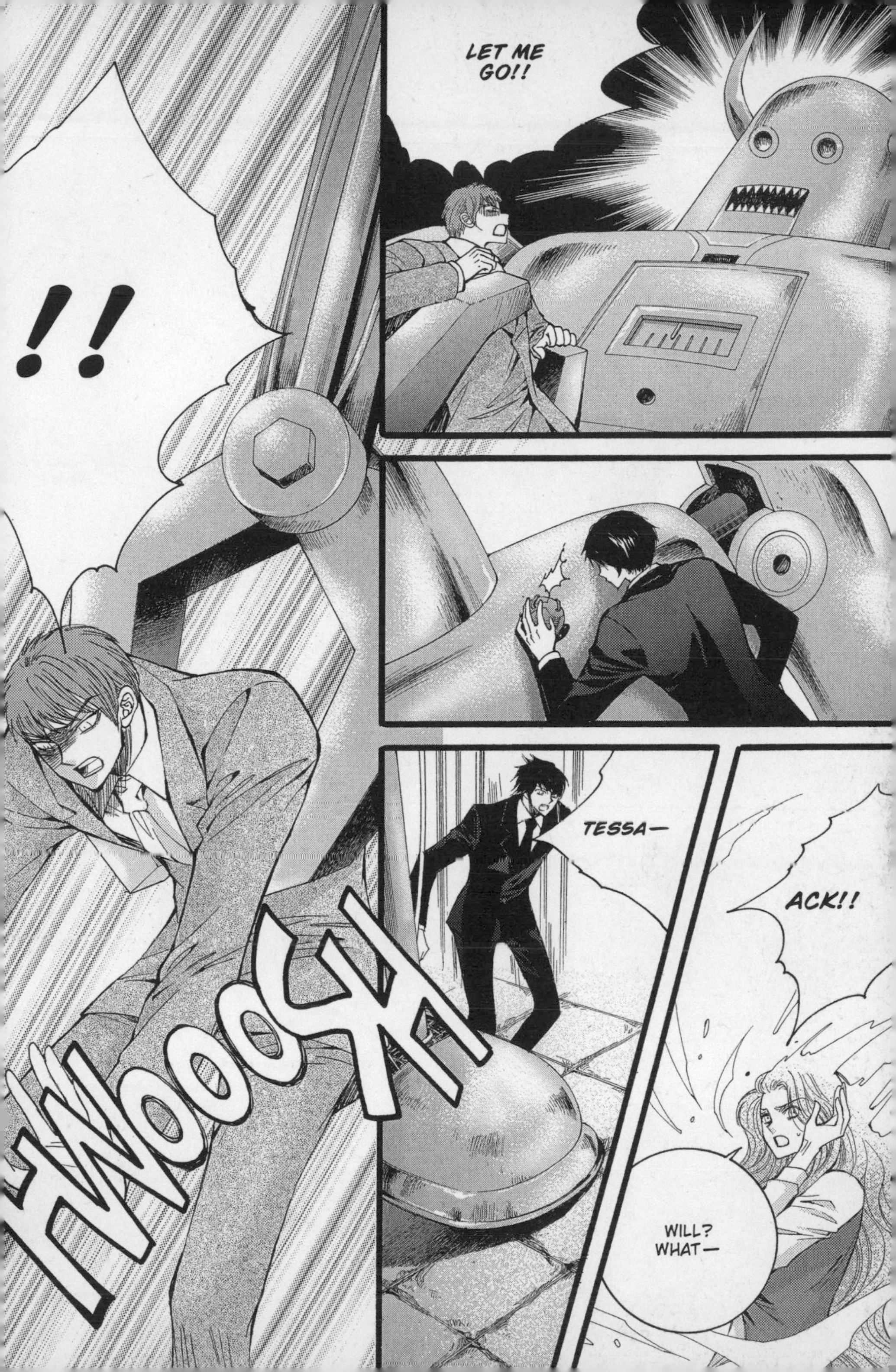
LET ME GO!!
!!
TESSA—
ACK!!
WILL? WHAT—
WHOOSH

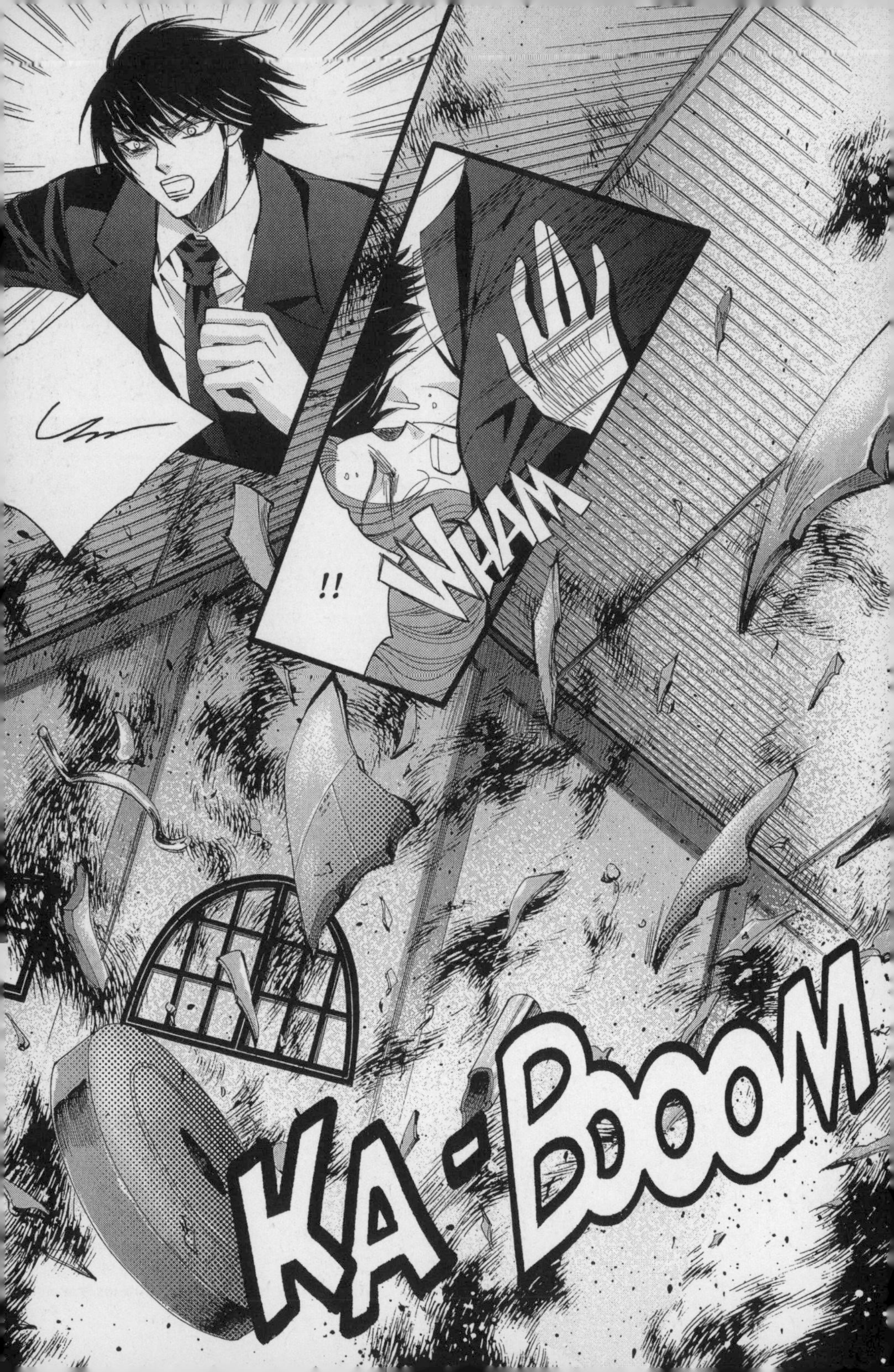

WHAM
!!
KA-BOOM

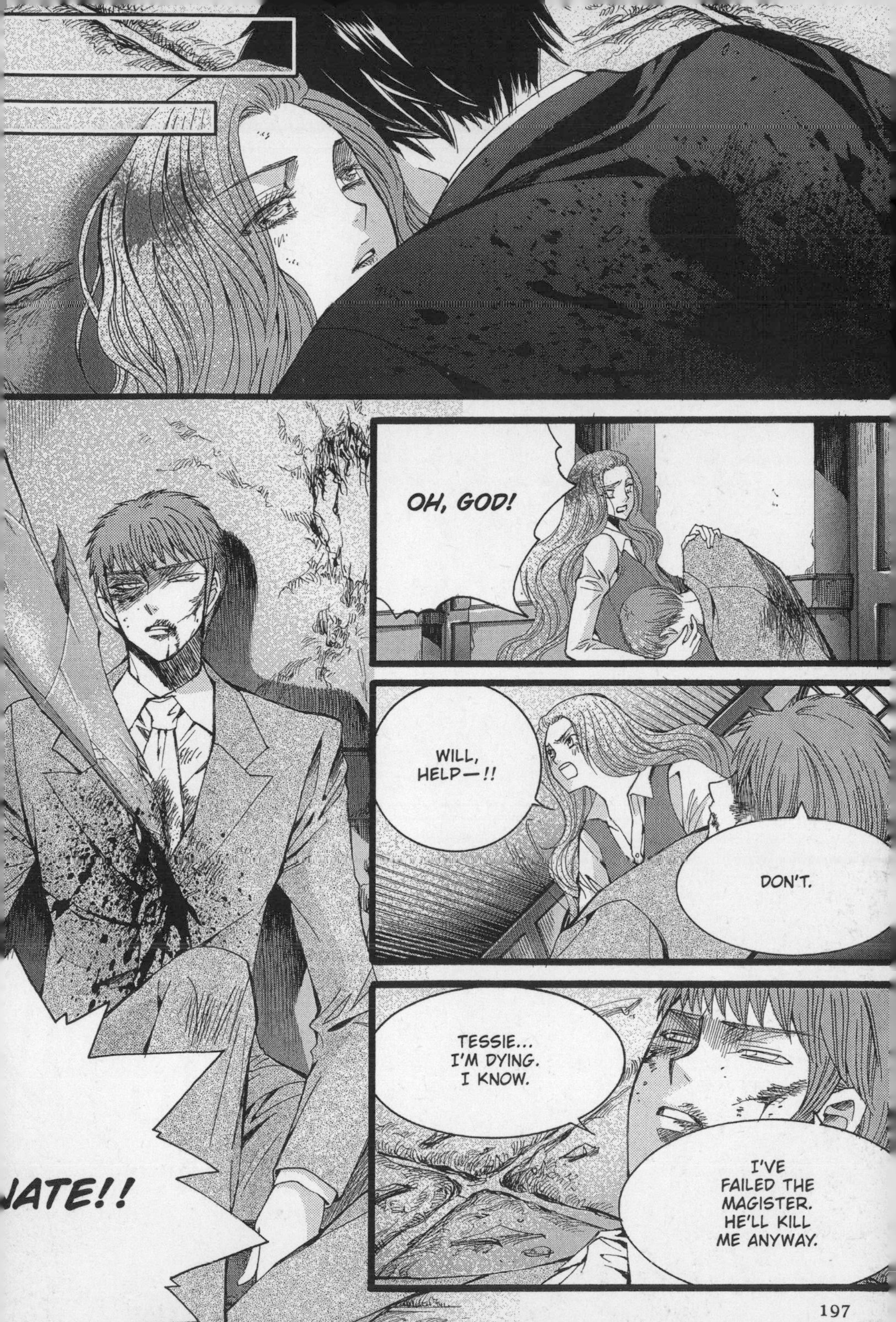
NATE!!
OH, GOD!
WILL, HELP—!!
DON'T.
TESSIE... I'M DYING. I KNOW.
I'VE FAILED THE MAGISTER. HE'LL KILL ME ANYWAY.

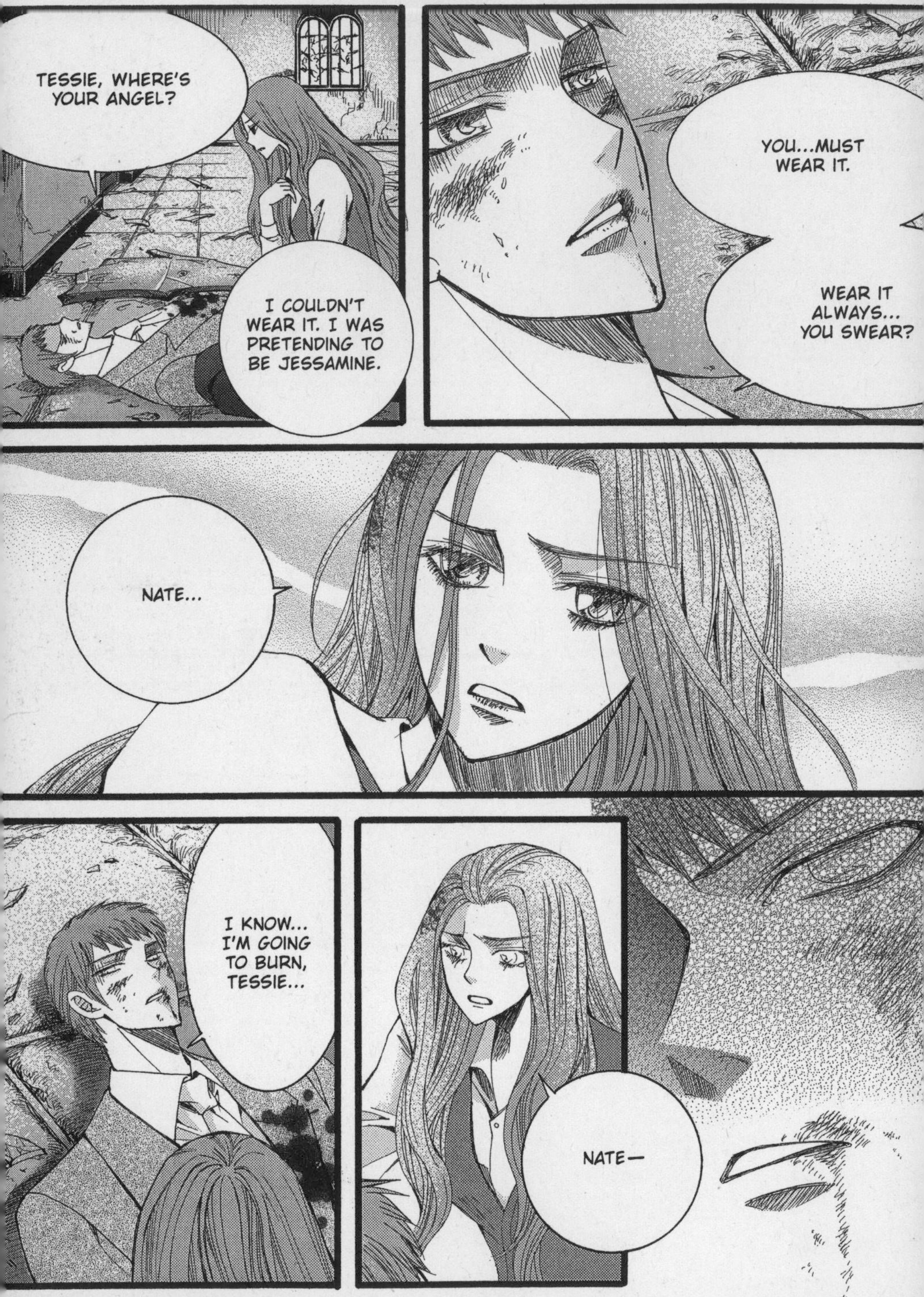
TESSIE, WHERE'S YOUR ANGEL?
I COULDN'T WEAR IT. I WAS PRETENDING TO BE JESSAMINE.
YOU...MUST WEAR IT.
WEAR IT ALWAYS... YOU SWEAR?
NATE...
I KNOW... I'M GOING TO BURN, TESSIE...
NATE—

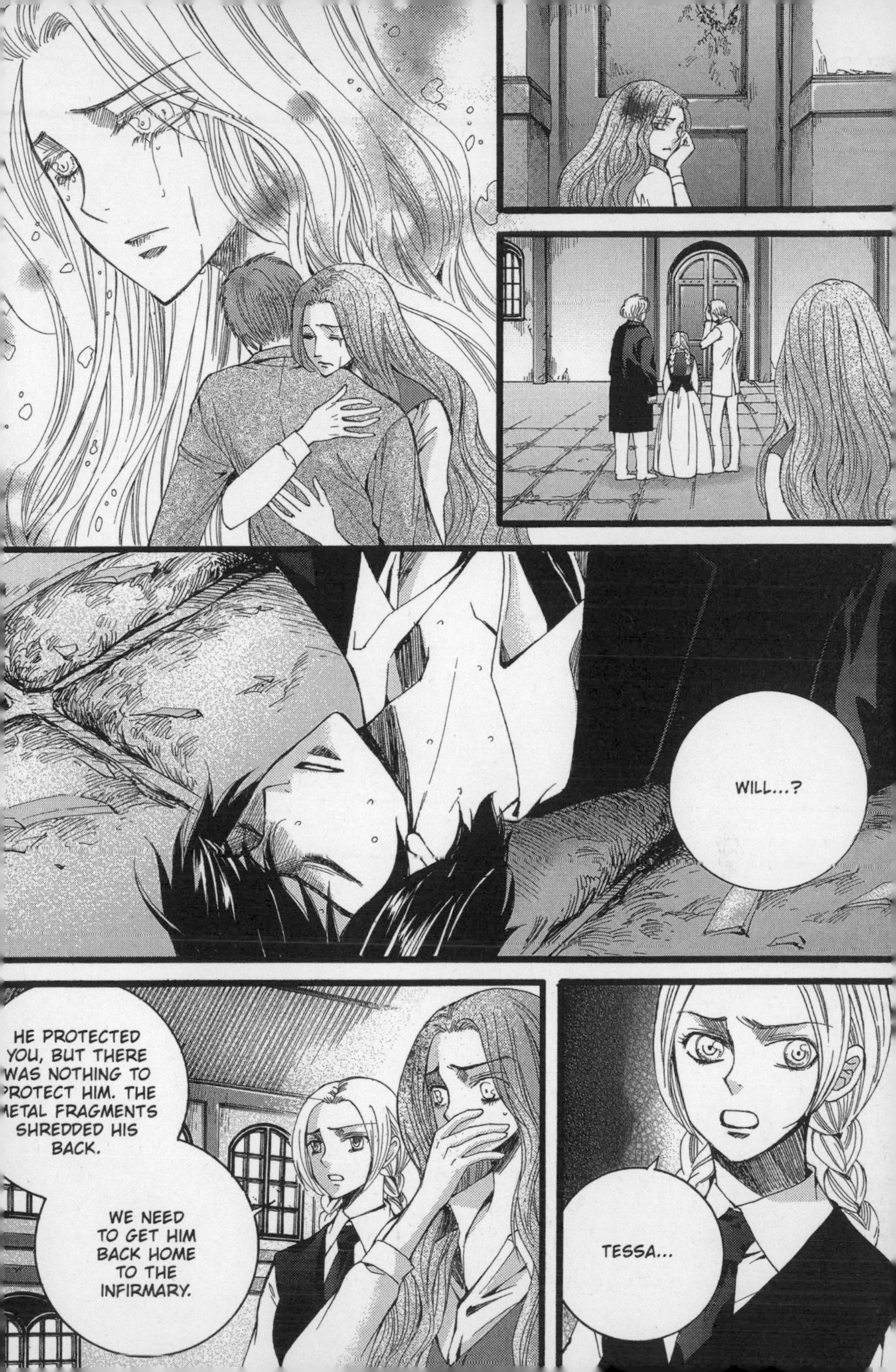
WILL...?
TESSA...
HE PROTECTED YOU, BUT THERE WAS NOTHING TO PROTECT HIM. THE METAL FRAGMENTS SHREDDED HIS BACK.
WE NEED TO GET HIM BACK HOME TO THE INFIRMARY.

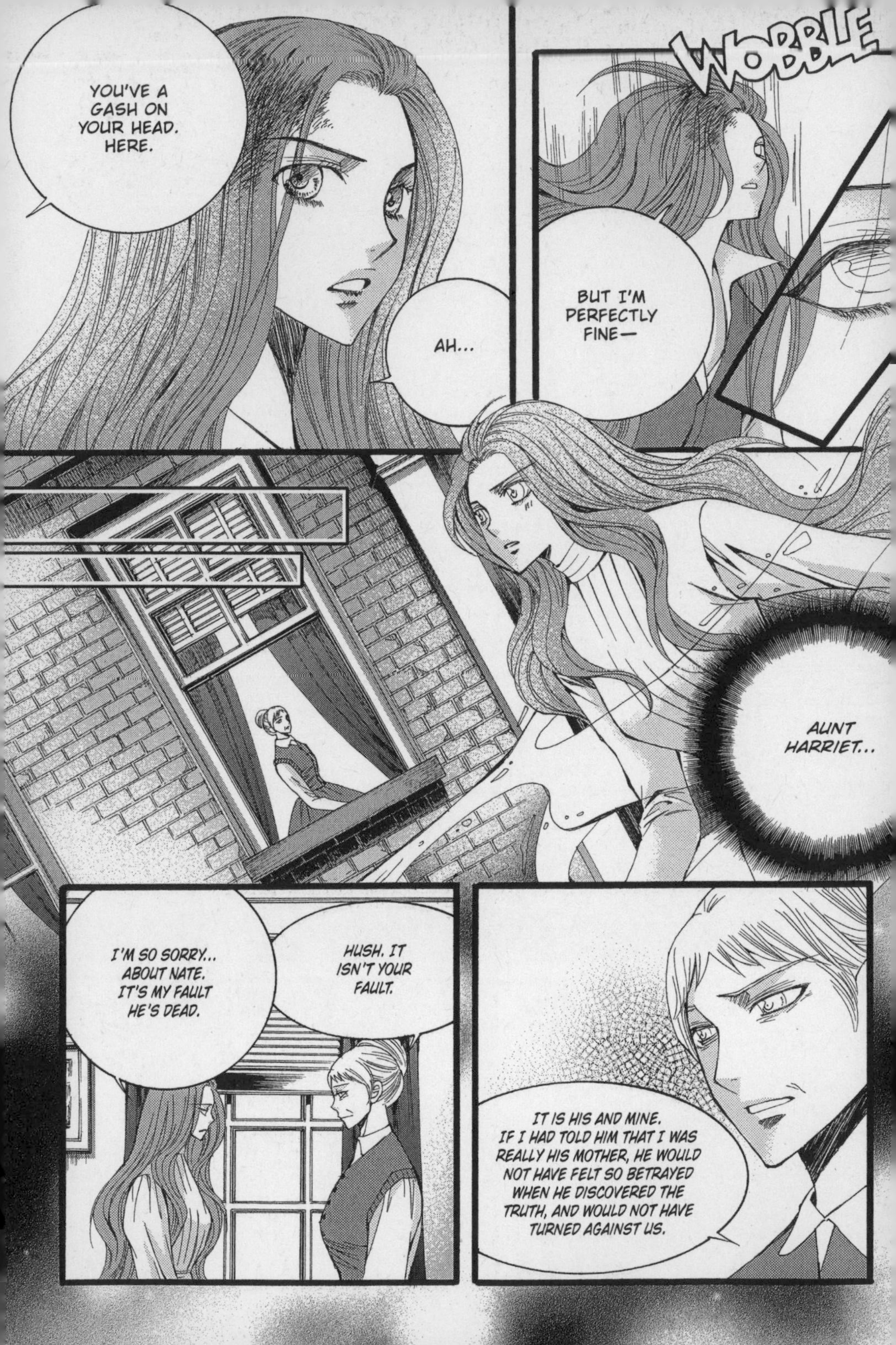
YOU'VE A GASH ON YOUR HEAD. HERE.
AH...
WOBBLE
BUT I'M PERFECTLY FINE—
AUNT HARRIET...
I'M SO SORRY... ABOUT NATE. IT'S MY FAULT HE'S DEAD.
HUSH. IT ISN'T YOUR FAULT.
IT IS HIS AND MINE. IF I HAD TOLD HIM THAT I WAS REALLY HIS MOTHER, HE WOULD NOT HAVE FELT SO BETRAYED WHEN HE DISCOVERED THE TRUTH, AND WOULD NOT HAVE TURNED AGAINST US.

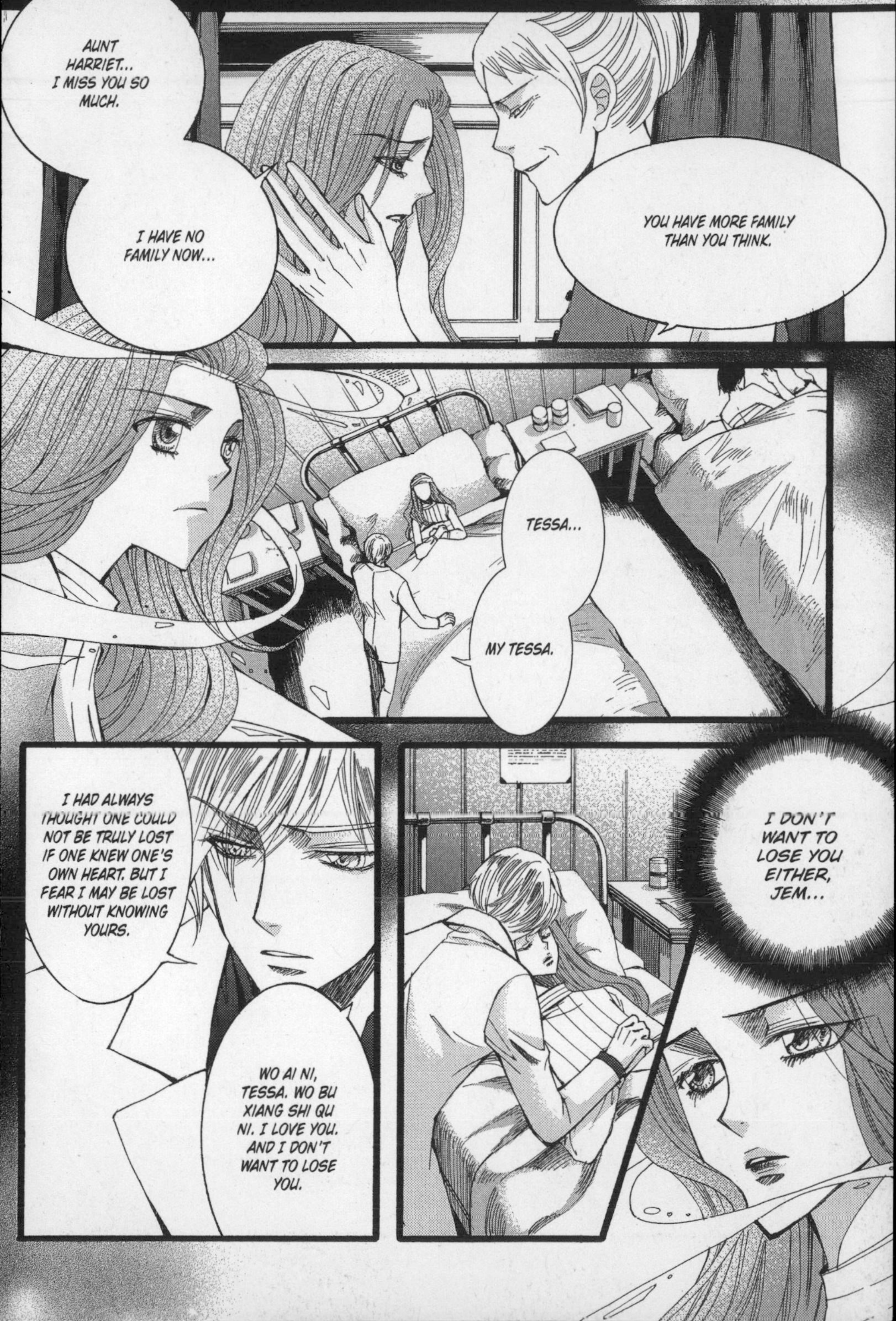
AUNT HARRIET... I MISS YOU SO MUCH.
I HAVE NO FAMILY NOW...
YOU HAVE MORE FAMILY THAN YOU THINK.
TESSA...
MY TESSA.
I HAD ALWAYS THOUGHT ONE COULD NOT BE TRULY LOST IF ONE KNEW ONE'S OWN HEART. BUT I FEAR I MAY BE LOST WITHOUT KNOWING YOURS.
WO AI NI, TESSA. WO BU XIANG SHI QU NI. I LOVE YOU. AND I DON'T WANT TO LOSE YOU.
I DON'T WANT TO LOSE YOU EITHER, JEM...

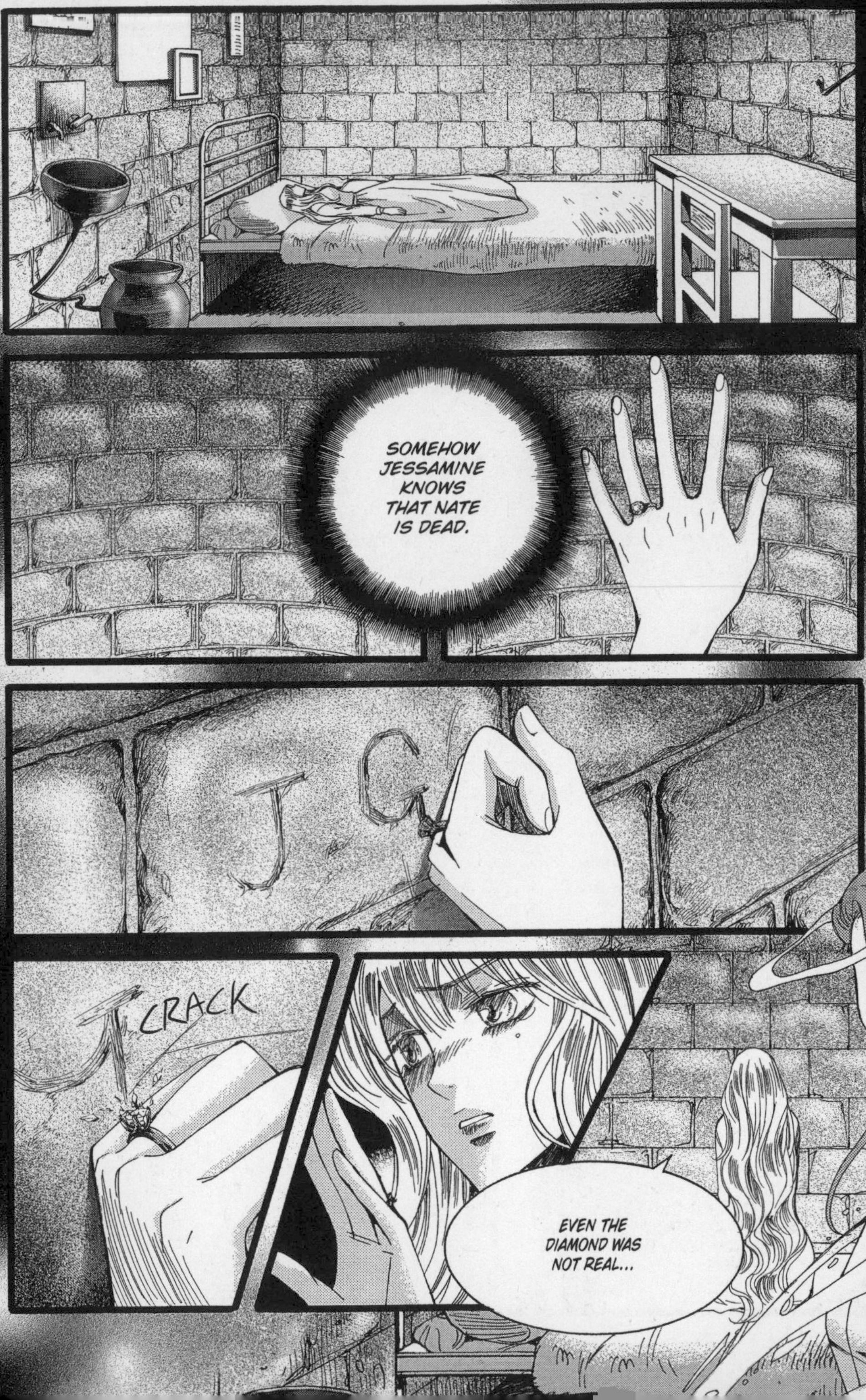
SOMEHOW JESSAMINE KNOWS THAT NATE IS DEAD.
CRACK
EVEN THE DIAMOND WAS NOT REAL...

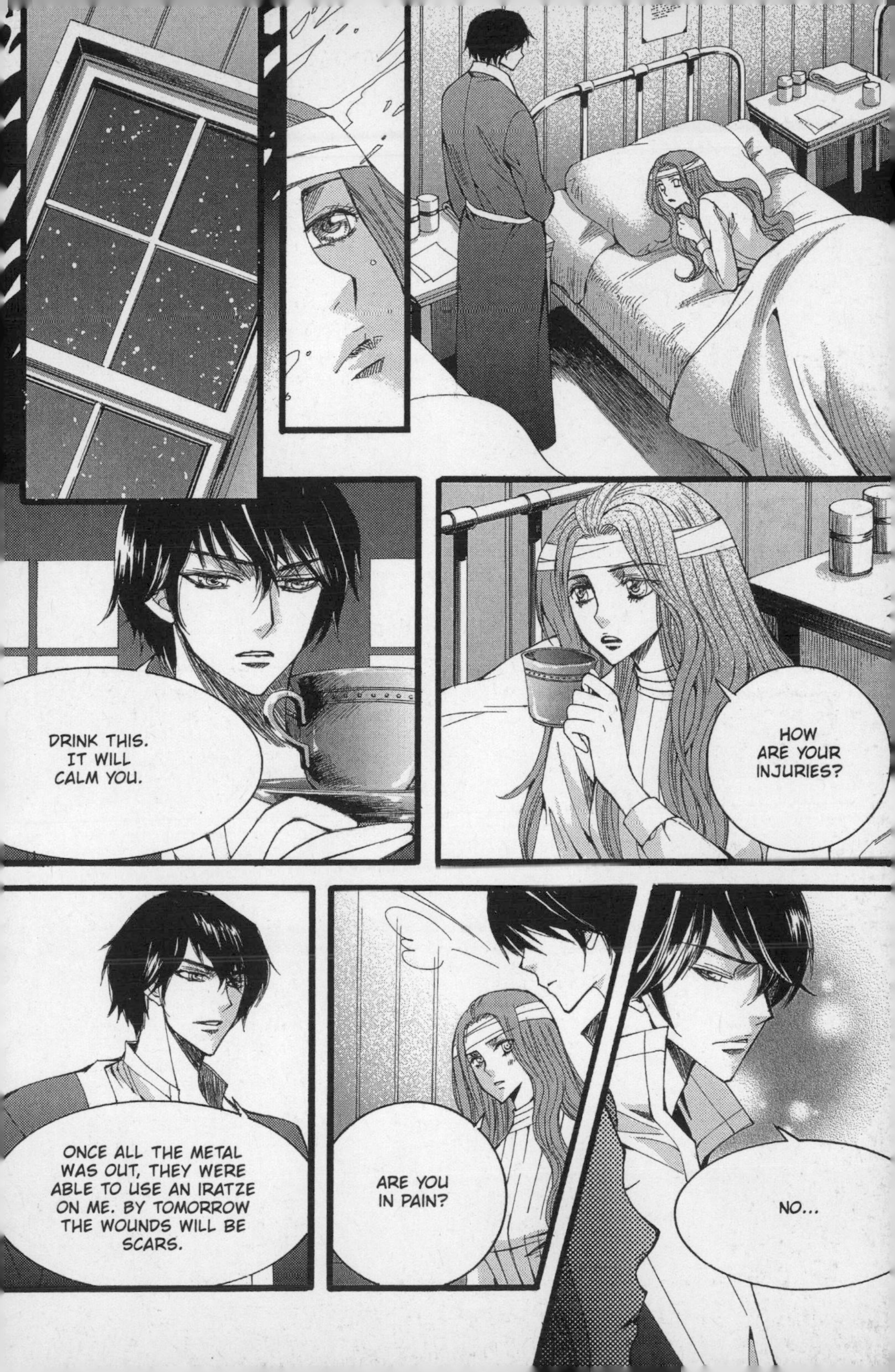
DRINK THIS. IT WILL CALM YOU.
HOW ARE YOUR INJURIES?
ONCE ALL THE METAL WAS OUT, THEY WERE ABLE TO USE AN IRATZE ON ME. BY TOMORROW THE WOUNDS WILL BE SCARS.
ARE YOU IN PAIN?
NO...

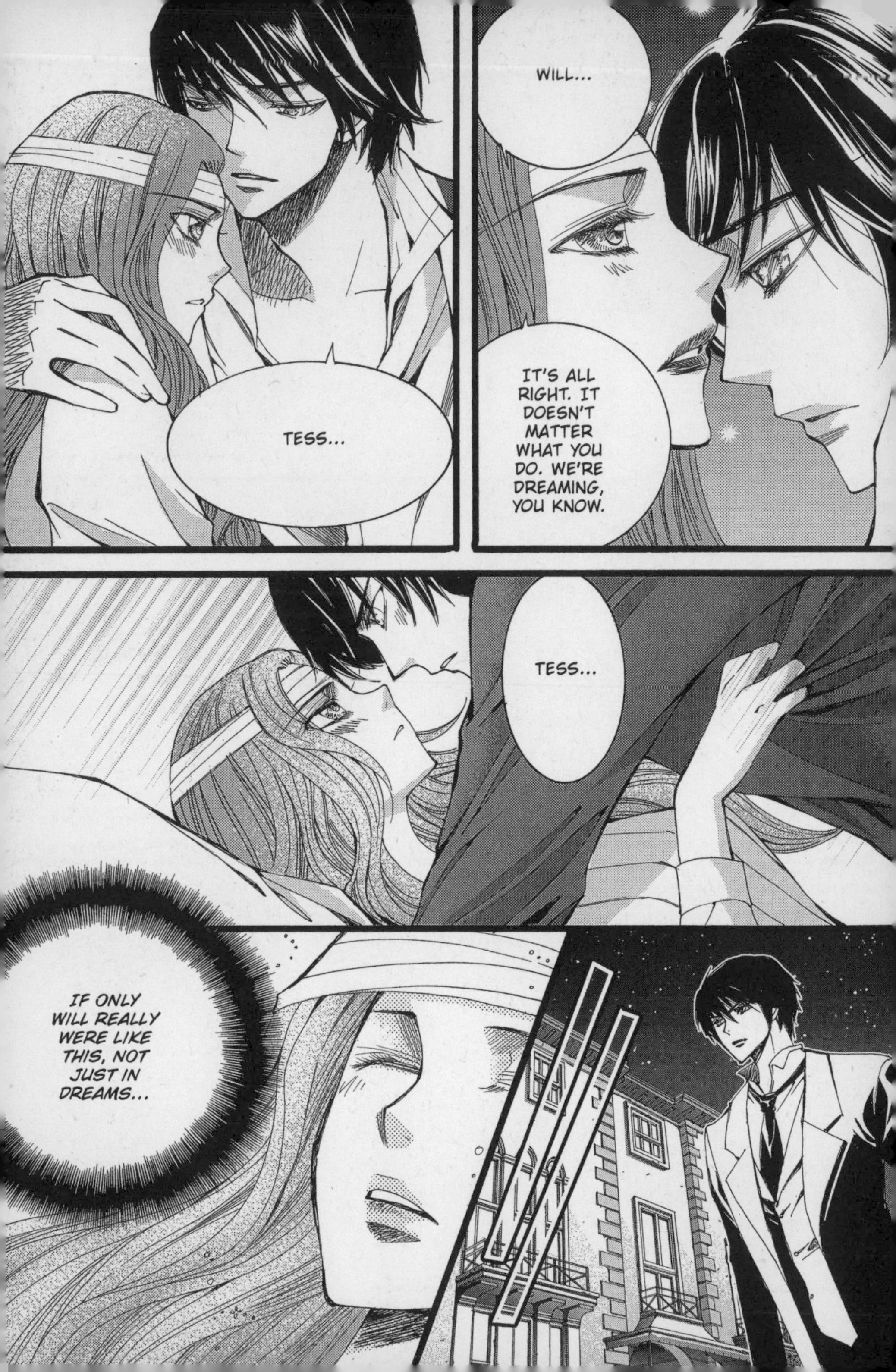
WILL...
IT'S ALL RIGHT. IT DOESN'T MATTER WHAT YOU DO. WE'RE DREAMING, YOU KNOW.
TESS...
TESS...
IF ONLY WILL REALLY WERE LIKE THIS, NOT JUST IN DREAMS...

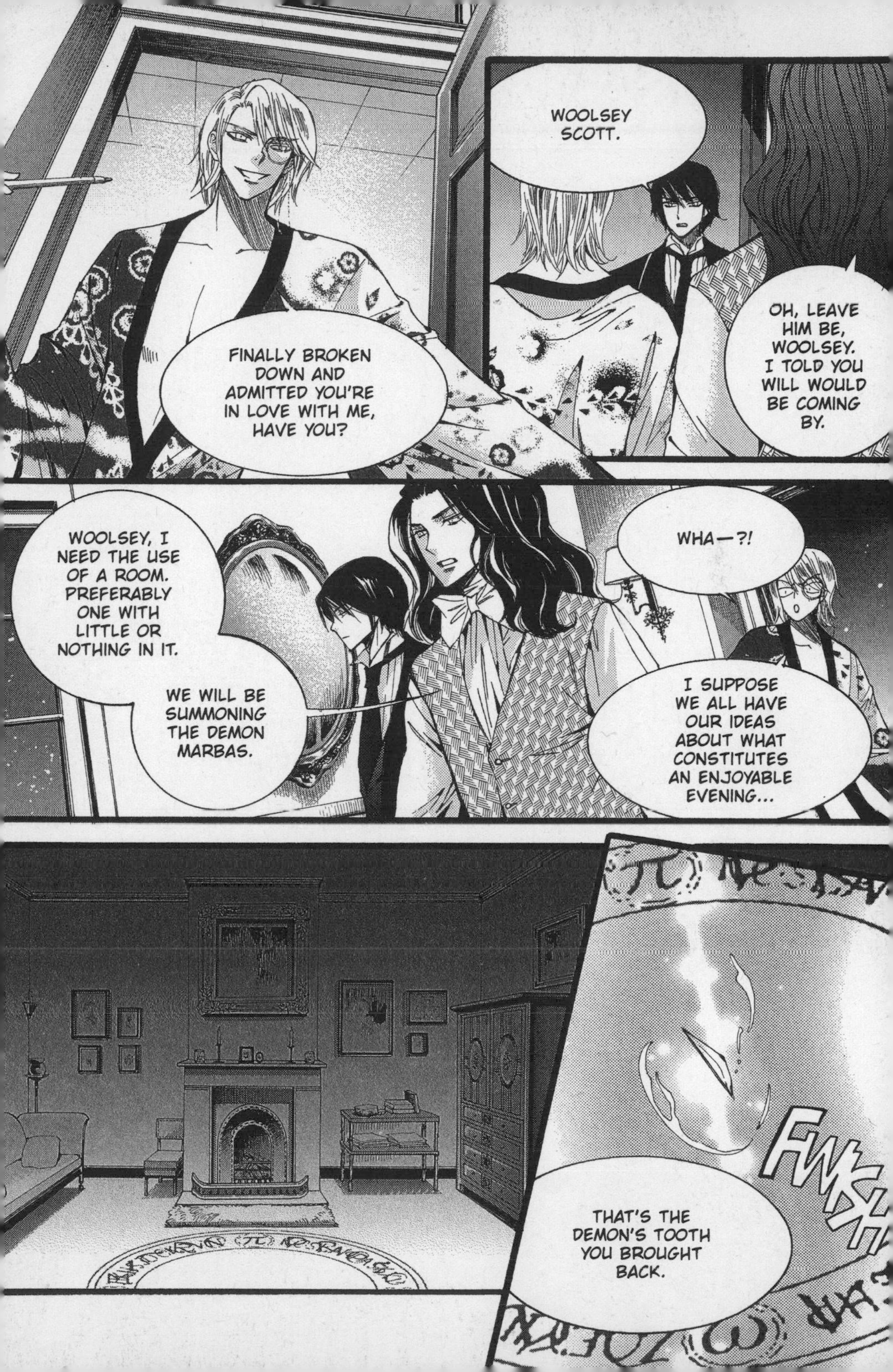
WOOLSEY SCOTT.
FINALLY BROKEN DOWN AND ADMITTED YOU'RE IN LOVE WITH ME, HAVE YOU?
OH, LEAVE HIM BE, WOOLSEY. I TOLD YOU WILL WOULD BE COMING BY.
WOOLSEY, I NEED THE USE OF A ROOM. PREFERABLY ONE WITH LITTLE OR NOTHING IN IT.
WE WILL BE SUMMONING THE DEMON MARBAS.
WHA—?!
I SUPPOSE WE ALL HAVE OUR IDEAS ABOUT WHAT CONSTITUTES AN ENJOYABLE EVENING...
FWSH
THAT'S THE DEMON'S TOOTH YOU BROUGHT BACK.

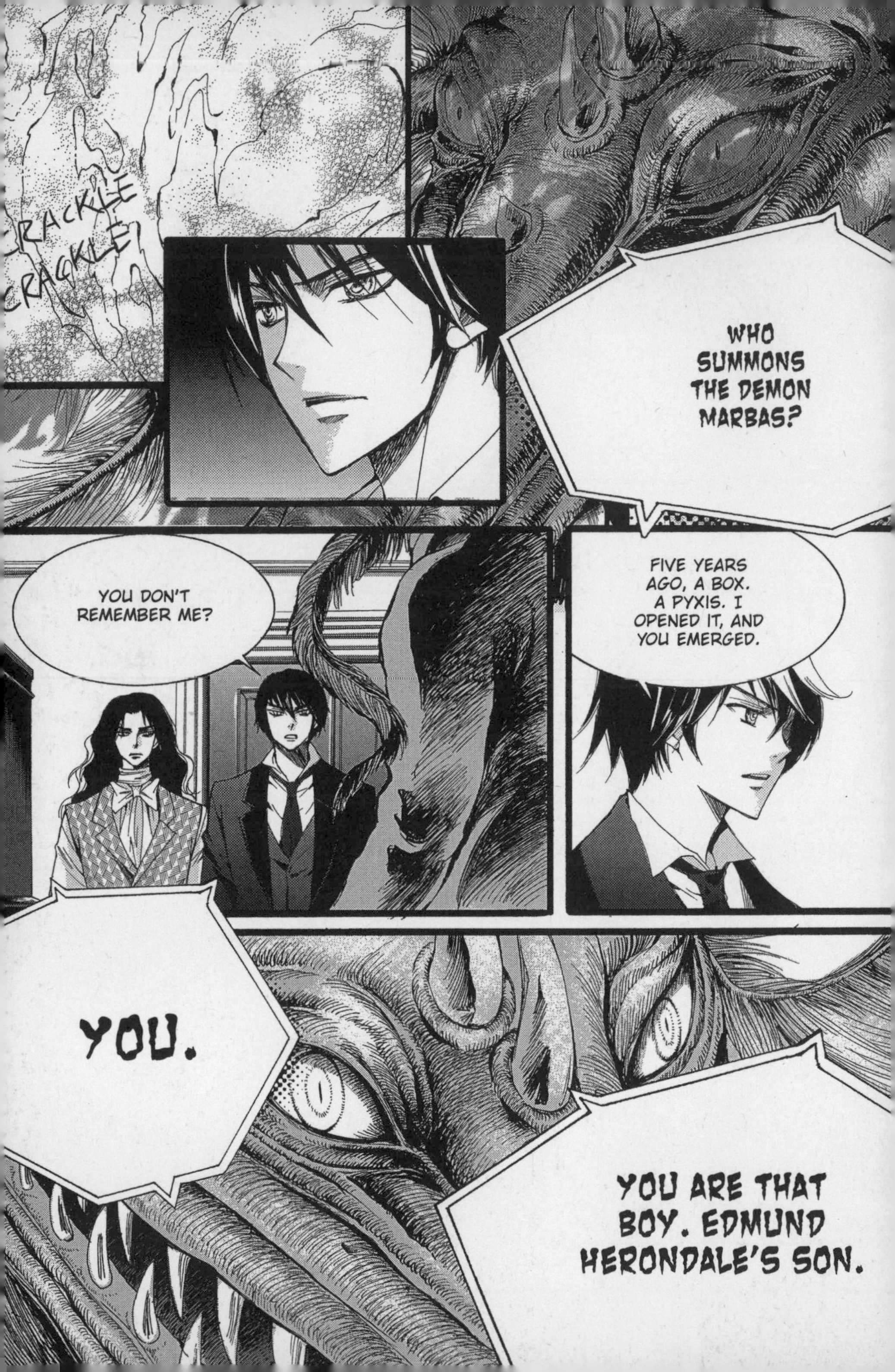
CRACKLE
CRACKLE
WHO SUMMONS THE DEMON MARBAS?
YOU DON'T REMEMBER ME?
FIVE YEARS AGO, A BOX. A PYXIS. I OPENED IT, AND YOU EMERGED.
YOU.
YOU ARE THAT BOY. EDMUND HERONDALE'S SON.

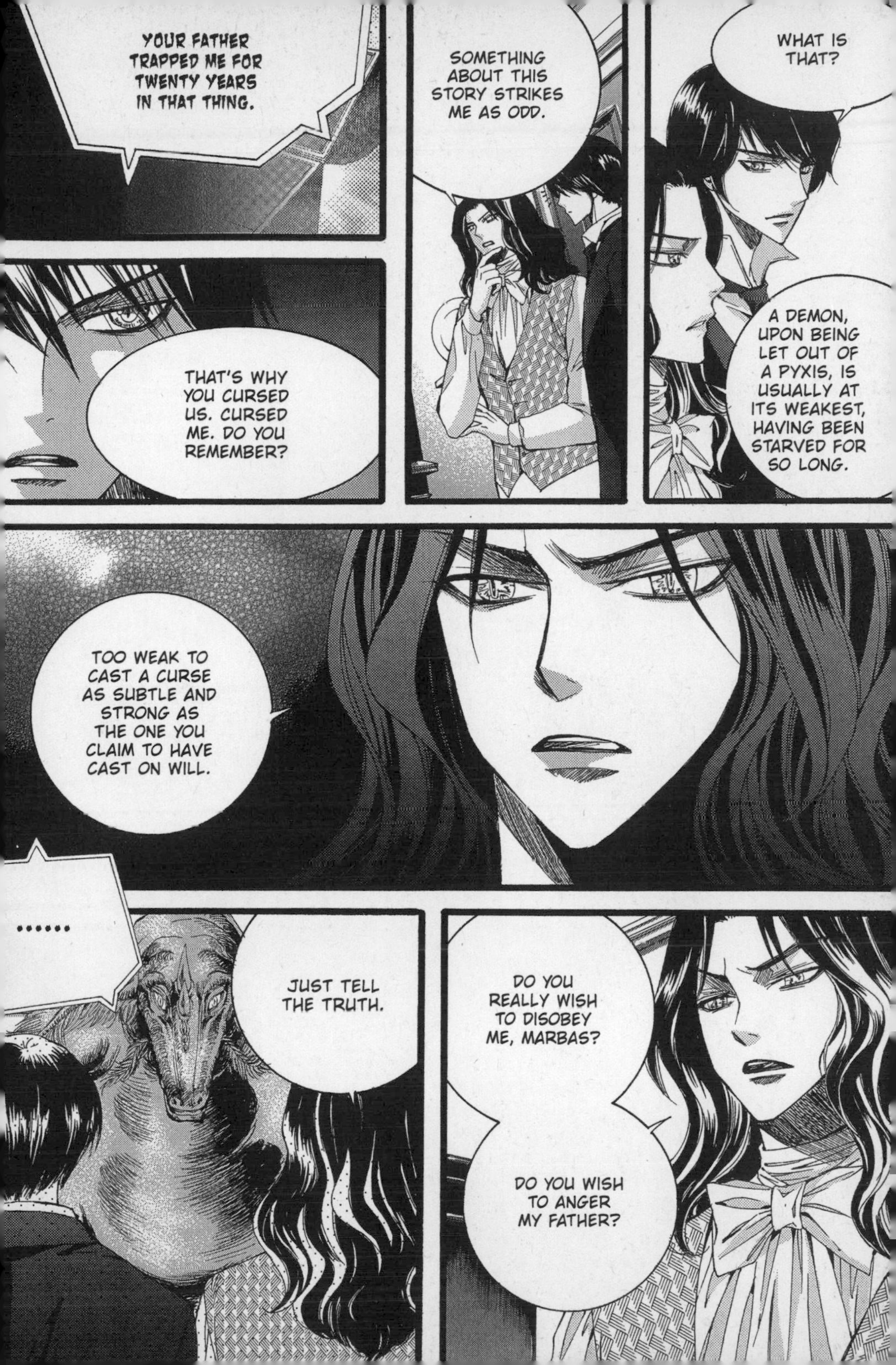
YOUR FATHER TRAPPED ME FOR TWENTY YEARS IN THAT THING.
SOMETHING ABOUT THIS STORY STRIKES ME AS ODD.
WHAT IS THAT?
THAT'S WHY YOU CURSED US. CURSED ME. DO YOU REMEMBER?
A DEMON, UPON BEING LET OUT OF A PYXIS, IS USUALLY AT ITS WEAKEST, HAVING BEEN STARVED FOR SO LONG.
TOO WEAK TO CAST A CURSE AS SUBTLE AND STRONG AS THE ONE YOU CLAIM TO HAVE CAST ON WILL.
......
JUST TELL THE TRUTH.
DO YOU REALLY WISH TO DISOBEY ME, MARBAS?
DO YOU WISH TO ANGER MY FATHER?

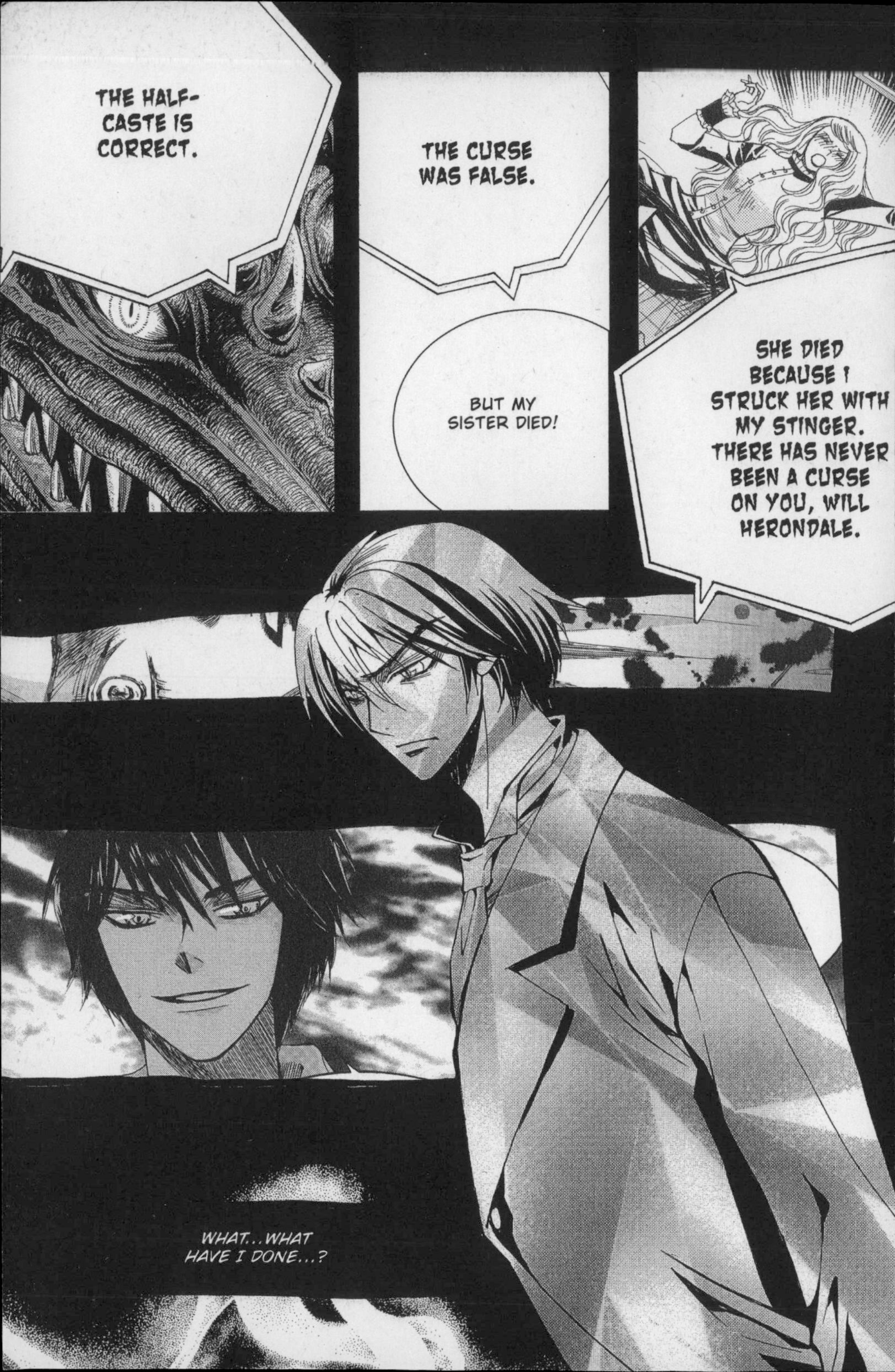
THE HALF-CASTE IS CORRECT.
THE CURSE WAS FALSE.
BUT MY SISTER DIED!
SHE DIED BECAUSE I STRUCK HER WITH MY STINGER. THERE HAS NEVER BEEN A CURSE ON YOU, WILL HERONDALE.
WHAT...WHAT HAVE I DONE...?

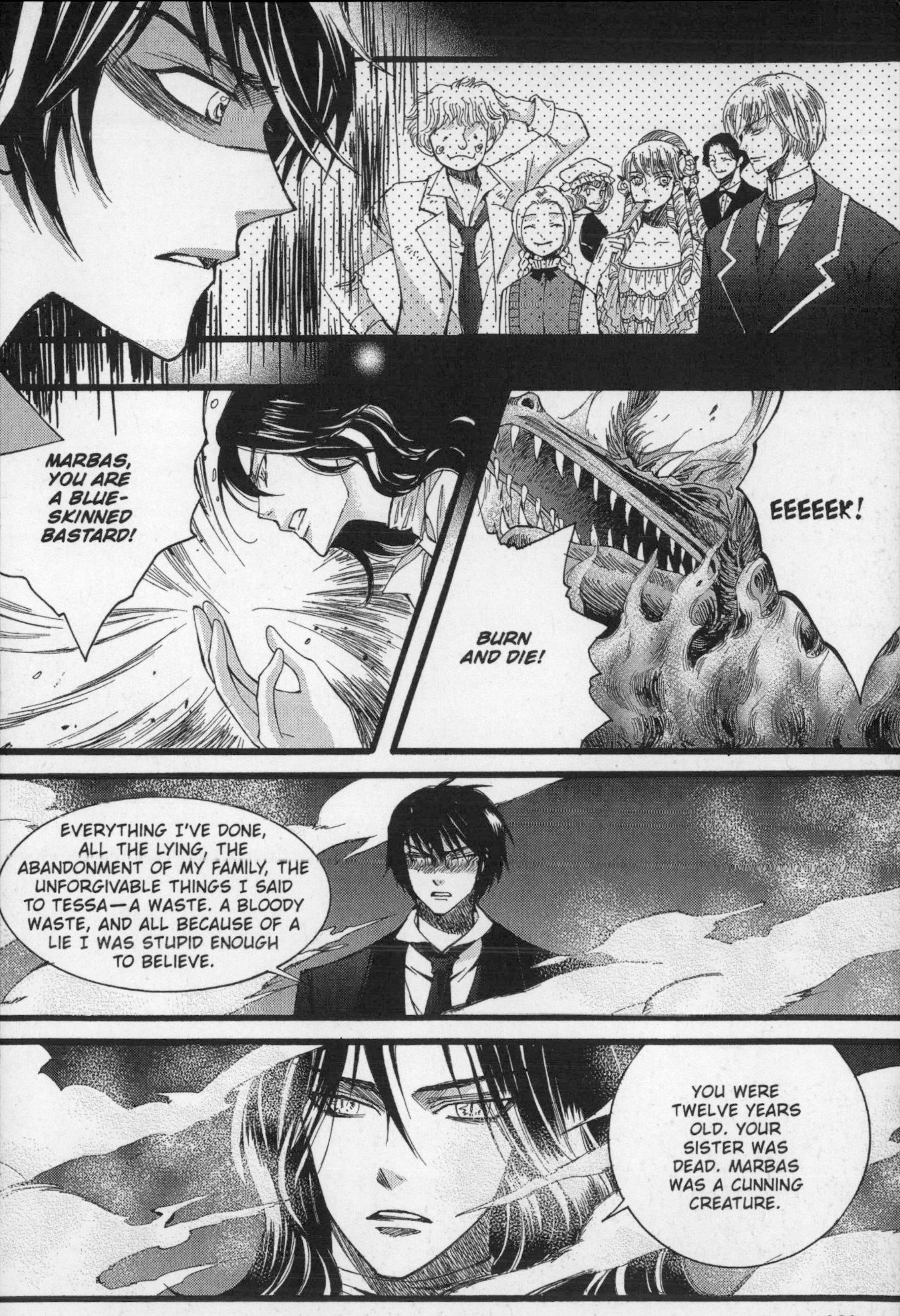
MARBAS, YOU ARE A BLUE-SKINNED BASTARD!
EEEEEK!
BURN AND DIE!
EVERYTHING I'VE DONE, ALL THE LYING, THE ABANDONMENT OF MY FAMILY, THE UNFORGIVABLE THINGS I SAID TO TESSA—A WASTE. A BLOODY WASTE, AND ALL BECAUSE OF A LIE I WAS STUPID ENOUGH TO BELIEVE.
YOU WERE TWELVE YEARS OLD. YOUR SISTER WAS DEAD. MARBAS WAS A CUNNING CREATURE.

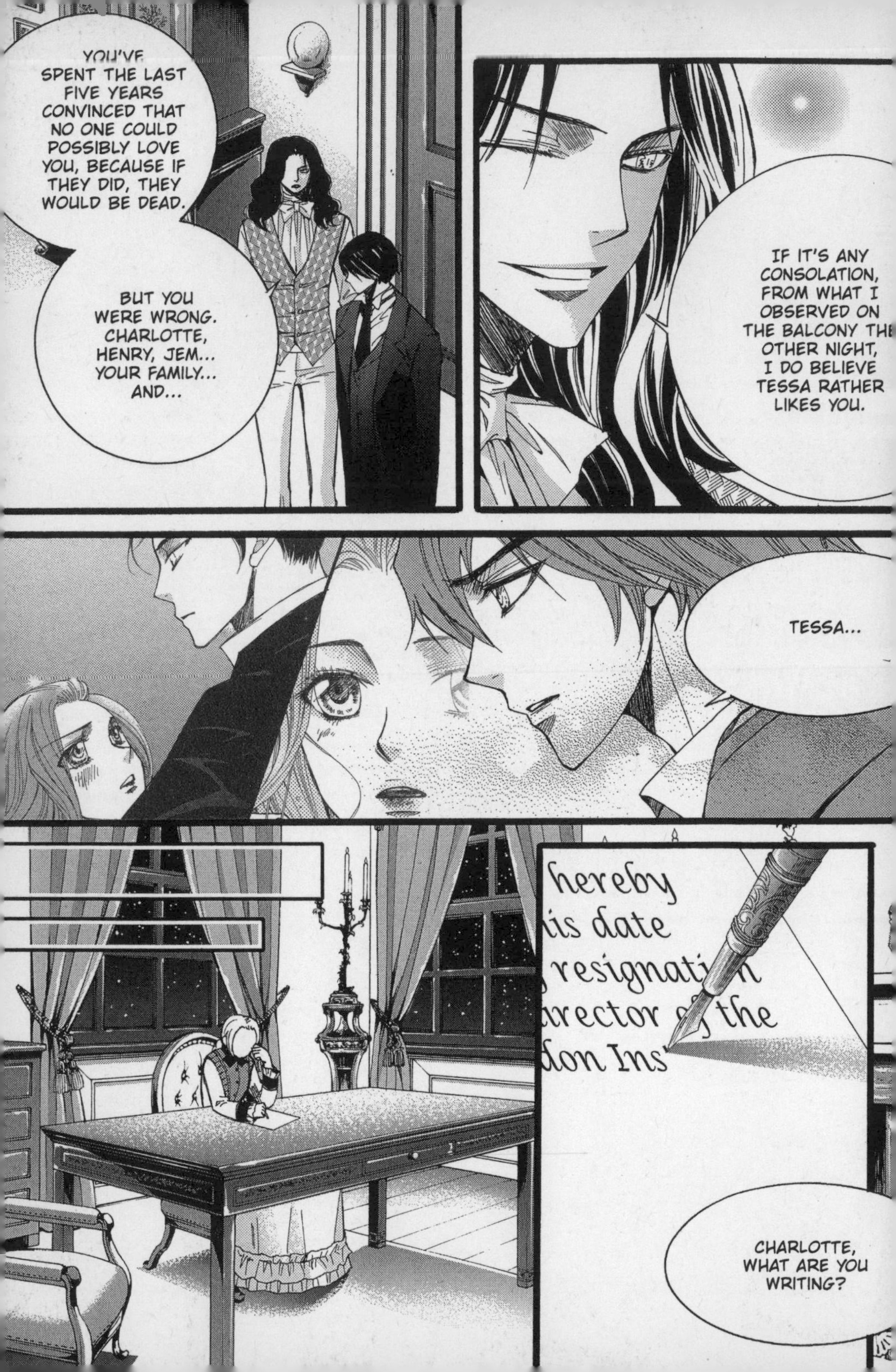
YOU'VE SPENT THE LAST FIVE YEARS CONVINCED THAT NO ONE COULD POSSIBLY LOVE YOU, BECAUSE IF THEY DID, THEY WOULD BE DEAD.
BUT YOU WERE WRONG. CHARLOTTE, HENRY, JEM... YOUR FAMILY... AND...
IF IT'S ANY CONSOLATION, FROM WHAT I OBSERVED ON THE BALCONY THE OTHER NIGHT, I DO BELIEVE TESSA RATHER LIKES YOU.
TESSA...
hereby
is date
resignation
rector of the
don Ins
CHARLOTTE, WHAT ARE YOU WRITING?

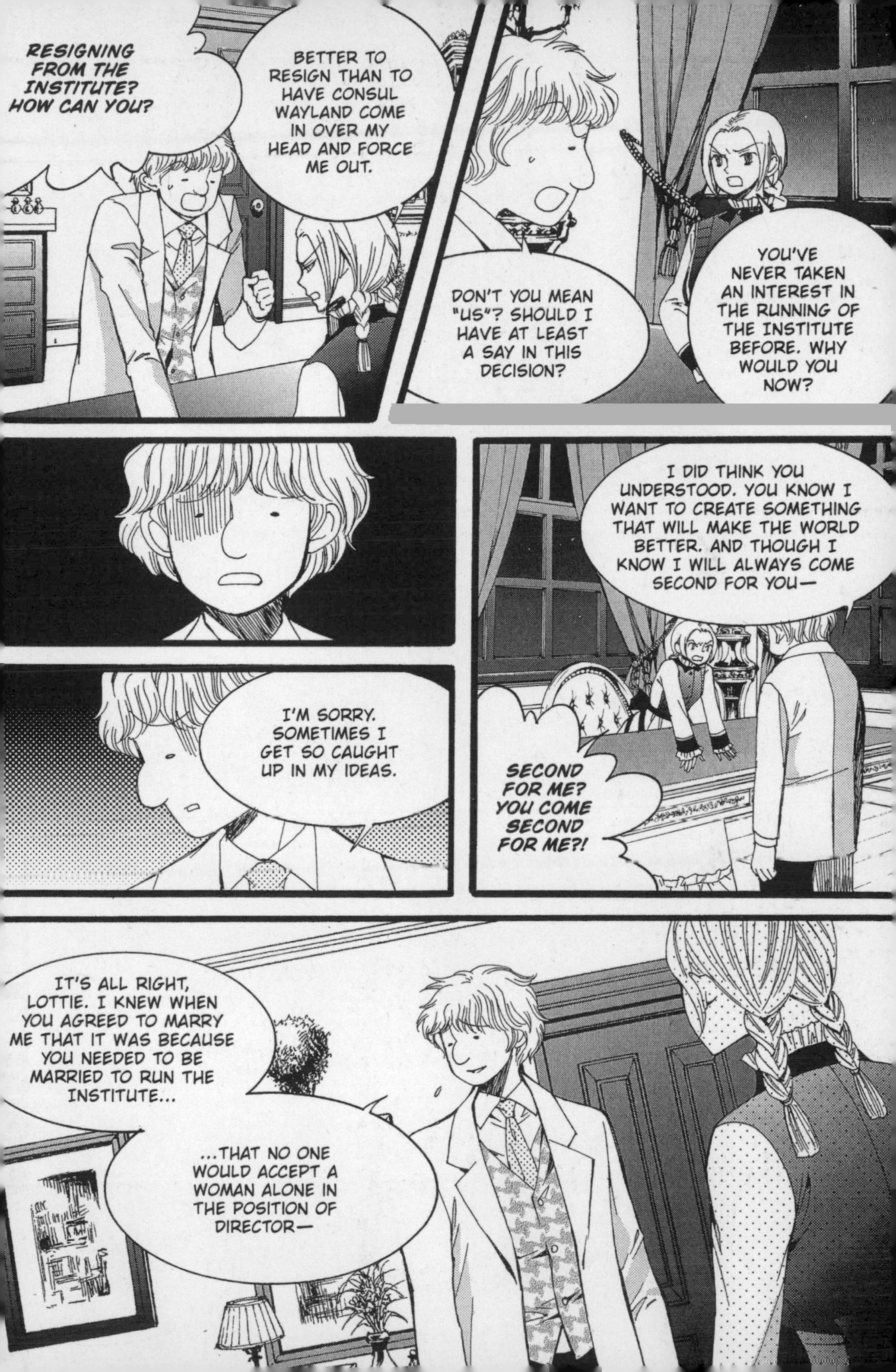
RESIGNING FROM THE INSTITUTE? HOW CAN YOU?
BETTER TO RESIGN THAN TO HAVE CONSUL WAYLAND COME IN OVER MY HEAD AND FORCE ME OUT.
DON'T YOU MEAN "US"? SHOULD I HAVE AT LEAST A SAY IN THIS DECISION?
YOU'VE NEVER TAKEN AN INTEREST IN THE RUNNING OF THE INSTITUTE BEFORE. WHY WOULD YOU NOW?
I DID THINK YOU UNDERSTOOD. YOU KNOW I WANT TO CREATE SOMETHING THAT WILL MAKE THE WORLD BETTER. AND THOUGH I KNOW I WILL ALWAYS COME SECOND FOR YOU—
SECOND FOR ME? YOU COME SECOND FOR ME?!
I'M SORRY. SOMETIMES I GET SO CAUGHT UP IN MY IDEAS.
IT'S ALL RIGHT, LOTTIE. I KNEW WHEN YOU AGREED TO MARRY ME THAT IT WAS BECAUSE YOU NEEDED TO BE MARRIED TO RUN THE INSTITUTE...
...THAT NO ONE WOULD ACCEPT A WOMAN ALONE IN THE POSITION OF DIRECTOR—

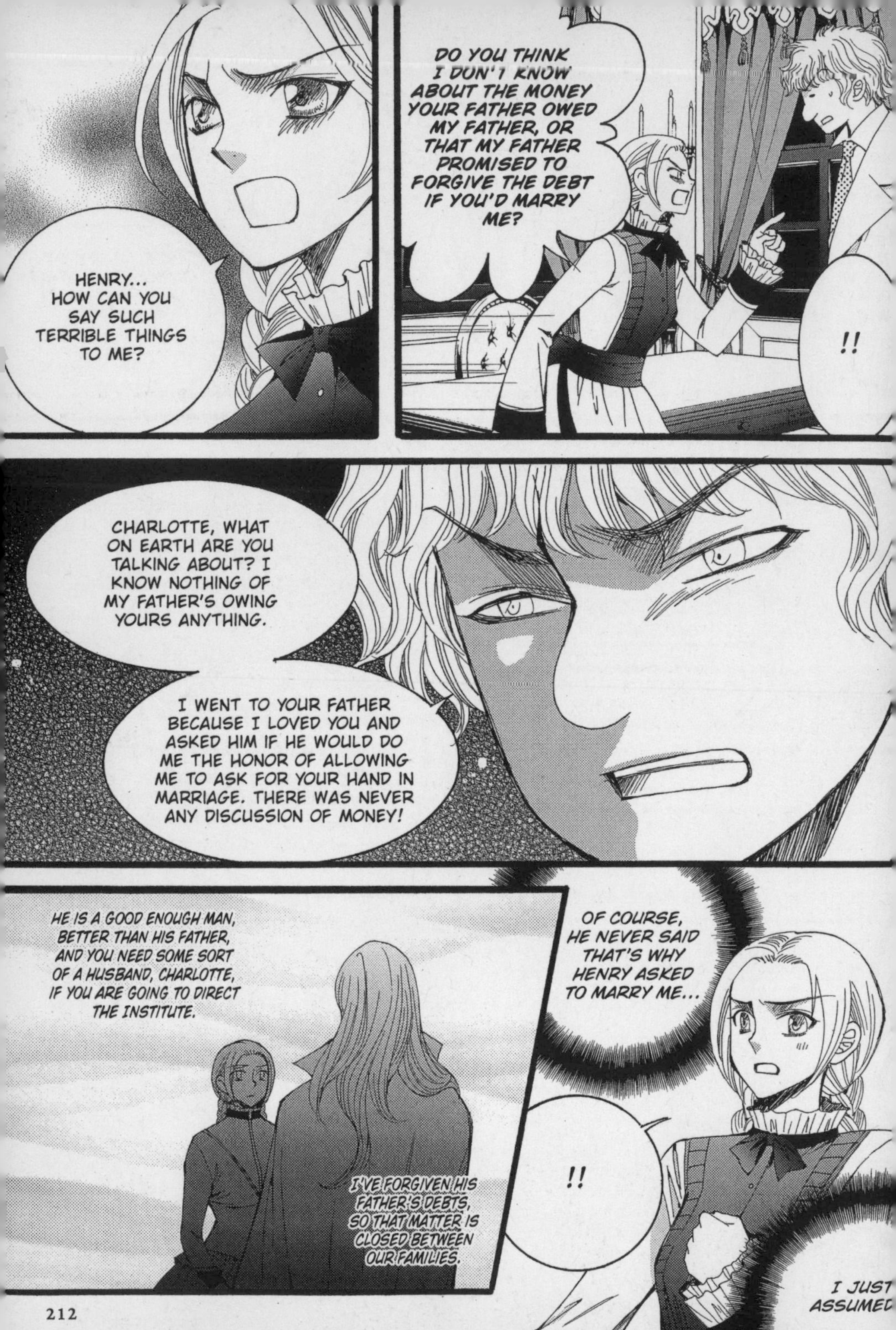
HENRY... HOW CAN YOU SAY SUCH TERRIBLE THINGS TO ME?
DO YOU THINK I DON'T KNOW ABOUT THE MONEY YOUR FATHER OWED MY FATHER, OR THAT MY FATHER PROMISED TO FORGIVE THE DEBT IF YOU'D MARRY ME?
!!
CHARLOTTE, WHAT ON EARTH ARE YOU TALKING ABOUT? I KNOW NOTHING OF MY FATHER'S OWING YOURS ANYTHING.
I WENT TO YOUR FATHER BECAUSE I LOVED YOU AND ASKED HIM IF HE WOULD DO ME THE HONOR OF ALLOWING ME TO ASK FOR YOUR HAND IN MARRIAGE. THERE WAS NEVER ANY DISCUSSION OF MONEY!
HE IS A GOOD ENOUGH MAN, BETTER THAN HIS FATHER, AND YOU NEED SOME SORT OF A HUSBAND, CHARLOTTE, IF YOU ARE GOING TO DIRECT THE INSTITUTE.
I'VE FORGIVEN HIS FATHER'S DEBTS, SO THAT MATTER IS CLOSED BETWEEN OUR FAMILIES.
OF COURSE, HE NEVER SAID THAT'S WHY HENRY ASKED TO MARRY ME...
!!
I JUST ASSUMED

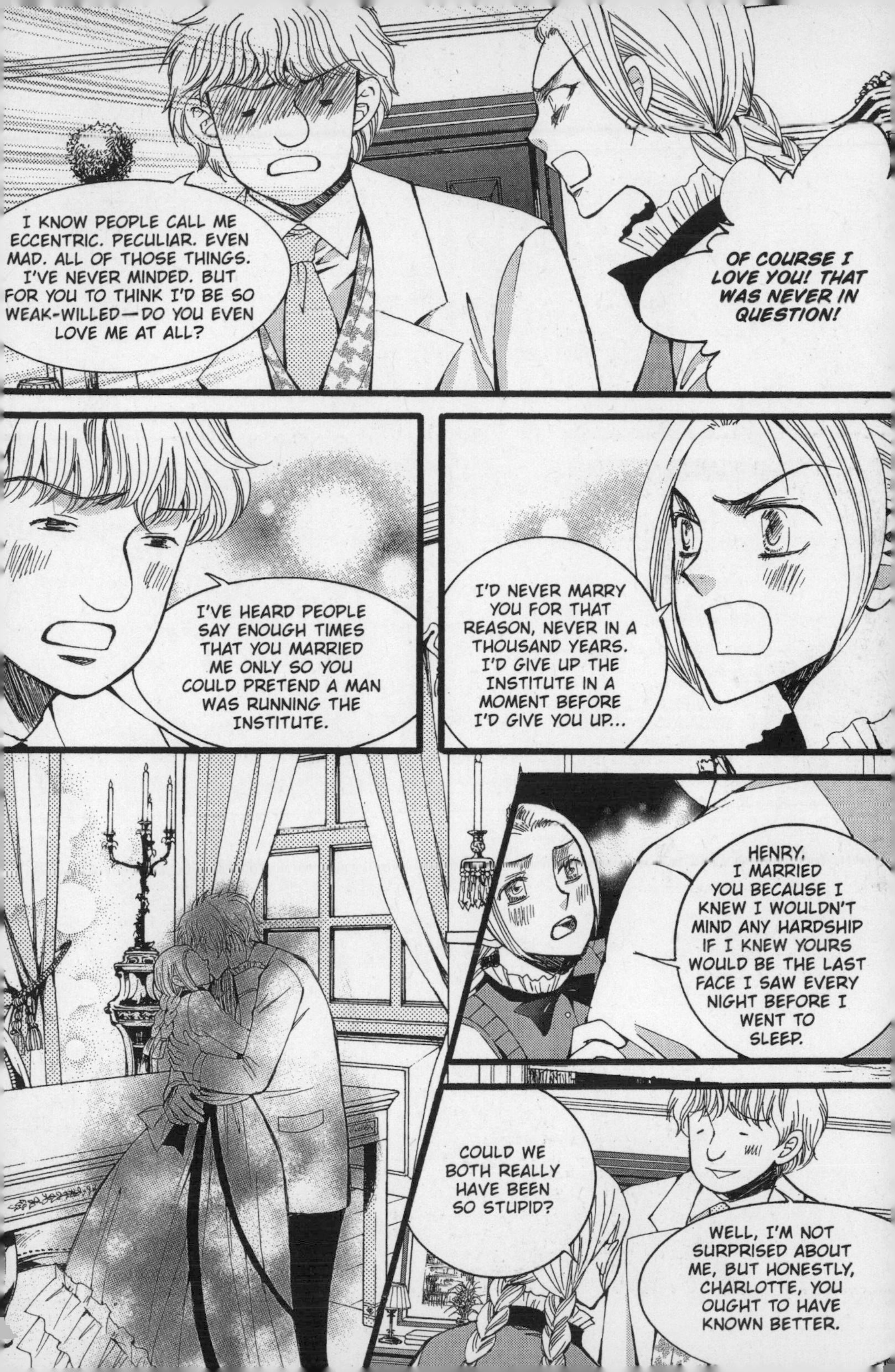
I KNOW PEOPLE CALL ME ECCENTRIC. PECULIAR. EVEN MAD. ALL OF THOSE THINGS. I'VE NEVER MINDED. BUT FOR YOU TO THINK I'D BE SO WEAK-WILLED—DO YOU EVEN LOVE ME AT ALL?
OF COURSE I LOVE YOU! THAT WAS NEVER IN QUESTION!
I'VE HEARD PEOPLE SAY ENOUGH TIMES THAT YOU MARRIED ME ONLY SO YOU COULD PRETEND A MAN WAS RUNNING THE INSTITUTE.
I'D NEVER MARRY YOU FOR THAT REASON, NEVER IN A THOUSAND YEARS. I'D GIVE UP THE INSTITUTE IN A MOMENT BEFORE I'D GIVE YOU UP...
HENRY. I MARRIED YOU BECAUSE I KNEW I WOULDN'T MIND ANY HARDSHIP IF I KNEW YOURS WOULD BE THE LAST FACE I SAW EVERY NIGHT BEFORE I WENT TO SLEEP.
COULD WE BOTH REALLY HAVE BEEN SO STUPID?
WELL, I'M NOT SURPRISED ABOUT ME, BUT HONESTLY, CHARLOTTE, YOU OUGHT TO HAVE KNOWN BETTER.

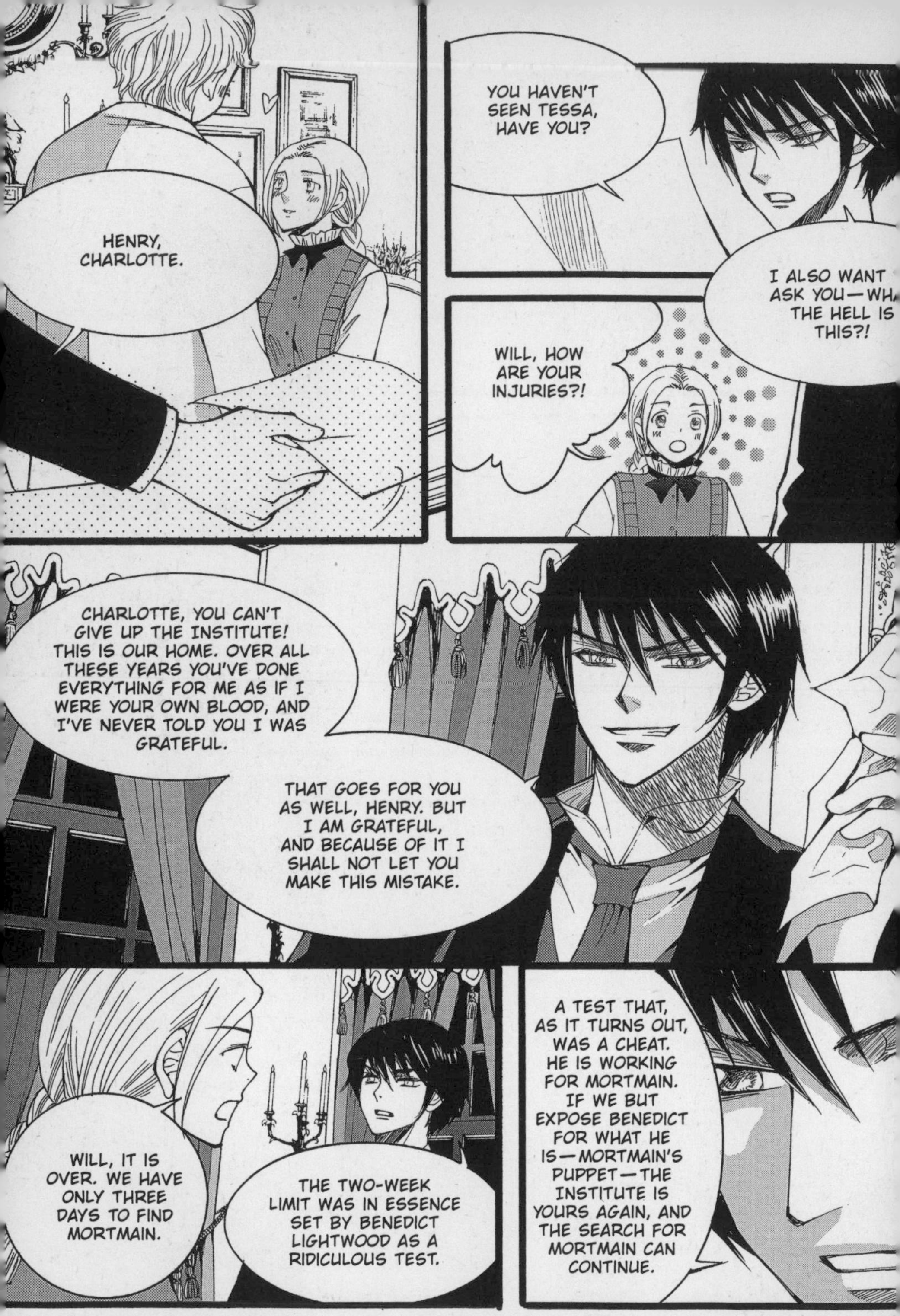
HENRY, CHARLOTTE.
YOU HAVEN'T SEEN TESSA, HAVE YOU?
WILL, HOW ARE YOUR INJURIES?!
I ALSO WANT ASK YOU—WH THE HELL IS THIS?!
CHARLOTTE, YOU CAN'T GIVE UP THE INSTITUTE! THIS IS OUR HOME. OVER ALL THESE YEARS YOU'VE DONE EVERYTHING FOR ME AS IF I WERE YOUR OWN BLOOD, AND I'VE NEVER TOLD YOU I WAS GRATEFUL.
THAT GOES FOR YOU AS WELL, HENRY. BUT I AM GRATEFUL, AND BECAUSE OF IT I SHALL NOT LET YOU MAKE THIS MISTAKE.
WILL, IT IS OVER. WE HAVE ONLY THREE DAYS TO FIND MORTMAIN.
THE TWO-WEEK LIMIT WAS IN ESSENCE SET BY BENEDICT LIGHTWOOD AS A RIDICULOUS TEST.
A TEST THAT, AS IT TURNS OUT, WAS A CHEAT. HE IS WORKING FOR MORTMAIN. IF WE BUT EXPOSE BENEDICT FOR WHAT HE IS—MORTMAIN'S PUPPET—THE INSTITUTE IS YOURS AGAIN, AND THE SEARCH FOR MORTMAIN CAN CONTINUE.

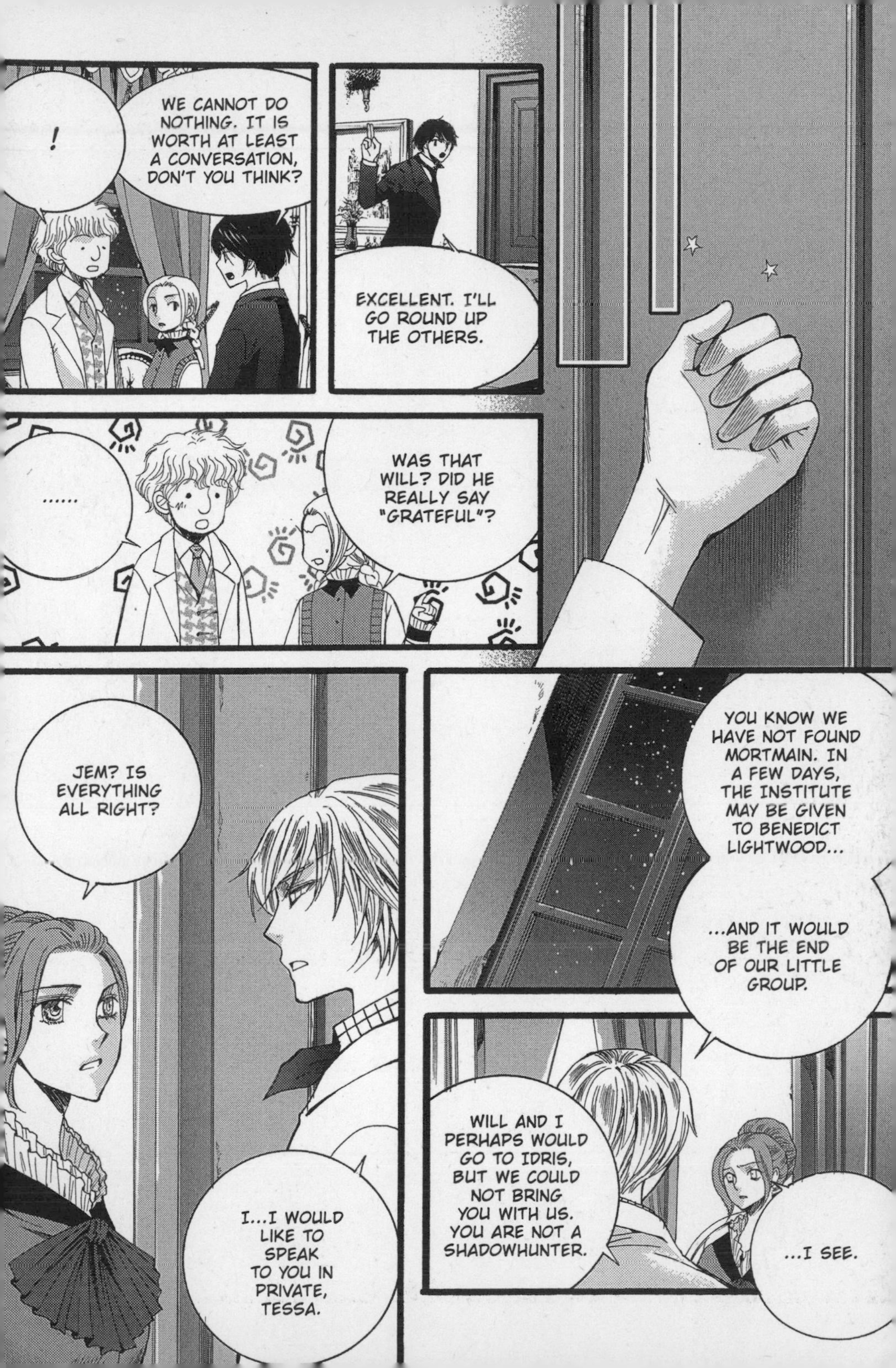
!
WE CANNOT DO NOTHING. IT IS WORTH AT LEAST A CONVERSATION, DON'T YOU THINK?
EXCELLENT. I'LL GO ROUND UP THE OTHERS.
......
WAS THAT WILL? DID HE REALLY SAY "GRATEFUL"?
JEM? IS EVERYTHING ALL RIGHT?
I...I WOULD LIKE TO SPEAK TO YOU IN PRIVATE, TESSA.
YOU KNOW WE HAVE NOT FOUND MORTMAIN. IN A FEW DAYS, THE INSTITUTE MAY BE GIVEN TO BENEDICT LIGHTWOOD...
...AND IT WOULD BE THE END OF OUR LITTLE GROUP.
WILL AND I PERHAPS WOULD GO TO IDRIS, BUT WE COULD NOT BRING YOU WITH US. YOU ARE NOT A SHADOWHUNTER.
...I SEE.

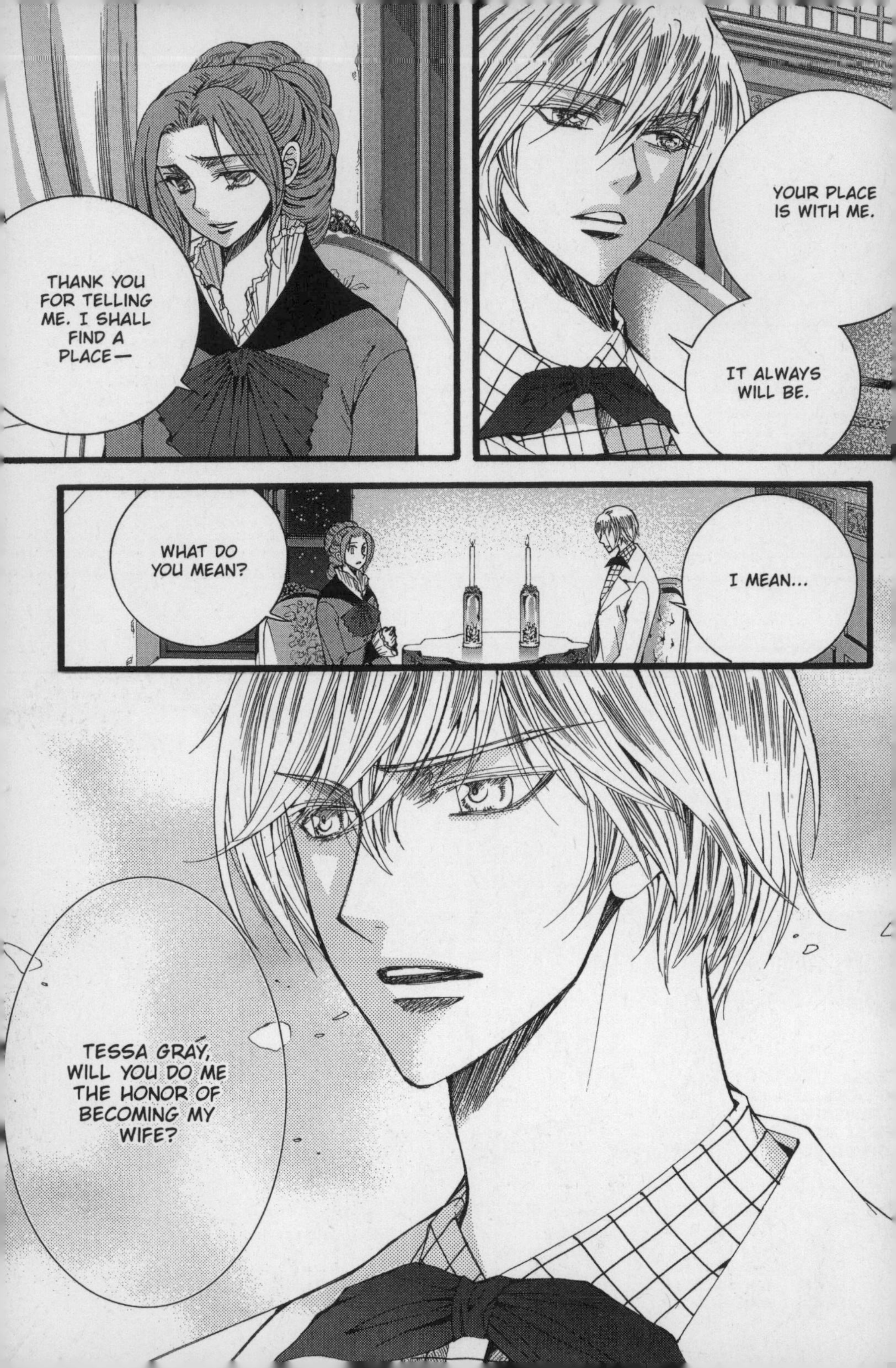
THANK YOU FOR TELLING ME. I SHALL FIND A PLACE—
YOUR PLACE IS WITH ME.
IT ALWAYS WILL BE.
WHAT DO YOU MEAN?
I MEAN...
TESSA GRAY, WILL YOU DO ME THE HONOR OF BECOMING MY WIFE?

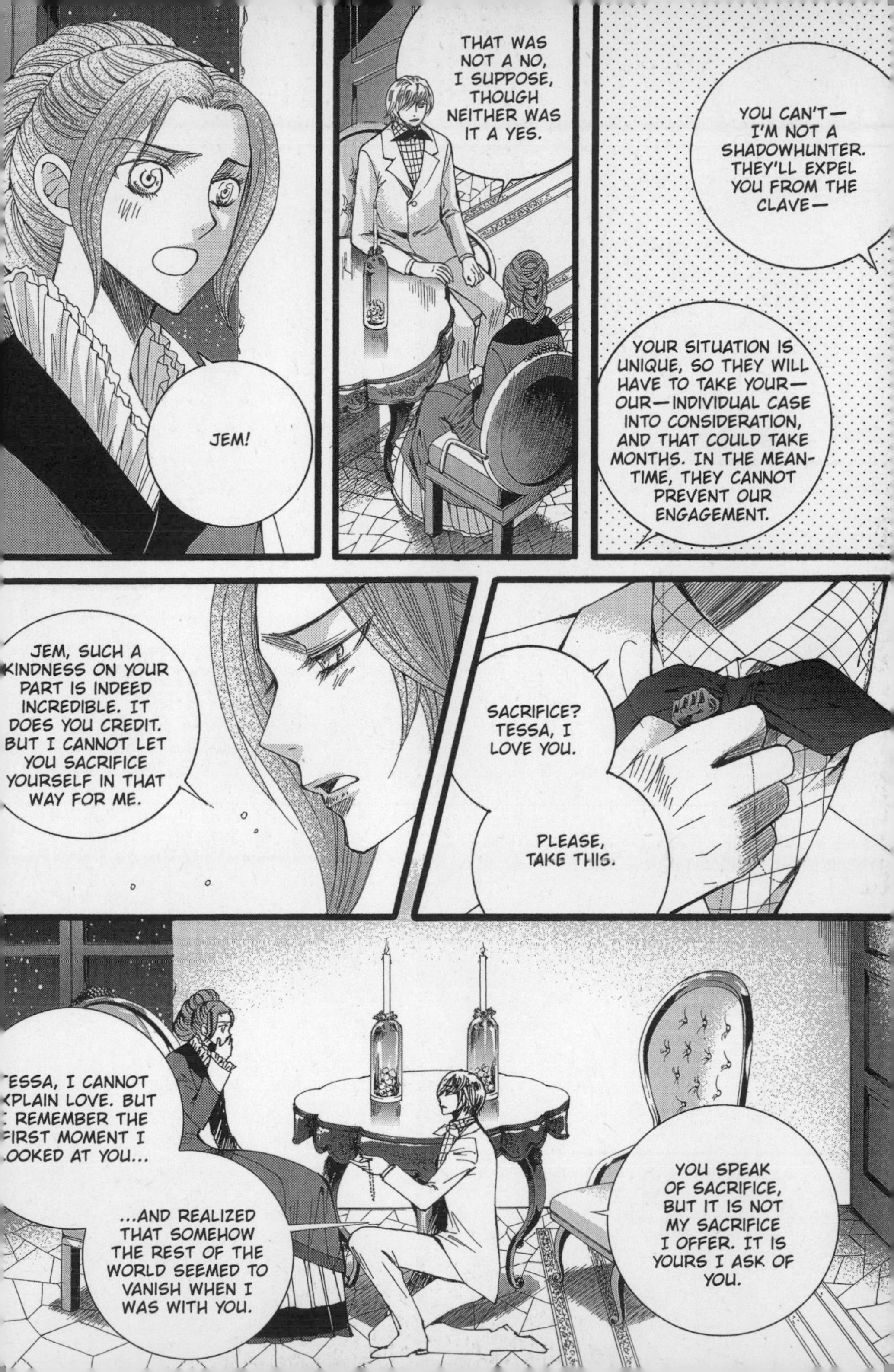
JEM!
THAT WAS NOT A NO, I SUPPOSE, THOUGH NEITHER WAS IT A YES.
YOU CAN'T— I'M NOT A SHADOWHUNTER. THEY'LL EXPEL YOU FROM THE CLAVE—
YOUR SITUATION IS UNIQUE, SO THEY WILL HAVE TO TAKE YOUR—OUR—INDIVIDUAL CASE INTO CONSIDERATION, AND THAT COULD TAKE MONTHS. IN THE MEAN-TIME, THEY CANNOT PREVENT OUR ENGAGEMENT.
JEM, SUCH A KINDNESS ON YOUR PART IS INDEED INCREDIBLE. IT DOES YOU CREDIT. BUT I CANNOT LET YOU SACRIFICE YOURSELF IN THAT WAY FOR ME.
SACRIFICE? TESSA, I LOVE YOU.
PLEASE, TAKE THIS.
TESSA, I CANNOT EXPLAIN LOVE. BUT I REMEMBER THE FIRST MOMENT I LOOKED AT YOU...
...AND REALIZED THAT SOMEHOW THE REST OF THE WORLD SEEMED TO VANISH WHEN I WAS WITH YOU.
YOU SPEAK OF SACRIFICE, BUT IT IS NOT MY SACRIFICE I OFFER. IT IS YOURS I ASK OF YOU.

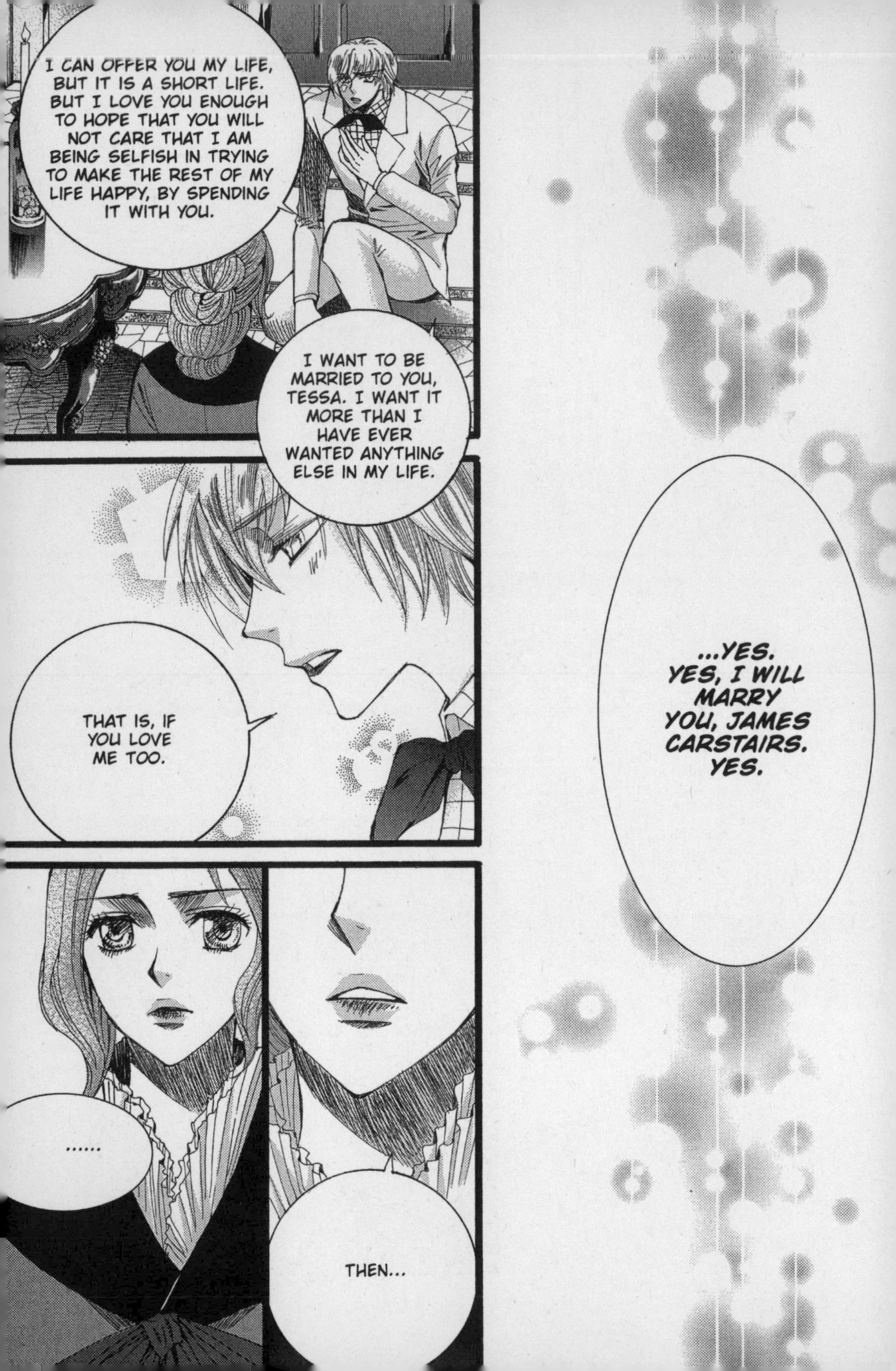
I CAN OFFER YOU MY LIFE, BUT IT IS A SHORT LIFE. BUT I LOVE YOU ENOUGH TO HOPE THAT YOU WILL NOT CARE THAT I AM BEING SELFISH IN TRYING TO MAKE THE REST OF MY LIFE HAPPY, BY SPENDING IT WITH YOU.
I WANT TO BE MARRIED TO YOU, TESSA. I WANT IT MORE THAN I HAVE EVER WANTED ANYTHING ELSE IN MY LIFE.
THAT IS, IF YOU LOVE ME TOO.
......
THEN...
...YES. YES, I WILL MARRY YOU, JAMES CARSTAIRS. YES.

THE INFERNAL DEVICES
CLOCKWORK PRINCE

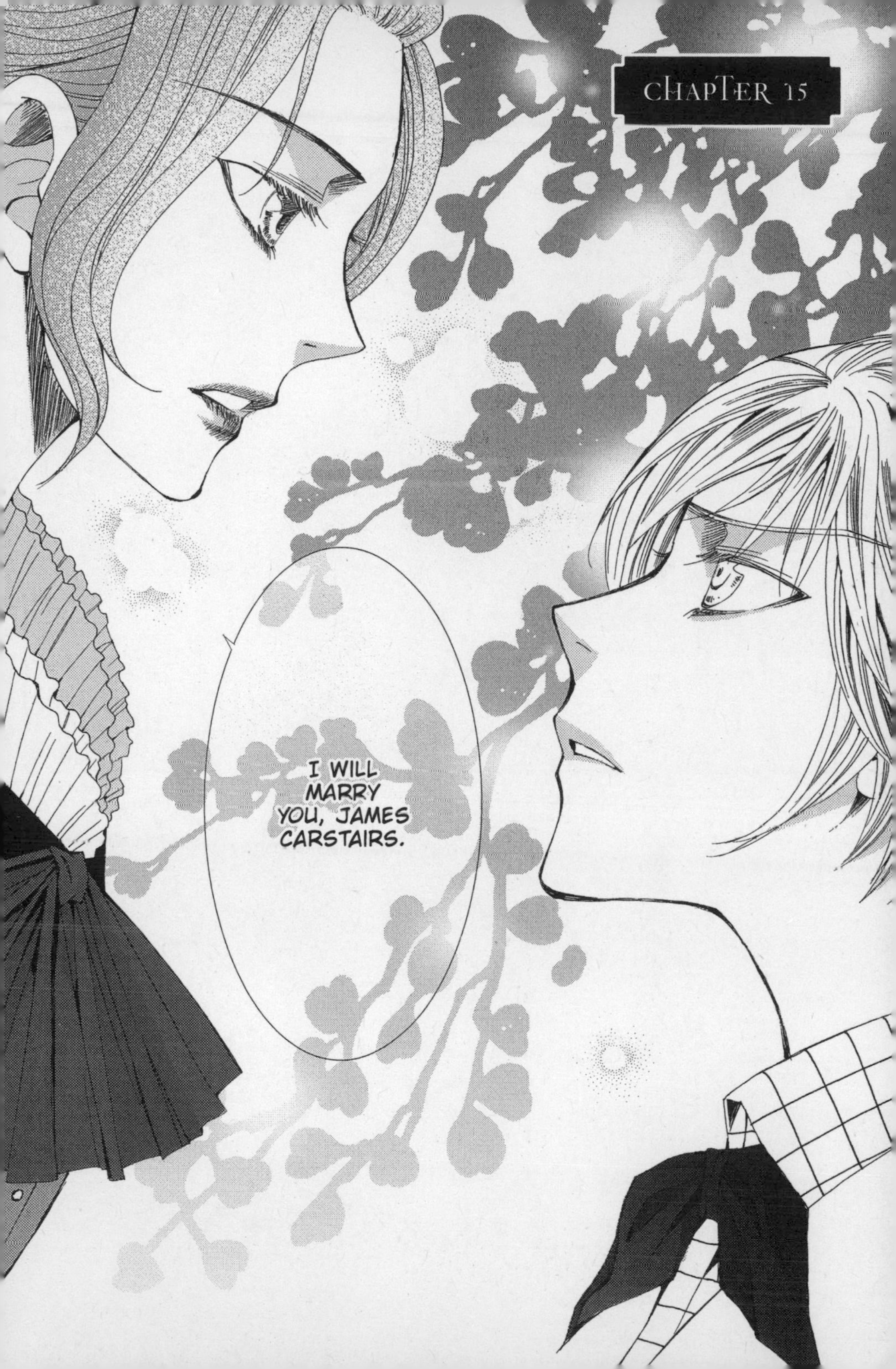
CHAPTER 15
I WILL MARRY YOU, JAMES CARSTAIRS.

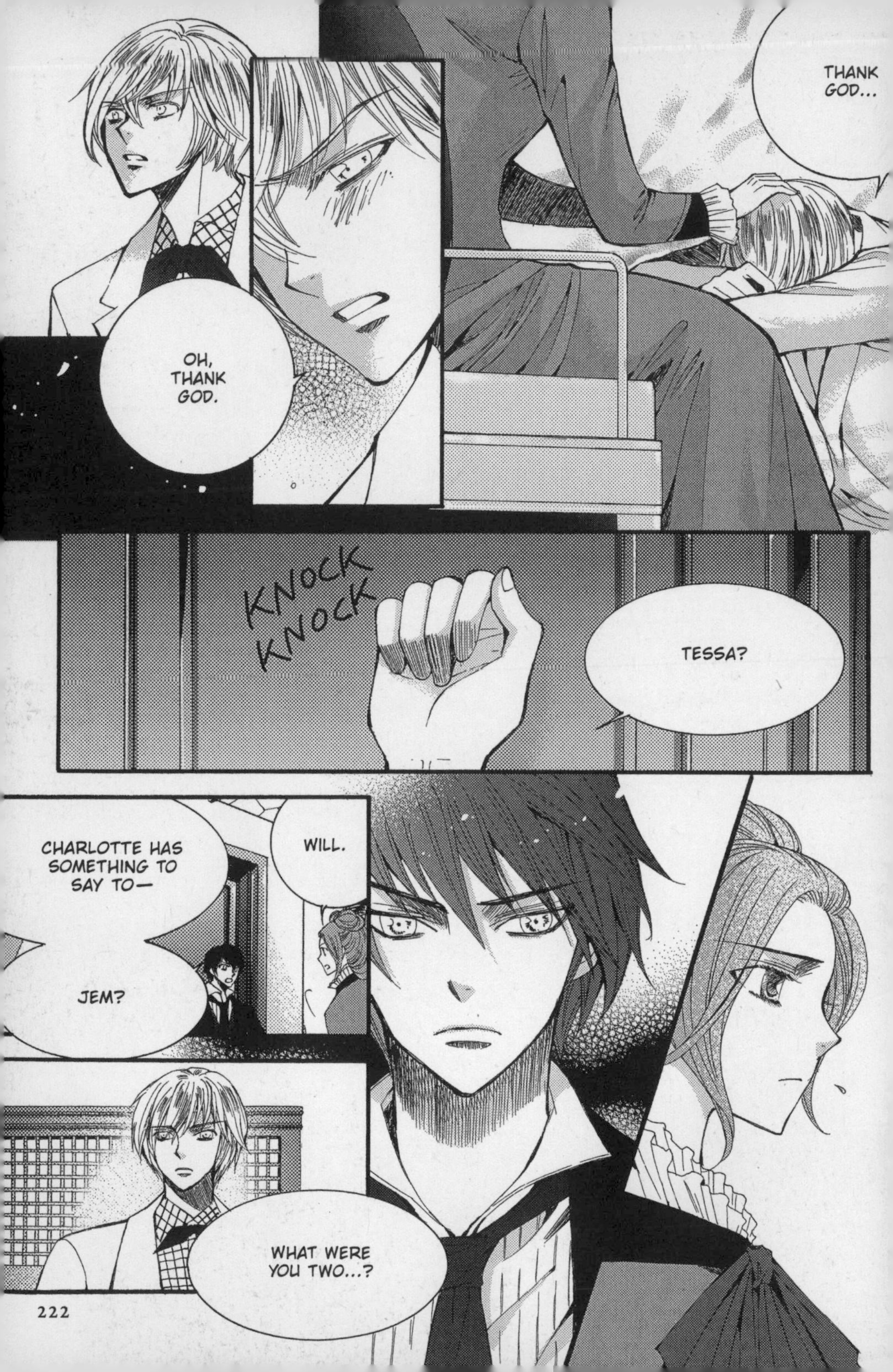
THANK GOD...
OH, THANK GOD.
KNOCK KNOCK
TESSA?
WILL.
CHARLOTTE HAS SOMETHING TO SAY TO—
JEM?
WHAT WERE YOU TWO...?

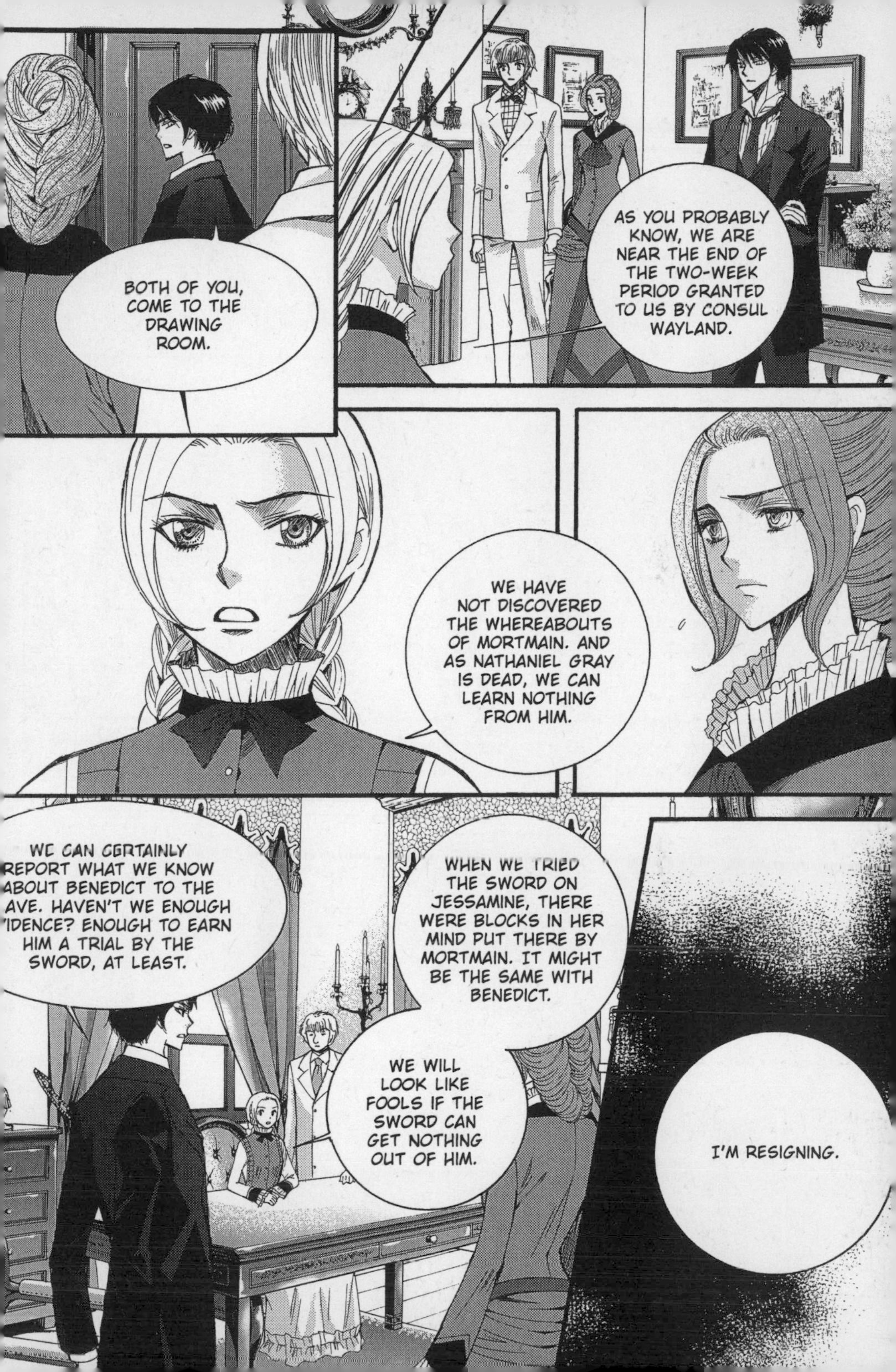
BOTH OF YOU, COME TO THE DRAWING ROOM.
AS YOU PROBABLY KNOW, WE ARE NEAR THE END OF THE TWO-WEEK PERIOD GRANTED TO US BY CONSUL WAYLAND.
WE HAVE NOT DISCOVERED THE WHEREABOUTS OF MORTMAIN. AND AS NATHANIEL GRAY IS DEAD, WE CAN LEARN NOTHING FROM HIM.
WE CAN CERTAINLY REPORT WHAT WE KNOW ABOUT BENEDICT TO THE AVE. HAVEN'T WE ENOUGH IDENCE? ENOUGH TO EARN HIM A TRIAL BY THE SWORD, AT LEAST.
WHEN WE TRIED THE SWORD ON JESSAMINE, THERE WERE BLOCKS IN HER MIND PUT THERE BY MORTMAIN. IT MIGHT BE THE SAME WITH BENEDICT.
WE WILL LOOK LIKE FOOLS IF THE SWORD CAN GET NOTHING OUT OF HIM.
I'M RESIGNING.

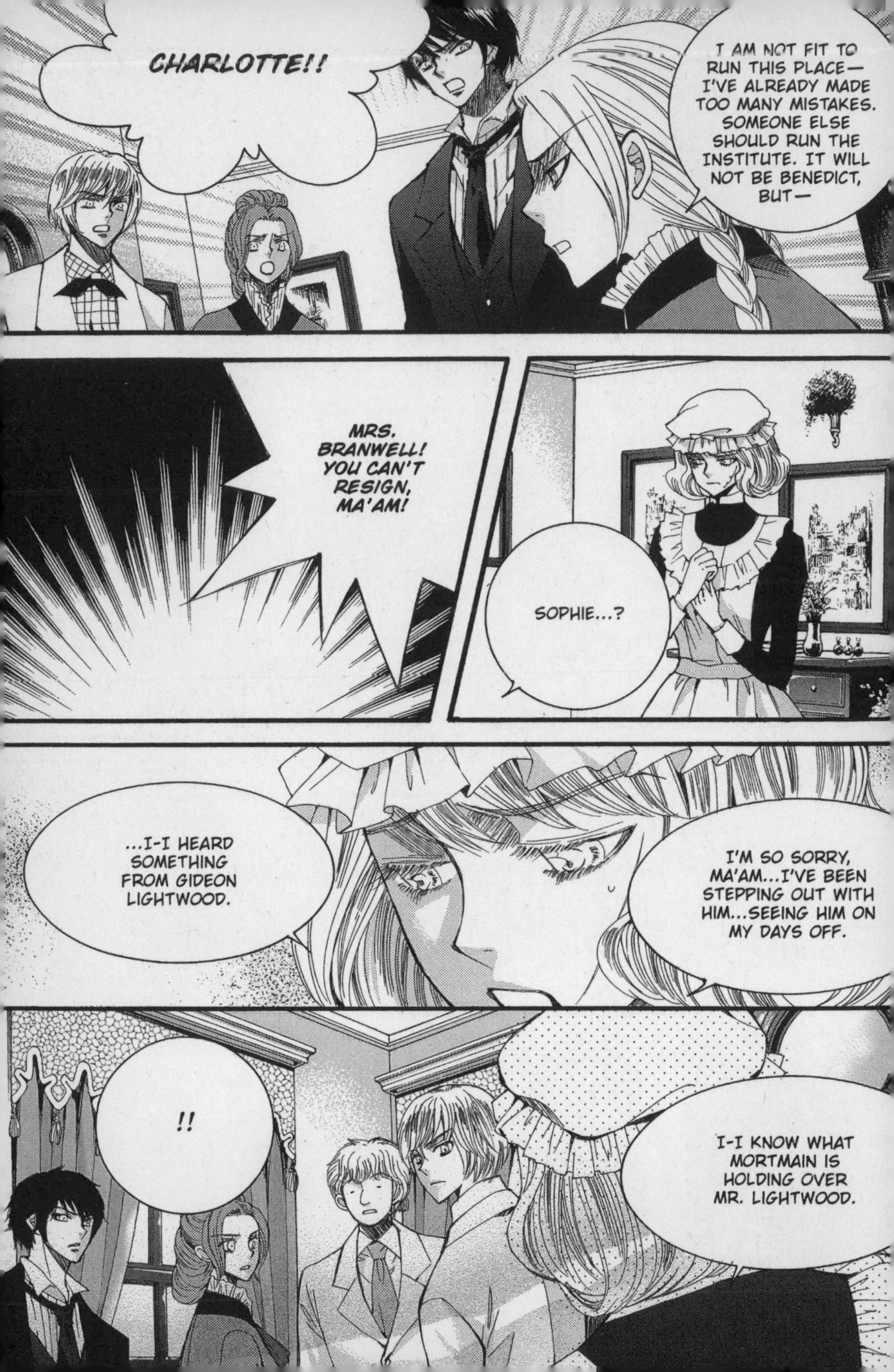
CHARLOTTE!!
I AM NOT FIT TO RUN THIS PLACE— I'VE ALREADY MADE TOO MANY MISTAKES. SOMEONE ELSE SHOULD RUN THE INSTITUTE. IT WILL NOT BE BENEDICT, BUT—
MRS. BRANWELL! YOU CAN'T RESIGN, MA'AM!
SOPHIE...?
...I-I HEARD SOMETHING FROM GIDEON LIGHTWOOD.
I'M SO SORRY, MA'AM...I'VE BEEN STEPPING OUT WITH HIM...SEEING HIM ON MY DAYS OFF.
!!
I-I KNOW WHAT MORTMAIN IS HOLDING OVER MR. LIGHTWOOD.

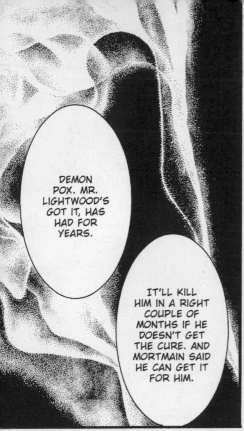

DEMON POX. MR. LIGHTWOOD'S GOT IT, HAS HAD FOR YEARS.

IT'LL KILL HIM IN A RIGHT COUPLE OF MONTHS IF HE DOESN'T GET THE CURE. AND MORTMAIN SAID HE CAN GET IT FOR HIM.

DEMON POX?!

BUT THE ONLY WAY YOU CAN CONTRACT DEMON POX IS BY HAVING IMPROPER RELATIONS WITH A DEMON—

BENEDICT WAS WITH A DEMON WOMAN AT THAT PARTY OF HIS!

RIGHT! THE ONE WHO HAD A SNAKE FOR A TONGUE!

!!

DON'T THE SYMPTOMS OF DEMON POX BEGIN WITH A SHIELD-SHAPED RASH ON ONE'S BACK THAT SPREADS OVER THE BODY, CREATING CRACKS AND FISSURES IN THE SKIN?

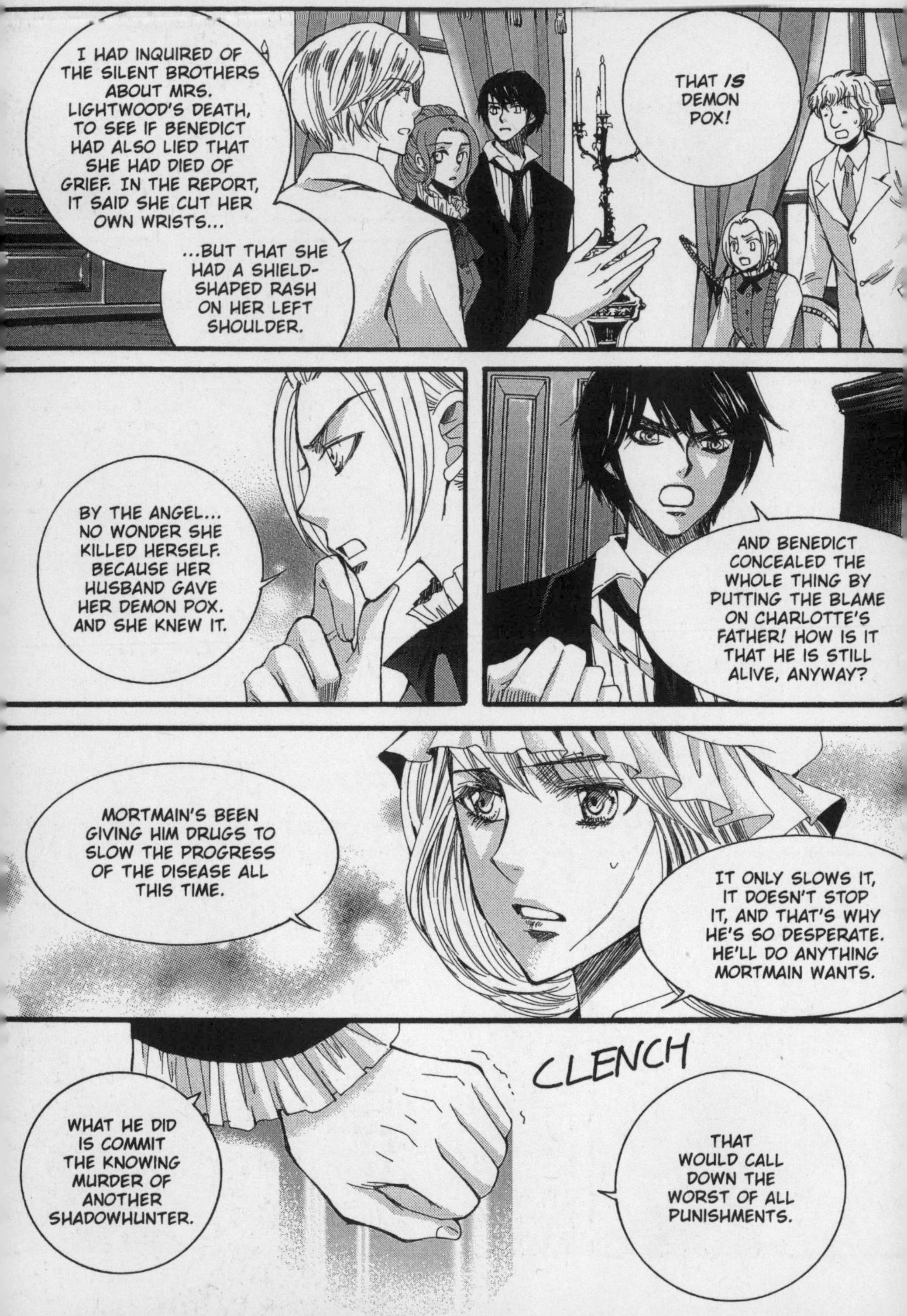
I HAD INQUIRED OF THE SILENT BROTHERS ABOUT MRS. LIGHTWOOD'S DEATH, TO SEE IF BENEDICT HAD ALSO LIED THAT SHE HAD DIED OF GRIEF. IN THE REPORT, IT SAID SHE CUT HER OWN WRISTS...
...BUT THAT SHE HAD A SHIELD-SHAPED RASH ON HER LEFT SHOULDER.
THAT *IS* DEMON POX!
BY THE ANGEL... NO WONDER SHE KILLED HERSELF. BECAUSE HER HUSBAND GAVE HER DEMON POX. AND SHE KNEW IT.
AND BENEDICT CONCEALED THE WHOLE THING BY PUTTING THE BLAME ON CHARLOTTE'S FATHER! HOW IS IT THAT HE IS STILL ALIVE, ANYWAY?
MORTMAIN'S BEEN GIVING HIM DRUGS TO SLOW THE PROGRESS OF THE DISEASE ALL THIS TIME.
IT ONLY SLOWS IT, IT DOESN'T STOP IT, AND THAT'S WHY HE'S SO DESPERATE. HE'LL DO ANYTHING MORTMAIN WANTS.
CLENCH
WHAT HE DID IS COMMIT THE KNOWING MURDER OF ANOTHER SHADOWHUNTER.
THAT WOULD CALL DOWN THE WORST OF ALL PUNISHMENTS.

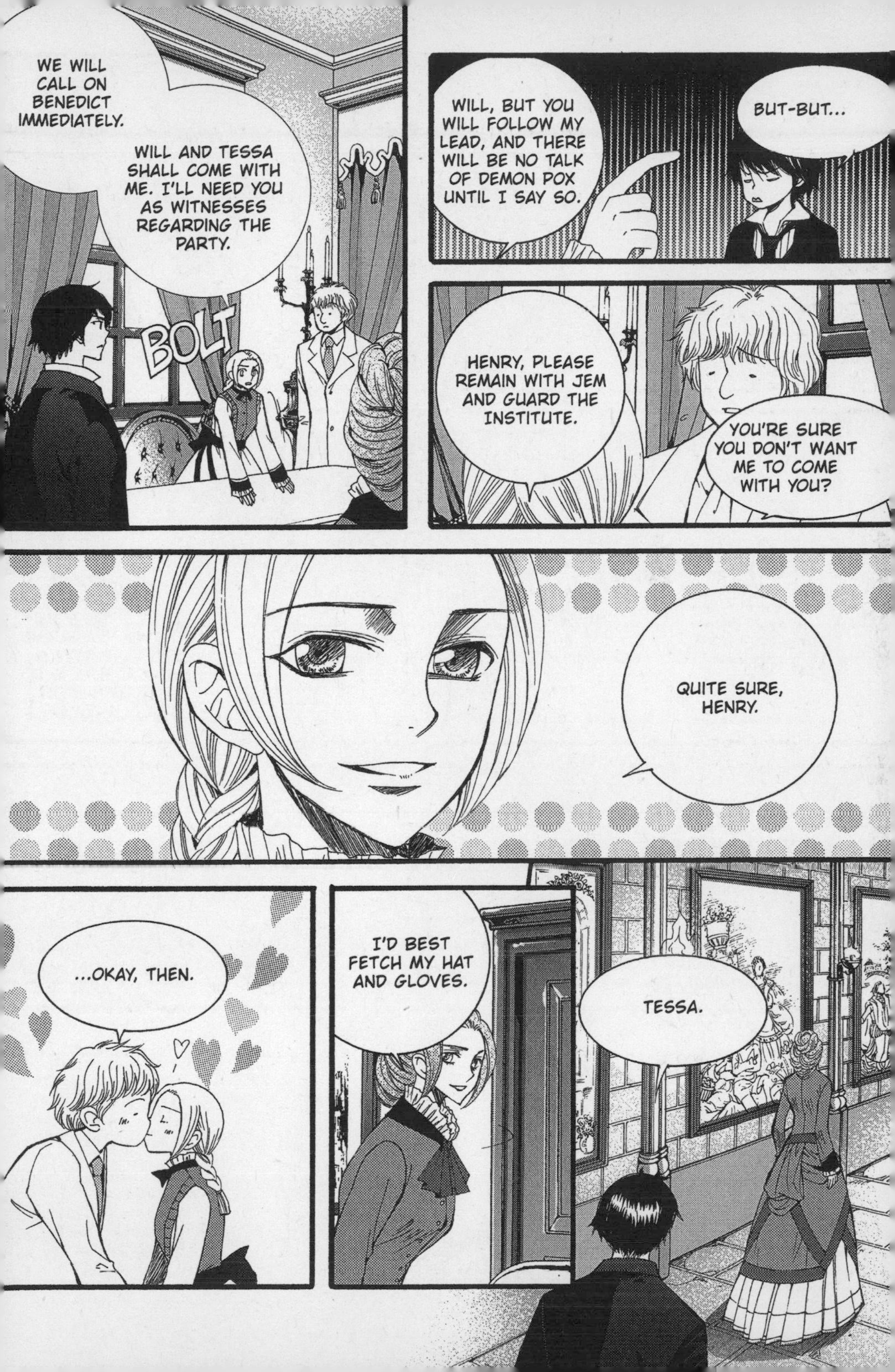
WE WILL CALL ON BENEDICT IMMEDIATELY.
WILL AND TESSA SHALL COME WITH ME. I'LL NEED YOU AS WITNESSES REGARDING THE PARTY.
BOLT
BUT-BUT...
WILL, BUT YOU WILL FOLLOW MY LEAD, AND THERE WILL BE NO TALK OF DEMON POX UNTIL I SAY SO.
HENRY, PLEASE REMAIN WITH JEM AND GUARD THE INSTITUTE.
YOU'RE SURE YOU DON'T WANT ME TO COME WITH YOU?
QUITE SURE, HENRY.
...OKAY, THEN.
I'D BEST FETCH MY HAT AND GLOVES.
TESSA.

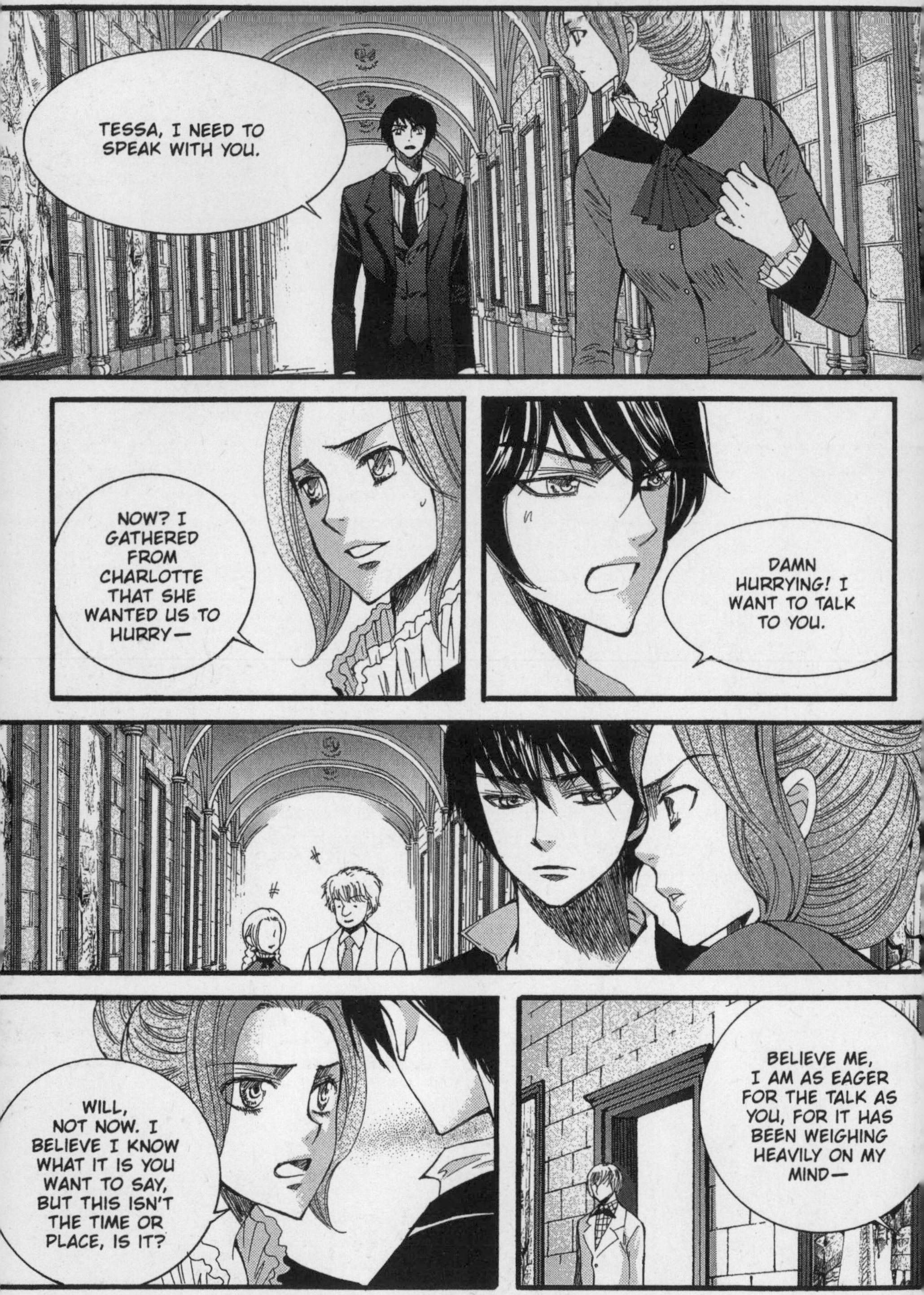
TESSA, I NEED TO SPEAK WITH YOU.
NOW? I GATHERED FROM CHARLOTTE THAT SHE WANTED US TO HURRY—
DAMN HURRYING! I WANT TO TALK TO YOU.
WILL, NOT NOW. I BELIEVE I KNOW WHAT IT IS YOU WANT TO SAY, BUT THIS ISN'T THE TIME OR PLACE, IS IT?
BELIEVE ME, I AM AS EAGER FOR THE TALK AS YOU, FOR IT HAS BEEN WEIGHING HEAVILY ON MY MIND—

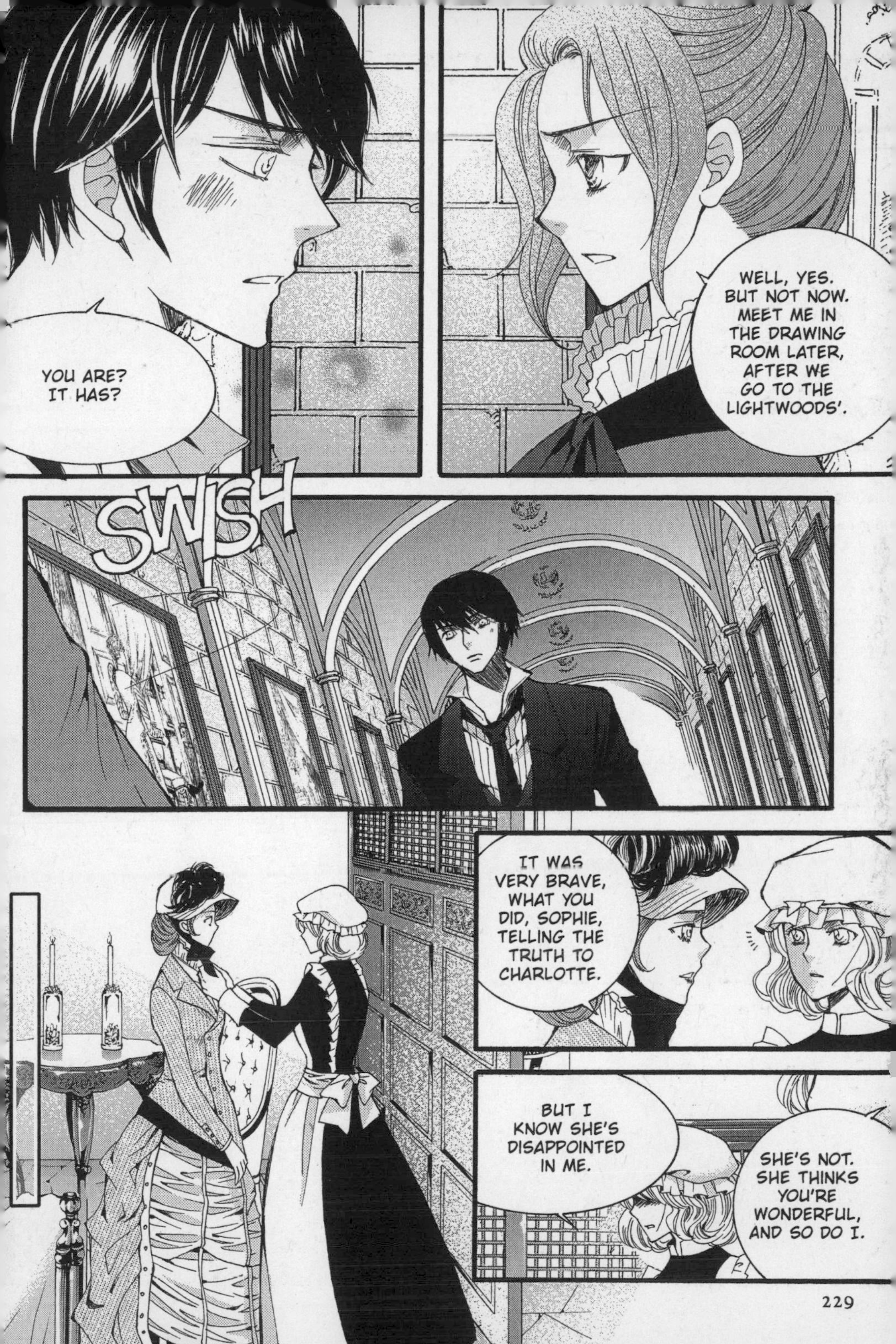
WELL, YES. BUT NOT NOW. MEET ME IN THE DRAWING ROOM LATER, AFTER WE GO TO THE LIGHTWOODS'.
YOU ARE? IT HAS?
SWISH
IT WAS VERY BRAVE, WHAT YOU DID, SOPHIE, TELLING THE TRUTH TO CHARLOTTE.
BUT I KNOW SHE'S DISAPPOINTED IN ME.
SHE'S NOT. SHE THINKS YOU'RE WONDERFUL, AND SO DO I.

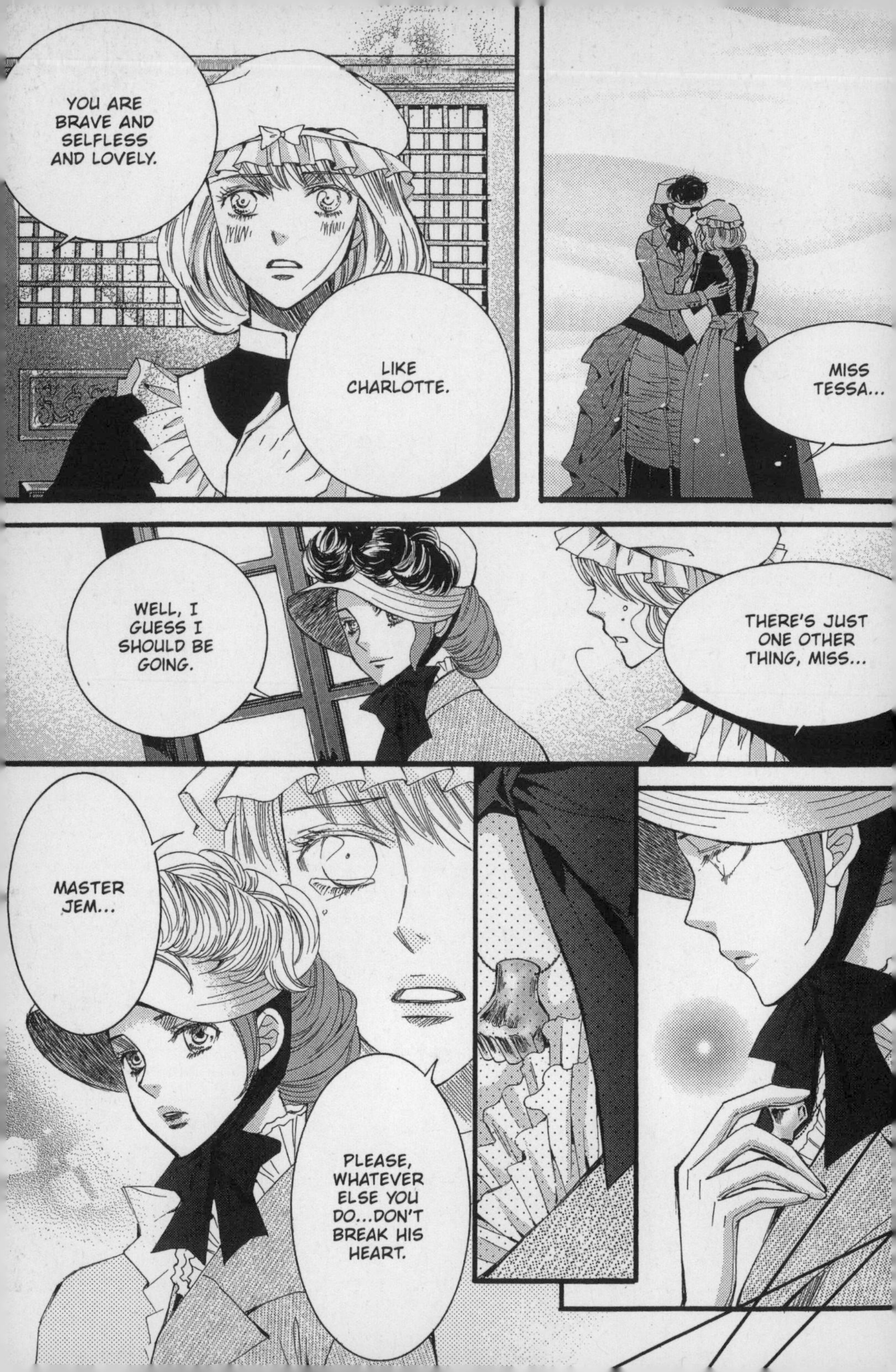
YOU ARE BRAVE AND SELFLESS AND LOVELY.
LIKE CHARLOTTE.
MISS TESSA...
WELL, I GUESS I SHOULD BE GOING.
THERE'S JUST ONE OTHER THING, MISS...
MASTER JEM...
PLEASE, WHATEVER ELSE YOU DO...DON'T BREAK HIS HEART.

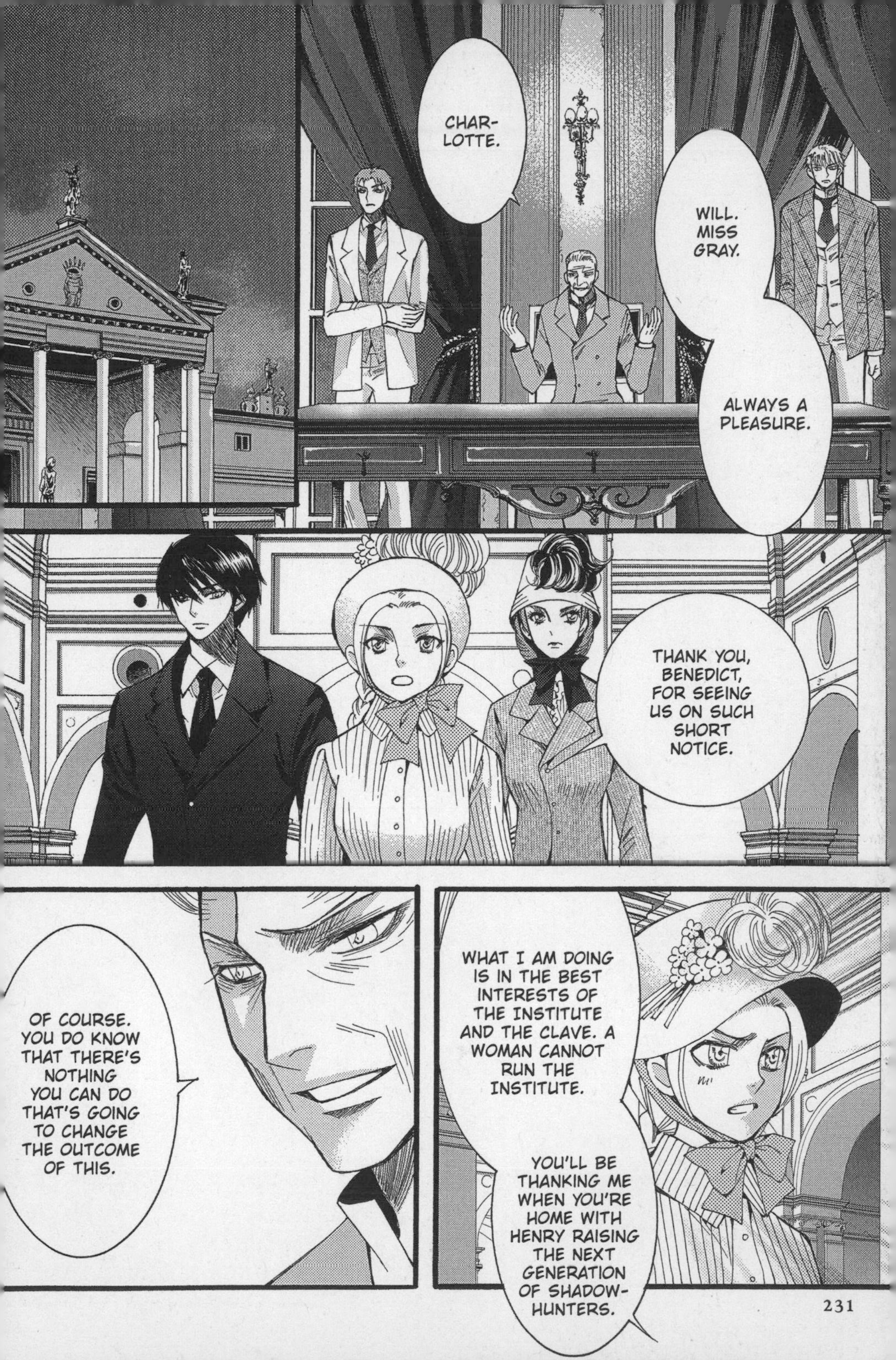
CHAR-LOTTE.
WILL. MISS GRAY.
ALWAYS A PLEASURE.
THANK YOU, BENEDICT, FOR SEEING US ON SUCH SHORT NOTICE.
OF COURSE. YOU DO KNOW THAT THERE'S NOTHING YOU CAN DO THAT'S GOING TO CHANGE THE OUTCOME OF THIS.
WHAT I AM DOING IS IN THE BEST INTERESTS OF THE INSTITUTE AND THE CLAVE. A WOMAN CANNOT RUN THE INSTITUTE.
YOU'LL BE THANKING ME WHEN YOU'RE HOME WITH HENRY RAISING THE NEXT GENERATION OF SHADOW-HUNTERS.

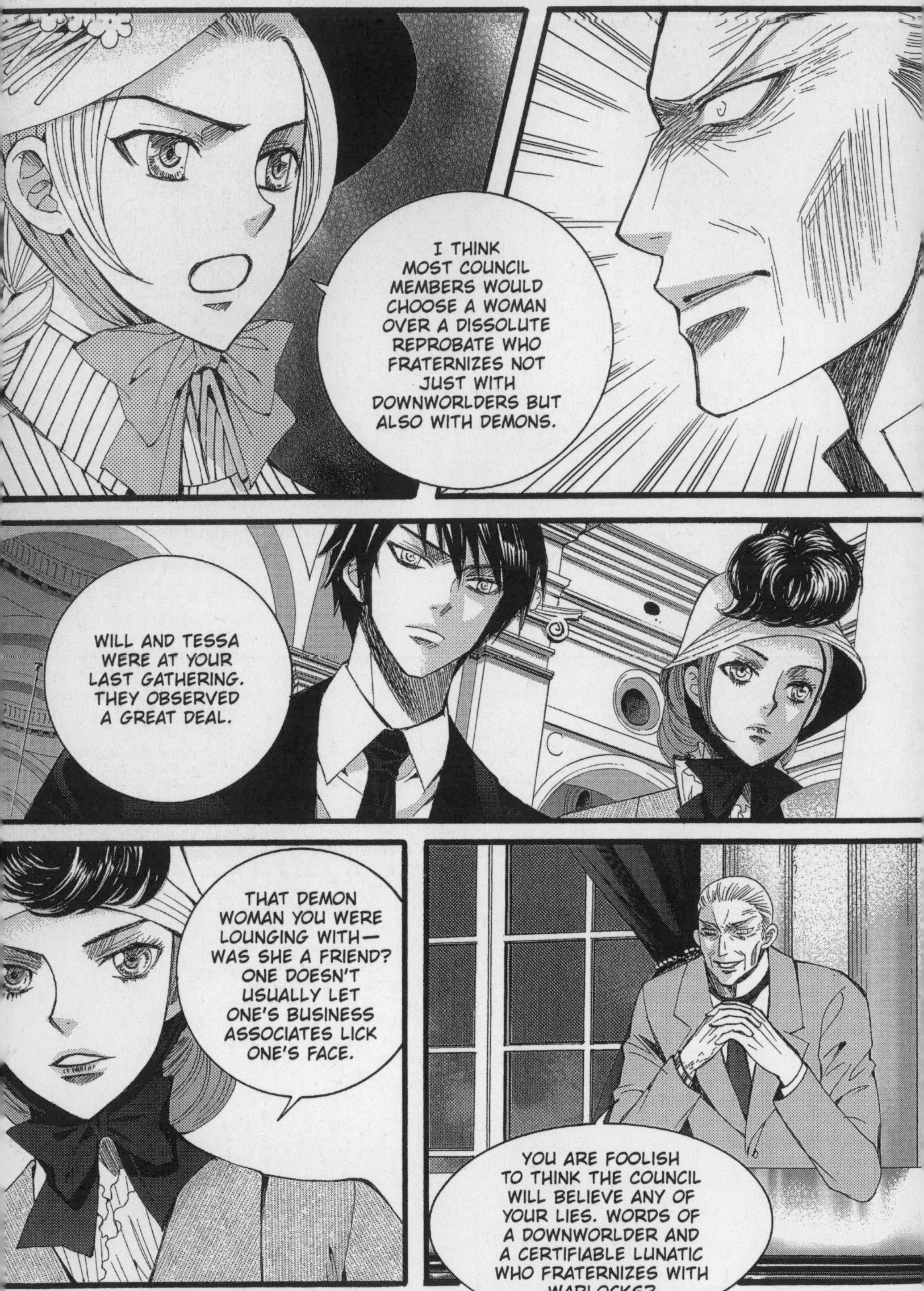
I THINK MOST COUNCIL MEMBERS WOULD CHOOSE A WOMAN OVER A DISSOLUTE REPROBATE WHO FRATERNIZES NOT JUST WITH DOWNWORLDERS BUT ALSO WITH DEMONS.
WILL AND TESSA WERE AT YOUR LAST GATHERING. THEY OBSERVED A GREAT DEAL.
THAT DEMON WOMAN YOU WERE LOUNGING WITH— WAS SHE A FRIEND? ONE DOESN'T USUALLY LET ONE'S BUSINESS ASSOCIATES LICK ONE'S FACE.
YOU ARE FOOLISH TO THINK THE COUNCIL WILL BELIEVE ANY OF YOUR LIES. WORDS OF A DOWNWORLDER AND A CERTIFIABLE LUNATIC WHO FRATERNIZES WITH WARLOCKS?

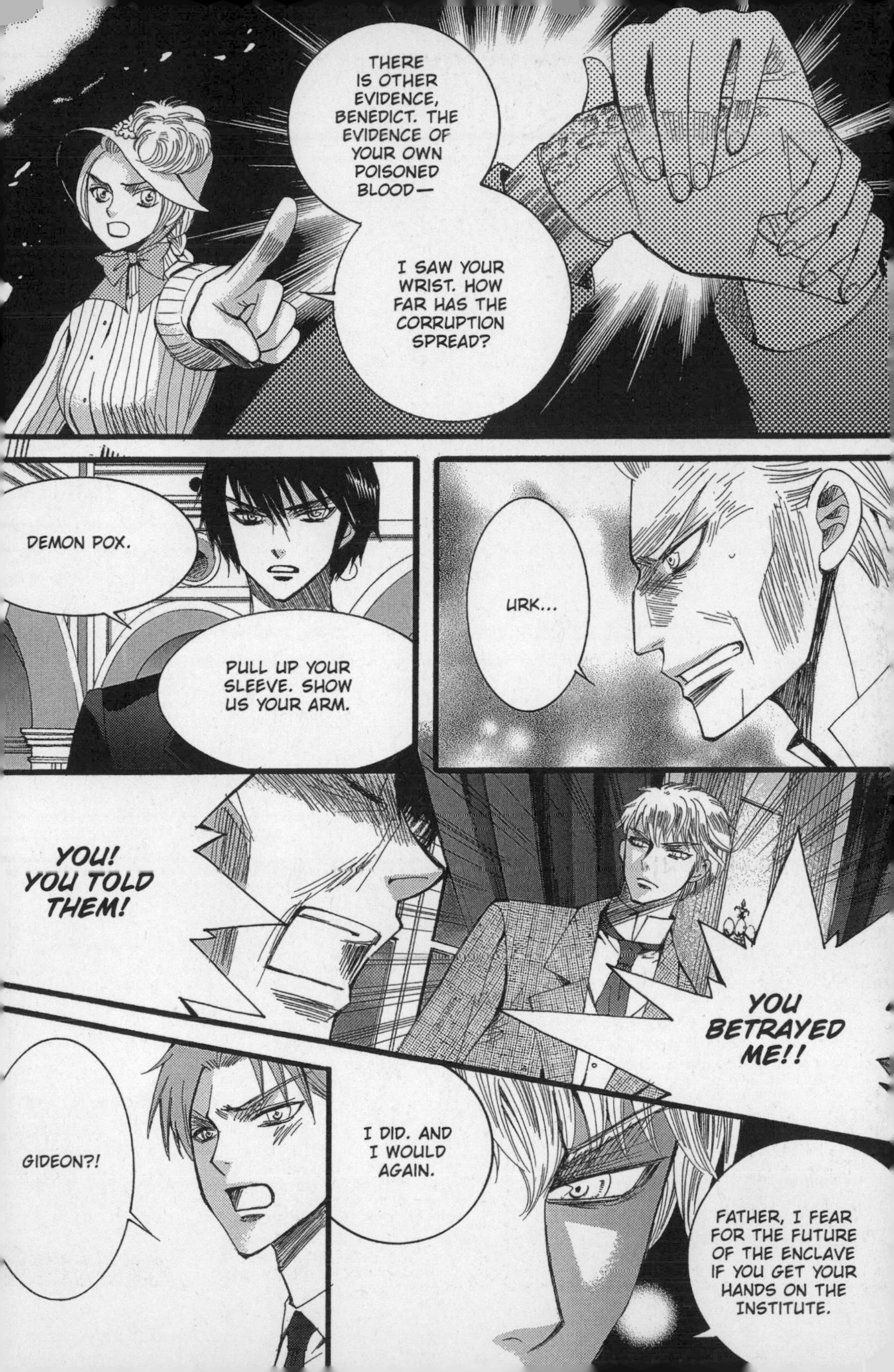
THERE IS OTHER EVIDENCE, BENEDICT. THE EVIDENCE OF YOUR OWN POISONED BLOOD—
I SAW YOUR WRIST. HOW FAR HAS THE CORRUPTION SPREAD?
DEMON POX.
PULL UP YOUR SLEEVE. SHOW US YOUR ARM.
URK...
YOU! YOU TOLD THEM!
YOU BETRAYED ME!!
GIDEON?!
I DID. AND I WOULD AGAIN.
FATHER, I FEAR FOR THE FUTURE OF THE ENCLAVE IF YOU GET YOUR HANDS ON THE INSTITUTE.

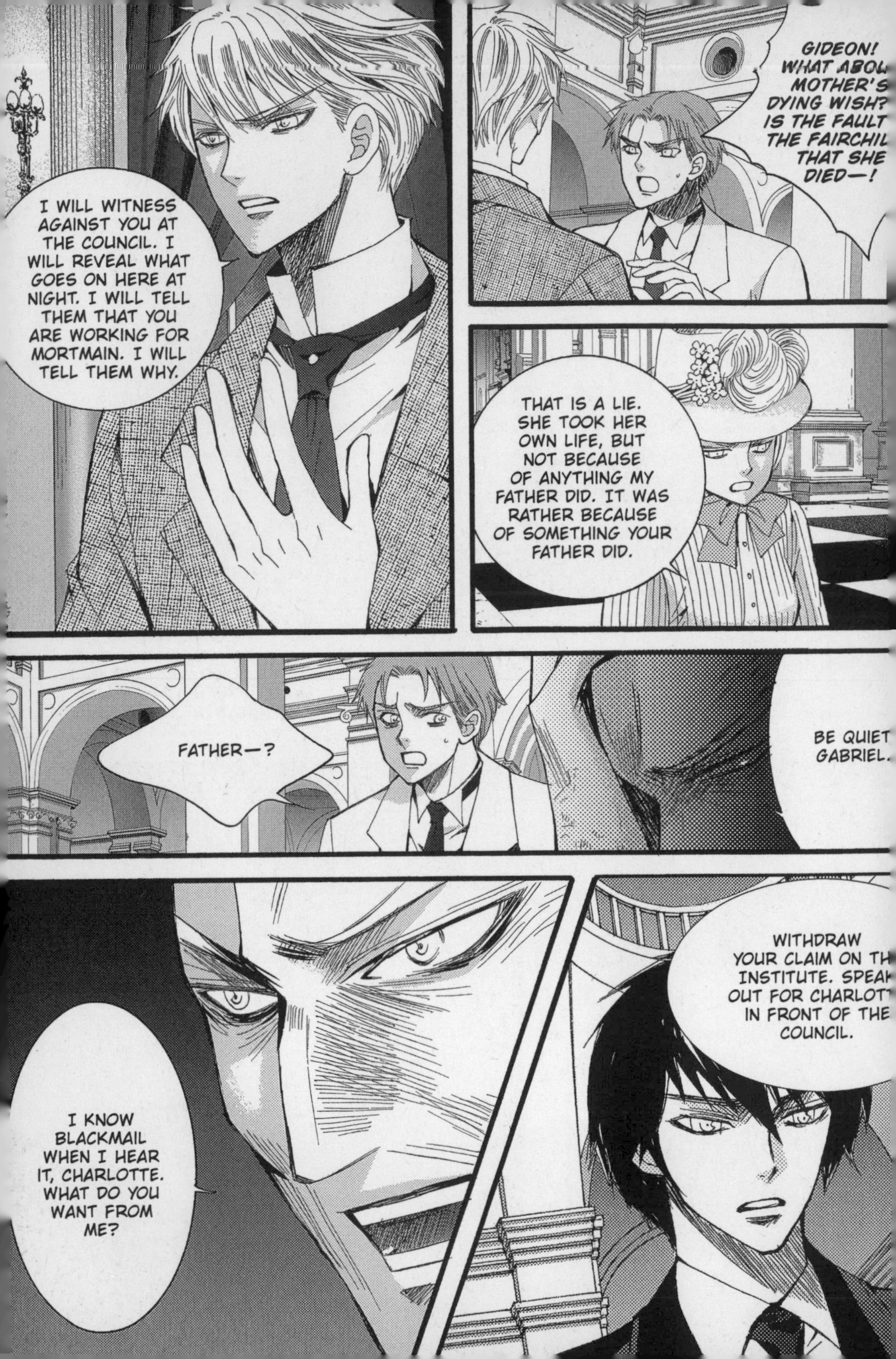
I WILL WITNESS AGAINST YOU AT THE COUNCIL. I WILL REVEAL WHAT GOES ON HERE AT NIGHT. I WILL TELL THEM THAT YOU ARE WORKING FOR MORTMAIN. I WILL TELL THEM WHY.
GIDEON! WHAT ABOU MOTHER'S DYING WISH? IS THE FAULT THE FAIRCHIL THAT SHE DIED—!
THAT IS A LIE. SHE TOOK HER OWN LIFE, BUT NOT BECAUSE OF ANYTHING MY FATHER DID. IT WAS RATHER BECAUSE OF SOMETHING YOUR FATHER DID.
FATHER—?
BE QUIET GABRIEL.
I KNOW BLACKMAIL WHEN I HEAR IT, CHARLOTTE. WHAT DO YOU WANT FROM ME?
WITHDRAW YOUR CLAIM ON TH INSTITUTE. SPEAK OUT FOR CHARLOTT IN FRONT OF THE COUNCIL.

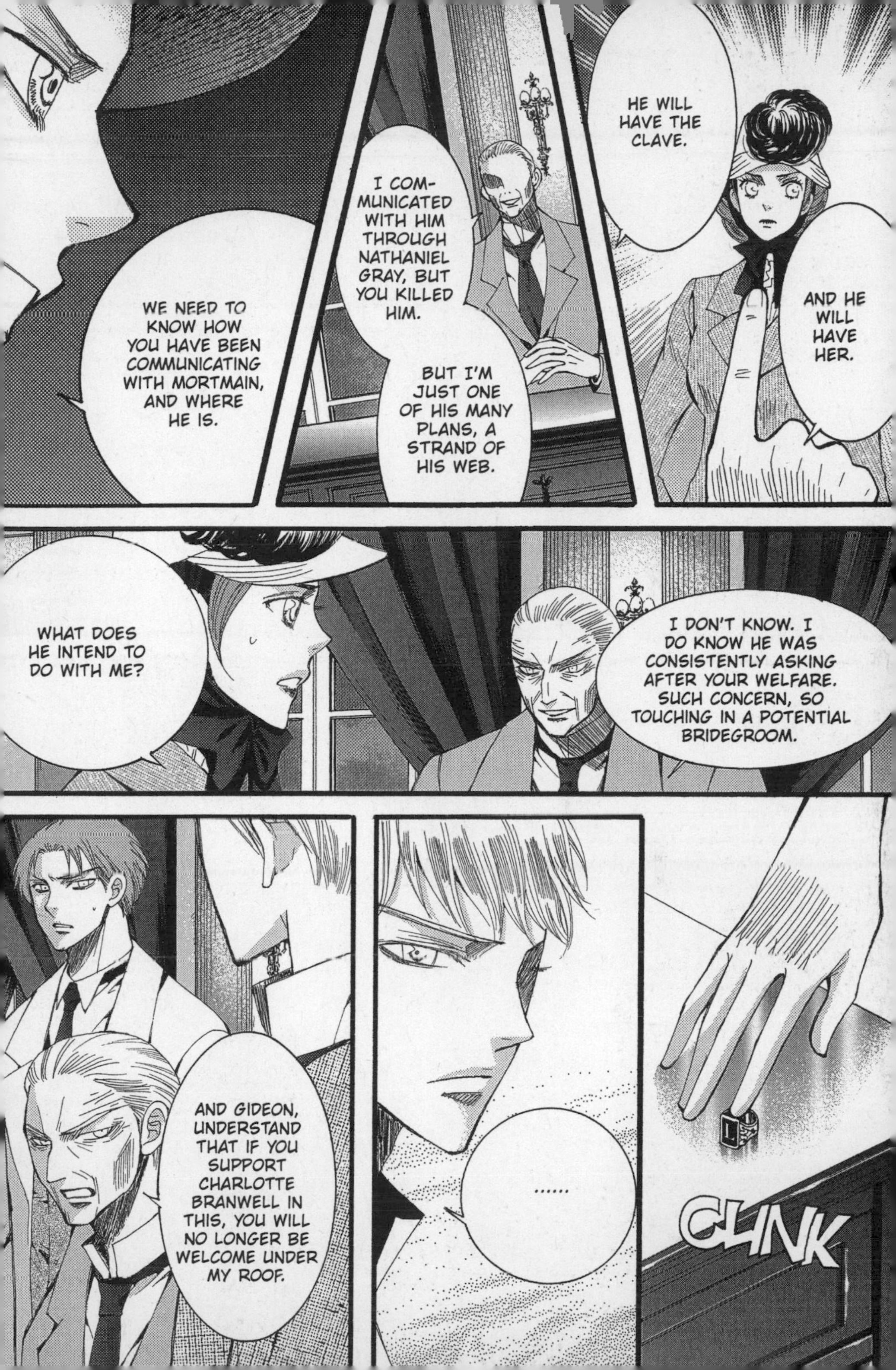
WE NEED TO KNOW HOW YOU HAVE BEEN COMMUNICATING WITH MORTMAIN, AND WHERE HE IS.
I COM-MUNICATED WITH HIM THROUGH NATHANIEL GRAY, BUT YOU KILLED HIM.
BUT I'M JUST ONE OF HIS MANY PLANS, A STRAND OF HIS WEB.
HE WILL HAVE THE CLAVE.
AND HE WILL HAVE HER.
WHAT DOES HE INTEND TO DO WITH ME?
I DON'T KNOW. I DO KNOW HE WAS CONSISTENTLY ASKING AFTER YOUR WELFARE. SUCH CONCERN, SO TOUCHING IN A POTENTIAL BRIDEGROOM.
AND GIDEON, UNDERSTAND THAT IF YOU SUPPORT CHARLOTTE BRANWELL IN THIS, YOU WILL NO LONGER BE WELCOME UNDER MY ROOF.
......
CLINK

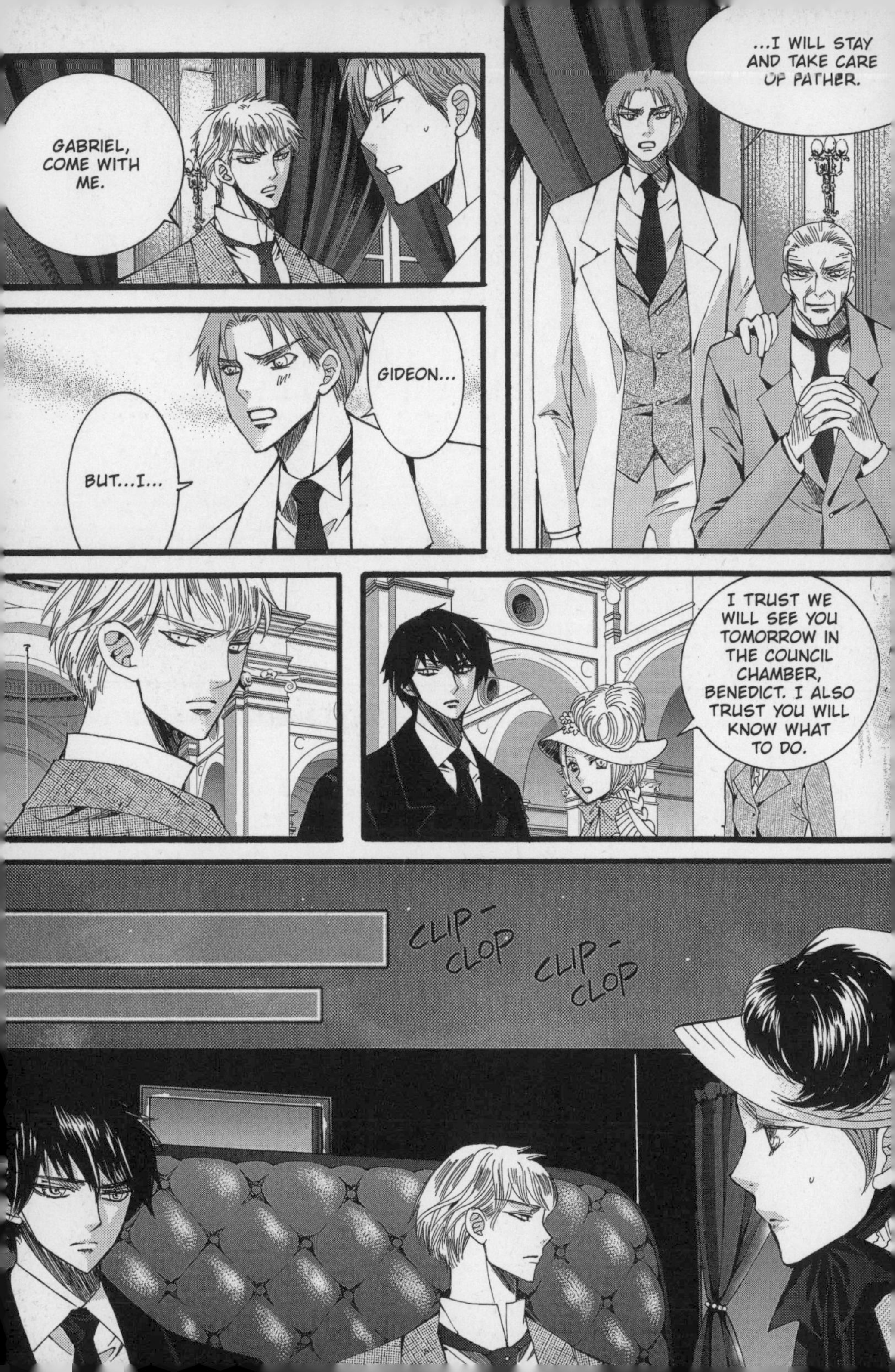
GABRIEL, COME WITH ME.
GIDEON...
BUT...I...
...I WILL STAY AND TAKE CARE OF FATHER.
I TRUST WE WILL SEE YOU TOMORROW IN THE COUNCIL CHAMBER, BENEDICT. I ALSO TRUST YOU WILL KNOW WHAT TO DO.
CLIP - CLOP
CLIP - CLOP

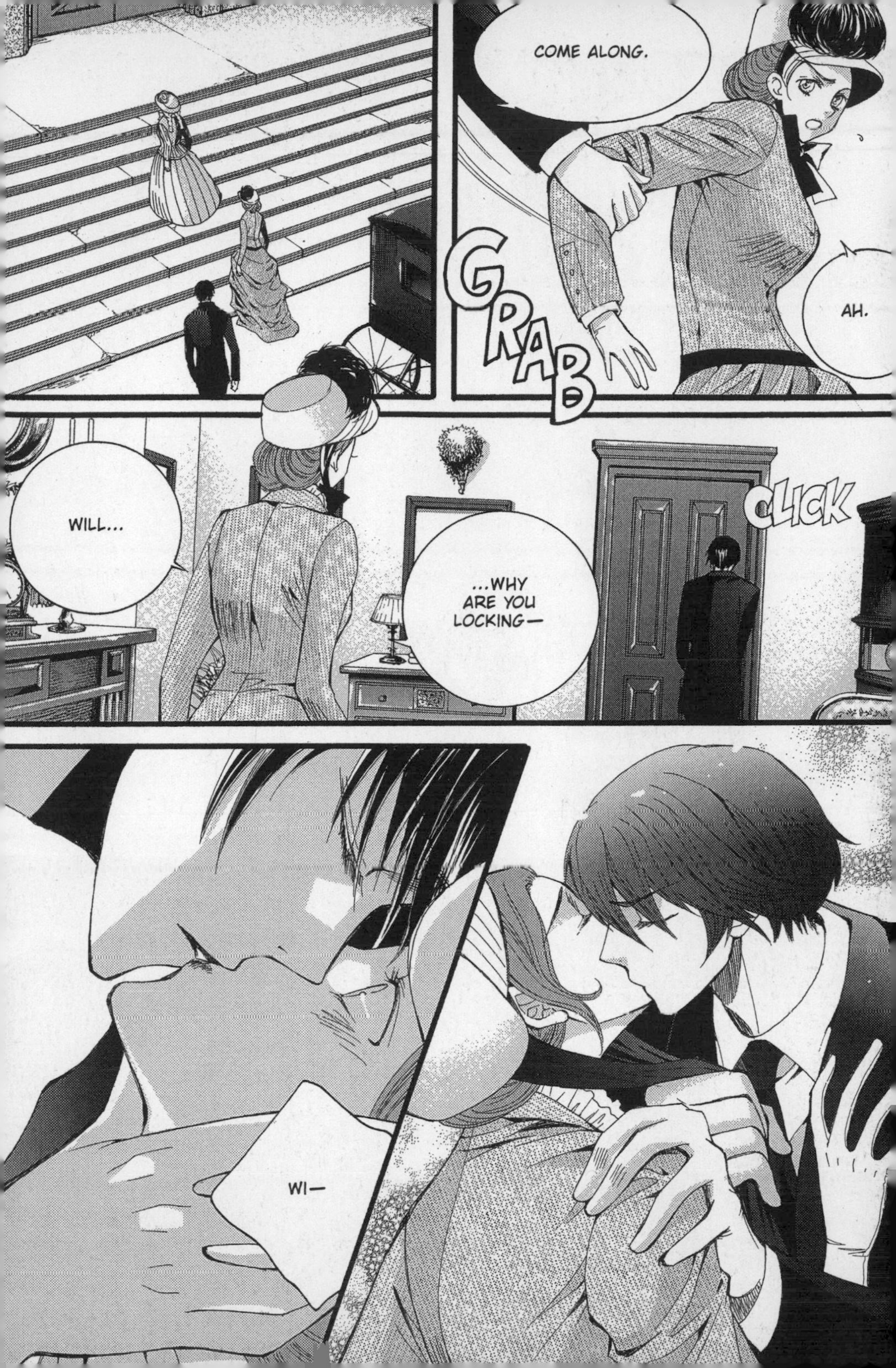
COME ALONG.
GRAB
AH.
WILL...
...WHY ARE YOU LOCKING—
CLICK
WI—

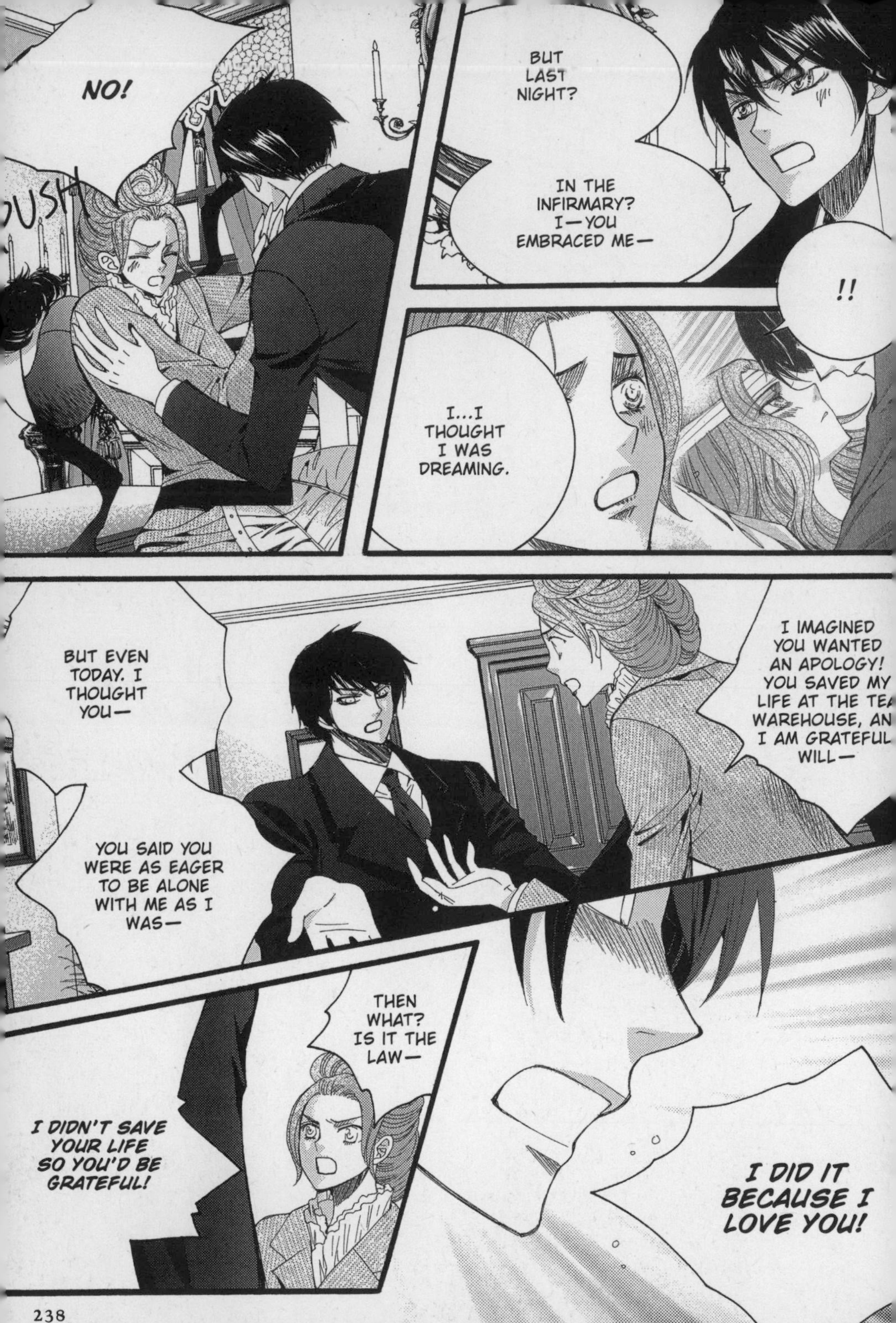
NO!
PUSH
BUT LAST NIGHT?
IN THE INFIRMARY? I—YOU EMBRACED ME—
!!
I...I THOUGHT I WAS DREAMING.
BUT EVEN TODAY. I THOUGHT YOU—
YOU SAID YOU WERE AS EAGER TO BE ALONE WITH ME AS I WAS—
I IMAGINED YOU WANTED AN APOLOGY! YOU SAVED MY LIFE AT THE TEA WAREHOUSE, AN I AM GRATEFUL WILL—
THEN WHAT? IS IT THE LAW—
I DIDN'T SAVE YOUR LIFE SO YOU'D BE GRATEFUL!
I DID IT BECAUSE I LOVE YOU!

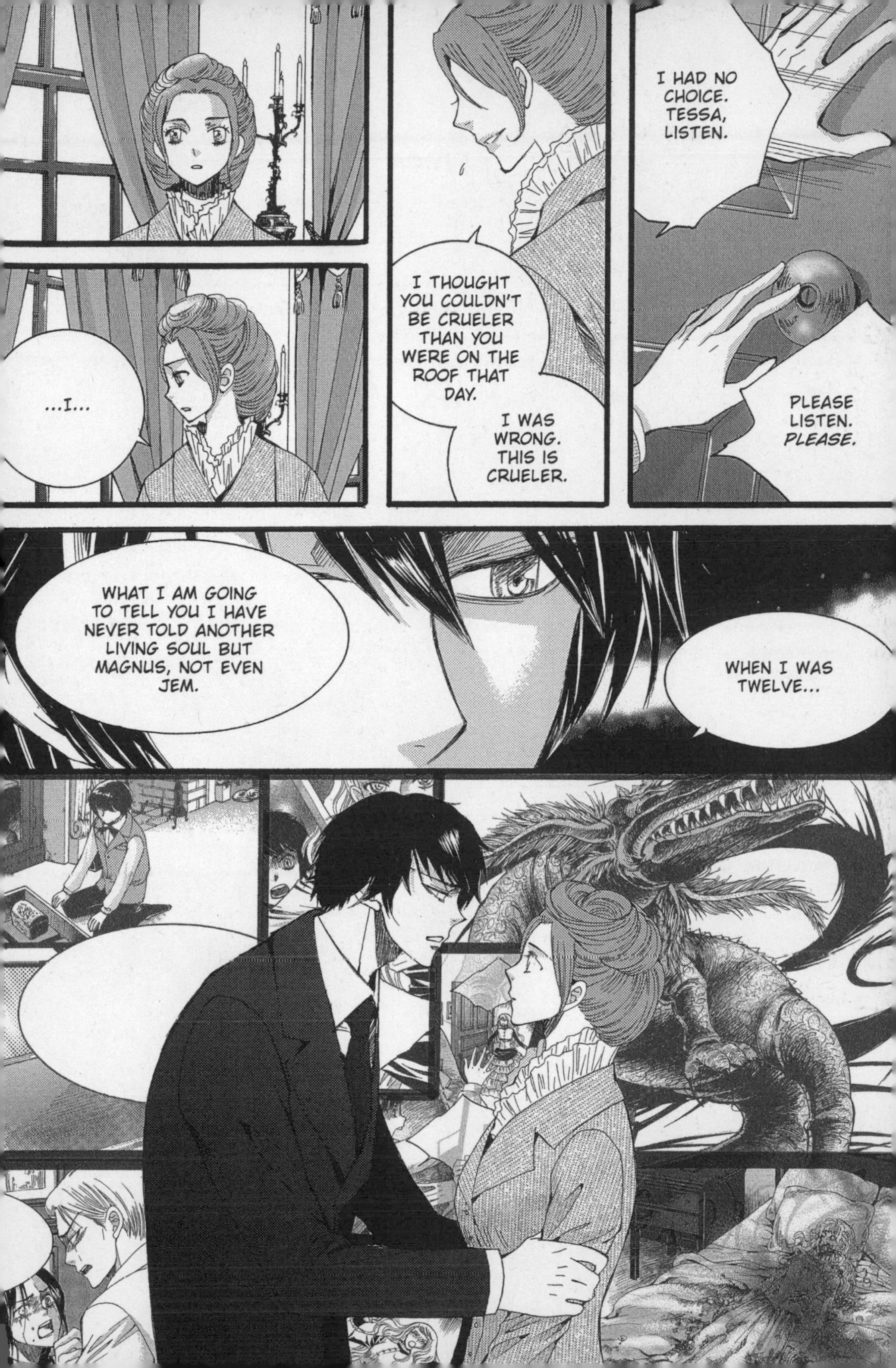
...I...
I THOUGHT YOU COULDN'T BE CRUELER THAN YOU WERE ON THE ROOF THAT DAY.
I WAS WRONG. THIS IS CRUELER.
I HAD NO CHOICE. TESSA, LISTEN.
PLEASE LISTEN. *PLEASE.*
WHAT I AM GOING TO TELL YOU I HAVE NEVER TOLD ANOTHER LIVING SOUL BUT MAGNUS, NOT EVEN JEM.
WHEN I WAS TWELVE...

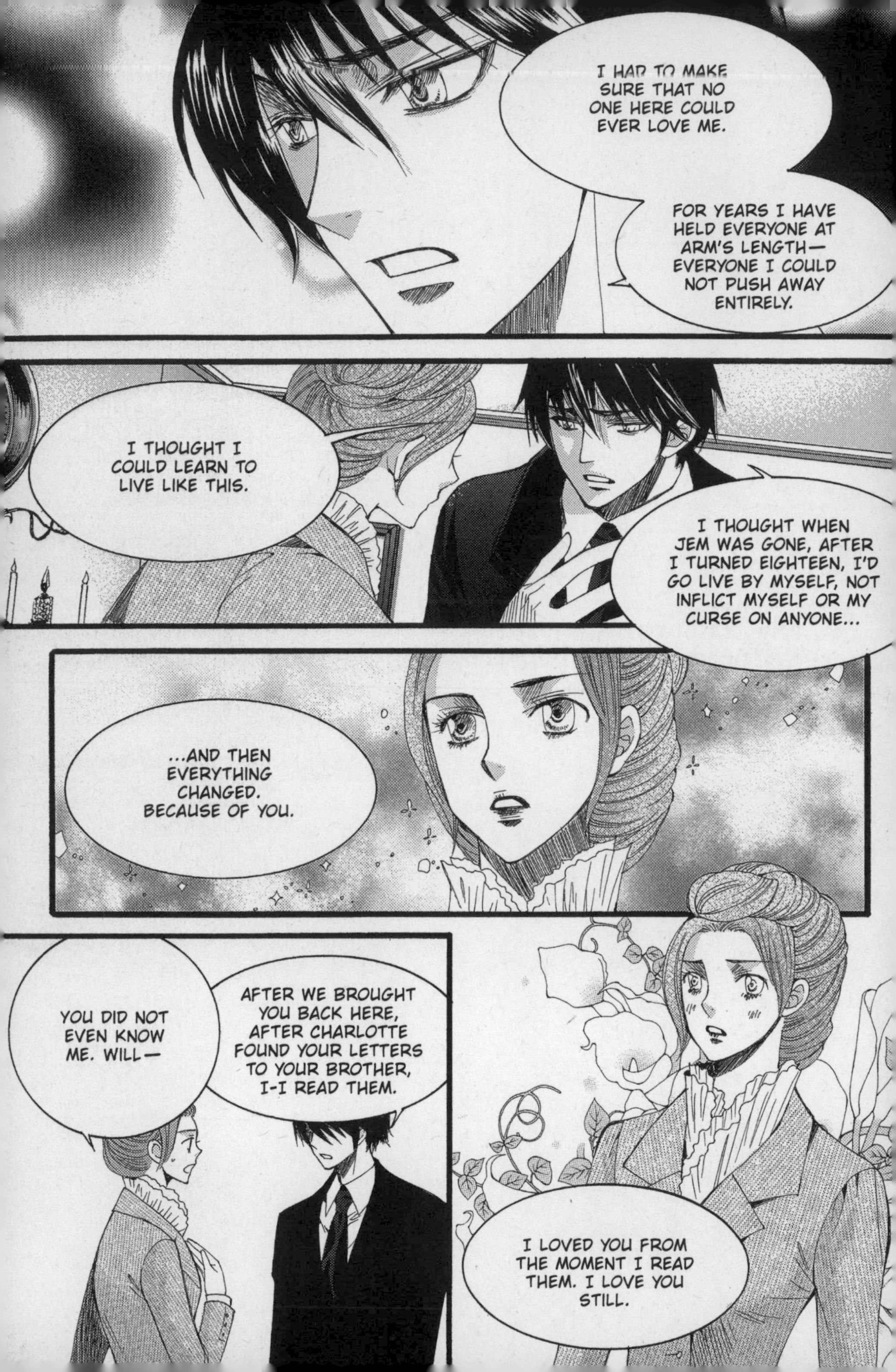
I HAD TO MAKE SURE THAT NO ONE HERE COULD EVER LOVE ME.
FOR YEARS I HAVE HELD EVERYONE AT ARM'S LENGTH— EVERYONE I COULD NOT PUSH AWAY ENTIRELY.
I THOUGHT WHEN JEM WAS GONE, AFTER I TURNED EIGHTEEN, I'D GO LIVE BY MYSELF, NOT INFLICT MYSELF OR MY CURSE ON ANYONE...
I THOUGHT I COULD LEARN TO LIVE LIKE THIS.
...AND THEN EVERYTHING CHANGED. BECAUSE OF YOU.
AFTER WE BROUGHT YOU BACK HERE, AFTER CHARLOTTE FOUND YOUR LETTERS TO YOUR BROTHER, I-I READ THEM.
YOU DID NOT EVEN KNOW ME. WILL—
I LOVED YOU FROM THE MOMENT I READ THEM. I LOVE YOU STILL.

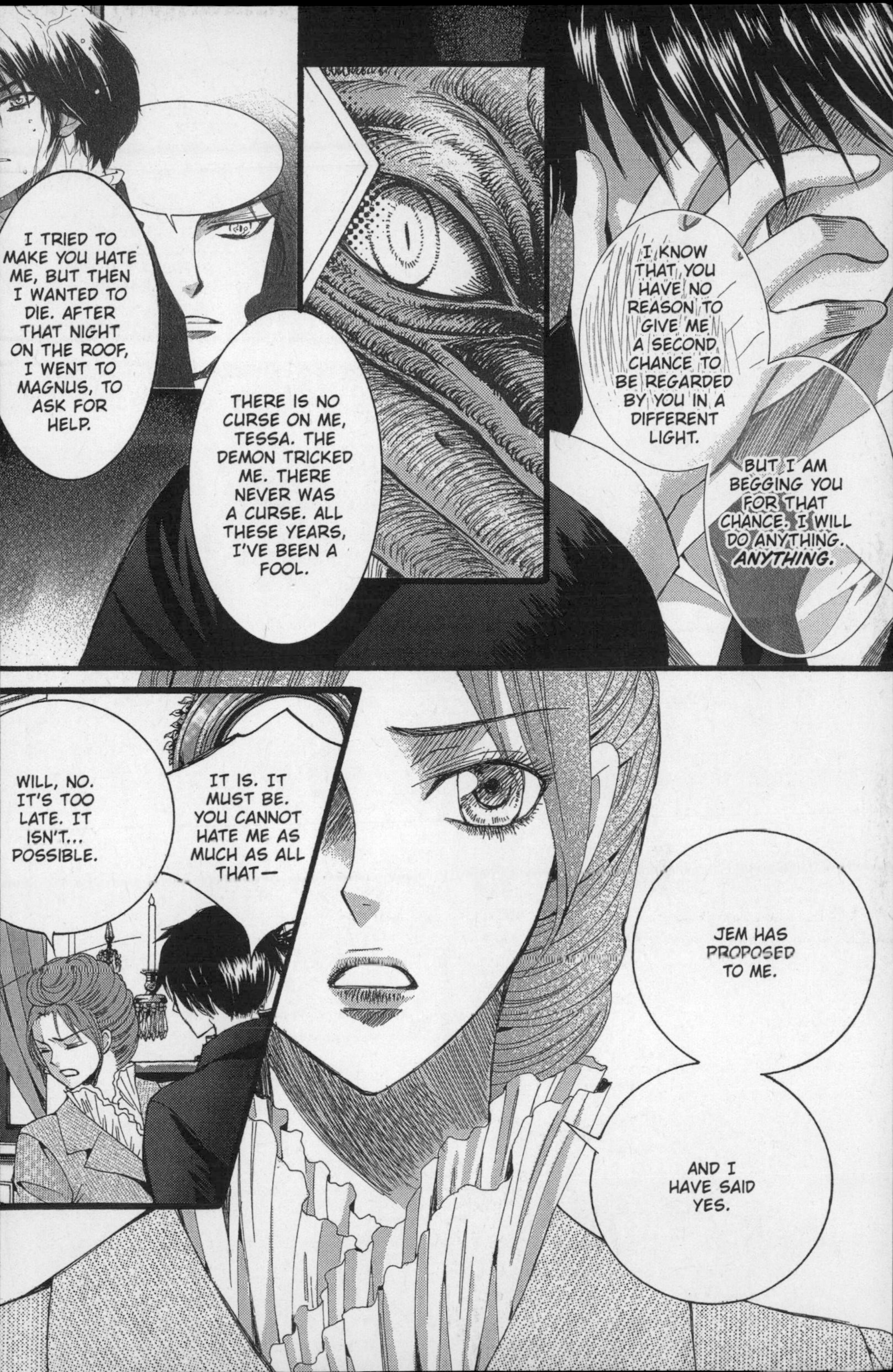
I TRIED TO MAKE YOU HATE ME, BUT THEN I WANTED TO DIE. AFTER THAT NIGHT ON THE ROOF, I WENT TO MAGNUS, TO ASK FOR HELP.
THERE IS NO CURSE ON ME, TESSA. THE DEMON TRICKED ME. THERE NEVER WAS A CURSE. ALL THESE YEARS, I'VE BEEN A FOOL.
I KNOW THAT YOU HAVE NO REASON TO GIVE ME A SECOND CHANCE TO BE REGARDED BY YOU IN A DIFFERENT LIGHT.
BUT I AM BEGGING YOU FOR THAT CHANCE. I WILL DO ANYTHING. ***ANYTHING.***
WILL, NO. IT'S TOO LATE. IT ISN'T... POSSIBLE.
IT IS. IT MUST BE. YOU CANNOT HATE ME AS MUCH AS ALL THAT—
JEM HAS PROPOSED TO ME.
AND I HAVE SAID YES.

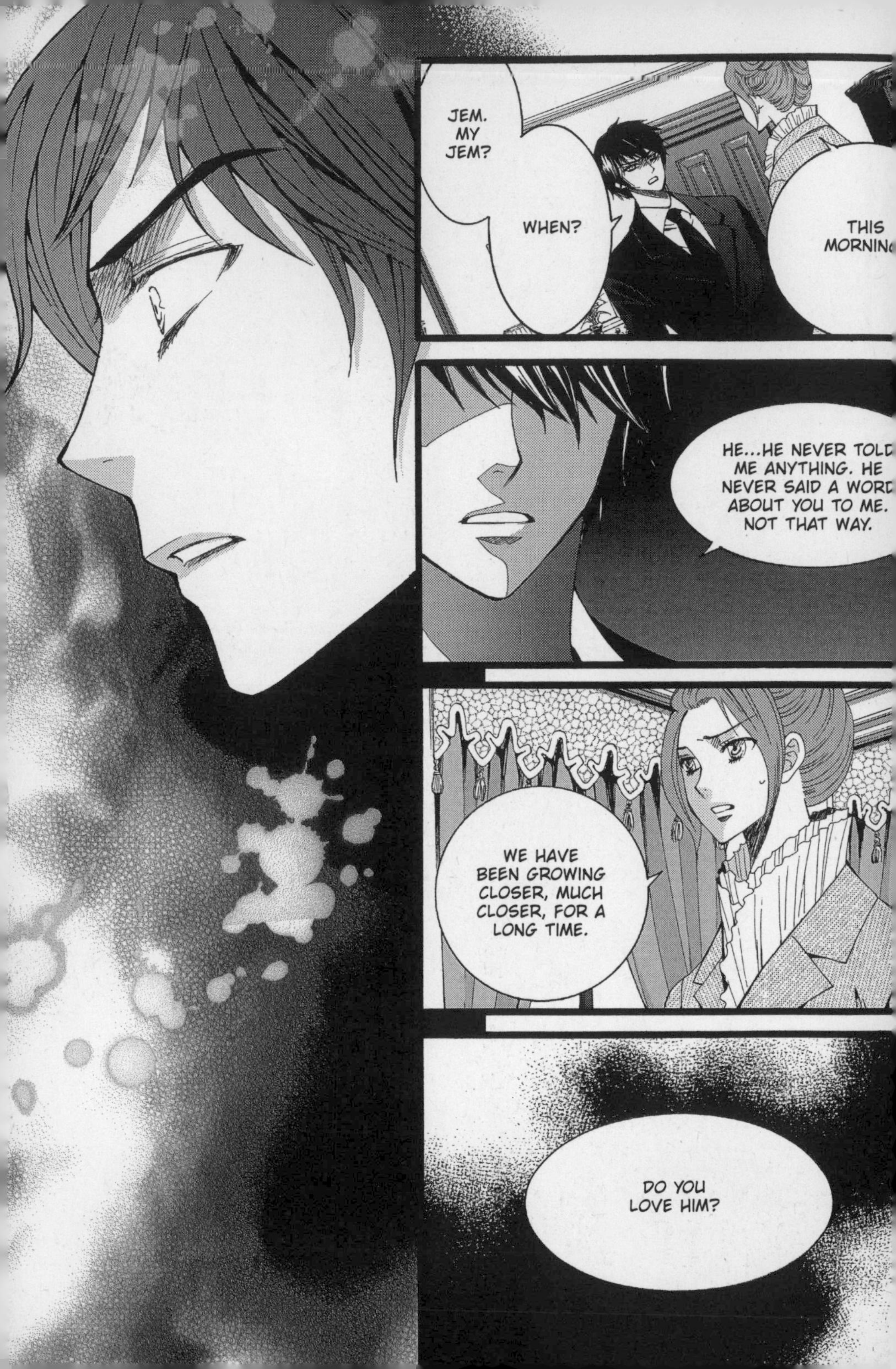
JEM. MY JEM?
WHEN?
THIS MORNING
HE...HE NEVER TOLD ME ANYTHING. HE NEVER SAID A WORD ABOUT YOU TO ME. NOT THAT WAY.
WE HAVE BEEN GROWING CLOSER, MUCH CLOSER, FOR A LONG TIME.
DO YOU LOVE HIM?

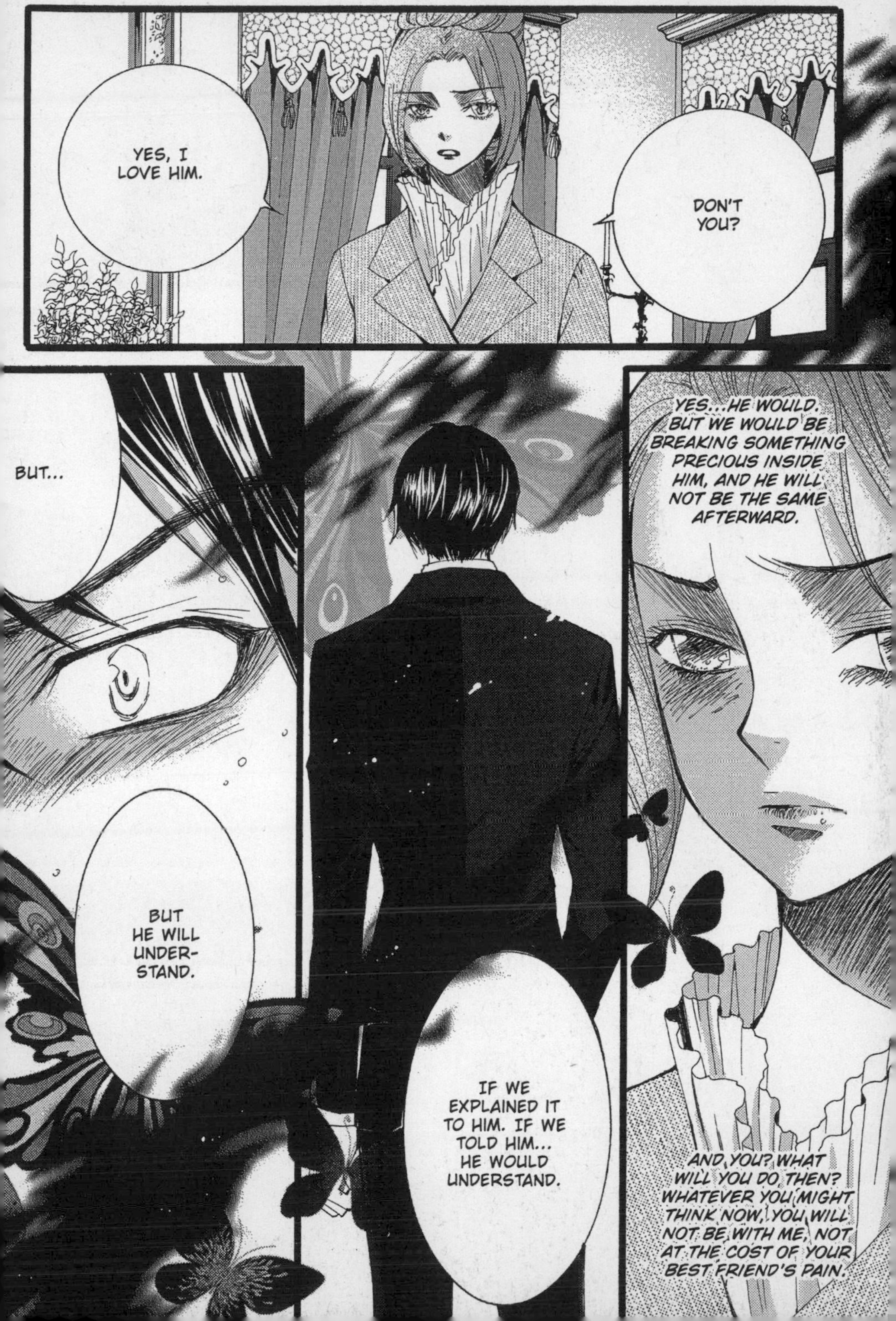
YES, I LOVE HIM.
DON'T YOU?
BUT...
BUT HE WILL UNDER-STAND.
IF WE EXPLAINED IT TO HIM. IF WE TOLD HIM... HE WOULD UNDERSTAND.
YES...HE WOULD. BUT WE WOULD BE BREAKING SOMETHING PRECIOUS INSIDE HIM, AND HE WILL NOT BE THE SAME AFTERWARD.
AND YOU? WHAT WILL YOU DO THEN? WHATEVER YOU MIGHT THINK NOW, YOU WILL NOT BE WITH ME, NOT AT THE COST OF YOUR BEST FRIEND'S PAIN.

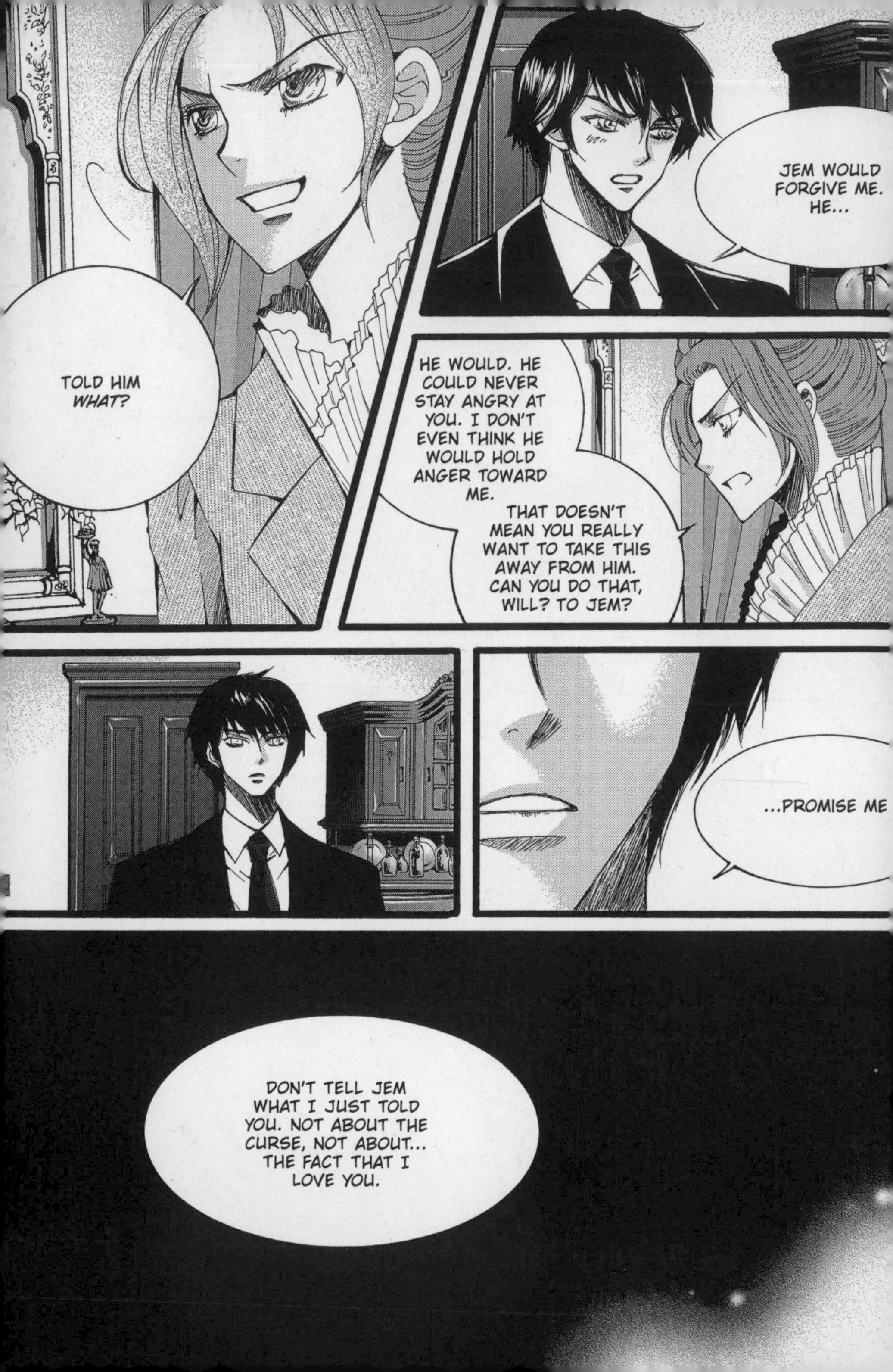
TOLD HIM *WHAT?*
JEM WOULD FORGIVE ME. HE...
HE WOULD. HE COULD NEVER STAY ANGRY AT YOU. I DON'T EVEN THINK HE WOULD HOLD ANGER TOWARD ME.
THAT DOESN'T MEAN YOU REALLY WANT TO TAKE THIS AWAY FROM HIM. CAN YOU DO THAT, WILL? TO JEM?
...PROMISE ME
DON'T TELL JEM WHAT I JUST TOLD YOU. NOT ABOUT THE CURSE, NOT ABOUT... THE FACT THAT I LOVE YOU.

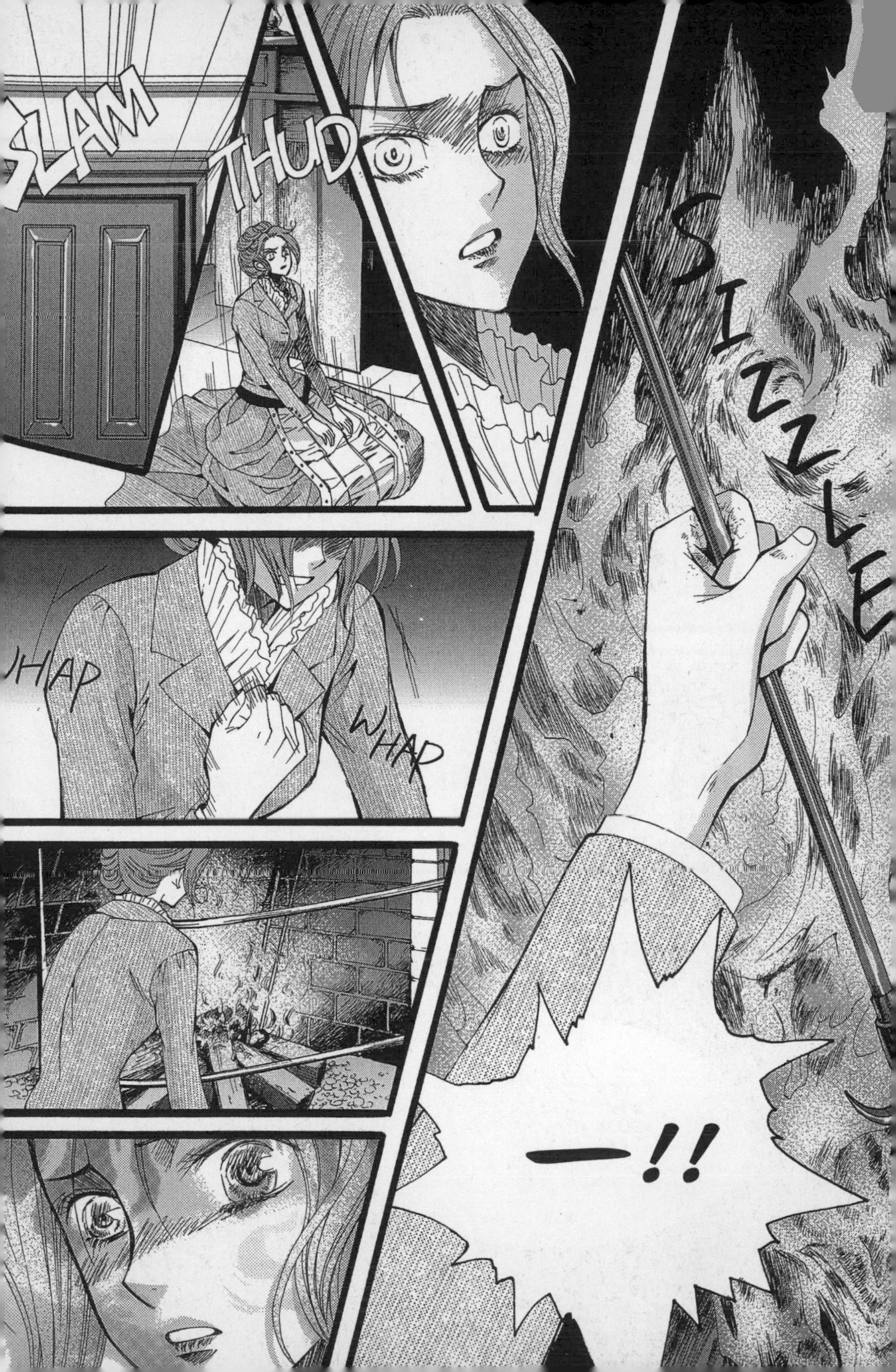
SLAM
THUD
SIZZLE
WHAP
WHAP
—!!

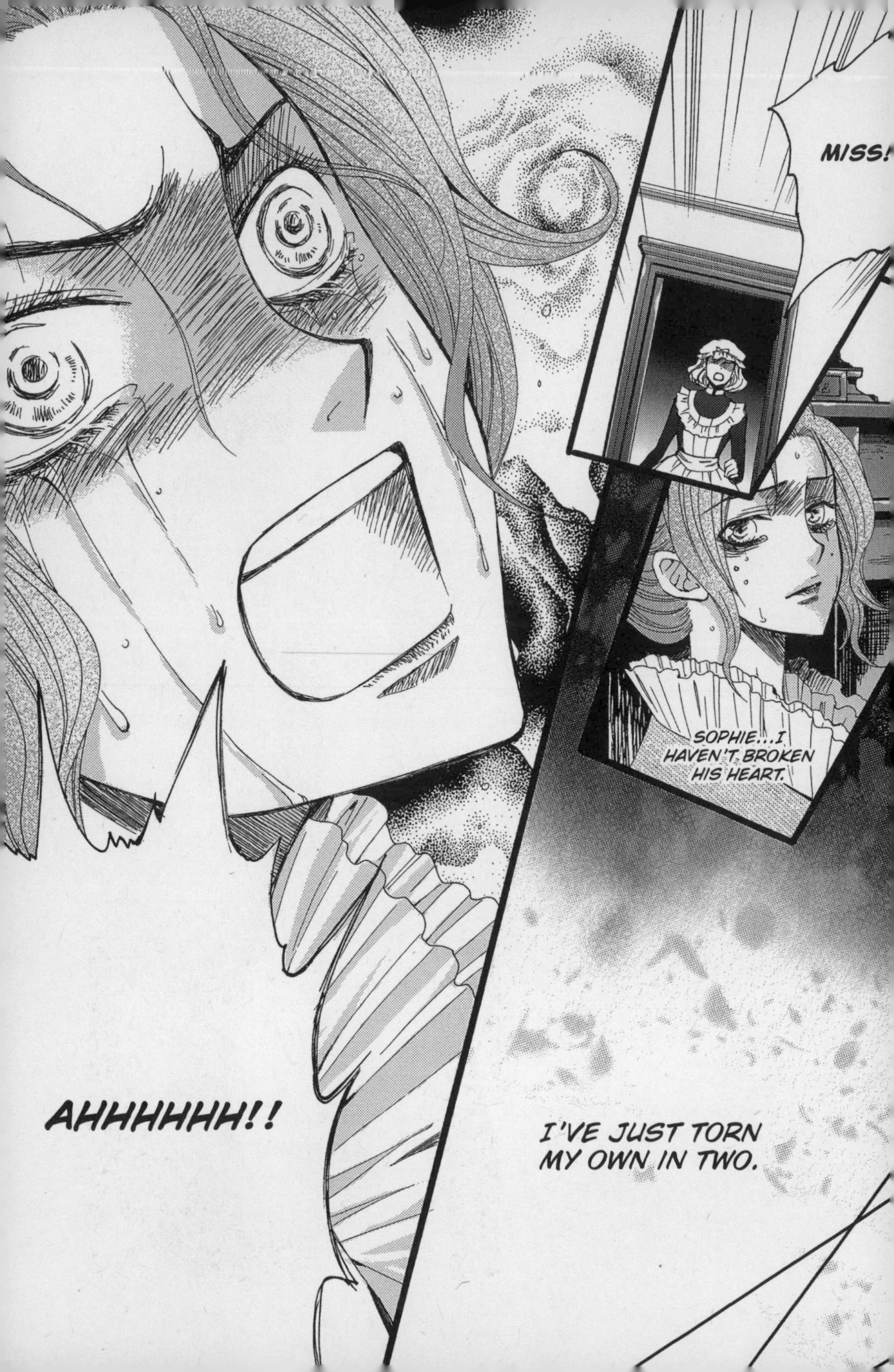
MISS!
SOPHIE...I HAVEN'T BROKEN HIS HEART.
I'VE JUST TORN MY OWN IN TWO.
AHHHHHH!!

THE INFERNAL DEVICES
CLOCKWORK PRINCE

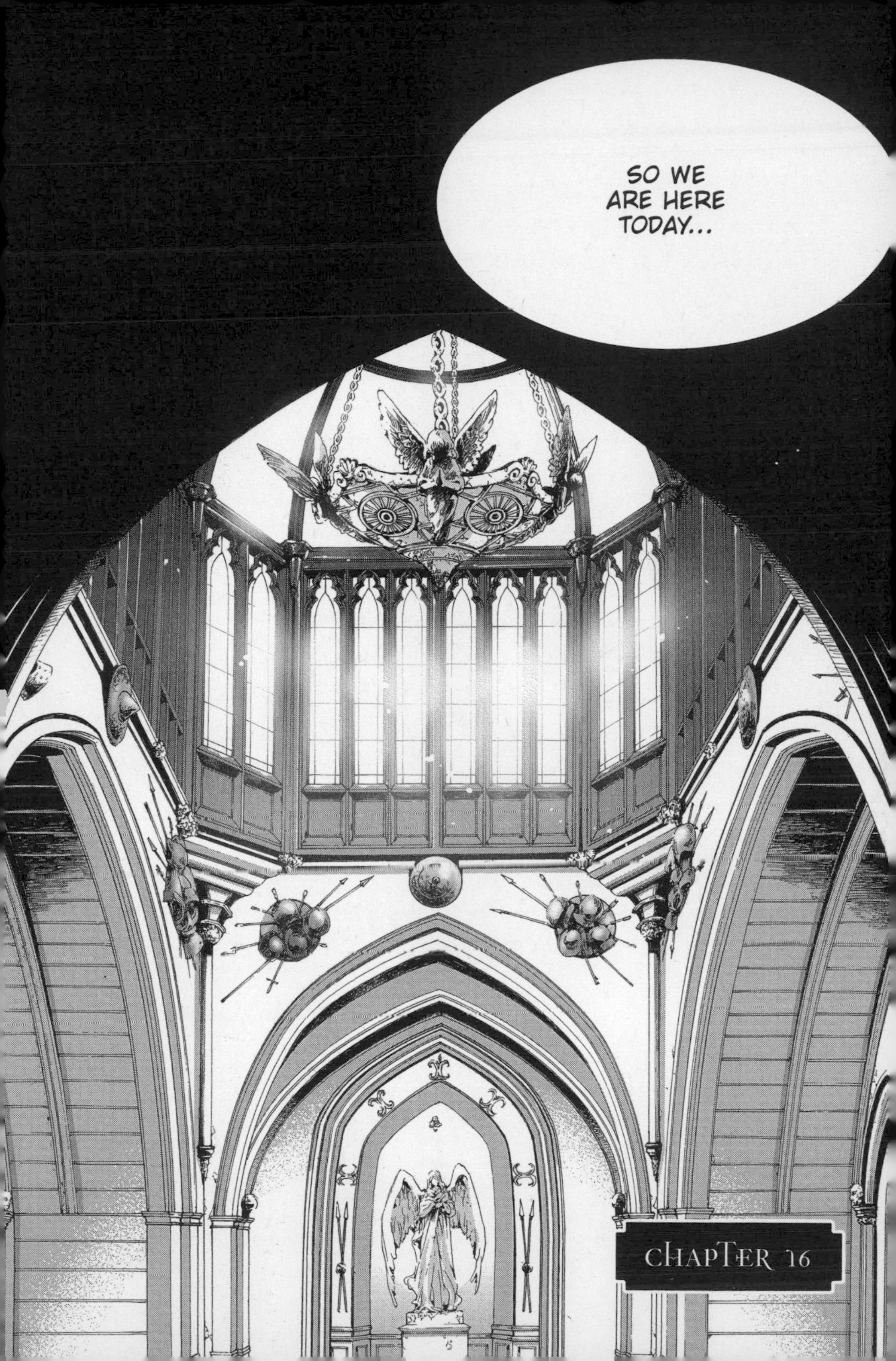
SO WE ARE HERE TODAY...
CHAPTER 16

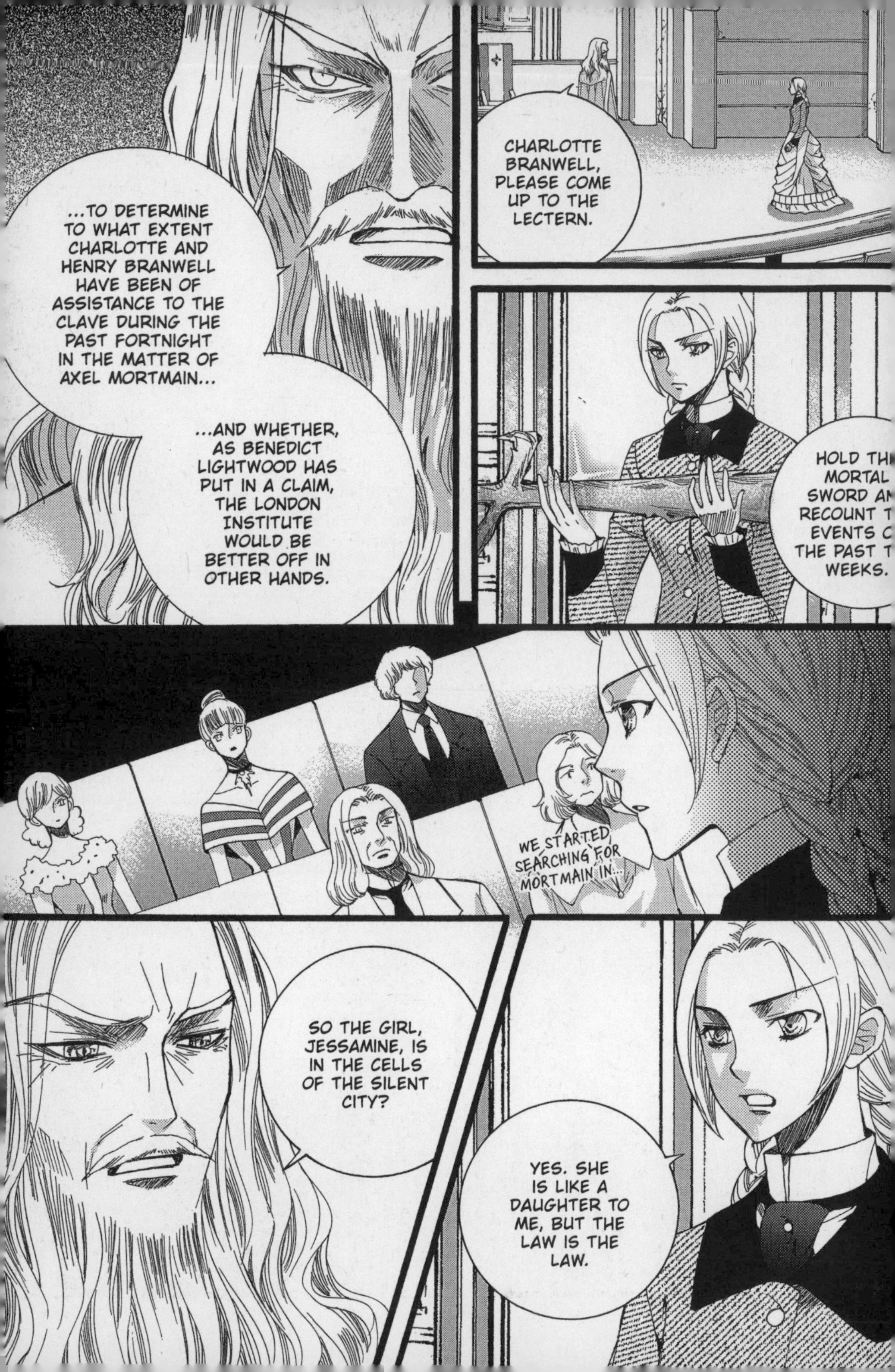
...TO DETERMINE TO WHAT EXTENT CHARLOTTE AND HENRY BRANWELL HAVE BEEN OF ASSISTANCE TO THE CLAVE DURING THE PAST FORTNIGHT IN THE MATTER OF AXEL MORTMAIN...
...AND WHETHER, AS BENEDICT LIGHTWOOD HAS PUT IN A CLAIM, THE LONDON INSTITUTE WOULD BE BETTER OFF IN OTHER HANDS.
CHARLOTTE BRANWELL, PLEASE COME UP TO THE LECTERN.
WE STARTED SEARCHING FOR MORTMAIN IN...
SO THE GIRL, JESSAMINE, IS IN THE CELLS OF THE SILENT CITY?
YES. SHE IS LIKE A DAUGHTER TO ME, BUT THE LAW IS THE LAW.

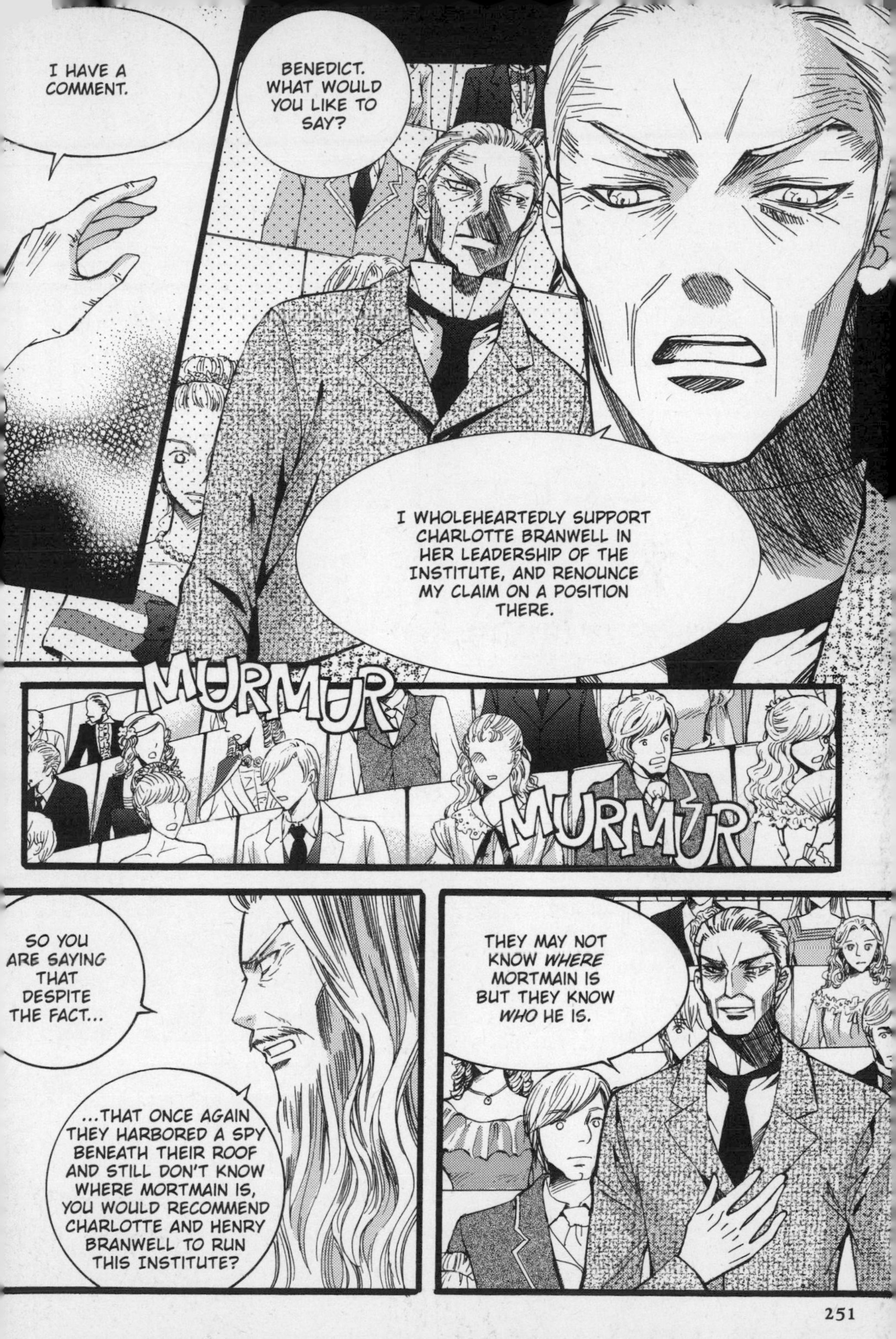
I HAVE A COMMENT.
BENEDICT. WHAT WOULD YOU LIKE TO SAY?
I WHOLEHEARTEDLY SUPPORT CHARLOTTE BRANWELL IN HER LEADERSHIP OF THE INSTITUTE, AND RENOUNCE MY CLAIM ON A POSITION THERE.
MURMUR
MURMUR
SO YOU ARE SAYING THAT DESPITE THE FACT...
...THAT ONCE AGAIN THEY HARBORED A SPY BENEATH THEIR ROOF AND STILL DON'T KNOW WHERE MORTMAIN IS, YOU WOULD RECOMMEND CHARLOTTE AND HENRY BRANWELL TO RUN THIS INSTITUTE?
THEY MAY NOT KNOW *WHERE* MORTMAIN IS BUT THEY KNOW *WHO* HE IS.

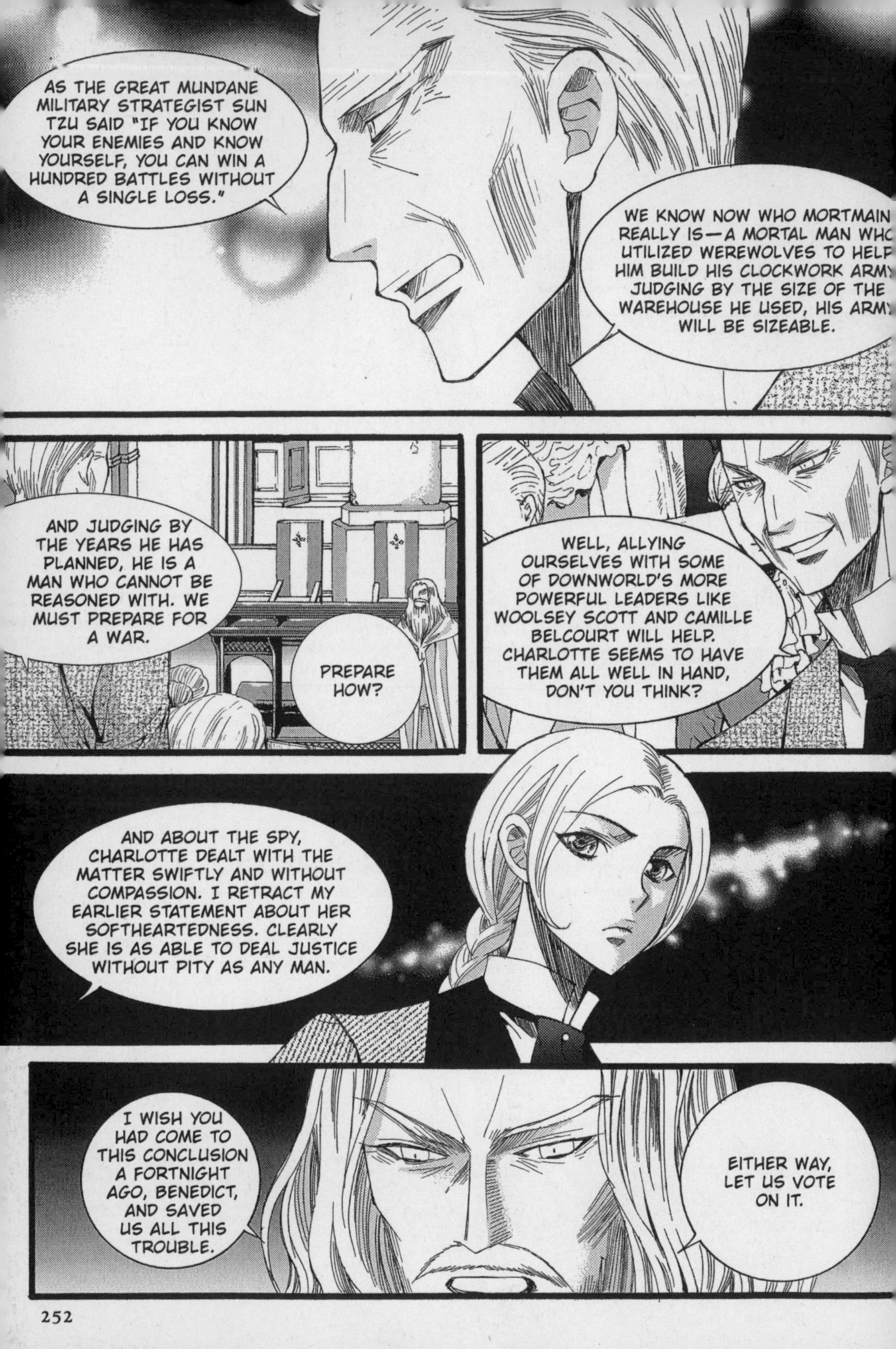
AS THE GREAT MUNDANE MILITARY STRATEGIST SUN TZU SAID "IF YOU KNOW YOUR ENEMIES AND KNOW YOURSELF, YOU CAN WIN A HUNDRED BATTLES WITHOUT A SINGLE LOSS."
WE KNOW NOW WHO MORTMAIN REALLY IS—A MORTAL MAN WHO UTILIZED WEREWOLVES TO HELP HIM BUILD HIS CLOCKWORK ARMY. JUDGING BY THE SIZE OF THE WAREHOUSE HE USED, HIS ARMY WILL BE SIZEABLE.
AND JUDGING BY THE YEARS HE HAS PLANNED, HE IS A MAN WHO CANNOT BE REASONED WITH. WE MUST PREPARE FOR A WAR.
PREPARE HOW?
WELL, ALLYING OURSELVES WITH SOME OF DOWNWORLD'S MORE POWERFUL LEADERS LIKE WOOLSEY SCOTT AND CAMILLE BELCOURT WILL HELP. CHARLOTTE SEEMS TO HAVE THEM ALL WELL IN HAND, DON'T YOU THINK?
AND ABOUT THE SPY, CHARLOTTE DEALT WITH THE MATTER SWIFTLY AND WITHOUT COMPASSION. I RETRACT MY EARLIER STATEMENT ABOUT HER SOFTHEARTEDNESS. CLEARLY SHE IS AS ABLE TO DEAL JUSTICE WITHOUT PITY AS ANY MAN.
I WISH YOU HAD COME TO THIS CONCLUSION A FORTNIGHT AGO, BENEDICT, AND SAVED US ALL THIS TROUBLE.
EITHER WAY, LET US VOTE ON IT.

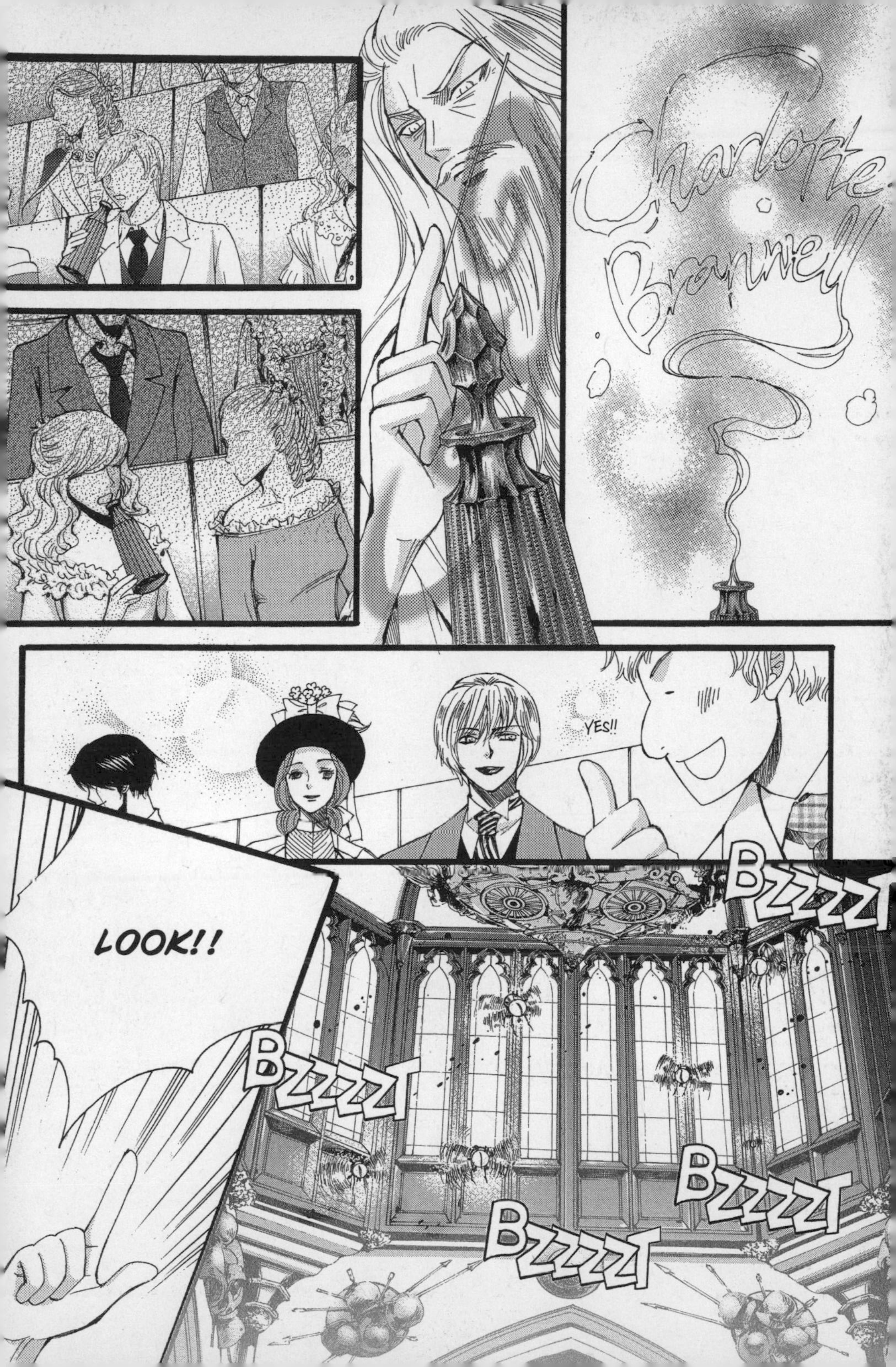
Charlotte Bramwell
YES!!
LOOK!!
BZZZZZT
BZZZZZT
BZZZZZT
BZZZZZT

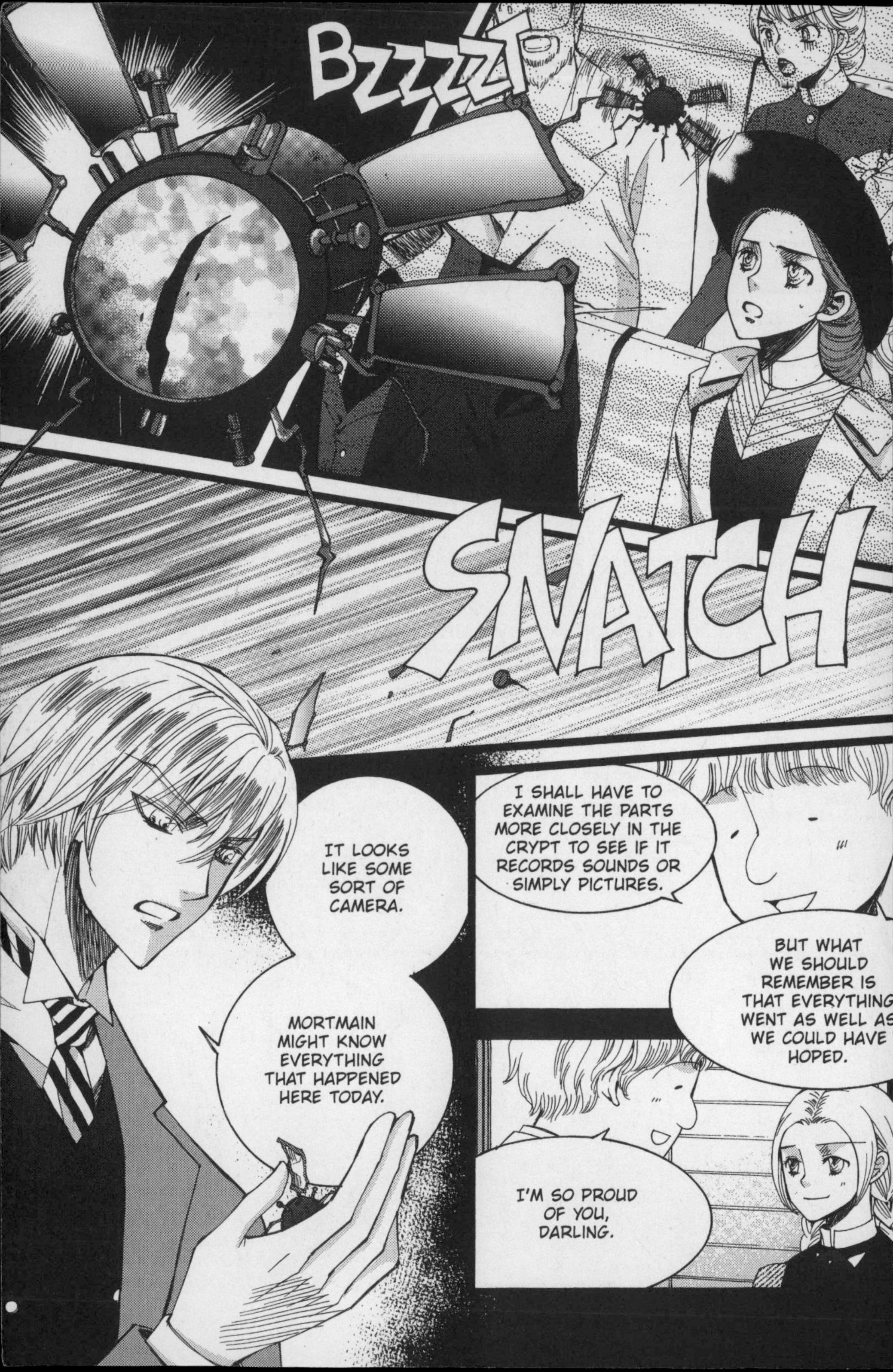
BZZZZZT
SNATCH
IT LOOKS LIKE SOME SORT OF CAMERA.
MORTMAIN MIGHT KNOW EVERYTHING THAT HAPPENED HERE TODAY.
I SHALL HAVE TO EXAMINE THE PARTS MORE CLOSELY IN THE CRYPT TO SEE IF IT RECORDS SOUNDS OR SIMPLY PICTURES.
BUT WHAT WE SHOULD REMEMBER IS THAT EVERYTHING WENT AS WELL AS WE COULD HAVE HOPED.
I'M SO PROUD OF YOU, DARLING.

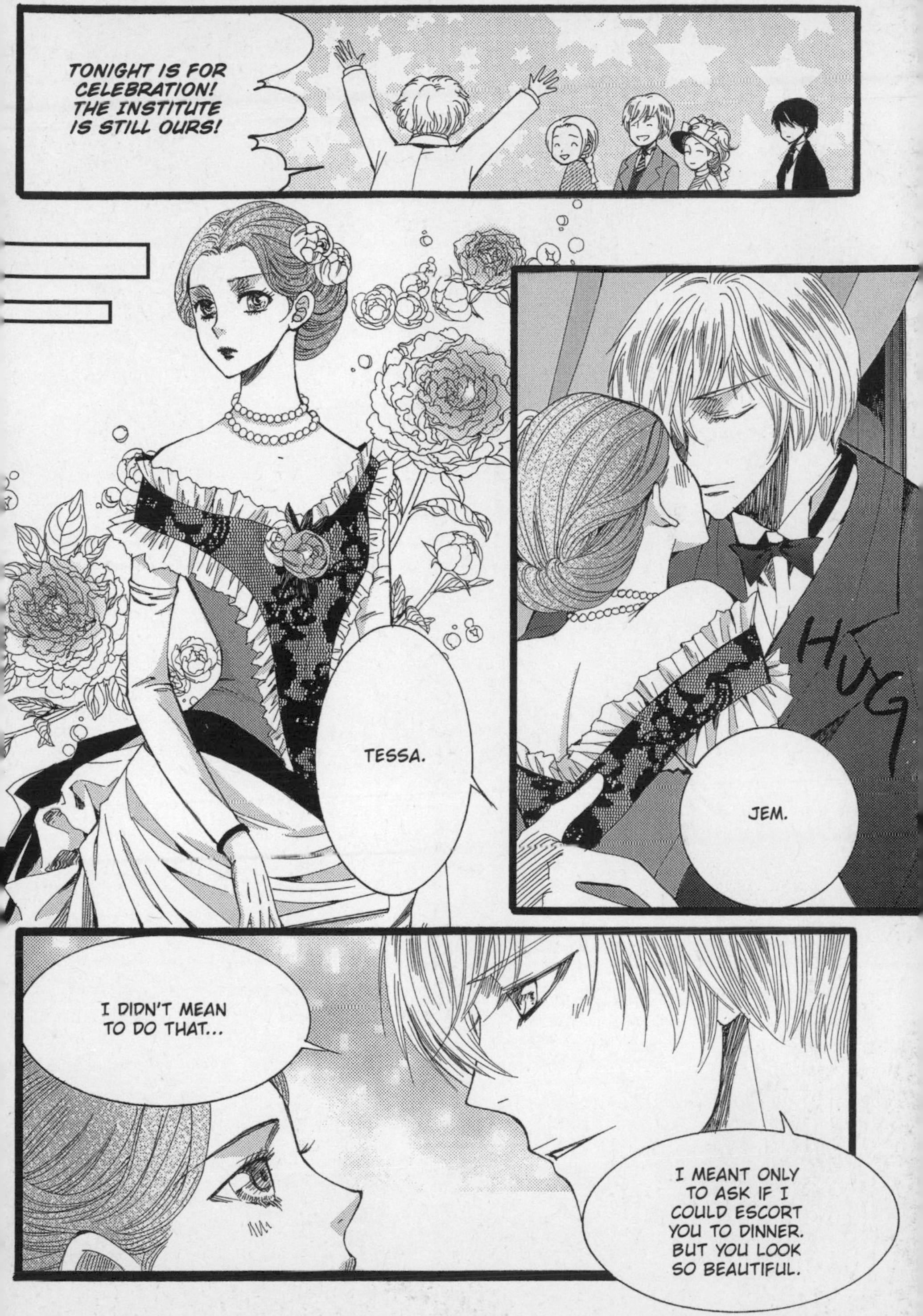
TONIGHT IS FOR CELEBRATION! THE INSTITUTE IS STILL OURS!
TESSA.
JEM.
HUG
I DIDN'T MEAN TO DO THAT...
I MEANT ONLY TO ASK IF I COULD ESCORT YOU TO DINNER. BUT YOU LOOK SO BEAUTIFUL.

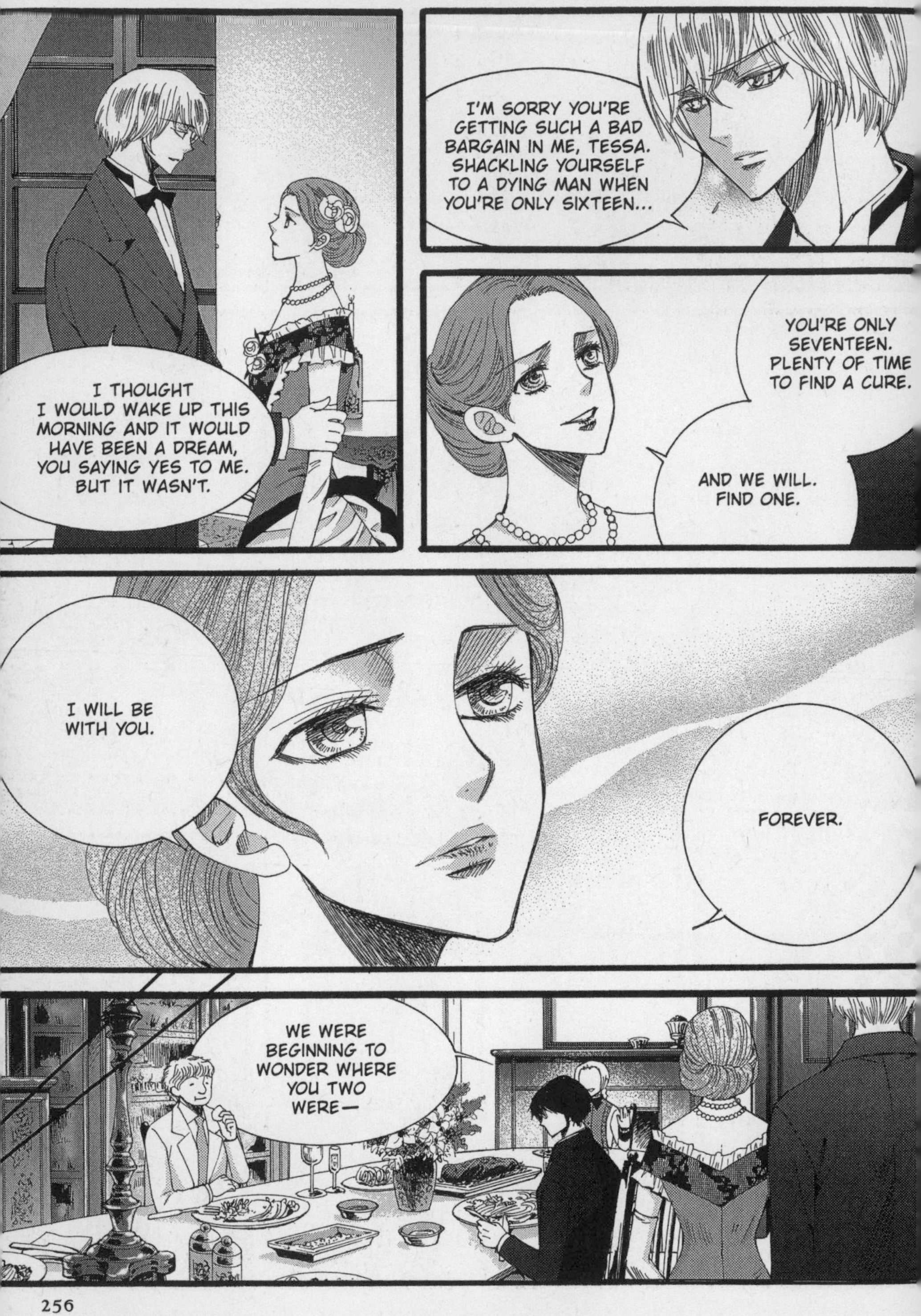

I THOUGHT I WOULD WAKE UP THIS MORNING AND IT WOULD HAVE BEEN A DREAM, YOU SAYING YES TO ME. BUT IT WASN'T.
I'M SORRY YOU'RE GETTING SUCH A BAD BARGAIN IN ME, TESSA. SHACKLING YOURSELF TO A DYING MAN WHEN YOU'RE ONLY SIXTEEN...
YOU'RE ONLY SEVENTEEN. PLENTY OF TIME TO FIND A CURE.
AND WE WILL. FIND ONE.
I WILL BE WITH YOU.
FOREVER.
WE WERE BEGINNING TO WONDER WHERE YOU TWO WERE—

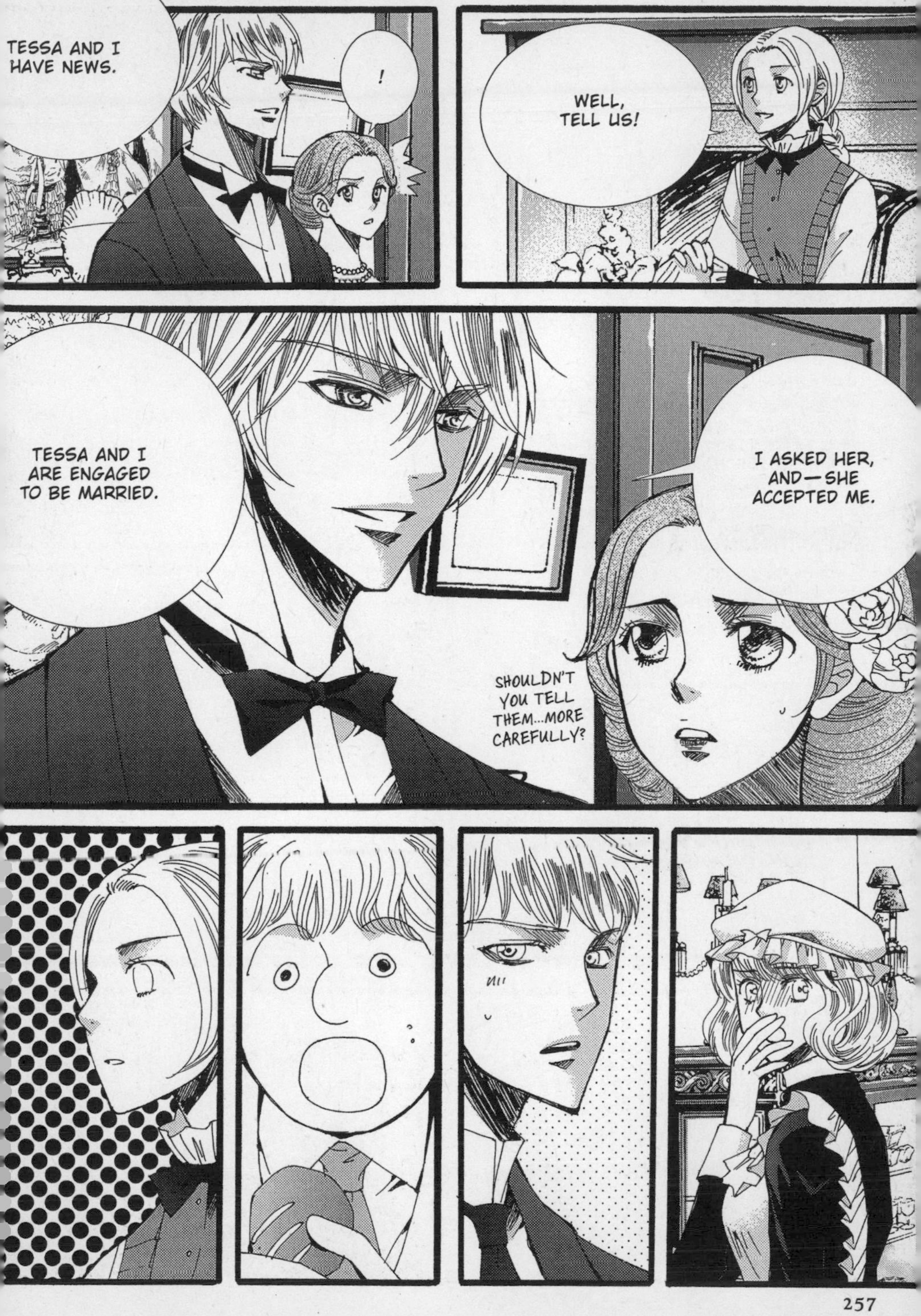
TESSA AND I HAVE NEWS.
!
WELL, TELL US!
TESSA AND I ARE ENGAGED TO BE MARRIED.
I ASKED HER, AND—SHE ACCEPTED ME.
SHOULDN'T YOU TELL THEM...MORE CAREFULLY?

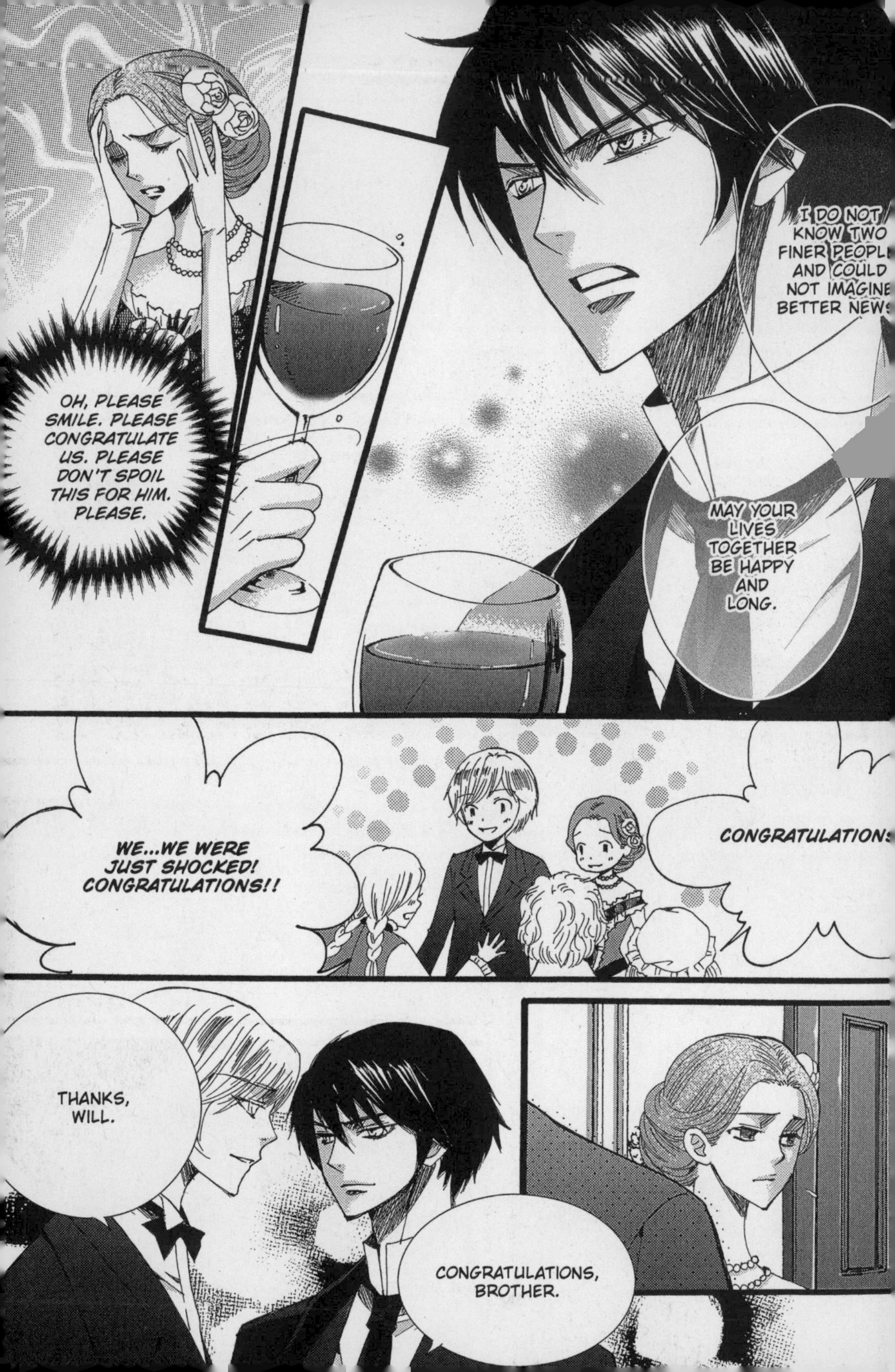
I DO NOT KNOW TWO FINER PEOPLE AND COULD NOT IMAGINE BETTER NEWS
MAY YOUR LIVES TOGETHER BE HAPPY AND LONG.
OH, PLEASE SMILE. PLEASE CONGRATULATE US. PLEASE DON'T SPOIL THIS FOR HIM. PLEASE.
CONGRATULATIONS
WE...WE WERE JUST SHOCKED! CONGRATULATIONS!!
THANKS, WILL.
CONGRATULATIONS, BROTHER.

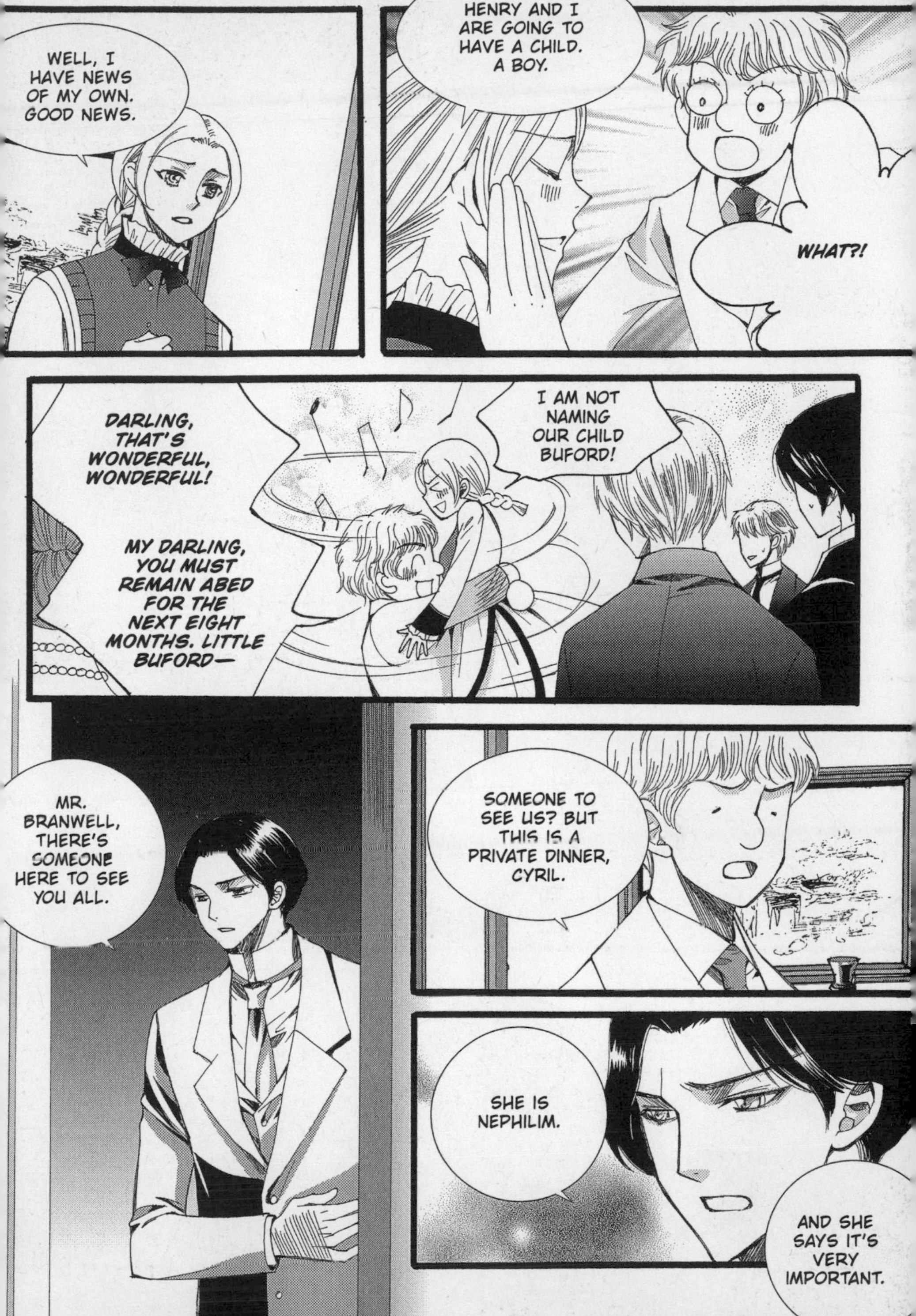
WELL, I HAVE NEWS OF MY OWN. GOOD NEWS.
HENRY AND I ARE GOING TO HAVE A CHILD. A BOY.
WHAT?!
DARLING, THAT'S WONDERFUL, WONDERFUL!
MY DARLING, YOU MUST REMAIN ABED FOR THE NEXT EIGHT MONTHS. LITTLE BUFORD—
I AM NOT NAMING OUR CHILD BUFORD!
MR. BRANWELL, THERE'S SOMEONE HERE TO SEE YOU ALL.
SOMEONE TO SEE US? BUT THIS IS A PRIVATE DINNER, CYRIL.
SHE IS NEPHILIM.
AND SHE SAYS IT'S VERY IMPORTANT.

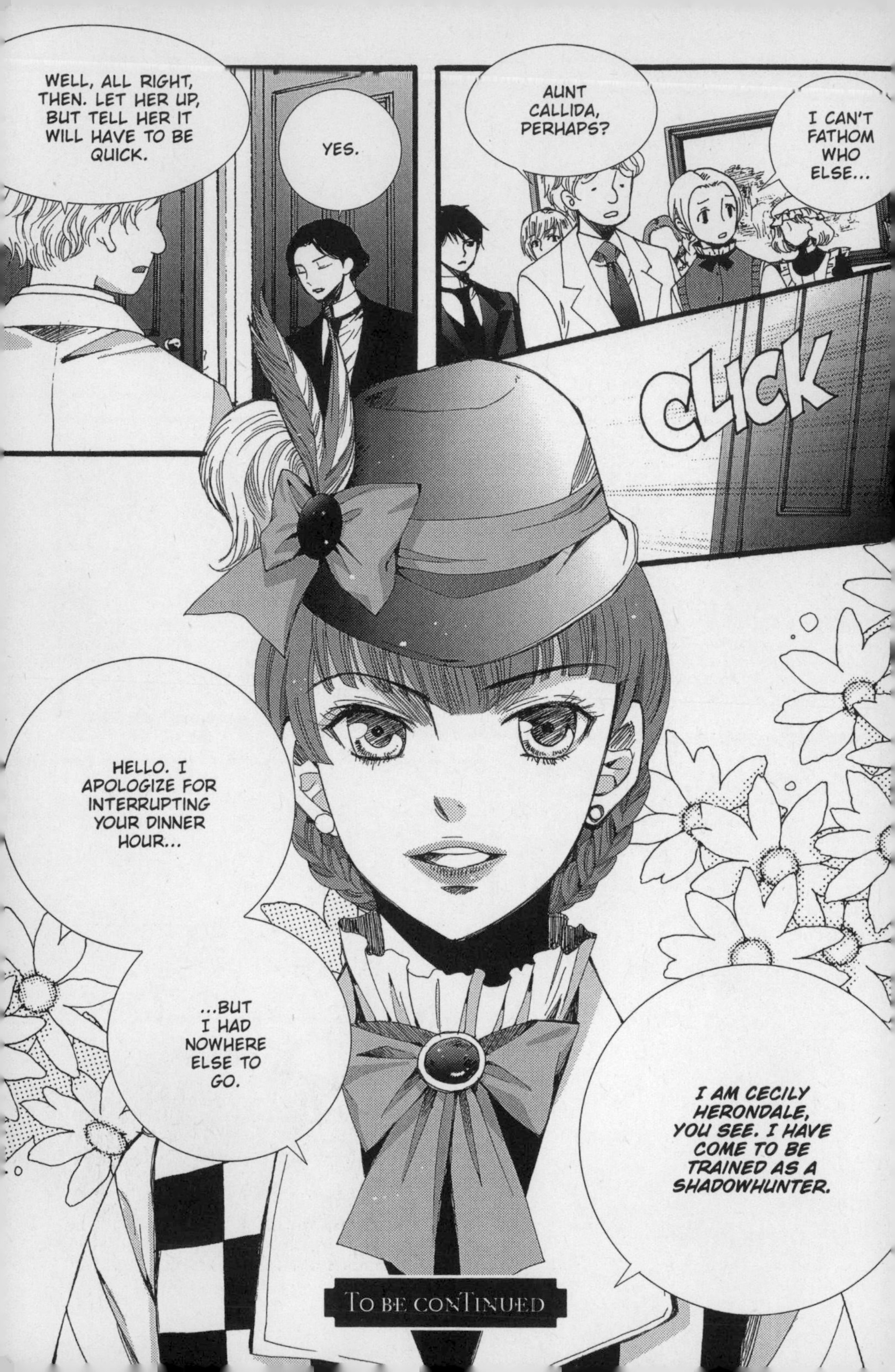
WELL, ALL RIGHT, THEN. LET HER UP, BUT TELL HER IT WILL HAVE TO BE QUICK.
YES.
AUNT CALLIDA, PERHAPS?
I CAN'T FATHOM WHO ELSE...
CLICK
HELLO. I APOLOGIZE FOR INTERRUPTING YOUR DINNER HOUR...
...BUT I HAD NOWHERE ELSE TO GO.
I AM CECILY HERONDALE, YOU SEE. I HAVE COME TO BE TRAINED AS A SHADOWHUNTER.
TO BE CONTINUED

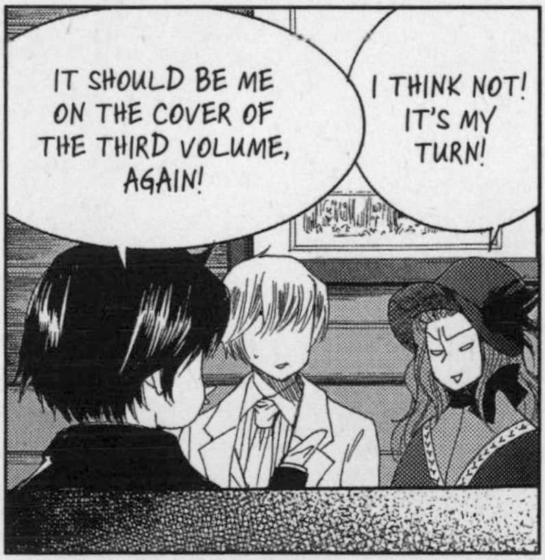
I THINK NOT! IT'S MY TURN!
IT SHOULD BE ME ON THE COVER OF THE THIRD VOLUME, AGAIN!

THE INFERNAL DEVICES: CLOCKWORK PRINCE

CASSANDRA CLARE
HYEKYUNG BAEK

Art and Adaptation: HyeKyung Baek

Lettering: JuYoun Lee

ORBIT

First published in Great Britain in 2013 by Orbit

A CIP catalogue record for this book is available from the British Library.

Yen Press is an imprint of Hachette Book Group, Inc. The Yen Press name and
logo are trademarks of Hachette Book Group, Inc.

First Yen Press Edition: September 2013

ISBN: 978-0-356-50269-4

Printed in the United States of America

Orbit
An imprint of
Little, Brown Book Group
100 Victoria Embankment
London EC4Y 0DY

An Hachette UK Company
www.hachette.co.uk

www.orbitbooks.net
www.yenpress.com